Mac OS® X Snow Leopard
IN DEPTH

Paul McFedries

que®

800 East 96th Street
Indianapolis, Indiana 46240

MAC OS® X SNOW LEOPARD IN DEPTH

ISBN-13: 978-0-7897-4229-2

ISBN-10: 0-7897-4229-2

Library of Congress Cataloging-in-Publication Data:

McFedries, Paul.

   Mac OS X Snow Leopard in depth / Paul McFedries.

       p. cm.

   Includes bibliographical references and index.

   ISBN 978-0-7897-4229-2

   1. Mac OS. 2. Operating systems (Computers) 3. Macintosh (Computer)—Programming. I. Title.

   QA76.76.O63M398155 2010

   005.4'46—dc22

                          2009030548

Printed in the United States of America

First Printing: September 2009

Trademarks

All terms mentioned in this book that are known to be trademarks or service marks have been appropriately capitalized. Que Publishing cannot attest to the accuracy of this information. Use of a term in this book should not be regarded as affecting the validity of any trademark or service mark.

Warning and Disclaimer

Every effort has been made to make this book as complete and as accurate as possible, but no warranty or fitness is implied. The information provided is on an "as is" basis. The author and the publisher shall have neither liability nor responsibility to any person or entity with respect to any loss or damages arising from the information contained in this book.

Bulk Sales

Que Publishing offers excellent discounts on this book when ordered in quantity for bulk purchases or special sales. For more information, please contact

   U.S. Corporate and Government Sales

   1-800-382-3419

   corpsales@pearsontechgroup.com

For sales outside of the U.S., please contact

   International Sales

   international@pearson.com

Associate Publisher
Greg Wiegand

Acquisitions Editor
Laura Norman

Development Editor
Dan Richcreek

Managing Editor
Patrick Kanouse

Project Editor
Mandie Frank

Copy Editor
Margaret Berson

Indexer
Tim Wright

Proofreader
Leslie Joseph

Technical Editor
Brian Hubbard

Publishing Coordinator
Cindy Teeters

Designer
Ann Jones

Compositor
Bronkella Publishing LLC

CONTENTS AT A GLANCE

CONTENTS

11 Managing Your Schedule 233

12 Working with Text and Graphics 249

III Living in a Connected World

13 Connecting Your Mac to the Internet 267

ABOUT THE AUTHOR

Paul McFedries is a Mac expert with more than 20 years experience with all flavors of Macs. Paul is a full-time technical writer and has been authoring computer books since 1991. He has more than 60 books to his credit, including a number of titles covering Macs, Mac OS X, and the iPhone. Paul has written many books for Que, including *Tweak It and Freak It: A Killer Guide to Making Windows Run Your Way*; *Build It. Fix It. Own It: A Beginner's Guide to Building and Upgrading a PC*; *Tricks of the Microsoft Office 2007 Gurus*; *Formulas and Functions with Microsoft Excel 2007*; *VBA for the 2007 Microsoft Office System*; and *Microsoft Office Access 2007 Forms, Reports, and Queries*. Paul's Mac titles include *Macs Portable Genius*, *Switching to a Mac Portable Genius*, *iPhone 3G S Portable Genius*, *Teach Yourself VISUALLY Macs*, and *Teach Yourself VISUALLY Mac OS X Snow Leopard*. Paul's books have sold more than three million copies worldwide.

However, all geek and no play makes Jack (and Paul) a dull boy. Paul's other interests include solving and writing cryptic crosswords, word play of all forms, reading, running, baking bread, and taking naps. Paul lives in Toronto with Karen, the love of his life, and Gypsy the kissing dog. They have no cats.

Paul is also the proprietor of Word Spy, a website devoted to recently coined words and phrases. Word Spy generates over a million page views each month, has won numerous awards, and has been mentioned or featured in such august publications as *The New York Times*, *The Wall Street Journal*, and *Time* Magazine. Paul invites you to join in the fun at http://www.wordspy.com/, or on Twitter at http://twitter.com/wordspy.

If you'd like to contact Paul, please feel free to drop by his website at http://www.mcfedries.com/ or via Twitter at http://twitter.com/paulmcf/.

DEDICATION

To Karen, as always, and of course to Gypsy, too!

ACKNOWLEDGMENTS

Being an author is the most wonderful vocation (I don't think of it as a job) I can imagine. I get to play with words, I get to talk about things I'm intensely interested in, and I get some big-time warm, fuzzy feelings when people write to me to tell me that, in some small way, something I've written has helped them.

Any book, but especially a book as big as this one, is the result of the efforts of many hard-working people. The Que editorial staff, in particular, never fail to impress me with their dedication, work ethic, and commitment to quality, and there are a few I'd like to thank personally: Acquisitions Editor Laura Norman, Development Editor Dan Richcreek, Project Editor Mandie Frank, Copy Editor Margaret Berson, and Technical Editor Brian Hubbard.

The members of the editorial team aren't the only people who had their fingers in this publishing pie. Flip back a few pages and you'll find a list of the designers, illustrators, indexers, and other professionals who worked long and hard to produce this book. I tip my authorial hat to all of them. I'd also like to thank the thousands and thousands of readers who have written to me over the years to offer book compliments and suggestions.

WE WANT TO HEAR FROM YOU!

As the reader of this book, *you* are our most important critic and commentator. We value your opinion and want to know what we're doing right, what we could do better, what areas you'd like to see us publish in, and any other words of wisdom you're willing to pass our way.

As an associate publisher for Que Publishing, I welcome your comments. You can email or write me directly to let me know what you did or didn't like about this book—as well as what we can do to make our books better.

Please note that I cannot help you with technical problems related to the topic of this book. We do have a User Services group, however, where I will forward specific technical questions related to the book.

When you write, please be sure to include this book's title and author as well as your name, email address, and phone number. I will carefully review your comments and share them with the author and editors who worked on the book.

Email: feedback@quepublishing.com

Mail: Greg Wiegand
           Associate Publisher
           Que Publishing
           800 East 96th Street
           Indianapolis, IN 46240 USA

READER SERVICES

Visit our website and register this book at www.informit.com/title/9780789742292 for convenient access to any updates, downloads, or errata that might be available for this book.

Introduction

Welcome to Mac OS X

You don't have to see too many of those ubiquitous "Mac versus PC" ads to get the basic idea: Macs are intuitive, easy to use, and they just work. That's all true, certainly, but it misses something important about the Mac, and particularly about Mac OS X, the Mac operating system: *easy* is not the same as *simple*. Easy means that you can accomplish tasks (and, importantly, *figure out* how to accomplish tasks) with a minimum of fuss and with no sign of bother. Simple, on the other hand, implies a kind of shallowness, a superficiality where all you get is a pretty interface. It implies, in other words, that Mac OS X has no depth.

Friend, I'm here today to tell you that Mac OS X most definitely has depth. We're talking here about one of the world's most sophisticated operating systems, with millions of lines of programming code behind it, dozens of free and powerful applications installed by default, and hundreds, nay *thousands* of options, settings, and preferences to warm the cockles of any system tweaker's geeky heart.

However, Apple has spent untold millions of dollars and tens of thousands of man (and woman) hours designing an interface that seems to serve just one purpose: to hide the depths of Mac OS X from view. That's fine if you just want to use your Mac to accomplish a few simple goals, such as surfing the Web, managing email, sending texts, and perhaps writing a thing or two. But if your goal is to get the most out of your Mac investment and to make your computing life more efficient and more effective, you need to get beyond the surface of Mac OS X and dive head-first into its depths. And the best way to do that is to have a guide at your side to show you the nooks and crannies, light up the dark corners, and dig up the buried treasures. This book is your guide to hidden depths of Mac OS X.

Welcome to *Mac OS X Snow Leopard In Depth*

This book has two fundamental purposes:

- To help you make the jump to Mac OS X as efficiently as possible

- To provide a reference for you to use as you continue to grow in your Mac OS X use

To accomplish the first purpose, this book is written in a straightforward style; you won't find any fluff here. The book is designed to help you *use* Mac OS X as efficiently and effectively as possible. Everything about the book is an attempt to make specific information accessible and applicable to your daily Mac life. You will find only the background information you need to understand how to apply specific techniques and technologies; the focus is on the information you need to apply what you learn to your own Mac.

To accomplish the second purpose, this book covers an extremely broad range of topics. In addition to coverage of the core functionality of the desktop, you get extensive coverage of topics to enable you to accomplish productive work with your Mac, such as surfing the Net, burning discs, and using Mac OS X's applications to accomplish specific tasks. This book also contains substantial amounts of information to help you add devices to expand your system so you can accomplish even more. Because Mac OS X has been designed to be networked, you learn how to use its capabilities in this area to connect with other Macs, as well as to Windows networks. You learn how to both prevent and solve OS X problems along the way.

How This Book Is Organized

This book consists of six parts, each of which contains at least four chapters. The following list provides an overview of this book's contents:

- **Part I, "Exploring Mac OS X"**—This part gets you started on the right foot. You learn the core operations of the OS, including the desktop, the Dock, and Finder. You also learn how to manage files and folder, search your Mac, set system preferences, and install applications.

- **Part II, "Getting Things Done with Snow Leopard's Applications"**—Mac OS X includes a number of useful applications, such as Safari, iTunes, QuickTime Player, Address Book, iCal, and others. In this part, you learn how to take advantage of these great applications.

- **Part III, "Living in a Connected World"**—Mac OS X has been designed to facilitate your interaction with networks and with the Internet. This part of the book explains how to configure Mac OS X for the Internet and how to use the tools it provides after you are connected. You also learn how to create and manage wired and wireless networks.

- **Part IV, "Delving Deeper into Mac OS X"**—After Parts I to III, you're ready to take your Mac OS X skills to a new level. In Part IV you learn how to manage user accounts; take control of your desktop with Exposé and Spaces; use fonts and accessibility options; use the powerful Automator application; take advantage of the Mac OS X notebook features; work with Dashboard and Widgets; and run Unix and Windows on your Mac.

- **Part V, "Working with Devices in Mac OS X"**—No Mac is an island; this part of the book helps you understand the input and output technologies supported by Mac OS X to enable you to select and add the peripheral devices you need.

- **Part VI, "Maintaining, Protecting, and Repairing Your Mac"**—As great as Mac OS X is, you still need to know how to minimize problems with good preventive maintenance actions and be able to effectively solve any problems you do experience. You should also learn how to use Mac OS X's extensive security features to protect your Mac.

Special Features

This book includes the following special features:

- **Chapter roadmaps**—At the beginning of each chapter, you will find a list of the top-level topics addressed in that chapter. This list will enable you to quickly see the type of information the chapter contains.

- **Troubleshooting**—Several chapters in the book have a section dedicated to troubleshooting specific problems related to the chapter's topic.

- **Notes**—Notes provide additional commentary or explanation that doesn't fit neatly into the surrounding text. You will find detailed explanations of how something works, alternative ways of performing a task, and comparisons between Mac OS X and previous versions of the OS.

- **Tips**—Tips help you work more efficiently by providing shortcuts or hints about alternative and faster ways of accomplishing a task.

- **Cautions**—These sidebars provide a warning to you about situations that involve possible danger to your Mac or its data.

- **Cross-references**—Many topics are connected to other topics in various ways. Cross-references help you link related information together, no matter where that information appears in the book. When another section is related to one you are reading, a cross-reference will direct you to a specific page in the book on which you will find related information.

Conventions

To make things as clear as possible, this book doesn't use many special conventions or formatting techniques to identify specific kinds of information. However, there are a few things you need to be aware of:

- Menu commands are referred to by starting with the menu name and moving down to the specific command while separating each layer with a comma. For example, rather than writing, "Open the Terminal menu, then select the Services command, then select the Mail command, and then select Mail Text," I use a shorthand technique. In this example, I would write, "Select Terminal, Services, Mail, Mail Text." This shorthand makes the command structure more clear and cuts back on the number of words you have to read.

- When you are working in the Terminal, the commands you enter and the output you see are in a `monospace font like this.`

- Variables that stand for text that is specific to you are usually in *italics*. For example, if I need to refer to your username in a specific location, I write, "Users/*username*, where *username* is your username," to indicate that you should look for your own information in place of the italicized phrase.

Who Should Use This Book

In this book, I've made certain assumptions about your specific experience with the Mac OS and your general comfort level with technology. The biggest assumption is that you are quite comfortable with the fundamentals of using the Mac OS. For example, you won't find any explanations of how to use a mouse, how to copy and move files, the basics of drag and drop, and so on. When there are significant differences in these basic tasks under Mac OS X as compared to the previous versions of the OS, you will find those differences explained, but probably not in enough detail to teach you how to do them if you have never done them before.

If you are completely new to computers, you will still find this book very useful, but you will also need a companion book that explains the fundamentals of using a Mac in more detail than is provided in this book, such as *Easy Mac OS X Leopard* (0-7897-3711-X).

If you have used previous versions of the Mac OS, such as Mac OS 9 or earlier versions of Mac OS X, and are comfortable with basic tasks, this book will help you make the jump to Mac OS X version 10.5 in a short time. It also will serve as a comprehensive reference for you as you explore this amazing operating system.

1

WORKING ON THE MAC OS X DESKTOP

The Mac OS X Desktop

When you start your Mac and log on to your user account, the first thing you will see is the Mac OS X desktop, which takes up the entire screen as shown in Figure 1.1. The default desktop is fairly sparse with only the Dock at the bottom of the screen and the menu bar at the top. This relative emptiness won't last long, however, because as you use Mac OS X, the desktop gets populated with icons, Finder windows, other application windows, dialogs, and the other objects that are part of day-to-day life in the Mac universe.

This chapter introduces you to all the main features of the Mac OS X desktop, so you'll have a solid base from which to explore the rest of the system in the chapters that follow.

➡ *Because the Dock is such an important part of Mac OS X, it has a chapter dedicated to it; **see** Chapter 2, "Getting to Know the Dock," p. 23.*

➡ *For information on viewing and using Finder windows, **see** Chapter 3, "Getting to Know Mac OS X Finder Windows," p. 37.*

Figure 1.1
The Mac OS X desktop is where you'll do almost all of your work on your Mac.

Working with Mac OS X Menus

One of the features that makes Mac OS X so easy to learn and use is the menu system. The menu bar that runs across the top of the desktop never moves, and the vast majority of the time it remains visible no matter how you move or size your open windows, so you always know where to find the menus. And although the left side of the menu bar changes depending on which application you're currently using, Mac OS X and its applications offer a remarkably consistent set of menus. This will help reduce the learning curve in all your OS X applications.

The next few sections take you on a tour of some of these common menus.

The Mac OS X Apple Menu

The Apple menu—marked by the apple icon in the top-left corner of the screen—is a crucial part of the Mac OS X interface, not only because of the familiarity of the apple icon, but also because this menu provides you with continuous access to a specific set of commands that doesn't change whether you are working on the desktop or within an application. The Mac OS X Apple menu contains the commands listed in Table 1.1.

Table 1.1   Commands on the Mac OS X Apple Menu

Command	What It Does
About This Mac	Opens a window showing the version of Mac OS X installed, the physical RAM installed, the number and type of processors, and the startup disk. You can also click Software Update to get the latest versions of Apple software, or click More Info to open the System Profiler to get more information about your Mac.
System Profiler	Hold down Option and click the Apple menu to see this command, which opens the System Profiler application.
Software Update	Opens the Software Update tool, which you can use to get the latest versions of the Apple software installed on your Mac.
Mac OS X Software	Opens your Mac's default web browser and loads the Mac OS X software downloads web page.
System Preferences	Opens the System Preferences application.
Dock	Displays a menu of commands that give you control over the Dock's settings for hiding, magnification, and position and enables you to open the Dock Preferences pane of the System Preferences application.
Recent Items	Displays a menu of the applications, documents, and servers that you have recently accessed. The menu is organized into three sections—Applications, Documents, and Servers—and you can select an item to open it. It also has the Clear Menu command, which removes everything from the menu.
Force Quit	Opens the Force Quit Applications window, which enables you to shut down a running application that's no longer responsive (for example, because it has crashed).
Force Quit Finder	Hold down Shift and click the Apple menu to see this command, which forces Finder to relaunch.
Sleep	Puts the Mac to sleep.
Restart	Restarts the Mac.
Shut Down	Shuts down the Mac.
Log Out *username*	Logs the current user (whose account name is *username*) off the Mac and opens the Login window.

Mac OS X Application Menus

The menu items on the left side of the Mac OS X menu bar (except for the Apple menu) change depending on which application currently has the focus. For example, if you're working in Finder you see seven menus: Finder, File, Edit, View, Go, Window, and Help, as shown in Figure 1.2.

Figure 1.2
When you're working in Finder, the menu bar displays the seven menu items shown here.

If you then switch to, say, Safari, the menu bar changes to show the eight menus associated with the Safari web browser: Safari, File, Edit, View, History, Bookmarks, Window, and Help, as shown in Figure 1.3.

Figure 1.3
If you switch to Safari, the menu bar changes to display the eight menu items shown here.

These menu sets are called *application menus*. The application menus provide the commands you use to control the application in which you're working. A standard set of commands is consistent among all Mac OS X applications—such as Cut, Copy, and Paste on the Edit menu—but specific applications can have additional commands on their Application menu. Every Mac OS X program has its own application menu located immediately to the right of the Apple menu. This *Application menu* always uses the name of the application itself. For example, Finder's Application menu is called Finder (see Figure 1.2), while Safari's Application menu is called Safari (see Figure 1.3).

The following commands are standard on every Application menu:

- **About *Application***—This command, where *Application* is the name of the active application, displays version information about the application. Some About windows also provide links to support sites, the publisher's website, and so on. The About Finder command displays the version of Finder you are using.

- **Preferences**—You use the Preferences command to set the preferences for an application. For example, you can use Finder's Preferences command to control specific properties of the desktop.

  ➡ *To learn about Finder Preferences, see "Changing the Desktop's Appearance," p. 17.*

- **Hide *Application***—This command (where *Application* is the name of the running application) hides the current application.

- **Hide Others**—This command hides all the running applications except the current one. This is useful if your desktop is cluttered with other application windows and you'd like to clean things up a bit to help you concentrate on the current application.

- **Show All**—This command unhides all previously hidden applications.

 tip

The keyboard shortcut for the Preferences command is ⌘-, and this shortcut works for all Apple applications and for most third-party programs.

 note

Hiding an application removes its windows and its menu bar from the desktop. The application continues to run and any processes that are under way continue. You can also minimize application windows, which places open windows on the Dock; the application's menu bar continues to appear while the application is active, even if its windows are minimized.

The Application menu of every program (except Finder) also contains the following commands:

- **Services**—This command provides commands that enable you to work with other applications from within the current application. For example, if you're using the TextEdit word processing application, its Services menu contains several commands that use the Grab application to capture something on the screen. After you capture the image, it's automatically pasted into the current TextEdit document. The commands available on the Services menu depend on the applications installed on your Mac and how those applications support the Services menu.

  ➡ *To learn more about using the Services command with Mac OS X applications,* **see** *"Working with Mac OS X Application Menus," p. 132.*

- **Quit** *Application*—This command (where *Application* is the name of the current program) shuts down the application.

Finder's Application menu (Finder menu) also has the Empty Trash and Secure Empty Trash commands, which are unique to its Application menu:

- **Empty Trash**—This command deletes any files or folders located in the Trash.

- **Secure Empty Trash**—This command deletes files located in the Trash *and* overwrites the disk space where those files were stored, so they can't be recovered. Because the Secure Empty Trash command overwrites disk space, it takes much longer to execute than does the Empty Trash command (however, because it works in the background, it shouldn't slow down your work).

Mac OS X File Menus

The File menu contains commands that enable you to work with files, folders, and discs. The specific commands you see on an application's File menu depend on the application. Most File menus have the New, Open, Save, Save As, Print, and Page Setup commands. Many other commands might appear on the File menu as well.

Finder's File menu offers the commands listed in Table 1.2.

tip

The keyboard shortcut for the Quit command is ⌘-Q. When you are working on the desktop, ⌘-Q doesn't do anything because you can't quit Finder. However, you can relaunch Finder using the Force Quit command.

note

The Mac OS X Compress command is one of the most useful Finder commands. This command enables you to create compressed files from any folders and files on your Mac. Even better, Mac OS X supports the ZIP compression format, which is the standard, native compression format on Windows computers. You no longer need a separate application to compress files. You can also expand any Zip file from the desktop by opening it.

Table 1.2   Commands on Finder's File Menu

Command	What It Does
New Finder Window	Opens a new Finder window
New Folder	Creates a new folder
New Smart Folder	Creates a new smart folder

Table 1.2 Continued

Command	What It Does
New Burn Folder	Creates a new folder intended to be burned onto a disc
Open	Opens the selected item
Open in New Window and Close	Opens the selected item in a new window and closes Finder window (hold down Option to see this command)
Open With	Enables you to open a selected file with a specific application
Print	Enables you to print a selected file
Close Window	Closes the active window
Close All	Closes all open windows (hold down Option to see this command)
Get Info	Opens the Info window
Compress	Compresses selected items and creates a .zip file to store the compressed versions in
Duplicate	Creates a duplicate of the selected item
Make Alias	Creates an alias of the selected item
Quick Look	Opens the Quick Look view for the selected item
Show Original	Exposes the original item for which an alias was created
Add to Sidebar	Adds an alias of the selected item to the Places Sidebar
Move to Trash	Moves the selected item to the Trash
Eject	Ejects the selected item (disc, disk image, server volume, and so on)
Burn	Burns the selected item to a disc
Find	Opens Finder's Find tool so you can locate files and folders
Label	Applies the label you choose to the selected items

Mac OS X Edit Menus

The Edit menu contains commands for working with data. When you're using most applications other than Finder, the commands that appear on the Edit menu are Cut, Copy, and Paste. Most applications also provide many more commands on this menu, such as Undo, Redo, Select All, and so on.

Finder's Edit menu is a bit different because you don't use Finder to edit documents. Its commands apply to files and folders instead. For example, when you select a file and choose Edit, Copy, the file is copied. You can move to a different location and choose Edit, Paste to place a copy of the selected item in the new location. Finder's Edit menu also has the Select All command, which selects everything in the active window; the Show Clipboard command, which shows what has been copied to the Clipboard; and the Special Characters command, which opens the Character palette.

Finder's View Menu

Finder's View menu contains the commands you use to view Finder windows.

➥ *To learn about using Finder's View commands,* **see** *Chapter 3, "Getting to Know Mac OS X Finder Windows," p. 7.*

Finder's Go Menu

Finder's Go menu contains commands that you use to navigate your system. Using the Go menu, you can navigate to the following locations:

- **Back or Forward**—Moves you through the windows in a chain of open Finder windows.

- **Enclosing Folder**—Moves you to the folder that contains the currently selected item.

- **Frequently Used Folders**—Commands such as Computer, Home, Applications, and Utilities move you to the specified folder.

- **Recent Folders**—Displays a list of the most recent folders you've used, and lets you select a folder to return to it. You can clear the Recent Folders menu by selecting Clear Menu.

- **Specific Folder**—Use the Go to Folder command to enter the path to a specific folder to open it.

- **Server**—Use the Connect to Server command to open a server on your network.

➥ *To learn how to use the Go menu to navigate folders,* **see** *"Changing Folders with the Go Menu," p. 54.*

➥ *To learn how to connect to servers,* **see** *"Accessing Shared Files from a Mac OS X Computer," p. 368.*

Mac OS X Window Menus

The Window menu provides commands you use to work with windows that are currently open. Common choices on the Window menu include the following:

- **Minimize**—This does the same thing as clicking the Minimize button in a window: It moves a window onto the Dock.

- **Zoom**—This does the same thing as the Maximize button: It makes the active window as large as it needs to be to display all the window's contents or to fill the desktop, whichever comes first. Choosing it again toggles the window back to its previous size.

- **Cycle Through Open Windows**—This moves you among the open windows, one at a time.

- **Bring All to Front**—This command brings all open windows to the front. For example, if you have a lot of open Finder windows and then switch to an application and then back to Finder, you might not see all your open Finder windows. If you use this command, they all come to the foreground so you can see them.

- **List of Open Windows**—The Window menu always displays a list of the windows open for the application providing that menu. You can switch to an open window by selecting it on the menu.

On the Window menu, the active window in the application you are currently using is marked with some sort of icon. The active Finder window is marked with a check mark; other applications might use a different indicator (for example, a diamond). Be aware that a window can be both active and minimized, in which case the active icon on the Window menu can help you identify the active window even if you can't see that window (because it's on the Dock).

If you hold the Option key down while you open the Window menu, you see two additional commands that replace default commands:

- **Minimize All**—This command replaces Minimize and it causes all open windows in the application, such as Finder, to be minimized and moved to the Dock.

- **Zoom All**—This command replaces the Zoom command and it makes all the active windows as large as they need to be to display the windows' contents or to fill the desktop, whichever comes first.

You might see more or fewer commands on the Window menu when you are working in specific applications.

Mac OS X Help Menus

Most applications provide a Help menu that enables you to open their help system. And, most applications provide help through the standard Mac OS X Help application. You can also use Spotlight to search your Mac for specific information.

Finder's Help menu contains two commands—Search and Mac Help.

You can use the Search box to use Spotlight to quickly search Finder and the Mac's Help for information in which you might be interested. To use this tool, select Help and type a search term in the Search box. As you type, the Help command is replaced by the results of the search, which appear in two groups:

- **Menu Items**—This is a list of commands in the menu system that match your search text. When you hover the mouse pointer over a command, the Help system opens the corresponding menu and points out the command, as shown in Figure 1.4. Click the command to run it.

- **Help Topics**—This is a list of Help system topics that match your search text. Click a topic to open it in a Help window.

To clear a search so you see the original two commands, click the Clear button (X) in the Search tool.

In Finder's Help menu, the Mac Help command opens the Mac Help application, which provides extensive help for many areas of Mac OS X. Even better, many applications you install integrate their help systems into the Mac OS X help system. This enables you to access plenty of help using the same tool.

Figure 1.4
Hovering the
mouse over a
menu item in
the search
results opens
the menu
and a large
floating
arrow points
out the item.

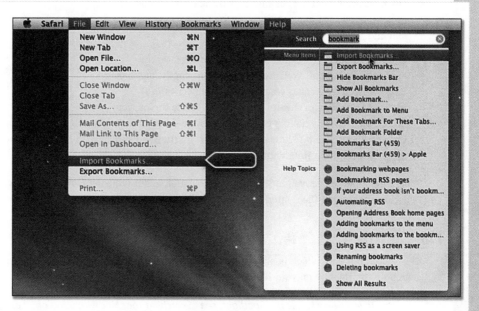

The Help application is based on HTML, so it works the same way web pages do. You can search for help and click links and buttons to access information and move around.

The Home button in the Help Center's toolbar takes you back to the current help's home page. If you click and hold the Home button, you see a list of all areas in which you can access help, such as AirPort Help, Mail Help, and so on. You can also view and choose these areas on the Help application's Library command.

When you have the Mac Help window open, there are a couple of tools you can use to help you find what you are looking for: the Index link and the Search box.

The Index link takes you to an index of topics listed alphabetically. From here you can click on a letter of the alphabet to move to a certain term or phrase.

The Search box invites you to Ask a Question; click inside the box, type a search term, and press Return to see the results that match your search text. The results window is organized into two areas, Help Topics and Support Articles:

- **Help Topics**—This area lists each help topic within the Help system that matches your search. By default, Help sorts this area by the Rank column, which is the Help system's judgment of how well a topic addresses your search criterion.

 tip

When you search for help, you frequently see the Tell Me More link. This link opens other pages that contain topics related to the one for which you searched.

 tip

You can also browse most help systems from their home pages. This is often an even better way to find a specific topic because you don't have to be concerned about using specific words as you do when you search for help.

Open a topic by double-clicking it or by selecting it and clicking Show. The topic appears in the window for viewing.

- **Support Articles**—This section lists the articles on the application's support website that the Help application has found for you (assuming your Mac can connect to the Internet to search for this information). Just like topics, you access an article by double-clicking it or by selecting it and clicking Show. The article is downloaded from the Web and appears within the Help window.

note

Articles on the Web are marked with the plus icon (+), and topics within the Help system are marked with the application's icon. For example, Mac OS X help topics are marked with the OS X icon (the "X").

Some help topics assist you in performing the action about which you are asking by providing hyperlinks that open the related application or resource.

The Spotlight Menu

The Spotlight menu, which is always located at the far right end of the menu bar, enables you to search for information on your Mac.

➡ *To learn how to use the Spotlight,* **see** *"Searching Your Mac with Spotlight," **p. 89**.*

Menu Extras

The *menu extras* are the icons that appear on the right side of the menu bar. The number of icons you see depends on the configuration of your Mac. (As you see throughout this book, there are many icons you can display here.) You use these icons to see the status of certain Mac features (such as your wireless network connection) and to configure other features. For example, you can use the volume icon to adjust the Mac's sound volume.

Mac OS X Contextual Menus

Mac OS X supports contextual menus. *Contextual menus* are pop-up menus that appear in various locations and contain commands specifically related to the context in which you are working. You can access contextual menus by pointing to an object that provides a contextual menu and clicking the right mouse button or holding down the Control key and clicking the left (or only, on a one-button mouse) mouse button. The contextual menu appears and you can select a command on it.

The desktop and Finder provide contextual menus, as do many applications, including those not provided by Apple. For example, the Microsoft Office application provides excellent support for contextual menus.

Table 1.3 provides a summary of a few of the more useful Finder contextual menu commands.

tip

Mac OS X supports a two-button mouse by default. You can open an item's contextual menu by right-clicking it. You can also program most multi-button input devices to perform a right-click. I strongly recommend that you use a mouse or trackball that has at least two buttons, if for no other reason than the convenience of opening contextual menus with one hand.

Table 1.3   Useful Finder Contextual Menu Commands

Object	Command	What It Does
Desktop	Change Desktop Background	Opens the Desktop & Screen Saver pane of the System Preferences application.
Desktop, Finder window	New Folder	Creates a new folder.
Desktop, Finder window, folder, file, volume	Get Info	Opens the Info window (this is covered in more detail later in this chapter).
Desktop, folder with no items selected	Show View Options	Opens the View options window for the desktop or the current folder.
Desktop, Finder window, folder,	Arrange By	Sorts the desktop icons or folder icons using the property that you specify (such as Name or Size).
Finder window	View	Switches the Finder window to the view you select.
Finder window	Clean Up	Arranges the Finder window icons into rows and columns.
File	Open With	Enables you to choose the application to use to open the selected file.
File	Quick Look	Opens the Quick Look tool (this is covered in more detail in Chapter 4; see "Getting a Quick Look at Things," p. xxx).
Folder	Paste item	Pastes the previously created copy of files or folders in the current location.
Folder, file	Color Label	Applies a label to the selected items.
Folder, file	Copy	Copies selected items.
Folder, file	Compress	Creates a Zip file containing the selected items.
Folder, file	Duplicate	Duplicates the selected items.
Folder, file	Make Alias	Creates an alias of the selected items.
Folder, file	Move to Trash	Moves the selected items to the Trash.
Folder, file	Open	Opens the selected item.
Mac OS X window toolbars	Customize Toolbar	Enables you to customize the current toolbar.
Mac OS X window toolbars	Toolbar Format commands	Use these to change the format of the toolbar, such as Text Only to hide the icons and display only text.
Mounted volume	Open Enclosing Folder	Opens the folder in which the selected item is stored.
Mounted volume	Rename	Enables you to rename the selected volume.
Sidebar item	Remove From Sidebar	Removes the selected item from the Places sidebar.

Finder's Action Menu

Every Finder window toolbar includes the Action menu, represented by a gear. This menu provides contextual commands that are similar to those you see on the contextual menus. When you select an item or view a folder, commands appropriate to that object appear on the menu (see Figure 1.5).

 note

Some applications, especially Apple applications, also provide an Action menu that is marked with the same gear icon.

Figure 1.5
The Action menu provides contextual commands; in this case, the commands are for the selected folder.

Working with the System Preferences Application

The System Preferences application enables you to configure options and settings for many areas of Mac OS X and some third-party applications and peripheral devices (see Figure 1.6). You can open the System Preferences utility in various ways, but the following two methods are the easiest:

- Select Apple, System Preferences.

- Click the System Preferences icon on the Dock.

The System Preferences window displays a collection of icons. To access the preferences for a specific area, click its icon. The System Preferences window changes to show a pane containing controls for that area. For example, if you click the Appearance icon, you see the Appearance preferences, as shown in Figure 1.7.

Figure 1.6
The System Preferences application enables you to configure and customize Mac OS X to suit your needs and personal preferences.

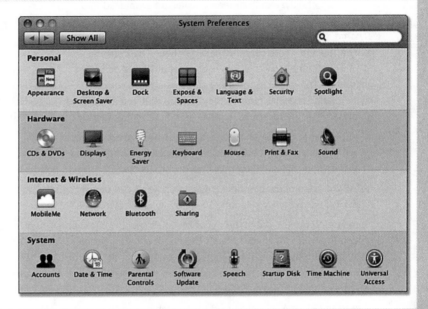

Figure 1.7
The Appearances pane of the System Preferences application enables you to customize various aspects of your system's visual appearance.

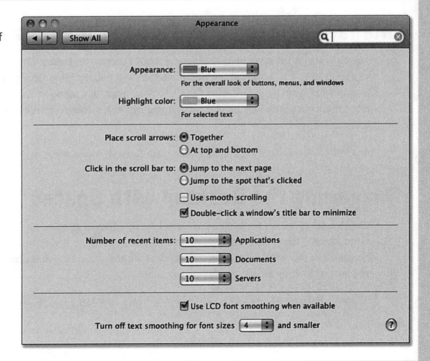

By default, the System Preferences icons are organized into four categories: Personal, Hardware, Internet & Wireless, and System. (If a third-party application or device has added icons, they appear in a fifth category called Other.) The Personal panes configure aspects of the user account that is currently logged in. The panes in the other three categories make system-wide changes (and so they require that you are logged in under or authenticate yourself as an administrator account).

If you prefer to display the icons in alphabetical order, select View, Organize Alphabetically. The categories disappear and the icons appear in alphabetical order (from left to right, top to bottom).

 note

Specific panes are covered in the parts of this book that explain the features they are related to. For example, the Accounts pane is explained in Chapter 21, Working with User Accounts."

After you have opened a pane, you can show all the panes of the window again by clicking the Show All button or by selecting View, Show All Preferences (⌘-L).

Some panes appear only when your Mac has specific capabilities, such as the Bluetooth pane, which appears only if your Mac is Bluetooth capable. When you add hardware or software to your system, additional panes can appear to enable you to configure the device or software you added. One example is the Ink pane, which appears when you attach a handwriting recognition device (such as a tablet) to your Mac.

Panes added by Apple-produced tools, such as the Bluetooth pane, appear within the related categories, such as Hardware. Panes added by third-party tools, such as keyboard customization panes, appear in the Other category.

Managing Open Windows with Exposé

As you work on the desktop, you'll open a lot of windows in Finder. Plus, each time you work with an application, you'll open at least one window, and usually more than one. All those windows add up to a lot of desktop clutter. Mac OS X's Exposé helps you manage open windows by being able to move them out of the way quickly so that you can easily focus on the specific windows you're interested in.

➥ *To learn about Exposé,* **see** *"Managing Open Windows with Exposé," p. 468.*

Managing the Desktop with Spaces

The Mac OS X Spaces feature enables you to create sets of applications and related windows and switch among those sets easily and quickly. Spaces are a great way to manage your desktop because you can work with groups of windows at the same time and change the context in which you are working by simply changing your space.

➥ *To learn about Spaces,* **see** *"Creating, Using, and Managing Spaces," p. 471.*

Customizing the Mac OS X Desktop

Although the default Mac OS X desktop is very nice to look at, you may want to customize it to suit your preferences. You can customize the appearance of your desktop in many ways, including the following:

- Change the clock

- Change mounted disk behavior

- Change the desktop icon size

- Change the desktop icon arrangement

- Set desktop pictures

 note

You can also change the Finder menu bar by adding menu extras to it, such as Displays, Volume, AirPort, and others. These menus are discussed in the related sections of this book. For example, you learn about the Displays menu in the section on configuring monitors using the Displays pane of the System Preferences application.

Changing the Clock Display

By default, Mac OS X provides a clock in the upper-right corner of the desktop. You can also configure the clock to be shown in a window that floats on the desktop if you prefer. You can control the appearance of the clock by using the System Preferences application:

1. Open the System Preferences application.

2. Click the Date & Time icon. The Date & Time pane appears.

3. Click the Clock tab (see Figure 1.8).

4. To hide the clock, deselect the Show the Date and Time in Menu Bar check box. Mac OS X removes the clock and disables all the clock options.

5. Select how you want the clock to be displayed:

- **Digital**—Select this option (it's the default) to see the time displayed as *hh:mm* AM/PM (where *hh* is the current hour and *mm* is the current minute).

- **Analog**—Select this option to display this time as a clock icon. Selecting this option disables most of the remaining clock check boxes, so skip to step 12.

 tip

A faster way to open the Date & Time pane is to click the menu bar clock and then click Date & Time Preferences.

tip

You can switch between the digital and analog clocks by clicking the menu bar clock and then clicking either View as Digital or View as Analog.

6. Select the Display the Time With Seconds check box to include the seconds in the display, so your digital display changes to *hh:mm:ss* AM/PM (where *ss* is the current second).

7. If you want the colon between the hour and minutes (and seconds, if you activated them in step 6) to blink on and off (somewhat like a real digital clock), select the Flash the Time Separators check box.

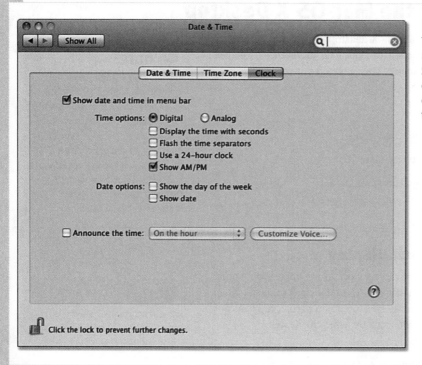

Figure 1.8
The Clock tab of the Date
& Time pane of the
System Preferences appli-
cation enables you to
customize the clock on
the desktop.

8. If you want to use a 24-hour clock, select the Use a 24-hour Clock check box. This means that a
   time such as 2:34 PM now appears as 14:34. (The Show AM/PM check box gets disabled if you
   select this option.)

9. If you want the AM/PM indicator to be shown when you use the 12-hour clock, select the Show
   AM/PM check box.

10. Select the Show the Day of the Week check box to include
    the day in the clock display.

11. Select the Show Date check box to include the date in the
    clock display.

12. If you want Mac OS X to announce the time, select the Announce the Time check box. Then
    select the time interval on the pop-up menu. Finally, click the Customize Voice button to select
    the voice used to announce the time.

tip

You can also display the date by
clicking the menu bar clock.

Changing the Desktop's Appearance

You can customize other aspects of the appearance of the desktop using the following steps:

1. Click an empty section of the desktop. This automatically switches you to Finder.

2. Select Finder, Preferences or press ⌘-, to open the Finder Preferences window.

3. Click the General tab.

4. Select the check boxes for the mounted items you want to appear on the desktop. Your choices are Hard Disks, External Disks, CDs, DVDs, iPods, and Connected Servers. If you deselect the check boxes, you don't see the items on your desktop; you can access these items through the Computer folder or within any Finder window. If you select the check boxes, the items appear on the desktop.

5. Close the Finder Preferences window.

6. Select View, Show View Options (or press ⌘-J) to open the Desktop dialog, which displays the view options window for the desktop.

7. Use the Desktop controls to configure how icons on the desktop appear. For example, click and drag the Icon Size slider to change how big the icons appear on the desktop.

   ➥ *To learn the details of these options, **see** "Customizing the Finder Window Views," **p. 62**.*

8. Close the Desktop dialog.

9. Right-click the desktop and then click Change Desktop Background to open the Desktop & Screen Saver pane of the System Preferences application. This pane has two tabs. The Desktop tab enables you to set your desktop picture; the Screen Saver tab enables you to configure the screen saver.

10. Click the Desktop tab (see Figure 1.9). The Image well shows the desktop picture currently being used. In the left pane of the window, the Source pane shows the available image collections. The right pane shows the images contained in the selected source.

11. Select the source containing the image you want to apply to the desktop. You have the following options:

    ▪ By default, Mac OS X includes several image collections (Desktop Pictures, Nature, Plants, Black & White, Abstract, and Solid Colors); these appear in the Apple collection at the top of the Source pane.

    ▪ Select the Solid Colors source to apply a color to the desktop.

 tip

If you just want to replace the current image with another one, drag the image you want to use onto the well. It replaces the image currently shown there and appears on the desktop immediately.

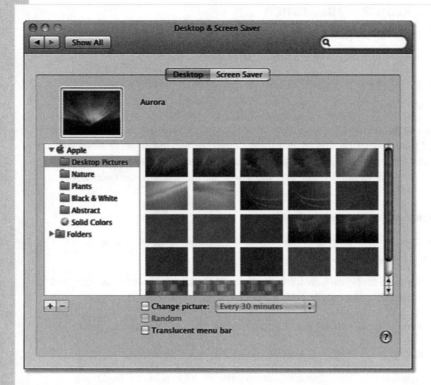

Figure 1.9
Use the Desktop tab to choose a picture or color to display on the Mac OS X desktop.

- The Folders source contains the Pictures folder from your Home folder. Click the Choose Folder option (+ sign at the bottom of the Source pane) to select another folder to use as a source of images.

- When you select a source, the images contained in the location appear in the preview pane in the right part of the window.

- When you select a folder, including the predefined ones, only the images at the root level of that folder are available on the preview pane. For example, if you select your Pictures folder, only the images that are loose in that folder are available. Any images contained within folders that are inside the Pictures folder are not available.

12. Apply the image to the desktop by clicking it on the preview pane. It appears in the Image well and on your desktop.

13. If you want to change desktop pictures automatically, select the Change Picture check box. The image in the well becomes the "recycle" icon to show that you have selected to have the system change images periodically. The images contained in the source selected in the Source pane will be applied to the desktop based on the criteria you configure.

14. Use the pop-up menu to select the time at which you want the images to be changed. The options include When Logging In, When Waking from Sleep, and a time interval from every five seconds to every day.

15. To have the images selected at random, select the Random Order check box. If you deselect this option, the images appear in the same order as they appear in the selected source (for example, alphabetically).

16. If you want the desktop image or color to show under the OS X menu bar, select the Translucent Menu Bar check box.

You can use just about any graphic file as a desktop image, such as JPEG, TIFF, and PICT files.

If you want to install images in the Apple collection in the Source pane so they appear by default, place them in the location Macintosh HD/Library/Desktop Pictures.

This folder contains the image sources that appear on the Desktop tab. You can add your images to the default folders, and they will appear in those sources. For example, if you add an image to Macintosh HD/Library/Desktop Pictures/Nature/, the image will appear when you click the Nature source in the Desktop tab. Unfortunately, you can't add sources to the Desktop tab by creating folders within the Desktop Pictures folder.

 note

If you use more than one monitor, each monitor has its own desktop picture. A Desktop Picture pane appears on each desktop. You use that pane to configure the desktop images on each monitor.

Restarting Your Mac

Although Mac OS X is very stable and you can generally leave it running for long periods, there are occasions when you need to restart your Mac to correct some problem. Also, occasionally, you'll need to restart your Mac after making system changes or installing new software.

You can restart Mac OS X in a couple of ways:

- Select Apple menu, Restart.

- On a notebook Mac, press the Power button briefly

Either way, select Restart in the resulting dialog box.

If Fast User Switching is enabled when you restart a Mac and other user accounts are logged in, you will see a warning dialog box. To be able to restart, you need to input an administrator user name and password and then click the Restart button.

➥ *To understand more about Fast User Switching, **see** "Enabling and Using Fast User Switching," p. 459.*

Shutting Down Your Mac

There isn't really much reason to turn a Mac off. Using the Energy Saver settings, you can configure your Mac to sleep when you aren't actively using it; this saves wear on the Mac's moving parts and theoretically saves energy (but I doubt it will make any difference in your electric bill!). Most of the time, when you're done working with your computer and you want to secure it, you should simply log out. This stops all the processes that are running and puts your Mac in a safe condition. Logging in is much faster because you don't have to wait for your computer to start up. Even better, select Login Window on the Fast User Switching menu to keep your account logged in and protected.

Still, if you are leaving your Mac for a long time, you might want to shut it down. You can do so in the following ways:

- Select Apple menu, Shut Down.

- On a notebook Mac, press the Power button briefly.

Either way, select Shut Down in the dialog box that appears.

If your Mac doesn't respond to any commands, you might need to perform a hard shutdown. Do so by pressing the Power key and holding it down until the Mac turns off. You won't have a chance to save any open files, so you should use this method only when all other options have failed and your Mac is locked up. A hard shutdown is definitely a last resort option, so use it only when you really need to.

Using Desktop Keyboard Shortcuts

Table 1.4 lists a few keyboard shortcuts that you may find useful when you're working with Finder.

Table 1.4   Keyboard Shortcuts for Finder

Keyboard Shortcut	Action
⌘-T	Add to Sidebar
Option-⌘-W	Close All
⌘-W	Close Window
⌘-K	Connect to Server
⌘-C	Copy item
⌘-X	Cut item
⌘-D	Duplicate
⌘-E	Eject
Shift-⌘-Delete	Empty Trash
Control-Eject	Display the Restart/Sleep/Shut Down confirmation dialog box
⌘-F	Find
Option-⌘-Esc	Force Quit
⌘-I	Get Info

Table 1.4 Continued

Keyboard Shortcut	Action
⌘-[	Go Back
⌘-]	Go Forward
Shift-⌘-A	Go to Applications Folder
Shift-⌘-C	Go to Computer Folder
⌘-up arrow	Go to Enclosing Folder
Shift-⌘-G	Go to Folder
Shift-⌘-H	Go to Home Folder
Shift-⌘-I	Go to iDisk Folder
Shift-⌘-K	Go to Network Folder
Shift-⌘-U	Go to Utilities Folder
⌘-H	Hide Finder
Option-⌘-T	Hide Toolbar
Shift-⌘-Q	Log Out (with confirmation)
Option-Shift-⌘-Q	Log Out (without confirmation)
⌘-?	Mac Help
⌘-L	Make Alias
⌘-M	Minimize Window
Option-⌘-M	Minimize All
⌘-Delete	Move to Trash
⌘-N	New Finder Window
Shift-⌘-N	New Folder
Option-⌘-N	New Smart Folder
⌘-O	Open
⌘-V	Paste item
⌘-,	Preferences
⌘-Y	Quick Look
Control-⌘-Eject	Restart (without confirmation, but you can save changes in open documents)
⌘-A	Select All
⌘-R	Show Original
⌘-J	Show View Options
Control-Option-⌘-Eject	Shut Down (without confirmation, but you can save changes in open documents)
Option-⌘-Eject	Sleep (without confirmation)
⌘-3	View as Columns
⌘-4	View as Cover Flow
⌘-1	View as Icons
⌘-2	View as List

2

GETTING TO KNOW THE DOCK

Introducing the Dock

When you see a picture of the Mac OS X desktop, one of the first things that leaps out at you is the colorful array of icons across the bottom of the screen. This is the Dock (see Figure 2.1), and it will be the starting point for many of your Mac adventures, so it's worth taking the time to get to know this important chunk of the Mac OS X landscape.

The first thing you need to know about the Dock is that it's actually split into two different sections. The dividing line is the Dock separator, the dotted line pointed out in Figure 2.1. The icons to the left of the separator represent applications. The icons to the right of the separator consist of your Documents and Downloads folders; icons for any open program, folder, and document windows that you have minimized; as well as the Trash/Eject icon.

The Dock is a versatile feature with many uses, but the following half-dozen are the most common and the most important:

- **Launching applications**—Clicking any Dock application icon immediately launches that application. (The application icons you see on the Dock aren't set in stone. As you learn a bit later—see "Adding an Icon to the Dock"—you can customize the Dock with icons for other applications, as well as for folders and documents.)

- **Restoring minimized windows**—Clicking any icon that represents a minimized program, folder, or document window immediately returns that window to the desktop.

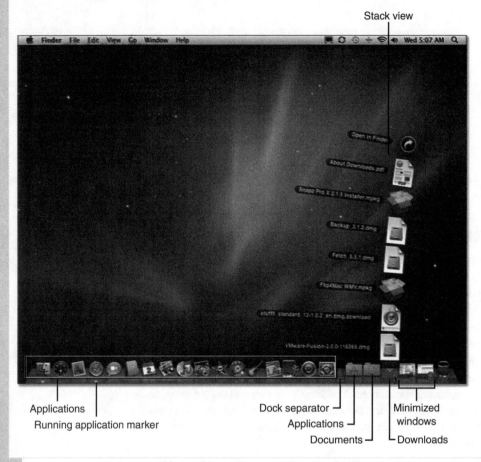

Figure 2.1
The Dock is an essential and iconic part of the Mac OS X interface.

- **Indicating the running applications**—When you click a Dock application icon, a small blue orb appears below the icon to indicate that the application is currently running (refer to Figure 2.1). If you launch any other application, that program's icon appears on the Dock along with the blue orb.

- **Providing application feedback**—The Dock also provides information about what's happening in running applications. For example, when you receive email, the Mail application's icon shows the number of messages you've received since you last read messages. Similarly, if an application requires your attention, its Dock icon bounces up and down.

- **Switching among open applications**—To switch to another running application, click its Dock icon. (You can also use the ⌘-Tab key and ⌘-Shift-Tab keyboard shortcuts to cycle through your running applications.)

- **Controlling an application**—Right-click (or Control-click with a one-button mouse) the icon of an open application to display a pop-up menu that lists commands such as Quit and Hide, as well as all the application's open windows; you can switch to a different window by selecting it from this menu.

 tip

You can also open a Dock icon's pop-up menu by clicking the Dock icon and holding down the mouse button. After a second or two, the Dock item's menu appears.

The default Dock is loaded with various icons, and the icon collection you see depends on the amount of horizontal screen space and the applications you have installed. For example, new Macs come with the iLife application suite installed, so the Docks on those Macs contain icons for iLife applications such as iPhoto, iMovie, and iDVD. If you're not sure what a Dock icon represents, hover the mouse pointer over the item and Mac OS X displays a ToolTip above the icon that shows the name of the item.

The default items on the Dock can include the following:

- **Finder**—If no Finder windows are currently open, the Finder icon opens a new Finder window that shows your default new Finder window location (which can be your Computer, Home folder, Documents folder, or just about any other location you choose). If at least one Finder window is open on the desktop, clicking the Finder icon while you're using another application takes you back to the Finder window that was most recently active.

  ➡ *To learn how to set your default new Finder window location,* ***see*** *"Configuring How New Finder Windows Open," p. 40.*

- **Dashboard**—This icon takes you to the Mac's Dashboard so you can use its widgets. You can also use its menu to access tools you can use to configure the Dashboard.

- **Mail**—Mail is Mac OS X's email application. When you receive email, an attention icon showing how many new messages you have received appears. If you open Mail's Dock icon menu while Mail is running, you can choose from several commands, such as Get New Mail and Compose New Message.

- **Safari**—This is Mac OS X's excellent web browser. Safari offers many great features, as you will learn later in this book. When you open the Safari Dock icon's menu, you can quickly jump to any web page that is open, among other things.

- **iChat**—This is Apple's instant messaging application, which you can use to communicate with others on your local network or over the Internet (it is compatible with AOL Instant Messenger and Google Talk) via text chats or audio/video conferencing.

- **Address Book**—Address Book is Mac OS X's contact manager application. You can store all sorts of information for everyone with whom you communicate, such as email addresses and phone numbers.

- **iCal**—You can use iCal to manage your calendar; it offers other cool features such as the ability to publish your calendar to the Web so other people can access it.

- **Preview**—The Preview application enables you to view photos, image files, PDFs, and other documents.

- **iTunes**—iTunes is the Mac's excellent digital music application. Its Dock menu offers selections you can use to control music playback.

- **Photo Booth**—If your Mac has a built in iSight camera or an attached digital camera or camcorder, you use Photo Booth to take a picture or record a video from the camera.

- **Time Machine**—Time Machine is the Mac OS X automated backup tool. When configured properly, the Time Machine icon in the Dock is how you can view the Time Machine interface and find the files and folders that you may have deleted.

➡ *To learn more about Time Machine,* **see** *"Backing Up Your Mac with Time Machine," p. 692.*

- **System Preferences**—The System Preferences application enables you to configure and customize various aspects of Mac OS X. You will be using it frequently, which is why its icon is included on the Dock by default.

- **Applications**—This icon represents the Applications folder in your Home directory, so it enables you to access your installed applications without having to open a Finder window.

- **Documents**—Mac OS X includes an icon on the Dock to take you to your Documents. Combined with the Stacks view, this is a very convenient way to get to the files you need.

The Stacks View

The Stacks view opens when you click on a folder in the Dock. Depending on the number of items in that folder, you will either see a vertical arc (or fan) of the icons in the folder (see Figure 2.1 for an example), or you will see a grid of the icons. You can also change the view by right-clicking (or holding down the Control key when clicking) on the folder in the Dock, then selecting an item in the View Content As section of the menu (Fan, Grid, List, or Automatic). Clicking an icon in the Stacks view will open that item.

- **Downloads**—This icon represents the Downloads folder located in your Home directory, which enables you to quickly access the items that you've recently downloaded from Safari and other applications.

- **Trash/Eject**—Use the Trash icon to delete applications, folders, and files. When the Trash contains files or folders, its icon includes crumpled paper so that you know the Trash is "full." When you click and drag an ejectable item such as an external hard disk, CD or DVD disc, or iPod, the Trash icon changes to the Eject symbol.

 tip

To have an application whose icon is on the Dock open automatically when you log in, open its Dock menu and choose Open at Login.

Using the Dock

I mentioned the half-dozen main uses for the Dock earlier, so let's take a closer look at some of those features. The next four sections take you through using the Dock to open items, switch windows, work with minimized items, and control items using the icon pop-up menus.

Opening Items with the Dock

Opening items using the Dock is straightforward: Click an icon to open whatever the item is. If the icon is for an application, that application opens (or becomes the active application if it's already running). If the item is a document, Mac OS X launches the application associated with that document type and then opens the document within that application. If the item is a folder, Mac OS X opens the folder in a new Finder window.

Unless the application is permanently installed on the Dock (in which case the icon remains in the same position), the icon for each application you open appears on the right edge of the application area of the Dock. As you open more applications, the existing application icons shift to the left and each icon becomes slightly smaller.

 note

When you click a non-running application's icon, you might notice that it "bounces" as the application opens. This lets you know that Mac OS X is busy opening your application. (The bouncing stops as soon as the application is fully loaded.) If all that bouncing bugs you, I'll show you how to turn it off later in this chapter (see "Customizing the Appearance and Behavior of the Dock").

Switching Windows

To switch to another running application, click that application's Dock icon.

If you'd prefer to use the keyboard to switch windows, press ⌘-Tab instead. As long as you hold down the ⌘ key, a menu appears across the center of the screen (see Figure 2.2). This menu displays an icon for each open application. The icons are listed in the order in which you have most recently used the applications, with the current application shown on the left side of the menu. With ⌘ held down, each time you press Tab, Mac OS X highlights the next icon in the menu and you see the application's name below its icon. When you release the ⌘ key, the currently highlighted icon's application becomes active (and visible, if it is hidden). You can move backward through the open applications on the menu by continuing to hold down the ⌘ key and pressing Shift-Tab.

If you press ⌘-Tab without holding down the ⌘ key, the menu won't appear; instead you switch immediately to the application you used before the current application. For example, suppose you checked your messages in Mail and then switched back to Word. If you press ⌘-Tab, you jump back into Mail; if you press ⌘-Tab again, you switch back to Word.

 note

If an application is open but the window in which you want to work is minimized, when you select that application with the ⌘-Tab shortcut, you will move into the application, but any windows that are minimized will not appear on the desktop because they are minimized. You have to click a minimized window's icon on the Dock for it to move back onto the desktop.

Figure 2.2
This menu of open applications appears when you hold down the ⌘ key and press the Tab key.

The Dock and Minimizing Windows

Unlike open applications, open documents don't automatically appear on the Dock. Document icons appear on the Dock only when you add them to the Dock manually or when you have minimized the document's window. Remember that when you open an application's menu in the Dock, you see a list of all the windows open in that application. You can then choose a listed window (such as a document window) to move into it.

When you minimize a window, it moves into the Dock as an
icon that shows a thumbnail view of the window. The icon for a minimized window behaves just as icons for other items do. To return a window to the desktop, click its icon on the Dock.

Minimized windows are marked with the related application's icon in the lower-right corner of the Dock icon so you can easily tell from which application the windows come. For example, minimized Finder windows have the Finder icon in the lower-right corner, minimized Safari icons have the Safari icon, and so on.

 note

Just as with all icons on the Dock, the names of folders, minimized windows, and documents are shown above their icons when you point to them.

When you minimize an application window, it is moved onto the Dock, just like any other window. However, when you hide an application, its open windows do not appear on the Dock. The hidden application's icon continues to be marked with the blue orb, so you know that the application is running. You can open a hidden application's Dock menu to jump into one of its open windows.

 tip

You can quickly minimize an open window by pressing ⌘-M.

Working with Icon Pop-Up Menus

Just as with an application's icon, if you point to a folder or a document icon on the Dock and right-click or Control-click it, a pop-up menu appears. What you see on this menu depends on what you clicked.

When you use Dock icon menus, the following outcomes are possible:

 tip

Remember that if you don't want to use the right button on your mouse or press the Control key while you click, just click an icon and hold down the mouse button. The menu will appear after a second or two.

- If you open the menu for the Finder Dock icon, the pop-up menu shows a list of all the open Finder windows, whether the windows are minimized or are on the desktop. Select a window on the menu to make it active. If you are working in another application, you can also select Hide to hide all open Finder windows.

- If you open the Dock menu for a closed application, folder, or document, you see the Show In Finder command, which opens a Finder window containing the item on which you clicked; the item is selected when the Finder window containing it appears. This can be a quick way to find out where something is located. You can also choose the Open command to open the item, the Open at Login command to have the item opened when you log in, and the Remove from Dock command to remove the icon from the Dock (only for icons that are actually stored on the Dock, of course).

- If you open the Dock menu for a folder, you can specify how the Stacks view should display the items in the folder. You can select to view the stack as a fan or a grid, and you can determine how the items should be sorted. The Stack view is a great way to make access to items within specific folders fast and easy.

- If you point to a URL reference or other item (such as a minimized document window) on the Dock, identification text appears above the icon to explain what the item is. If the icon is for a document, you can open the document by selecting Open on its Dock menu.

tip

If you fill the Dock with several open applications, documents, and folders, it can be a nuisance to switch to each item and close it. Instead, log out (either select Apple menu, Log Out, or press Shift-⌘-Q). When you log out, all open applications are shut down, all documents are closed, and all minimized folder windows are removed from the Dock. When you log back in, the Dock is back to normal. All Finder windows that were on the Dock are gone from there, but they remain open on the desktop. Hold down the Option key and click the Close box of one of the open windows to close them all.

■ If you open the Dock menu for an open application, you see some basic commands, including Quit. You also see a list of open windows; you can quickly jump to an open window by selecting it. Some applications also enable you to control what is happening from the Dock menu. For example, when iTunes is open, you can control music playback by using its Dock menu.

When you quit an open application, its icon disappears from the Dock—unless you have added that application to the Dock so that it always appears there. Minimized windows disappear from the Dock when you maximize them or when you close the application from which the document window comes.

Customizing the Dock

The default Dock is certainly useful enough, but if you want to get the most out of this powerful resource, you need to customize the Dock to include the items that you use most often and to organize the Dock to suit your style and the way you work. You can move Dock icons to make them more easily accessible; you can add applications, folders, and documents to the Dock to get one-click access to your favorite items; and you can remove Dock icons that you no longer need.

Moving Icons on the Dock

You can change the location of any Dock icon by dragging it left or right. When you drag an icon between two others, they slide apart to make room for the icon you're moving. However, you can't move most icons across the Dock separator; for example, you can't move an application icon to the right side of the Dock.

The Dock has two icons you can't move at all: Finder and Trash/Eject. The Finder icon always appears on the left end of the Dock (or top if you use a vertical Dock), and the Trash is always on the right end (or bottom if you use a vertical Dock). Other than these two end points, you can change all the other icons on the Dock as much as you like.

 tip

You can add multiple items to the Dock at the same time by holding down the ⌘ key while you select each item you want to add to the Dock and then drag it there.

Adding an Icon to the Dock

You can add applications, folders, and files to the Dock so it contains the items you want. Drag the item you want to add down to the Dock and drop it where you want it to be installed. Application icons must be placed to the left of the Dock separator, and all others (folders and files) are placed on the right side. Just as when you move icons on the Dock, when you add items between other icons already installed on it, the other icons slide apart to make room for them. When you add an item to the Dock, an alias to that item is created and you see its icon on the Dock.

 tip

If you move the icon of an open application that isn't installed on the Dock, that icon moves to the location to which you drag it and becomes installed on the Dock. You can add multiple items to the Dock at the same time by holding down the ⌘ key while you select each item you want to add to the Dock and then drag it there.

Removing Items from the Dock

You can remove an icon from the Dock by dragging it up onto the desktop. When you do this, the icon disappears in a puff of digital smoke and no longer appears on the Dock. Because the icons on the Dock are aliases, removing them doesn't affect the applications or files that those aliases represent.

If you drag a minimized window from the Dock, it snaps back to the Dock when you release the mouse button. You remove minimized windows from the Dock by maximizing or closing them.

 tip

When you open an application whose icon is not installed on the Dock, its Dock menu includes the Keep in Dock command. If you choose this, the icon is added to the Dock.

Adding Folders to the Dock

You can also add any folder to the Dock; when you click a folder's Dock icon, the contents of the folder are displayed in the Stack view by default. (To use the Folder view, instead, Control-click or right-click the folder icon and then click Folder.)

When you place a folder on the Dock, you can click its Dock icon to list the contents of that folder (refer to Figure 2.3), and you can click Open in Finder to display the folders's contents in a new Finder window.

Figure 2.3
Click a folder icon on the Dock to see the contents of that folder, such as the Pictures folder shown here.

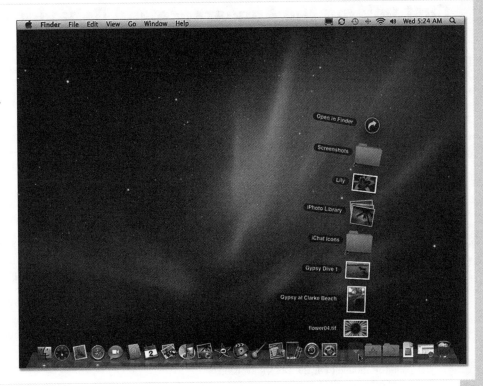

This feature is one of the most useful that the Dock offers. You can use it to create custom menus containing anything on your Mac (literally). Here are some ideas:

- Add your Home directory to the Dock so you can easily move to an item within it.

- Add your project folders to the Dock so you can easily get to the files you need for the project on which you are working.

- Create a folder that has aliases to your frequently used programs or documents. After you place that folder on the Dock, you will be able to get to those items very quickly.

You might find that adding folders to the Dock is even more useful than adding application or file icons to it. Remember that you can make more room on the Dock by removing items that you don't use from it. For example, you might choose to remove most or all of the application icons from the Dock and instead add the Applications folder to it.

 note

Although adding folders to the Dock is useful, it can be easier and just as useful to add folders to the sidebar in Finder windows. The benefit to adding folders to the Dock is that you can access them without bringing the Finder to the front.

Customizing the Appearance and Behavior of the Dock

The Dock offers several options you can change to suit your preferences. You can also change various aspects of its appearance, as follows:

- **Size**—You can change the default or current size of the Dock.

- **Magnification**—The magnification effect causes items on the Dock to be magnified when you point to them. This can make identifying items easier, especially when many items are on the Dock or when it is small (see Figure 2.4). You can set the amount of magnification that is used.

- **Hide/Show**—The Dock does consume some screen space. Because it is always topmost, it can get in the way when you are working near its location on the screen. You can set the Dock so that it is hidden except when you point to it. When this behavior is enabled and you point to the Dock's location, it pops onto the desktop and you can use it. When you move off the Dock, it is hidden again.

If the Dock is hidden, you need to hover a moment in the area of the screen in which it is located before it will appear. This prevents the Dock from popping up when you are working in a document near the edge of the screen and pass the mouse over the Dock's location.

 note

If you hide the Dock, that doesn't mean it won't try to catch your eye when a running application requires your attention. If the Dock is hidden when this occurs (say, an error dialog pops up), the application's icon will bounce up and down until you switch to that application to see what it needs.

- **Dock location**—The Dock can appear at its default location on the bottom of the screen, or you can move it to the left or right side of the desktop.

- **Minimize Effect**—You can choose either the Genie Effect (windows minimize to the Dock using a swirling effect reminiscent of a genie going back into its lamp) or the Scale Effect (windows minimize to the Dock by gradually getting smaller).

- **Icon animation**—You already know about this one because it is on by default. When you click an application's icon to open that application, the icon bounces to show you that the application is opening.

 note

The amount of magnification is not relative to the size of the Dock. For example, the magnified icons are the same size whether the Dock is large or small. Of course, because the Dock size is different, the magnified icons do make more contrast with a smaller Dock, but that is only because of the comparison your eye makes.

Figure 2.4
The magnification effect makes identifying items easier, although the magnification level of this particular Dock would be a bit much for most Mac users.

You can control these settings using the Dock pane of the System Preferences utility by doing the following:

1. Open the System Preferences application by clicking its icon on the Dock.

2. Click Dock to open the Dock pane of the utility (see Figure 2.5).

3. Use the Size slider to set the default size of the Dock. Using the Size slider changes the size of the Dock as well as the items on it. The best practice is to configure the Dock with the items you want it to contain. Then, use this slider to set its size when it contains those items. As you add items to it, it gets wider or taller until it fills the screen. After the Dock has expanded to the width of the screen, the items on it get smaller as you add more items to the Dock.

 tip

You can also open the Dock preferences pane by selecting Apple menu, Dock, Dock Preferences. The Dock command on the Apple menu also enables you to quickly turn Dock magnification and hiding on or off; you can also change its location by selecting the location where you want it to be.

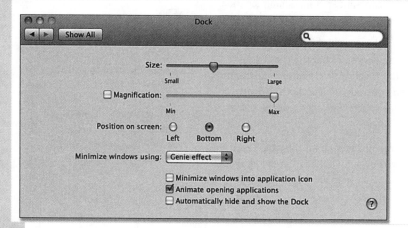

Figure 2.5
Use the Dock pane of the
System Preferences util-
ity to configure the
appearance and behavior
of the Dock.

4. Activate the Magnification check box to turn on Dock magnification, and then use the slider to set the amount of
magnification.

5. Click the Left, Bottom, or Right radio button to set the
Dock's location on the desktop.

6. In the Minimize Windows Using pop-up menu, choose the
minimize/maximize effect; the options are Genie Effect or
Scale Effect.

7. If you activate the Minimize Windows Into Application Icon
check box, Mac OS X no longer adds minimized windows
to the right side of the Dock (which is great for reducing Dock clutter). To restore a minimized
window, Control-click or right-click the application icon and then click the window title.

8. If you prefer that application icons not bounce when the application opens, deactivate the
Animate Opening Applications check box.

9. Activate the Automatically Hide and Show the Dock check box if you want the Dock to be visible
only when you move the mouse pointer to the bottom of the screen.

All Dock settings are specific to each user account, meaning that each user can have her own items
installed on her Dock, configure the Dock to be hidden, and so on. One user's Dock settings do not
affect any other user's Dock.

 tip

You can also change the size of the
Dock by pointing to the line that divides
the application side of the Dock from
the document and folder side. When
you do so, the cursor becomes a horizontal line with vertical arrows pointing
from the top and bottom sides. Drag
this cursor up to make the Dock larger
or down to make it smaller.

Using Dock Keyboard Shortcuts

Dock-related keyboard shortcuts are listed in Table 2.1.

Table 2.1 Keyboard Shortcuts for the Dock

Action	Keyboard Shortcut
Turn hiding off or on	Option-⌘-D
Move to the next open application	⌘-Tab
Move to the previous open application	Shift-⌘-Tab
Minimize a window	⌘-M
Highlight/unhighlight the Dock	Control-F3
Move among Dock items when it is highlighted	Left/Right arrow keys

 note

If you're using a notebook Mac, you might need to press the Function key (fn) to cause its function keys to act like true function keys. For example, on some mobile Macs, the F3 key controls volume unless you press the fn key, in which case it acts like the F3 key.

3

GETTING TO KNOW MAC OS X FINDER WINDOWS

Learning Finder Window Basics

You'll spend most of your Mac OS X time doing things that are creative, fun, entertaining, and educational, which is as it should be, because your Mac is eminently suited to all of those worthy activities. However, you'll also spend a significant amount of Mac OS X time on activities that are, to be honest, not so fun and interesting. I'm talking here about the day-to-day tasks associated with your files, folders, discs, removable drives, and hard drives. This is the less glamorous and cool side of Mac OS X, but it's a side you can't avoid.

Fortunately, these workaday Mac chores are made easier by Finder, which is the application you use to work with everything from files to drives. This section introduces you to all the basic Finder techniques you'll need. To get you started, Figure 3.1 points out the major features of a typical Finder window.

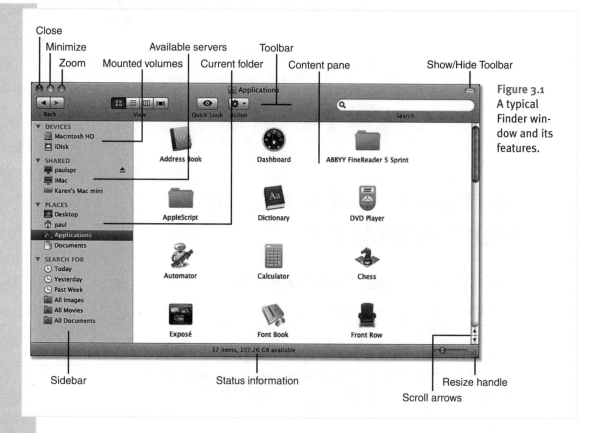

Figure 3.1
A typical Finder window and its features.

Opening Finder Windows

You can open Finder windows in several ways. If you click the Finder icon on the Dock, one of two things can happen:

- If no Finder windows are currently open, a new Finder window appears showing the contents of the default location you select (initially, this is your Home folder, but you can select any folder you'd like).

- If at least one Finder window is already open, Finder displays the window you used most recently.

You can also open a new Finder window by selecting File, New Finder Window (⌘-N). When you open a new Finder window, you see the contents of your default location (this is initially set to be your Home folder).

The Mac OS X Finder uses a web-like model in that each new Finder window you open starts a "chain" of windows (thus, the Back and Forward buttons in the Finder window toolbar). The first window in every new chain you start by using the New Finder Window command is always the folder you define as the default. You can have many window chains open at the same time, which is another similarity to web windows. (You can quickly jump into specific folders using the toolbar, the Sidebar, the Go menu, and keyboard shortcuts.)

➥ *To learn how to navigate Finder windows,* ***see*** *"Navigating Finder Windows,"* ***p. 50.***

By default, when you open an item (such as a folder), its contents replace the contents of the previous item that appeared in the Finder window you were viewing. (You can change this behavior globally with a preference setting.) You can also override this behavior so the new Finder window is separate from the first one by holding down the ⌘ key while you double-click an icon. This opens a new chain of Finder windows, with the contents of the item you opened displayed in the first window.

 tip

This default behavior assumes that the toolbar and Sidebar are shown in a Finder window. If not, opening a folder always opens a new, separate chain of Finder windows.

After you have one Finder window open, you can open other Finder windows (either in the same chain of windows or by starting a new chain) to view the contents of a different folder, volume, disc, and so on. To view the contents of a folder, volume, or disc shown in the current Finder window, double-click the icon for the item you want to open, or select an item and select File, Open (or press ⌘-O). The contents of the item you opened replace the window's current contents and the name shown at the top of the window becomes the name of the item you opened.

You can also choose different views for Finder windows. When you open a new Finder window, it always assumes the view you selected the last time you viewed that item in a Finder window. You'll learn more about Mac OS X Finder window views later in this chapter.

To reiterate this sometimes confusing behavior of Mac OS X windows, the view in which a new window opens is determined by the view you used for that window the last time you viewed it. In other words, windows retain their view settings, even if the window from which you opened a separate Finder window is different. For example, if you viewed the Applications folder in List view, it appears in List view whenever you open it in a new Finder window until you change the view in which it appears.

Along the left edge of every Finder window is the Sidebar. This handy tool consists of several sections. In the Devices section are all the volumes mounted on your Mac, including hard disk volumes, disk image volumes, your iDisk, CDs, DVDs, and so on. The Shared section will display icons for the servers that are available on your local area network (LAN). In the Places section of the sidebar are some of the folders in your Home folder and the Applications folder. You can add any folders, applications, documents, or other files to or remove them from this area to completely customize it. Finally, the Search For section of the sidebar allows you to quickly find content based on predetermined searches, and you can also store smart folders and Spotlight searches here. The purpose of the Sidebar is to enable you to quickly open a Finder window that displays the contents of any item it contains.

note

If you select an item while a Finder window is in the Column view, its contents are displayed in a new column.

 tip

If you hold down the ⌘ key while you click an item in the Sidebar, that item opens in a new Finder window chain. If you hold down the Option key when you click an item in the Sidebar, that item opens in a new Finder window and the previous window closes.

When you select a volume or folder in the Sidebar, its contents appear in the Finder window. The currently selected item is highlighted, so you can easily tell what is selected. (The name of the currently selected item appears at the top of the window as well.) If you select a document or application, that item opens just as it does when you double-click it.

Configuring How New Finder Windows Open

To configure how Finder windows open, perform the following steps:

1. Select Finder, Preferences or press ⌘-,. When the Finder Preferences window opens, click the General tab if it isn't selected already (see Figure 3.2).

Figure 3.2
Use the General pane of the Finder Preferences window to configure how new Finder windows open.

2. On the New Finder Windows Open pop-up menu, select the location where you want new Finder window chains you open to start.

On the pop-up menu, you see various volumes mounted on your Mac along with your Home and Documents folders. To choose one of these as the starting location for new Finder window chains, simply select it on the menu.

To select a location not shown on the pop-up menu, choose Other. Then use the Choose a Folder dialog box to move to and choose the folder that you want to be your starting place. Navigating such dialog boxes is very much like navigating in a Finder window in the Column view.

3. If you prefer that when you open an item, the item's contents always appear in a new Finder window chain, activate the Always Open Folders in a New Window check box. However, because this option can lead to a proliferation of Finder windows, I recommend that you leave this option off. (Remember that you can always open a new Finder window chain by holding down the ⌘ key when you double-click an item.) A better way to view content is to use the Column view, which enables you to quickly move to any location, as you will see later in this chapter.

➥ *To learn more about Mac OS X folders,* **see** *"Understanding the Standard Mac OS X Folders," p. 71.*

 note

One of the nice features of Mac OS X is that most preference changes are made in real time—you don't have to close the Preferences window to see the results of your changes. For example, when you make the change in the previous steps, the window-opening behavior becomes active as soon as you make a selection on the pop-up menu. A good habit is to leave preference windows open as you make changes and close the windows only when you are happy with all the changes you have made.

Working with Spring-Loaded Folders

Mac OS X Finder windows can be *spring-loaded* (this feature is turned on by default), meaning that they pop open when you drag an item onto a closed folder. This enables you to quickly place an item within nested folders without having to open each folder individually. Simply drag an item onto a closed folder so the folder is highlighted and "springs" open. After the delay time (which you can set) has passed, the highlighted folder opens in a separate Finder window chain (unless you are viewing the window in Column view, in which case a new column appears for the item onto which you are dragging the item). You can then drag the item onto the next folder and continue the process until you have placed it in its final destination. When you release the mouse button, what happens depends on the Finder preference you have selected. If new folders open in the same Finder window, you remain in the location in which you placed the item. If new folders always open in a new Finder window, you return to the window in which you started (however, the destination folder will remain open in its Finder window).

 tip

You can cause a folder to spring open immediately by pressing the spacebar when you drag an item onto a closed folder.

You can configure your Mac's spring-loaded behavior by following these steps:

1. Click the General tab in the Finder Preferences dialog box.

2. Activate the Spring-Loaded Folders and Windows check box to turn this feature back on if you have turned it off (it is on by default).

3. Use the Delay slider to set the amount of delay time (the time between when you drag an item onto a folder and when that folder springs open).

Scrolling Finder Windows

When the contents of a Finder window can't be shown in the amount of space the window currently has, you use the scrollbars to view contents that are out of sight. You have the following options:

- Drag the scrollbars.

- Click above or below or to the left or right of the bar to scroll one screen's worth at a time.

- Click the scroll arrows.

- Press the Page Up and Page Down keys to scroll vertically.

- Press the Home key to jump to the top of the window or the End key to jump to the bottom.

- Use the arrow keys or Tab (and Shift-Tab) to move among the items in the window (which also scrolls the window when you move outside the current view).

 note

The length of the scrollbar is proportional to the amount of the window you can see in the view. For example, if most of the scrollbar is filled in with color, you can view most of the window's contents. If the colored portion is relatively small, you can't view very much of the window's content.

You can modify several aspects of scrolling behavior. You can change the location of the scroll arrows. Also, rather than moving an entire page each time you click above, below, to the left, or to the right of a scrollbar, you can set the scrolling such that you move to the relative location you click instead. You can also turn on smooth scrolling, which smoothes out the appearance of a window when you scroll in it. Follow these steps to modify these scrolling features:

1. Open the System Preferences application.

2. In the Personal section, click Appearance.

3. Choose one of the following options to change the location of the scroll arrows:

   - **Together**—Select this option to place the scroll arrows beside each other, either at the bottom of a vertical scrollbar (see Figure 3.1, earlier), or to the right of a horizontal scroll bar.

   - **At Top and Bottom**—Select this option to place the scroll arrows above and below a vertical scrollbar (see Figure 3.3) or to the left and right of a horizontal scrollbar.

4. Choose one of the following options to change how scrolling works when you click in the scrollbar:

   - **Jump to the Next Page**—Select this radio button to scroll a screen at a time.

   - **Jump to the Spot That's Clicked**—Select this radio button to move to a position in the window that's relative to where you click in the scrollbar.

5. Activate the Use Smooth Scrolling check box to turn on smooth scrolling.

 tip

This is a good chance to practice Mac OS X preference-setting techniques. Make your changes to the Appearance pane, but leave the System Preferences application open. Click in a Finder window; your changes immediately become active. If you are satisfied, jump back to the System Preferences application and quit it. If not, jump back into the Appearance pane and continue making changes until you are satisfied.

Scroll arrows

Figure 3.3
You can con-
figure Finder
to place the
scroll arrows
at opposite
ends of a
scrollbar.

Resizing Finder Windows

To change the size of a window, drag its Resize handle (pointed out earlier in Figure 3.1) until the window is the size you want it to be.

You can also use the Zoom button to make a window large enough to display all the items it contains or until it fills the screen, whichever comes first. Click the button and the window jumps to the size it needs to be to show all the items it contains or until it fills the available screen space. Click the button again to return it to its previous size.

You can also use this button to quickly swap between two sizes for a window. Make the window a size you like. When you click the Zoom button, it expands to its maximum size. Click the button again and it returns to the previous size. Each time you click the Zoom button, the window returns to the size it was previously (either the maximum size or the size you set).

If you have a lot of Finder windows open on the Desktop, you can use this resizing behavior to make working between multiple windows more convenient. Select an open window and make it the size you want it to be so it is out of the way and you can store many windows of this size on your desktop; make it just large enough that you can see the window's title. You can click the Zoom button to open the window to work in it. Then, click the Zoom button again to return the window to its small size. Use the button to toggle between the two sizes. When you need to work in the window, make it large by clicking the Zoom button. When you are done, click the button again to make it small. You might find this even more convenient than minimizing windows (which you'll learn about shortly).

Resizing the Panes of Finder Windows

As you learned earlier, Finder windows have two panes. The left pane is the Sidebar, whereas the right pane is the Contents pane, which displays the contents of the item you are viewing in the Finder window. You can change the relative size of the Sidebar by dragging the line that is located between the two panes. Drag this to the left and the Sidebar takes up less room in the window. Drag it to the right and the Sidebar takes up more window space.

The Sidebar retains your settings as long as you work within the same Finder window chain. When you open a new chain, the Sidebar becomes its default size.

Closing, Minimizing, and Maximizing Finder Windows

Among the most distinctive features of Mac OS X are the three stoplight-type controls located in the upper-left corner of windows (refer to Figure 3.1). The red button (on the far left) closes the window. The gold button (in the middle) minimizes the window, which shrinks it and moves it to the right side of the Dock. The green button maximizes the window, which makes it as large as it needs to be to display all the items in the window until that window fills the screen (and returns it to the previous size, as you learned in the previous section).

⇒ *To learn how to use the Dock,* **see** *Chapter 2, "Getting to know the Dock," p. 23.*

The Close, Minimize, and Zoom buttons work even if the window on which they appear is not active. For example, you can close a window that is in the background by clicking its Close button without making the window active first. (When you point to a button on an inactive window, the button becomes colored so that you know it is active, even though the window itself is not.)

 tip

It's also possible to configure Mac OS X to minimize a window by double-clicking in its title bar. To set this up open the Appearance pane of the System Preferences application and activate the Double-Clicking a Window's Title Bar to Minimize check box

 tip

You can close all open Finder windows by holding down the Option key while you click the Close button in one of the open windows.

Moving Finder Windows

You can move a Finder window around the desktop by dragging its title bar or its status bar.

Using the Finder Window Views

note

If the Sidebar is collapsed, you can't move the window by dragging its status bar. Only the title bar is visible to be able to move the window.

You can display the contents of a Finder window in four different views: Icon, List, Column, and Cover Flow.

Using the Icon View

You can view Finder windows in the Icon view by clicking the Icon view button in the toolbar; by selecting View, As Icons; or by pressing ⌘-1. The objects in the window become icons, as shown in Figure 3.4.

Figure 3.4
A folder window in Icon view.

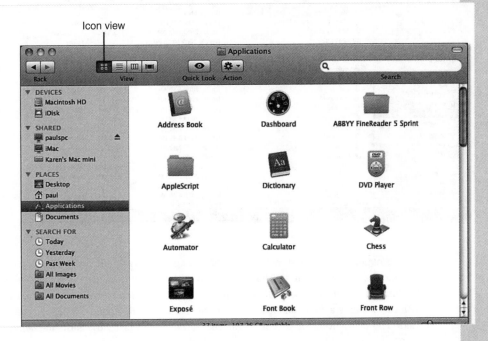

➡ *You can customize the Icon view for Finder windows. **See** "Customizing Finder Windows," p. 56.*

If you find that a window in the Icon view is messy, you can use the Clean Up command (View, Clean Up) to straighten up the window for you. This command neatly arranges icons so they line up in an orderly fashion.

To arrange icons by a specific criterion, select View, Arrange By, and then select the criterion by which you want the window's icons ordered. Your options are the following: Name, Date Modified, Date Created, Size, Kind, or Label.

 tip

If you select one or more icons and open the View menu, you'll see that the command is now Clean Up Selection. This places the selected items back in an orderly location.

Although the Icon view is clearly the most pleasing view to look at, it is one of the least useful in terms of the information you see.

Using the List View

The List view presents more information than does the Icon view (see Figure 3.5). To switch to the List view, click the List view button; select View, as List; or press ⌘-2.

PART 1

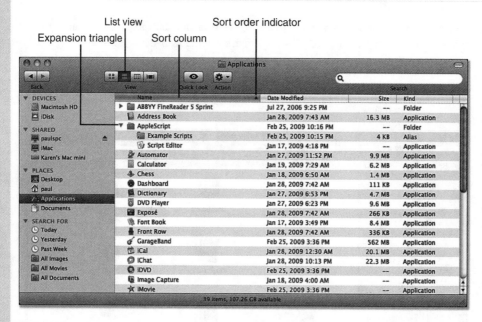

Expansion triangle | List view | Sort column | Sort order indicator

Figure 3.5
List view—At the top of the window are the same controls that are visible in the Icon view. However, the lower part of the window contains more information than is available in the Icon view.

The information in the List view is organized into columns, with a header at the top of the column indicating the information in it. The information in the List view is always sorted—you can select the column that is used to sort the contents of the window. You can also determine the order in which the columns appear, change the width of columns, and expand or collapse the contents of folders. The information for each item you see in the default List view is the following:

- **Name**—This is the filename for files, the folder name for folders, the volume name for volumes, and so on.

- **Date Modified**—The most recent date and time on which the object was changed. If the date is recent, it's indicated by a relative term, such as "Yesterday."

- **Size**—The size of the item, in kilobytes (KB), megabytes (MB), or gigabytes (GB). By default, the size of folders is not calculated (you can set Mac OS X to calculate folder sizes if that information is important to you).

- **Kind**—The type of object it is, such as folder, document, application, volume, and so on.

➥ *You can customize the List view for a single window or for all windows.* ***See*** *"Customizing Finder Windows," p. 56.*

The column by which the window is sorted is highlighted with the highlight color (blue or graphite). To change the sort column, click the column heading of the column by which you want the list to be sorted. That heading is highlighted and the list is re-sorted by that criterion. At the right edge of the column heading for the column by which the window is sorted, you see the Sort order indicator. This shows you in which direction the list is sorted. For example, if the list is sorted by the Name column, an up arrow indicates that the list is sorted alphabetically and a down arrow indicates that the list is sorted in reverse alphabetical order. To change the direction of the sort, click the Column heading—the list is sorted in the opposite order (from ascending to descending or from descending to ascending).

You can resize a column by moving the pointer to the right edge of the column heading cell and clicking. When you do, the cursor changes from the pointer to a vertical line with outward-facing arrows on each side of it. When you see this cursor, drag the column border to resize the column.

You can change the order in which columns appear by dragging the column heading of the column you want to move and dropping it in the new location. The columns reshuffle and then appear in the order you have indicated.

One of the other benefits of the List view is that you can expand the contents of a folder so you can view them without having to open the folder's window first. To do this, click the right-facing expansion triangle next to the folder's name (see Figure 3.5). The folder expands, and its contents are listed in the window. Click the triangle again to collapse the folder down to its icon.

 note

You can't change the location of the Name column; it is always the first column in a window in List view.

 tip

When you Option-click the expansion triangle for a collapsed folder, the folder and all the folders it contains are expanded. When you Option-click the expansion triangle for an expanded folder, the folder and all its contents are collapsed again.

Using the Column View

You can use the Coloumn view to quickly see and navigate levels of the hierarchy (see Figure 3.6). To switch to the Column view, click the Column view button on the toolbar; select View, as Columns; or press ⌘-3.

As you might suspect, in the Column view, the window is organized into columns, with each column representing a level of the file organization hierarchy. The leftmost column shows the highest level you can see, each column to its right shows the next level down the structure, and the column on the far right shows the lowest level you can see. When you select a file, the rightmost column shows a preview of the selected file. The "path" at which you are looking is indicated by the highlighted items in each column.

 note

One reason the Column view is so important is that you use this view to navigate within Open, Save, and other dialog boxes. When you are using the Column view in dialog boxes, it works just as it does in Finder windows.

Folder icons have a right-facing arrow at the right edge of the column in which they appear, to indicate that when you select them, their contents appear in the column to the immediate right.

Column view

Preview of selected item

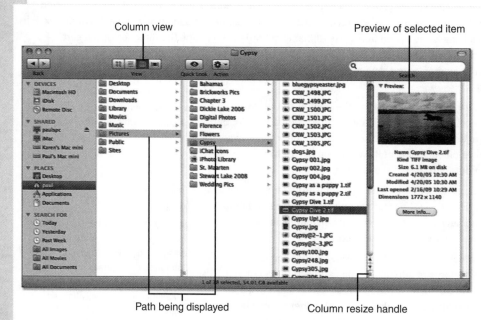

Figure 3.6
The Column view is a great way to see the hierarchical organization of folders and files.

Path being displayed

Column resize handle

For example, put a Finder window in the Column view and click your Home folder on the Sidebar to see its contents. The Home folder's contents are shown in the first column in the window. If you click one of the folders in your Home folder, it becomes highlighted and its contents appear in one of the middle columns. As you select folders within folders, their contents appear in the column to their right. This continues all the way down into a folder until it contains no more folders.

You can move down into the hierarchy by clicking the item about which you want more detail. The column to the right of the item on which you click shows the contents of what you click. If you click something in the right column and the window is not large enough to display the contents of all the columns, the view shifts and the columns appear to move to the left. You can use this approach to quickly see the contents of any folder on your Mac, no matter how far down in the hierarchy it is stored.

 tip

One of the best reasons to use the Column view is that you can move inside a window with the arrow keys on the keyboard. This is the fastest way to move among the folders and files on your Mac.

When there are more columns than can be displayed in the window, you can use the horizontal scrollbars to view all the columns. Scrolling to the left moves up the hierarchy, whereas scrolling to the right moves down the hierarchy. You can also make the window larger to view more columns at the same time.

You can resize the width of the columns in a window by dragging the resize handle located in the lower-right corner of each column. Each column in a window can have a different width.

When you click a file to select it, the far-right column shows a large icon or a preview of the file and information about that file is displayed (refer to Figure 3.6).

If you click document files for which Mac OS X can create a preview, you see the preview in the column. If the file you select has dynamic content, you can play that content in the preview that you see in the Column view. For example, if you select a QuickTime movie, you can click the play or pause button that appears over the preview when you move your mouse above it to watch the movie without opening the file. Certain types of text files are also displayed so you can read them (arrows appear on the preview to enable you to read the entire document). You can also see large thumbnail views of graphics stored in certain formats. For those items that Mac OS X cannot create previews of (an application is one example), you see a large icon instead of a preview.

 note

If you switch from the Column view to one of the other views, the contents of the folder you most recently selected are shown in the window.

If you prefer not to see the preview, there are two ways to hide it. You can hide it in individual windows or you can hide it by using View Options.

To hide the preview in specific windows, click the Expansion triangle next to the word Preview that appears just above the preview of a selected file in the Preview pane. This hides all previews for the current window and shows detailed information about the item that is selected, along with the More info button (which opens the Info window that you will learn about later).

➥ *To learn about the Column view's View Options,* **see** *"Customizing the Column View," p. 65.*

Using the Cover Flow View

Cover Flow provides a very interactive way to view previews of the files in a folder (see Figure 3.7). The Cover Flow view is especially useful if you are navigating a folder of photos or videos.

With a Finder window set to the Cover Flow view, you will see two panes. On the top is the actual Cover Flow preview of the files in the folder. The bottom pane is a list view of that same folder. Note that with the lower pane in list view, you can use the same steps to change the view as you do in a regular list view Finder window. For instance, you can sort by a different column or change the sort order.

The most noticeable feature of the Cover Flow view is the ability to scroll through the items in the folder. If you have a folder of photos, this view allows you to see a preview of each photo to find the one you are looking for. Resize the Finder window so that the Cover Flow preview area is big enough to see the preview. As you drag the Cover Flow scroll bar, the previews of the items in the folder flow in the direction you are scrolling. When you stop scrolling, the item that is selected displays at a slightly larger size than the other previews and is centered in the top pane. The name of the file is are displayed under the preview.

Browsing a folder that has QuickTime movies provides a preview of the movie. When you select a QuickTime movie and move the mouse over the preview, a play button appears on the preview. When you click the play button the movie will start to play in the Cover Flow preview pane. Move your mouse over the preview again and a stop button appears. While a movie is playing, the other files no longer show previews of those documents; once you move the Cover Flow scroll bar the previews will appear again.

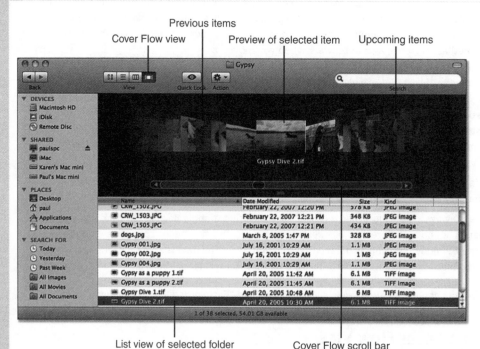

Previous items

Cover Flow view   Preview of selected item   Upcoming items

List view of selected folder   Cover Flow scroll bar

Figure 3.7
The Cover Flow view provides a very interactive way to preview photos and videos in a folder.

Navigating Finder Windows

The chores associated with Finder—moving and copying files, creating folders, renaming items, and so on—are necessary, but are not among the more exciting features of Mac OS X. Your goal in any Finder session should be to perform your tasks as quickly as possible so that you're soon back to more productive pursuits. One way to speed things up in Finder is to know how to navigate the interface and the contents of your Mac. The next few sections show you how to do just that.

Using the Keyboard to Select Items in a Finder Window

Although you can use the mouse to point to and click items to select them (or double-click to open them), moving to items and selecting them using the keyboard can be faster. There are two basic ways to navigate inside a window using the keyboard.

You can type an item's name to move to and select it. The OS matches item names as you type, so most of the time you don't need to type the item's whole name to move to it (for example, typing **mp3** moves you to the first item whose name begins with mp3). The more of the name you type, the more specific your movement becomes.

You can also move among items using the Tab and arrow keys. How this works depends on the view you are using for the windows.

Selecting Items in the Icon View

When you are in the Icon view, pressing the Tab key selects the next item according to alphabetical order. Holding down the Shift key while you press Tab moves you among the items in reverse alphabetical order.

You can also use the arrow keys to move to and select items. The keys work just as you might expect. The up-arrow key moves you up the window, the right-arrow key moves you right, and so on.

The window scrolls automatically to keep the items you select in view.

Selecting Items in the List View

When a window is shown in List view, you can use the up- and down-arrow keys to move up and down the list of items in the window.

When you select an item, you can use the right-arrow key to expand it and the left-arrow key to collapse it.

 tip

The Option key works with the arrow keys as well. If you hold down the Option key and press the right-arrow key, all the folders within the selected folder are expanded as well.

Selecting Items in the Column View

In the Column view, the right-arrow key moves you down the hierarchy, whereas the left-arrow key moves you up the hierarchy. The up- and down-arrow keys enable you to move up and down within a selected folder (which appears in a column).

Using these keys, you can move around your folders rapidly. As you move through the structure using these keys, the window scrolls so that you always see the currently selected item. It maintains your view at all times so you can quickly jump into different areas without scrolling manually.

When you get used to it, using the keyboard in combination with the Column view is one of the fastest ways to navigate Mac OS X Finder windows.

 tip

After you have selected an item, press ⌘-down arrow to open it. For example, when you select an application and press these keys, the application launches.

Selecting Items in the Cover Flow View

Using your keyboard in Cover Flow view is very similar to List view. In fact, because the List view is present at the bottom of the Cover Flow Finder window, when you use the keyboard you will see the results in that pane as well. Using the right arrow, down arrow, or Tab key will move you to the next item. The left arrow, up arrow, and Shift-Tab will move you to the previous item. If you select a folder and hold the ⌘ key while pressing the down arrow, you will move into that folder.

Selecting Items with the Search Tool

The Finder window toolbar's Search tool transforms a folder into a smart folder. You can set the criterion used and the smart folder finds all folders and files that meet this criterion and displays them in the folder's Finder window. To search for files or folders, perform the following steps:

1. Open a Finder window.

2. Type the text or numbers for which you want to search in the Finder window Search box. As you type, the Finder starts finding folders and files that meet your search criterion and displays them for you (see Figure 3.8).

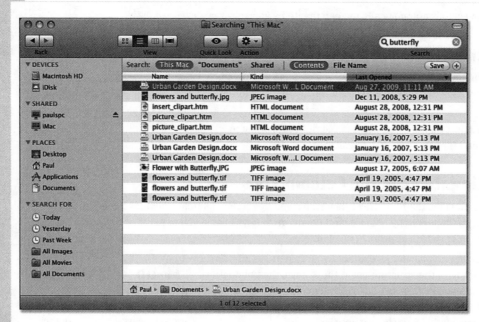

Figure 3.8
A smart folder gets its name for good reason; as you type something in the Search tool, files and folders that match what you type are displayed in the Finder window.

The locations of the items listed can be scoped by choosing the location in which you are interested. These are shown at the top of the window. From left to right they are This Mac, the location you were viewing when you started the search, and Shared.

3. Select the location in which you want to see items that match your search. For example, to find items anywhere on your computer, click This Mac. To narrow the search to your previous location, click its button. The window is refreshed and you will see items that match your search criterion that are in the location you selected.

4. When you find an item in which you are interested, click in the Contents pane and use the up- and down-arrow keys to select the item in the upper pane. Its location appears in the lower pane of the window (see Figure 3.8).

5. To add more criteria to the search, click the Add button (+) next to the Save button. Use the resulting sheet to choose and configure additional search attributes.

 tip

You can save a smart folder by clicking the Save button and using the Save sheet to name it, choose a save location, and indicate if you want it to be added to the Sidebar. After you've saved a search, you can run it again by opening it.

To clear the search and return to the previous Finder window, click the Clear Search button, which is the "x" located in the right end of the Search tool.

➥ *To learn more about Smart folders,* ***see*** *"Searching Your Mac with Smart Folders," **p. 97**.*

Navigating Up and Down the Folder Structure

There are several ways to move up and down the folder structure within Finder windows. You can use the keyboard as discussed in the previous section. You can also use the icons in the Sidebar as well as the Path pop-up menu. The Go menu enables you to jump to specific folders quickly.

Changing Folders with the Sidebar

The Finder's Sidebar is a fast way to change the folder displayed in the current Finder window. The sidebar contains icons that take you to specific folders. As mentioned earlier, the Sidebar contains several sections. In the Devices section are all the volumes mounted on your Mac, including hard disk volumes, disk image volumes, your iDisk, CDs, DVDs, and so on. The Shared section will display icons for the servers that are available on your local area network (LAN). In the Places section of the Sidebar are some of the folders in your Home folder and the Applications folder. You can add any folders, applications, documents, or other files or remove them from this area to completely customize it. Finally, the Search For section of the sidebar allows you to quickly find content base upon predetermined searches, and you can also store smart folders and Spotlight searches here. The purpose of the Sidebar is to enable you to quickly open a Finder window that displays the contents of any item it contains.

➥ *To learn how to customize the sidebar,* ***see*** *"Customizing the Sidebar," **p. 56**.*

To view the contents of an item shown in the sidebar, simply click its icon. The right pane of the Finder window shows the contents of the item you select. For example, if you click your Home folder (the icon with your user account short name as its name), you'll see the contents of your Home folder in the Contents pane of the Finder window.

Navigating Folders Using the Back and Forward Buttons

Click the Back button on the toolbar to move back to the previous Finder window in the current Finder window chain. You can continue to click the Back button as many times as you want until you reach the first window you viewed using the current Finder window chain; at that point, the Back button is grayed out. Similarly, the Forward button moves you forward in a chain of Finder windows. You can also use the Go, Back and the Go, Forward commands to move back in the chain or forward in the chain, respectively.

 tip

You can press ⌘-[to move back and ⌘-] to move forward.

➥ *To learn how to customize the Finder toolbar,* ***see*** *"Customizing the Toolbar," **p. 59**.*

If you open a new Finder window, the Back and Forward buttons are grayed out because there is no window to move back or forward to. Opening a new Finder window starts a new chain of windows, so both buttons are disabled. As soon as you open a second window within the same Finder window chain, the Back button becomes active. If you move back along that chain of windows, the Forward button becomes active.

Changing Folders with the Path Pop-Up Menu

The Path pop-up menu enables you to quickly move up and down the folder structure of your Mac. To change folders, hold down the ⌘ key and click the window name in the title bar of a Finder window. When you do so, you see all the folders from the one currently displayed in the window up to the Computer folder (where Computer is the name of your Mac; this is the highest level on your Mac). Select a folder from the menu and the Finder window displays the folder you chose.

You can add the Path button to your toolbar so you can select a folder without using the ⌘ key.

➡ *To learn how to add buttons to the Finder toolbar,* **see** *"Customizing the Toolbar," p. 59.*

 tip

You can also move up the folder structure one folder at a time by pressing ⌘-up arrow, which is the keyboard shortcut for the Enclosing Folder command that moves to the folder enclosing the item you are currently viewing.

Changing Folders with the Go Menu

The Finder's Go menu enables you to move into many areas of your Mac. The menu is divided into several areas that contain various kinds of options.

At the top of the menu are the Back and Forward commands, which do the same thing as the Back and Forward buttons on the toolbar.

Just under these commands is the Enclosing Folder command. When you are displaying an item in a Finder window and press ⌘-up arrow or select Go, Enclosing Folder, the folder that contains the currently selected item is shown in the Finder window.

You can also use the Finder's Go menu to open specific folders. To do so, open the Go menu and select the folder you want to view. Its contents replace those shown in the active Finder window (if no Finder windows are active, the folder's contents appear in a new Finder window). For example, to display your Home folder, select Go, Home.

 tip

Keyboard shortcuts are available for the specific folders on the Go menu. See the "Finder Window Keyboard Shortcuts" section at the end of this chapter for a list of these shortcuts.

If you select Go, Recent Folders, you can quickly move back to one of the folders you have recently viewed (you can set the number of recent folders on this list using the Appearance pane of the System Preferences application).

You can also move to a folder using the Go to Folder command. Select Go, Go to Folder to see the Go to Folder dialog

 tip

To clear the list of recent folders, choose Go, Recent Folder, Clear Menu.

box (see Figure 3.9). You can type a pathname in this dialog box and click Go to open a Finder window for that folder. Following are some tips on how to type pathnames:

- Pathnames are case sensitive.

- A slash (/) separates each level in the path.

- Almost all paths should begin and end with the slash (/).

- The exception to the previous rule is when you want to move to a specific user's Home folder, in which case you can just type ~*username*/, where *username* is the short name for the user's account.

- If the path begins with the folder on which Mac OS X is stored, you can skip that folder name and start the path beginning with the next level. If it is on another volume, you can include that volume's name at the beginning of the path.

 note

Although you should be careful to use the proper case in pathnames, sometimes it doesn't make a difference. For example, the path to the Mac OS X System folder can be /SYSTEM/, /system/, or /System/. Sometimes, however, the case of the path you type must match exactly, so it is good practice to always match the case of the folder names you type.

Figure 3.9
This Go to Folder dialog box shows the path to the iTunes Music folder within my Home folder.

Go to the folder:

~paul/Music/iTunes/iTunes Music

Cancel   Go

Table 3.1 provides some examples of paths you would enter in the Go to Folder dialog box to move to specific folders.

Table 3.1 Paths to Specific Folders

Location	Path
A folder called Documents on a volume named Mirror	/Mirror/Documents/
The Documents folder in the Home folder for the user account with the short name paul	~paul/Documents/
The Mac OS X System folder	/System/
A folder called Books located in the Documents folder in the user paul's Home folder	~paul/Documents/Books

The following are some additional tips for the Go to Folder command:

- You can open the Go to Folder dialog box by pressing ⌘-Shift-G. Type the path and press Return to move there.

- If you are patient when you type, Mac OS X will try to match the path you are typing and complete it for you. This usually

 tip

Although pathnames should end in /, you don't really have to type the last /. If it is needed, Mac OS X adds it for you. If not, the path works without it.

takes more time than typing it yourself, but if the path is
filled in for you, press Return to accept the path entered
for you to move there.

- The most recent path you have typed remains in the Go to
  Folder dialog box; you can modify this path to move to a
  different folder.

> **note**
>
> You can use the Connect to Server
> command to move to folders located
> on your network.

➡ *To learn how to connect to servers,* ***see*** *"Accessing Shared Files from a Mac OS X Computer,"*
   p. 368.

Changing Folders with the Keyboard

One of the cool navigation features of Mac OS X is the capability to move up and down the folder structure using only the
keyboard. Use the previous tips to select an item, and then
press ⌘-down arrow to move into the item, such as a folder,
an application, a document, and so on. For example, if you use
the Tab key to select an application icon and then press ⌘-
down arrow, that application opens. Similarly, if you press this
key combination when you have a folder selected, the contents of that folder are shown in its previous view state.

To move up the folder structure, press ⌘-up arrow.

> **note**
>
> This technique also works in the
> Column view to open applications or
> documents. When you are viewing
> folders and volumes, you don't need
> to hold down the ⌘ key because, in
> the Column view, the contents of a
> folder or volume are displayed when
> you select it.

Customizing Finder Windows

My goal in this chapter has been to get you comfortable enough with Finder that you don't waste
precious time on boring but necessary tasks such as working with files, folders, and discs. One of
the best ways to become efficient with Finder is to set up the application to suit the way you work.
You do that by customizing aspects of the Finder interface such as the Sidebar, the toolbar, the status bar, and the various Finder views. The next few sections take you through all of Finder's customization options.

Customizing the Sidebar

The Sidebar provides a convenient way to access the mounted volumes on your Mac along with
specific folders, documents, and applications (see Figure 3.10). As mentioned earlier, the Devices
section of the sidebar shows all the mounted volumes on your Mac; the Shared section shows
servers you are connected to; and the Search For section shows saved searches and smart folders.
By default, the Places section of the Sidebar shows several of the folders within your Home folder
and the Applications folder, but you can add or remove folders, documents, or applications to this
area to customize it.

Figure 3.10
The Sidebar makes getting into any mounted volume on your Mac or into specific folders easy.

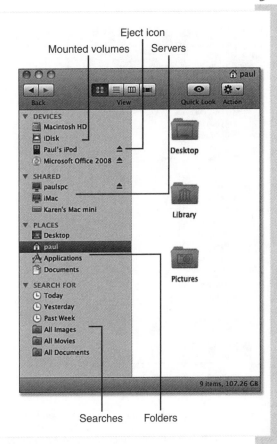

Eject icon

Mounted volumes   Servers

Searches   Folders

To view the contents of a volume or folder, click it—its contents appear in the Content pane of the Finder window. For volumes, a button enables you to perform an action. For example, when you have an ejectable volume, such as a disk image or DVD, you can click an Eject button. When you have inserted a blank CD or DVD, you can click the Burn button that appears next to a Burnable folder to burn the disc.

 tip

You can also store files in the Places section of the Sidebar. Clicking a file icon on the Sidebar opens the file.

Setting the Default Items in the Sidebar

Finder preferences determine which items appear in the Sidebar. To set them, follow these steps:

1. Select Finder, Preferences or press ⌘-,.

2. Click the Sidebar tab (see Figure 3.11).

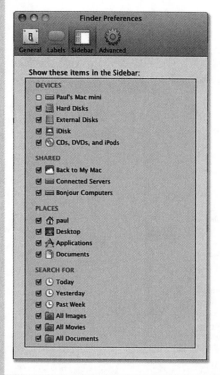

Figure 3.11
Use the Sidebar pane of the Finder Preferences window to configure the default items in the sidebar.

3. Activate the check box next to each item you want to appear in the Sidebar.

4. Deactivate the check box next to each item you don't want to appear in the Sidebar.

The next time you view a Finder window, its sidebar contains the items you specified. These selections only impact default items; anything you've added or removed manually is not impacted.

Organizing Your Sidebar

You can further organize the Sidebar by doing the following tasks:

- You can add any folder or file to the Places section of the Sidebar by dragging it into that section.

- You can also add a folder or file to the sidebar by selecting it and selecting File, Add to Sidebar or pressing ⌘-T.

- You can remove folders from the sidebar by dragging them out of the sidebar. When you do, they disappear in a puff of smoke. Of course, the original item isn't affected.

 note

If you remove an item whose check box is checked on the Sidebar pane of the Finder Preferences window, that folder is removed and its check box becomes unchecked in the Preferences window.

- Resize the Sidebar to make it fill up more or less of the Finder window (your change lasts only as long as the current Finder window chain).

- Show or hide the Sidebar by clicking the Show/Hide Toolbar button in the upper-right corner of Finder windows.

- Drag icons up and down within the Places section of the Sidebar to reorganize them.

Customizing the Toolbar

Along the top of Finder windows, you see the toolbar. This toolbar contains the Back and Forward buttons, the View buttons, the Action menu (covered in a later section), Quick Look button, and the Search tool. As with the sidebar, you can customize many aspects of this toolbar. You can show or hide it and customize the tools it contains.

 note

Many applications, especially those that come with Mac OS X, also provide a Mac OS X toolbar in their windows. You can use these same techniques to work with many of those toolbars.

Showing or Hiding the Toolbar

You can hide or show the toolbar in a Finder window in any of the following ways:

- Click the Show/Hide Toolbar button in the upper-right corner of the Finder window.

- Select View, Hide Toolbar or View, Show Toolbar.

- Press Option-⌘-T.

The state of the toolbar controls how new Finder windows open when they are viewed in the Icon or List view. If the toolbar is displayed, new Finder windows open according to the preferences you set using the Finder Preferences dialog box. If the toolbar is hidden, new Finder windows always open in a separate window.

When you open a new Finder window from a window in which the toolbar is hidden (for example, by holding down the Option key when you open a new Finder window), the toolbar is hidden in the new window. When you open a Finder window from a window in which the toolbar is shown, the toolbar is shown in the new window as well.

The toolbar state in currently open Finder windows is independent. For example, you can show the toolbar in one Finder window while it is hidden in another. In fact, if you have two Finder windows for the same folder open at the same time, you can hide the toolbar in one window while it is shown in the other.

Changing the Tools on the Toolbar

The default toolbar contains various useful buttons, but you can customize its content by adding tools to it or removing tools from it by doing the following:

1. Open a Finder window.

2. Select View, Customize Toolbar. The Toolbar customization sheet appears (see Figure 3.12).

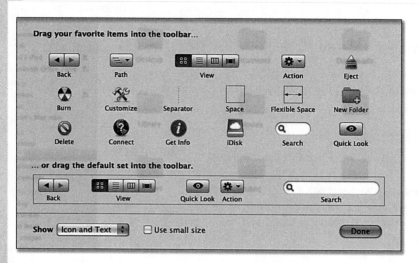

Figure 3.12
You can add buttons to or remove them from the toolbar using the Customize Toolbar sheet.

3. To add a button to the toolbar, drag it from the sheet to the toolbar, placing it in the location where you want it. (Table 3.2 lists the available buttons and what they do.)

   When you move a button between two current buttons on the toolbar, existing buttons slide apart to make room for the new button.

4. Remove a button from the toolbar by dragging it off the toolbar.

5. Change the location of the icons by dragging them. You can move buttons and menus that you add as well as those that are installed by default.

6. Use the Show pop-up menu to determine whether the buttons have text and an icon, text only, or an icon only.

7. To use the small icon size, activate the Use Small Size check box.

8. Click Done.

 note

If you place more buttons on the toolbar than can be shown in the current window's width, a set of double arrows appears at the right edge of the toolbar. Click this to pop up a menu showing the additional buttons.

 tip

You can return to the default toolbar by dragging the default toolbar set onto the toolbar from the Customize Toolbar sheet.

 tip

You can rotate the toolbar among its views, such as Icon and Text, Icon Only, and so on, by holding down ⌘ while you click the Show/Hide Toolbar button.

Table 3.2   Useful Toolbar Buttons

Button Name	What It Does
Back/Forward	Moves you back or forward in a chain of Finder windows.
Path	Pops up a menu that shows the path to the current folder. You can select a folder on the pop-up menu to move there.
View	Changes the view for the current window.
Action	Provides a pop-up menu with access to various context-sensitive commands.
Eject	Enables you to eject items, such as mounted volumes, discs, and so on, from the desktop.
Burn	Enables you to burn a CD or DVD from a burnable folder.
Customize	Enables you to open the Customize Toolbar sheet.
Separator	A graphic element you can use to organize your toolbar.
Space	Adds a block of space to the toolbar.
Flexible Space	Adds a block of flexible space to the toolbar.
New Folder	Creates a new folder.
Delete	Deletes the selected item.
Connect	Opens the Connect to Server dialog box.
Get Info	Opens the Get Info window for a selected item.
iDisk	Accesses your iDisk.
Search	Enables you to search Finder windows.
Quick Look	Opens a floating window to preview or provide information about the selected item. If you have selected a folder, you will be shown details about the contents of the folder. Selecting a document will provide a preview of that file.

Customizing the Status Bar

The status bar provides status information for the current folder, volume, or whatever else is being displayed in the Finder window. Mostly, the status bar provides information about the number of items in the window and the amount of free space on the current volume.

Where the status bar is displayed depends on whether the toolbar is shown.

If the toolbar is shown, the status bar information is displayed at the bottom of the window. For example, if you are viewing a folder, the number of items it contains and the amount of space available on the drive on which it is stored will be shown.

 tip

If you add more buttons than can be displayed and then want to remove some of the buttons you can't see (you see the double arrows instead), you have to make the window wider so that you can see the button on the toolbar to remove it; you can't remove a button from the pop-up menu. You can also temporarily remove other buttons until you can see the one you want to remove.

If the toolbar is hidden, the status bar appears immediately under the title bar (see Figure 3.13). As with the toolbar, you can hide or show the status bar using the View menu. Unlike the toolbar, however, the contents of the status bar can't be changed.

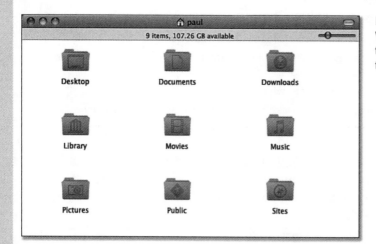

Figure 3.13
When the toolbar is hidden, the status bar appears immediately under the title bar.

Customizing the Finder Window Views

For each view type of Finder window view, you can set default or global view preferences that affect all windows you open using that view type. You can then set options for individual windows to override the default settings for that view type for that specific window. For example, one of the customization options for the List view is the data you see in the window. You can choose to display the Comments column for a window in List view. If you set this as a default preference, each time you open a new window in List view, you see the Comments column. If there is a window in which you don't want to see the Comments column, you can change the preferences for that window so the Comments column is not displayed.

When you set a default preference, it affects all windows shown in that view. When you change a window's preference, it affects only the current window.

Customizing the Icon View

Set your default preferences for the Icon view using the following steps:

1. Open a Finder window in the Icon view so you can preview the preferences you will set.

2. Select View, Show View Options or press ⌘-J. The View Options window appears (see Figure 3.14). You use this window to set both default and window settings. At the top of the window is the name of the folder you are currently viewing.

3. Use the Icon Size slider to set the relative size of the icons you see. As you move the slider, the icons in the open window reflect the size you set. When you are happy with the size of the icons, release the slider.

4. Use the Grid Spacing pop-up menu to set the size of the grid used to keep icons organized in the window.

Figure 3.14
The View Options window enables you to customize Finder window views.

5. Use the Text Size pop-up menu to set the size of the icon labels.

6. In the Label Position area, select the location of icon labels: Bottom or Right.

7. Activate the Show Item Info check box to see information for the items in a window. The information you see depends on the items being displayed. For example, when the window shows volumes, you see the total space on the volume and the free space on each volume. When you view folders, you see the number of items in that folder. When you see files, information about the file is shown, such as the sizes of image files.

8. Deactivate the Show Icon Preview check box if you don't want Mac OS X to create a preview of the file in the file's icon even if the file type doesn't include one by default. By default, graphic file icons contain a preview of the file's content within the icon. Some types of files don't include this icon information and their icon doesn't contain a preview. To see this preview, leave this check box activated.

9. Use the Arrange By pop-up menu to select the criterion by which you want icons grouped on the pop-up menu. None is selected by default, and your other options are Name, Date Modified, Date Created, Size, Kind, and Label. Choose Snap to Grid to keep icons organized by the window's invisible grid.

 note

When you select Snap to Grid, a small grid icon will appear at the bottom left corner of the Finder window.

 tip

You can also modify the view of the desktop, which is always in Icon view. Click anywhere on the desktop and open the View Options window. You can then set the icon size, text size, and other options just like a folder window (except for the folder background, which is set using the Desktop pane of the System Preferences Utility).

10. Select a folder background option:

    - **White**—This options gets you the standard white background.

    - **Color**—Use the Color placeholder to open the Color Picker to select the background color you want to use.

    - **Picture**—To select a picture to use as the background, either drag a picture file from a Finder window and drop it on the picture placeholder, or click the picture placeholder and then use the Select a Picture dialog box to select a background image.

12. Click Use As Defaults.

 note

Supported image formats for a background image include PICT, TIFF, and JPEG. The background image you choose appears in folders you view using the default icon settings. This does not affect any image you are using as a background image on your desktop.

After you have made these settings, any window you view in Icon view is displayed using your default preferences unless you override the global settings by setting a window's preference.

To change the preferences for an individual window, do the following:

1. Open the window you want to view and put it in the Icon view.

2. Open the View Options window by selecting View, Show View Options (or press ⌘-J).

3. Use the controls to set the Icon view preferences for the window you opened in step 1 (see the previous steps for help).

This window uses the preferences you set for it until you change them.

 tip

You can leave the View Options window open while you select other windows. If you do so, the name shown at the top of the dialog box changes, as do the controls you see if the window you select is in a view different from the current one.

Customizing the List View

Customizing List view works pretty much the same way as Icon view, except that you have different options.

Set your default List view preferences using the following steps:

1. Open a Finder window in List view.

2. Open the View Options window (⌘-J).

3. Select the radio button for the icon size you want to use.

4. Select the text size using the Text Size pop-up menu.

5. In the Show Columns area, activate the check boxes next to the data columns you want to be displayed in List view. The default data are Date Modified, Size, and Kind. The other data available are Date Created, Version, Comments, and Label.

6. Activate the Use Relative Dates check box if you want to use relative dates, which means you see date values that are relative to today (such as Yesterday or Past Week) for some dates rather than the full date for all dates.

7. Activate the Calculate All Sizes check box if you want the size of folders to be displayed in the Size column. This option uses extra computing power, especially for those folders that contain many folders and files. You should usually leave this box unchecked unless folder size information is critical to you.

8. Activate the Show Icon Preview check box to have the Finder display a preview icon of a selected item, rather than a generic icon.

9. Click Use As Defaults.

Every window you see in List view uses these options, unless you override the settings for a particular window.

Overriding the default options for a specific window is analogous to what you do for the Icon view. Open the window, open the View Options window, and use the controls to set the view options for the current window.

Customizing the Column View

The Column view has fewer customization options than the other views. The Column view preferences you set apply to all windows in the Column view. You can customize the column view by doing the following:

1. Open a Finder window in Column view.

2. Open the View Options window (⌘-J).

3. Select the text size using the Text Size pop-up menu.

4. Deactivate the Show Icons check box to hide the icons in the window.

5. Deactivate the Show Icon Preview check box to have the Finder display a generic icon instead of a preview icon of a selected item.

6. Deactivate the Show Preview Column check box if you prefer not to see the preview of a file you have selected in the window.

7. Use the Arrange By pop-up menu to select the criterion by which you want icons grouped on the pop-up menu: Name, Date Modified, Date Created, Size, Kind, or Label.

 note

The Finder remembers the view you used the last time you opened a specific window and maintains that view each time you open that window—until you change that window's view. If you want a specific folder to always open in a particular view, click the check box at the top of the View Options dialog box to do so.

Similarly, you can't tell the Finder to apply the default view preferences to all windows at the same time. If you have changed the view preferences for individual windows, you have to reapply the default view preferences to that window if you want to use them (by using the View Options window).

Customizing the Cover Flow View

The view options for Cover Flow windows are identical to the options you have for a List view. Because the Cover Flow view includes a list view in the bottom pane, it is beneficial to be able to set these options.

Set your default Cover Flow view preferences using the following steps:

1. Open a Finder window in Cover Flow view.

2. Open the View Options window (⌘-J).

3. Select the radio button for the icon size you want to use.

4. Select the text size using the Text Size pop-up menu.

5. In the Show Columns area, activate the check boxes next to the data columns you want to be displayed in List view. The default data are Date Modified, Size, and Kind. The other data available are Date Created, Version, Comments, and Label.

6. Activate the Use Relative Dates check box if you want to use relative dates, which means you see date values that are relative to today (such as Yesterday or Past Week) for some dates rather than the full date for all dates.

7. Activate the Calculate All Sizes check box if you want the size of folders to be displayed in the Size column. This option uses extra computing power, especially for those folders that contain many folders and files. You should usually leave this box unchecked unless folder size information is critical to you.

8. Activate the Show Icon Preview check box to have the Finder display a preview icon of a selected item, rather than a generic icon.

9. Click Use As Defaults.

Working with the Finder Window's Action Pop-Up Menu

One of the default tools on the Finder window toolbar is the Action pop-up menu (see Figure 3.15). This menu provides access to context-sensitive commands, which means that commands on the menu depend on the item you have selected on the desktop. For example, when you select a file and open the menu, you see commands including New Folder, Open, Open With, Move to Trash, Get Info, Compress, Burn, Duplicate, Make Alias, Quick Look, Copy, Show View Options, and Label.

 note

As you probably suspect, the commands on the Action pop-up menu are similar to the commands on an item's contextual menu, which you can open by pointing to an item, holding down the Control key, and clicking the item (or right-clicking the item if you use a two-button mouse). If you do this, you'll see a couple more options on the contextual menu that you will learn about later in this book.

Figure 3.15
The com-
mands on
the Action
pop-up menu
change
depending
on the items
you have
selected.

To use a command on the menu, select the item on which you want to use the command, open the menu, and select the command you want to use.

Organizing Folder Items with Labels

Labels enable you to color-code and text-code files and folders as a means of identifying and organizing them. For example, you can assign all the folders for a specific project using the same label. In addition to making the relationship between these folders clearer, you can choose to group items within a window by label, which keeps them near one another as well. You can also use Smart Folders to automatically gather files and folders that have the same label.

Setting Up Labels

You can assign text to the color labels by following these steps:

1. Open the Finder Preferences window.

2. Click the Labels button to open the Labels pane, which contains the seven label colors. Next to each color is its text label, which by default is the name of the color.

3. Edit the text labels for each color to match your label needs. For example, you can replace the color with the name of a project.

Applying Labels

You can apply labels to a folder or file by following these steps:

1. Select the items to which you want to apply a label.

2. Open the Action pop-up menu or the contextual menu.

3. Select the label you want to apply to the selected labels.

When an item has a label applied to it and you view the enclosing folder in Icon view, its name is highlighted in the label's color. When you view a window in the Cover Flow, Columns, or List view, a large dot filled with the label color appears next to the item you have labeled. If you view a window in the List view and select to show the Label column, the label text appears in the Label column for the item.

 tip

If you view a window in Icon view, you can choose to keep items grouped by label. This keeps all the files with which you have associated a specific location together in the window.

Finder Window Keyboard Shortcuts

Table 3.3 lists keyboard shortcuts for working with Finder windows.

Table 3.3 Keyboard Shortcuts for Finder Windows

Menu	Action	Keyboard Shortcut
None	Opens an item on the sidebar and closes the current window	Option-click
None	Opens an item on the sidebar in a new Finder window	⌘-click
None	Closes all open Finder windows	Option-click the Close button
None	Opens an item in a new Finder window	⌘-double-click a folder
Finder	Preferences	⌘-,
File	New Finder Window	⌘-N
File	New Folder	Shift-⌘-N
File	New Smart Folder	Option-⌘-N
File	Open	⌘-O
File	Close Window	⌘-W
File	Get Info	⌘-I
File	Duplicate	⌘-D
File	Make Alias	⌘-L
File	Quick Look	⌘-Y
File	Show Original	⌘-R
File	Add to Sidebar	⌘-T
View	as Icons	⌘-1

Table 3.3 Continued

Menu	Action	Keyboard Shortcut
View	as List	⌘-2
View	as Columns	⌘-3
View	as Cover Flow	⌘-4
View	Show/Hide Toolbar	Option-⌘-T
View	Show/Hide View Options	⌘-J
Go	Back	⌘-[
Go	Forward	⌘-]
Go	Enclosing Folder	⌘-up arrow
Go	Computer	Shift-⌘-C
Go	Home	Shift-⌘-H
Go	Desktop	Shift-⌘-D
Go	Network	Shift-⌘-K
Go	iDisk, My iDisk	Shift-⌘-I
Go	Applications	Shift-⌘-A
Go	Utilities	Shift-⌘-U
Go	Go to Folder	Shift-⌘-G
Go	Connect to Server	⌘-K
Window	Minimize Window	⌘-M
Window	Cycle Through Windows	⌘-`

MANAGING FILES AND FOLDERS

Understanding the Standard Mac OS X Folders

I'm going to assume you want to minimize the amount of time you spend working with files and folders in Mac OS X (because you have more important or interesting or fun things to do with your Mac). To that end, it helps to familiarize yourself with the standard Mac OS X folders, so you can navigate your Mac quickly and efficiently.

Fortunately, there are only a few folders that you need to know about, and the next few sections break those folders down into two main categories: system folders and user folders.

Mac OS X System Folders

Your Mac comes with two main folders that provide access to the Mac OS X system-level files and folders: the Computer folder and the Mac OS X startup volume.

The Computer Folder

The Computer folder is the highest-level folder on your Mac. It shows the volumes mounted on your machine, including hard drives, drive partitions, disk images, external hard disks, DVDs, CD-ROMs, network connections, iPods, and more (see Figure 4.1). To access the Computer folder in any Finder window select Go, Computer, or press Shift-⌘-C. The name of the Computer folder is the name of your Mac.

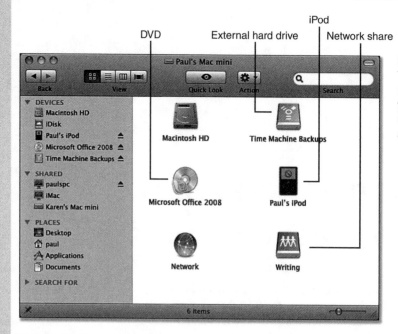

DVD   External hard drive   iPod   Network share

Figure 4.1
The Mac OS X Computer folder represents all the contents of your machine as well as the network resources you can access.

The Mac OS X Startup Volume

The Computer folder includes the folder in which Mac OS X is installed, which is known generically as the Mac OS X startup volume, but is given the default name Macintosh HD. By default, your startup volume folder contains the following four folders that are part of the Mac OS X installation:

- **Applications**—Under Mac OS X, all applications are stored in this folder.

  ➥ *To learn how to install applications, **see** Chapter 7, "Installing and Using Mac OS X Applications," p. 127.*

- **Library**—The Library folder contains many subfolders that provide resources to support applications, hardware devices, and other items you add to your Mac. This library folder contains the system folders that can be modified.

- **System**—This folder contains the Library folder that provides the core operating system software for Mac OS X. The items in this folder can't be modified except by installation applications, system updaters, or using the root account.

- **Users**—The Users folder contains the Home folder for each user for whom an account has been created. The Home folder of the user currently logged in has the Home icon; the Home folders for the rest of the users have plain folder icons. If you have deleted user accounts, it also contains a folder called Deleted Users that contains a disk image for each deleted user account (if you elected to keep the user's resources when you deleted his folder).

Mac OS X User Folders

Each user account on your Mac has a Home folder. This folder contains other folders that are used to store private files, public files, and system resources (such as preferences and password keychains) for that user account. With two exceptions (the Public and Site folders), only someone logged in under a user account can access the folders in that user account's Home folder.

➥ *To learn about the root account,* ***see*** *"Enabling the Root User Account," p. 461.*

By default, a user's Home folder contains the folders shown in Figure 4.2. However, the user can create additional folders within the Home folder. And, of course, users can create additional folders within the default folders contained in the Home folder as well. Any folders created with a Home folder take on the security settings of that folder. For example, if a user creates a folder within the Documents folder, that folder can only be accessed by that user.

caution

The exception to the general rule about accessing the folders in another user's Home folder is the *root* account. The root user account can access everything on your Mac and is outside the normal security provided by user accounts. You should use the root account only in special situations, and you really need to understand it before you use it.

Figure 4.2
Every user account on your Mac has a Home folder; this folder contains folders that only that user can access (except for the Public and Sites folders).

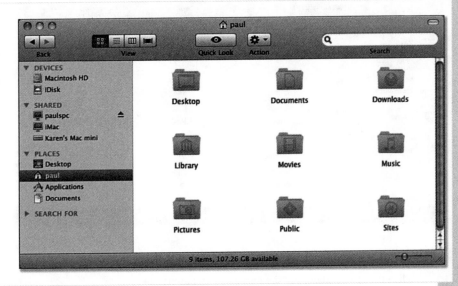

Most of these folders are easy to understand because they are used to organize a user's files. For example, the Documents folder is the default location in which the user stores documents he creates. The Desktop folder contains items that are stored on that user's desktop (which, by the way, means that each user account has a unique desktop), and so on.

Some applications will automatically select a folder when storing files. For example, when you add music files to your iTunes Library, they are stored in the iTunes folder within the Music folder. Likewise, when you create movies with iMovie, they are stored in the Movies folder.

Only someone logged in under a user account can access the contents of the folders in that user's Home folder—except for the Public and Sites folders that can be accessed by anyone using your Mac. Locked folders have an icon that includes a red circle with a minus sign (see Figure 4.3). If someone other than those who have permission attempts to open one of these protected folders, they only see a warning message and not any of the contents of the protected folder. Accessible folders in another user's directory have the plain folder icon, which means their contents are available to that user. Unlocked default folders in the current user's Home directory have the decorative Mac OS X icons (refer to Figure 4.2). (Folders you create within your Home folder will have the generic folder icon but will be protected in the same way as its default folders.)

🔘 tip

You can quickly tell which user account is active by looking at the Home directory icon in the Finder window's Places sidebar, which is always located at the left side of Finder windows. It looks like a house for the current user's Home folder; the other Home directory icons are plain folders. The short name for a user account appears in the title bar of that user's Home folder (in Figure 4.2, the currently logged in account is called paul).

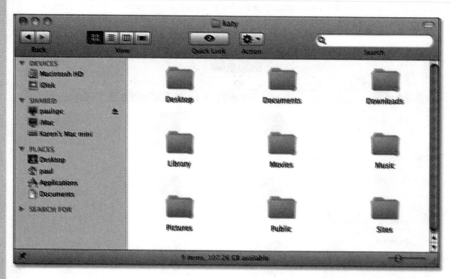

Figure 4.3
When you view another user's Home directory, the protected folders are marked with the minus icon to indicate that their contents are inaccessible to you.

There are four folders in each Home folder that don't behave like the others; those are the Public, Sites, Library, and Desktop folders.

The Public Folder

A user's Public folder is accessible by users logged in under any account. Its purpose is to enable users to share files that are stored within different user accounts on the same computer. To share your files with other users, simply store them

🔍 note

Notice in Figure 4.3 that the title of the window shown is "katy." This is the name of another user account; you can tell that it isn't the one currently logged in because it doesn't appear in the Places sidebar nor does its icon look like a house.

in your Public folder. Other users can then open your Public folder to get to those files. Likewise, to access files other users have shared with you, you can open their Public folder.

To access the files and folders in another user's Public folder, perform the following steps:

1. In Finder, click the Mac OS X startup volume (usually Macintosh HD).

2. Open the Users folder.

3. Open the Home folder for the user who has a file you want to share.

4. Open the Public folder and use the files contained within it.

> **tip**
>
> You can open a file or folder within another user's Public folder, or you can drag the file to your own folder to make a copy of it.

Within the Public folder, you will also see a Drop Box folder (see Figure 4.4). Other users can place items into this folder, but no one else can open it. This is useful when you want others to transfer items to you but don't want all the other users to be able to see what has been shared.

Figure 4.4
In this example, I've opened another user's Public folder; I can work with any files it contains (as can other users) or I can place files in the Drop Box folder.

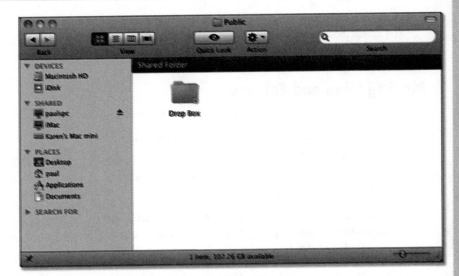

The Sites Folder

The Sites folder contains files for each user's website. Part of each user account's resources is a website that can be accessed over a local network, from another user's account, or from the Internet (depending on how the Mac's Internet access is configured). You place the files for a user's website in the Sites folder to publish that site.

The Library Folder

The Library folder is the only folder in the Home directory that is not intended for document storage. It contains items related to the configuration of the user account and all the system-related files for that account. For example, user and application preferences are stored here, as are font collections, addresses, password keychains, and so on. Basically, any file that affects how the system works or looks that is specific to a user account is stored in the Library directory. You won't usually access this folder unless you are troubleshooting problems.

The Desktop Folder

The user's Desktop folder contains the items the user has placed on his desktop. Each user can have as much or as little on his desktop as he likes. When another user logs in, she sees only the contents of her desktop folder on the desktop.

Working with Files and Folders

Performing file and folder chores is never fun or glamorous, but it's necessary work no matter how you spend the rest of your Mac time. Fortunately there are only a few key techniques to learn, and Mac OS X makes them as painless as possible.

Moving Files and Folders

When you need to move a file or folder to a new destination, follow these steps:

1. Open the folder that contains the item you want to move.

2. If the destination volume or folder isn't listed on the Sidebar, open a second Finder window and use it to display the destination volume or folder.

3. Click and drag the item you want to move and then drop it on the destination (either an item in the Sidebar or a separate Finder window).

 note

The Column view is one of the more useful for moving files and folders around because it gives you a good view of the entire hierarchy of the volume you are working with.

When you move an object over a folder, it becomes highlighted so you can easily see in which folder the item you are moving will be placed. This is especially useful when you are viewing Finder windows in the Column view. Similarly, when you drag something over a folder on the Places section of the sidebar, the folder will be highlighted so it is clear which folder the object will be moved into when you release the mouse button.

Copying Files and Folders

If you want to place a copy of a file or folder in a new destination, Mac OS X gives you two choices:

- Follow the same steps as outlined earlier for moving a file or folder in the previous section, except hold down the Option key when you drag and drop the item.

■ Select the item, select Edit, Copy, switch to the destination volume or folder, and then select Edit, Paste Item.

If you want to create a duplicate of a file or folder (that is, make a copy of the item in its current location), select the item and then select File, Duplicate (or press ⌘-D).

Creating and Naming Folders

The purpose of folders under Mac OS X is to enable you to organize files. You can create a new folder by using the New Folder command (such as File, New Folder, or ⌘-Shift-N). The new folder will be created in your current location. Immediately after you create it, its name will be editable so you can simply type the name of the new folder.

Naming a folder is mostly a matter of personal preference; the maximum number of characters that you can use in a folder name is 256. Of course, you aren't likely to ever use a folder name that long because it would be very difficult to read, but at least you have a lot of flexibility with folder names.

To name a folder or edit its current name, select the folder and press Return. The folder's name becomes highlighted and you can create a new name.

Naming Files

Naming files is very similar to naming folders, with one exception. The underlying architecture of the Mac OS X uses *filename extensions*—for example, .txt at the end of a text document filename.

File extensions are a code that helps identify a file's type and thus the application used to view or edit that file. Many Mac OS X applications also use filename extensions; the OS uses these extensions to launch the appropriate application for that document when you open the file.

➡ *To understand more about filename extensions under Mac OS X,* **see** *"Saving Documents in Mac OS X," p. 143.*

When you name a document from within an application that uses filename extensions, the correct extension is appended automatically to the filename you enter. However, when you rename files on the desktop or in a Finder window, you need to be aware of a filename's extension if it has one (not all applications use an extension).

A complication in this is that you can choose to show or hide filename extensions on a file-by-file basis or at the system level. However, filename extensions are almost always in use, whether you can see them or not. Hiding them simply hides them from your view.

You can use the Info tool to associate applications with specific files, so the lack of a proper filename extension is not a significant problem.

➡ *To learn how to associate files with specific applications,* **see** *"Opening Documents in Mac OS X," p. 135.*

If you want to rename a file that has an extension, you should leave the extension as it is. If you change or remove the extension, the application you use to open the file might not be launched automatically when you try to open the file.

The filename extensions you see under Mac OS X include some of the three- or four-letter filename extensions with which you are no doubt familiar, such as .doc, .xls, .html, .jpg, .tiff, and so on. However, there are many, many more filename extensions you will encounter. Some are relatively short, whereas others (particularly those in the system) can be quite long. There isn't really any apparent rhyme or reason to these filename extensions so you just have to learn them as you go. Because you will mostly deal with filename exten-sions that are appended by an application when you save a document, this isn't a critical task. However, as you delve deeper into the system, you will become more familiar with many of the sometimes bizarre-looking filename extensions Mac OS X uses.

 note

Depending on the file type, some files open properly even if you do remove or change the file's exten-sion. But it is better to be safe, so you should usually leave the file extension as you find it.

You can choose to hide or show filename extensions globally or on an item-by-item basis. To config-ure filename extensions globally, use the following steps

1. Select Finder, Preferences to open the Finder Preferences window.

2. Click the Advanced icon.

3. To globally show filename extensions, activate the Show All File Extensions check box.

➥ *To learn how to show or hide filename extensions for specific items,* **see** *"Working with Name and Extension Information,"* **p. 83.**

Creating and Using Aliases

An alias is a pointer to a file, folder, or volume. Open an alias and the original item opens. The ben-efit of aliases is that you can place them anywhere on your Mac because they are very small in file size, so you can use them with little storage penalty.

There are several ways to create an alias, including

- Select an item and select File, Make Alias.

- Select an item and press ⌘-L.

- Hold down the Option and ⌘ keys while you drag an item.

- Open the Action menu for an item and select Make Alias.

- Open the contextual menu for an item and select Make Alias.

After you create an alias, you can work with it much as you can the original. For example, you can open it or move it to a new location.

Occasionally, you might need to find the original from which an alias was created. For example, if you create an alias to an application, you might want to be able to move to that application in the Finder. To do this, follow these steps:

1. Select the alias.

2. Select File, Show Original (or press ⌘-R). A Finder window containing the original item opens.

Occasionally, an alias *breaks*, meaning your Mac loses track of the original to which the alias points. The most common situation is that you have deleted the original, but it can happen for other reasons as well. When you attempt to open a broken alias, you will see a warning dialog box that provides the following three options:

- **Delete Alias**—If you click this button, the alias is deleted.

- **Fix Alias**—If you click this one, you can use the Fix Alias dialog box to select another file to which you want the alias to point.

- **OK**—If you click OK, the dialog box disappears and no changes are made to the alias.

Trashing Files and Folders

Since its inception, the Mac's Trash can has been the place where you move files and folders that you no longer want so that you can delete them from your computer. Under Mac OS X, the Trash is located at the right end or bottom of the Dock.

To move something to the Trash, use one of the following methods:

- Drag the item to the Trash on the Dock. When you are over the Trash icon, it is highlighted so you know you are in the right place.

- Select an item, open its contextual menu, and select Move to Trash.

- Select an item and choose File, Move to Trash.

- Select an item and press ⌘-Delete.

After you have placed an item in the Trash, you can access it again by clicking the Trash icon on the Dock. A Finder window displaying the Trash folder opens, and you can work with the items it contains.

When you want to delete the items in the Trash, do so in one of the following ways:

- Select Finder, Empty Trash. In the confirmation dialog box, click either OK (or press Return) to empty the Trash or Cancel to stop the process. You can skip the confirmation dialog box by holding down the Option key while you select Empty Trash.

- Open the Trash's Dock contextual menu and select Empty Trash on the resulting pop-up menu.

- Press Shift-⌘-Delete. In the confirmation dialog box, click either OK (or press Return) to empty the Trash or Cancel to stop the process. You can skip the confirmation dialog box by pressing Option-Shift-⌘-Delete instead.

To permanently disable the warning dialog box when you empty the Trash, perform the following steps:

1. Select Finder, Preferences to open the Finder Preferences window.

2. Click the Advanced icon.

3. Deactivate the Show Warning Before Emptying the Trash check box. The warning will no longer appear, no matter how you empty the Trash.

You can also securely delete items from the Trash. When you do this, the data that makes up those items is overwritten so it can't be recovered. To perform a secure delete, place items in the Trash and select Finder, Secure Empty Trash.

Creating and Using Burn Folders

Burn folders are a special type of folder that are designed to help you move files and folders onto CD or DVD more easily. One of the differences between a regular folder and a burn folder is that everything you move into a burn folder becomes an alias. This means you can build a CD or DVD without disturbing the location of the items that you want to put on disc. Simply create a burn folder and place items into it. When you are ready to burn a disc, you can do so quite easily.

To create a burn folder choose File, New Burn Folder. When the new folder appears, you will see it has the radioactive icon and the name "Burn Folder." The name is highlighted, so you can rename it immediately. Do so and press Return to save the new name.

After you have created a burn folder, move the files and folders that you want to place on a disc into it. As you move files and folders into it, aliases to the original items are created inside the burn folder. Continue placing items inside the folder until you have moved all the files you want to place on disc into it (see Figure 4.5).

You can organize files and folders within a burn folder just like other folders with which you work. For example, you can create new "regular" folders within the burn folder and place items within those folders.

When you are ready to burn a disc from the burn folder, view the folder and click its Burn button. You are prompted to insert a disc; in this prompt, you'll see the amount of space needed to burn the files on a disc. When your Mac mounts a disc that is ready to burn, you see the Burn prompt. Enter the name of the disc (it defaults to the name of the Burn folder), choose the burn speed on the Burn Speed pop-up menu, and click Burn. A progress bar appears and the disc is burned.

 tip

You can use burn folders as a backup mechanism. For example, suppose you want to back up your iPhoto Library to DVD. Create a burn folder and place your Pictures folder in it. To create a fresh backup of your library, burn the folder. (You don't need to move the files into it again because the aliases are updated automatically.)

 tip

For quick access, add a burn folder to the Places section of the sidebar so you can get into it easily to add more files to it.

 note

Unfortunately, using a Burn folder supports burning to a disc in a single session. After you burn a folder to a disc, that disc is closed and can't be burned to again (unless it is an erasable disc, in which case you can erase its contents). Hopefully, someday the Finder will allow multi-session burns so you can add files to a disc you have burned.

Figure 4.5
A burn folder contains aliases to items you place in it along with the black bar containing the folder name and Burn button shown at the top of its window.

You can quickly burn the contents of a burn folder at any time by repeating these steps; such as when you want to refresh your backups of important files.

Getting Information on Items

The Info window is a tool you use to learn about various items on your desktop and in Finder windows. For some items, you can also control specific aspects of how those items work and how they can be used.

You can access all the tools in the Info window from a single pane by using its expansion triangles. The window is organized into sections; you expose a section by clicking its expansion triangle. You can have multiple information windows open at the same time (which is helpful when you want to compare items).

The Info window has slightly different features and information for each of the following groups:

- Folders and volumes

- Applications

- Documents

The sections you see for each type of item is described in Table 4.1.

 note

You might wonder why it is better to create and use a burn folder than it is just to place files and folders directly on a disc. If you are only going to burn a disc once, there isn't a lot of benefit to creating a burn folder because it is just as easy to insert a blank disc into your burner and add files and folders to it. Burn folders become valuable when you want to re-create a disc, such as to refresh a backup or to make multiple copies of the same disc. Or, you might want to use them to organize files you are going to burn later in the order they will be on the disc.

Table 4.1   Sections of the Get Info Window

Section	Applicable Items	Information/Tools It Provides
Spotlight Comments	Folders and volumes; applications; files	Enables you to enter comments that will be searched when you use Spotlight or choose this as a criterion for a smart folder search.
General	Folders and volumes; applications; files	Provides identification information about the item, such as its path, type, and significant dates.
More Info	Folders and volumes; applications; files	Provides additional information about an item such as the date on which it was last opened, resolution information (for images), and so on.
Name & Extension	Folders and volumes; applications; files	Gives the full item name, including its filename extension if applicable.
Preview	Folders and volumes; applications; files	Shows the icon of everything except files. For files, a preview of the file's content is provided (this is the same preview the Column view provides).
Open with	Files	Enables you to select an application with which to open a file. You can also set the application used for all files of the same type.
Sharing & Permissions	Folders and volumes; applications; files	Enables you to configure the access permissions for an item.

Examples of how to use each of these parts of the Info Window are provided in the following sections.

Working with the Spotlight Comments Information

The Spotlight Comments section enables you to add comments to a selected item:

1. Open the Info window for the item in which you are interested.

2. Expand the Spotlight Comments section.

3. Enter your comments in the field. The comments you enter remain with the item, and you can read them by either expanding the Comments section or adding the Comments column to the List view and viewing a Finder window in that view.

 tip

You can use the Comments field as a search criterion for a smart folder. This can be useful to create and easily gather a group of related items together in a smart folder.

Working with General Information

The General section of the Info window is used mostly to provide detailed information about an item. However, for specific items, you can also use the controls it provides:

1. Select the item you are interested in and choose File, Get Info or press ⌘-I. The Info window appears.

2. Expand the General section if it isn't expanded by default.

3. View the information provided at the top of the window.

4. Use any tools that appear to configure the item.

 tip

You can also use the Actions pop-up menu or contextual menu to open the Info window.

Depending on the item you select, you have the following choices:

- You can select the Locked check box that appears when the selected item is a document, a folder, or an application to prevent the item from being changed.

- You can use the Stationery Pad check box to convert a selected document into a template.

- If the selected item is an alias, you can associate it with a different file by using the Select New Original button and then choosing the file you want it to point to.

- You can apply a color label by clicking the color you want to apply to the item. Click the "x" button to remove a label from the item.

Working with More Info Information

The More Info section provides a variety of data that depends on the kind of item about which you are viewing information. For example, when you have selected an image file, this section displays resolution information. For most items, you see the date on which the item was last opened. In some cases, Mac OS X can't generate any more information for an item in which case you'll see No Info in this section. To view more info for an item, do the following:

1. Select the item and press ⌘-I. The Info window will open.

2. Expand the More Info section.

Working with Name and Extension Information

The Name & Extension section enables you to view and change the name of the selected item:

1. Select the item you are interested in and press ⌘-I. The Info window appears.

2. Expand the Name & Extension section.

3. Edit the item name in the Name & Extension field that appears. Remember to add or edit filename extensions as appropriate (volumes and folders don't have filename extensions).

note

Applications have the filename extension .app.

When you are displaying Name & Extension information for a document, the Hide Extension check box is enabled. When you activate this check box, the filename extension for the file is hidden in Finder windows. This check box is overridden by the Finder's file extension preference. If you activate the Show All File Extensions check box in the Finder Preferences window (as described earlier in this chapter), filename extensions are shown regardless of the state of the Hide Extension check box for an individual file. The Finder preference must be unchecked for this box to hide or show a file's filename extension.

Working with Preview Information

The Preview section provides a preview of the selected item. For everything except documents, this preview is simply the item's icon. However, when you use this feature on a document, you get a preview of the item's content, just as you do when you view a Finder window in Column view. If the content is dynamic, such as a QuickTime movie, you can view or hear that content from the Preview section:

1. Select the item you are interested in and press ⌘-I to open the Info window.

2. Expand the Preview section.

3. Use the Preview section to preview the item's content. For example, use the controls to view the item if it is a QuickTime movie. If you selected an image, you can view a preview of the image.

 tip

You can have more than one section of the Info window expanded at the same time. In fact, you can have as few as none expanded, or you can have all of them expanded.

For documents for which Mac OS X can't generate a preview, you see the appropriate icon instead.

Working with Open With Information

You can use the Open With section to determine which application is used to open a file:

1. Select the document you are interested in and press ⌘-I.

2. Expand the Open With section.

3. Select the application with which you want the file to be opened on the pop-up menu; the application currently associated with the document is shown in the pop-up menu. The suggested applications appear on the menu by default. If you want to select an application that is not shown on the pop-up menu, click Other and select the application you want to be used.

4. If you want all files of the same type to be opened with the application you selected, click the Change All button.

Working with Sharing & Permissions Information

The Sharing & Permissions section is used to configure access to the item (see Figure 4.6). This area enables you to control who has access to an item, as well as defining the type of access provided.

Figure 4.6
The Sharing & Permissions section of the Information window is an important security tool whether you share your Mac directly or across a network.

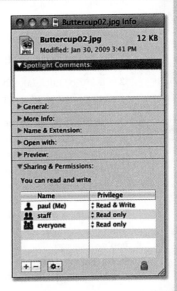

➡ To learn how to configure access to an item, *see* "Understanding and Setting Permissions,"
p. 377.

Working with the Inspector

When you work with the Info window, each item has its own window. This is nice because you can display the Info window for multiple items at the same time. However, it can get tedious when you don't want to do this because you have to select each item, open its Info window, and then close the Info window when you are done.

You can use the Inspector to see information about the *currently selected* item rather than the one that was selected when you opened the Info window. This is handy because you can leave the Inspector open and as you select items, their information is displayed. You don't clutter up your desktop with a lot of Info windows and you don't have to keep opening the Info window for items.

To open the Inspector, hold the Option key down and choose File, Show Inspector or press Option–⌘-I. The Inspector window appears. It looks just like the Info window except it has square corners instead of rounded ones. As you select items on the desktop, the information in the Inspector changes to reflect the currently selected item.

Getting a Quick Look at Things

The Finder's Quick Look command enables you to examine an item without opening an application. For example, if you see a number of image files, but don't know what they are, you can select them and use the Quick Look command to view them without having to wait for an application to launch and then viewing the images in separate windows. To use the Quick Look command, perform the following steps:

1. Select the items about which you want a quick look.

2. Click the Quick Look button in the Finder toolbar. The Quick Look window appears (see Figure 4.7).

3. Use the controls at the bottom of the Quick Look window to view the selected items. The controls you see depend on the items you selected. For example, if you select a group of images, you can play them in a slideshow, view an index sheet, and so on. To view the Quick Look in full screen, click the Full screen button.

> **tip**
>
> You can also choose File, Quick Look or press ⌘-Y to open the Quick Look window.

If you select a group of different kinds of objects at the same time, you can see each object's information in the window by clicking the right-facing arrow. The window updates for each object you've selected. The information shown in the Quick Look window depends on the kind of object in focus. For example, you see images in image files, the contents of text documents, and so on. For some objects, you only see an icon, such as volumes or files for which Mac OS X can't display a preview.

Figure 4.7
The Quick Look window enables you to see what selected objects are without opening an application to view them. The tools you see at the bottom of the Quick Look window will change based on the items you are viewing.

Browsing and
slide show controls

Full
screen

Add to iPhoto

Index sheet

5

SEARCHING YOUR MAC

Looking for Things on Your Mac: A Modern Approach

It's hard to believe that only a few years ago we spent much of our Mac time deleting or archiving unneeded or old files because we were in constant danger of running out of room on our hard disks. Now, with new Macs routinely shipping with hundreds of gigabytes of hard disk real estate, getting rid of files is no longer an issue because we have plenty of room to store everything, even things we don't need.

Of course, this kind of digital pack rat behavior leads to a completely different problem: *finding* things. With a typical hard disk now home to thousands of our files, locating the document you need without wasting huge amounts of time is becoming increasingly problematic. Not only that, but these days we also have our data scattered across multiple types of information: documents, email messages, web pages, contacts, appointments, and more. Clearly, the days of locating information by browsing are long over. We need newer, faster, more efficient ways to find the data we want. Fortunately, Mac OS X includes not one, but *two* powerful tools you can use to find what you need on your Mac: Spotlight and Smart folders.

Searching Your Mac with Spotlight

One of the best features of Mac OS X is an amazingly powerful and yet easy-to-use tool for finding things on your Mac, regardless of what kind of "thing" it is. This tool is called Spotlight and it enables you to search your entire Mac quickly and easily.

The secret to Spotlight's success is that it doesn't simply examine filenames or file contents when it searches your Mac. It does those things, for sure, but it also goes a lot deeper by examining the various attributes associated with every file. These attributes include things like the email addresses and subject lines associated with email messages, the album name and song title for a music track, lens data such as aperture and exposure time for a photo, and so on. These attributes—which are also called *metadata*, because they're data that describe data—enable you to perform incredibly targeted searches that help you quickly and efficiently find exactly what you're looking for.

Best of all, Spotlight searches aren't restricted to just your documents. A Spotlight search will also return applications, folders, email messages, bookmarks, contact information, even system preferences, so all your Mac is available for searching.

Configuring Spotlight

Although Spotlight is extremely simple to use as is, you can get more out of it by configuring Spotlight so that it works the way you prefer. Follow these steps to configure Spotlight's preferences:

1. Open System Preferences.

2. Click Spotlight. By default, the Search Results tab is selected (see Figure 5.1).

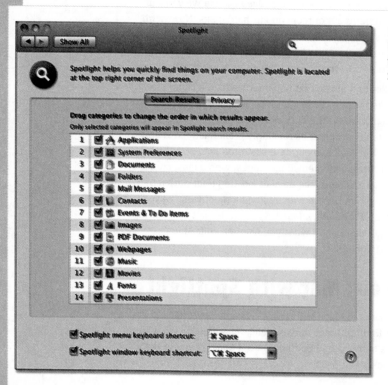

Figure 5.1
Use the Spotlight pane to configure the items for which Spotlight will search.

3. Deactivate the check box beside each item you don't want included in your Spotlight search results. For example, if you never search for fonts, deactivate the Fonts check box.

4. Set the keyboard shortcut you use to launch Spotlight using the Spotlight Menu Keyboard Shortcut check box and pop-up menu. The default is ⌘-spacebar, but you can change this to be a function key if you prefer.

5. Use the Spotlight Window Keyboard Shortcut check box and pop-up menu to configure the keys you use to move into the Spotlight search results window. The default is ⌘-Option-spacebar, but you can use the pop-up menu to choose a function key instead.

6. Click the Privacy tab. You use this pane to select areas of your Mac that you don't want Spotlight to search. For example, if you keep sensitive documents in a particular folder, you might want to block that folder from Spotlight searches.

7. Click the Add button (+) at the bottom of the pane. The Choose Folder sheet appears.

8. Move to the folder you want to shield, select it, and click Choose. That folder is added to the list and won't be included in Spotlight searches.

9. Repeat steps 7 and 8 until you have protected all your sensitive folders.

Searching with Spotlight

With Spotlight configured to your liking, you're ready to use it to search your Mac from the desktop.

To show you just how easy it is to use Spotlight, here's a quick-and-dirty set of steps that you'll use most of the time:

1. Click the Spotlight icon (the magnifying glass) in the upper-right corner of your desktop, or press ⌘-spacebar. The Spotlight search bar appears.

2. Type your search text. Mac OS X immediately displays the matching items, organized by category.

3. If you see the item you're looking for, click it to open it.

That's all there is to it. Spotlight really is that easy. However, Spotlight also has hidden depths, so you should also know how to tap into its powerful features. To get started down that road, here's a more in-depth look at the search process:

1. Click the Spotlight icon (the magnifying glass) in the upper-right corner of your desktop, or press the Spotlight menu keyboard shortcut (⌘-spacebar by default). The Spotlight search bar appears (see Figure 5.2).

Figure 5.2
Click the Spotlight icon to display the Spotlight search bar.

2. Type your search criterion in the search bar. As you type, Spotlight immediately begins searching your Mac and presents results in the Spotlight results window (see Figure 5.3). Here are
some things to notice:

- At the top of the window is the Show All item, which
  you learn about in the next step.

- Just under Show All is the Top Hit, which is the item
  that Spotlight believes best matched your search criterion.

- Under Top Hit, the remaining results are organized by
  type, including Applications, System Preferences,
  Documents, Folders, Mail Messages, and so on.

 tip

You are probably used to typing a
search term and then pressing the
Return key. If you do this, you will be
taken automatically to the Top Hit
item. Try not to press the Return key,
so you can see all of the matching
results.

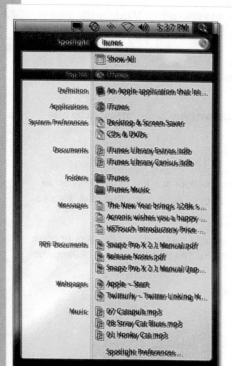

Figure 5.3
This search has found many items that are associated with the
"itunes" criterion, including applications, preferences, documents, a Dictionary definition, and so on.

3. To open an item on the results list, select it. For example, if you select a document, it opens. If you select a folder, a Finder window opens so you can view its contents. If you select an application, it launches. When you switch to the item, Spotlight hides so you can more easily work with the result you selected.

4. To return to the search results, click the Spotlight icon again. Your previous search results appear because Spotlight remembers your search until you indicate that you are done with it.

 note

If you used the Spotlight preference pane to prevent a type from being included in Spotlight searches, that category doesn't get searched and so won't appear in the results window.

The results shown in the initial Spotlight window might be limited if there are a large number of them; as mentioned previously, the first item on the results list is the Show All option. This option presents every item that meets your search criterion.

5. To show all the results of a search, click Show All. The Spotlight window appears (see Figure 5.4). The Spotlight window behaves much like a Finder window, which is really what it is. For example, you can sort the window, change its view, and so on.

Figure 5.4
You can use the Spotlight window to display all of your search results and to change how they are listed.

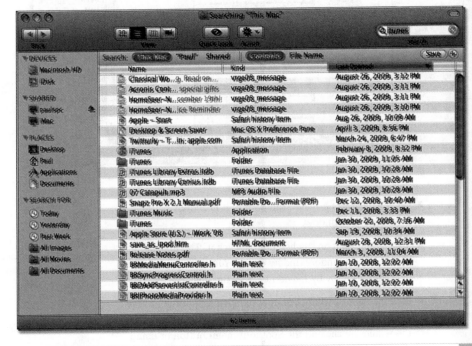

The Spotlight window has many features, including the following:

- Click the Quick Look button to display a preview of an item (see Figure 5.5). You can use the quick view area to preview some items. For example, you can listen to audio files, watch movies, and so on. Click the arrow button at the bottom of the Quick Look window to show the preview at full screen size.

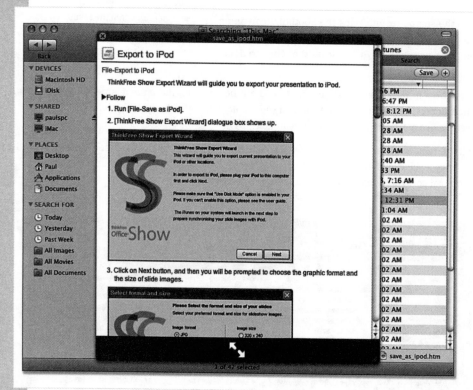

Figure 5.5
Here, the Quick Look button has been clicked to see a preview of a web page.

- When you select a result, the path to it is shown at the bottom of the window.

- To open an item on the list, double-click it. The appropriate application or Finder window opens. You can return to the Spotlight window by moving back to the desktop.

- Minimize the Spotlight window to move it out of your way while you look at an item you found. You can jump back to the results by clicking the Spotlight menu button or using the keyboard shortcuts for the menu or window.

To clear a Spotlight search, click the "x" in the Spotlight search tool or close the Spotlight window.

tip
You can move back to the Spotlight window or open it any time using the keyboard shortcut, which is Option-⌘-spacebar by default.

tip
Take advantage of Exposé (see Chapter 22) as you work with Spotlight results because that feature makes it easy to manage multiple open windows.

Saving Spotlight Searches

You can save Spotlight searches and run them again at any time.

1. Use the information in the previous section to perform a Spotlight search and open the Spotlight window.

2. Configure the results as you want to see them.

3. Click the Save button near the top-right portion of the Spotlight window.

4. Name the search and specify where to save it. The default is Saved Searches.

5. To add the saved search to the Sidebar, activate the Add to Sidebar check box.

6. Press Return to save it.

To run a saved search, you have two choices:

- If you activated the Add to Sidebar check box, click the search's icon in the Search For section of the Sidebar.

- If you didn't activate the Add to Sidebar check box, open a Finder window, select your home folder, open Library, open Saved Searches, and then launch the search icon.

When you save a Spotlight search, you save the search criterion, not the results. So, if new information that meets the search criterion has been added to your Mac, the next time you run the search, that information appears in the results.

 tip

To edit a saved search, first run the search as described in this section. Once the search results appear, click the Action menu and then select Show Search Criteria. The criteria for your search appear, and you can then edit those criteria (as described in the next section). When you have completed your changes, click the Save button.

Using Spotlight to Create Complex Searches

When you use Spotlight, you'll probably get a lot of results. Because its searches are broad, the results are wide-ranging and might or might not be easy to work with. Perform the following steps to create and save complex searches:

1. Open a saved search.

2. Click the Action menu and choose Show Search Criteria. The search criteria bar is added to the Spotlight window (see Figure 5.6).

3. On the location bar, choose where the search should take place. For example, by default the search will take place across your entire Mac. To limit the search to just your Home folder, click your username in the location bar. Select whether the Spotlight should just return file names that match your search or also search the content of those files.

4. Use the search criteria bar to fine tune your search. Click the first pop-up menu to select an attribute, such as Last Modified Date. The search criteria bar will then change to show specific things to search for related to that attribute.

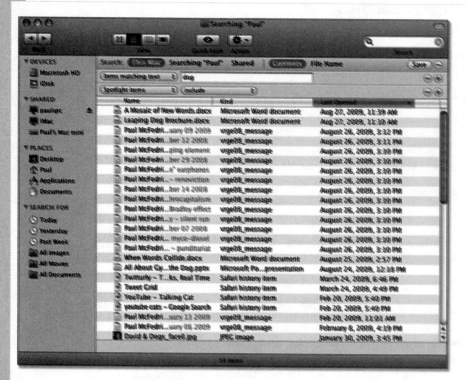

Figure 5.6
Use the search criteria and the search location bars to create complex Spotlight searches.

5. Click the Add button (+). Another search criterion appears.

6. Repeat step 4 to configure the new criterion.

7. Repeat steps 5 and 6 until you've added all the criteria to the search that you want it to include (see Figure 5.7).

8. The search runs as you make the changes to the search criteria, and you see the results in the Spotlight window.

9. Click the Save button so that you can run this search again. You can rerun the search at any time by selecting it in the Search For section of the Sidebar.

Figure 5.7
This search looks for images in my Home folder that include text "dog."

Adding Spotlight Information to Folders and Files

You can use the Finder's Info window to add metadata to files and folders so you can find them with Spotlight searches.

1. Use Finder to select an item.

2. Select File, Get Info or press ⌘-I to open the Info window.

3. Expand the Spotlight Comments section.

4. Use the Spotlight Comments box to type any extra information you want to associate with the file or folder. Your Mac searches the information you add when you perform Spotlight searches.

Searching Your Mac with Smart Folders

The Finder enables you to create smart folders. A smart folder displays its contents based on search criteria that you define, as opposed to a "regular" folder that displays items that have been manually placed within it. Even better, you can save smart folders so that you can repeat searches simply by refreshing the smart folders you create.

Just like Spotlight, smart folders search metadata so that there are many kinds of criteria you can use to search your Mac. Because of this, you can search by many different kinds of information, including the content of files and many attributes that aren't even displayed in the Finder.

Smart folders, the Finder's File, Find command (press ⌘-F), and the Spotlight window are all identical. You may get there in different ways, but the window, and the things you can do with it, are the same. As you further define your search criteria for a smart folder, you can save them to the Search For section of the Sidebar.

Creating and Saving a Smart Folder

To search your Mac using a smart folder, perform the following steps:

1. Choose File, New Smart Folder or press Option-⌘-N. A new smart folder appears.

2. Choose the location in which you want to search by clicking the appropriate Search location button. To search your entire Mac, click the This Mac button. To limit the search to your Home folder, click your short username. To search servers to which you are connected over a network, click Shared.

   Next, you need to build the specific criteria that you want to use for the search.

3. Click the Add button (+) to show the first Search Criteria bar, which shows Kind by default.

4. Choose the first criterion by which you want to limit your search. For example, to limit the search by the date something was last changed, choose Last Modified Date. If you choose the Other option, you'll see a sheet that enables you to select from a very large number of options (see Figure 5.8). You can browse this list to see all of the criteria that are possible. A brief description is provided in the sheet for these options. To choose a criterion on this list, select it and click OK.

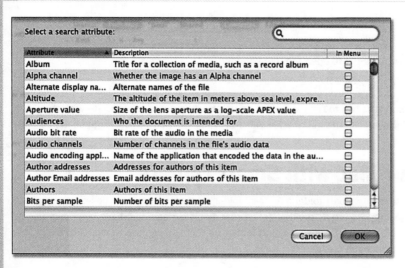

Figure 5.8
When you choose Other on a Search Criteria pop-up menu, you can choose from any of the possible search criteria.

After you have selected a criterion, controls appropriate for that criterion will appear. For example, when you choose a text criterion, a text box will appear. When you select a date criterion, a pop-up menu of options appears. If you choose Kind, a list of kinds of files appears as a pop-up menu.

5. Configure the criterion you selected by entering text, making a choice from the pop-up menu, and so on.

   In some cases, making a choice will result in additional tools you can use to configure the criterion. For example, if you choose Before for a date criterion, a date box will appear so that you can enter a date.

 tip

You can search for a criterion by typing text in the Search box at the top of the Other sheet. As you type, the criteria shown in the sheet will be limited to those that match your search. To add a criterion to the Search Criteria pop-up menu, select it and check the Add to Favorites check box.

6. If an additional tool has appeared, such as a date box, complete the data for the criterion.

   As you define criteria, the location you selected will be searched and items that meet the current search criteria will be shown in the Results section of the folder.

7. Click the Add button, which is the "+" at the end of each criterion's row, to add another criterion to the search

8. Configure the next criterion with the same steps you did to configure the first one (steps 3 through 6).

9. To remove a criterion from the search, click the Remove button, which is the "-" at the end of each criterion's row. That criterion is removed from the smart folder and will no longer impact the search.

10. Continue adding, configuring, or removing criteria until you have fully defined your search (see Figure 5.9).

Figure 5.9
This search will find all documents modified today whose contents include the term "neologism."

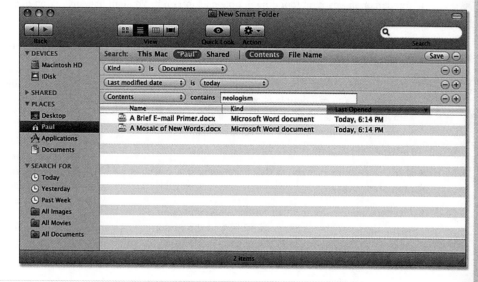

11. When the search is configured, click the Save button. You see a Save sheet.

12. Name your search, choose a location in which to save it, and determine whether it will be added to the Search For section of the Sidebar by checking or unchecking the Add To Sidebar check box, and then click Save (see Figure 5.10).

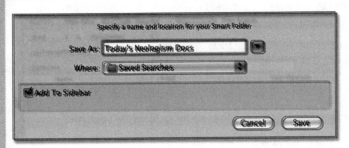

Figure 5.10
You can name and save the smart folders that you create so that you can repeat searches easily.

You return to the smart folder, which is named with the name you entered. If you opted to have the search added to the Search For section of the Sidebar, you see it there as well.

Following are some points to ponder when you are working with smart folders:

■ If you don't want to limit your search, don't configure any search criteria. Instead just type the text or numbers for which you want to search in the Search box at the top of the smart folder's window. This can be literally anything from text contained in documents, resolution of images, dates associated with documents, people's names, and so on. As you start to type, your Mac begins its search and documents, folders, bookmarks, and anything else that meets your search text appear in the results section of the folder.

■ You can open any item found by double-clicking on it. You can use any action or contextual commands on items as well, just as you can in a regular folder.

■ If you click the Quick Look button (the "eye") associated with an item, you see a preview of it in a new window.

■ When you select an item in the results area, the path to its location is shown at the bottom of the window. You can double-click on any part of the path shown to open that part. For example, if the Pictures folder is part of the path shown, double-click on the Pictures icon to open that folder.

■ If you close a smart folder without first saving it, you're prompted to do so.

■ After you have saved a smart folder, when you open it again, the search tools are not visible. Use the Action menu to select Show Search Criteria to see the search parameters again.

tip

Want to find all the documents on your Mac that have changed recently so you can back them up? Create and save a smart folder with search criteria of Last Modified Since Yesterday and Kind Documents. The results will display all documents that have changed since yesterday.

- The default save location for smart folder searches is the Saved Searches folder located at /~username/Library/Saved Searches where /~username is your username. If you want to remove searches, open this folder and delete any smart folder files you want to remove from your computer. If you also added the smart folder to your Sidebar, you'll need to remove its icon by dragging it off the sidebar.

Using Smart Folders

After you have created a smart folder, you can perform the search again by opening the smart folder. If you choose to add it to the Search For section of your Sidebar, click its icon. You see the current results of the search.

The smart folder's window always shows the most current results of a search.

There are several ways to search with a saved smart folder:

- Place the smart folder in the Search For section of the Sidebar and click its icon.

- Drag the smart folder from its saved location onto the Dock. You can run the search by clicking the icon on the Dock.

- Select a smart folder's icon and choose File, Open or press ⌘-O.

- Double-click the smart folder's icon.

 note

When you save a smart folder, you save the search criteria, not the results. This means that each time you use the smart folder, the search is repeated. If something has changed such that an item now meets the search criteria, it will appear in the smart folder.

 tip

For immediate access to all your smart folders without cluttering up your Sidebar, store all the searches in one folder and add that folder to the Dock. Right-click the folder and you can immediately select any smart folder to open it.

Changing Smart Folders

You can change an existing smart folder, such as to change one or more of its search criteria.

1. Open the smart folder you want to change. The results are shown, but the tools to edit your search do not appear.

2. Click the Action menu and section Show Search Criteria.

3. Reconfigure the search by changing existing criteria, adding new ones, or removing them. You can also change the search location.

4. Click Save. The smart folder now contains the revised search criteria.

Keeping Your Mac Organized

You can make things easier to find on your Mac if you keep your files and information organized in logical ways and then are consistent about how you store data on your Mac. Often, this will eliminate the need to search because you'll already know where to find what you're looking for.

Following are some pointers you might want to consider to reduce the time and effort you have to spend looking for information:

- **Folders in the Finder** Your Home folder includes some default folders, such as Documents, Music, and so on, that you can use to organize files and other information. These should be just a start for you; create folders within these folders to further organize your files. There's really no limit to the number of folders you can create, and using the Column view, you can quickly get to any level of folder.

- **Folders within applications** Many applications, including iTunes, Address Book, iPhoto, and so on, enable you to create folders to organize data in those applications. Making good use of these tools often reduces the searches you need to do because you know where information is stored.

- **Names** Use meaningful names when you create files and folders. For example, when you are working on a project, apply the same prefix to all the folders and files associated with that project. When you view a Finder window in list or columns view, the files will naturally group themselves by the project prefix.

- **Trash** Get rid of files and folders when you are done using them. The more junk you have on your Mac, the harder it is to find things in which you are interested.

SETTING SYSTEM PREFERENCES

Taking a Tour of the System Preferences

If you want to learn Mac OS X in depth, as I hope to show you in this book, you have to go beyond the superficial features and tools that the interface provides and get under the hood to tinker with the non-obvious settings and options. In Mac OS X, this means (at least in part), tackling the System Preferences application, which is a powerful and important tool that you use to control how your Mac OS X system works and looks. With a thorough understanding of what you can do with System Preferences, you'll be in great shape not only to learn Mac OS X in depth, but also to fully customize and configure Mac OS X to suit the way you work and your personal tastes. This chapter gives you that thorough understanding.

To open System Preferences, you have two choices:

- Click the System Preferences icon in the Dock.

- Pull down the Apple menu and select System Preferences.

Figure 6.1 shows a default System Preferences window, which on this Mac displays 26 total preferences icons.

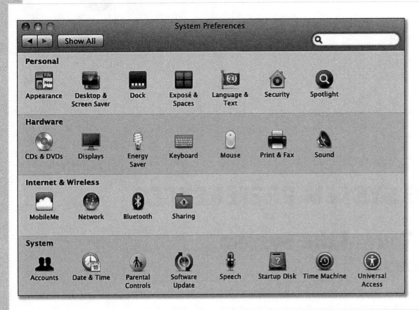

Figure 6.1
The default System Preferences window is home to more than two dozen preference panes.

Table 6.1 provides a summary of each pane and tells you where in this book you can learn more about it.

Table 6.1   System Preferences Application Panes

Category	Pane	What It Does	Where You Can Learn More About It
Personal	Appearance	Controls several aspects of how your desktop looks, how scrolling happens, the number of recent items to display, and font smoothing	"Setting Appearance Preferences," p. 107
Personal	Desktop & Screen Saver	Sets the desktop picture and configures the screen saver	"Setting Desktop Pictures and Choosing a Screen Saver," p. 109
Personal	Dock	Controls how the Dock looks and works	"Customizing the Appearance and Behavior of the Dock," p. 32
Personal	Exposé & Spaces	Enables you to set hot keys for Exposé and to configure spaces on your Mac	"Managing Your Desktop with Exposé and Spaces," p. 465
Personal	Languages and Text	Configures the languages and formats your system uses	"Setting International Preferences," p. 116
Personal	Security	Enables you to protect your Mac with FileVault, a firewall, and system security controls	"Securing Your Mac," p.705

Table 6.1 Continued

Category	Pane	What It Does	Where You Can Learn More About It
Personal	Spotlight	Configures how Spotlight works	"Configuring Spotlight," p. 90
Hardware	Bluetooth	Configures Bluetooth communication between your Mac and other devices	"Choosing, Installing, and Using Bluetooth Devices," p. 601 (Chapter 30); note that this pane appears only if your Mac is Bluetooth capable.
Hardware	CDs & DVDs	Sets default behaviors when you work with CDs or DVDs	"Setting Default Disc Behaviors," p. 120
Hardware	Displays	Configures the settings of displays connected to your Mac	"Configuring a Mac's Display," p. 612
Hardware	Energy Saver	Manages your Mac's poweruse	"Managing Your Mobile Mac's Power," p. 549
Hardware	Ink	Controls the Ink handwriting recognition system when you connect a tablet device to your Mac	Use this pane to configure how your Mac recognizes your handwriting as input if you use a tablet input device; this pane appears only if you have a tablet device connected to your Mac.
Hardware	Keyboard	Configures keyboards you use	"Working with Mice, Keyboards, and Other Input Devices," p. 591
Hardware	Mouse	Configures mice you use	"Working with Mice, Keyboards, and Other Input Devices," p. 591
Hardware	Trackpad	Configures the trackpad on a notebook Mac	"Working with Mice, Keyboards, and Other Input Devices," p. 591
Hardware	Print & Fax	Configures printers your Mac can access and provides fax settings	"Installing, Configuring, and Using Printers," p. 635
Hardware	Sound	Provides the settings you use to manage your Mac's sound	"Working with Your Mac's Sound," p. 625
Internet & Network	MobileMe	Use this pane to set up and manage your MobileMe account	"Using MobileMe to Integrate a Mac onto the Internet," p. 421
Internet & Network	Network	This pane enables you to configure a Mac for network access	"Wired Networking with Mac OS X," p. 361 "Wireless Networking with Mac OS X," p. 385
Internet & Network	Sharing	Enables you to share your Mac's services and Internet connection over a network	"Configuring and Using File Sharing," p. 364 "Sharing an Internet Account with Mac OS X," p. 411

Table 6.1 Continued

Category	Pane	What It Does	Where You Can Learn More About It
System	Accounts	Enables you to create and manage user accounts	"Working with User Accounts," p. 441
System	Date & Time	Sets your Mac's date and time	"Configuring Your Mac's Date and Time," p. 120
System	Parental Controls	Enables you to customize the access specific user accounts have to your Mac's resources and allows you to limit someone's time on a Mac	"Securing Your Mac," p. 705
System	Software Update	Keeps your version of Mac OS X and Apple applications current	"Using Software Update to Maintain Your System Software," p. 672
System	Speech	Configures speech recognition and text to speech settings	"Making Your Mac Accessible to Everyone," p. 495
System	Startup Disk	Configures your Mac's startup volume	"Choosing a Startup Volume with System Preferences," p. 123
System	Time Machine	Configures a backup system for your Mac's data	"Backing Up Your Mac," p. 689
System	Universal Access	Enables you to make your Mac more accessible to those who have disabilities	"Making Your Mac Accessible to Everyone," p. 495
Other	As Installed	The Other section appears when you've added hardware or software to your system that has a preference component. After you install the hardware or software, its preference pane will be shown in the Other section.	Documentation or help system provided with hardware or software

The following are some tips to work with the System Preferences application:

- You can open a pane by selecting it on the application's View menu.

- Right-click on the System Preferences application's icon on the Dock and choose a pane on the pop-up menu to work with it.

- To see all the panes again, select View, Show All Preferences; press ⌘-L; or click the Show All button on the System Preferences application's toolbar.

 note

You might see more or fewer panes in the System Preferences application than are listed in Table 6.1 depending on the hardware and software you have installed. For example, if your Mac doesn't support Bluetooth hardware, you won't see the Bluetooth pane.

- You can search for a pane by typing text in the System Preferences application's Search tool. (You can move into the tool by clicking in it; selecting View, Search; or pressing ⌘-F.) As you type, the panes that meet your search will become "spotlighted" and the rest of the panes will be darkened.

- If you prefer that the panes be listed alphabetically rather than by category, select View, Organize Alphabetically. The System Preferences application will be reorganized and the panes will appear alphabetically from the upper left to the bottom right.

- Use the toolbar's Back and Forward buttons to move among panes you have opened.

Setting Appearance Preferences

How your Mac's desktop looks is likely an important thing; because you are going to be looking at it so much, it should look as pleasing to you as possible. Likewise, it should work in the way that makes the most sense to you. You can use the Appearance pane of the System Preferences application to configure certain aspects of how Mac OS X looks and works. And if the default colors provided in the pane aren't to your liking, you can use the Color Picker to add colors you'd like to see.

Using the Appearance Pane

Use the Appearance pane of the System Preferences application to control several basic settings for your system. This pane is organized into four sections. From top to bottom, they control basic appearance settings, scroll behavior, the number of recent items tracked, and font smoothing (see Figure 6.2).

The Appearance pop-up menu includes these options:

- Select Blue if you want color in the buttons, menus, and windows.

- Select Graphite if you want to mute the color so the color elements are gray instead.

- Use the Highlight Color pop-up menu to select the highlight color. You can choose one of the default colors on the pop-up menu or choose Other to open the Color Picker, which is described in the next section.

Use the Place Scroll Arrows radio buttons to set the following scrolling behaviors:

- Choose the Together radio button to place the scroll arrows together.

- Choose the At Top and Bottom radio button to have a scroll arrow placed at each end of the scrollbar.

- Select Jump to Here to cause a window to jump to the relative position in the scrollbar on which you click or Jump to the Next Page to scroll a page at a time when you click above or below the scroll box.

- If you want scrolling to be smooth (instead of jumping when you scroll, your Mac kind of strolls to the new location), check the Use Smooth Scrolling check box.

- Activate the Double-Click a Window's Title Bar to Minimize check box if you want to be able to minimize a window by double-clicking its title bar.

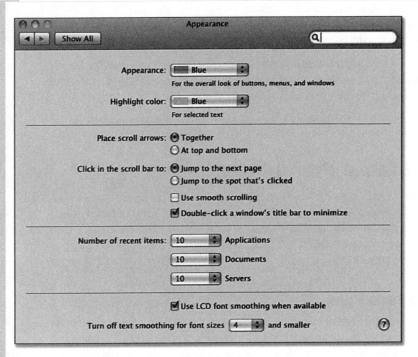

Figure 6.2
The Appearance pane can be used to configure several different aspects of how Mac OS X looks and works.

Set the number of recent items tracked on the Apple menu for applications, documents, and servers using the Number of Recent Items pop-up menus. You can track as few as none or as many as 50 recent items with a number of choices in between.

The bottom section of the pane provides the controls you use to configure how font smoothing is enabled on your Mac. *Font smoothing* (known as antialiasing for graphics) reduces the jaggies that occur when you view certain fonts onscreen; this is most noticeable when you use larger sizes or thick fonts or when you apply bold or other formatting. Font smoothing is always turned on, but you can configure it specifically for your system:

1. Open the Appearance pane of the System Preferences application.

2. Activate the Use LCD Font Smoothing When Available check box.

3. Because the effect of smoothing is less noticeable at small font sizes, your system can save some wasted processing power by not smoothing fonts displayed at small sizes. Select the font size at or below which text smoothing is disabled, using the Turn Off Text Smoothing for Font Sizes X and Smaller pop-up menu. The default value is 4 points, but you might not even notice if you increase this value slightly.

Using the Color Picker to Choose Colors

There are many areas in which you choose to use colors for certain things, such as when you apply colors to text or apply a color to the background of a Finder window. To apply colors, you use the Color Picker, which you can open by choosing Other on the Highlight Color pop-up menu on the Appearance pane (see Figure 6.3). Within applications, you use the Colors panel to apply colors to text and images, and it works in the same way as the Color Picker.

 tip

How you open the Colors panel depends on the application you are using. However, in some applications, such as TextEdit, you can open it by pressing Shift-⌘-C.

Figure 6.3
The Color Picker enables you to create and apply custom colors to selected elements, such as to the background of a Finder window or the color your Mac uses to highlight interface elements.

The five modes in the Color Picker are represented by the five buttons along the top of the window. From left to right they are the Color Wheel, Color Sliders (including Gray Scale, RGB [Red Green Blue], CMYK [Cyan Magenta Yellow Black], and HSB [Hue Saturation Balance], Color Palettes, Image Palettes, and Crayons. Each of these modes work similarly. Select the mode you want to use, and the controls in the Color Picker window change to reflect the mode you are in. Use the mode's controls to select or configure a color to apply. When you want to apply the color to the selected object, click it.

 tip

You can add the configured color to the list of favorite colors at the bottom of the window by dragging the color from the top of the dialog box to the boxes at the bottom so you can easily apply the color again in the future.

If you click the Magnifying Glass icon, the pointer turns into a magnifying glass. If you move this over an area and click, the color in that area appears in the current color box of the Color Picker.

Setting Desktop Pictures and Choosing a Screen Saver

Setting a desktop picture is a great way to personalize your Mac and make it more pleasing to look at; using a screen saver is a good way to protect your screen from damage that can be caused by a static image being displayed on it for a long period of time. You can use the Desktop & Screen Saver pane of the System Preferences application to configure both these aspects of your system.

 note

The Colors panel you see within particular applications might have the same or slightly different modes.

Choosing Desktop Pictures

You use the Desktop tab of the Desktop & Screen Saver pane of the System Preferences application to configure a desktop picture (see Figure 6.4). You can choose to use one of Mac OS X's default images, any image or folder of images in your Pictures folder, any image or folder of images located elsewhere, or any photos you have in your iPhoto Library. You can use images in just about any image format as desktop pictures, such as TIFF, JPG, and so on.

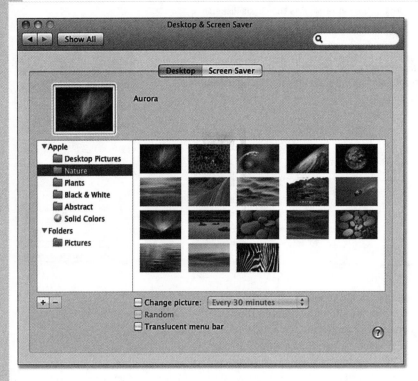

Figure 6.4
Although you probably won't see your desktop picture all that much if you have a lot of windows open, it's nice to have something pleasant to look at from time to time.

Configuring desktop pictures is easy:

1. Select the Desktop tab. At the top of the tab, you see the current desktop picture in the Image well and the name of the image next to the Image well. Beneath that on the left side of pane is the list of available sources of pictures. On the right side of the pane are the pictures in the source that is selected on the left side of the pane.

2. Choose the image source that you want to use on the desktop by selecting it on the Source list. There are a number of default sources including Desktop Pictures, Nature, Plants, and so on. Choose Folders, Pictures to use the

 tip

If your Mac is connected to multiple displays, the desktop on each display can have its own desktop picture. When you open the Desktop tab, a pane will appear on each display. Use each screen's pane to configure its desktop picture; the desktop picture on each display is independent so you can have the picture on one display be dynamic while the picture on the other is static.

Pictures folder in your Home folder as the source. You can add any other folder as a source by clicking the Add Source (+) button at the bottom of the pane. After you select a source, its images appear in the right part of the pane (see Figure 6.5).

Figure 6.5
Here I've selected a folder with photos from a recent vacation.

3. To use one of the images being shown, select it. The image you select will be placed on the desktop.

4. To have your Mac rotate the desktop picture among those in the selected source, activate the Change Picture check box and choose the amount of time each picture should be displayed on the pop-up menu; there are many options including each time you log in, when waking up from sleep, and various times from every five seconds to every day. If you want the images to be selected at random, activate the Random check box; if you leave this deactivated, the images will be used in the same order as they are in the source. When you do this, the Image well will be filled with an icon that indicates that images will be rotated. The first image is selected and placed on the desktop and is changed according to the timing you selected.

 tip

You can also place a single image on the desktop by dragging it from Finder onto the Image well.

 tip

To remove an image source from the list, select it and click the Remove Source button (-).

Configuring a Screen Saver

Mac OS X was the first version of the Mac OS that included a built-in screen saver. Many Mac users enjoy having a screen saver, and Mac OS X's version provides the features you would expect. The quality and style with which the screen saver displays images are quite nice. It can be especially nice when you use your own images.

You use the Screen Saver tab of the Desktop & Screen Saver pane of the System Preferences application to configure a screen saver for your computer (see Figure 6.6).

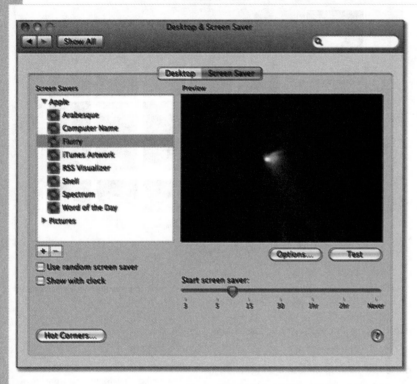

Figure 6.6
You can use one of Mac OS X's built-in screen saver modules, create your own screen saver, or add a screen saver that someone else created.

Display Sleep Time

If you really want to protect your screen, use the Energy Saver pane to set a display sleep time. Display sleep actually turns off the display mechanism, which saves the screen. Of course, a blank screen isn't nearly as interesting as the screen saver.

To be safe when it comes to the health of your Mac's display, you should keep the display sleep setting at a relatively short amount of time so it sleeps when you aren't actively using your Mac. This will prevent possible damage to your display more effectively than the screen saver does.

Along the left side of the pane, you see two general categories of screen saver modules you can use. The Apple group includes modules provided by Apple, such as Flurry or iTunes Artwork. The Pictures section includes sources of photos that can be used as a screen saver module, including photos from your iPhoto Library. The Preview pane shows a preview of the selected module and you see various controls you can use to configure and test the module you select; these work similarly for all the modules.

Using a Built-in Screen Saver Module

The general steps for using one of Mac OS X's built-in modules are the following:

1. Display the Screen Saver tab.

2. If you want your Mac to randomly select and use a screen saver, activate the Use Random Screen Saver check box and skip to step 9. Each time the screen saver activates, your Mac will select a different module to use.

3. Select the screen saver module you want to use from the Screen Savers list; you see a preview in the Preview window.

4. Click the Options button to set various parameters for the screen saver you select. The options that are available depend on the specific module you select. Some modules don't have options and the Options button will be disabled.

5. If you select a module that uses photos, use the Display Style buttons to choose how the photos are displayed. You can choose a Mosaic style, Collage style, or you can have each image presented using transition effects to create a slideshow.

6. If you want the clock to be displayed along with the screen saver, activate the Show with Clock check box. The time will appear on screen along with the screen saver images.

7. If your Mac is connected to multiple displays, but you want the screen saver to be shown only on the main display, activate the Main Screen Only check box. The images will be displayed on the display with the Mac title bar; other displays will be blank.

8. Test the screen saver by clicking the Test button. The images that are part of the screen saver are rendered and displayed with the configuration options you selected.

 note

Most of the default Mac OS screen saver modules use standard images Apple has provided. One of them— the iTunes Artwork module—is more interesting, however. It creates a screen saver using the artwork associated with albums in your iTunes Music Library. When you select this module, the artwork is gathered from iTunes automatically and the album covers appear in a large square consisting of subsquares, each of which rotates through various album covers.

 note

If you use multiple displays, a different image from the selected screen saver module is shown on each display.

9. Use the Start Screen Saver slider to set the idle time that must pass before the screen saver is activated.

10. Click the Hot Corners button.

11. On the resulting sheet, select the corners to which you can move the mouse to manually start or disable the screen saver. Select the action you want to occur on the pop-up menu located at the corner you want to configure and click OK. For example, if you select Start Screen Saver on the pop-up menu located in the upper-left corner of the sheet, you can start the screen saver by moving the cursor to the upper-left corner of the display. The default is to have no action occur at any corner.

 note

If the display sleep time set on the Energy Saver pane is less than the time you set in step 9, you will never see the screen saver because the display will sleep before the screen saver is activated. If this is the case, a warning appears on the Screen Saver tab pane and a button enables you to jump to the Energy Saver pane. You can either decrease the time for the screen saver to activate or increase the time for Display sleep.

Creating a Custom Screen Saver Module

Some of the built-in modules are pretty cool (I especially like iTunes Artwork), but you can have even more fun by creating or using a custom module. There are several ways to do this:

- Create a screen saver from a folder of pictures.

- Create a screen saver from a MobileMe member's gallery.

- Create a screen saver that displays an RSS feed.

- Use a screen saver you download from the Internet.

The next four sections take you through the details.

Creating a Screen Saver from a Folder of Pictures

To create a screen saver from your own images, use the following steps:

1. Create a folder containing the images you want to use. The images can be in the standard image formats, such as JPG or TIFF.

2. Open the Screen Saver tab and select the Add icon (+).

3. Select Add Folder of Pictures.

3. Use the Choose Folder sheet to move to and select the folder containing the images you want to use.

4. Click Choose.

5. Use the other controls on the tab to configure the screen saver. You have the same display options as for the built-in screen saver modules.

You can choose to use the images within your Pictures folder by selecting it on the list of screen savers. Only the images located in the root folder (not within folders that are inside the Pictures folder) are used. You configure the screen saver using the same steps you use for other options.

If you have installed and use iPhoto, you can choose any images in your iPhoto Photo Library as a screen saver by selecting Library, which is located under the Choose Folder module. You can also select any photo album you have created in iPhoto as a screen saver by selecting it on the list that appears under the Photo Library on the screen saver list.

Creating a Screen Saver from a MobileMe Gallery

To create a screen saver from a MobileMe gallery, follow these steps:

1. Open the Screen Saver tab and select the Add icon (+).

2. Select Add MobileMe Gallery. System Preferences prompts you for a MobileMe member name.

3. Type the member name and click OK. System Preferences retrieves a list of albums, as shown in Figure 6.7.

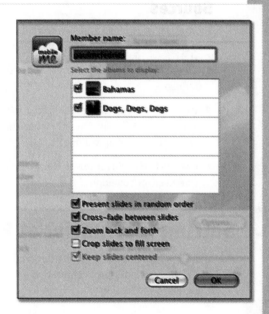

Figure 6.7
You can create a screen saver from the image in a MobileMe gallery.

4. Activate the check boxes beside each gallery you want to use.

5. Use the other check boxes to set the slide show options.

6. Click OK.

7. Use the other controls on the tab to configure the screen saver. You have the same display options as for the built-in screen saver modules.

Creating a Screen Saver from an RSS Feed

If you know of an RSS feed that includes pictures, you can uses the feed images for your screen saver. Here are the steps to follow:

1. Open the Screen Saver tab and select the Add icon (+).

2. Select Add RSS Feed. System Preferences prompts you for the RSS feed address.

3. Type the feed URL and click OK. System Preferences retrieves the feed images.

4. Use the other controls on the tab to configure the screen saver. You have the same display options as for the built-in screen saver modules.

Using Screen Savers Acquired from the Internet and Other Sources

You can also download screen savers from the Internet or obtain them from other sources. Screen saver modules have the .saver filename extension. To do this, follow these steps:

1. Download the screen saver you want to use and prepare it for use.

2. Place the .saver file in the directory *Mac OS X*/Library/Screen Savers, where *Mac OS X* is the name of the startup volume.

3. Use the Screen Saver tab to choose and configure the screen saver you added.

note

You can browse Apple's screen savers from the Screen Saver tab. Click the Add icon (+) and then select Browse Screen Savers.

Setting International Preferences

Mac OS X includes support for a large number of languages; language behaviors; and date, time, and number formats. You control these properties through the Language & Text pane of the System Preferences application (see Figure 6.8).

Figure 6.8
You can use the Language & Text pane of the System Preferences application to control various language and format properties based on a language and the conventions of particular nations.

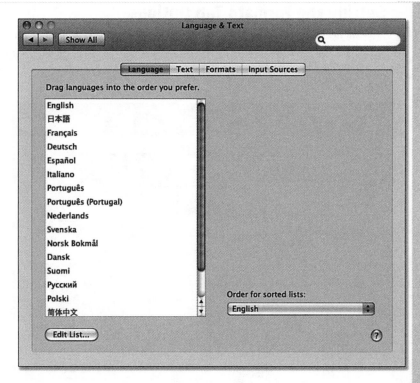

Setting the Language Tab Options

Use the Language tab to configure the languages you want to use. The Languages list shows the languages that are currently active. You can drag these languages up and down in the list to set the preferred order in which you want to use them on menus and in dialog boxes. If you click the Edit List button, a sheet will appear on which you can choose the languages that appear in the Languages list by unchecking the Show check boxes for the languages you don't want to use (the languages on this list are those that were installed when you installed Mac OS X). After you click OK, the languages whose check boxes you unchecked will no longer appear on the language list. Use the Order for Sorted Lists pop-up menu to choose the language by which lists will be sorted.

 note

Changes you make to language settings will become active in the Finder the next time you log in.

Setting the Formats Tab Options

Use the Formats tab to configure the format of the dates, times, and numbers used on your Mac. When you open this tab, you see a section for each of these areas along with the Region pop-up menu (see Figure 6.9).

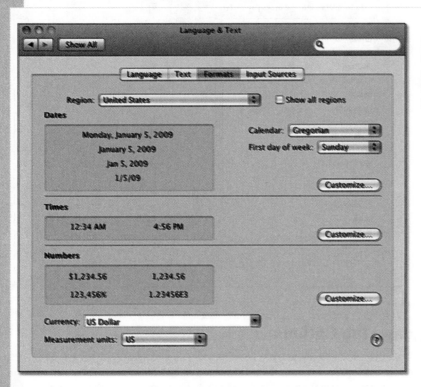

Figure 6.9
Use the Formats tab of the International pane to set the format of dates, times, and numbers for your system.

Choosing a Region

Select the region setting for your Mac on the Region pop-up menu. By default, you see region choices that relate to the languages you have installed. If you want to see all possible region options, check the Show All Regions check box. When you make a selection, default formats for the region you selected are applied to each setting area (dates, times, and numbers).

After you have set general format preferences via the Region pop-up menu, you can customize the format in each area.

 note

The options described in the following paragraphs are for the United States region. If you choose a different region, different options might be available to you, but they can be set using similar steps.

Customizing Date Options

In the Dates section, click the Customize button. The Customize Dates sheet will appear. Use the controls on this sheet to set the date formats displayed in Finder windows and other locations. There are four general date formats: Short, Medium, Long, and Full. Use the pop-up menus, check boxes, and text fields to set the format for each type of date. Choose the date format you want to configure on the Show pop-up menu. The default format will be shown in the box below the pop-up menu. Click each element, such as the month, to customize it. For example, you can customize the month format by selecting the abbreviated form. Drag the elements around to change the order in which they appear. If you want to add more elements to the default format you selected, drag them from the Date Elements section of the sheet to the location in which you want the elements to appear. Repeat these steps to configure each of the date format options (such as for the Short format). Click OK to save your settings and close the sheet. On the Calendar pop-up menu, choose the calendar you want to use, such as Gregorian or Japanese.

 tip

To remove an element from the date or time customization, select it and press the Delete key.

Customizing Time Options

In the Times section, click the Customize button. The Customize Times sheet will appear. Choose the time format you want to configure on the Show pop-up menu. The default format will be shown in the box below the pop-up menu. Click each element, such as the minute, to customize it. For example, you can customize the minute display by choosing to show the leading 0 or not. Drag the elements around to change the order in which they appear. If you want to add more elements to the default format you selected, drag them from the Time Elements section of the sheet to the location in which you want the elements to appear. Repeat these steps to configure each of the time format options (such as for the Short format). To determine the modifier that is displayed when the time is before or after noon, enter the modifier in the Before Noon and After Noon boxes. Click OK to save your settings and close the sheet.

note

The settings you make in the Dates and Times sheets affect the format of these values in the Finder and other locations. They do not affect the clock display; you control the format of the clock using the Time & Date pane.

Is time really important to you? With Mac OS X, you can choose to display milliseconds by adding the Milliseconds element to one of the standard time formats.

Customizing Number Formats

You can see the format of numbers using the region you have selected in the Numbers section. You can click Customize to configure your own number and currency separators, or you can select default formats using the following two controls.

 note

When you make changes to a standard format, the selection on the Region pop-up menu becomes Custom to indicate that you have customized your settings.

- Use the Currency pop-up menu to choose the currency format you want to use, such as US Dollar or Euro.

- Use the Measurement Units pop-up menu to select the default measurement units used (U.S. [aka English] or Metric).

Setting the Input Sources Tab Options

Use the Input Sources tab to control and configure the Input menu that can appear on the menu bar.

➡ *To learn how to configure the Character Palette, **see** "Working with the Character Viewer," p. 491.*

➡ *To learn how to configure a keyboard for different languages, **see** "Configuring a Keyboard," p. 593.*

Setting Default Disc Behaviors

Use the CDs & DVDs pane of the System Preferences application to determine your Mac's default behaviors when you insert a disc (see Figure 6.10).

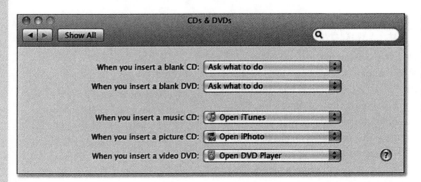

Figure 6.10
The CDs & DVDs pane of the System Preferences application enables you to determine what your Mac does when you insert a disc into it.

You set a behavior for your Mac when you insert a music CD, picture CD, or video DVD. On the pop-up menu for each of these, you'll see a similar set of commands. At the top of the menu is a list of all applications that Mac OS X thinks might be suitable for the type of disc you insert. Choose the application that you want to be used by default; for example, you can choose DVD Player or Front Row for video DVDs. To select an application not on the list, choose Open Other Application and then choose the application you want to be used. To have an AppleScript run, choose Run Script and then select the script you want to be used. To have your Mac do nothing, choose Ignore.

The next time you insert a disc, your Mac will take the default action that you set.

Configuring Your Mac's Date and Time

The Date & Time pane of the System Preferences application enables you to set and maintain your system's time and date (see Figure 6.11). You can set the time and date manually, or you can use a network timeserver to set and maintain your system's time and date for you.

Figure 6.11
The Date & Time pane enables you to determine how your Mac keeps track of time.

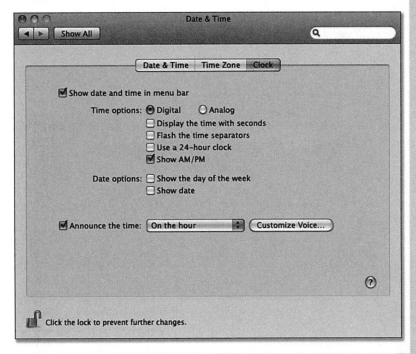

To set your system's date and time, do the following:

1. Open the Date & Time pane.

2. Click the Time Zone tab.

3. Use either of the following methods to set the time zone:

   ■ Activate the Set Time Zone Automatically Using Current Location to have Mac OS X do all the work for you.

   ■ Use the map to set your time zone (see Figure 6.12). Drag the highlight bar over your location to select the correct time zone. Then use the Closest City pop-up menu to select the specific time zone for the area in which you are located.

note

If you specified a MobileMe account when you installed Mac OS X, the time zone information has been configured for you.

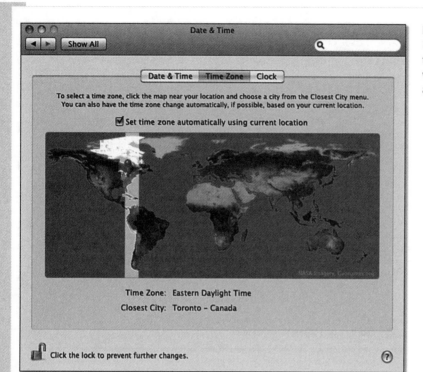

Figure 6.12
Use the Time Zone tools to set the time zone in which you and your Mac are currently located.

4. Click the Date & Time tab.

5. Choose how you want to set the time:

   - If you are going to use a network timeserver to maintain the time and date for your machine, activate the Set Date & Time Automatically check box and select the timeserver you want to use on the drop-down list. The options you see depend on where you are. Apple provides three primary timeservers, one for the Americas, one for Asia, and one for Europe. Select the server that is appropriate for your location.

   - If you want to set the time and date manually, deactivate the Set Date & Time Automatically check box. There are easy-to-understand controls that you use to set the date and time. You can use the Calendar tool to choose a date, type a date in the date box, or use the arrows next to it to select a date. You can then use similar controls to set the time.

 note

You have to be connected to the Internet to use one of Mac OS X's built-in timeservers. Similarly, you must be connected to a local network to use a timeserver located on that network.

 note

You can find the official time for any time zone in the United States at www.time.gov. Of course, this is useful only if you live in the United States and can handle the time being off by as much as 0.1 seconds.

➥ To learn how to use the Clock tab to configure the desktop clock, **see** *"Changing the Clock Display," p. 15.*

Controlling System Startup

Under Mac OS X, there are several ways to configure and control the startup process. The most straightforward way is to use the Startup Disk pane of the System Preferences application to select a startup volume. There are other ways you can control system startup as well, such as selecting a startup volume during the startup process, starting up in the single-user mode, and starting up in the verbose mode.

Choosing a Startup Volume with System Preferences

The Startup Disk pane of the System Preferences application enables you to select a startup volume (see Figure 6.13). Open the pane to see a list of the valid startup volumes on your machine. Select the volume from which you want to start up and click Restart. You are prompted to confirm this action by clicking the Restart button. Your selection is saved and your Mac restarts from the volume you selected.

Figure 6.13
The Startup Disk pane allows you to select a startup volume for your Mac.

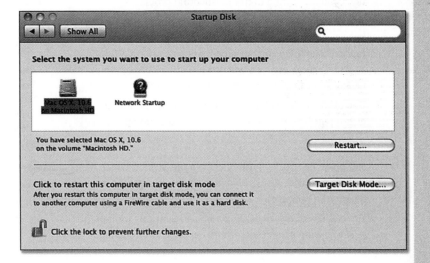

If you want your Mac to start up in Target Disk mode so it acts as if it is only a hard disk, click Target Disk Mode and then click Restart at the prompt sheet.

➡ *To learn more about Target Disk Mode,* **see** *"Starting Up in Target Disk Mode,"* **p. 125.**

 tip

For troubleshooting purposes, it's a good idea to install Mac OS X on more than one volume. Use one of these as your working startup volume. Don't use the other one except for troubleshooting purposes. This can be a great help when you are having trouble with your Mac.

Choosing a Startup Volume During Startup

During the startup process, you can select the startup volume by holding down the Option key while the machine is starting up. As the Mac starts up, you see icons for each of the valid startup volumes on your machine. The currently selected startup volume is highlighted. You can select a startup volume by clicking the arrow below the volume's icon. The Mac will then start up from the volume you selected.

Starting Up in Single-User Mode

The single-user mode starts up your Mac in a Unix-like environment. In this environment, you can run Unix commands outside of Mac OS X. This can be useful in a couple of situations, mostly related to troubleshooting problems.

To start up in single-user mode, hold down ⌘-S while the machine is starting up. Many system messages appear and report on how the startup process is proceeding. When the startup is complete, you will see the root# Unix prompt. This means you can start entering Unix commands.

One of the more useful things you can do is to run the Unix disk-repair function, which is fsck. At the prompt, type

/sbin/fsck -y

and press Return. The utility checks the disk on which Mac OS X is installed. Any problems it finds are reported and repaired (if possible).

You can use many other Unix commands at this prompt, just as if you were using the Terminal application from inside Mac OS X.

> ➡ *To learn more about using Unix commands,* **see** *Chapter 26, "Working with the Mac OS X Command Line," p. 531.*

To resume the startup process in Mac OS X, type the command **reboot** and press Return. Additional, even more arcane Unix messages appear and then the normal Mac OS X startup process continues. When that process is complete, you end up at the Login window or directly in the Mac OS X desktop, depending on how your Login preferences are configured.

 note

Single-user mode is also called *Console mode.*

 caution

When you start up in single-user mode, you will be using the root account. Under this account, you can do anything to the files on your Mac. Some actions you perform under the root account can't be undone, so be careful that you don't do something you didn't mean to do.

 note

During the startup process, you are likely to see some information that doesn't make a lot of sense to you unless you are fluent in Unix and in the arcane system messages you see. You might also see some odd error messages, but typically I wouldn't worry about them too much. However, if you have particular problems you are trying to solve, some of these messages might provide valuable clues for you.

 note

If the startup disk is Journaled, type /**sbin**/**fsck -yf** to force the utility to run.

 tip

If you want to eject a disc when you restart your Mac, hold down the mouse button while you restart.

Starting Up in Verbose Mode

If you hold down ⌘-V while your Mac is starting up, you start up in the verbose mode. In this mode, you see all sorts of system messages while the machine starts up. The difference between verbose mode and single-user mode is that the verbose mode is not interactive. All you can do is view the system messages; you can't control what happens. Many of the messages you see will probably be incomprehensible, but some are not (particularly messages about specific system processes starting up). This mode is likely to be useful to you only in troubleshooting. And even then, the single-user mode is probably more useful because it gives you some control over what is happening.

Starting Up in Safe Mode

If you are having trouble starting up your Mac, try starting in Safe mode. When you do this, you'll start up in a basic system where many features and peripherals are disabled. However, this can be useful when you are troubleshooting problems. To start up in Safe mode, start or restart your Mac. When the startup sound plays, hold down the Shift key. When you see the spinning progress indicator underneath the Apple logo, release the Shift key. You will then start up in Safe mode.

Starting Up in Target Disk Mode

If you'd like to connect two computers together so you can easily move files between them, you can use FireWire to have one computer act like a mounted volume on another. The computer you want to use as a disk must be started up in Target Disk mode.

First, configure the Mac you want to use as a disk to start in Target Disk mode. Open the Startup Disk pane of the System Preferences application, and click the Target Disk Mode button located at the bottom of the pane. Click Restart at the prompt. When the Mac restarts, you'll see a FireWire symbol on its screen. This indicates that it is in Target Disk mode.

Connect the Mac to another one using a FireWire cable. The Target Disk Mac will appear as a mounted disk on the second Mac. You can then use its hard drive just like one installed on the second machine. For example, you can move files to it, install software on it, and so on.

To return the Mac to normal condition, press and hold the Power button until the Mac shuts down. Disconnect the FireWire cable and then press the Power button again to restart it normally.

 note

Target Disk Mode is different than networking computers because the computer that is operating in Target Disk mode works like a hard drive instead of like a computer. You can't use it to do anything beyond what an external drive can do.

 tip

Using Target Disk mode can be an easy way to back up all the files on a mobile Mac. Restart the mobile Mac in Target Disk mode and connect it to a desktop machine with some free hard drive space. Drag all the files from the mobile Mac onto the disk on which you want to store the backed-up files.

Using Other Startup Options

Table 6.2 lists various startup options and their keyboard shortcuts.

Table 6.2 Mac OS X Startup Options

Startup Option	How to Select It
Prevent automatic login	Hold the left Shift key and mouse button down when you see the progress bar during the startup process.
Start up from a computer connected via FireWire in Target Disk Mode	Hold T down during startup.
Eject a CD during the startup process	Hold down the mouse button during startup.

7

INSTALLING AND USING MAC OS X APPLICATIONS

Understanding Mac OS X Application Types

Although you're free to spend your time in Mac OS X tweaking system preferences and fiddling with files, I assume you've got more productive, creative, or fun things to do. In Mac OS X, this means launching applications that enable you to work, create, or play.

You might think that an application is an application, but that's not the case under Mac OS X. In fact, your Mac can run *five* different types of applications:

- **Cocoa applications**—These applications are written using the Cocoa programming architecture, which means they take full advantage of the advanced features that Mac OS X provides. Most new Mac OS X applications are based on Cocoa, and many applications written for previous versions of the Mac OS have been rewritten in Cocoa.

- **Carbon applications**—These applications are written using the Carbon programming environment, which is designed to take advantage of the Mac OS X architecture. Many Carbon programs are existing applications that have been ported over to Mac OS X—in Mac OS X lingo, they have been *carbonized*. Because carbonizing an application requires considerably fewer resources than creating a Cocoa application does, most Mac OS X applications were carbonized Mac OS 9 applications early in Mac OS X's life. As Mac OS X has continued to mature, most applications have been written or rewritten specifically for Mac OS X.

- **Windows applications**—With an Intel Mac, you can run Windows applications in a number of ways. Mac OS X Snow Leopard includes Boot Camp, a tool that allows you to install Windows XP or Vista and then boot your Mac from that operating system. Programs from Parallels, VMware, and others provide the ability to have a Windows operating system running at the same time as Mac OS X.

  ➥ *To learn about running Windows applications,* **see** *Chapter 29, "Running Windows and Windows Applications,"* **p. 577***.

- **Java applications**—These are applications written in the Java and Java 2 programming languages. Because Java is a platform-independent programming language, the same applications work on Windows, Macintosh, and other platforms. You mostly encounter Java applications on the Web, but you will find some standalone Java applications as well.

- **Unix applications**—These are applications created for the Unix operating system, but you can run many Unix applications on your Mac because Mac OS X is based on a variation of Unix. Some of these applications have to be recompiled to run on the Mac, but most will work as they are. Of course, you will need to run them from the command line (unless you install a graphical user interface for the Unix subsystem). Because Unix is such a prevalent OS, thousands of Unix applications are available for you to use.

> **note**
>
> The X11 environment that is installed with Mac OS X provides a graphical interface for Unix applications. If you run Unix applications regularly, you can use this environment by launching the X11 application in the Application/Utilities folder.

Installing Mac OS X Applications

In Mac OS X, there are two common methods for installing applications:

- **Drag and drop**—With this method, you drag the application file (it's usually just one file or folder) and drop it on the location where you want to install the application, which is almost always the Applications folder.

- **Installer**—With this method, you install the application using an installation program that comes with the application. Most applications use the standard Mac OS X Installation application as their installation mechanism. These applications are provided as package files, which have the file extension `.pkg`.

If you're the only person who uses your Mac, the location where you install an application isn't all that important, although it's always a good idea to install all or most of your applications in a single location (such as the Applications folder). However, if you share your Mac with other people and have set up multiple user accounts, you need to give a bit more thought to where applications get installed. There are two locations to consider:

- **The Applications folder**—Install an application here if you want the application to be accessible to everyone who uses your Mac. Note, however, that to install an application into the Applications folder, you must be logged in as an administrator or know an administrator user name and password. Most applications that use an installer are installed in the Applications folder, and you usually don't have the option to install them elsewhere.

tip

You can also use the Parental Controls pane of the System Preferences application to limit access to specific applications. See Chapter 37, "Securing a Mac."

- **The Home folder**—Install an application in a user's Home folder if you want only that person to use the application. Because most applications default to the Applications folder, you can usually only install to a user's Home folder with applications that use the drag-and-drop installation method.

These installation locations are appropriate only for Mac OS X (carbonized or Cocoa) applications. You install Unix or other types of applications in locations that are appropriate for those types of applications.

When you try to install an application, you might see an error message stating that you don't have sufficient privileges. To install an application in the Applications folder, you must be logged in as an administrator. If you can't log in as an administrator, try installing the application in your Home folder instead.

note

The only difference between the behavior of .smi and .dmg files is that .smi files automatically mount on your desktop when you launch them. Disk image files use Apple's Disk Utility software to mount— because this application is installed on your Mac by default, these files behave quite similarly and you probably won't notice any difference between them. However, you could use a .smi file even if Disk Utility wasn't installed on your machine, whereas you can't use a .dmg file without the Disk Utility application.

Installing Mac OS X Applications with Drag and Drop

Under Mac OS X, applications can be provided as *bundles*. A bundle is a collection of the executable files and other resources required for an application. An application bundle can be presented to you as a single icon, which makes the drag-and-drop installation technique possible. Instead of having to deal with an installer application or a bunch of individual files, you can easily act on an entire application bundle by acting on its single icon.

Installing applications that use the drag-and-drop method is especially simple. Most of these applications are provided as self-mounting image (.smi) or disk image (.dmg) files. This means that the file behaves just as if it were a volume you mount on your desktop.

Many Mac OS X applications use this method, making installation of these applications very easy.

note

Some applications don't even provide a .smi or .dmg file. After you download and uncompress the file, you'll see the application's folder immediately. Drag this folder and drop it on the Applications folder (or wherever the application requires to be installed).

Here are the general steps to follow to install an application via drag and drop using a .smi or .dmg file:

1. Download and, if necessary, uncompress the .smi or .dmg file.

2. If the file isn't mounted on your Mac automatically, double-click the file (which is likely a .dmg file). Its volume is mounted on your desktop.

3. Open the resulting volume and drag the application's folder or file to the appropriate directory on your Mac, which in most cases is the Applications folder.

4. Unmount the mounted volume by selecting it and pressing ⌘-E (or select File, Eject).

If you won't need to install the application again, you can trash .smi or .dmg files. However, it's possible you may need to reinstall the application if problems arise with your Mac or with the application itself, so I recommend keeping the original file. If disk space is tight, consider archiving the original file to a flash drive, memory card, or CD or DVD.

➥ *To learn how to download files from the Web and prepare them for use,* *see* *"Downloading and Preparing Files," p. 308.*

Installing Mac OS X Applications Using an Installer

Mac OS X applications that use the Installer application come in package files, which have the extension .pkg. Here are the general steps to follow to install an application via the installer method using a .pkg file:

1. Download and prepare the file containing the application you want to install.

2. Mount the disk image and open it.

3. Double-click the .pkg file.

4. Work through the steps in the installer application.

 tip

If you want to save a little disk space, save the compressed .sit or .zip files that you download instead of the uncompressed .dmg files. When you want to access the .dmg files again, you can uncompress the .sit or .zip files. You don't need to save both versions. The .dmg file is slightly more convenient than the .sit or .zip file, but it also requires slightly more disk space.

 caution

Some companies remove the installers for one version from their website when the next version is released. In such cases, you might not be able to download and install the application again without paying an upgrade fee to get the new version. Therefore, the only way to ensure that you'll be able to reinstall the same version of an application you downloaded and licensed is to keep the original installer files. You should also keep any updates you download and install for that version.

 note

When you download an application that comes in a .pkg file, it often is included in a .dmg or .smi file. This usually means that there are extra files that the developer wants to include with the application but doesn't want installed with the application (such as readme files).

 note

Some installations require that you authenticate yourself as an administrator before you can begin the installation—even if you are already logged in as the administrator.

Launching Mac OS X Applications

There are many ways to launch Mac OS X applications, including the following:

- Double-click the application's icon.

- Single-click an application's icon on the Dock or the Finder Sidebar.

- Double-click a document of a file type that's associated with the application.

- Select the application in a Finder window and select the Finder's Open command (⌘-O).

- Open an alias to the application, such as one stored on your desktop.

- Drag and drop a document onto an application's icon (or an alias's icon).

- Select an application's icon or alias and press ⌘-down arrow.

- Launch the application from within another application. (For example, you can launch a web browser by clicking a URL in an email program.)

- Add the application to the Login Items window so it is launched automatically when you log in.

- Launch the application from a script created by the Automator, AppleScript, or another scripting utility.

One of the most powerful methods—although it's underused by many Mac users—is to launch an application by drag and drop. The drag-and-drop approach is especially efficient when you want to open a document with an application that wasn't used to create it initially. For example, if you receive a plain-text file and double-click it, it opens in TextEdit. If you want to open it in Word instead, you can drag and drop the document onto Word's icon, and Mac OS X uses Word to open the file. Otherwise, you'd have to first open Word, use the Open command, maneuver to the text file, and then open it.

If the file type is compatible with the application on which you drag it, the application icon becomes highlighted to indicate that it is a compatible file.

 tip

To unmount a disk image, click the Eject button next to it in the Sidebar; select it and select File, Eject; or select it and press ⌘-E.

 note

The first time you launch an application under Mac OS X, you will see a dialog box that explains you are opening the application for this first time. In this dialog box, you'll see the name of the application that is trying to open, along with tools you can use to control it. The primary purpose of this is to warn you when an application first opens so you can confirm it is a legitimate application and not some Trojan horse or other application that is trying to launch without your knowledge. If you want to proceed with opening the application, click Open. If you aren't sure about the application, stop the process and check it out before opening it again.

 tip

You can force an application to attempt to open a document with which it is not compatible by holding down the Option and ⌘ keys while you drag the document onto the application's icon. If the application is capable of opening files of that type, the file is opened. If not, either the application still launches but no document window appears, or the document window appears and is filled with garbage.

You can also use drag and drop to open documents using applications installed on the Dock. Drag the file you want to open onto the application's Dock icon. If the application is capable of opening the document, the application's icon becomes highlighted. When you release the mouse button to drop the document, the application launches and the document is opened.

If a file opens, but what appears onscreen is a bunch of gobbledygook, it means that the file contains data the application can't interpret. Use the Info window for the document to associate a different application with the document; using an application that Mac OS X lists as a recommended application makes it more likely it will open successfully. You can also try opening the document from within an application rather than from the Finder.

 tip

When you try to open a document by dragging its icon on top of an application's icon, the icon might not highlight. This happens when you try to open a document for which the application is not recommended. You can force it to open by holding down the Option-⌘ keys while you drag the document's icon onto the application's icon. You can also associate an application with a document using the document's Info window (see "Using the Info Window to Associate Documents with an Application," later in this chapter).

Using Standard Mac OS X Application Menus

Mac OS X applications follow certain conventions when it comes to the menus they provide. Although applications can provide more menus than the core set of standard menus, they're not supposed to provide fewer.

⚠ caution

The information in this section is based on standard Mac OS X menus for Cocoa applications. Carbonized applications might not follow the typical application menus. For example, all carbonized applications provide an Application menu, but not all provide Cocoa's Format menu.

Working with Mac OS X Application Menus

All Mac OS X applications have an application menu, which provides the commands you use to control the application itself as well as to interact with the OS (see Figure 7.1).

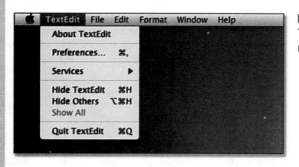

Figure 7.1
This TextEdit menu is typical of the application menu provided by Mac OS X applications.

Here are some standard commands that you should see on the application menu for most applications:

- About—Usually shows the name and version number of the application.

- Preferences—Displays the application's preferences.

- Services—Provides access to commands in other applications (see the detailed discussion that follows).

- Hide/Show—Hides or displays the application's windows.

- Quit—Shuts down the application.

One of the more interesting commands on the application menu is the Services command, which gives you access to functions provided by other applications. Although the Services command isn't supported by all applications, it can be quite useful in those applications that do support it.

There are various uses for the Services command, but as an example, suppose you are having trouble understanding an error message you are getting in a certain application and you want to send an email to the technical support organization to get some help. That email might be a lot more meaningful if you can include an image of the actual error dialog box that you see with your explanation. Using the Services commands from within the Mail application, you can do just that:

1. Display the dialog box you want to capture (such as an error message that pops up on your screen).

2. Without doing anything in the dialog box (for example, don't click the OK button), launch Mail by clicking its icon on the Dock.

3. Create a new email message and click inside the body of the message.

4. Select Mail, Services, Capture Timed Screen.

5. Bring the dialog box you want to capture to the front by clicking its window.

6. Wait for Grab's timer to go off (it lasts for 10 seconds).

7. Move back into the Mail application. The screen that Grab captured is pasted into the new email message.

8. Finish your message and send it.

The specific commands offered on the Services menu depend on the application you're using and the data you're working with. Most Apple applications do provide some services, but even with those, support for Services can be spotty. The only way to know is to explore the Services menu for the applications you use.

 note

Some third-party applications can add their own commands to the Services menu. For example, QuicKeys, which enables you to create and run macros, adds a command to the Services menu that enables you to create a macro from within any application.

Even though the TextEdit application that comes with Mac OS X isn't all that great for word processing, it does provide a great example of how many Services commands can be supported. Table 7.1 provides a list of some of the Services commands available in TextEdit.

Table 7.1 Sample Commands on the TextEdit Services Menu

Services Command	What It Does
Add to iTunes as a Spoken Track	Adds the selected text as a spoken track in iTunes
Make New Mail Note	Creates a new Mail note
Make New Sticky Note	Creates a new sticky note
Capture Selection from Screen	Enables you to capture screen shots and paste them into the current document
Import Image	Enables you to import images from an imaging device, such as a digital camera, connected to your Mac
Look Up in Dictionary	Looks up the selected word in the Dictionary application
Search with Google	Searches for the selected text on www.google.com
New Email To Address	Creates a new Mail message addressed to the selected address
New Email With Selection	Creates a new Mail message with the selected text as the message body
New Note With Selection	Creates a new Mail note from the selected text

Working with Mac OS X File Menus

The Mac OS X File menu provides the commands you use to work with files. Most of these are fairly obvious, such as New, Open, Save, Save As, and so on.

Working with Mac OS X Edit Menus

Although all applications should provide an Edit menu, the commands on this menu can vary widely from application to application. At the least, the Cut, Copy, and Paste commands will appear on this menu. There might be others as well, such as Find, Spelling, Speech, and so on. As with the File menu, these commands should be familiar to you unless you are new to using a Mac.

Working with Mac OS X Format Menus

As you might expect from its name, the Format menu provides commands that enable you to format the file with which you are working. The specific commands on the Format menu depend on the particular application you are using.

One of the most useful commands on most applications' Format menus is the Font command. This command enables you to work with the fonts you use in a document (see Figure 7.2). In addition to the commands you expect to see, such as Bold, Italic, and so on, you also will see the Show Fonts command, which opens the Font panel.

 note

The Mac OS X Format menu, including the Fonts panel, is available only in Cocoa applications that are designed to use it. Many Mac OS X applications provide format and font commands that are specific to those applications.

Figure 7.2
TextEdit's Font command is typical of this command on many applications' Format menus.

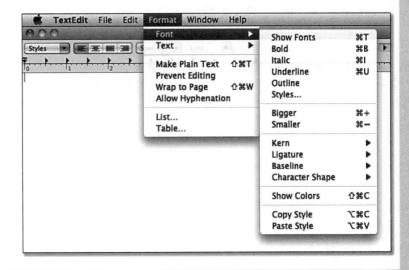

 To learn how to install, manage, and use fonts, **see** Chapter 23, "Managing and Using Fonts," p. 477.

Opening Documents in Mac OS X

Using most applications involves opening documents; Mac OS X offers several features that applications can use to make opening documents fast and easy.

There are several ways in which you can open documents:

- Select the document's icon in a Finder window and select the Finder's Open command (press ⌘-O).

- Double-click a document's icon in the Finder.

- Single-click a document's icon on the Dock or Sidebar.

- Drag a document icon or alias onto an application's icon or alias (on the desktop, in a Finder window, or on the Dock).

- Select the document's icon or alias and press ⌘-down arrow.

- Open the document using an Automator application, AppleScript, or other macro.

- Open a compatible application and use its Open command to open a document.

> **note**
>
> If you see the document's icon on the Dock, an alias to that document has been placed there. If you see a thumbnail of the document's window on the Dock, that document is open and its window has been minimized. In either case, single-clicking the icon causes the document to open so you can work on it.

Most of these techniques are simple. The Mac OS X Open dialog box is a good model of all the file selection dialog boxes you will encounter, so you should get very familiar with the way in which it works. Also, you need to understand how you can associate documents with specific applications so you can determine which application opens when you open a document.

Using the Mac OS X Open Dialog Box

The Open dialog box is modeled after a standard Finder window, which means that you navigate an Open dialog box in the same way you navigate Finder windows. This makes sense since both serve a similar purpose (enabling you to access files and folders).

Different applications can add features to the Open dialog box for specific purposes, but most Open dialog boxes offer a similar set of features.

Figure 7.3 shows a typical Open dialog box .

 note

Many dialog boxes, although not called Open, are actually the Open dialog box with the name modified to suit the specific purpose at hand. These dialog boxes have names such as Choose a Picture, Choose a File, and so on. However, they all work in basically the same way and offer similar features as the Open dialog box.

Forward/
Back   List view

Icon   ┌ Column view
view

Location pop-up menu

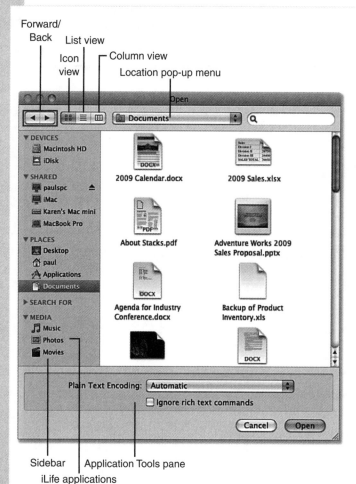

Figure 7.3
This Open dialog box, from TextEdit, is typical of those offered by Mac OS X applications.

Sidebar │ Application Tools pane
iLife applications

An Open dialog box offers navigation features that are similar to those of Finder windows. For example, the Sidebar in an Open dialog box enables you to choose the location from which you want to open a file. Just as in a Finder window, when you select a place, its contents appear in the center pane of the window.

You can also choose to view this pane in the Icon, List, or the Columns view; again, these views are the same as when you are viewing Finder windows. You can also use the Icon button's pop-up menu to configure how icons appear in the dialog box. You can use the Forward and Back buttons to move back to locations you viewed previously.

➡ *To learn how to work with Finder windows, **see** Chapter 3, "Getting to Know Mac OS X Finder Windows," p. 37.*

The Media section of the Sidebar allows you to quickly access files that you have stored in your iLife applications. When you click on one of these familiar icons, you will be able to select a file from that application. This can be helpful, as the path to these files is often complex.

The folder shown in the Location pop-up menu is the currently selected folder whose contents are displayed in the pane. For example, if Documents is shown in the Location pop-up menu, the Documents folder is selected and its contents are displayed. If you have selected the Columns view, the contents of the location selection on the Location pop-up menu appears in the leftmost column.

You can also use the Location pop-up menu to quickly access many areas of your Mac, from your current location up to the volume on which Mac OS X is installed (see Figure 7.4).

Figure 7.4
The Location pop-up menu in the Open dialog box enables you to move "up" from your current location or to choose from places you've been recently.

If you use the Icon or List views, to open a file or folder you either select it and then click Open, or double-click the file or folder. If you use the Columns view and select a folder, that folder becomes selected and you see its contents in the pane to the right of the folder. You can then select a folder or document it contains. In either view, you can select a document and double-click it or click Open.

You can change the Open dialog box in several ways, including the following:

- Change the view.

- Use the resize handle to make the dialog box larger or smaller.

- Click the Maximize button to make the dialog box its maximum size, such as to fill up the screen.

- Drag the dialog box around the screen. Because the Open dialog box is an independent window, you can move it around to move it out of the way.

 note

The Maximize button is not included in the Open dialog box under all applications—typically, only Cocoa applications include this feature.

The Open dialog box might contain application-specific controls. For example, in Figure 7.3, you saw the Plain Text Encoding pop-up menu that lets you choose the type of encoding you want to use. In the Application Tools pane, you'll also see different tools depending on the application in which you are working. As you locate and open files or documents, you should be aware of these additional options and apply them as needed.

Determining the Application That Opens When You Open a Document

When you open a document, the system determines which application should be used to open that file (other than when you open a document from within an application using its Open command, of course). Typically, the document's creator opens if it is installed on your Mac, such as Microsoft Word opening a `.doc` or `.docx` file.

When you're opening a file from outside an application, several factors determine which application opens when you open a document, including the document's file type and creator information, as well as the file's filename extension. Mac OS X does a good job evaluating these properties to ensure that the correct application opens.

However, there might be situations in which you want to use a different application than the one the system selects, or you might not have the application that was used to create the document. In such cases, you can choose the application in which a document opens.

You can also change the association for all files of a specific type to determine which application opens when you open any file of that type.

There are three ways to associate document types with the applications used to open them: using the Info window; using a document's contextual menu; and using a document's file extension.

Using the Info Window to Associate Documents with an Application

You can use the Open With section of the Info window to determine which application is used to open a file.

1. Select the document you are interested in and press ⌘-I. The Info window appears.

2. Expand the Open With section. The application with which the document is currently associated is shown on the pop-up menu. The associated application is called the default application—the text (default) appears after the application name when you open the pop-up menu.

3. Open the pop-up menu. You will see all the applications the system recognizes as being able to open the document, along with the Other selection (see Figure 7.5).

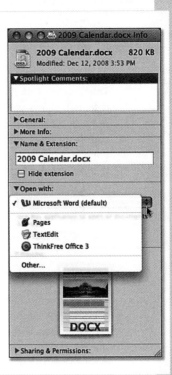

Figure 7.5
This menu lists all the applications Mac OS X thinks you can use to open the document.

4. If one of the listed applications is the one you want to associate with the document, choose it on the menu. The document is opened with that application the next time you open it.

5. If you want to select an application not shown on the pop-up menu, select Other. The Choose Other Application sheet appears (see Figure 7.6).

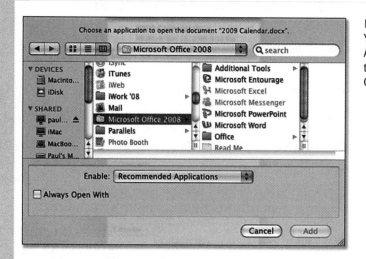

Figure 7.6
You can use the Choose Other Application sheet to select applications to open a document, even if Mac OS X doesn't recommend them.

The Choose Other Application sheet moves to the Applications directory automatically, and by default, it shows you only the recommended applications, which are those that Mac OS X recognizes as being compatible with the document. This set of applications might or might not be the same as you saw on the pop-up menu in the Info window. Mac OS X recognizes that some applications that can open files of that type might not really be intended to work with files of that type and so doesn't show them in the pop-up menu. However, they might be active in the Choose Other Application dialog box. Applications Mac OS X doesn't think can be used at all are grayed out.

 tip

If you want to permanently change the application used to open the document, activate the Always Open With box.

6. To make all applications active, select All Applications from the Enable pop-up menu.

7. Use the sheet's controls to move to the application you want to select, select it, and click Add. After you click Add, you return to the Info window and the application you selected appears in the window. That application is used the next time you open the file.

If you choose an application that Mac OS X isn't sure can open files of the selected type, you see a warning saying so in the sheet after you select the application. You can proceed even when you see the warning, but you might get unexpected results.

 caution

Just because you told Mac OS X to use a specific application, even if it is the one that Mac OS X recommended, that doesn't mean you'll actually be able to open the document with the application you select. If you try to open the document and generate error messages, you need to go back and select an application that can handle the type of file you are working with.

You can also use the Info window to associate all files of a specific type with an application. Here's how:

1. Use the previous steps to associate a file of the type you want to associate with an application. After you have changed the application association, the Change All button becomes active.

2. Click the Change All button. You see a warning dialog box that explains what you are about to do; for example, it lists the document types you are changing and the application with which you will associate documents of that type (see Figure 7.7).

 tip

Even though Mac OS X tries to recommend applications that are appropriate for the selected document, it doesn't always do a great job. In those situations, use the All Applications command on the Enable pop-up menu to add the application you want to use for the document.

Figure 7.7
This warning dialog box provides the information you need to ensure that the file association you are creating is the correct one.

3. If you're sure that you want to make the change, click Continue. All files of the selected type become associated with the application you selected. The application you selected becomes the default application for all documents of that type.

Using a Contextual Menu to Open a Document with a Specific Application

You can also use a file's contextual menu to determine which application is used to open it. Here are the steps to follow:

1. Select a document that you want to open with a specific application.

2. Hold down the Control key and click the file to open its contextual menu.

3. Select Open With. Another menu appears that lists all the applications the system recognizes as being compatible with the document you are trying to open. The application currently associated with the document is marked as the default (see Figure 7.8).

Figure 7.8
This menu provides the same controls as the Open With section of a document's Info window.

4. Select the application you want to use to open the document. If you want to use an application that's not on the list, select Other and use the Choose Other Application sheet to select the application. (See the preceding section for detailed information on how this sheet works.) The document opens in the application you selected.

When you use this technique, the document is associated with the application only if you save the document from within that application. If you simply open it and view it, the previous application continues to be associated with the document.

If you want the file to always be opened with a different application, even if you don't make any changes to it, open the contextual menu and then press the Option key. The Open With command becomes the Always Open With command. After you choose an application, the file is associated with that application and always opens in it.

 note

Setting an application for all files with a specific type and creator combination does not override any documents for which you have set a specific application. For example, suppose you set the application to use for a specific document. Then, using another document, you change the application used for documents of that type and creator to be a different application. The first document would still open with the specific application you selected previously.

 tip

You can also access the same Open, Open With, and Always Open With commands on the Action pop-up menu in the Finder window's toolbar.

Using Filename Extensions to Associate Documents with Applications

You can also try to change the application associated with a specific document by changing the document's filename extension. For example, to associate QuickTime Player with a document, you would change its extension to .mov. When you do so, the file's icon might change to reflect that extension and the document opens with the application that extension is associated with. But this doesn't always happen. To do this, use the following steps:

1. Edit the filename extension of the file you want to associate with an application so the extension is unique to that application. For example, you can change .rtf to .doc to associate a file with Microsoft Word.

   The filename extension you use must be specific to an application for this to work. For example, some filename extensions, such as .tiff, can be associated with many applications. You must use the Info window or contextual menu to change the association for such files.

   A warning dialog box appears (see Figure 7.9). In this dialog box, you see two buttons: One keeps the file's current filename extension, and other causes the new one to be used.

Figure 7.9
When you change a filename extension, you have to confirm the change by clicking the Use button in a dialog box like this one.

Are you sure you want to change the extension from ".rtf" to ".doc"?

If you make this change, your document may open in a different application.

[Keep .rtf] [Use .doc]

2. Click the Use button; the filename extension is changed. The file is associated with the application currently associated with files that have the filename extension you chose to use. (If you click the Keep button, nothing is changed.)

Changing the filename extension does not override a selection you have made with the Info window. If you associate an application with a document by using the Info window tools and then subsequently change the filename extension, the choice you made with the Info window overrides the filename extension and determines the application used to open that document.

Saving Documents in Mac OS X

When you use applications, you will also be saving documents frequently. Fortunately, Save sheets or dialog boxes under Mac OS X are also similar to Finder windows, just like Open sheets or dialog boxes.

The specific Save sheet or dialog box you see depends on the application you are using. Cocoa and some carbonized

 note

You can resize the Save sheet using its Resize handle; its size is independent of the document window from which it comes, but it always remains attached to the top of that window.

applications use the Save sheet that is described in this section. Some carbonized applications use the older Save dialog boxes.

A typical Mac OS X Save sheet is shown in Figure 7.10.

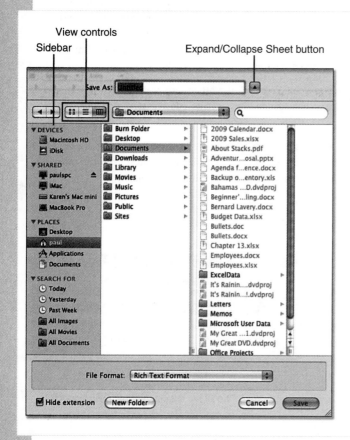

View controls

Sidebar

Expand/Collapse Sheet button

Figure 7.10
Under Mac OS X, the Save sheet sticks to the current document's window; otherwise, it looks and works similarly to the Open dialog box.

The sheet contains the Save As text box in which you enter the filename. If you click the Expand/Collapse button, the sheet expands so you see a window that is very similar to the Open dialog box you learned about in the previous section. If you click this button again, you see the collapsed version of the sheet.

Save sheets and Open dialog boxes look and work very similarly, but a couple of items on Save sheets aren't on Open dialog boxes, so you need to pay attention to them.

One is the Format pop-up menu, which is sometimes called File Format depending on the application in which you are

 note

One of the benefits of a sheet is that an open sheet will not prevent you from working with other documents, even within the same application. The sheet stays with the document to which it is attached. You can open, work with, and save other documents without closing the sheet.

working. You use this pop-up menu to choose the format of the file you are saving.

The other is the Hide Extension check box. If you activate this check box, the filename extension is hidden. If you deactivate this check box, which I recommend that you do, the filename extension is shown in the Save As box. Because filename extensions are important clues about how a document will open, you should generally choose to display them.

Some applications work in an opposite way: Instead of the Hide Extension check box, their Save sheets include the Append File Extension check box. When you activate this check box, the filename extension is added to the file's name.

In some applications' Save As sheet, you will see additional controls, such as an Options button that enables you to configure options for the file format you select.

Understanding Filenames and Filename Extensions

Filename extensions are an important aspect of saving documents under Mac OS X. Filename extensions consist of a period and two or more characters that are added to the end of the filename. When you save a document, most Cocoa and carbonized applications automatically append the correct filename extension for the type of file you are saving. Mac OS X uses the filename extension to associate the file with a particular application.

The addition of filename extensions to Mac filenames can be confusing because one of the Mac's strengths has traditionally been the lack of such extensions. However, because most applications tack the appropriate filename extension onto the filename you enter automatically, you generally don't have to worry about them.

Most Mac OS X files have a filename extension, including documents, system resources, and so on. In fact, a bewildering number of filename extensions exist under Mac OS X, and because it is based on the Unix operating system, Mac filename extensions are not limited to a certain number of characters. However, most document filename extensions consist of three or four characters. Some examples are shown in Table 7.2.

tip

Creating a new folder (using the New Folder button) in the Save As sheet can be a bit confusing. The new folder is created in the currently selected directory, which is shown in the Location pop-up menu. Because viewing multiple levels of the hierarchy using the Columns view controls is easy, you might be creating a new folder in a location you didn't realize you had selected. Before using that command, double-check the Location pop-up menu to ensure that you have selected the correct location in which to create the new folder.

note

In fact, if an extension is left off a filename, the Mac still uses the file creator and type information to open the file in a compatible application. However, you should include filename extensions for all documents you save.

Table 7.2   Examples of Mac Document Filename Extensions

Filename Extension	What It Stands For	Default Application Associated with It
`.mov`	Movie	QuickTime Player
`.tiff`	Tagged Interchange File Format	Preview
`.rtfd`	Rich Text Formatted Document	TextEdit
`.rtf`	Rich Text Format	TextEdit
`.jpg` or `.jpeg`	Joint Photographic Experts Group	Preview
`.pdf`	Portable Document Format	Preview
`.html`	Hypertext Markup Language	Default web browser (such as Safari)
`.doc` or `.docx`	Microsoft Word Document	Word
`.xls` or `.xlsx`	Microsoft Excel Spreadsheet	Excel
`.mp3`	Motion Picture Experts Group, Audio Layer 3	iTunes

System Filename Extensions

Although dealing with document filename extensions is fairly straightforward, dealing with system filename extensions can get really ugly. Some are straightforward, such as `.app` for applications and `.dock` for docklings, but many seem to be gibberish. Usually, you can just take system filename extensions as they are (because you can't change them), and sometimes you can even figure out what they stand for. For example, the `.kext` filename extension stands for kernel extension, which is an extension to the operating system software.

One system filename extension that is useful to know is `.plist`. It indicates a preference file, as in `com.apple.iTunes.plist`, which is the preferences for the iTunes application.

At the top of the Save sheet, you enter the filename you want to use. Under Mac OS X, you can use long filenames—up to 255 characters, including the filename extension and the period between the filename extension and the filename itself (so be sure to allow room for the filename extension when you enter a filename). When you save a document in many applications, the appropriate filename extension is added to the filename automatically (you won't see it if the Hide extension check box is checked). As mentioned previously, in some applications, you have to check a box to add the filename extension to the filename.

 note

If you intend to share your files with people who use older operating systems (such as Mac OS 9), you need to keep the name under 31 characters, including the filename extension the application will add to the name you enter. Similarly, if you want to share your files with Windows computer users, you need to ensure that the filename extension used is comprehensible to Windows PCs.

Viewing or Hiding Filename Extensions

Under Mac OS X, you have the option to view or hide filename extensions. However, filename extensions are usually used whether you can see them or not. Generally, I recommend that you always view them because they provide valuable information.

You can choose to hide filename extensions for specific files, or you can set the Finder to always display filename extensions for all files (regardless of the filename extension setting for a specific file).

You can show or hide the filename extensions for specific files by using the following steps:

1. In a Finder window, select the file for which you want to hide the filename extension.

2. Open the Info window.

3. Expand the Name & Extension section.

4. Activate the Hide Extension check box. (To show the extension for a file, deactivate this check box.)

5. Close the Info window.

To override the filename extension display setting for every file, use the following steps:

1. Open the Finder Preferences window.

2. Click the Advanced button to make the Advanced pane appear.

3. Activate the Show All File Extensions check box.

4. Close the Finder Preferences window.

Filename extensions will always be shown, regardless of the Hide Extension check box in the Info window.

Under most applications, the filename extension status (hidden or not) for specific files is saved, even when you use the Finder preferences to always display filename extensions. If you turn off Show All File Extensions again, the filename extensions for any files you have hidden become hidden again.

Some applications, especially carbonized applications, don't automatically add filename extensions unless the appropriate check box is checked in the Save sheet.

<div class="sidebar">

note

Some applications provide a File Format pop-up menu in the Save As sheet that you can use to choose the file format in which you want to save the document. Sometimes, the options on it are disabled. In such cases, look for the Save To command. This command enables you to save one file type to another type. The Save To dialog box looks and works exactly as the Save As sheet does, except that the options on the File Format pop-up menu are enabled.

tip

You can edit a file's name and filename extension in the box in the Name & Extension pane of the Info window.

</div>

Saving Documents as PDFs

One of the many benefits of Mac OS X is that the Portable Document Format (PDF) is a native format. This means you can create a PDF from *any* application without using Adobe's Acrobat or Distiller (although those tools offer some special features that are not available to Mac OS X natively).

PDF documents are useful for two primary reasons. First, they retain their appearance regardless of the fonts and applications installed on the viewing computer. Second, PDF documents can be viewed natively in Mac OS X (using the Preview application) or by Adobe's free Reader application (which is available for all platforms). These reasons make PDF the ideal format for distributing and viewing documents electronically.

PDFs also retain their formatting when they are printed. This makes PDF a good way to distribute documents that you know the recipient will want in hard copy. You can email a PDF and the receiver can print it. Unlike faxing, in which the document format degrades significantly, when the recipient prints the PDF, it will look as good as it does when you send it.

An additional benefit to PDFs is that they can't be easily modified. When you send a PDF to someone, he will have a difficult time changing it (it can't be changed at all without special tools). So, PDFs are also a good way to secure documents you provide to others.

To create a PDF version of a document, you use the Print command to "print" the document to a PDF file:

1. Create your document using the appropriate application.

2. Save the document.

3. Select File, Print to open the Print sheet.

4. Open the PDF drop-down menu and select Save as PDF.

5. Use the Save dialog box (it's not a sheet when you save to PDF) to name the file and choose a location. You can also add identification information and configure security options.

6. Click Save.

A PDF file is created in the location you specify. This document can be viewed using the Preview application or with Adobe Reader.

➡ *To learn about using Preview to view PDFs,* ***see*** *"Using Preview to Read PDFs,"* ***p. 256.***

➡ *To learn more about creating PDFs,* ***see*** *"Creating a PDF Files,"* ***p. 649.***

 note

You probably noticed that the Print dialog box is also a sheet. This means you can leave it open and work with other documents in the same or different applications.

 note

You can also choose to print documents in the PostScript file format. To do this, select Save as PostScript on the PDF drop-down menu on the Print sheet. Then use the Save to File sheet to choose a location and save the document.

PLAYING AND MANAGING MUSIC WITH ITUNES

Listening to Music

iTunes is a multimedia marvel that supports visual media such as movies and TV shows. However, iTunes is better known for its audio features, including its support for podcasts, audiobooks, Internet radio, and mobile phone ringtones, and it's best known for its flexible and powerful music features. I only have so much room to cover iTunes here, so I'm going to focus on these music features, including ripping audio CDs, navigating the Music library, adding tags and lyrics, viewing album artwork, managing playlists, and more.

Let's begin with the most basic iTunes task: listening to music. Follow these steps to listen to music with iTunes:

1. If you want to listen to an audio CD, insert the CD into your Mac. If iTunes asks whether you want to import the CD, click No. (See "Ripping Music from Audio CDs," later in this chapter, to learn how to import tracks from an audio CD.) By default, iTunes automatically connects to the Internet and attempts to identify a CD you have inserted. If it finds it, it displays the CD's information, including the CD name, track names, times, artist, and genre, in the Content pane. If iTunes finds information for a CD, it remembers that information and displays it each time you insert the CD.

2. Use the Source list on the left side of the iTunes window to choose the source that contains the music you want to listen to. This will usually be the Music library, but if you inserted an audio CD in step 1, select the CD when it appears in the Source list. At the bottom of

the iTunes window is the Source Information display. This shows you the total number of songs in the source, how long it plays, and the total disc space used.

3. Click the Play button in the upper-left corner of the window (when playing, this becomes the Pause button). (You can also select Controls, Play or press the spacebar.) As a song plays, a speaker icon appears next to it in the Content pane to indicate it is the current song, and information about that song appears in the Information window (see Figure 8.1).

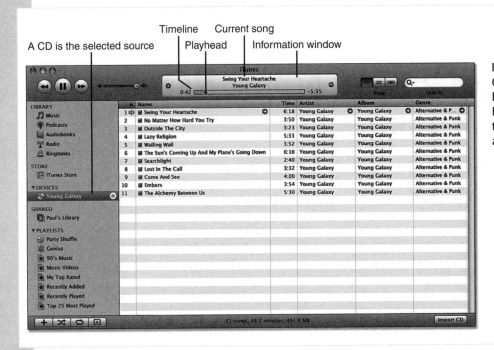

Timeline   Current song

A CD is the selected source   Playhead   Information window

Figure 8.1
Click the Play button to begin playing the selected audio source.

4. Control the volume of the sound by dragging the Volume slider to the left to turn it down or to the right to turn it up. You can also control the volume by pressing the ⌘-up arrow and ⌘-down arrow keys. To toggle the sound off and on, press Option+⌘+down arrow.

5. To pause a song, click the Pause button. (You can also select Controls, Pause or press the spacebar.)

There are a lot of other ways to control tunes, as the following list shows:

- Double-click any song to play it.

- When a song is playing and you click and hold the Rewind or Fast Forward button, the song rewinds or fast-forwards until you release the button.

 note

Using the Volume slider within iTunes changes the volume of iTunes relative to your system's volume. If you can't make the music loud or quiet enough, set your system volume level and then change the iTunes volume with the slider.

- When a song is playing, drag the playhead on the timeline (see Figure 8.1) to the right to move ahead in the song or to the left to move back in a song. When you release the playhead, the song resumes playing at that point.

- When a song is playing, click on the timeline at the point you want the song to play. The playhead jumps to the point on which you clicked, and the song plays from that position.

- If a song is not playing or a song is playing but you single-click (but don't hold down) the Rewind or Fast Forward button, the previous or next song, respectively, is selected. (If the previous song was playing, the next one starts to play when you jump to it.) You can also select Controls, Next (or press ⌘-Right arrow) or Controls, Previous (or press ⌘-Left arrow) to move to the next or the previous song.

- To remove a CD, select it in the Source list and select Controls, Eject Disc. (You can also press ⌘-E, click the Eject button that appears next to the CD on the Source list, or press the Eject button on your keyboard.)

Viewing Information While Listening to Tunes

You can view different information in the Information window, such as the name, artist, and album of the currently playing song. When you first view this window, it contains a timeline bar that represents the total length of the song being played. A black diamond (the playhead) indicates the relative position of the music you are hearing at any point in time compared to the total length of the song.

At the top of the Information window is a line of text that shows the song currently playing (even if it is paused). What appears on the second line of text changes over time; it rotates between the artist name and the album name. You can freeze this display on a specific attribute, such as album name, by clicking the text. Each time you click, the information changes from album to artist to album again. Whichever one you last clicked remains showing in the window.

Underneath the album, artist, and song name line is the timeline. The value shown on the left end of the timeline is always the time position of the playhead. As a song plays, the playhead moves to the right; the portion of the timeline representing the amount of song that has been played is shaded (everything to the left of the playhead). The value shown on the right end of the timeline can be either the total time of the track or the track's remaining time (indicated by a negative value). You can choose the value that is displayed by clicking the time; if total time is shown, it becomes remaining time and the reverse.

 note

When you freeze information in the Information window, it remains frozen until the next track is played, at which point it starts rotating again.

 note

When you play a CD containing music from various artists, the artist will be shown on the top line of text next to the song name for each song. The artist displayed on the lower line of text will be Various Artists.

If you click the Show Current Song button, which is the curved arrow located at the right side of the Information window (see Figure 8.2), the song currently playing is selected in the Content pane; this is indicated by blue highlighting. This can be handy when you are working with other music sources while listening to a song because you can click this button to quickly return to the song that is playing.

Finally, if you click the Change Display button (see Figure 8.2), the display becomes a graphical representation of the volume levels at various frequency groups. You can return to the song information by clicking the button again.

 note

The Information window changes based on the context of what you are doing. You have seen how it works when you listen to music. When you rip music to your Library (see "Ripping Music from Audio CDs," later in this chapter), the information and tools you see in the Information window are related to the import process. Similarly, when you burn a CD, the Information window shows burn-related data and tools.

Change Display   Show Current Song

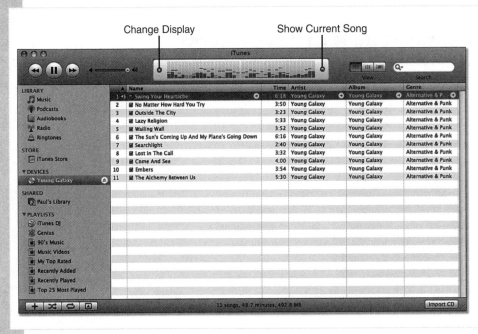

Figure 8.2
Click the Change Display icon to display the volume levels in the Information window.

Controlling the Order of Tunes

Playing a source from start to finish and controlling the volume are useful and required tasks, but with iTunes you can take control of your music so that you hear only what you want to hear, in the order in which you want to hear it. The following sections show you how iTunes lets you take control of your tunes. For example, in the next section you'll learn how to choose the songs you want to hear.

Let's face it—you probably don't like every song on a CD no matter how much you like the CD on the whole. With iTunes, you can choose the songs that play when you play a source. You can cause a song to be skipped by deactivating its check box. When the source plays, every song whose check box is deactivated is skipped.

To have iTunes include and thus play the song again the next time you play the source, activate its check box again.

iTunes determines the order in which songs play by the order in which they are shown in the Content pane, starting from the top of the pane and moving toward the bottom. By default, songs are listed and therefore play in the order they appear on a CD, from track 1 to the last track on the disc. However, you can make songs in a source play in any order you choose. There are a couple of ways to do this.

You can change the order in which songs are listed in the Content pane (and thus the order in which they play) by dragging the songs up or down (you can't do this when the Music is the source). When you change the order of the songs in the pane, you change the order in which they play.

You can also change the order of tracks by sorting the Content pane by the various attributes shown, such as Track Number, Song Name, Time, Artist, and so on. You can do this by clicking the column heading of the attribute by which you want to sort the list. When you do so, the tracks are sorted by that column. To change the direction of the sort (from ascending to descending or from descending to ascending), click the Sort Order triangle; the sort direction is reversed and the songs will be reordered accordingly. Just as they do when you move songs around manually, they will play in the order in which they are listed in the pane. (This isn't so useful when you listen to a CD because many of the attributes, such as artist, genre, and album are the same. However, when you use playlists or display more attributes, this can be very handy.)

The column on which the pane is sorted is indicated by the column heading being highlighted in blue—this defaults to the first column, which is the Track Number (which, by the way, is the only unnamed column because it applies only to audio CDs and to no other sources; see Figure 8.2). (When a CD is the source, the Track Number column is always the first or leftmost column in the Content pane.) When you select a different column, its heading becomes blue to show that it is the current sort column.

You can also tell which column is the current sort column by the Sort Order triangle. It appears only in the sort column. When the triangle points down, the sort is descending. When the triangle points up, the sort is ascending.

 tip

Along with a CD's information, iTunes remembers the settings you make for a CD and reuses them each time you insert and play the CD. This includes skipping songs, changing the order in which they play, and so on.

note

If you have manually reordered a CD by dragging songs up and down in the Content pane, that order is remembered and used when you sort the CD by the first column (Track Number). To put songs back in their original order, drag them so that track 1 is at the top, track 2 is next, and so on.

Playing Music Randomly

For a little variety, you can have iTunes play songs in a source randomly using its Shuffle feature: click the Shuffle button located at the bottom of the window (second one from the left) or select Controls, Shuffle, Turn On Shuffle. The songs are reordered in the Content pane and play in the order in which they are listed (which should be in a random fashion). The Shuffle button is highlighted in blue to indicate that it is active.

To return the source to the order you have set for it (or its original order if you haven't changed it), click the Shuffle button again or select Controls, Shuffle, Turn Off Shuffle.

By default, Shuffle works by randomly shuffling songs. To change this, select Controls, Shuffle, and then select one of the following commands:

- **By Songs**—Choose this option if you want songs to be shuffled randomly.

- **By Albums**—Choose this option to randomly select an album, play all its songs, and then randomly choose the next album to play.

- **By Groupings**—Choose this option if you want iTunes to randomly choose groupings of songs to play (such as compilations).

Repeating Tracks

Sometimes, you just can't get enough of the music to which you are listening. In that case, you can set iTunes to repeat an entire source or to repeat only a single song. To repeat your tunes, check out these pointers:

- To have iTunes repeat an entire source, select Controls, Repeat, All or click the Repeat button located at the bottom of the window (third one from the left). The Repeat button becomes highlighted to show you that it is active, and the source repeats when you play it.

- To repeat only the selected song, select Controls, Repeat, One or click the Repeat button a second time. A "1" appears on the Repeat button to indicate that only the current song will be repeated.

- To turn off the repeat function, select Controls, Repeat, Off or click the Repeat button until it is no longer highlighted in blue.

 tip

Using Repeat, you might hear a song you don't like all that much more than once. Remember to deactivate the Select check box for any songs you don't want to hear. They are skipped no matter how you play the source.

Controlling iTunes from the Dock

The iTunes icon on the Mac OS X Dock enables you to control iTunes at any time, even when the iTunes window is in the background, when its window is minimized, or when the application is hidden. When you Control-click the iTunes Dock icon (or right-click if you have a two-button mouse), the iTunes menu appears (see Figure 8.3). At the top of this menu is the iTunes command, which moves you into the iTunes window. Just under that is the Now Playing section that provides information about the song currently playing (if no music is selected or playing, you won't see this section). You can control iTunes by selecting a command on the iTunes Dock menu. For example, you can pause the music by selecting Pause. After you select a command, the menu disappears and you can get back to what you were doing.

 tip

If you use iTunes as much as I do, you'll want the application running all the time. Open the iTunes Dock menu and select the Open at Login command. This adds iTunes to your list of Login items so it opens each time you log in to your Mac.

Figure 8.3
Use the Dock menu to control iTunes even when you can't see the application.

Controlling iTunes with the iTunes Widget

First, configure the iTunes widget to appear when you use the Dashboard (see Chapter 28) by performing the following steps:

➥ *To learn more about the Dashboard,* ***see*** *"Working with Dashboard and Widgets," **p. 561**.*

1. Open the Dashboard.

2. Click the plus sign (+) located in the lower-left corner of the desktop. The Dashboard bar appears.

3. Drag the iTunes widget from the bar onto the location on your desktop where you want it to be when you open the Dashboard.

4. Close the Dashboard.

When you want to use the iTunes widget, open the Dashboard. Your widgets appear, including the iTunes widget (see Figure 8.4). Some of the controls look slightly different than they do within iTunes, but they work in the same way. Use the controls, such as rotating the Volume wheel to change volume, and then hide the Dashboard again by pressing its key or clicking someplace else.

Figure 8.4
The iTunes widget is another way to control iTunes when you aren't working with the application directly.

One control that isn't so obvious is the one that enables you to select a music source from within the iTunes widget. Open the widget and wait for a moment or two. An *i* appears at the bottom of the widget near its center. Click this button and you see the Select a Playlist pop-up menu. Choose a playlist on this menu and click Done. You can play the source you selected by clicking the widget's Play button and control the music with the widget's other controls.

Customizing iTunes

You can configure iTunes in various ways to suit your style. I discuss iTunes preferences throughout this chapter, but let's take a look here at the general preferences and the playback preferences. To display with the iTunes preferences, select iTunes, Preferences (or press ⌘-,).

Setting General iTunes Preferences

On the General pane of the iTunes Preferences dialog box are several settings you might want to use:

- **Library Name**—When you share music across a network, use this field to name your Library so other users know what it is.

- **Show**—Use the Show check boxes to determine if specific sources appear on the Source List. For example, to hide the Ringtones source, deactivate its check box.

- **Source Text**—Use this drop-down list to change the font size of the sources shown in the Source list. The options are Small (default) and Large.

- **List Text**—This setting changes the size of the text used in the Content pane. Again, your options are Small and Large.

- **When You Insert a CD**—Use this pop-up menu to choose what iTunes does when you insert a CD into your Mac's optical drive. The default is Ask to Import CD. If you always click Yes when iTunes asks to import the CD, choose Import CD in this list to avoid the dialog box each time you insert a CD. To learn about the Import Settings button, see "Configuring iTunes to Import Music," later in this chapter.

- **Automatically Retrieve CD Track Names from Internet**—When this check box is activated, iTunes looks for CD data online as soon as you insert a CD.

- **Check for new software updates automatically**—This check box controls whether iTunes checks for updates and lets you know when they are available. Because it is a good idea to use the current version, you should leave this check box activated. Mac OS X's Software Update feature also checks for iTunes updates.

Setting iTunes Playback Preferences

You can use iTunes Playback preferences to control how your music plays. For example, you can get rid of the gap of silence between songs or make songs play back at a consistent volume level. You can take advantage of these features by using the Playback pane of the iTunes Preferences dialog box. On this pane, you can configure the following preferences for your music (see Figure 8.5):

Figure 8.5
Control how your music sounds with the Playback preferences.

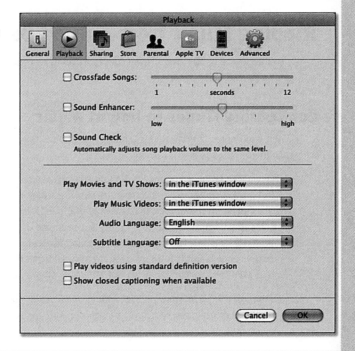

- **Crossfade Songs**—This effect causes one song to fade out and the next one to fade in smoothly, eliminating the gaps of silence between songs. To turn it on, activate the Crossfade Songs check box and use the slider to see the amount of fade time. If you move the slider to the left, songs fade out more quickly. If you set it to 0, there is no fading and as soon as one song ends, the next one starts. If you move the slider to the right, songs overlap; as one song starts to fade out, the next start to fade in so you hear them both at the same time. Click OK to put the new setting into effect.

 note

The Crossfade Songs setting does not impact audio CDs. Because there is a physical gap between tracks on the CD, iTunes can't do anything about it. This setting applies to other sources, such as your Music source and playlists.

- **Sound Enhancer**—This effect is iTunes' attempt to add depth and enliven the quality of your music. The actual result of this effect is a bit difficult to describe, so the best thing to do is try it for yourself. Activate the Sound Enhancer check box and use the slider to set the relative amount of enhancement. Click OK and then listen to some music. It if sounds better to you, increase the amount of the effect. If not, decrease it or turn it off.

- **Sound Check**—This effect sets the relative volume level of all songs to be the same. It is useful if you have changed the relative volume level of songs and want to have all your music play at the same volume level. To implement this effect, activate the Sound Check option and click OK.

Ripping Music from Audio CDs

If you have audio CDs, you'll want to import them to your iTunes Library so the music they contain is always available to you.

Configuring iTunes to Import Music

When you import CDs into your Library, you choose the encoding format you use. The options are as follows:

- **MP3**—MP3 is the acronym for the audio compression scheme called *Moving Picture Experts Group (MPEG) audio layer 3*. The revolutionary aspect of the MP3 encoding scheme is that music data can be stored in files that are only about 1/12 the size of unencoded digital music without a noticeable degradation in the quality of the music. A typical music CD consumes about 650MB of storage space, but the same music encoded in the MP3 format shrinks down to about 55MB. Put another way, a single 3.5-minute song shrinks from 35MB on audio CD down to a paltry 3MB or so in MP3 format. The small size of MP3 files opened up a world of possibilities.

  Although the MP3 format is still widely used, when you work with iTunes, you're better off using one of the newer formats it supports, such as AAC.

■ **AAC**—The primary successor to MP3 is called *Advanced Audio Coding (AAC)*. This format is part of the larger MPEG-4 specification. Its basic purpose is the same as that of the MP3 format: to deliver excellent sound quality while keeping file sizes small. However, the AAC format is a newer and better format in that it can be used to produce files that have better quality than MP3 at even smaller file sizes.

The AAC format also enables content producers to add copy protection schemes to their music. Typically, these schemes won't have any impact on you (unless of course, you are trying to do something you shouldn't).

One of the most important aspects of the AAC format is that all the music in the iTunes Store is stored in it; when you purchase music from the store, it is added to your computer in this format.

■ **WAV**—The *Windows Waveform (WAV)* audio format is a standard on Windows computers. It has been widely used for various kinds of audio, but because it does not offer the same benefits in terms of quality versus file size as the MP3 or AAC formats do, it is mostly used for sound effects or clips people have recorded from various sources. Millions of WAV files are available on the Internet that you can play and download.

You can load WAV files into iTunes, and you can even use iTunes to convert files into the WAV format. However, because MP3 and AAC are much newer and better file formats, you aren't likely to want to do this very often.

■ **AIFF**—The *Audio Interchange File Format (AIFF)* provides relatively high-quality sound, but its file sizes are larger than MP3 or AAC. As you can probably guess from its name, this format was originally used to exchange audio among various platforms and applications.

As with the WAV format, MP3 and AAC formats provide a trade-off between better sound quality versus file size, so you aren't likely to use the AIFF format very often. The most typical situation in which you might want to use it is when you want to move some music or sound from your iTunes collection into a different application that does not support MP3 or AAC.

■ **Apple Lossless**—The goal of this format is maximum sound quality. As a result, files in this format are larger than they are in AAC or MP3. However, Apple Lossless files are slightly smaller than AIFF or WAV files. If you have a sophisticated ear, high-quality sound systems, and discriminating taste in music (whatever that means), you might find this format to be the best for you. However, because storing music in this format requires a lot more space on your computer and on an iPod, you will probably use the AAC or MP3 format more often.

Before you start importing music to your Library, choose the import options (mainly format and quality levels) you want to use. Here are the steps to follow:

1. Select iTunes, Preferences, display the General tab, and then click Import Settings to open the Import Settings dialog box (see Figure 8.6).

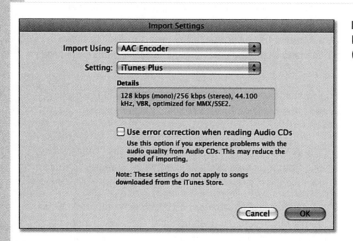

Figure 8.6
Here, you can see that the AAC format (the AAC Encoder) is selected.

2. Select the format in which you want to add music to your Library on the Import Using menu. For example, to use the AAC format, select AAC Encoder. To use the MP3 format, select MP3 Encoder. Or, select Apple Lossless Encoder to maximize the quality of your music.

3. Select the quality level of the encoder you want to use on the Setting menu. The options you see in this list depend on the format you selected in step 2. If you chose AAC Encoder, you have four quality options: High Quality, iTunes Plus, Spoken Podcast, and Custom. If you chose MP3 Encoder, you have four options: Good Quality, High Quality, Higher Quality, and Custom. If you selected the Apple Lossless Encoder, you have only the Automatic option.

   In the Details box, you see a summary of the settings you have selected. For example, you see the data rate of the encoder, such as 128Kbps, and the processor for which the encoder has been optimized.

4. Activate the Use Error Correction When Reading Audio CDs check box to cause iTunes to more closely control the encoding process. You should use this option only if you notice problems with the music you add to your Library, such as cracking or popping sounds. If that happens, activate this check box and try the import process again.

5. Click OK to return to the General tab.

 note

The Custom option enables you to configure specific settings the encoder uses. If you want to check it out, select Custom on the Setting menu and explore the options you see.

 tip

In most cases, choosing an encoder isn't a difficult decision. If hard drive space is a factor for you, you use an iPod, or you don't have the ears of a music expert, the AAC encoder is the way to go. If you demand perfection, use the Apple Lossless Encoder.

6. Activate the Automatically Retrieve CD Track Names From Internet check box to have iTunes download information about a CD so that information is added to the Library when you import the CD.

7. Click OK to put the settings into effect.

Adding Audio CDs to Your Library

Use these steps to add a CD to your Library:

1. Insert the CD you want to add to your Library. iTunes attempts to identify it. When it does, the CD appears in the Source list and is selected. Depending on your importing preferences, you may be presented with a dialog box to import the CD. You can click Yes to have iTunes import all of the songs automatically, or No so that you can determine what you want to import.

2. If there are songs you don't want to add to the Library, deactivate their check boxes; only songs with their check boxes activated are imported. Unless you really hate a song or disk space is at a premium, it is generally better to import all the songs on a CD. If you don't like to hear specific songs, you can use the check box in another source, such as in your Library, to cause those songs to be skipped when you play that source.

3. Click the Import CD button. The import process starts (see Figure 8.7).

Songs that have been imported

Song currently being imported   Import information   Stop button

Figure 8.7
iTunes in the middle of importing a music CD.

Deactivated songs are not imported

The Information window shows information related to the import process, such as the name of the song currently being imported and the rate at which the import process is happening.

The rate of the import process depends on the hardware you are using, the import settings, and other tasks your computer might be performing. In most cases, the import process occurs at a much greater rate than the playing process. For example, with moderate hardware, you can usually achieve import rates exceeding 7x, meaning 7 minutes of music can be imported in 1 minute of time.

An orange circle with a squiggly line inside it marks the song currently being imported. When a song has been imported, it is marked with a green circle containing a check mark.

If you want to stop the import process for some reason, click the Stop button (the small *x* within a circle) in the Information window.

When the process is complete, you hear a tone, and all the songs are marked with the Import Complete icon.

During the import process, you don't have to listen to what you are importing. You can select a different source, such as a playlist, and play it while the CD is being imported. This slows the import speed slightly, but probably not enough to bother you.

4. Eject the CD when the import process is complete. You can put the CD away somewhere because you probably won't need to use it again.

Adding Audio CDs to the iTunes Library Quickly

The import process moves along pretty quickly, but you can make it even faster by following these steps:

1. Gather a pile of your CDs in a location close to your Mac.

2. Choose your import preferences (encoder and quality), as described earlier.

3. Select iTunes, Preferences, and display the General tab.

4. In the When You Insert a CD pop-up menu, select Import CD and Eject. This causes iTunes to begin the import process immediately when you insert a CD. When the import process is complete, the CD is ejected automatically, too.

5. Click OK to close the dialog box.

6. Insert the first CD you want to import. iTunes starts importing it automatically. When the process is complete, the CD is ejected automatically.

7. Insert the next CD you want to import. Again, iTunes imports the music and ejects the disc when it is done.

8. Repeat step 7 until all the CDs you want to be able to use in iTunes have been imported.

 tip

When you are finished importing your CDs, you might want to reset the When You Insert a CD menu to Show Songs to prevent accidentally importing a CD more than once.

Adding Music from Other Sources to Your iTunes Music Library

While audio CDs are likely to be a major source of the music you add to your Library, they certainly don't need to be the only one. You can purchase music from the iTunes Store easily and quickly. And, you can add any audio file to your Library, such as files you download from the Internet.

Purchasing Music from the iTunes Store

When you select the iTunes Store source, you move to Apple's online iTunes Store (see Figure 8.8). You can use the various links, buttons, and search tool to find music in which you are interested. You can then preview that music; adding the music to your Library is as simple as clicking the Buy Now button for albums or individual songs. Once downloaded, the music is added to your Library and you can listen to it and use it mostly like music you import from CD. (There are some limitations imposed by the copyright protection, but you aren't likely to encounter those.) All the music you purchase is also stored in the Purchased playlist.

Figure 8.8
The iTunes Store offers a lot of great music, not to mention videos and podcasts.

Importing Audio Files into Your Library

Another potential source of music for your Library is the Internet. There are millions of audio files there, and you can download these files and add them to your Library.

1. Locate the files you want to add to your Library. For example, find the MP3 files on your hard drive or go to a website that has audio files, such as MP3 files, and download them to your computer.

2. Select File, Add to Library. You see the Add To Library dialog box.

3. Use the dialog box to move to and select the folder containing the files you want to add or to select the files you want to add to the Library.

4. Click Open. The files you selected are imported into your Library.

Browsing and Searching Your Music Library

It won't be long until you have a large Library with many kinds of music in it. In fact, you are likely to have so much music in the Library that you won't be able to find songs you are interested in just by scrolling up and down the screen. In this section, you learn how to find music in your Library, first by browsing and then by searching. When you browse, you can choose to use three views: List, Grid, and Cover Flow.

Browsing in the Library with the List View

The Browser enables you to find music by browsing:

1. Click the List view button, which is the View button closest to the Information window.

2. Select Music on the Source list. This focuses iTunes' attention on the music content in your collection.

3. If you don't see the Browser, select View, Browser (or press ⌘-B). The Browser appears between the Information window and the Content pane (see Figure 8.9). The Browser has three columns: Genre, Artist, and Album. The columns start on the left with the most general category, Genre, and end on the right with the most specific category, which is Album.

Figure 8.9
The Browser offers a good way to find songs in your Library.

If you don't see the Genre column in the Browser, open the General pane of the iTunes Preferences dialog box and activate the Show Genre When Browsing check box.

The contents of the path selected in the Browser are shown in the Content pane that now occupies the area below the Browser. At the top of each Browser column is the All option, which shows all the contents of that category. For example, when All is selected in the Genre column, you see the contents of all the genres for which you have music in the Library.

4. To start browsing your Library, select the genre in which you are interested by clicking it. When you do so, the categories in the other two columns are scoped down to include only the artists and albums that are part of that genre.

5. To further limit the browse, click an artist in which you are interested in the Artist column. The Album column will be scoped down to show only those albums for the artist selected in the Artist column (see Figure 8.10). Also, the Content pane shows the songs on the albums listed in the Album column.

 note

The Source information at the bottom of the window always reflects the selections you've made in the Browser.

Figure 8.10
You can narrow your browsing by selecting a genre and then an artist.

6. To get down to the most narrow browse possible, select the album in which you are interested in the Album column. The Content pane shows the tracks on the selected album.

7. When you have selected the genre, artist, and album categories in which you are interested, you can scroll in the Content pane to see all the tracks included in the music you are browsing.

To make the browse results less narrow again, select All in one of the Browser's columns. For example, to browse all your music again, click All in the Genre column.

I hope you can see that you can use the Browser to quickly scan your Library to locate music you want to hear or work with. As you use the Browser more, you come to rely on it to get you to a group of songs quickly and easily.

Browsing in the Library Using the Grid View

The List view is useful, but it doesn't really provide you with a good sense of the collections of music you browse because the tracks appear in a list with no respect to how the tracks are collected. Use the Grid view to browse the Music source while seeing the groups of music you are browsing:

1. Click the Grid view button, which is the middle View button. The music in the Content pane is grouped by album or collection and you'll see the artwork associated with each group.

2. Select a grid by clicking a category button: Albums (see Figure 8.11), Artists, Genres, or Composers.

Figure 8.11
Using the Grid view, you get to see how the music you are browsing is grouped, along with its artwork.

Browsing in the Library with the Cover Flow View

I admit that browsing music only in a digital format does lose something when compared to looking through a collection of CDs. There's something appealing about flipping through a set of CDs, especially when you stumble upon one you haven't listened to in a while. If you like to do this, the Cover Flow view will appeal to you. To use it to browse your music, perform the following steps:

1. Click the Cover Flow view button, which is the rightmost View button. The Browser is replaced by the Cover Flow browser (see Figure 8.12). Here, you see the album art associated with the music you're browsing; this looks similar to a collection of CDs. The album facing the screen directly is associated with the music at the top of the Content pane (this is the music currently in focus). You see the album name and artist just below the album in focus. The covers to the right of this one represent music lower in the Content pane, whereas the covers to the left represent music higher in the Content pane.

Figure 8.12
The Cover Flow view enables you to flip through your music collection to browse it.

2. To browse ahead in your music, click an album cover to the right of the one in focus; to browse back in your music, click a cover to the left of the one in focus. The farther to the left or right you click, the more covers you jump ahead or back, depending on which direction you click. For example, if you click on an album immediately next to the one in focus, you move ahead or back one album. If you click all the way to edge of the screen, you jump ahead or back by multiple albums.

As albums come into focus, you see their content at the top of the Content pane.

3. When music comes into focus that you want to hear, double-click it to start playing it.

 tip

You can also use the scroll bar and scroll box to browse your music. Click the right arrow button at the right end of the scrollbar or drag the scroll box to the right to move ahead, or use the left arrow button or drag the scroll box to the left to move back. The scroll tools enable you to browse even a large collection of music quickly. But it isn't quite as fun as using the flip technique.

As you flip through albums, music you happen to be playing continues to play as you bring other music into focus. If you don't play the music you are browsing, after a couple of seconds of inactivity the covers flip back to the music currently playing so that it comes back into focus.

To see a full screen browser with playback controls, click the Full Screen button, which is just to the right of the scroll bar. The desktop is replaced by a full screen browser; use the controls at the bottom to control playback or browse the source (see Figure 8.13).

Figure 8.13
The Full Screen browser is nice to look at, but you can't use anything else on your Mac while it appears.

Searching Your Music Library

You can use iTunes Search tool to search for specific content. You can search for content (music, audiobooks, video, and so on) by any of the following criteria:

- Artist

- Album

- Composer

- Song (track name)

To search for music in your Library, perform the following steps:

1. Select the source you want to search. (For example, click the Music source to search your entire music collection.) As you might surmise, you can search any source in the Source list—such as a CD, playlist, and so on—by selecting it and then performing a search.

2. To choose a specific attribute by which to search, such as Album, click the Magnifying Glass icon and choose the search attribute on the drop-down list that appears. If you don't choose a specific attribute, All is used, which searches all the available attributes.

3. Type the data for which you want to search in the Search tool. As you type, iTunes searches the selected source and presents the songs that meet your criterion in the Content pane. It does this on the fly, so the search narrows with each keystroke. As you type more text or numbers, the search becomes more specific.

4. Keep typing until the search becomes as narrow as you need it to be to find the content in which you are interested.

5. To refine your search by attribute, open the Magnifying Glass icon and choose the attribute to which you want to limit the search. For example, if you want to see only results that have your search term as the Artist attribute, choose Artist. The search results are limited to only those tracks that match the current criteria (what you typed and the attribute you selected).

 tip

The current search attribute is marked with a check mark on the Magnifying Glass drop-down list.

By the way, searching works the same way regardless of the current view.

After you have found content with a search, you can play it, add it to playlists, and so on.

To clear your search, click the Clear Search button that appears in the Search tool after you have typed in it. The songs shown in the Content pane are again determined by your selections in the current view.

Removing Tunes from the Music Library

Not all that glitters is gold, nor are all tunes that are digital good. Sometimes, a song is so bad that it just isn't worth the hard disk space it consumes. To remove songs from your Library, ditch them with the following steps:

1. Find the songs you want to delete by browsing or searching.

2. Select the songs you want to trash. They become highlighted to show you they are selected

3. Press the Delete key. You are prompted to confirm that you really want to delete the song you have selected.

 tip

Remember that you can stop a song from playing by deactivating its check box in the Content pane. If you aren't sure you want to dump a song permanently, use that method instead so you can always listen to the song again if you change your mind about it.

4. If you see the warning prompt, click Remove to confirm the deletion. You see another prompt asking whether you want the selected files to be moved to the Trash or you want to keep the files on your computer. (If you have disabled the warning prompt, you move directly to the second dialog box.)

5. Click Move to Trash to move the files so you can get rid of them entirely. The selected songs are deleted from your Library, and their song files are moved to the Trash. The next time you empty that receptacle, those songs are gone forever.

   If you just want to remove the references to files from the iTunes Library but not delete the song files, click Keep Files. The songs are removed from the Library, but the song files remain in their current locations (and so you could always add the songs to your Library again later).

You should never delete music you purchased from the iTunes Store unless you are absolutely sure you never want it again or you have that music backed up elsewhere. You can download music you purchased from the store only one time. After that, you have to pay for it to download it again.

Of course, songs you delete probably might not really be gone forever. You can always add them back to the Library again by repeating the same steps you used to place them in there the first time. This assumes you have a copy somewhere, such as on a CD or stored in some other location. If you imported the music from your hard disk and had iTunes move the song's files to your iTunes Music folder, your only copy resides in your iTunes Library, so make sure you have such music backed up before you delete it if you might ever want it again.

Understanding and Using Tags

Browsing and searching music is fast and easy, even if you have thousands of songs in your Library. This functionality is enabled because each track in your Library has data—also called *tags*—that categorize and identify that track for you. Genre, artist, and album are just three of the possible tags for each track in iTunes. There are many more items of information that iTunes manages.

Tags fall into two groups: tags that iTunes assigns for you and that you can't change, and tags that you or iTunes assigns and that you can change.

Tags that iTunes assigns and that you can view but can't change include the following:

- **Kind**—This identifies the type of file the track is, such as Protected AAC audio file, AAC audio file, MP3, and so on.

- **Size**—The amount of disk space required to store the track.

- **Bit Rate**—The quality level at which the track was encoded. Larger numbers, such as 128Kbps, mean the track was encoded at a higher quality level (and also has a relatively larger file size).

- **Sample Rate**—The rate at which the music was sampled when it was captured.

- **Date Modified**—The date on which the track file was last changed.

- **Play Count**—The number of times the track has been played.

- **Last Played**—The last time the track was played.

- **Profile**—A categorization of the track's complexity.

- **Format**—The format in which the track was encoded, such as MPEG-1, Layer 3.

- **Channels**—Whether the track is stereo or mono.

- **Encoded with**—The tools used to encode the track, such as the version of iTunes used, the version of QuickTime, and so on. This applies only when you use iTunes to encode the track.

 note

Not all tracks have all the data fields listed. You will see only data that is applicable to a specific track. For example, only music purchased from the iTunes Store has information about the purchase.

- **ID3 Tag**—ID3 tags are data formatted according to a set of specifications. If a track's data has been formatted with this specification, the ID3 version number will be shown.

- **Purchased by, Account Name, and FairPlay Version**—If a track was purchased from the iTunes Store, this information identifies who purchased the music and which account was used. The FairPlay version information relates to the means by which the track is protected.

- **Owner, Narrator, Published**—This information is provided for audiobooks that you add to your Library, such as those from Audible.com. The owner is whoever purchased the book. The narrator is who reads the book. Published identifies when the book was published.

- **Where**—This shows a path to the track's file on your computer along with its filename.

Tags collected for songs that you can change include the following:

- **Name**—This is the name of the track.

- **Artist**—The person or group who performs the track.

- **Album Artist**—Often used to indicate Various Artists for soundtracks and other compilation albums.

- **Album**—The name of the album or compilation from which the song comes.

- **Grouping**—This is a label you can assign to group tracks together. You can then organize tracks by their group, collect them in playlists, and so on.

- **Composer**—The person who is credited with composing the track.

- **Comments**—This is a free-form text field in which you can make comments about a track.

- **Genre**—This associates a track with its genre, such as Jazz or Classical.

- **Year**—The year the track was created.

- **Track Number**—The track's position on the CD from which it came, such as "2 of 12."

- **Disc Number**—The number of the CD or DVD. This is meaningful for multiple-disc sets.

- **BPM**—The track's beats per minute.

- **Part of a Compilation**—When activated, this check box indicates that the track is part of a compilation, meaning a CD or other grouping that contains tracks from a variety of artists.

When you add a song to your Library, no matter how you add it, iTunes adds as much of this data as it can find for each song.

When you insert a CD, iTunes attempts to get that CD's information from an online CD database, which is why it connects to the Internet. If iTunes finds the CD in this database, the information for that CD is applied to the CD and carried into the Library if you import the tracks from that CD into iTunes. If you purchase music from the iTunes Store, it also contains many of these tags. If content you add to your Library doesn't have tags, you'll have to add them yourself (which isn't hard to do, as you'll soon see).

Even if content you add does have tags, you can add or change the data in the previous list.

So, why should you care about all these tags? There are a couple of reasons.

First, as you already know from Chapter 5, "Searching Your Mac," you can use tags to find music you're interested in.

Second, you can use tags to determine which tracks are included in your playlists. For example, you can configure a playlist to include the last 25 songs you have played from the Jazz genre. This is just a basic example—you can get much more sophisticated than this. In fact, you can include several combinations of tags as criteria in playlists to create interesting sets of music to listen to.

When you view music in the Browser and in the Content pane, all the information you see results from the tags associated with that music, such as artist, title, album, time, kind, and so on. You can also view tags in other contexts.

Viewing Tags in the Info Window

To view the Info window, select a track in your Library and select File, Get Info or press ⌘-I. The Info window appears; at the top of the window, you see the name of the track whose information you are viewing (see Figure 8.14). This window has six panes that apply to music and a seventh that can be used with video content.

The Summary pane provides a summary view of the track's tags that you can't change on the tab, starting at the top with any album art associated with the track and including its name, length, artist, and album. In the center part of the pane, you see the data that iTunes manages. (You can view this data, but you can't change it.) At the bottom of the pane, you can see the path to the track's file on your computer.

When you click the Info tab, you see the tags you can change.

The other three panes of the window that relate to music content—Sorting, Options, Lyrics, and Artwork—are used to configure specific aspects of a track.

You can view information for other tracks in the selected source without closing the window. Click Next to move to the next track in the source you are viewing (such as your Music) or Previous to move to the previous track. When you do so, the next or previous track's information is displayed in the Info window.

Figure 8.14
The Info window enables you to view the tags associated with tracks, and you can change many of them.

Labeling a Track in the Info Window

Typically, if you have imported a CD or purchased music from the iTunes Store, you shouldn't change the data that came from the source, such as name, artist, album, track number, and so on. Occasionally, a CD's information will include an error when it is added (such as a misspelling in the artist's name); you'll probably want to fix such mistakes. You can certainly add data to empty fields.

You can use the Info window to change a track's tags, as you can see in the following steps:

1. Open the Info window for the track that has tags you want to add or change.

2. Click the Info tab.

3. Enter or change the information shown in the various fields. For example, you can change the track's name or artist. Or you might want to add comments about the track in the Comments box.

4. To change a track's genre, select the new genre from the Genre menu.

5. When you are done entering or changing tags, click OK. The Info window closes, and any changes you made are saved.

 tip

If a genre by which you want to classify music isn't listed on the menu, you can add it to the menu by selecting Custom on the menu and then typing the genre you want to add. That genre will be added to the menu and associated with the current track. You can use the genres you create in this way just as you do the default genres.

Tagging Multiple Tracks at the Same Time

You can change some tags, such as Genre, for a group of tracks at the same time. This can be a faster way to enter tags because you can change multiple tracks in one window. Here are the steps to follow:

1. Select the tracks whose tags you want to change.

2. Open the Info window. You're prompted to confirm that you want to change the information for a group of tracks.

3. Click Yes to clear the prompt. The Multiple Item Information window appears (see Figure 8.15). The information and tools in this window work in the same way as they do for individual tracks. The difference is that the information and settings apply to all the tracks you have selected.

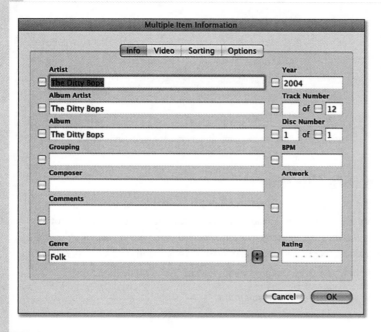

Figure 8.15
You can use this window to change the data for multiple tracks at the same time.

4. Enter data in the fields, make changes to existing data, or use the other tools to configure the tracks you have selected. As you change information, the check box next to the tag becomes activated to show that you are changing that tag for all the selected tracks.

5. When you are finished making changes, click OK. The window closes, and the changes you made will be saved.

Most of the fields in the Multiple Item Information dialog box are pretty straightforward, such as Artist, Album, and so on.

 tip

Many iTunes dialog boxes have a check box you can activate to prevent the dialog from being displayed again. For example, if you don't want to be warned when you use the Multiple Item Information tool, activate the Do Not Ask Me Again check box.

You'll learn about others when you read about changing a track's options later in this chapter. The same options apply as for an individual track; you can just change multiple tracks at the same time by using the Multiple Item Information dialog box.

Setting Tags in the Content Pane

You can also edit tags within the Content pane:

1. Click once on a track to select it.

2. Click once on the tag you want to edit. The tag is highlighted to show that it is ready to be edited.

3. Type the new information, choose a value on the tag's drop-down list (such as to set equalization for a track), or click to set a value (for example, to rate a track).

4. Press Return. The changes you made are saved.

Changing Sorting Tags

By default, iTunes uses and tracks default tags for sorting purposes, such as its title, artist, and so on. However, you can add sorting tags in case the default tags aren't sufficient. To do this, perform the following steps:

1. Select a track, open the Info window, and click the Sorting tab.

2. Enter the information by which you want iTunes to sort the track in the related Sort fields. For example, enter information in the Sort Artist field. You can change the name of the artist for sorting purposes without changing the name of the artist that is associated with the track on audio CD or from the iTunes Store.

3. Click OK. When you sort music, any information you entered in the Sort fields is used instead of the default tags.

Configuring a Track's Options

You can configure a number of options for the tracks in your Library, including the following:

- **Volume Adjustment**—You can change a track's relative volume so it is either louder or quieter than normal. This is useful if you like to listen to tracks recorded at a variety of volume levels, because the volume remains somewhat similar as you move from track to track.

- **Equalizer Preset**—You can use the iTunes Equalizer to configure the relative volume of sound frequencies. When you set an Equalizer preset for a track, the settings in that preset will be used each time the track plays.

- **Rating**—You can give tracks a rating from one to five stars. You can use ratings in various ways, for example, to create criteria for playlists (for example, include only my five-star songs) or to sort the Content pane.

■ **Start and Stop Time**—You can configure tracks to start or stop playing at specific times in the track. This can be useful if you don't want to hear all of a track, for example, when a track has an introduction you don't want to hear each time it plays.

■ **Remember Playback Position**—When this option is enabled, iTunes (and an iPod) starts playing a track from the point at which you last played it. This is an incredibly useful option for tracks that are audio books, podcasts, or videos because you can stop playing that content and do something else, such as listen to or watch other content. When you come back to a track with this option enabled, iTunes and an iPod will pick up where you left off. This prevents you from hearing or seeing the same content again or from searching for the point at which you stopped listening or watching.

■ **Skip when Shuffling**—If this option is enabled for a track, the track is skipped when you play iTunes in the Shuffle mode. This is useful for tracks you don't want to hear when you shuffle (such as those that make sense only in the content of the album from which they come) or for content that doesn't make sense when you shuffle (such as episodes of a podcast or an audio book).

■ **Part of a gapless album**—Some tracks are designed to be heard with no gap between them, such as those from a live album. When a track is part of such an album, activating this option removes any gap between songs. iTunes recognizes most gapless albums automatically, but you can manually configure this setting if you need to.

> **note**
>
> iTunes is pretty smart and makes your listening and viewing life as easy as possible. For example, when you add podcasts, video, or audio books from the iTunes Store to your Library, the Playback Position, Skip, and Gapless options are set appropriately. If you add this kind of content from other sources, you should make sure these options are set the way you want them to be.

Configuring Track Options in the Info Window

You can configure a track's options in the Info window by performing the following steps:

1. Select the track whose options you want to set.

2. Open the Info window.

3. Click the Options tab (see Figure 8.16).

4. To set the track's relative volume, drag the Volume Adjustment slider to the left to make the track quieter or to the right to make it louder.

5. To apply an equalizer preset to the track, choose the preset you want to be used when the track plays on the Equalizer Preset menu. On this menu, you see a large number of presets that are available to you. When you choose one, the track's playback is adjusted accordingly. For example, if you choose Bass Booster, the relative volume of the bass frequencies is increased.

Figure 8.16
Using the Options tab, you configure a track's optional settings.

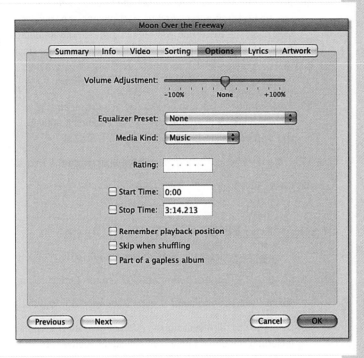

6. To rate the track, click the dot representing the number of stars you want to give it in the Rating field. For example, to give the track three stars, click the center (third) dot. Stars appear up to the point at which you click. In other words, before you click, you see a dot. After you click a dot, it becomes a star, as do the rest of the stars to its left.

7. To set a track's start time, activate the Start Time check box and enter a time in the format *minutes:seconds*. When you play the track, it starts playing at the time you enter. The default value is 0:00, which makes sense because that is the starting point for a track.

8. To set a stop time, activate the Stop Time check box and enter a time in the format *minutes:seconds*. When you play the track, it stops playing at the time you enter. The default stop time is the total track length, which also makes sense. Notice that the default stop time is very precise, even going to two decimal places beyond a second.

 tip

If you want to configure options for a group of tracks, select those tracks and open the Info window. Use the resulting Multiple Song Information window to make changes to all the tracks at the same time.

 note

When you set a start or stop time, you don't change the track file in any way. You can play the whole track again by deactivating the Start Time or Stop Time check box.

9. If you want iTunes to remember the point at which you stopped playing a track and to start playing the track at that point the next time you play it, activate the Remember Playback Position check box. If you always want the track to start playing at the current Start Time, leave the box deactivated.

10. If you want the track to be skipped when you shuffle (when the track is an audio book, for example), activate the Skip When Shuffling check box.

tip

To determine the start or stop times you want to use, play the track and use the times displayed when the playhead is at the position where you want the track to start or stop playing.

11. If the track is part of a gapless album, activate the Part of a Gapless Album check box.

12. Click OK.

Rating Tracks in the Content Pane

You can also rate tracks in the Content pane. To do so, follow these steps:

1. Scroll in the Content pane until you see the Rating column.

2. Select the track you want to rate. Dots appear in the Rating column for that track.

3. Click the dot representing the number of stars you want to give the track. The dots up to and including the one on which you clicked become stars.

Working with Lyrics

In the Info window, you've seen that there is a Lyrics tab. As you probably can guess, you can store lyrics, or any other text for that matter, for a track on this tab. You can then view the text you store there by using the Info window, or you can display the lyrics on an iPod.

Adding Lyrics to a Track

The first step is to find or create the lyrics you want to associate with a track. Although it might be a lot of fun figuring out the lyrics for tracks by listening to them and writing them down yourself, I'm going to assume you have better things to do with your time. In that case, it's easy to look up lyrics for most artists on the Web.

Most of the lyrics available on the Web come from a person who listened to the music (as opposed to the published source). This means that there can be errors in the lyrics you find. You can correct them yourself or look for a more reliable source.

You can then copy and paste the lyrics you find onto the Lyrics tab. Here's how:

1. Open your web browser and move to www.google.com.

2. Search for *artistname* and lyrics, where *artistname* is the name of the artist with which the track is associated. The result is likely to be several sites that provide lyrics for that artist.

3. Click a link to move to one of the sites. These sites typically organize lyrics by album.

4. Find the track for which you want lyrics, and click it. The lyrics appear.

5. Select the lyrics and copy them to your Mac's Clipboard.

Now that you have the lyrics, you can apply them to a track by performing the following steps:

1. In iTunes, open the Info window for the track whose lyrics you just copied.

2. Click the Lyrics tab.

3. Paste the lyrics you copied into the Lyrics pane (see Figure 8.17).

Figure 8.17
I've pasted the lyrics for the song Mushaboom into the Lyrics tab.

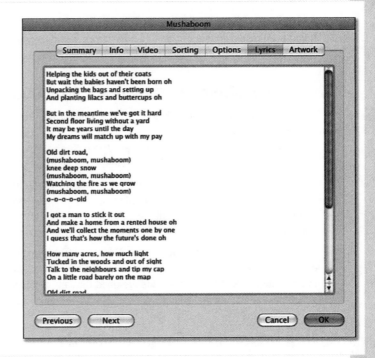

4. Click OK. The lyrics are saved with the track.

Viewing Lyrics for a Track

After you have added lyrics for a track, you can view those lyrics in iTunes by selecting the track and opening the Lyrics pane of the Info window.

 tip
You can also view lyrics on newer iPod models by clicking the Select button until the lyrics are displayed on its screen.

Adding and Viewing Album Artwork

Many CD and album covers are works of art, and it would be a shame never to see them just because your music has gone digital. With iTunes, you don't need to miss out, because you can associate artwork with tracks and display that artwork in the iTunes window.

To enjoy artwork with your tunes, you need to first associate artwork with your music. There are a number of ways to do this. All the music you purchase from the iTunes Store includes artwork, so any music you buy has artwork automatically. And, if you have an iTunes Store account, iTunes can be configured to automatically download artwork for music you add to your Library in other ways, such as when you import an audio CD. If the artwork for music isn't in the iTunes Store because the music itself isn't there, you can add artwork to music manually or semi-automatically.

After artwork has been added to your music, you can easily view it in iTunes.

If you burn discs for your music, having artwork associated with your music is good because you can use iTunes to print jewel case covers that include this art.

Configuring iTunes to Download Album Artwork Automatically

One of the cool features of iTunes is that it automatically downloads artwork from the iTunes Store. As you read earlier, when you purchase music from the store, its art comes with it. What you might not expect is that as long as you have an iTunes Store account, iTunes also downloads art associated with music you add to the Library from other sources, such as audio CDs you import.

After you have an iTunes Store account, open the iTunes Preferences dialog box, click the Store tab, activate the Automatically Download Missing Album Artwork check box, and click OK. iTunes automatically retrieves artwork for all the albums in your Library that it can. As you add other music to your Library by importing it, iTunes retrieves any artwork it can automatically.

The limitation to this feature is that for iTunes to automatically download an album's artwork, that album must be available in the iTunes Store. This isn't a big limitation because a huge amount of music is available there, so the odds are good that any music you add to your Library will be there, which means most of your music will get artwork automatically.

Adding Artwork for Songs Manually

If music isn't available in the iTunes Store, you can add it manually. Or you might want to associate artwork that isn't the default album cover with a track. For example, you might want to add the artist's picture or some other meaningful graphic to tracks.

You can add one or more pieces of art to tracks by using the following steps:

1. Prepare the artwork you are going to associate with a track. You can use graphics in the usual formats, such as JPG, TIFF, GIF, and so on.

 tip

You can often find album artwork on Amazon.com by searching for the artist, album, or song title. Click the album art and save the image to your Mac so you can use it in iTunes using the process below.

2. Select the track you want to work with.

3. Open the Info window and then click the Artwork tab (see Figure 8.18). If the selected track has artwork with it, you see it in the Artwork pane.

Figure 8.18
You use the Artwork pane to add artwork to a song.

4. Click Add. A dialog box that enables you to choose an image appears.

5. Select the image you want to associate with the track.

6. Click Choose. The image is added to the Artwork pane of the Info window.

   You can use the slider under the image box to change the size of the previews you see on the Artwork pane. Drag the slider to the right to make the image larger or to the left to make it smaller. This doesn't change the image; instead, it only impacts the size of the image as you currently see it in the Info window. This is especially useful when you associate a lot of images with a track because you can see them all at the same time.

7. Repeat steps 4–6 to continue adding images to the Artwork pane until you have added all the images for a track.

8. To change the order of the images, drag them around in the image box. If a track has more than one graphic, place the image that you want to be the default on the left side of the image box.

9. Click OK. The window closes and the images are saved with the song.

 tip

You can also add artwork to a track by dragging the image file from your desktop onto the Artwork pane of the Info window or onto the Artwork pane of the iTunes window (select View, Show Artwork Pane, or press ⌘-G).

Viewing Album Artwork

To view a track's artwork, do one of the following:

- In List View (or in Grid view when you're viewing a particular album, artist, or composer), select View, Show Artwork Column (or press ⌘-G) to add the Artwork column (see Figure 8.19).

- Click the Show/Hide Artwork button, which is the fourth button from the left under the Source list. The Artwork pane appears and displays the artwork associated with either the currently playing song or the currently selected song (see Figure 8.19). At the top of the artwork, you see Selected Item, which indicates you are viewing the artwork associated with the selected track, or Now Playing, which indicates you are viewing artwork associated with the track currently playing.

Figure 8.19
You can view the artwork associated with a track in the Artwork pane.

Artwork pane
Show/Hide Artwork

- Move the pointer over the artwork and click when the pointer becomes the hand icon to see a larger version in a separate window. The title of the window is the name of the track with which the artwork is associated.

- To choose between viewing artwork associated with the selected track or the track currently playing, click the arrow button or text at the top of the Artwork pane. The artwork changes to the other option (for example, if you click Now Playing, it becomes Selected Song), and you see the appropriate artwork for that track.

- If you select the Now Playing option, the artwork changes in the Artwork pane and in the separate art window as the next track plays (unless, of course, the tracks use the same artwork, and even then the track title in the separate artwork window will change). When nothing is playing or selected, you see a message saying so in the Artwork pane.

- If the track has more than one piece of artwork associated with it, click the arrows that appear at the top of the pane to see each piece of art. You can click on each image to open it in a separate window too.

Customizing the Content Pane

There are a number of ways to customize the columns (tags) that appear in the Content pane. What's more, you can customize the Content pane for each source. The customization you have done for a source (such as a CD or playlist) is saved and used each time you view that source.

You can select the tags (columns) that are shown for a source by using the following steps:

1. Select the source whose Content pane you want to customize. Its contents appear in the Content pane.

2. Select View, View Options or press ⌘-J. You see the View Options dialog box (see Figure 8.20). At the top of the dialog box, you see the name of the source for which you are configuring the Content pane. You also see all the available columns that can be displayed. If a column's check box is activated, that column is displayed; if not, it won't be shown.

Figure 8.20
You can set the columns shown in the Content pane with the View Options dialog box.

3. Activate the check boxes next to the columns you want to see.

4. Deactivate the check boxes next to the columns you don't want to see.

5. Click OK. When you return to the Content pane, only the columns you selected are shown for the source.

Not all columns apply to all types of content. For example, the Season column is intended for TV shows to display what season a particular track (episode) appeared in. iTunes doesn't limit the columns available in the View Options dialog box based on the source you've selected. If you include a column for a source that doesn't really apply, just open the View Options dialog box again and deactivate its check box.

Following are some other ways to customize the Content pane:

- You can change the width of columns in the Content pane by pointing to the line that marks the right boundary of the column in the column heading section. When you do, the cursor becomes a vertical line with arrows pointing to the left and right. Drag this to the left to make a column narrower or to the right to make it wider. The rest of the columns move to accommodate the change.

- You can change the order in which columns appear by dragging a column heading to the left or to the right. When you release the mouse button, the column assumes its new position and the other columns move to accommodate it.

- You can sort the Content pane by any of the columns shown, by clicking the column heading by which you want the pane to be sorted. The tracks are sorted according to that criterion, and the column heading is highlighted to show it is the current sort column. To change the direction of the sort, click the Sort Order triangle, which appears only in the Sort column. When you play a source, the tracks play according to the order in which they are sorted in the Content pane, starting from the top of the pane and playing toward the bottom (unless you have the Shuffle feature turned on, of course).

Building and Listening to Standard Playlists

Although they aren't as smart as their younger siblings (smart playlists), standard playlists are definitely useful because you can choose the songs included in them and the order in which those songs play.

Creating a Standard Playlist

You have two ways to create a playlist. One is to create a playlist that is empty (meaning it doesn't include any songs). The other is to choose songs and then create a playlist that includes those songs.

The place you start depends on what you have in mind. If you want to create a collection of songs but aren't sure which specific songs you want to start with, create an empty playlist. If you know of at least some of the songs you are going to include, select them first and then create the playlist. Either way, you'll end up in the same place.

Creating an Empty Standard Playlist

You can create an empty playlist from within iTunes by using any of the following techniques:

- Select File, New Playlist.

- Press ⌘-N.

- Click the Create Playlist button, which is the + icon at the bottom of the Source list.

Whichever method you use will result in an empty playlist whose name is highlighted to show you that it is ready for you to edit. Type a name for the playlist and press Return. The playlist is renamed and selected. The Content pane is empty because you haven't added any songs to the playlist yet. You will learn how to do that later in this section.

Creating a Standard Playlist with Songs in It

If you know some songs you want to place in a playlist, you can create the playlist so it includes those songs as soon as you create it. Here are the steps to follow:

1. Browse or search the Library to find the songs you want to be included in the playlist. For example, you can browse for all the songs in a specific genre or search for music by a specific artist.

2. In the Content pane, select the songs you want to place in the playlist.

3. Choose File, New Playlist from Selection. A new playlist appears on the Source list and is selected. Its name is highlighted to indicate that you can edit it, and you see the songs you selected in the Content pane.

   iTunes attempts to name the playlist by looking for a common denominator in the group of songs you selected. For example, if all the songs are from the same artist, that artist's name is the playlist's name. Similarly, if the songs are all from the same album, the playlist's name is the artist's and album's names. Sometimes iTunes picks an appropriate name, and sometimes it doesn't.

 tip

iTunes keeps playlists in the Source pane in alphabetical order within each group (standard and smart playlists). So, when you rename a playlist, it jumps to the location in the standard playlist section on the Source list to be where it belongs.

 tip

You can select a group of songs that are next to one another by clicking the first song, holding down the Shift key, and then clicking the last song. You can select multiple songs that aren't next to one another by holding down ⌘ key while you click them.

 tip

When you add a new album to your Library, use this technique to quickly create a playlist to make it easy to listen to. Select all the songs in the album and then use the New Playlist from Selection command. You can use the resulting playlist to easily select the new album for your listening pleasure.

 tip

For still another way to create a playlist, try this: Select a group of songs and drag them onto the Source list. When you do so, iTunes does the same thing it does when you create a playlist using the steps in this section.

4. While the playlist name is highlighted, edit the name as needed and then press Return. The playlist is ready to listen to and for you to add more songs.

Adding Songs to a Playlist

The whole point of creating a playlist is to add songs to it. Whether you created an empty playlist or one that already has some songs in it, the steps to add songs are the same:

1. Select the Music source.

2. Browse or search the Music source (or other source) so that songs you want to add to the playlist are shown in the Content pane.

3. Select the tracks you want to add to the playlist by clicking them (remember the techniques to select multiple tracks at the same time).

4. Drag the selected songs from the Content pane onto the playlist to which you want to add them. As you drag, you see the songs you have selected in a ghost image attached to the pointer. When the playlist becomes highlighted and the cursor includes a plus sign (+), release the mouse button. The songs are added to the playlist.

5. Repeat steps 2–4 until you have added all the songs you want to include in the playlist.

6. Select the playlist on the Source list. Its songs appear in the Content pane. Information about the playlist, such as its playing time, appears in the Source Information area at the bottom of the iTunes window.

Removing Songs from a Playlist

If you decide you don't want one or more songs included in a playlist, select the songs you want to remove in the playlist's Content pane and press the Delete key. A warning prompt appears. Click Yes and the songs are deleted from the playlist.

 tip

You can also move songs from one playlist to another one. Just select a playlist containing tracks you want to add to the playlist instead of the Library in step 1.

 tip

You can add the same song to a playlist as many times as you'd like to hear it.

 tip

If you double-click a playlist, it opens in a separate window. You can drag songs onto this window to add them to the playlist. This is helpful when you have a lot of playlists and other items on your Source list because you can arrange the iTunes window and the playlist window so you can see both easily at the same time.

 note

The Source Information area becomes very important when you are creating a CD because you can use this to make sure a playlist will fit onto a CD.

 tip

You can add a song to a standard playlist by opening its contextual menu, choosing Add to Playlist, and then choosing the playlist to which you want to add that song.

Setting the Order in Which a Playlist's Songs Play

Just like other sources, the order in which a playlist's songs play is determined by the order in which they appear in the Content pane (the first song is the one at the top of the window, the second is the next one down, and so on). You can drag songs up on the list to make them play earlier or down in the list to make them play later.

You can also change the order in which songs will play by sorting the playlist by its columns. You do this by clicking the column title in the column by which you want the Content pane sorted. You can set the columns that appear for a playlist by selecting View, View Options, as you learned to do earlier.

Listening to a Standard Playlist

After you have created a playlist, you can listen to it by selecting it on the Source list and using the same controls you use to listen to other sources. You can even search in and browse playlists just as you can the Library or CDs. (That's the real beauty of iTunes; it works the same way no matter what the selected source is!)

Deleting a Standard Playlist

If you decide you no longer want a playlist, you can delete it by selecting the playlist on the Source list and pressing the Delete key. A prompt appears; click Yes and the playlist is removed from the Source list. Even though you've deleted the playlist, the songs in the playlist remain in the Library or in other playlists for your listening pleasure.

Building and Using Smart Playlists

The basic purpose of a smart playlist is the same as a standard playlist—that is, to contain a collection of tracks to which you can listen, put on a CD, and so on. However, the path smart playlists take to this end is completely different from that of standard playlists. Rather than choose specific songs as you do in a standard playlist, you tell iTunes the kind of tracks you want in your smart playlist and it picks out the tracks for you and places them in the playlist. For example, suppose you want to create a playlist that contains all your classical music. Rather than picking out all the songs in your Library that have the Classical genre

 note

When you delete a song from a playlist, it *isn't* deleted from the Library. It remains there so you can add it to a different playlist or listen to it from the Library. Of course, if it is included in other playlists, it isn't removed from those either.

 note

You can't sort a playlist by dragging songs up or down unless the playlist is sorted by the Track Number column (always the first column in the Content pane unless you are viewing the Library, in which case it is always the first column with information in it). If songs bounce back when you try to reorder them, click the Track Number column to make it the sort column. Then you'll be able to drag songs around to change their order.

note

The only time tracks or other content are actually removed from your Library is when you delete them while the Music source is selected. You should do this only when you are absolutely sure you won't want those tracks again. If you are working with playlists, deleting tracks removes them from only the current playlist so you can always add them again later if you change your mind.

(as you would do to create a standard playlist), you can use a smart playlist to tell iTunes to select all the classical music for you. The application then gathers all the music with the Classical genre and places that music in a smart playlist.

Understanding Why Smart Playlists Are Called Smart

You create a smart playlist by defining a set of criteria based on any number of tags. After you have created these criteria, iTunes chooses songs that match those tags and places them in the playlist. For example, suppose you are a big-time Elvis fan and regularly add Elvis music to your Library. You could create a playlist and manually drag your new Elvis tunes to that playlist. But by using a smart playlist instead, you could define the playlist to include all your Elvis music. Anytime you add more Elvis music to your Library, that music is added to the playlist automatically so it always contains all the Elvis music in your Library.

You can also base a smart playlist on more than one attribute at the same time. Going back to the Elvis example, you could add the condition that you want only those songs you have rated four stars or higher so the smart playlist contains only your favorite Elvis songs.

As the previous example shows, smart playlists can be dynamic; iTunes calls this *live updating*. When a smart playlist is set to be live, iTunes changes its contents over time to match changes to the music in your Library. If this feature isn't set for a smart playlist, that playlist contains only those songs that met the criteria at the time the playlist was created.

Finally, you can also link a smart playlist's conditions by the logical expression All or Any. If you use an All logical expression, all the conditions must be true for a song to be included in the smart playlist. If you use the Any option, only one of the conditions has to be met for a song to be included in the smart playlist.

Creating a Smart Playlist

You can create a smart playlist by performing the following steps:

1. Select File, New Smart Playlist or hold down the Option key and click the New Playlist button, which becomes the New Smart Playlist button when the Option key is pressed down. You see the Smart Playlist dialog box (see Figure 8.21).

 tip

You can also create a new smart playlist by pressing Option-⌘-N.

2. In the Tag menu, select the first tag you want the smart playlist to be based on. For example, you can select Artist, Genre, My Rating, or Year, among many others. The Operator menu is updated with operators that are applicable to the attribute you select. For example, if you select Artist, the Operator menu includes text operators such as Contains or Starts With, whereas if you select Bit Rate, the Operator menu includes numeric operators such as Is or Is Greater Than.

3. In the Operator menu, select the operator you want to use. For example, if you want to match data exactly, select the Is operator. If you want the condition to be more loose, select an operator such as Contains or Is Less Than.

Tag menu   Operator menu   Condition box

Remove Condition

Add Condition

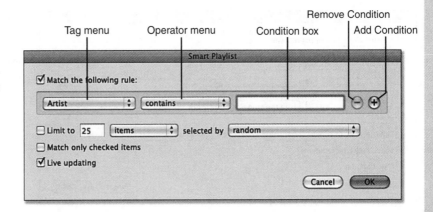

Figure 8.21
The Smart Playlist dialog box enables you to create playlists based on a single tag or on many of them.

4. Use the Condition box to type the condition you want to match. The more you type, the more specific the condition is. As an example, if you select Artist in step 1, select Contains in step 2, and type Elvis in this step, the playlist finds all songs that include Elvis, Elvis Presley, Elvis Costello, Red Elvises, and so on. If you type Elvis Presley in the Condition box, instead, iTunes includes only songs whose artist includes the full phrase *Elvis Presley*, such as Elvis Presley, Elvis Presley and His Back-up Band, and so on.

5. To add another condition to the smart playlist, click the Add Condition button. A new, empty condition appears. At the top of the dialog box, the Match menu also appears.

6. In the second condition's Tag menu, select the second tag on which you want the smart playlist to be based. For example, if you want to include songs from a specific genre, select Genre on the menu.

7. In the second condition's Operator menu, select the operator you want to use.

8. Use the Condition box to type the condition you want to match.

9. Repeat steps 5–8 to add more conditions to the playlist until you have all the conditions you want to include (see Figure 8.22).

 note

As you make selections on the Attribute menu and type conditions in the Condition box, iTunes will attempt to automatically match what you type to tags in your Library. For example, if your Library includes Elvis music and you use Artist as an attribute, iTunes will enter Elvis Presley in the Condition box for you when you start typing "Elvis."

 tip

If you want to remove a condition from a smart playlist, click the Remove button (the minus sign) for the condition you want to remove.

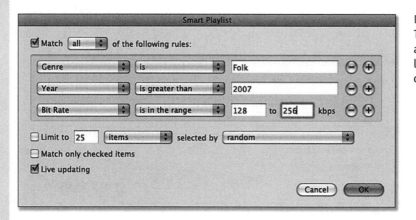

Figure 8.22
This smart playlist is approaching the genius level; it now includes three conditions.

10. In the Match pop-up menu, select All if all the conditions must be met for a track to be included in the smart playlist, or select Any if only one of them must be met. For example, you could create a smart playlist based on multiple Artist conditions and the playlist would feature music by those artists. In this case, you would choose Any so that if a song were associated with *any* of the artists for which you created a condition, it would be included in the playlist. As a contrasting example, if you want the playlist to include songs you have rated as three stars or better by a specific artist, you would include both of these conditions and then select All in the menu so that both conditions would have to be met for a song to be included (a song is both by the artist and is rated with three or more stars).

11. If you want to limit the playlist, activate the Limit To check box. If you don't want to set a limit on the playlist, leave the check box deactivated and skip to step 15.

12. Use the Limit To pop-up menu to select the parameter you want to use to limit the playlist; by default, this menu has Items selected. Your choices include the number of songs (Items on the menu), the time the playlist will play (Minutes or Hours), and the size of the files the playlist contains (MB or GB).

13. Type the data appropriate for the limit you selected in the Limit To box. For example, if you selected Minutes in the menu, type the maximum length of the playlist in minutes in the box. If you selected Items, enter the maximum number of songs that can be included in the playlist.

 note

If you include more than one condition based on the same tag, you usually don't want to use the All option because the conditions will likely be mutually exclusive, and using the All option will result in no songs being included in the playlist because no song will be able to meet all the conditions at the same time.

tip

Limiting a playlist by disk space is useful when you want to do something else with that playlist, such as burning a CD. You could set the playlist to be limited to 700MB to ensure all its songs will fit on one disc. (The exact limit depends on the specific drive and disc media you use.)

14. Select how you want iTunes to choose the songs it includes based on the limit you selected by using the Selected By menu. This menu has many options, including Random, Most Recently Played, and Most Recently Added.

15. If you want the playlist to include only songs whose check box in the Content pane is activated, activate the Match Only Checked Items check box. If you leave this check box deactivated, iTunes includes all songs that meet the playlist's conditions, even if you have deactivated their check boxes in the Content pane.

16. If you want the playlist to be dynamic, meaning that iTunes updates its contents over time, leave the Live Updating check box activated. If you deactivate this check box, the playlist includes only those songs that meet the playlist's conditions when you create it.

17. Click OK to create the playlist. iTunes adds the smart playlist to the Source list, and its name is ready for you to edit. Also, the songs in your Library that match the criteria in the playlist are added to it and the current contents of the playlist are shown in the Content pane.

18. Type the playlist's name and press Return. The smart playlist is complete.

Listening to a Smart Playlist

Listening to a smart playlist is just like listening to other sources: You select it on the Source list and use the playback controls to listen to it. The one difference is that, if a smart playlist is set to be live, its contents can change over time.

Changing a Smart Playlist

To change the contents of a smart playlist, you change the smart playlist's criteria (remember that iTunes automatically places tracks in a smart playlist based on your criteria). Use the following steps to do this:

1. Select the smart playlist you want to change.

2. Select File, Edit Smart Playlist. The Smart Playlist dialog box appears, and the playlist's current criteria are shown.

3. Use the techniques you learned when you created a playlist to change its criteria. For example, you can remove conditions by clicking their Remove buttons. You can also add more conditions or change the other settings for the playlist.

4. Click OK. Your changes are saved and the contents of the playlist are updated to match the current criteria.

 note

Just as with other sources, when you select a smart playlist, its information is shown in the Source Information section at the bottom of the window. This can be useful if you want to create a CD or just to see how big the playlist is (by number of songs, time, or file size). Remember, though, that because a smart playlist's contents can change over time, its source information can also change over time. So, just because a smart playlist fits on a CD today doesn't mean it still will tomorrow (or even later today).

 tip

You can also edit a smart playlist by selecting it and opening the Info window (which also opens the Smart Playlist dialog box). Plus, you can open the playlist's contextual menu by right-clicking (two-button mouse) or Control-clicking it (one-button mouse) and selecting Edit Smart Playlist.

You can also change a smart playlist by using the same techniques you use on other sources such as sorting it, selecting the columns you see when you view it, and so on.

 tip

To delete a smart playlist, select it on the Source list and press Delete. Confirm the deletion at the prompt (if you see it), and the playlist is removed from the Source list.

9

PLAYING AND MANAGING MOVIES AND DIGITAL VIDEO

Playing Digital Video with QuickTime

Apple's QuickTime is the technology your Mac uses to handle dynamic data. *Dynamic data* simply means data that changes over time. This includes video, audio, and other such media. In fact, QuickTime technology and the QuickTime framework enable all the iLife applications, including iTunes. Without QuickTime, using Mac OS X wouldn't be nearly as interesting as it is.

Under Mac OS X, except for viewing QuickTime movies on your computer and on the Web, you likely won't deal with QuickTime directly very often. But, in addition to knowing how to handle those tasks, you should have a good understanding of the QuickTime technology.

Since its introduction, Apple's QuickTime has been one of the most successful multimedia standards on any platform. In fact, it has been so successful that it is also widely used on Windows computers; QuickTime movies on Windows play the same way they do on the Mac. QuickTime has also been widely adopted on the Web, with many websites serving video and animation files as QuickTime movies. And, like on the Mac, QuickTime technology drives iTunes on Windows computers.

Although you are most likely to encounter QuickTime movies on the Web, you will encounter them in many other places, including interactive games, reference titles, entertainment titles, learning tools, and of course web pages.

Opening QuickTime Player

QuickTime Player is the basic application you use to view QuickTime content stored on your computer or in the QuickTime format on CD or DVD, such as those you create using iMovie. Although the appearance of the QuickTime Player controls varies a bit among these contexts, the controls you use to watch movies work similarly.

To launch QuickTime Player, open it from within the Applications folder.

Watching QuickTime Movies Stored Locally

If you use a VCR, CD player, or DVD player, you won't have any trouble using the QuickTime Player controls to view QuickTime content. Find a QuickTime movie on your hard drive or on a disc and open it. QuickTime Player launches and you see the QuickTime Player window (see Figure 9.1).

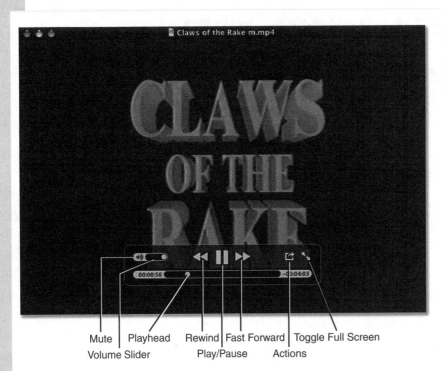

Figure 9.1
The QuickTime Player window provides the basic controls you use to watch QuickTime movies.

Mute | Playhead   Rewind | Fast Forward | Toggle Full Screen
Volume Slider   Play/Pause   Actions

Most of the controls in the QuickTime Player window are easy to understand. For example, the Rewind button plays the movie in reverse, the Fast Forward button plays the movie in fast forward mode, and so on.

However, you need to become familiar with the less obvious parts of the QuickTime Player window, especially if you have

 tip

QuickTime movie files use the extension `.mov`. If you don't know where a QuickTime movie is, use Spotlight to search for files with this extension.

never worked with digital video before. The current frame is shown in the viewing window (if you haven't played the movie, it is the first frame in the movie). Just below the viewing window is the movie's Timeline bar (also known as the Scrubber bar). This represents the total length of the movie. The location of the playhead shows where in the movie the current frame is located. As you play a movie, the playhead moves to the right in the Timeline bar so that it always shows the location of the frame displayed in the viewing window.

Control the size of the movie using the commands on the View menu. You can view it at Full Screen, Actual Size, or Fit to Screen. Increasing the size of a movie beyond the size at which it was created sometimes decreases its image quality and frame rate. With some movies, this is hardly noticeable; with others, increasing the size can make them unwatchable. You can experiment to see which size is the best compromise for a particular movie on your specific system.

Click the Play button (or press the spacebar) to view the movie and use the Volume slider to adjust its sound level.

➡ *QuickTime Player offers many keyboard shortcuts; to learn which shortcuts are available, **see** "Using QuickTime Player Keyboard Shortcuts," **p. 197**.*

If the movie contains chapter markers, such as those you can add to your iMovie projects, jump to a specific chapter in the movie by opening the Chapter pop-up menu and selecting the chapter you want to view. If you are playing the movie when you use this menu, you will jump to the chapter you selected and the movie will continue to play. If it isn't playing, you'll see the first frame in the chapter you selected.

You can move to any point in the movie by dragging the playhead to the frame you want to view.

You can get more information about a movie by selecting Window, Show Movie Inspector. In the resulting window, you see technical information about the movie, such as its format, resolution, and size.

You can cause a movie to loop so that it plays over and over again by selecting View, Loop or by pressing ⌘-L.

You can also change the size of the QuickTime Player window using the Resize handle. The window remains in proportion to the size in which the movie was created. If you hold down the Shift key, you can resize the window any way you want (with sometimes amusing effects on the movie itself). You can quickly return a movie to its default size by selecting View, Actual Size or by pressing ⌘-1.

To mute a movie, click the speaker icon at the left edge of the Volume slider.

When you minimize a movie you are watching, it moves onto the Dock and continues to play.

note

QuickTime movies can also be inserted into many types of documents, such as Word files, presentations, and so on. When you view such a file, you will see a "mini" QuickTime controller that enables you to watch the movie embedded in a particular document. Applications can add or remove controls to customize the interface you see in that application, but when you understand how to view movies with the QuickTime Player, you won't have any trouble with these other controllers.

Watching QuickTime Movies Stored on the Web

QuickTime is a major format for movies on the Web. Using the QuickTime plug-in, you can watch QuickTime movies from within a web browser, such as Safari. When you do so, you use controls that are similar to those in the QuickTime Player application.

One of the best places to view QuickTime movies is at Apple's Movie Trailer site. Here, you can view trailers for the latest creations from Hollywood.

To view a movie or video online, you have two choices:

- If you know the address of the movie file, select File, Open URL (or press ⌘-U), type the address in the Movie URL text box, and then click OK.

- Use Safari to surf to the page that contains the movie you want to view, and then click the link to the movie.

The movie will start to download. As soon as enough has been downloaded that it can play without interruption the rest of the way, it will begin to play. The movie will appear in a window that contains QuickTime controls you can use to watch the trailer (see Figure 9.2). (Note that if you open an HD version, the QuickTime Player application will launch for you to watch the trailer.) If you use a fast connection and use the Instant-On feature, this happens quickly. If you use a slow connection or have configured a delay using the Instant-On slider, it can take longer. You can see how much of a movie has been downloaded by looking at the dark shaded part of the Timeline bar. Use the QuickTime controls listed in Table 9.1 to control playback.

caution

If you use a slow Internet connection, watching movies, such as the movie trailers on the Apple website, can be an exercise in patience. High-quality movie files are *big*. Watching them on the Web, even with the streaming feature and the MPEG-4 format, can take more time than it is worth. If you use a slow connection, try watching some movies to see whether you can tolerate the length of time it takes to download enough of the movie so you can begin watching it. If you can, great. If not, you might have to find smaller movies to watch or, even better, move up to a faster connection. You can also use the Instant-On preference to configure the delay before a movie begins to play.

Figure 9.2
You can use QuickTime Player to view movies online.

Depending on how the movie is presented, you might not see the window shown in Figure 9.2. For example, some QuickTime content will play in the iTunes window. Others, especially those that offer full-screen versions, will provide a customized playback window or will play in the QuickTime Player.

Using QuickTime Player Keyboard Shortcuts

Some useful QuickTime Player keyboard shortcuts are shown in Table 9.1.

> **tip**
>
> You can start a movie at any time by pressing the spacebar. If you don't wait for the automatic start, the movie might stop before it finishes if it runs out of downloaded movie before it gets to the end.

Table 9.1   Keyboard Shortcuts for QuickTime Player

Menu	Action	Keyboard Shortcut
File	Close Player window	⌘-W
File	Open URL	⌘-U
None	Move playhead backward one frame	Left arrow
None	Move playhead forward one frame	Right arrow
None	Pause movie (movie playing)	Spacebar
None	Play movie (movie paused)	Spacebar
None	Turn down volume	Down arrow
None	Turn up volume	Up arrow
None	Turn volume to maximum	Shift-Option-up arrow
None	Turn volume to minimum	Shift-Option-down arrow
View	Loop	⌘-L
View	Play movie at actual size	⌘-1
View	Play movie and fit to screen	⌘-3
View	Play movie and fill screen	⌘-4
View	Play movie in panoramic view	⌘-5
View	Increase the window size	⌘-+
View	Decrease the window size	⌘--
View	Play movie at full screen	⌘-F
Window	Show Movie Inspector	⌘-I

Watching DVD Movies with DVD Player

DVDs are a great way to watch movies, TV shows, and other content. Because they are digital, the image and sound quality of DVD movies is superb (well, except for poorly produced ones, that is). And the digital format enables special features that can't be duplicated with other means, such as videotape. For example, with DVD movies, you can get true 5-, 6-, or even 7-track soundtracks to provide unbelievable surround sound and sound fidelity. Plus, DVDs usually have a lot of features—missing scenes, trailers, and so on.

Mac OS X supports the playback of DVD movies with its DVD Player application. When you insert a DVD, your Mac automatically starts the DVD Player application. In most cases, DVD Player will enter into Full Screen mode and start playing your DVD. Moving your mouse to the top of the screen reveals the Image bar, along with the menu bar (see Figure 9.3). Moving your mouse to the bottom of the screen reveals the Controller. Your movie plays in the Viewer, which is the main part of your screen.

Image bar

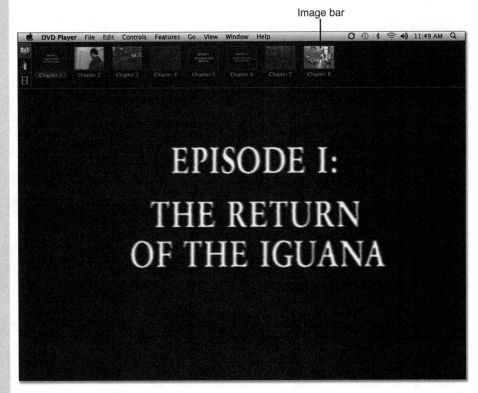

Figure 9.3
With DVD Player, you can enjoy all the amazing content available on DVD.

In Full Screen mode, the Mac OS interface disappears and you can see only the DVD content and the DVD windows you choose to display by moving the mouse to reveal them. If you need to resize the window so that you can have your movie running while you work on other things, move your mouse to the top of the screen to reveal the menu bar and use the View menu to change the window size. Your options include Half Size, Actual Size, Double Size, and Fit to Screen.

 note

When you view a movie at a size other than full screen, DVD Player will have a separate Viewer window, a Controller that you can move around to different locations on the screen, and the ability to open a window to see the Chapters/Bookmarks/Video Clips.

➥ *To learn how to add digital sound to your Mac, **see***
*Chapter 32, "Working with Your Mac's Sound," **p. 625.***

The Controller contains the controls you use to watch movies (see Figure 9.4).

 note

To really enjoy DVD content, you should connect your Mac to a digital sound system.

Figure 9.4
The Controller does just what you think: It enables you to control DVD playback.

DVD menu controls   Playback controls   Player Settings └─ Disc information
Volume slider   Streams/Closed Captioning

The Player settings and Streams/Closed Captioning buttons provide additional control over what you hear and see from your DVD. Clicking on the Streams/Closed Captioning button presents you with a menu to select different languages, subtitles, closed captioning, and viewing angles.

If you have used a standard DVD player or VCR, the DVD Player controls will be easy to understand. To play and control a movie, use the following steps:

1. Insert the DVD into your Mac's DVD drive. After a moment, the DVD is mounted on the machine. By default, DVD Player opens and begins to play the DVD. Depending on the DVD, the disc's main menu might appear or you might be prompted to select a soundtrack or other features.

 tip

To configure what action your Mac takes when you insert a DVD, use the CDs & DVDs pane of the System Preferences application.

2. Select the menu option you want, such as Play Movie, by clicking it. You can also use the arrow keys to move among the menu options and then press Return to select an option. The movie begins to play in the Viewer. When you activate a control, the upper-left corner of the Viewer briefly displays an icon or text describing the control you used most recently (such as Play).

3. Use the commands on the View menu to control the size of the Viewer.

4. To bring the Controller back, move the pointer, press a key, or press Option-⌘-C.

5. If you move the pointer to the bottom of the screen, the Controller will appear displaying the Timeline bar. At the left end, you see the current position of the playhead while at the right end you see the time remaining. You can drag the playhead to move to a different position in the movie.

6. Use any of the controls on the Player settings button on the Controller to modify how the DVD Player application displays your movie. You can modify the video zoom and color, as well as display an audio equalizer using the small triangle at the top-right corner of the Player settings window.

Following are some other DVD playback notes:

- **DVD menus**—All DVD movies include a menu that provides access to the content of the disc and its special features. You can highlight and select commands on these menus using the keyboard's arrow buttons, using the mouse to point to them, or using the mouse to point to them on the Controller. You can move back to the most recent menu you viewed by clicking the menu button on the Controller; selecting Go, DVD Menu; or pressing ⌘-d. Depending on how the DVD is structured, clicking the title button might take you to the same place or it might move you to the DVD's main menu.

- **Use the Controller to quickly change the movie's settings**—For example, you can control subtitles, closed captioning, and select different angles (when available) from the Streams/Closed Captioning button.

 tip

Click in the Disc information section on the Controller to cycle through the available data, such as chapter, remaining time, and so on. Click the Title or Chapter text to change the display to the related information.

 note

If you're running a fairly powerful Mac and you minimize the Viewer, it moves into the Dock and the movie continues to play. Be sure to take a look at the DVD Player preferences and deactivate the Pause Playback option (it's in the Player tab) when the viewer is minimized.

 tip

You can also control a movie by selecting onscreen controls with the mouse.

 tip

When you move to a menu and then back to the DVD, you will move back to the same spot at which you were viewing the DVD when you selected the menu command.

- **Scan forward or backward**—When you scan forward or backward, you can control the rate of the scan by selecting Controls, Scan Rate, and then the rate at which you want to scan (such as 8x speed). DVD Player supports scan rates up to 32x, which is really fast. The scan rate you select controls both forward and backward scanning.

- **Go menu**—Many commands are available on this menu that you can use to quickly access various areas on the DVD, including the DVD menu, the beginning of the disc, the content you were viewing the last time you played the disc, bookmarks, titles, chapters, and so on.

- **Bookmarks**—You can use this feature to mark specific areas of a DVD so you can quickly return to them. When viewing content to which you want to add a bookmark, select Controls, New Bookmark. In the New Bookmark sheet, name the bookmark and click Add. You can return to that bookmark by selecting Go, Bookmarks, *Bookmarkname*, where *Bookmarkname* is the name of a bookmark you have created. You can also jump to a bookmark by selecting it on the Bookmark menu on the Image bar or by using the Bookmarks window. (You learn more about bookmarks later in this chapter.)

- **Chapters**—Most DVD content is organized by chapter. Moving your mouse to the top of the screen will reveal the Image bar; click on the icon of a book to see the chapters on your DVD. Choose Go, Chapter Number to jump to a chapter. You can also choose Window, Chapters (⌘-B) to move into the Chapters window on which you can click a chapter's thumbnail to jump to it.

 tip

If thumbnails don't appear for the chapters, open the Action pop-up menu and choose Generate Missing Thumbnails.

- **Keyboard commands work best**—As you watch movies, you will find that the best way to control them is using the keyboard. Most of the major functions in the player have keyboard shortcuts. For the best DVD experience, learn to use these shortcuts.

➥ *To learn about bookmarks,* **see** *"Working with Bookmarks,"* **p. 207**.

➥ *To learn the many keyboard shortcuts for playback and configuration DVD Player offers,* **see** *"Using DVD Player Keyboard Shortcuts,"* **p. 210**.

Configuring DVD Player

DVD Player is a relatively simple application, but you can do some configuration to make it work the way you want it to. The DVD Player preferences window has six panes: Player, Disc Setup, Full Screen, Windows, Previously Viewed, and High Definition. These preference settings are summarized in Table 9.2.

 note

You can't control a movie while the Preferences dialog box is open.

Table 9.2 DVD Player Preferences

Pane	Preference	Effect
Player	When DVD Player Opens: Enter Full Screen Mode	These preferences determine which action DVD Player takes when it opens. Because it is typically in the Full Screen mode when you watch a movie, this preference selects the Full Screen mode automatically when a DVD is mounted on your desktop and DVD Player starts (which it does by default when a DVD containing movie content is mounted on your Mac).
Player	When DVD Player Opens: Start Playing Disc	If you want discs to start playing when DVD Player opens, leave this check box activated.
Player	When DVD Player Is Inactive: Pause Playback	Activate this check box to have DVD Player pause the playback, when you switch to another program.
Player	When a Disc Is Inserted: Start Playing Disc	Leave this check box activated to have DVD Player automatically start the playback as soon as you insert the DVD.
Player	When Playing Using a Battery	On a notebook Mac, leave this check box activated to have DVD Player put the DVD drive into sleep mode when you switch to batteries.
Player	When Muted: Show Closed Captioning	Leave this check box activated to have DVD Player automatically turn on the DVD's closed captioning when you mute the volume.
Player	During iChat with Audio: Mute Audio or Pause Playback	Use these radio buttons to determine which action DVD Player takes when you enter a chat session. You can have DVD Player either mute its audio or pause the playback of the DVD.
Player	When Viewer Is Minimized: Pause Playback	If you select this preference, when you minimize the viewer (and it moves onto the Dock), the pause function is selected automatically. This is handy when you need to move DVD Player out of the way to do something else (for example, when your editor calls and you need to act as if you are working). When you return to the DVD Player window, you can start viewing at the same point you left off.
Disc Setup	Language: Audio	Use this pop-up menu to choose the default audio track for discs you play. If you choose Use Disc Default, DVD Player will start with the default audio track for the disc. If you choose a language, it will try to start with that instead.
Disc Setup	Language: Subtitle	Use this pop-up menu to set the default Subtitle options.
Disc Setup	Language: DVD Menu	This option sets the default menu language for discs you view.

Table 9.2 Continued

Pane	Preference	Effect
Disc Setup	Internet: Enable DVD@ccess Web Links	Many DVDs offer content on the Web. Use this preference to enable or disable links on DVDs you view.
Disc Setup	Audio Output	Use this pop-up menu to choose the output sound source for DVD playback. If you have only one sound option, your only choice is System Sound Output. If you have more than one option, you can choose the sound output you want to use on this menu.
Disc Setup	Disable Dolby Dynamic Range Compression	If your Mac supports digital audio out, use the pop-up menu to select Digital Out to take advantage of that output, such as 5.1 digital surround sound. Use the check box to determine whether dynamic range compression is used (this evens out the volume level of a disc).
Full Screen	Hide Controller If Inactive for x Seconds	Use this to control the automatic hiding of the separate Controller window when you aren't using it. By default, the Controller window is hidden after 10 seconds. You can change this time or turn off the feature if you want to manually hide and show the Controller window.
Full Screen	Dim Other Displays While Playing	If you have more than one monitor connected to your Mac, this preference causes all of them except the one on which the DVD is being shown to go black while you are playing a DVD.
Full Screen	Remain in Full Screen When DVD Player Is Inactive	If you want DVD Player to remain in Full Screen mode whenever it is inactive, activate this box. By default, DVD Player switches to Maximum Size mode when you move to the Finder or another application. With this preference active, it remains in Full Screen mode instead.
Full Screen	Use Current Video Size in Full Screen	If you activate this check box, DVD Player leaves the movie at its current size when you switch to full screen. Use this when you are viewing low-resolution content whose quality looks poor at large sizes.
Full Screen	Kiosk Mode (Disable Menu Bar)	Activate this check box if you want to disable the DVD Player menu bar.
Full Screen	Allow Screensaver on DVD Menu In Kiosk Mode	When you enable this preference, you are operating in kiosk mode, and the disc is playing on a menu screen, your Mac's screen saver will activate. This prevents a static image on the DVD menu from appearing on your display for a long time (possibly damaging the display).

Table 9.2 Continued

Pane	Preference	Effect
Windows	Display Status Information	The status information appears at the top of the Viewer and provides information about what is happening, such as when you click a control.
Windows	Fade Controller When Hiding	To have the Controller window fade slowly out of existence when it hides, activate this box. With it deactivated, the Controller blinks out of existence. (Your Mac must support Quartz Extreme for this to happen.)
Windows	Closed Captioned, Text	Use this button to set the color of text used when Closed Captioning is displayed.
Windows	Closed Captioned, Background	Use this button to set the color of the background over which Closed Captioning text is displayed.
Windows	Closed Captioned, Transparency	Use this slider to set the transparency of the Closed Captioned text box.
Windows	Closed Captioned, Font	Use the Font pop-up menu to choose the font for Closed Caption text.
Windows	Closed Captioned, Font, Size for Separate Window	Use this box to enter the font size when Closed Captioned text appears in a separate window.
Previously Viewed	Start Playing Discs from: Beginning; Last Position Played; Default Bookmark; or Always Ask	Choose the radio button to select the location from which you want discs to start playing. For example, if you choose Last Position Played, a disc will start playing at the same point you stopped playing the last time you viewed it.
Previously Viewed	Always Use Disc Settings for: Audio Equalizer; Video Color; or Video Zoom	DVD Player includes tools you can use to adjust the audio, video color, and zoom settings for a disc. If you want DVD Player to use disc settings for these, activate the appropriate box for the setting you want to always use from the disc. If you deactivate a box, you can configure the related setting manually (you learn how later in this chapter).
High Definition	For Standard Definition: Actual Video Size or Disc Default	Use these radio buttons to determine how DVD Player handles discs in the standard definition format. Choose Disc Default to have DVD Player use the disc's default size; choose Actual Video Size to use the current size of the Viewer.
High Definition	For High Definition: Actual Video Size; 720 Height; or 1080 Height	Use these radio buttons to determine how DVD Player handles discs in the high definition format. Choose 720 Height or 1080 Height to specify the viewer height in pixels; choose Actual Video Size to use the current size of the Viewer.

Working with Disc Info

You can use the Disc Info window to rename a disc and set an image to display in the Viewer window when the disc isn't playing, such as an image from the DVD. Here's how:

1. Insert the DVD you want to work with.

2. Move to the frame in the DVD that you want to display when the DVD is stopped—this image will be shown instead of a black Viewer window.

3. Select File, Get Disc Info. The Disc Info window will appear. This window has four panes. The Info pane provides detailed information about the disc including its audio and video formats, media type, and so on.

4. To rename a disc, type the name of the disc in the Title box. This doesn't actually change the disc, but Mac OS X will substitute the name you enter for the disc's name when it appears at the top of the separate Viewer window. Because discs are often named according to filename limitations, it's often better to have DVD Player use a more meaningful name.

5. Click Jacket Picture. The image that appears in the image well is the image that will be shown on the screen when you stop playback. In most cases, this is the image from the DVD's case. However, you can set this to be the frame at which you are currently located by clicking Current Frame. You can also choose a different graphic by clicking Choose and selecting the graphic you want to use instead (see Figure 9.5). You can return the image to the disc jacket's image by clicking Disc Jacket Picture.

6. Click the Regions icon to open the Regions pane. All DVDs are encoded with specific geographic regions. Likewise, all DVD players are encoded with a region. In order for a disc to be played, the player and disc's region must be the same. On the Regions tab, you see the disc's region and the drive's region. When you insert a disc from a different region, you'll be prompted to change the region setting for the drive to match so that you can play the disc.

 tip

If you watch a TV series on DVD and choose the Last Position Played preference, it can be somewhat confusing for you because when you insert a new disc, DVD Player will sometimes resume playing from a point that you haven't viewed previously. This happens because the markers on the discs for different episodes during the same season might be the same. Thus, DVD Player can't tell the difference between discs within the same season or series and moves to the same spot on the new disc where you left off on the previous one. If this happens, just select Go, DVD Menu to move to the disc's menu. Then you can choose which part you want to view.

 caution

Many DVDs that claim to offer DVD-ROM or web content are not compatible with the Mac. However, you can often open these DVDs via the Finder to access some of this additional content.

 caution

You can only change the region four times, so you should be sure you want to change the drive's region setting because after you've hit the limit, you won't be able to change it again and you'll only be able to play discs from that region from that point on. At the bottom of the Regions pane, you see how many region changes you have left.

Figure 9.5
When this disc is stopped, the image shown in the image well will be displayed in the Viewer.

7. Click the Parental Control icon to open that pane. When you've enabled Parental Controls for a user account, you can use the controls on this pane to determine what happens when the disc is inserted. For example, you can require authorization before the disc will be able to be played.

8. Click OK. The Disc Info window closes and any changes you made are saved. All your settings are remembered for the specific disc. For example, the name you gave the disc will be the title of the Viewer window. When you stop the disc, the image you selected will be shown in the Viewer.

Using Closed Captioning

Closed Captioning presents text on the screen for the speaking parts and some sound effect portions of a disc's soundtrack. You can control Closed Captioning for a disc using the following pointers:

- Turn on Closed Captioning by selecting Features, Closed Captioning, Turn On. You can also press Option-⌘-T or you can select Streams/Closed Captioning from the Controller when viewing your DVD in Full Screen mode.

- To have the Closed Captioning appear in a window separate from the Viewer, select Features, Closed Captioning, Separate Window. (Remember that you can configure this window using preferences you learned about earlier in this chapter.) When you play this disc, the Closed Captioning will appear in a window called Closed Caption.

- Turn off Closed Captioning by selecting Features, Closed Captioning, Turn Off. You can also press Option-⌘-T.

 note

If you have Closed Captioning displayed in a separate window, when you close the Closed Caption window, the Closed Captioning will move back into the Viewer window.

Working with Bookmarks

Bookmarks enable you to set locations within a disc and move back to them easily. Bookmarks work just like chapters on a disc, except that you set them rather than the disc's producer.

Setting Bookmarks

To set a bookmark, perform the following steps:

1. Move to the point at which you want to set a bookmark.

2. Select Controls, New Bookmark or press ⌘-=. The disc will be paused and the New Bookmark sheet will appear.

3. Name the bookmark. You can name the bookmark almost anything you want.

4. If you want the bookmark to be the default for the disc, activate the Make Default Bookmark check box.

5. Click Add. The bookmark will be added for the disc.

Using Bookmarks

There are a number of ways to work with the bookmarks you create, including the following:

- To jump to a bookmark, select Go, Bookmarks, *bookmarkname*, where *bookmarkname* is the name of a bookmark you have created. You'll move to the bookmarked frame and the disc will play from there (if it was playing when you selected the bookmark).

- When viewing a DVD in Full Screen mode, move your mouse to the top of the screen to reveal the Image bar. Click the icon at the left end of the Image bar that looks like a bookmark; the Image bar will display the bookmarks you have created for the movie.

- Select Window, Bookmarks. The Bookmarks window will open. Here, you'll see a list of all the bookmarks you have set for a disc.

- Double-click a bookmark in the window to jump to it.

- Click the Add button (+) to add a new bookmark.

- Select a bookmark and click the Delete button (-) to delete it.

- Open the Action menu and select Show Thumbnails. A thumbnail will be shown for each bookmark.

- Select a bookmark and open the Action menu. Select Rename and then rename the bookmark, or select Delete to delete it.

- If you make a bookmark the default, you can use the Default bookmark preference to have the disc always start playing from the bookmark each time you view it.

Working with Video Clips

You can mark video clips from DVDs you view and watch them. For example, there might be scenes you love to watch over and over. You can mark these segments as video clips and then easily view them anytime you want.

Capturing a Video Clip

To create a video clip, perform the following steps:

1. Move to the point at which you want the video clip to start.

2. Select Controls, New Video Clip or press ⌘-. The new Video Clip sheet appears, and the start time is set to the current location (see Figure 9.6).

 note

The term "video clip" is a bit misleading. You aren't actually creating a clip. Instead, you are marking a portion of the DVD as a clip so that you can watch that clip easily. It isn't really a clip, which implies that you are saving the clip as a QuickTime movie or some other object that you could use in another application.

Figure 9.6
Using the Video Clip sheet, you can create custom video clips for a disc.

3. Use the playback controls or playhead to move the point at which you want the video clip to end.

4. Click the Set button next to the End preview window. The end point of the clip is set.

5. Name the clip.

6. Click Save. The sheet closes and the clip is saved.

 tip

You can use the same steps to set the starting point of the clip as well. The default start is set to be the current frame.

Working with Video Clips

There are a number of ways to work with video clips you create, including the following:

- To jump to a video clip, select Go, Video Clips, *videoclipname*, where *videoclipname* is the name of a video clip you have created. The clip will play; when it starts, you will see its name in the upper-left corner of the window. When the clip is done, it will stop playing and you'll see the complete message.

- To exit clip mode, select Go, Video Clips, Exit Clip Mode.

- To repeat a clip, select Go, Video Clips, Repeat Clip.

- When viewing a DVD in Full Screen mode, move your mouse to the top of the screen to reveal the Image bar. Click the icon at the left end of the Image bar that looks like a film strip; the Image bar will display the video clips you have created for the movie.

- Select Window, Video Clips. The Video Clips window opens. In this window, you'll see the video clips you have created for a disc.

- Double-click a video clip in the window to play it.

- Click the Add button (+) to add a new clip.

- Select a clip and click the Delete button (-) to delete it.

- Open the Action menu and select Show Thumbnails. A thumbnail will be shown for each clip.

- Select a clip and open the Action menu. Select Rename and then rename the bookmark, or select Delete to delete it. Select Exit Clip Mode to move back to regular playing mode or Repeat Clip to repeat the video clip.

Using the DVD Player Timer

The Timer feature will cause a specific action to be performed when an event happens. For example, if you tend to fall asleep watching DVDs, you can configure the Timer to put your Mac to sleep at a specific time.

To configure the Timer, do the following:

1. Insert a DVD.

2. Select Controls, Timer, Set Timer or press ⌘-T. The Timer sheet appears.

3. Choose the action you want to be performed on the Action pop-up menu. The options are Quit DVD Player, Sleep, Shut Down, and Log Out.

4. Use the radio buttons to set when the action you selected will happen. The options are in a specific amount of time or when the DVD ends.

5. Click OK. You return to the Viewer and the Timer On message is displayed briefly. When the time you specified occurs, the action you selected will be done.

Following are a few other Timer tricks:

- Select Controls, Timer, Display Timer to cause the current time remaining and action to be performed to appear on the screen. It disappears again after a few seconds.

- Select Controls, Timer, Pause to pause the timer.

- Select Controls, Timer, Cancel Timer or press Option-⌘-. to stop the timer.

Setting Custom Playback Size

You can customize the size of the video shown in the Viewer window by using the Video Zoom controls.

1. Select Window, Video Zoom. The Video Zoom window appears.

2. Activate the On check box to turn on the Video Zoom.

3. Use the sliders to set the width and height of the video.

4. If you want to maintain the video's aspect ratio, activate the Lock Aspect Ratio check box. When you move one slider, the other will also move to keep the same proportion between the two dimensions.

Configuring DVD Player Audio

DVD Player also includes a built-in graphic equalizer so you can customize audio playback for your DVDs and sound system. Here's how:

1. Select Window, Audio Equalizer. The Audio Equalizer window appears.

2. Turn it on by clicking the On check box.

3. Use the sliders to set the relative volume levels of various frequencies.

Using DVD Player Keyboard Shortcuts

Table 9.3 contains keyboard shortcuts for DVD Player.

 note

Some discs prevent you from resizing video. If this is the case, you will get the NOT PERMITTED message when you try to use the Video Zoom function.

 note

Using the Video Zoom tool changes the size of the video being displayed in the Viewer window, not the size of the Viewer window itself. To change the size of the Viewer, use the commands on the View menu.

 tip

Open the pop-up menu located in the upper-right corner of the window for additional options, such as presets including Standard Display – Widescreen Movie. You can also create your own presets.

 tip

Just like the Video Zoom and Video Color tools, you can use the Audio Equalizer's pop-up menu to work with presets. Also, you can open any of these tools from the same window by selecting the tool with which you want to work from the pop-up menu in the window's title bar.

Table 9.3   Keyboard Shortcuts for DVD Player

Menu	Action	Keyboard Shortcut
	Highlight DVD menu options	Up, down, left, right arrows Tab; Shift-Tab
	Select DVD menu options	Return
Controls	Scan Backwards	Shift-⌘-left arrow
Controls	Scan Forward	Shift-⌘-right arrow
Controls	Close/Open Control Drawer	⌘-]
Controls	Closed Captioning, Turn On/Off	Option-⌘-T
Controls	Eject DVD	⌘-E
Controls	Mute	Option-⌘-down arrow
Controls	New Bookmark	⌘-=
Controls	New Video Clip	⌘--
Controls	Play/Pause	Spacebar
Controls	Stop	⌘-.
Controls	Timer, Cancel Timer	Option-⌘-.
Controls	Timer, Set Timer	⌘-T
Controls	Volume Down	⌘-down arrow
Controls	Volume Up	⌘-up arrow
DVD Player	Preferences	⌘-,
File	Get Disc Info	⌘-I
Go	DVD Menu	⌘-D
Go	Next Chapter	Right arrow
Go	Beginning of Disc	Shift-⌘-D
Go	Previous Chapter	Left arrow
Go	Switch To Finder	Option-⌘-F
View	Enter/Exit Full Screen	⌘-F
View	Half Size	⌘-0
View	Actual Size	⌘-1
View	Double Size	⌘-2
View	Fit to Screen	⌘-3
Window	Show/Hide Controller	Option-⌘-C

10

MANAGING YOUR CONTACTS

Getting to Know Address Book

Although I imagine there are quite a few people who still use a physical address book, the practice has a decidedly anachronistic feel to it these days. That's particularly true for Mac users, who have the Address Book application a mere click away. Address Book is a contact management application, which means you can use it to store all kinds of information about the people you know and work with. With Address Book you can track basic data such as the person's name, company name, phone numbers, email addresses, and physical address, but Address Book also supports a wide array of contact data, including instant messaging (IM) user names, job title, website URL, birthday, maiden name, and lots more.

Address Book acts as the central contact database for Mac OS X, so other applications can dip into this database whenever they need contact data. For example, you can use Address Book to select recipients for an outgoing message in Mail, and you can select contacts for an IM conversation in iChat.

Address Book is based on *virtual cards*, or *vCards*. A vCard is a kind of electronic business card that stores contact data. vCard is a standard contact file format, so you can drag and drop vCards between applications to transfer the information contained on that card. You can

 tip

Address Book is not the only application that can work with vCards. Many other applications can use vCards. For example, Microsoft Entourage can read vCards, so you can provide your vCard to someone who uses that application and that person can easily add your contact information to her contact database. Microsoft Outlook, the dominant email, calendar, and contact information application on Windows computers, also supports vCards.

also share vCards with other users to exchange information. For example, you can drag someone else's vCard onto your Address Book to quickly add that person's information to your contacts.

Exploring Address Book

You launch Address Book by clicking the Address Book icon on the Dock or by opening the Applications folder and double-clicking the Address Book icon. When you open Address Book, you see that its window consists of three columns. The first two columns are:

- The Group column shows All Contact by default but you also see Last Input if you're imported and the groups you create later on will also appear here (see "Working with Address Groups," later in this chapter).

- The Name column lists each card in your Address Book, listed alphabetically.

The rest of the Address Book window displays the data for the card that you've selected in the Name column (see Figure 10.1). Before you add any contact information, your Address Book includes a card for you and one for Apple. You can build your Address Book over time so that it includes all your contacts.

> **note**
>
> The contact information entered for you is whatever you provided when you registered your copy of Mac OS X. If you entered a username and password for an Apple ID account when you installed Mac OS X, your contact information is retrieved from your Apple account as well.

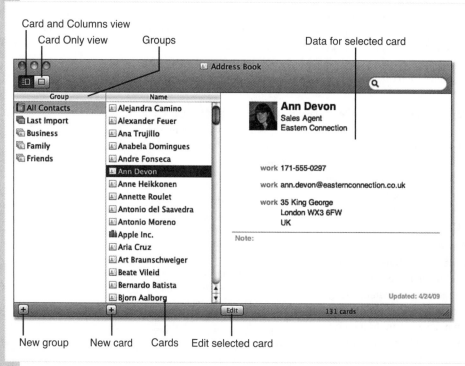

Figure 10.1
The Address Book is a powerful tool you can use to manage all your contact information.

Just above the Group column are buttons you can use to control the look and features of Address Book:

- **Card and Columns view**—Click this button (or press ⌘-1) to present Address Book's default view (the Group and Name columns and the current card data).

- **Card Only view**—Click this button (or press ⌘-2) to show only the current card data. Address Book's back and forward arrows enable you to navigate the cards in this view.

In the upper-left corner of each card is an image well that you can use to place an image for your contact, such as a photo of the person for whom you created the card or the logo for a company (such as the apple for Apple). You can add a photo to a card by dragging a photo onto this well. The photo you use can be a JPEG, GIF, TIFF, or PDF file and should be 64×64 pixels.

 note

When you send email to or receive email using Mail from a contact who has an image in the related Address Book card, that image appears in the email.

The card marked with a silhouette is your card. This is important because your card can be used to add your contact information in various locations automatically.

Although Address Book provides the standard functions you expect, such as email addresses and phone numbers, the information in Address Book is dynamic. For example, when a contact's card includes an email address, you can click the address to send the contact email. When you include a URL for a contact, you can click it to visit that web page, and when the contact has a MobileMe account, you can open the contact's iDisk. You can also use the contact's card to chat with the person using iChat and visit the contact's website from within Safari. Address Book information is also accessible in many other places, such as when you are faxing documents using Mac OS X's built-in fax capability.

The information in Address Book is extremely flexible. The fields displayed for each contact can be configured individually. When you display a card, only the fields that contain information are displayed. For example, compare Figure 10.1 and Figure 10.2 to see how Address Book has reconfigured the card display for cards with different amounts of information.

Finding Information in Address Book

To locate information within Address Book itself, you can browse your contacts or search for specific contacts.

To search for a contact's information, type your criteria in Address Book's Search box. You can enter text found in any of the contact's information, including name, address, home page, and so on. As you type, the list of names shown in the Name column is narrowed so it includes only those contacts whose data contains the text you enter. If you see the contact whose information you want to view, select the card. The contact's card is displayed, and you can see the contact's information.

To view all your contacts again, click the X button that appears in the Search box when you perform a search.

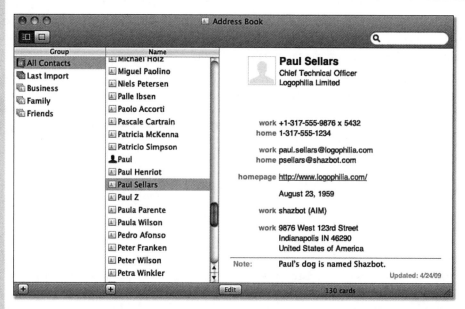

Address Book

Figure 10.2
Address Book supports many fields, so you can populate a contact with lots of useful information.

Using Information in Address Book

When working with the Address Book, you can do the following tasks:

- **Send an email**—To send an email to one of your contacts, view the contact to which you want to send an email. Then click the label next to the email address to which you want to send an email. A pop-up menu appears. Select Send Email (see Figure 10.3). Your default email application will open and a new message addressed to the contact.

- **Visit the contact's website or home page**—Click a URL shown on the card. (Alternatively, click the label next to a website you want to visit, and then click Open URL.) Your default web browser opens and displays the website.

- **View a map to an address**—Click the label next to an address and select Map This Address from the resulting pop-up menu. Your default web browser opens and displays the Google Maps website. A map to the selected address is then displayed.

- **Copy a mailing label**—Click the label next to a physical address and then click Copy Mailing Label to copy the address. You can then paste the address into an application, such as a program you use to create envelopes or mailing labels.

> 🔍 **note**
>
> When you click a data label, such as an email or physical address, the pop-up menu that appears has different commands for different items. For example, when you open an email address pop-up menu, one of the options is Send Email. However, if you click a physical address, you see different options including Map This Address, which enables you to retrieve a map for the address.

Figure 10.3
Click an email address label to display the Send Email command.

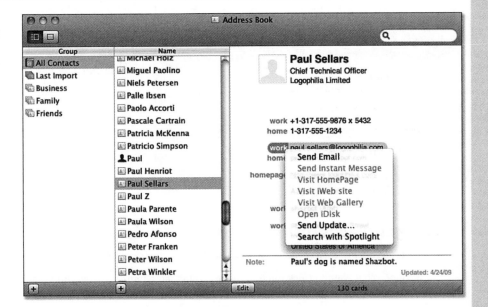

- **Open an iDisk**—If the contact has a MobileMe account and you have added the contact's MobileMe email address to the card, you can open the person's iDisk by clicking the label next to the MobileMe email address and selecting Open iDisk. The contact's iDisk will open in a new Finder window.

- **Scroll through your contacts**—Select Card, Next Card (or press ⌘-]) or select Card, Previous Card (or press ⌘-[) to browse through your contacts.

- **Edit your contacts**—Click the Edit button to move into the Edit mode (more on this later in the chapter).

Configuring Your Address Book

You can configure several aspects of the Address Book by using its Preferences dialog box (see Figure 10.4). To open this dialog box, select Address Book, Preferences or press ⌘-,.

 note

Oddly, the Open iDisk command is only enabled for MobileMe addresses that use the .mac domain, not the new .me domain. Also, the pop-up menu for a MobileMe address includes a Visit HomePage command that used to display the HomePage for a .Mac account. HomePages are no longer supported by MobileMe, so choosing the Visit HomePage command produces an error.

 tip

Explore the contextual menus for various card elements along with the options in the menus to discover even more Address Book commands.

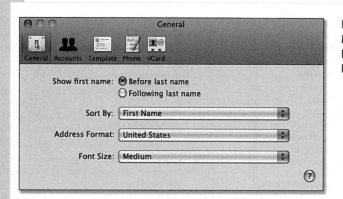

Figure 10.4
Maximize the benefits of your Address Book by customizing it using the Preferences dialog box.

Configuring Address Book General Preferences

Using the General tab of the Preferences dialog box, you can configure the following preferences:

- **Show First Name**—Click the Before Last Name radio button to have Address Book display contact information in the first name, last name format. Click the Following Last Name radio button to display contacts in the last name, first name format.

- **Sort By**—Use this pop-up menu to specify how you want Address Book to sort the Cards column: by First Name or by Last Name.

- **Address Format**—Use this pop-up menu to select the address format you want to use by country.

- **Font Size**—Use this pop-up menu to select the Small, Medium, or Large font size for the information shown in the Address Book window.

Configuring Address Book Accounts Preferences

You can use the Account tab of the Preferences dialog box to configure the following preferences:

- **Synchronization via MobileMe**—If you use more than one Mac and have a MobileMe account, you can keep your Address Book synchronized on all your computers. Activate the Synchronize with MobileMe check box and click the MobileMe button. You'll move to the MobileMe pane of the System Preferences application, where you can configure your options.

   ➡ *To learn how to use MobileMe to synchronize information, **see** "Using MobileMe to Integrate a Mac onto the Internet," p. 421.*

- **Synchronization with Yahoo!**—If you have a Yahoo! account, activate this check box to synchronize the contacts in that account with your Address Book. Enter your Yahoo! ID and password and click OK to connect to your Yahoo! account.

■ **Synchronization with Google**—If you have a Google account, activate this check box to synchronize the contacts in that account with your Address Book. Enter your Google ID and password and click OK to connect to your Google account.

Customizing Your Address Book Card Template

You can customize the information and layout of the cards in your Address Book.

Open the Address Book Preferences window and click the Template button to open the Template preferences pane.

To change the layout of and the information contained on the cards in your Address Book, you can do any of the following:

> **note**
>
> Address Book can also work with Lightweight Directory Access Protocol (LDAP) directories, which can provide address information over a network. Explaining how to use such directories is beyond the scope of this chapter. If you need help, see the administrator of the network that is providing one or more LDAP directories to you.

■ **Add fields**—Use the Add Field pop-up menu at the top of the dialog box to add fields to the cards in your Address Book. To add a field, select it on the menu. The field will be added and it will be greyed out on the pop-up menu to indicate that it is part of the current template.

■ **Remove fields**—Click the minus sign next to a field to remove it from the card.

■ **Add more fields of the same kind**—Click the plus sign next to a field to add another field of the same type to the card.

> **tip**
>
> You can also edit the card template by selecting Card, Add Field, Edit Template.

■ **Change a field's label**—Use the pop-up menu next to a field's label to change that label. You can select one of the labels on the menu or select Custom and create a custom label.

Using these tools, you can customize the contents of cards and the specific fields they contain as much as you like. Because Address Book displays only those fields that contain data (when you view a card), you don't need to be concerned about having too many fields on your cards because on each card, you'll only see those fields that contain data.

Configuring Address Book's Phone Number Format

You can change the phone number format used in Address Book by using the following steps:

1. Open the Phone pane of the Address Book Preferences dialog box.

2. To have Address Book format phone numbers automatically, activate the Automatically Format Phone Numbers check box. With this active, Address Book will automatically add hyphens, periods, or other formatting elements to phone numbers when you enter them on a card.

3. If you activate the check box mentioned in the previous step, use the Formats pop-up menu to select the format that should be used.

Choosing vCard Preferences

On the vCard pane of the Address Book Preferences dialog box, you can set the following preferences:

 tip

You can create custom phone number formats by clicking the down arrow next to the Formats pop-up menu, which opens a pane showing the configured formats. Select one and click Edit to change it. To add a new format, click the plus sign. To remove a format, select it and click the minus sign.

- **vCard Format**—Click the 3.0 radio button to use the newer vCard format. Click the 2.1 radio button to use an older version of the vCard standard.

- **vCard 2.1 Encoding**—Use the Encoding pop-up menu to choose the encoding you want to use, such as Western (Mac OS Roman). This is only used with the older 2.1 vCard format.

- **Enable Private Me Card**—You can use this option to hide information on your vCard so that information won't be exported when you provide your vCard to someone else. To do so, activate this check box. Edit your card and deactivate the check boxes for the data that you don't want to include on your vCard when you share it.

- **Export Notes in vCards**—If you activate this check box, when you export vCards, any notes you have entered for a card are exported with the card. If you put information in the notes on cards, be careful with this one because any information you put in notes will be exported with the vCards!

- **Export Photos in vCards**—If you activate this check box, when you export vCards, any vCards you export that contain photos will have those photos included when you export them.

Sharing Your Address Book with MobileMe Users

You can share your Address Book information with other people who use MobileMe. To do so, perform the following steps:

1. Open the Accounts pane of the Address Book Preferences dialog box.

2. Click the Sharing tab.

3. Activate the Share Your Address Book check box.

4. Click the Add button (+). The information in your Address Book will appear in the resulting sheet.

5. Select the people who use MobileMe with whom you'd like to share your Address Book and click OK. You'll move back to the Sharing tab and the people whom you selected will be shown in the list.

6. Activate the Allow Editing check box for those people whom you want to be able to change information in your Address Book.

7. Select the people you have added and click the Send Invitation button. An email will be created and addressed to those people. This email will contain the link they need to be able to access your Address Book information.

 tip

To remove someone from the list of people who can access your Address Book, select his name on the list and click the Remove button (-).

Adding Contacts to Your Address Book

Obviously, before an address book is of much value, it has to have some information in it. There are several ways to get information into your Address Book:

- Edit your own address card.

- Add contacts manually.

- Add a contact from an email message you have received.

- Import a contact's vCard.

- Import contacts from an email application.

- Synchronize your Exchange Google, or Yahoo! account contacts with your Address Book.

Editing Your Own Address Card

The first time you open Address Book, a card is created for you automatically based on the information you entered when you installed Mac OS X. If you entered one or more email addresses when you installed Mac OS X, those addresses are included in your address card automatically. You should edit this card, mostly so that you can easily send your contact information to other people simply by sending them your vCard.

 note

Another place your card's information is used is for Safari's AutoFill feature. When you complete a form on the Web, your card's information is used if you choose to enable Safari's AutoFill feature.

You can jump to your card by selecting Card, Go to My Card. Your card will be selected. Your card's icon has a silhouette next to your name. When you select your name in the Name column, your card appears; its image well is marked with the text me.

If you want to create a different card for yourself for some reason, you can create a new card and enter your contact information in it. After you have created your new card, select it and select Card, Make This My Card (this is disabled if you have already selected your card).

 tip

You can export a vCard by viewing it and selecting File, Export, Export vCard. Select a location, name the vCard, and click Save.

You can edit your own card using the same steps you use to edit any other cards (editing cards is explained shortly).

Adding Contacts Manually

As you might expect, you can add people to your Address Book by inputting their information manually.

To manually add an address, do the following:

1. Click the Plus button in the Name column; select File, New Card; or press ⌘-N to see a new, empty address card. The first name is highlighted by default so you can edit it immediately (see Figure 10.5). The fields on the card are those that are defined in your current template.

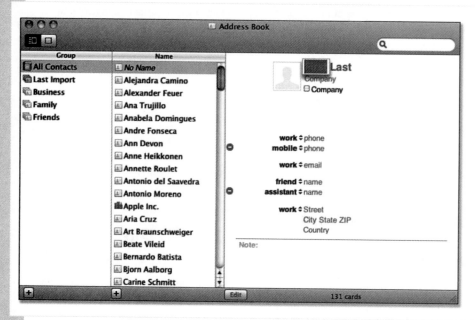

Figure 10.5
This is a new card, ready for the contact's information.

2. Input the first name.

3. Press Tab to move to and select the Last field, and then enter the contact's last name.

4. Press Tab to move to and select the Company field, and then enter the person's company information if applicable.

5. If you want the company to be listed above the name, activate the Company check box.

6. Press Tab to move to and select the first contact information, which is work phone by default.

7. Click the menu icon to reveal the label pop-up menu (see Figure 10.6).

8. Select the label for the contact information, such as home.

 note

Two entries on the label pop-up menu require some explanation. The selection called other inserts the label other. If you select Custom, you can create a custom label for a field.

Figure 10.6
Use this pop-up menu to label contact information.

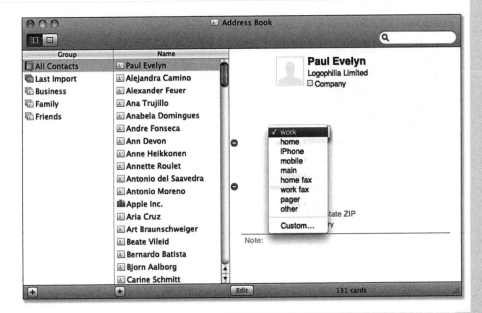

9. Enter the contact information, such as a work phone number if you chose the label work.

10. Continue tabbing to each field on the card, selecting the label for that field and editing the information to fill in the rest of the card.

11. If the contact has a home page, select the home page field and enter the URL of the home page with which you want to associate the contact.

12. If you want to remove fields from the card, click the Remove Field button (the minus sign) next to the field you want to remove. The field is removed from the current card only.

13. If you want to add more fields of the same type to the card, click the Add Field button (+) next to one of the existing fields. After you have added a field, you can edit it in the same way as the default fields. Similar to removing a field from a card, when you add a field to the card, it is added on the current card only.

➡ *To learn how to add a field to all cards in the Address Book,* **see** *"Customizing Your Address Book Card Template," p. 219.*

14. If you have an image you want to associate with the contact, drag the image onto the contact's image well. (You can add images in the usual graphics formats, such as JPEG or TIFF.) When you are over the image well, the cursor changes to a green circle with a plus sign in it. Release the mouse button and you see the image in a new window (see Figure 10.7).

Figure 10.7
When you drop a picture on the photo well, Address Book displays the image in this window.

15. Use the slider at the bottom of the window to crop the image.

16. When the image appears as you want it, click the Set button.

17. Add notes for the card by clicking next to the Note label and typing the note.

18. Click the Edit button to move out of the Edit mode. Your new card is now ready to use.

Adding a Contact from an Email Message

You can create a contact in your Address Book by adding the sender's information from an email message to it. To add a contact from an email that you receive in the Mail application, do the following:

1. Use Mail to open an email message from the person whom you want to add to your Address Book.

2. Select Message, Add Sender to Address Book (or press Shift-⌘-Y). The person's name and email address are entered on a new address card.

 tip

When you are editing a card, you can double-click an image or the image well to open the image editing window. You can also select Card, Choose Custom Image to open the same window. In that window, click the Choose button to move to and select an image to display in the window. If you have a camera, such as an iSight camera, connected to your Mac, click the camera button to capture the image being taken by the camera. With either an imported or captured photo you can apply Photo Booth effects by clicking the effects gallery button.

Using vCards to Add Contacts to Your Address Book

The benefit to using a vCard is that you can add a lot of information about a contact with very little work on your part. When you receive a vCard from someone, use the following steps to add that person's address card to your Address Book:

1. Drag the vCard onto the Name column in Address Book.

2. Click OK when prompted. The vCard will be added to your Address Book.

3. Select the card and click the Edit button.

4. Edit the information as needed (you learn how to edit cards later in this chapter).

 note

When you import vCards to your Address Book, the group called Last Import always contains the cards you most recently added.

 note

vCard files have the filename extension .vcf (virtual card file).

Importing Contacts from Another Application

If you have used another email application in the past, you probably have an Address Book or Contact database in that application. If that application supports vCards, you can easily export vCards from the application and then add them to the Address Book.

As an example of how this works, the following steps show you how to export contacts from Microsoft's Entourage email application and then add those contacts to the Address Book. Because Entourage supports vCards, you can create vCards for your Entourage contacts and then import those contacts into the Address Book:

1. Create a folder to temporarily store the vCards you export from Entourage. You will probably want this folder visible on the Desktop or in the Dock so you can access it easily.

2. Open Entourage.

3. Click the Address Book button to move into the Address Book mode.

4. Drag the contacts for whom you want to create vCards from the Entourage window onto the folder you created in step 1, and drop them in that folder. A vCard is created for each of your Entourage contacts.

 note

If you drag an Entourage group to create a vCard, a text clipping file is created instead. You need to re-create your groups within Address Book.

5. Open Address Book.

6. Drag the vCards from the folder in which you stored them onto the Name column. The contacts you added are now available for you to use and edit.

It is unlikely that all the information in your current address book or contact list will make it into the Address Book application. For example, if you have added Category information for your Entourage contact list, that information is not imported into the Address Book. After you have imported contacts into the Address Book, you should activate them so you know exactly what information made it in, and what didn't. If you lost any important information, you might have to spend some time re-creating it within Address Book.

Editing Contacts in Your Address Book

note

When you import addresses into your Address Book and it finds duplicates, you have the opportunity to review the addresses you are adding so you can remove the duplicated entries. You can also merge the multiple entries together.

To edit an address in your Address Book, use the following steps:

1. In Address Book, view the card containing the information you want to edit.

2. Click the Edit button. Address Book moves into the Edit mode. The first name is selected and is ready to edit.

3. Use the same steps to change the information on the card that you do to create a card (see the earlier section on creating cards for the details).

Many of the data fields have pop-up menus containing the data field's label. You can open these menus and select a new label for that field. The changes you make by doing this affect only the current address card; this means you can configure the information for a specific card independent of other cards. For example, if you know someone who has three mobile phones, you can select mobile as the label for three of the fields on that person's address card. You can also select Custom to create custom field labels for existing or new fields.

tip

You can use the Add Field button on the Template pane of the Address Book Preferences dialog box to add fields to the card. You can also add fields by using the Card, Add Field command. On the Add Field menu, you can select the type of field you want to add.

You can quickly swap the last name with the first name for the card by viewing the card and selecting Card, Swap First/Last Name.

To remove an image from a card, view the card and select Card, Clear Custom Image.

note

After you add a field, you can't remove it. You can only delete its data so that it doesn't appear on the card any more.

If you don't want a field's data to appear on a card, select the data and click the Delete data button (the minus sign). The data is replaced with the type of data it is, such as Email for an email address. The data does not appear on the card when it is viewed.

To delete a card from the Address Book, select it and press Delete. Click Yes in the resulting prompt and the card is removed from Address Book.

tip

You can view a card in an independent window by viewing it and selecting Card, Open in Separate Window (or by pressing ⌘-I). You can also edit a card when it is displayed in a separate window.

Working with Address Groups

Address groups (just called *groups* in Address Book) enable you to email multiple people using a single object. Working with an address group is similar to working with other address cards in your Address Book.

There are two types of groups. A group is a collection of cards that you add to the group manually. A smart group defines a set of criteria; cards that meet these criteria are added to the group automatically.

Creating and Configuring a Basic Address Group

Creating an address group is simple, as you can see in the following steps:

1. Click the New Group button, which is the plus sign in the Group column; select File, New Group; or press Shift-⌘-N. You will see a new group in the Group column, and the name of the group will be selected and ready to edit.

2. Change the group's name to something meaningful and press Return.

3. Click All in the Group column to view all the cards in the Address Book.

4. Search or browse for the cards you want to add to your Address Book.

5. Drag the cards you want to be included in the group onto the group's icon in the Group column. Those cards become part of the group.

 tip

You can create a new group and add selected address cards to it by first selecting the cards you want to place in the new group and selecting File, New Group From Selection. A new group is created and includes the cards you selected.

You can view a group by selecting it on the Group column. The Name column shows only those cards that are included in the group. You work with the cards in a group just as you do individual cards. For example, you can edit a card, use it to send email to that individual, and so on.

To remove a card from a group, view the group, select the card you want to remove, and press Delete. After you confirm the action, the card is removed from the group. However, the card still exists in the Address Book.

You can also export a group as a vCard. Select the group, Control-click it or right-click with a two-button mouse, and select Export Group vCard. Select a location, name the card, and click Save. You can use the group's vCard in the same way you use vCards for individuals.

If any of the cards you add to a group includes more than one email address, you can edit the mailing list for the group to set the specific addresses that are used:

1. Select the group for which you want to configure the mailing list.

2. Select Edit, Edit Distribution List. The Edit Distribution List dialog box will appear.

3. Select the email address you want to use for an individual by clicking it. The address that will be used appears in bold; other addresses are grayed out to show that they won't be used.

4. Click OK. When you send a message to the group, the addresses you selected are used.

tip

You can change all the email addresses used for the group to be of the same kind by selecting a type on the Change All Labels pop-up menu. For example, to use only home email addresses, select home.

Creating a Smart Address Group

You can use the Smart Groups feature to have Address Book populate a group based on criteria you define rather than manually placing contacts in the group. Smart groups work just like other smart objects, such as smart playlists in iTunes or smart photo albums in iPhoto. To create a smart address group, perform the following steps:

1. Choose File, New Smart Group or press Option-⌘-N. The Smart Address Book sheet appears (see Figure 10.8).

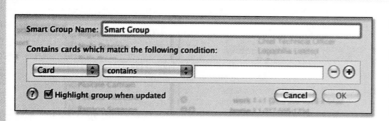

Figure 10.8
To create a smart address group, define the criteria for contacts that you want included in the group and Address Book will put them there automatically.

2. Enter the name for the group in the Smart Group Name field.

3. On the first pop-up menu, choose the field on which you want to base the first criterion. For example, to base it on last name, choose Other and then choose Last. Choose Card to base on the criterion on any data on a card.

4. On the second pop-up menu, choose the operator for the condition, such as contains, is, and so on.

5. In the box, type the data for the condition, such as the last name.

6. To add another condition, click the Add Condition button (the plus sign). An empty condition is created.

7. Configure the new condition by repeating steps 3–5.

8. Continue adding conditions until you have all that you want to use.

9. Choose the pop-up menu at the top of the sheet to choose All if all the conditions you configured have to be met to have a card included in the group or Any if you want a card included as long as it meets at least one condition.

10. Activate the Highlight Group When Updated check box if you want Address Book to highlight the group when any changes are made to it. Because Address Book automatically includes or excludes cards in the group based on it conditions, it's not obvious when the group changes. Use this setting if you want to know whenever a smart group changes.

11. Click OK. The smart group is created and any cards that meet its criteria are added to it automatically.

Following are a few tidbits about smart groups:

- To change the contents of a smart group, open its contextual menu and choose Edit Smart Group. The Smart Group criteria sheet will appear. Use that sheet to change the group's conditions. When you click OK, the group's content will reflect its current conditions.

- To remove a condition from a smart group, edit it and click the Remove Condition button (the minus sign) next to the condition you want to delete. That condition no longer impacts the cards included in the group.

- You can perform similar tasks with a smart group that you can with basic groups, such as sending email to the group.

Getting More Out of Address Book

To complete your look at the Address Book application, the rest of this chapters takes you through a few useful techniques, including selecting and printing contacts, using the Address Book widget, subscribing to another person's address book, and using Address Book keyboard shortcuts.

Addressing Email

There are several ways in which you can address email to people in your Address Book:

- View the contact to whom you want to send a message and click the label for the email address you want to use. Select Send Email on the pop-up menu.

- Drag the contact's vCard to the To, Cc, or Bcc box of a Mail email message.

- Open a group's contextual menu and select "Send email to *groupname*," where *groupname* is the name of the group you clicked.

- Drag a group's vCard to the To, Cc, or Bcc box of a Mail email message.

 note

When you send email from the Address Book, the email application used is your default email application.

Printing Your Address Book

As you work with your Address Book, you might want to print it to take it with you, to print address labels, and so on. When you print from the Address Book, you have the following four layout options:

- **Envelopes**—This option prints envelopes for your contacts.

- **Lists**—This option prints the cards you select in a list. You can select the attributes that are included on the list for each card.

- **Pocket Address Book**—This option prints a small version of your Address Book that is designed to be carried.

- **Mailing Labels**—This prints the cards as mailing labels.

To print the Address Book as a list, use the following steps:

1. Select the cards you want to print. To print the entire Address Book, select All in the Groups column.

2. Select File, Print or press ⌘-P. The Print dialog box opens. The first time you go to print in Address Book, the dialog box is collapsed; click on the downward-facing arrow at the right to expand the dialog box and see all of the options.

3. On the Style pop-up menu, select Lists.

4. Configure the printer, presets, paper size, and orientation just as you do with any print job.

5. Select the attributes you want included for each card by activating their check boxes. You will see a preview of the list in the left side of the dialog box.

6. Select the font size on the Font Size pop-up menu.

7. Print the list.

To print mailing labels, use the following steps:

1. Select the cards you want to print. To print the entire Address Book, select All in the Groups column.

2. Select File, Print or press ⌘-P. The Print dialog box opens.

3. On the Style pop-up menu, select Mailing Labels.

4. Click the Layout tab.

5. If you are printing on standard Avery or DYMO labels, select the label type on the Page pop-up menu. If you are creating a custom label, select Define Custom instead; in the Layout Name sheet that appears, enter the name of the label you are creating and click OK. As you make choices, a preview of the labels will appear in the left pane of the dialog box.

6. If you selected a standard label, select the specific label number you are printing on the label number drop-down list that appears next to the Page pop-up menu. If you selected Define Custom in the previous step, use the controls under the Layout tab to design the label, such as by defining the margins, number of rows and columns, and the gutters.

7. Click the Label tab.

8. Select the address type for which you want to print labels on the Addresses pop-up menu. If you want to print labels for all addresses, select All.

9. On the Print In pop-up menu, select how you want the labels to be sorted. The options are Alphabetical Order and Postal Code Order.

10. If you want to include the contact's company name on their label, activate the Company check box. If you want country to be included on the labels, activate the Country check box. If you don't want your own country to be included, activate the Except My Country check box.

11. Click the Color box and use the Color Picker to select the color of the text on the labels.

12. Click the Image Set button to place an image on the labels.

13. Click the Font Set button to open the Font panel and select the font you want to use on the labels.

14. Activate the labels in the preview pane.

15. Print the labels.

> **note**
>
> The other two types of printing can be done in a similar way. Choose the type of print job you want to do on the Style pop-up menu and use the controls in the dialog box to configure the print job.

Using the Address Book Widget

You can also access your Address Book through the Address Book widget.

➡ *To learn how to use the Address Book widget, **see** "Using the Address Book Widget," **p. 565**.*

Subscribing to an Address Book

If other MobileMe users have shared their Address Book with you, you can subscribe to it to view or edit its information by using the following steps:

1. Select File, Subscribe to Address Book.

2. In the resulting sheet, enter the MobileMe user's username and click OK. You'll be able to view the other user's Address Book information, and you can edit it if you have permission to do so.

Using Address Book Keyboard Shortcuts

Table 10.1 shows keyboard shortcuts for the Address Book application.

Table 10.1 Keyboard Shortcuts for the Address Book

Action	Keyboard Shortcut
Address Book Help	⌘-?
Edit Card	⌘-L
Hide Address Book	⌘-H
Import vCards	⌘-O
Merge Selected Cards	⌘-|
Minimize Address Book Window	⌘-M

Table 10.1   Continued

Action	Keyboard Shortcut
Move Between Fields on an Address	Tab and Shift-Tab
New Card	⌘-N
New Group	Shift-⌘-N
New Smart Group	Option-⌘-N
Next Card	⌘-]
Open in Separate Window	⌘-I
Preferences	⌘-,
Previous Card	⌘-[
Mark as a Company	⌘-\
View Card and Columns	⌘-1
View Card Only	⌘-2
View Directories	⌘-3

MANAGING YOUR SCHEDULE

Managing Your Calendar with iCal

It seems almost redundant to describe modern life as "busy." Everyone is working harder, cramming more appointments and meetings into already-packed schedules, and somehow finding the time to get their regular work done between crises. As many a management consultant has advised over the years (charging exorbitant fees to do so), the key to surviving this helter-skelter, pell-mell pace is *time management*. And although there are as many theories about time management as there are consultants, one of the keys is that you should always try to make the best use of the time available. Although that often comes down to self-discipline and prioritizing your tasks, an efficient scheduling system can sure help.

That's where Mac OS X's iCal application feature comes in. It's a sort of electronic secretary that, although it won't get coffee for you, will at least help you keep your affairs in order. iCal is a simple electronic day-planner you can use to keep track of appointments, meetings, tasks, and other commitments. You can also maintain multiple calendars at the same time, such as a work calendar and a home calendar, and you can share your calendar with others, so coordinating activities is much easier. iCal even lets you access other people's calendars to see how your schedule meshes with theirs.

Getting to Know iCal

To get started with iCal, click the iCal icon in the Dock. Figure 11.1 shows the iCal window that appears, and points out a few of the more interesting features.

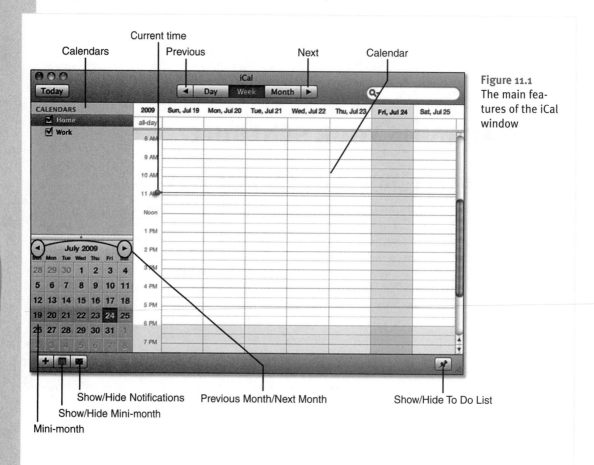

Current time

Calendars

Previous

Next

Calendar

Figure 11.1
The main features of the iCal window

Show/Hide Notifications   Previous Month/Next Month   Show/Hide To Do List

Show/Hide Mini-month

Mini-month

The iCal window is divided into three main areas:

- **Calendars**—This is the area on the upper-left side of the iCal window. In this pane, you see the two default calendars—Home and Work—as well as each calendar you create yourself and any calendar you've subscribed to. If a calendar's check box is activated, iCal displays its events; you can hide a calendar's events by deactivating its check box.

- **Mini-month**—This is the area on the lower-left side of the iCal window, which shows you a month at a glance. You can toggle the Mini-month on and off by clicking the Show/Hide Mini-month button (pointed out in Figure 11.1). You can also use this area to display the Notifications pane, which shows you information about notifications. You can toggle the Notifications pane on and off by clicking the Show/Hide Notifications button (see Figure 11.1).

> **tip**
>
> You can drag the Mini-month pane's top border up to display more months or down to show fewer.

- **Calendar**—This area takes up the bulk of the iCal window, and it's where iCal displays your events. The area with the white background defines your day, and the areas with the shaded background are outside of your day (although you can still schedule events in those times). See "Configuring iCal," later in this chapter, to learn how to change the day's start and end times.

➥ *You can also access your calendar information via the Dashboard iCal widget. To learn about the Calendar widget, **see** "Using the iCal Widget," p. 566.*

Navigating the Calendar

Before you create an event in iCal, you must first select the date on which the event occurs. iCal gives you three ways to navigate to a particular date:

- **Use the Mini-month**—In the Mini-month, click the Next Month button (see Figure 11.1) until the month of your event appears. If you go too far, click the Previous Month button to move back to the month you want. Then click the date on which the event occurs.

- **Go to a specific date**—Select View, Go to Date (or press Shift-⌘-T) to open the Go to Date dialog box, shown in Figure 11.2. Use the Date text box to type the date you want using the format mm/dd/yyyy, and then click Show. iCal displays the date in the calendar.

Figure 11.2
Use the Go to Date dialog box to navigate to specific date.

- **Scroll through the calendar**—First click the calendar view you want to use for scrolling: Day (or press ⌘-1), Week (or press ⌘-2), or Month (or press ⌘-3). Then click Next (see Figure 11.1) to go forward by a day, week, or month, or click Previous to go back by a day, week, or month.

> **tip**
>
> You can always return to the current day on your calendar by clicking the Today button or by pressing ⌘-T.

Configuring iCal

iCal is good to go right out of the box, but the application does offer a few preferences that you might want to configure. Select iCal, Preferences to see the General tab of the iCal Preferences dialog box, shown in Figure 11.3.

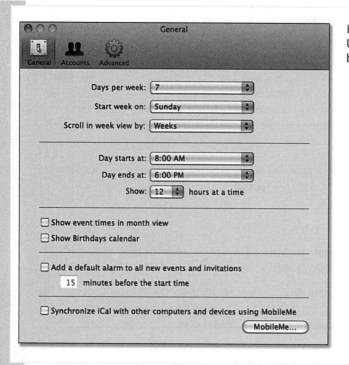

Figure 11.3
Use the General tab to configure some basic iCal preferences.

Here's a summary of the preferences available on the General tab:

- **Days per Week**—Use this pop-up menu to set the number of days you want to see when you switch to iCal's Week view. The default is all seven days, but if you only want to see Monday through Friday, choose 5 in the menu.

- **Start Week On**—Use this pop-up menu to specify the day of the week that appears first when you switch iCal to Week view.

- **Scroll in Week View By**—Use this pop-up menu to determine how iCal scrolls when you switch to Week view. By default, clicking the Next and Previous buttons scrolls one week at a time. Choose Days in the menu if you prefer to scroll just one day at a time.

- **Day Starts At**—Use this pop-up menu to set the start time for the calendar day (the default is 8:00 AM).

- **Day Ends At**—Use this pop-up menu to set the end time for the calendar day (the default is 6:00 PM).

- **Show X Hours at a Time**—Use this pop-up menu to specify how many hours iCal displays in the calendar pane.

- **Show Event Times in Month View**—If you activate this check box, iCal displays the time next to events when you switch iCal to the Month view.

- **Show Birthdays Calendar**—If you have stored birthdays for your contacts in the Address Book, activate this check box to display the Birthday calendar that shows those birthdays.

- **Add a Default Alarm to All New Events and Invitations**—Activate this check box to have iCal automatically add an alarm to each event to remind you when the event is due. Use the text box to specify how many minutes before the default event the alarm should go off.

- **Synchronize iCal with Other Computers and Devices Using MobileMe**—Activate this check box to synchronize your calendar information with your MobileMe account. Use the Synchronize My Calendars with Other Computers and Devices Using MobileMe check box and the MobileMe button to configure this.

  ➡ *To learn how to synchronize information on multiple machines,* **see** *"Using MobileMe to Integrate a Mac onto the Internet,"* **p. 421.**

The Advanced pane of the iCal Preferences dialog box (see Figure 11.4) offers the following options:

- **Turn on Time Zone Support**—Activate this check box to turn on iCal's Time Zone Support feature, which enables the application to add time zone information to your calendar. You can then associate events with specific time zones and change the time zone for which you are viewing events. This feature is most useful when you are using iCal while traveling. As you change time zones, you can set iCal to use the time zone you are currently in. Then, it adjusts the time for each event so it is appropriate to the time zone you are in.

- **Hide To Do Items That Are Due After the Dates Visible in the Calendar**—Activate this check box to hide any To Do items that don't need to be done during the period you are currently viewing or that have been completed prior to the current time being displayed.

- **Hide To Do Items X Days After They Have Been Completed**—Activate this check box to have iCal automatically hide To Do items after they are completed. Use the text box to set the number of days that must pass before iCal hides completed items.

- **Delete Events X Days After They Have Passed**—Activate this check box to have iCal automatically delete Events after they have occurred. Use the text box to set the number of days that must pass before iCal deletes past events.

- **Delete To Do Items X Days After They Have Been Completed**—Activate this check box to have iCal automatically delete To Do items after you have completed them. Use the text box to set the number of days that must pass before iCal deletes completed items.

- **Turn Off All Alarms**—If you activate this check box, iCal turns off all alarms so that you're never reminded about an event or invitation.

 note

If you want to use iCal as a means to document tasks you have done and events in which you have participated, leave the two Delete check boxes deactivated to ensure that these items are maintained in iCal.

- **Open Events in Separate Windows**—Activate this check box to open an event in its own window when you double-click it. Normally iCal displays the event information within the iCal window.

- **Ask Before Sending Changes to Events**—When this check box is activated and you make changes to an event that's part of a shared calendar, iCal asks if you want to send those changes to anyone who is subscribed to that calendar. If you always send your changes, deactivate this check box to avoid the prompt.

- **Automatically Retrieve Invitations from Mail**—Activate this check box if you use Mail and want iCal invitations you receive to be retrieved automatically. This features makes it easy to schedule events with other people who use iCal or a compatible application because you can send invitations to them and they can accept (or not) and you'll be notified of their decision.

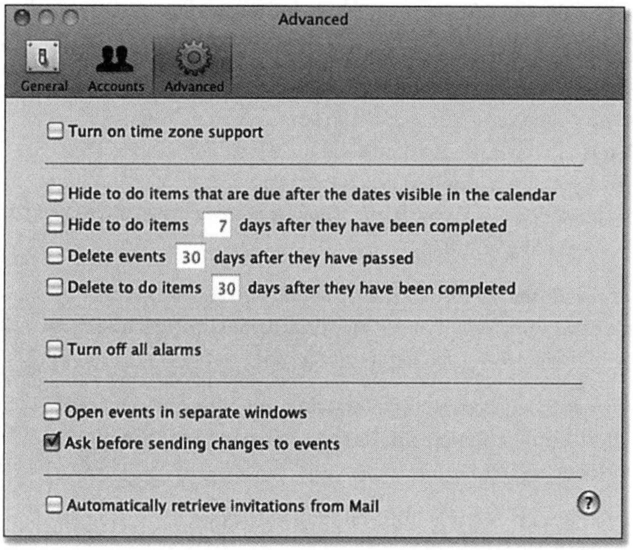

Figure 11.4
More iCal preferences are available in the Advanced tab.

Use the Accounts pane of the iCal Preferences dialog box to configure access to calendars available to you via CalDAV services on a network, as well as calendars available through Exchange 2007, Google, and Yahoo! This pane enables you to configure the information you need to access these calendars so they will be displayed within iCal. You need to have access to the server addresses, user names, and passwords to access this information and then use the Accounts preferences to configure iCal to access that information. You aren't likely to use this unless your Mac is connected to an organization's network, in which case you will need to contact your network administrator to be able to configure iCal to access this information.

Creating, Configuring, and Working with Calendars

As you read earlier, you can manage multiple calendars within the iCal application. iCal already comes with separate calendars for home and work activities, but you might want to create extra calendars for special projects, freelance work, school activities, and so on. Each calendar can include its own events and To Do items. To create a new calendar, do the following steps:

1. Click the New Calendar button. (You can also press Option-⌘-N or select File, New Calendar.) A new, untitled calendar appears in the Calendar pane.

2. Enter the name of the new calendar and press Return.

3. Select the new calendar and then select Edit, Get Info (or press ⌘-I). The calendar info sheet opens. At the top of the sheet, the name of the calendar is shown so that you know which calendar you are getting information about.

4. Enter a description of the calendar.

5. Use the Color pop-up menu to associate a color with the calendar. When you add events to the calendar, they appear in the color you select. Having different colors for different calendars is useful because you can easily see which events came from which calendars when you are viewing multiple calendars at the same time.

6. If you do not want alarms to be displayed for the items on just this calendar, activate the Ignore Alarms check box.

7. Click the Publish button to share your iCal calendar with others using either MobileMe or a private server.

➥ *To learn how to publish your calendar,* **see** *"Publishing Your iCal Calendar,"* **p. 245.**

To include a calendar's events and To Do items in the calendar being displayed, activate its check box. If you deactivate a calendar's box, its events and To Do items are hidden (you can activate its box to see its events and To Do items again).

To remove a calendar, select it and press Delete. The calendar, along with all its events and To Do items, will be removed from iCal. Most of the time, you're better off hiding a calendar because it won't appear in iCal any more, but you can still access its information at any time. When you delete a calendar, all of its information is deleted with it.

Working with Events

You can use iCal to track life events of all kinds. You can associate events with specific calendars, set reminders, and so on. To create an event, do the following steps:

1. Select the calendar and then the day on which you want the event to appear.

2. Select File, New Event (or press ⌘-N). A new one-hour event appears on the selected date; the event starts at the top of the next hour.

3. Type the name of the event and press Return.

4. Double-click on the event to see the Info sheet. When you first double-click an event after creating it, you see the event details; subsequent double-clicks only display the basic information, and you need to click the Edit button to see the details.

tip

You can also create an event by dragging over the time on the day which the event occurs.

5. Enter information about the location of the event by clicking the word None next to Location that appears under the event's title.

6. Activate the All-Day check box if the event is an all-day event.

tip

You can also change or set the date of the event using the From and To fields.

7. If it isn't an all-day event, use the From and To fields to set a start and end time for the event.

8. If the time zone is enabled, choose the time zone for the event on the Time Zone pop-up menu.

9. If you want the event to repeat, use the Repeat pop-up menu. You can choose a standard frequency for the event or select Custom to set a custom frequency. When you choose a frequency, the End pop-up menu appears. Use this to choose an end date for the repeating event.

10. If you want to change the calendar on which the event appears, use the Calendar pop-up menu to choose the calendar on which you want the event to appear.

11. If you want to set an alarm for the event, use the Alarm pop-up menu. Your options for the alarm are the following: None, which has no alarm; Message, which displays a text message; Message with Sound, which displays a text message and plays a sound; Email, which causes an email to be sent to an address you select; Open File, which opens a file of your choice; or Run Script, which causes a script you select to run. If you select an alarm with sound, the sound pop-up menu appears. If you choose any type of alarm, a pop-up menu that enables you to set the alarm time appears. If you select Email, a pop-up menu that enables you to select the email address to which the alarm should be sent appears.

You can set multiple alarms for an event by configuring the first alarm and then clicking the second "alarm" pop-up menu that gets created automatically. Use the alarm configuration tools to configure the second alarm. You can repeat this as many times as you need to set as many alarms as you want.

tip

The email addresses that appear on the Alert pop-up menus for events or To Do items are those that are on your card in the Address Book application. To add more addresses, add them to your card in Address Book.

12. Select the sound for the alarm if applicable and the amount of time before the event that you want the alarm to be activated.

13. Set the time for the alarm using the lowest pop-up menu in the Alarm section. The times you can choose are all relative to the event start time, such as 1 hour before.

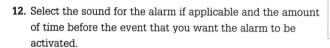

14. Enter attendees for the event in the Attendees field. You can type in names or drag them from your Address Book. To show people in your Address Book, select Window, Address Panel (Option-⌘-A). You can drag people from the Addresses window onto the "attendees" list. You can enter multiple attendees by dragging each onto the attendees field.

15. You can add attachments to a calendar item so that you can access items you need for that event. Click on Add File and use the resulting Open dialog box to navigate to and select the file. Click Open and the file will be attached to the event.

16. If a URL is associated with the event, enter it in the URL field.

17. Enter any notes about the event in the Notes field.

18. Review the event and make any necessary changes; you can then click Done to save the event (see Figure 11.5).

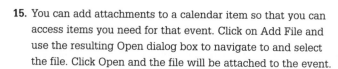

note

If your calendar is on a CalDAV or Exchange server, you can view attendee availability by clicking the Show Availability button that appears on the Info sheet. You can also reserve rooms and meeting equipment for your event.

Figure 11.5
A completed event ready for scheduling.

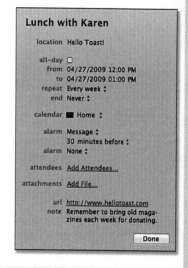

19. If you want to send email invitations for the event to the people on the attendees list, open the detail of the event again and click in the area where the attendees are listed. The Done button changes to Send; click the Send button. This is active only if you added attendees with email addresses to the event. After you've clicked Send, an email will be created in your default email application and the event will be attached to it. Depending on the email application you use, the email may send automatically. The people who receive these invitations can easily add the event to their own calendars by accepting them.

To view or change the details of an event, double-click the event in the calendar and then click the Edit button. Make changes to the event as needed and the changes are saved automatically.

Here are some additional tips for working with events:

- You can change the date on which an event occurs by dragging it from one date in the calendar to another.

- You can change the calendar on which an event occurs by opening its contextual menu (Control-click the event) and selecting the event's new calendar.

- You can duplicate an event by opening its contextual menu and selecting Duplicate; selecting Edit, Duplicate; or pressing ⌘-D. You can drag the copy onto a different date.

- You can email an event to others by opening its contextual menu and selecting Mail Event. (This is the same action that happens when you click the Send button for an event. The difference is that you can address the email that is created to anyone. When you click Send, the email is sent to only those people listed as attendees for the event.) Your default email application will open and the event will be included as an attachment. The recipient can then click the attachment, which has the extension .ics, onto iCal to add it to her calendar.

- If you use the Send command, as people add the event to their calendars, you'll see a green check next to their names. This indicates that the attendee has accepted the event by adding it to his calendar. This tracking doesn't occur when you use the Mail event command.

- When you change an aspect of a repeated event, such as the alarm, you'll be prompted to make the change to all the events or only to the current one. If you choose only the current one, the current event is detached from the series and will no longer be connected to the other instances of the same event. This will be indicated by (Detached Event) being appended to the frequency shown in the Repeat section for the event.

- Several of the data elements for events have contextual menus to enable you to perform actions. For example, if you click the alarm element, you can add more alarms or remove an existing alarm. If you add a URL, you can use its contextual menu to visit that website.

- As you configure an event, icons will appear at the top of the event on the calendar to indicate when an alarm has been set, whether the event is a repeating event, and so on.

- If you have turned on the time zone feature, the "time zone" pop-up menu appears in the Info sheet when you view the event. You can use this to set the time zone for the event. This is especially useful if you will be inviting people who are not in your current time zone. If they've enabled time zones in iCal, the event will be adjusted on their calendar automatically for their time zone.

Working with Your To Do List

To create a To Do item, use the following steps:

1. Select the calendar to which you want to add the To Do item.

2. Select File, New To Do (or press ⌘-K). A new To Do item appears on the To Do list and the name is selected.

3. Type the name of the To Do item and press Return.

4. Double-click the To Do to open the Info sheet. Information about the To Do item appears.

5. Use the Priority pop-up menu to set the To Do item's priority. As you set priorities, To Do items will be sorted on the To Do list accordingly.

6. If the event has a due date, activate the Due Date check box and use the date fields that appear to set the due date.

7. If you want to set an alarm for the event, open the Alarm pop-up menu and select the alarm you want to set (this is only enabled when the To Do item has a due date). The options are the same as those for an event.

8. If you want to use a different calendar, select the calendar using the Calendar pop-up menu.

9. If a URL is associated with the To Do item, enter it in the URL field.

10. Enter any notes for the To Do item in the Notes field. Figure 11.6 shows a completed To Do item.

11. Click Close.

Figure 11.6
A completed To Do item.

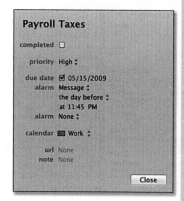

Following are some tips for working with To Do items:

- You can change a To Do item by double-clicking it to open the Info sheet. Then use the tools to change the item's information; these work just like when you create a To Do item.

- When you have completed a To Do item, mark it as complete by activating the check box next to its name on the To Do list or by activating the Completed check box on the Info sheet. (Remember that you can show or hide the To Do list.)

- The priority of To Do items is indicated by the number of bars that appear to the right of their names on the To Do items list (see Figure 11.7).

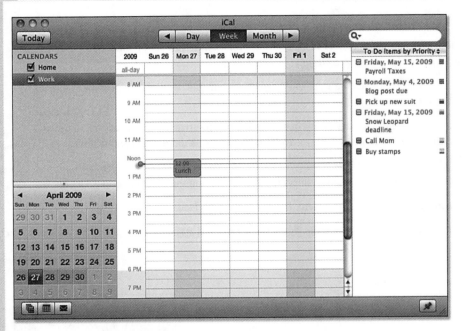

Figure 11.7
The priority of items on your To Do list is indicated by the number of bars shown next to its name.

- Sort the order in which To Do items appear on the list using the pop-up menu at the top of the To Do pane. You can sort the list by due date, priority, title, calendar, or manually.

- On the To Do pop-up menu, choose Hide Items After the Calendar view if you only want to see To Do items related to the days you are currently viewing. When this option is not selected, you'll see all your upcoming To Do items.

- If you want to see all of the items you've completed, open the To Do pop-up menu and choose Show All Completed Items.

- Open a To Do item's contextual menu to duplicate it, change the calendar with which it is associated, mark its priority, email it, or change the sort order for the To Do items pane.

- When the due date for an item is the current date or the due date has passed, its Complete check box becomes a warning icon to indicate that the item is overdue. You can activate the warning icon to mark the item as complete.

 tip

When you email an event or a To Do item to someone, the recipient can add the item to his calendar by clicking its link or by dragging it onto the iCal window. If the recipient uses Mail and their preferences are set to add invitations to iCal automatically, the iCal information will be added to their calendar when they receive your email.

Printing from iCal

From iCal, you can print calendars that show events, To Do items with due dates, mini-months, and your calendar keys (showing the calendars with which events and To Do items are associated). Open the Print dialog box to view and set the straightforward options for printing calendar information (see Figure 11.8). For example, you can choose the date range you want to print, which calendars are included, and the specific items you want to be included.

Figure 11.8
iCal offers flexible printing options.

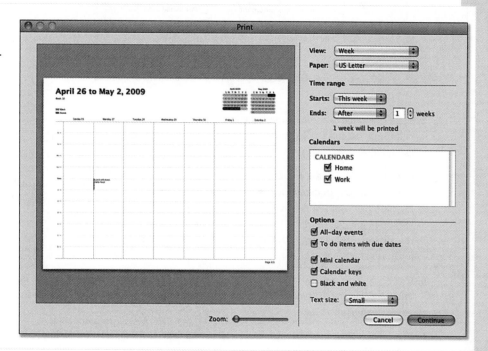

Publishing Your iCal Calendar

One of the cool things about iCal is that you can publish your calendars online so other people can view them. You can choose to share an iCal calendar via your MobileMe account or use any other server.

To publish your calendar, use the following steps:

1. Select the calendar you want to share.

2. Select Calendar, Publish. The Publish sheet appears (see Figure 11.9).

 tip

Because you can access a shared calendar over the Web, sharing your calendar provides a way for you to view your calendar even if your Mac isn't available. As long as you can access the Web, you can get to and view your calendar.

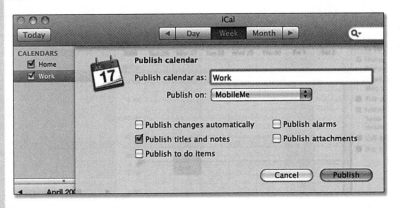

Figure 11.9
You can easily publish your calendars via MobileMe.

3. Type the name of the calendar as you want it to appear online; by default the calendar's name is entered, but you can change this if you want to.

4. Choose how you want to publish the calendar on the Publish On pop-up menu. Select MobileMe to use your MobileMe account or A Private Server to choose a different server. If you choose the latter option, you need to enter the server's URL along with your username and password for that server.

> **note**
>
> If you haven't configured your MobileMe account when you start to publish your calendar using MobileMe, you will be prompted to do so.

5. If you want changes you make to your calendar to be published automatically, activate the Publish Changes Automatically check box. In most cases, you should activate this so your calendar is always up-to-date.

6. If you want both the title and notes associated with an item to be published, activate the Publish Titles and Notes check box.

7. If you want the alarms and To Do items to be published, activate the Publish Alarms and Publish To Do Items check boxes. You can also publish attachments that are associated with events on your calendar.

8. Click Publish. When the calendar has been published, you will see the confirmation dialog box. This dialog box provides the URL for the calendar and enables you to visit the calendar online or send an email announcing the calendar.

9. Click the button for the action you want to take, such as OK to close the dialog box and return to iCal or Visit Page to see the calendar online.

Following are some more pointers on publishing your calendars online:

- When a calendar is published, the published icon (which looks like a dot radiating waves) appears next to the calendar's name.

- If you open a published calendar's contextual menu, you see several interesting commands. These include Unpublish, which removes the calendar from the Web; Send Publish Email, which enables you to send an email announcing the published calendar and its URL; Copy URL to Clipboard, which copies the calendar's URL to the Clipboard so you can easily paste it into documents; Refresh, which publishes any changes you have made to the calendar; and Change Location, which enables you to move the calendar to a different site.

- People can subscribe to your shared calendars so they appear in their iCal windows. More on this in the next section.

- You can view your own shared calendar at any time from any computer by moving to its URL. This is a great way to maintain access to your own calendar when you aren't at your Mac.

- You can change a shared calendar by selecting and opening the Info drawer. Use the controls in the drawer to make changes to the calendar's publishing settings.

Subscribing to Other Calendars

You can subscribe to other people's personal calendars or public calendars to add them to your iCal window.

Subscribing to Personal Calendars

You can add other personal calendars to your iCal window by doing the following steps:

1. Select Calendar, Subscribe (Option-⌘-S). The Subscribe sheet appears.

2. Enter the URL for the calendar to which you want to subscribe and click Subscribe. The Subscribing configuration sheet appears.

3. Enter the title that you want to be used for the calendar in iCal. You can also add a description for the calendar and select which color the items for the calendar should be. If you need to change the URL for the calendar you can edit it here, as well.

4. If you want the calendar's information to be refreshed automatically, select the frequency at which you want the refresh to occur on the pop-up menu.

5. If you don't want the calendar's alarms to appear in your iCal window, activate the Remove Alarms check box.

6. If you don't want the calendar's To Do items to show up in your iCal window, activate the Remove To Do Items check box. You usually don't want to display the To Do items on a calendar to which you are subscribing unless you have To Do items on it.

 tip

If you are part of a family of iCal users, each person can publish their own calendar and subscribe to each family member's calendar. This provides a great way for everyone in the family to know what's happening in each other's schedule because all they have to do is look in iCal to see all the calendars at the same time.

7. If you don't want the calendar's attachments showing up in your iCal window, activate the Remove Attachments check box.

8. Click OK. The calendar is added to your iCal window, and you can view it just like your own calendars. iCal creates a Subscriptions section in the Calendars pane and displays the new calendar here. If you set the calendar to be refreshed automatically (refer to step 4), it is kept current for you too.

tip

If you don't set a calendar to be refreshed automatically, you can refresh it manually by opening its contextual menu and selecting Refresh.

Subscribing to Public Calendars

note

You can't make any changes to a calendar to which you are subscribed. You can only view it.

Many public calendars are available to which you can subscribe. For example, most professional sports teams have calendars that show games and other events. You can also find DVD release calendars, TV schedules, and many other types of calendars to subscribe to. Just like personal calendars, when you subscribe to public calendars, the events on those calendars are shown in your iCal window. To find and subscribe to public calendars, do the following steps:

1. Use Safari to go to one of several iCal sharing sites, such as iCalShare.com.

2. Use the search tool or browse through the available calendars that are published on the site. When you find a calendar you want to subscribe to, select it and view the information page. At the bottom are several links; click on Subscribe. You move into iCal and the Subscribe To sheet appears. The URL information is filled in automatically.

3. Click Subscribe. The Subscribe To configuration sheet appears.

4. Review the subscription options and change them as needed.

5. Click OK. The calendar will be added to your iCal window, and you can view its events.

tip

If you don't set a calendar to be refreshed automatically, you can refresh it manually by opening its contextual menu and selecting Refresh.

WORKING WITH TEXT AND GRAPHICS

The Mac OS X Text and Graphics Applications

All operating systems enable you to expand your system by installing new applications, and of course Mac OS X is no exception. However, one of the hallmarks of a good operating system is that it ships with a decent collection of applications that cover the most common computing tasks. Again, Mac OS X fits the bill here by offering a few native applications that enable you to work with text and graphics. Sure, you can install iLife (if it didn't come preinstalled on your new Mac), iWork, Microsoft Office, Adobe Acrobat, and many other third-party applications to help you with your text and graphics chores, but if your budget's tight or you just want to stick with your Mac's default applications for now, Mac OS X won't disappoint. This chapter covers several useful text and graphics applications that come with Mac OS X. These include TextEdit, Preview, Image Capture, and Grab.

Word Processing with TextEdit

Judging by the name alone, the TextEdit application sounds like a text editor. And while TextEdit can do text-only documents without breaking a sweat, TextEdit is really a full-fledged word processor that can probably handle most of what you use a word processor for. (In this section I assume you've used a similar application before, so I won't go into the basics of creating a document.) To get TextEdit on the desktop, press ⌘-Space to open the Spotlight menu, type **textedit** (actually, you probably only have to type **te** or **tex**) and then select TextEdit in the results.

(Alternatively, open Finder and select Applications, TextEdit.) Figure 12.1 shows the surprisingly Spartan interface that TextEdit presents to the world.

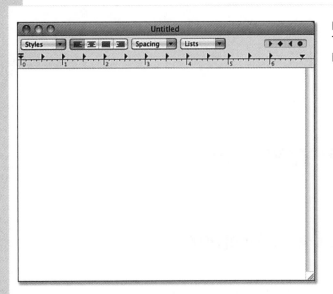

Figure 12.1
TextEdit packs some powerful features in a plain-looking package.

However, check out the following list of features that you might not spot at first glance:

- **File formats**—TextEdit is compatible with a number of document file formats. Its basic file format is the Rich Text Format (RTF), but it supports many others including: HTML, web archive, and most importantly, various flavors of Word. You can save or open documents in any of these formats.

- **Formatting**—TextEdit's Format menu includes the Font command (see Figure 12.2), which enables you to apply a large variety of formatting to text, including using the Mac OS X Font panel (the Show Fonts command in Figure 12.2).

- **Styles**—Styles are collections of formatting elements that you can save and reapply to text by choosing the appropriate style name. To create a style, enter text and format it as you want the style to be saved and select it. Then, open the Styles pop-up menu located on the left side of the TextEdit toolbar and choose Other. The Styles sheet appears; click Add To Favorites; in the resulting sheet, enter a name for the style, and configure whether you want the font and ruler to be included as part of the file. After you click Add, the style you created will be added to the Styles pop-up menu and you can reapply it to text easily by selecting the text and choosing the style on the pop-up menu.

  After you've defined styles, you can easily select text in the document with that style by selecting an instance of the style, choosing Other on the Styles menu, and clicking Select. You can then choose to select text within the document or within an existing selection. When the text is selected, you can make changes to it consistently throughout a document.

Figure 12.2
TextEdit's Format, Font command offers a wealth of text formatting options.

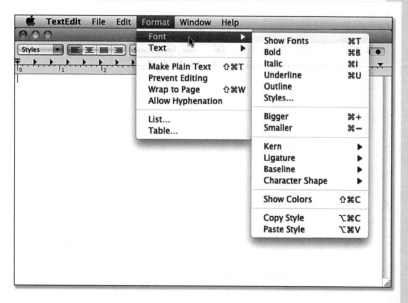

To remove a style, open the Styles menu and choose Other. Select the Favorite Styles radio button, use the pop-up menu to select the style you want to delete, (see Figure 12.3), and then click Remove From Favorites.

Figure 12.3
The Styles sheet enables you to preview and select text based on the styles defined.

- **Tables**—Like other word processors, TextEdit supports the creation of tables. To insert a table into a document, choose Format, Table. The Table tool appears (see Figure 12.4). Use the tool to define the number of rows and columns, the alignment (vertical and horizontal), cell border and color, and cell background and color. You can also create nested tables. After you've created your table, you can drag the borders of cells to resize them. You can also use styles and apply the other formatting tools to a table's content.

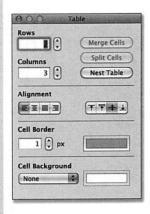

Figure 12.4
The Table tool enables you to create tables in your TextEdit documents.

- **Lists**—Using the List tool, you can create a variety of lists. To start a list, open the toolbar's Lists menu and choose the style of bullet you want to use in the list. You can choose from symbols, such as bullets, or organized lists, such as numbers for a numbered list. Each time you press Return, a new list item will be created using the bullet style you selected. To end the list, choose None on the Lists menu or press Return twice.

  If you choose Other on the Lists menu, a sheet appears in which you can define custom lists by adding a prefix, choosing a bullet, and adding a suffix.

- **HTML Creation**—You can use TextEdit to create or edit HTML documents for web pages. You can save any document in HTML; if you use TextEdit's tables and lists, those elements will be maintained and formatted properly in the resulting web page.

- **Spelling and Grammar** —TextEdit has a full-featured spell checker, which can check as you type or on a entire document. It's available on the Edit menu. If you open the Spelling and Grammar tool, you can choose to have grammar checked when you check spelling.

- **Hyperlinks**—Select some text and then select the Edit, Add Link command to add a hyperlink to your TextEdit document.

If you find TextEdit useful, check out its preferences. You can use these to set default formats, formatting, options (including spell checking and page numbering), and open/save settings.

Previewing Documents

As its name implies, Preview's primary function is to let you preview documents. In the context of Preview, *documents* include many kinds of files, such as image files, PDFs, and many more. Preview is useful for viewing a wide variety of documents and allows you to make some minor editing changes to some of those documents.

 note
Preview is Mac OS X's default PDF viewing application.

Working with Images in Preview

Many of the image file types you commonly use under Mac OS X are configured to open in Preview by default.

To open and view images in Preview, use the following steps:

1. In Finder, select one or more image files, and then select File, Open. Preview opens and you see the selected image in the Preview window (see Figure 12.5). You see the other open images in the Sidebar. If the image doesn't fill the Preview window, you see gray borders around it.

 note

Preview might not be the default application for viewing image, PDF, or other files. If not, you can open any image file by first opening Preview and then using the Open command, or by setting Preview to be the application associated with a specific image file.

➡ *To learn how to associate files with an application, **see** "Determining the Application That Opens When You Open a Document," **p. 138**.*

Figure 12.5
Preview enables you to view images and perform some basic image editing tasks.

2. Use the tools in the toolbar to control how the images appear, such as the Zoom In button to make the image larger.

tip

If an application other than Preview opens when you open an image file, open the file's contextual menu and select Open With, Preview.

Many of Preview's commands are straightforward, such as the Zoom To Fit command, which sizes the current image so it fills the Preview window. If you have used any graphics application, you won't have any trouble with these basic viewing commands.

Preview also features the Sidebar, which is useful when you are working with more than one image at a time. Each image appears as a thumbnail in the Sidebar. Select an image's thumbnail to view it in the Preview window.

You can open and close the Sidebar by clicking the Sidebar button on the toolbar; by selecting View, Sidebar; or by pressing Shift-⌘-D. You can change the size of the thumbnails in the Sidebar by dragging the right edge of the Sidebar; use the Action pop-up menu to change how the images in the Sidebar are organized.

To get information about an image, choose Tools, Show Inspector (or press ⌘-I). In the Inspector window, you see various information about the image, such as its resolution, type, file size, and so on (see Figure 12.6). Click the More Info tab, which has the *i* icon, to get even more detailed information. You can use the third tab, which has the magnifying glass icon, to associate keywords with an image; you can use these keywords to find images using Spotlight.

 tip

To zoom in on part of an image, select the part on which you want to zoom and select View, Zoom to Selection (or press ⌘-*). To remove the selection box, click the image outside of the box.

 note

If you open images one at a time, a Preview window will open for each image file.

 tip

You can customize Preview's toolbar just as you can in many other Mac OS X applications, including the Finder.

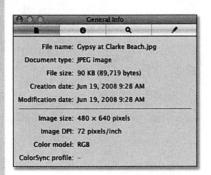

Figure 12.6
Preview's Inspector provides detailed information about an image.

To perform basic image correction on an image, choose Tools, Adjust Color (or press Option-⌘-C). Use the resulting Adjust Color tool to change exposure, white- and black-point, saturation, contrast, and other aspects of an image (see Figure 12.7). You can use the Sepia slider to apply the sepia effect to an image.

Figure 12.7
Use the Adjust Color tool to improve your image.

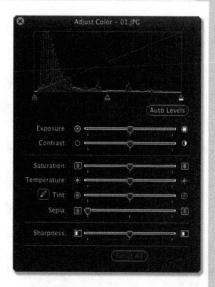

You can resize an image by choosing Tools, Adjust Size. In the resulting sheet, you can change the image's dimensions based on pixels or inches.

Cropping is one of the most basic and useful image-editing options. Fortunately, you can use Preview to easily crop images, as you can see in the following steps:

1. Open the image you want to crop.

2. Choose the selection tool you want to use on the Select pop-up menu and drag in the image to select the portion of the image you want to keep (see Figure 12.8).

3. To adjust the selected part of the image, drag the selection box around or resize it by either dragging a corner or dragging the resize handle located in the center of each side of the selection box.

4. When you have the part of the image you want to keep selected, select Tools, Crop or press ⌘-K. Preview removes the portions of the image that lie outside the selection box.

 tip

To keep the selection box proportional to the original image, hold down the Shift key while you drag.

 tip

You can restore the most recently saved version of an image by selecting File, Revert to Saved.

Figure 12.8
Select the portion of the image you want to keep before you use the Crop command.

Using Preview to Read PDFs

Portable Document Format (PDF) files are a common way to distribute electronic documents. You are likely to encounter many PDFs on the Web, as file attachments to emails, and so on. Preview is Mac OS X's default PDF viewer.

➡ *You can create your own PDF documents. To learn how,* **see** *"Saving Documents as PDFs," **p.** 148.*

To view a PDF with Preview, do the following:

1. In Finder, select the PDF document and then select File, Open. The PDF document appears in Preview.

2. Open Preview's Sidebar. The Sidebar has four views: Contact Sheet, Thumbnails, Table of Contents, and Annotations, each of which has its own button in the toolbar at the bottom of the Sidebar. To see the document's table of contents, click the Table of Contents button on Sidebar's toolbar. You see the document's table of contents; you can expand or collapse sections by clicking their expansion triangles (see Figure 12.9).

Figure 12.9
You can click a section in the table of contents to jump to it.

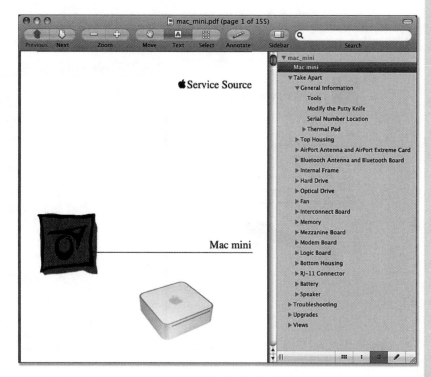

3. To view the document via thumbnails, click the Thumbnails button; click a thumbnail to move to a specific page.

4. Move to pages one at a time by clicking the Next or Previous button in the toolbar or by pressing the Page Down or Page Up keys.

5. Adjust the display of a PDF document by using the commands shown when you select View, PDF Display. The options include Single Page, which shows the document page-by-page; Two Pages, which shows two pages at a time; and so on.

6. You can add notes to your PDF by selecting text and annotating it. Choose the Text selection tool on the Preview toolbar and select the text you want to annotate. On the Preview toolbar, click Annotate to display the Annotations toolbar, as shown at the bottom of Figure 12.10. Click the type of marking you want to apply, such as highlighting or strikethrough. Or, choose an annotation, such as a box or oval. You can use both types of tools on the same page, and you can include multiple annotations on the same page.

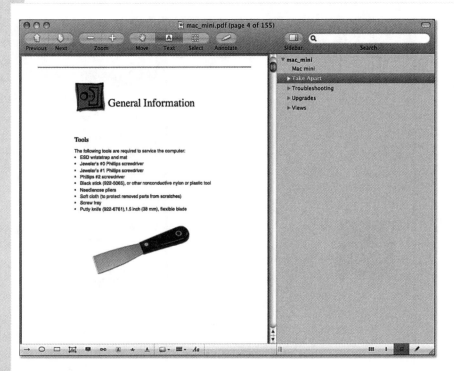

Figure 12.10
You can annotate
PDF documents
using Preview's
Annotation toolbar.

7. To move around inside a document, select Tools, Move Tool, click the Move tool on the toolbar, or press ⌘-1. The cursor will become the hand and you can drag around a page to move it within the Preview window (unless the entire page fills the window, in which case you can't do this).

8. To select text so you can copy and paste it into other documents, select Tools, Text Tool or press ⌘-2. Select the text you want to copy and select Edit, Copy. The text will be moved to the Clipboard, from which you can paste it into other documents, such as TextEdit. (A PDF's security settings determine whether you can do this or not.)

9. To select parts of a page using a selection box, select Tools, Select Tool or press ⌘-3. Drag on the page to select part of it. You can then copy that part and paste it into other documents. To remove the selection box, choose a different tool.

10. To add a bookmark to a PDF, move to the location at which you want to set a bookmark and select Bookmarks, Add Bookmark or press ⌘-D. In the resulting sheet, name the bookmark and click Add. You can return to this point in the document at any time by selecting it on the Bookmarks menu.

11. To search a PDF document, type the text for which you want to search in the Search box that appears at the right end of the Toolbar. As you type, Preview will search the document for your search text. When it finds the first instance, the page on which it appears will be shown and the occurrence of the search term is highlighted. In the Sidebar, each occurrence of the search term appears on the list of results (at the top of the list, you will see how many occurrences there are in the document). When you click an occurrence, the page on which it appears is shown in the Preview window and the search term is highlighted on the page.

12. If you made annotations to the document, save it before you close it.

 tip

Check out the Inspector when you are working with PDF documents. It has four tabs, which provide lots of information about and control over the PDF document.

Viewing a Slideshow in Preview

iPhoto, iDVD, and iMovie can be used to create slideshows. Although not nearly as sophisticated as those applications, you can create a basic slideshow in Preview by performing the following steps:

1. Use Preview to open the image files you want to view in a slideshow.

2. Select View, Slideshow, or press Shift-⌘-F. The Preview interface will disappear and the images will be displayed as a slideshow.

3. Move the mouse and a set of controls appears at the bottom of the screen (see Figure 12.11). From left to right, the buttons are

   ■ **Back**—Moves the slideshow back one image

   ■ **Pause/Play**—Pauses or plays the slideshow

   ■ **Next**—Moves to the next image

   ■ **Index Sheet**—Displays thumbnails of each image so you can click one to move to that image

   ■ **Fit to Screen/Actual Size**—Adjusts the size of the image to fill the screen or be the actual size

   ■ **Add to iPhoto**—Adds the image to the iPhoto library. Note that you only see this button if you have iPhoto installed on your Mac.

   ■ **Close**—Stops the slideshow

4. Use the appropriate buttons to control the slideshow.

5. When you are done, click the Close button or press Esc. You move back to the standard Preview window.

Figure 12.11
Preview's
slideshows
aren't fancy,
but they are
a quick way
to view a
batch of
images.

Using Preview to Convert Files to Different Formats

One of the nice things you can do in Preview is to convert an image from one format to another. Here's how:

1. Open the image you want to save in a different format.

2. Select File, Save As. The Save As sheet appears.

3. Select the file format in which you want to save the file from the Format pop-up menu (see Figure 12.12).

4. If the format you selected has options, use the slider, check boxes, or other controls to configure its settings.

5. Rename the file, choose a save location, and then click Save. A new file in the format you selected will be created.

Figure 12.12
One of Preview's most useful functions is its ability to convert image files to different formats.

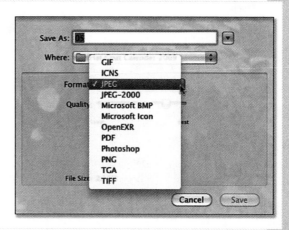

Setting Preview Preferences

You can configure several Preview preferences to tweak Preview to suit your needs. These options are summarized in Table 12.1.

Table 12.1 Preview Preferences

Tab	Preference	What It Does
General	When Opening Files: Open All Files in One Window	No matter how you open files (one at a time or many at once), they all appear in the same window and you can use the Sidebar to work with them.
General	When Opening Files: Open Groups of Files in the Same Window	When you open multiple images at the same time, they all appear in the same window and you can use the Sidebar to work with them.
General	When Opening Files: Open Each File in its Own Window	No matter how many images you open at once, they each appear in a separate Preview window.
General	Window Background	Sets the color of the area outside an image in the Preview window (the default is gray).
Images	Initial Image Scale: Actual Size	Opens images at their default sizes.

Table 12.1 Continued

Tab	Preference	What It Does
Images	Initial Image Scale: Scale Large Images to Fit Window	Automatically zooms out in large images so the entire image is displayed in the Preview window.
Images	Define 100% Scale as: 1 Image Pixel Equals 1 Screen Pixel	Defines full scaling as a one-to-one correspondence between each image pixel and each screen pixel.
Images	Define 100% Scale as: Size on Screen Equals Size on Printout	Defines full scaling as a correspondence between the actual size of the image and the size of the image on screen.
PDF	Initial Document Scale	Choose Use Scale Of and enter a value to cause Preview to use the scale value you enter when you open a PDF; choose Size to Fit to automatically scale the PDF to fit the Preview window.
PDF	Define 100% Scale as: 1 Point Equals 1 Screen Pixel	Defines full scaling as a one-to-one correspondence between each PDF point and each screen pixel.
PDF	Define 100% Scale as: Size on Screen Equals Size on Printout	Defines full scaling as a correspondence between the actual size of the PDF and the size of the PDF on screen.
PDF	On Opening Documents: Show Sidebar Only for Table of Contents	Causes Preview to open the Sidebar only when a PDF has a table of contents element included in it.
PDF	On Opening Documents: Start on Last Page Viewed	Causes Preview to display the page you last viewed when you most recently opened the PDF.
PDF	Viewing Documents: Smooth Text and Line Art	Activate this check box to configure Preview to use antialiasing techniques to smooth the PDF's text and line art.
PDF	Viewing Documents: Use Logical Page Numbers	Activate this check box to configure Preview to show the correct overall page numbers in a document, including the front matter pages (which might be numbered with Roman numerals or another numbering scheme).
PDF	Annotations: Add Name to Annotations	Activate this check box to configure Preview to track who makes annotations to a PDF.

Table 12.1   Preview Preferences

Tab	Preference	What It Does
PDF	Annotations: Name	Use this text box to type the name you want Preview to add to the annotations when it tracks them.
Bookmarks		This pane shows all the bookmarks that have been created using Preview; for each, the label, file, and page are shown.
Bookmarks	Remove	Select a bookmark and click Remove to delete it from the document in which it was created.

Capturing Images

Mac OS X was designed to work with digital images; it includes the basic Image Capture application, which provides a consistent interface for various models of digital cameras. Its single purpose is to download images from digital devices (cameras, scanners, and so on) to your Mac. If you have iLife installed, when you are working with a digital camera, you are better off using iPhoto to download images because it has more powerful tools and enables you to build and organize your image library. Still, Image Capture has a few tricks up its sleeves and might be the best way to scan images.

 note

The more technical name for PTP is ISO 12740.

Image Capture works with devices that support the Picture Transfer Protocol (PTP). If you aren't sure whether your device supports this protocol, activate the manufacturer's website and product specifications to see whether your particular model supports PTP. Fortunately, almost all modern digital imaging devices do.

Image Capture can be configured so it automatically downloads images when you plug your camera or scanner into your Mac. By default, Mac OS X is configured to open iPhoto when it detects a camera. You can change this behavior with the Image Capture Preferences command.

note

Image Capture works pretty much the same way, whether you are downloading images from a scanner or a camera. However, your best bet is to use iPhoto to download images from your camera so you have all its photo-related tools at your fingertips.

Using Image Capture to Download Images from a Camera to Your Mac

If you don't have iPhoto installed on your Mac, you can use Image Capture to download images from a camera to your Mac so you can work with them, such as viewing them or creating a simple slideshow in Preview. Use the following steps to get images from a camera to your Mac:

1. Connect your camera to your Mac using its USB cable.

2. Power up your camera (if it has a mode selector to communicate with a computer, choose that mode—most cameras switch to this mode automatically). If you haven't configured Image Capture to open automatically, open it (Applications folder). If you have configured Image Capture to open automatically, it will do so when your Mac detects the camera. You will see the Image Capture window (see Figure 12.13). The application communicates with the camera to determine how many images need to be downloaded. When the camera is ready to begin downloading images, the Import and Import All buttons become active (see Figure 12.13).

 note

If iPhoto is installed on your Mac, by default your Mac opens iPhoto when you connect a camera to it. You can allow that to happen and then open Image Capture. Both applications can be running at the same time. You can also change the Image Capture preferences to specify that Image Capture should open when you connect your camera to your Mac.

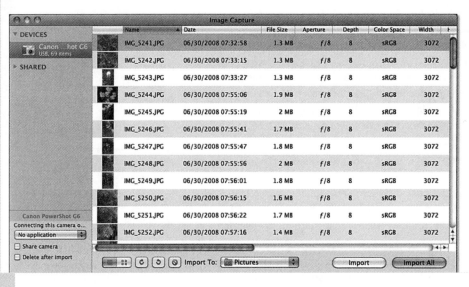

Figure 12.13
When you connect a supported camera to your Mac, Image Capture displays the number of images that are ready to be downloaded.

3. Select the folder into which you want the images to be downloaded on the Import To pop-up menu. By default, Image Capture selects the Pictures folder. You can select Other on the menu to choose a different folder to which to save images instead.

4. You now have two choices:

   - To download all the images on the camera, click Import All.

   - To download only some of the images, select the images and then click Import.

note

If your camera is not recognized by Image Capture, it probably does not support PTP. In that case, you have to use the camera's software to download images from it.

The images you download are saved into the appropriate directories in your Home folder or in the folder you selected on the Import To pop-up menu. For example, photos are downloaded to the Pictures directory. As the images are downloaded, you see the progress in the Image Capture status bar. When the application is done downloading images, it moves to the background, and the directories into which it downloaded images are opened. After the images have been downloaded, a Finder window containing the images you downloaded opens so you can work with them.

 note

If your camera has QuickTime movies on it, those are placed in the Movies directory in your Home directory. Likewise, sounds are placed in the Music directory.

Troubleshooting Image Capture

If Image Capture doesn't recognize your camera when connected to your Mac, it is most likely that Mac OS X does not support the camera you are using, probably because your camera does not use PTP. In this case, you can try to obtain Mac OS X–compatible software for your camera and use that to download images. You will probably have to use software that came with the camera to download its images to your Mac.

 tip

You can connect multiple cameras to your Mac at the same time. To choose the one with which you want to work, use the Camera pop-up menu.

In rare cases, a cable or hardware problem might exist. Use the Apple System Profiler to ensure that your Mac is capable of communicating with the camera.

➡ *To learn about the System Profiler, **see** "Using System Profiler to Create a System Profile," p. 737.*

Capturing Screen Images

In many instances, capturing an image of what is happening on your Mac's screen is useful. One example is if you are writing instructions about how to do a particular task, for example, when you are writing your own book about Mac OS X. Another is when you want to capture an error message or some other anomaly you want to be able to explain to someone (for example, you might want to capture the image of an error dialog box so you can email it when you try to get technical support).

With Mac OS X, you have two built-in ways to capture screen images. One is to use keyboard commands. The other is to use the Grab application.

Capturing Screen Images with Keyboard Shortcuts

Mac OS X includes keyboard commands you can use to capture desktop images. After you capture an image, it is stored on your desktop as a Portable Network Graphics (PNG) file and is called Picture X.png, where X is a sequential number. You have the following three options:

- Shift-⌘-3 captures the entire desktop.

- Shift-⌘-4 changes the pointer to a plus sign. Drag this pointer to select the part of the screen you want to capture. When you release the mouse button, an image of the selected area is captured.

- Shift-⌘-4-spacebar enables you to capture a window, menu bar, Dock, or other area of the screen. First, open the area you want to capture, such as a window or menu. When you press the key combination, a large camera pointer icon appears. Move this icon over the area that you want to capture, which becomes highlighted. Click the mouse button to capture the image.

 tip

To choose not to capture an image after you have pressed these key combinations, press Escape. If you want to save an image to the Clipboard so you can easily paste it into a document, hold down Control while you press the keys for the kind of screenshot you want to take.

Capturing Screen Images with Grab

Mac OS X includes the Grab application. As its name implies, using Grab, you can "grab" an image of your Mac's desktop. There are several options you can use to capture a specific image. To capture a desktop image, follow these steps:

1. Open Grab (Applications/Utilities).

2. Select the Capture mode you want for your screenshot using the Capture menu. Your options are as follows:

   - Selection captures an area of the screen you select.

   - Window captures the active window.

   - Screen captures the entire screen.

   - Timed Screen provides a timer so you can set up a screen before it is captured (so you have time to switch to a window and open a menu before the image is captured, for example).

3. Follow the instructions you see. For example, if you select Timed Screen, the Timed Screen Grab dialog box appears. Then open the area you want to capture, such as a document window with a menu open. When you are ready to take the shot, click Start Timer in the Timed Screen Grab dialog box and get the window as you want it to be captured. After 10 seconds have passed, Grab captures the image.

   When the capture is complete, you see a new window containing the image you captured.

4. To see the size of the image you captured and its color depth, select Inspector from the Edit menu or press ⌘-1. The Inspector window appears and you see information about the image.

5. Save the image. Grab's default file format is TIFF.

The images you capture with Grab are just like images you create in other ways. You can open them in image-editing applications, preview them in Preview, print them, and so on.

 tip

Grab's capturing capabilities are provided to the OS so that other applications can use them. For example, if you are working in a Carbon or Cocoa application, you can easily grab an image of its screen by selecting the Services command from that application's menu. Then, select Grab and select the type of grab from the menu. When you release the mouse button, the image you captured is displayed. How it is displayed depends on the application from which you captured it. For example, if you grab an image while you are using TextEdit, a Rich Text Format (RTF) file is created.

CONNECTING YOUR MAC TO THE INTERNET

Connecting Your Mac Directly to the Internet

In many cases, connecting your Mac to the Internet is straightforward. The vast majority of Macs (and *all* new Macs) are configured right of out of the box to access an Internet connection shared over a network. So if your network already has an Internet connection through a router or gateway, all you have to do is connect your Mac to the network—either using a wired connection to the router or to a switch connected to the router, or using a wireless connection—and your Mac will have Internet access within seconds. That's pretty sweet, but it only happens if you've already done the legwork to get your network Internet-enabled. If you haven't got that far yet, I explain everything in detail in Chapter 19, "Sharing an Internet Connection."

This chapter is mostly about a different Internet connection scenario: where you connect your Mac to the Internet directly, either using a dial-up connection or a broadband connection. I'm assuming here that you've already done the necessary prep work for choosing an Internet service provider (ISP) and that you've got an account set up with the ISP. The rest of this chapter shows you how to take the info provided by the ISP and turn it into a functioning Internet connection.

Gathering the Internet Connection Data

If you use a broadband account of some sort, the provider sometimes installs any needed hardware for you, such as a cable modem, and configures your machine to use it (although self-install kits are becoming more common). If you use a dial-up account, you usually receive instructions about how to configure that account; some providers, such as EarthLink, provide software that does the installation and configuration for you.

Even if the provider handles the initial installation and configuration for your account, you still need to understand how to configure your account yourself. You should try to understand the configuration information related to your account. You at least should ensure that you have all the information you need to configure your account for the inevitable situation in which you must reconfigure it on your machine.

Gathering Dial-Up Internet Connection Data

If you have a dial-up account, you only need the following bits of information to set up a connection:

- **Phone number**—All dial-up accounts come with a phone number that you use to reach your ISP. Some ISPs offer different numbers for different modem speeds, so be sure you get the phone number that matches your modem.

- **Username**—Also called the *account name*. You need a username to log on to your account when you make the connection. You probably chose your own username when you established your account, although many ISPs assign a username.

- **Password**—You also need to specify your account password when you make the connection. Again, many ISPs assign passwords, but you may have been given the option to choose your own.

Your dial-up USP will also provide you with the particulars for setting up your email account, which is covered in Chapter 15, "Managing Your Email."

➥ **See** *"Configuring Email Accounts," p. 317*.

 caution

Be wary about any dedicated "front-end" software a provider might want to install on your machine. Most of the time, this software consists of an application that gives you a specialized interface for using the service. This software is almost never necessary and can cause problems for you. It is better to just use the configuration information the provider gives you and then use Mac OS X software to access the Internet.

 tip

If your provider offers more than one way to connect, such as via a cable modem and a backup dial-up account, be sure you get the information you need for all connection methods available to you.

 tip

Make sure that you collect and organize the information you need to access your account. You will need to reconfigure your Mac at some point and, if you don't have the information handy, this will be harder than it needs to be. One way to do this is to configure your account and after you are sure it works properly, you can take screenshots (Shift-⌘-3) of the various configuration screens. This enables you to quickly re-create your specific configuration. Of course, you should also keep copies of any information your provider gives you.

Gathering Broadband Internet Connection Data

The following data is required to configure your Mac for broadband Internet access:

- **Type of configuration**—This information tells your computer which protocol to use to connect to the Internet. If you are using a broadband connection, several possibilities exist, which include a static IP address, Dynamic Host Configuration Protocol (DHCP), PPP over Ethernet (PPPoE), DHCP with a fixed IP address, or the Bootstrap Protocol (BootP). A static IP address means that your Mac always has the same IP address. When you use DHCP, your provider assigns your Mac an IP address along with most of the other information you need to connect; this is the most common type and is also the easiest to configure. PPPoE is most often used for DSL accounts. DHCP with a fixed IP address means that your IP address is fixed, but the DHCP server provides the other information for you. BootP access is used for "diskless" machines that use a server to provide the operating system.

- **IP address, subnet mask, and router**—These addresses locate your machine on the Internet and provide it with its address. Most broadband accounts use dynamic IP addressing, which simply means that your Mac has an IP address assigned each time it connects rather than having a static address. If you have a manual or static IP address, it never changes and is permanently assigned to your machine. When you have a static IP address, you also need the subnet mask and router; with dynamic addressing, this information is provided by the server.

- **DHCP client ID**—If you use DHCP access, you sometimes have a client ID name for your computer. In most situations this is optional; however, if your provider includes a DHCP Client ID with your account, you need to use it. If you are configuring an account using a local DHCP server, you probably don't have to use a client ID.

- **Domain name server**—A domain name server (DNS) translates the addresses the computers use into language that we humans can usually understand. The DNS enables you to use an address such as www.companyname.com rather than having to deal with a series of numbers such as 192.169.x.x. The DNS number you need from your provider will be something such as 192.169.x.x. Ideally, your provider will include several DNS addresses so you have a backup in case the primary DNS fails. (If your DNS fails, you won't be able to access websites unless you know their numeric IP addresses.)

- **Search domain**—This information is related to the particular part of the provider's network on which you are located. It is usually optional. You might be provided with more than one search domain.

- **Usernames and passwords**—These are the two pieces of information that uniquely identify you and enable you to access your account. You probably chose your own username when you established your account. Your password might or might not have been assigned by the ISP.

  You might have more than one username or password. Sometimes, your ISP gives you one username and password that enable you to connect to the Internet and another set (or maybe just a different password or username) to let you use your email account. Make sure that you know which is which and use the right ones in the right setting fields. If you use a PPPoE account, your username is your account name.

- **Email account information**—You will be given your email address (probably something such as username@isp.net). You will also need an address for the server that receives your mail (this often has a "pop" in it, such as pop.isp.net). The third piece of information you need is the address of the server that sends your mail (this often has "smtp" in it, such as smtp.isp.net). Some broadband accounts have simpler server configuration for both sides, such as mail.isp.net.

- **Web customer support address**—If your account offers additional services, such as multiple email accounts, obtain the information you need to access that site so you can manage your account.

> **note**
>
> In some cases, you might not need a username and password to access the Internet. For example, if you have a static IP address, you don't need a username and password to connect to the Internet. However, you will need a username and password to access your email accounts. You usually don't have a username and password for cable access either, because the physical location of the modem determines whether the access is valid or not.

Most broadband providers include the modem hardware (such as a cable modem) you use to connect with your account. In some cases, they also install the hardware for you. However, you can usually supply your own hardware if you prefer (this is usually less expensive over the long haul). And, many providers offer "self-install" kits at local retailers. These kits include the hardware, software, and instructions you need to install the service yourself. (One benefit to these kits is that you don't have to wait all day for the cable guy to show up!)

If you need to install the modem you will be using, do so. In the case of an Ethernet-based connection, this requires you to connect the modem to your Mac's Ethernet port or the WAN port on your network hub and then connect the modem to the source (the cable that comes into your house).

Connecting Your Mac with Dial-Up Internet Access

If you decided to go the dial-up route, either because you don't have access to broadband service in your area, or because your Internet needs are simple, you'll be happy to know that configuring your Mac for dial-up Net access and making the connection are also simple.

Configuring Your Mac for Dial-Up Internet Access

With your dial-up account information at hand, follow these steps to set up the connection:

1. If you have an external dial-up modem, connect that modem to your Mac and turn it on, if necessary. If this is the first time you've connected to the modem, your Mac displays a message letting you know that it has detected the modem (see Figure 13.1); click Network Preferences and then skip to step 5.

2. Click System Preferences in the Dock.

3. Click Network. The Network preferences appear.

4. In the list of network interfaces, click your modem.

Figure 13.1
This dialog appears whenever you connect a modem that you haven't yet configured.

5. Use the Telephone Number text box to type your ISP's dial-up phone number.

6. Use the Account Name and Password text boxes to enter your dial-up account's logon data.

7. If you want to control the modem from the menu bar, activate the Show Modem Status in Menu Bar check box.

8. Click Apply to configure the modem. Figure 13.2 shows a configured modem ready for action.

Figure 13.2
Click your modem in the Network preferences and then configure your dial-up account data.

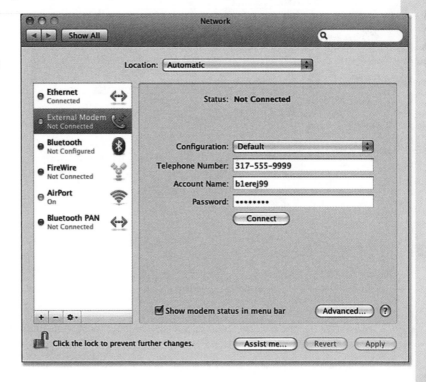

Making the Dial-Up Connection

With your dial-up account configured on your Mac, you have two ways to initiate the connection:

- In the Network preferences pane, click your modem and then click Connect.

- If you have the modem status icon in the menu bar, click the icon and then click Connect *Modem*, where *Modem* is the name of your modem interface (such as External Modem).

Your Mac makes the connection through your modem and then changes the modem status to Connected, which you see in the Network preferences and in the modem status icon in the menu bar, which also shows the total connection time as shown in Figure 13.3.

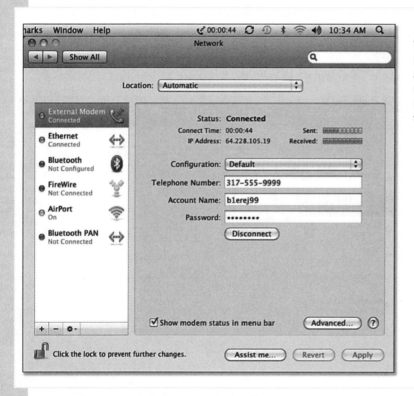

Figure 13.3
When your Mac is connected to a dial-up Internet account, you see the connection status in the Network preferences and in the modem status icon.

When you're done with the Internet, you should disconnect immediately to avoid running up your connection time:

- In the Network preferences pane, click your modem and then click Disconnect.

- If you have the modem status icon in the menu bar, click the icon and then click Disconnect *Modem*, where *Modem* is the name of your modem interface.

Configuring Your Mac for Broadband Internet Access

Providing the details of configuring every type of broadband Internet account is beyond the scope of this chapter, but some examples of configuring cable and DSL connections should enable you to configure your particular account.

You can configure multiple sets of Internet configurations for your machine so that you can switch between them easily. And, you can have multiple accounts configured and active on a machine at the same time (they will be used according to the priority you determine). This is useful when you use your Mac in different locations—for example, with a MacBook that you use at a work location and at home or while traveling. Another case in which this is useful is if you have several ways of connecting from the same location, such as via a cable modem or dial-up account. You use the Location Manager to manage the Internet configurations on your machine. If you envision needing to do this, you should set up a location before configuring it. If you will need only one set of configurations, you don't need to use the Location Manager. Also, a single location can include multiple configurations, such as Ethernet and wireless connections to a network connected to a cable modem.

➡ *To learn how to configure and use locations, **see** "Configuring and Using Locations," p. 557.*

The Internet accounts you configure on your Mac will be available to all users who have accounts on your machine.

Connecting Your Mac to the Broadband Modem

➡ *To learn how to install and use a wired hub to share an Internet account, **see** Chapter 17, "Wired Networking with Mac OS X," p. 361.*

➡ *To learn how to install and use an AirPort base station as a hub, **see** Chapter 18, "Wireless Networking with Mac OS X," p. 385.*

➡ *To learn how to protect your Mac from Internet attacks, **see** "Defending Your Mac from Internet Attacks," p. 720*

Configuring an Internet account for Ethernet connection is usu-

 note

When you install Mac OS X, the Internet Setup Assistant leads you through the configuration of your Internet account. You can launch the Internet Setup Assistant at other times to walk you through the configuration process by clicking the Assist Me button on the Network pane of the System Preferences application.

If you use a provider that includes configuration software with your account, such as EarthLink, you can configure your account by using that software. In this section, you learn how to configure your account manually.

 caution

Here's another caution about any specific access software a provider might give you to access the Internet. This software tends to be more problematic than it is worth, especially if it is web-based. When you get an account and such software is provided, ask the provider whether it is required.

 caution

As soon as you connect your Mac to the Internet with an always-on connection, especially one with a fixed IP address, your Mac will be subject to attacks from hackers. You shouldn't directly connect a Mac to the Internet unless you have some type of firewall protection in place; fortunately, Mac OS X includes a built-in firewall.

However, best practice is to install a hub between your Mac and the modem. Most hubs offer protection and also enable you to share an Internet account.

ally simple. The three main options you use for an Ethernet-based Internet account are Manual IP Settings, DHCP Server, and PPPoE. DHCP Server is the most likely option you will use. However, your ISP will tell you which option is appropriate for your connection.

Connect your Mac's Ethernet port to the broadband modem's Ethernet port or to the hub to which the broadband modem is connected. Then, configure the OS to use that connection.

 note

Some broadband modems connect to a USB port rather than an Ethernet port, but configuring the account on your Mac works in the same way.

Configuring TCP/IP Using a DHCP Server

If your provider provides access through a DHCP server, configuring your account is straightforward.

To configure your account, do the following:

1. Open the Network pane of the System Preferences application.

2. From the Services list on the left side of the pane, select Ethernet.

3. Select Using DHCP from the Configure menu.

4. If you have a DHCP Client ID (your ISP will tell you if this is the case), click the Advanced button and select the TCP/IP tab. You can then enter it in the DHCP Client ID field. (If you are using a DHCP server on a local network, you can probably leave this field empty. In most cases, you can leave this field empty even when you are using an ISP to gain Internet access.) Click OK to return to the Services list and the configuration of the Ethernet service.

note

Many local area networks provide Internet access by installing a DHCP server on the network and connecting that server to the Internet (often with a T-1 line). In such cases, you can configure your Mac to use that DHCP server to connect to the Internet just as you can when you deal directly with an ISP for an account.

5. If you have DNS and search domain information, enter it in the appropriate fields (these are optional when you use a DHCP server and in most cases, you will leave these fields empty). You might see information in these fields already; Mac OS X will try to obtain the information from your ISP automatically.

6. If you are on a network that uses a proxy server, click the Advanced button, select the Proxies tab, and configure the proxies for your network.

➡ *For more information about proxy servers, **see** "Understanding and Configuring Proxy Servers," p. 275.*

7. Click Apply to save your changes.

8. Open an Internet application, such as a web browser. If you can access Internet resources, your configuration is complete.

If you are unable to access Internet resources after configuring your account with a DHCP server, see "Troubleshooting the Connection," later in this chapter.

Configuring Static TCP/IP Settings

If your provider supplies a static or manual address for you, use the following steps to configure it:

1. Open the Network pane of the System Preferences application.

2. From the Services list, select Ethernet.

3. Select Manually from the Configure pop-up menu.

4. Enter the IP Address, Subnet Mask, Router, DNS, and Search Domains information your ISP provided in the appropriate fields.

6. Click Apply to save your changes.

7. Open an Internet application, such as a web browser. If you can access Internet resources, your configuration is complete.

If you are unable to access Internet resources after configuring your account manually, see "Troubleshooting the Connection," later in this chapter.

Understanding and Configuring Proxy Servers

A *proxy server* is a server that sits between end-user computers on a network and the Internet. All Internet traffic of a specific type (such as HTTP for web pages) passes through a specific proxy server. There can be separate proxy servers for each type of service (such as HTTP, FTP, and so on), or a network can use a single proxy server for all Internet services.

When a machine on the network requests a resource (such as a web page), the proxy server downloads the resource and serves it to the machine as if the resources originated from the proxy server itself (although the user doesn't notice that the page is being served by the proxy server instead of the server hosting the requested page).

Proxy servers serve two main purposes:

- **They can improve speed in some cases**—Because the Internet resources are downloaded to the proxy server and then served to users on the local network, after the first access, subsequent accesses to that resource are much faster. This is true because the resource must be downloaded from the Internet to the proxy server only once; from there, it can be served to users on the local network rather than downloading it from the Internet each time.

- **They can be used to filter requests**—Because all information from the Internet flows through a proxy server, that server can be set to block access to specific Internet resources.

 note

You can also use a static IP address with the router being assigned dynamically. If this is the case for you, select Using DHCP with Manual Address instead of Manually. The rest of the steps are the same, except you don't configure the router because that is done for you by the DHCP router.

 note

IPv4 is the current Internet protocol standard in almost situations. However, IPv6 is a newer standard that is being used in some research institutions. If you need to configure a connection based on IPv6, you can do so by clicking the Advanced button and using the Configure IPv6 section of the resulting sheet to configure the service. In most cases, the automatic settings should work fine, but you can also enter manual settings if you need to.

If you are on a network that uses proxy servers, you use the Proxies tab of the Advanced section for the Network pane of the System Preferences application to configure them. You configure a proxy for a specific service by activating the check box for that service and entering the proxy address and port in the appropriate fields. Typically, you obtain the proxy server information you need from your network administrator.

Configuring a PPPoE Account

Configuring a PPPoE account is more complicated than the other Ethernet options, but it still doesn't take more than a few minutes:

1. Open the Network pane of the System Preferences application.

2. From the Services list, select Ethernet.

3. Use the Configure pop-up menu to select Create PPPoE Service. You are prompted to provide a name for the service.

4. Enter a name and click Done.

5. The new service you just created and named is now shown on the Services list and you can use the right side of the Network pane to configure the service (see Figure 13.4).

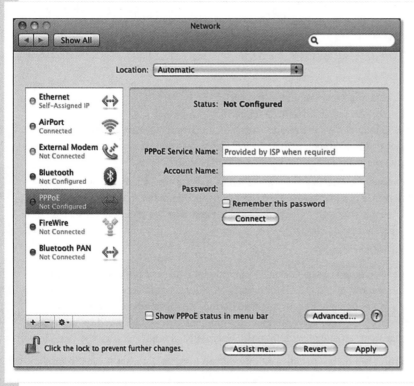

Figure 13.4
Create a new service to configure a PPP over Ethernet connection.

6. Enter the service name in the PPPoE Service Name field. (This is also optional.)

7. Enter your access account name in the Account Name field.

8. Enter your access password in the Password field; again, this might be different from your email account password. If you leave this field empty, you must enter your password each time you connect.

9. Activate the Remember This Password check box to enable other user accounts to access the account without entering the connection password.

10. Activate the Show PPPoE Status in Menu Bar check box. This puts a menu on the menu bar that you can use to control your PPPoE connection.

11. Click the Advanced button and select the PPP tab to view the Session Options. Use the controls on this sheet to configure your Internet access.

12. In most cases, you should activate the Connect Automatically When Needed check box. This enables your Mac to automatically connect to the Internet when it needs to (such as when you launch an Internet application such as Safari).

13. Use the next four check boxes to control how your Mac monitors your connection:

   ■ **Prompt Every X Minutes to Maintain Connection**—Activate this check box if you want to be prompted when your Mac is connected but is not actively using the connection, and enter the time after which you want to be prompted to maintain the connection.

   ■ **Disconnect If Idle for X Minutes**—Activate this check box if you want your Mac to automatically disconnect after your connection has been idle for a period of time, and enter the idle time in the text box.

   ■ **Disconnect When User Logs Out**—Most users should leave this check box activated so that the connection is broken when the current user logs out of the machine.

   ■ **Disconnect When Switching User Accounts**—Leave this check box activated if you want the connection to be shut down when a different user account becomes active.

14. Click OK to close the PPPoE Options sheet, and then click Apply to save your changes.

You can test your account by opening an Internet application, such as a web browser (assuming you enabled your Mac to connect automatically). If you are able to access Internet resources, your configuration is complete. Or, you can use the application that you use to manually connect and disconnect from your account, which is Internet Connect. Do the following:

1. Open the Network pane of the System Preferences application.

2. Select the PPoE service you created from the Services list. You will see the PPPoE account information you configured earlier.

3. Click the Connect button. You will see the status of the connection in the window. If your connection is successful, you will see the connected message and status information in the lower part of the Internet Connect window.

4. Click Disconnect to shut down the connection.

5. Quit System Preferences.

If you are able to connect successfully, you can use Internet applications, such as your email and web browser. You can monitor and control your connection from the PPPoE status menu on the menu bar.

If you aren't able to connect to the Internet, see "Troubleshooting the Connection," later in this chapter.

Troubleshooting the Connection

The most common cause of problems connecting with an Ethernet account is an incorrect configuration. Still, there can be other problems as well. The following guidelines should help you troubleshoot problems you experience when trying to connect with an Ethernet-based connection:

- If you are using a modem (such as a cable modem), make sure that the modem you are using is powered up and properly connected to your Mac, either directly or through a network. Most modems have power, PC link, and activity lights. If any of these don't indicate the proper status, check your modem installation.

- If your Mac gets its access through a network, power down the modem and hub (such as an AirPort Base Station) and wait for about 20 seconds. Then turn each device back on. Many times, resetting a modem and hub in this way will restore the Internet connection.

- Make sure that the ISP services are currently available. Most broadband connections are very reliable, but they can go down from time to time. Usually, ISPs provide a status hotline you can call to see whether problems with service have been reported in your area. If there are problems, you will have to wait for the provider to correct them before you will be able to connect (in these situations, it is nice to have a backup account, such as a dial-up account).

- If your Mac gets its access through a network, remove the Mac from the network, connect it directly to the modem, and reconfigure the Mac as needed to access the account directly (it's a good idea to save a location with this configuration for troubleshooting purposes). Don't do this unless the Mac is protected with the Mac OS X firewall as it may get hacked if the connection works. If the connection works, you know the problem is with the network, in which case, you'll need to troubleshoot the network. If the connection doesn't work, you know the issue is with the modem, the configuration, or the connection itself.

- Work through the configuration steps for your account again, being especially careful to activate all the configuration information you enter.

- If you are using a DHCP server, see whether you can obtain static settings for your account. Sometimes, you will be able to connect to an account with static settings when the automatic

(DHCP) settings fail. If you use DHCP, select the Ethernet service in the Network preferences and then check the IP address that appears. If you see one that starts with 169, that means your Mac is not obtaining an IP address from the provider and so won't be able to connect to the Internet. You must either figure out why it isn't able to obtain an IP address from your ISP, or use a manual IP address.

- If you use a DHCP service and something changes, your Mac's IP address can become invalid. When this happens, you lose your Internet connection. You can force the system to get a new address by clicking the Advanced button for the service, opening the TCP/IP tab and clicking the Renew DHCP Lease button. This attempts to obtain a new IP address and might solve the problem.

- If you are still unable to connect, contact the service provider or network administrator from whom you obtain your service. Confirm that you are using the correct installation information for your account. If you are, ask for assistance in troubleshooting the connection from the provider's end.

Getting Help

Be aware that you might get flak from your ISP's technical support when you tell them you are using a Mac. Because the Mac has a smaller number of users, the tech support person to whom you talk will probably have less experience with Macs than with Windows machines. Also, many technical support people, such as those with cable companies, are overloaded and will try to get you off the line as soon as possible. If your problem doesn't fit into a checklist, they might want to stop before your problem is solved. Try to stay positive; you might have to be assertive (not aggressive) to get the support you need. Sometimes, it is better to explore the support area of a provider's website (which, of course, assumes that you can connect in some fashion, perhaps from another computer) before calling for help.

Managing Multiple Internet Accounts

If the Internet is vital to you, such as for business purposes, you might have more than one Internet account you access in different ways. For example, you might use a cable modem as your primary access and maintain a dial-up account as a backup. You can maintain multiple Internet accounts on a single Mac.

You can manage the network ports and associated Internet accounts on your machine through the Services list on the Network pane of the System Preferences application.

Three network ports are shown by default. Active ports are indicated by a green circle next to the service name and will say Connected, while inactive ports have a red circle and will say Not Connected. The order in which the ports are listed determines which port is tried first when a connection is needed. Each of these ports could be configured with a different Internet connection so that if the connection on one port is not available, the connections on the other ports will be used.

To configure multiple accounts, do the following:

1. Open the Network pane of the System Preferences application.

2. Select the port you want to be your primary connection method on the Services list.

3. Configure that port for the related account (see the previous sections in this chapter for details). For example, configure your machine to use an Ethernet network to connect to the Internet.

4. Apply your changes to save the configuration of the port.

5. Make sure the connection you configured is turned on (it has a green circle) and that it is at the top of the Services list. If it is not the first connection listed, use the Action menu at the bottom of the Services list and select Set Service Order. A sheet will appear with the list of connection types (see Figure 13.5). Drag the connection you just configured to the top of the list, and change the order of the other services as well. Click OK to save your changes and return to the Network pane of the System Preferences application.

Figure 13.5
Use the Service Order list to specify the order in which network connections should be established.

6. From the Services list, select the port you want to be the second connection option, such as AirPort.

7. Configure the Internet connection for that port.

8. Make sure that the port is turned on; it should appear second in the Services.

9. Continue configuring the Internet connections on each port that you want to be active. Use the Set Services Order option of the Action menu to arrange the ports on the list in the order in which you want them to be used.

10. Click Apply and then quit the System Preferences application.

When your machine needs to connect to the Internet, it tries the ports and associated Internet accounts you specified in the order in which they are listed from top to bottom. Following are some other points about managing multiple connections:

- **You can have more than one configuration of the same port.** To create a new instance of a port, click the New button at the bottom of the Services list. Name the port and then select the type of port it is (Ethernet, AirPort, and so on). Click OK and the new port appears on the list. You can configure it in the same way as the default ports.

- **You can duplicate a port configuration.** This can be useful when you are configuring more than one port of the same type. Select the connection you want to duplicate in the Service list and click on the Action menu to select Duplicate Service. Provide a new name and click Duplicate. Your new connection will be listed in the Service list and ready for you to configure.

- **You can edit a port's name by selecting Rename Service on that connection's Action menu.**

 tip

Inactive ports will appear on the Services list. You can permanently delete a port by using the Delete button at the bottom of the Services list. If you find you need that port again, just use the Add button at the bottom of the Services list to create it again.

You can also maintain multiple sets of network and Internet configurations that you create and maintain through the Location Manager. For example, if you use a MacBook, you might have a configuration when you use the machine from home, another when you use it from work, and so on.

➡ *To learn how to configure and use locations,* ***see*** *"Configuring and Using Locations,"* ***p. 557****.*

14

SURFING THE WEB

Configuring Safari Preferences

The default web browser for Mac OS X is the excellent Safari application, one of the best browsers around, which may be why most Mac users stick with Safari rather than switching to a third-party browser such as Firefox. This chapter shows you how to browse the Web using Safari, but let's first take a tour of Safari's most useful preferences so that you can get it set up the way you want before heading out on the Web. Later sections in this chapter cover Safari's preferences for bookmarks, RSS feeds, tabs, and the AutoFill feature.

To get started, select Safari, Preferences (or press ⌘-) to open Safari's preferences dialog box.

Configuring Safari's General Preferences

In the Safari preferences dialog box, click the General button to open the General pane (see Figure 14.1). The general preferences are explained in the following list:

- **Default Web Browser**—Use this pop-up menu to choose your default web browser, which is the browser Mac OS X will use to view web pages and to open web links. Initially, Safari is the option selected on the pop-up menu. However, you can choose Select and then pick another browser that you've installed on your Mac. This sets your browser preference for all areas of the OS.

- **New Windows Open With**—Use this pop-up menu to choose what happens when you open a new Safari window. The options are Home Page, Empty Page, Same Page, or Bookmarks. In most cases, Empty Page is the best choice because it doesn't cause Safari to download a page that you probably don't want to view anyway. However, if you frequently use bookmarks to move to a new page, that can be a useful option as well.

- **New Tabs Open With**—Use this pop-up menu to configure what Safari loads into a new tab: Top Sites, the Home Page; an Empty Page; the Same Page (that is, the page that's in the current tab); or your Safari Bookmarks.

- **Home Page**—Type a URL in this text box to set it as your home page. Alternatively, you can move to the page you want to be your home page, open the General pane, and click Set to Current Page. The home page is displayed when you use the Home button or if you have it set to be displayed when you open a new Safari window or a new tab. If you leave the field blank, moving to the home page opens a new empty page.

- **Remove History Items**—Use this menu to choose when Safari deletes items from your history list, which is a log of the pages you've visited. The options range from one day to one year or Manually (which means you want to delete history items yourself).

- **Save Downloaded Files To**—Use this pop-up menu to select the folder where you want Safari to save the files that you download. Mac OS X gives each user account a Downloads folder, and it's a good idea to store your downloads there so you always know where to find them.

> **note**
>
> Setting a file download location, similar to choosing a default web browser, affects the OS—not just Safari. For example, if you use a download tool that uses your download location preference, such as Mail, that application uses the preference you set within Safari.

- **Remove Download List Items**—Use this pop-up menu to choose when items are removed from the Downloads window (you'll learn about that later).

- **Open "Safe" Files After Downloading**—Activate this check box (it is activated by default) to allow Safari to automatically open downloaded files that can't harm your Mac, such as images, movies, text file, sound files, and other content files. For all other files, particularly files that might cause damage to your system, such as applications, macros, and other suspicious files, you must open them manually after you download them.

- **Open Links from Applications**—You use these radio buttons to determine how Safari handles links in documents such as email messages. If you select the In a New Window radio button, a new Safari window opens and displays the page at which the link points; if you select In a New Tab in the Current Window, instead, the content at which the link points opens within a new tab in the current window.

Figure 14.1
The General pane enables you to configure important Safari behaviors.

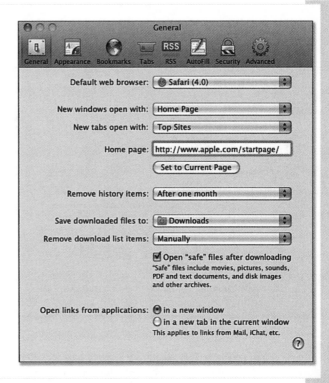

Configuring Safari's Appearance Preferences

Click the Appearance tab in the Safari Preferences dialog box to move to the Appearance pane. Here you can set the standard font, fixed-width font, and default encoding that is used when pages are displayed. (If a page uses a built-in style sheet, your options might be overridden by the style sheet, but most of the time, your preferences will be used.) To select a font, click the related Select button and use the Font panel to configure the font. To choose an encoding method, use the pop-up menu.

If you don't want images to be displayed when a page is opened, deactivate the Display Images When the Page Opens check box. If you use a slow connection, you might want to deactivate this check box so you don't waste time downloading images you aren't interested in.

Configuring Safari's Security Preferences

Safari has a number of good security features, some of which you can configure on the Security pane of the Safari Preferences dialog box (see Figure 14.2).

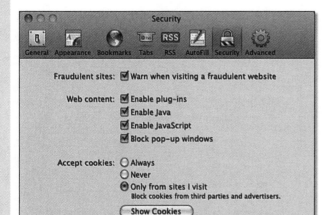

First, leave the Fraudulent Sites check box activated so that Safari will warn you if you surf to a phishing site or some other site that isn't what it claims to be.

The Web Content controls determine whether certain types of content are enabled. These controls include:

- **Enable Plug-Ins**—Determines whether any Safari plug-ins, such as those for QuickTime, Flash, and so on, are enabled. If you disable the plug-ins, content that requires them is not displayed. I recommend you leave this check box activated because most content that requires such plug-ins is safe. And, except for the plug-ins installed by default, you will choose the plug-ins you want to install.

- **Enable Java and Enable JavaScript**—Java and JavaScript are two programming languages that can be used to execute complex operations within the Safari browser. For example, if you use a bank service, it likely uses JavaScript to deliver its functionality. Again, you should typically allow these types of content.

- **Block Pop-Up Windows**—If you have ever been annoyed by the numerous and obnoxious pop-up windows that appear when you visit some websites, you might think that this is the single best feature of Safari. If this option is activated, Safari does not allow a web page to open additional windows. This means that all pop-up windows that point to different URLs are blocked and you never have to see them.

tip

If you block pop-up windows and a site that needs them doesn't work properly, you can enable them again by selecting Safari, Block Pop-Up Windows or by pressing Shift-⌘-K. This toggles the pop-up window setting, so you can also use it to quickly allow pop-ups if you generally prevent them.

Although blocking pop-up windows is mostly a good thing, some pop-up windows actually provide useful information and are necessary to get the most out of a website. If you block them, a site might not work well, or at all.

You use the Cookies radio buttons to determine how Safari deals with cookies it encounters. Typically, the Only from Sites I Visit radio button is the best setting because cookies often provide a useful service for the sites you intentionally visit, such as shopping sites. If you want to block all cookies, click Never. I don't recommend that you use the Always option.

To see the cookies that have been accepted, click the Show Cookies button. A sheet appears that shows you all the cookies that have been downloaded to your Mac (prepare to be astounded at their number!). In addition to the information you see about the cookies, you can select cookies and either click Remove to delete them or click Remove All to delete all the cookies on your Mac. It's not a bad idea to review this list from time to time and delete any cookies you can't recognize (or at least recognize where they came from). If a site needs a cookie to function, it will create it again, although you might lose some of your customized information on that site.

Cookies

On the Web, *cookies* are small text files websites use to track information about you. When you visit a site that uses cookies, the site can check the cookies it previously installed on your machine to serve you or capture more information about you. For example, a cookie can contain areas of interest so you are automatically taken to spots on the site that are more likely to generate a purchase from you.

Most cookies are harmless and some even serve a good purpose, but you do need to be aware that a lot of information about you and what you do on the Web is captured whether you know it or not. If this thought bothers you, select the Never radio button so cookies are never accepted. If you do this, be aware that some sites might not work for you or you might have to spend more time re-entering information, such as a username, each time you visit a site.

If you want Safari to warn you when you send nonsecure information from a secure site, leave the Ask Before Sending a Non-Secure Form from a Secure Website check box activated.

Configuring Safari's Advanced Preferences

To see Safari's Advanced preferences, click the Advanced tab on the Safari Preferences dialog box. The Advanced preferences consist of universal access, style sheet options, and proxy settings.

Use the Universal Access controls to set a minimum font size or to control Tab key behavior.

If you have a style sheet you want Safari to use, you can add it by selecting Other on the Style Sheet pop-up menu and then selecting the sheet you want to install. If you add more than one sheet, you can select that sheet you want to use on the Style Sheet pop-up menu.

 note

Cascading style sheets can be used to determine the formatting for web pages. Many pages use these sheets. If not, a page is presented based on Safari's own interpretation of the HTML and the other code of which the page is composed.

You can use the Proxies button to access the Proxies tab of the Network pane of the System Preferences application.

Browsing the Web with Safari

I'm going to assume that you're comfortable with the basics of using Safari, such as using its buttons, navigating the Web by clicking links and entering URLs in the Address bar, and so on. In this section, you learn about some of Safari's great features that might not be quite so obvious.

Configuring Safari's Window

By default, Safari's window is pretty standard looking. However, using the options on the View menu, you can customize the Safari browser experience to suit your preferences. On that menu, you have the following options:

- **Back/Forward**—The Back and Forward buttons do just what you expect.

- **Top Sites**—This button displays the Top Sites window.

- **Home**—This button takes you back to your home page.

- **New Tab**—This button creates a new tab.

- **History**—This button displays the History list.

- **Bookmarks**—This button displays the Bookmarks window.

- **Add Bookmark**—Use this to show or hide the Add Bookmark button.

- **Bookmarks Bar**—This button toggles the Bookmarks Bar on and off.

- **AutoFill**—If you click the AutoFill button, a form is completed with information from your card in your Address Book (more on this feature later).

- **Zoom**—These buttons enable you to increase or decrease the size of text being displayed on a page (if you have ever squinted while trying to read a page designed for Windows computers, you know why increasing the size of text on a page can be a good thing!).

- **Open in Dashboard**—This button enables you to capture all or part of a web page as a widget on the Dashboard. More on this tool later in this chapter.

- **Mail**—This button creates a new Mail message with the current page title as the subject line, and a link to the page in the message body.

- **Print**—Use this to print the page being displayed.

- **Downloads**—This button displays the Downloads window.

- **Report Bug**—When you click this button, you can send a bug report about Safari to Apple.

- **Address**—This tool can be used to enter or show a URL.

tip

Some of the optional tools are also available as commands on the View menu, such as Reload Page, Make Text Bigger, and so on.

- **Google Search**—The Google Search tool is a great way to search for information, as you will learn in a later section.

Figure 14.3
You can customize the Safari toolbar by dragging items from this sheet and dropping them on the toolbar.

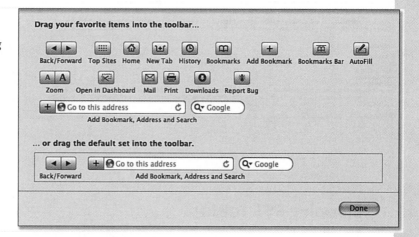

Browsing and Configuring RSS Feeds

Safari supports Rich Site Summary (RSS) web feeds. RSS feeds provide a summary of articles and other information on a web-site so you can more efficiently browse information and then drill down into the information in which you are interested (see Figure 14.4). On an RSS feed page, you see a headline for each element on the page. You can scroll up and down the page to browse the headlines. When you find something interesting, click the headline or the Read More link. You'll move to the arti-cle on a regular web page and can read its information. When you are done, click the SnapBack or RSS button to return to the RSS feed.

note

The articles you move to from some RSS feeds will cause the SnapBack button, RSS button, or both to appear in the Address bar. It doesn't matter which button you use—both will return you to the RSS feed.

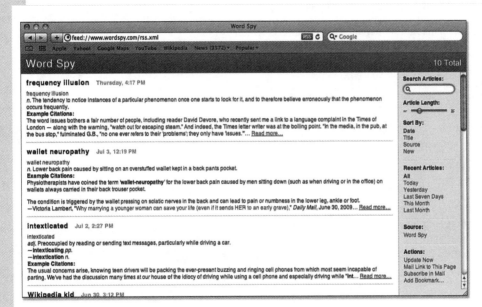

Figure 14.4
A typical RSS
feed page.

Browsing RSS Feeds

In addition to these handy features, there are several other things you need to know about RSS feeds:

- The URL for an RSS feed will start with `feed://` rather than `http://`. When an RSS feed is loaded into your browser, you'll also see the RSS button at the right end of the Address bar.

- When you view a regular website and the RSS button appears in the Address bar, an RSS feed is available for that website. Click the RSS button to view the RSS feed.

- Use the Search Articles tool to search the contents of the feed. If you enter a search term and then create a bookmark, your search will be saved as a bookmark so you can repeat it easily.

- Use the Article Length slider to set the length of the summaries you see on a feed page. With the slider all the way to the right, you see the full entry. If you move the slider all the way to the left, you only see the headline, the first few words of the entry, and the date for each story.

- Use the scope tools to configure the contents of the RSS page. For example, you can sort the articles using the Sort By options. You can choose the timeline for the articles you see with the Recent Articles options, for example, by choosing Today to see only articles that are published on the current day.

- The source of information for an RSS feed is shown in the Source area.

- Any actions available for the feed, such as a link to enable you to email it, are shown in the Actions area.

- Safari includes a number of bookmarked RSS feeds by default. To view these, choose Bookmarks, Show All Bookmarks. Then click the All RSS Feeds collection.

- Safari can automatically check for updates to RSS feeds and add them to the feed page. When new articles appear for a feed, the number of new articles is shown next to the feed's bookmark in the Bookmarks bar.

- You can view all the RSS feeds referenced in a bookmark folder that contains them by selecting Bookmarks, Bookmarks Bar, View All RSS Articles. In the resulting page, you see all the RSS feeds from all bookmarks in that folder (see Figure 14.5).

Figure 14.5
If you choose View All RSS Articles, you see a page containing articles from all the RSS feeds in that folder of bookmarks.

➡ *To learn how to read RSS feeds in Mail,* **see** *"Working with RSS Feeds," p. 345.*

Configuring Safari's RSS Preferences

There are many aspects of working with RSS feeds that you can configure using the RSS tab of the Safari Preferences dialog box (see Figure 14.6):

- Set the default RSS reader on the Default RSS Reader pop-up menu. If you want to use something other than Safari or Mail, choose Select and then navigate to and choose the application you want to use to read RSS feeds.

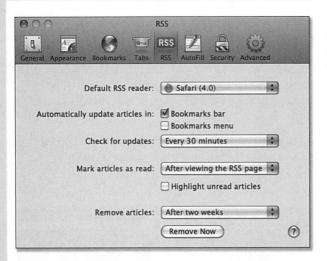

Figure 14.6
Use the RSS pane of the Safari Preferences dialog box to customize the way RSS feeds work.

- Use the Bookmarks Bar and Bookmarks Menu check boxes to tell Safari if you want the RSS feeds in these areas to be updated automatically. If you activate at least one of these, use the Check for Updates pop-up menu to set how frequently Safari updates the activated items. The options are Every 30 Minutes, Every Day, Every Hour, and Never (select Never if you don't want articles to ever be automatically downloaded to your Mac).

- If you want new articles highlighted with a color, activate the Highlight New Articles check box.

- If you want RSS articles automatically removed after a specific amount of time, choose the time on the Remove Articles pop-up menu. The times available range from after one day to never.

- To remove all articles, click the Remove Now button. If you click Remove Now in the resulting prompt, all RSS articles that have been downloaded to your Mac will be deleted.

Searching with Safari

Of course, you can use Safari to access the many web search engines available, such as Yahoo, Lycos, and so on. You do this by visiting that search engine's site.

However, you can access one of the best search engines, Google, directly from the Safari Address bar. This enables some great features, most notably the SnapBack button.

To search the Web using the built-in Google search tool, do the following:

 note

If you don't see the Google Search tool, make sure the Address bar is displayed and that the Google search tool has been added to the Address Bar (it is by default).

1. Type your search text in the Search tool and press Return. You jump to Google and the results of your search are displayed (see Figure 14.7).

2. Use a link on the results page to move to a page that looks promising (see Figure 14.8).

Figure 14.7
Safari's built-in search tool enables you to quickly search on Google.

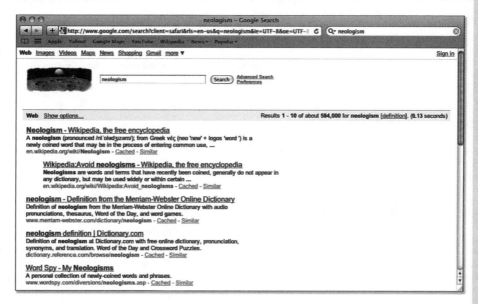

Figure 14.8
The SnapBack button enables you to return to the Google search results page.

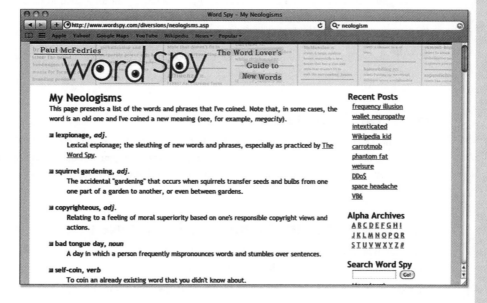

3. To return to the results page so you can try other links, click the SnapBack button; select History, Search Results SnapBack; or press Option-⌘-S.

Performing a Google search from within Safari is fast and easy. Here are few tips:

- To repeat a previous search, click the magnifying glass icon in the search tool; then on the pop-up menu, select the search you want to repeat.

- To clear the searches you have performed, click the magnifying glass icon in the search tool; then on the pop-up menu, select Clear Recent Searches.

- To clear the current search (when the Google page is being displayed), click the x button inside the search field.

Using Safari SnapBack

Using the SnapBack button when you search with the Google search tool is great, but you can also use this feature when you are browsing. Safari marks the first page you visit on any site as the SnapBack page. As you move to other pages on the site, you can return to the SnapBack page by clicking the SnapBack button shown at the end of the URL of the page you are currently viewing. You then move back to the SnapBack page for that site.

Here are two more SnapBack tips:

- You can mark a page to be the SnapBack page for a site by either selecting History, Mark Page for SnapBack or pressing Option-⌘-K. Whenever you click the SnapBack button, you return to this page. (If you don't set a SnapBack page, you return to the first page on the site.)

- You can also return to the SnapBack page by selecting History, Search Results SnapBack or pressing Option-⌘-S.

Using Safari Bookmarks

Like all other browsers, Safari enables you to bookmark web pages so you can easily return to them. And, also similar to other browsers, Safari provides tools you can use to organize your bookmarks. However, Safari's bookmark tools are more refined and powerful than most of the browsers I've used.

Configuring Safari Bookmarks Preferences

Open the Bookmarks pane of the Safari Preferences dialog box to configure your bookmark preferences. On this pane, you have the following options:

- **Bookmarks Bar**—The three Include check boxes determine whether Top Sites, Address Book and Bonjour sites are accessible from the Bookmarks bar.

  If you make your Address Book available from the Bookmarks bar, you can access any websites associated with cards in your Address Book by selecting the site you want to visit on the

Address Book menu. This is a very cool way to quickly access the website for anyone or any company in your Address Book.

Similarly, you can make all the Bonjour computers that provide services Safari can access available via the Bonjour menu. This enables you to quickly move to web, FTP, or other resources on your local network.

- **Bookmarks Menu**—This area enables you to add your Address Book and Bonjour sites to the Bookmarks menu. Additionally, you can include all the Bookmarks bar's bookmarks on the Bookmarks menu by activating the Include Bookmarks Bar check box.

- **Collections**—Safari uses the term *collections* for groups of bookmarks. You can use collections to organize bookmarks; a number of collections are included by default. You use the Bookmarks window to work with these (this is covered later in this section).

- **Synchronize**—If you use machines in different locations, you might find yourself adding bookmarks on one machine and not being able to use those bookmarks when you are working on another machine. If you have a MobileMe account, you can synchronize your bookmarks across many machines so they all have the same set. To do this, activate the Synchronize Bookmarks with Other Computers Using MobileMe check box and click the MobileMe button. The MobileMe pane of the System Preferences application opens and you can use the Sync tab to configure synchronization.

  ➡ *To learn how to configure MobileMe synchronization,* ***see*** *"Using MobileMe to Synchronize Important Information on Multiple Macs," **p. 435**.*

Accessing Safari Bookmarks

You can use bookmarks in the following ways:

- Click a bookmark on the Bookmarks bar.

- Select a bookmark on the Bookmarks menu.

- Press ⌘-1 to move to the first bookmark on the Bookmarks bar (not counting menu items on the bar), ⌘-2 to move to the second one, and so on up to ⌘-9 to move to the ninth one listed on the Bookmarks bar. This only works for bookmarks, not for folders. If an item is a folder, you must select it using the mouse.

- Open the Bookmarks window and double-click a bookmark.

- Open the Address Book or Bonjour menu on the Bookmarks bar and select a site to visit.

- Open a bookmark's contextual menu and select either Open, Open in New Window or Open in New Tab.

Setting Safari Bookmarks

You can bookmark web pages with the following steps:

1. Move to the page you want to bookmark.

2. Select Bookmarks, Add Bookmark or press ⌘-D. The Add Bookmark sheet opens.

3. Edit the name of the bookmark. You can use the default name, change it, or replace it with one of your choosing.

4. On the pop-up menu, select the location in which you want the bookmark to be stored. You can select Bookmarks Bar to add the bookmark to the Bookmarks bar, any folder to place the bookmark in that folder, or Bookmarks Menu to place the bookmark on the Bookmarks menu.

5. Click Add or press Return. The bookmark will be added in the location you selected.

 tip

You can add a bookmark to the Bookmarks bar by dragging across the URL in the Address bar and dropping it on the Bookmarks bar. In the resulting name sheet, edit the name of the bookmark and click OK. The bookmark will be added to the Bookmarks bar so you can access it from there.

Organizing Safari Bookmarks

Use Safari's Bookmark tools to organize your bookmarks. You can determine the location of bookmarks, place them in folders to create hierarchical bookmark menus, rename them, and so on. To do these tasks, open the Bookmarks window by clicking the Bookmarks button at the left end of the Bookmarks bar, by selecting Bookmarks, Show All Bookmarks, or by pressing Option-⌘-B. The Bookmarks window opens (see Figure 14.9).

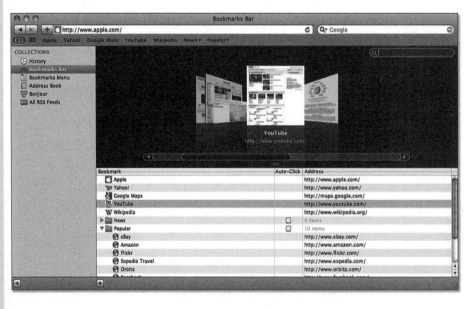

Figure 14.9
The Bookmarks window enables you to organize your bookmarks.

In the left pane of the window is the list of collections (groups or folders of bookmarks). At the top of the list is the History collection, which contains a list of sites you have visited, followed by the Bookmarks Bar and Bookmarks Menu collections that contain the bookmarks in those areas. Under those are the Address Book and Bonjour collections. At the bottom is the All RSS Feeds collection that contains all your RSS feeds. If you create your own bookmark folders, they get added on to the bottom of this list.

To view the contents of a collection, select it. The bookmarks it contains are shown in the right pane. For each bookmark, its name and address will be shown. If an item in the collection is a folder, you will see the folder along with its expansion triangle; click this to expand the folder's contents.

Organizing bookmarks is straightforward:

- Move bookmarks from one collection to another by dragging them onto the collection in which you want to place them. For example, to move a bookmark from the Bookmarks bar to the Bookmarks menu, drag it from the Bookmarks Bar collection to the Bookmarks Menu collection.

- Create new collections by clicking the New Collection button (the +) at the bottom of the Collections pane.

- Create a new folder in a collection by clicking the New Folder button (the "+") at the bottom of the Bookmarks pane.

- Rename a collection, folder, or bookmark by selecting it, opening the contextual menu, and selecting Edit Name.

- Change the URL for a bookmark by selecting it, opening the contextual menu, and selecting Edit Address.

- Move to a URL by double-clicking it or opening its contextual menu and choosing Open, Open in New Window, or Open in New Tab at the end of this sentence.

- Add a folder to the Bookmarks Bar or Bookmarks Menu collections by selecting Add Bookmark Folder from the Bookmarks menu. Then place bookmarks in the folder you created. When you select the folder in either location, a pop-up menu appears to enable you to quickly select any bookmarks in that folder.

- If you activate the Auto-Click check box for a folder, all the bookmarks in that folder will open, with each bookmark appearing in a separate tab, when you click the folder's button on the Bookmarks bar or choose it on a menu.

- Search your bookmarks using the Search tool at the top of the Bookmarks pane. Using the Magnifying Glass pop-up menu, you can choose to search in the selected collection or in all collections. After you've searched, you can scope the results by clicking the button with the name of the collection you are searching or All to show the bookmarks in all collections.

 tip

Put the bookmarks you use most often on the Bookmarks bar or Bookmarks menu because you can get to them most quickly there (if you have so many that they become cluttered, use folders to keep them organized). In the next section, you learn a technique that enables you to open an entire folder of bookmarks with a single click.

■ Delete a collection, folder, or bookmark by selecting it and pressing Delete or by opening its contextual menu and choosing Delete. If you delete a folder or collection, you will also delete any bookmarks contained in those items.

Using Safari Tabs

If you have spent any time on the Web, you have no doubt seen the benefits of having many web browser windows open at the same time. Of course, you can do this with Safari by selecting File, New Window or pressing ⌘-N. If you have done this, you also know that after opening more than a couple of windows, moving back to specific windows can be cumbersome. That is where Safari's Tabs feature comes in. You can open many pages within the same window; each web page appears as a tab. You then select the tab to view that page.

Configuring Tabs

First, configure the Tab feature by opening the Tabs pane of the Safari preferences dialog box (see Figure 14.10).

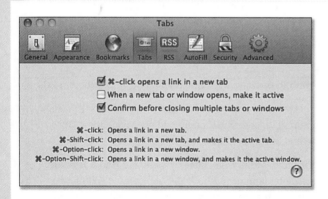

Figure 14.10
Configure tabs to open many windows on the Web in a single Safari window.

To configure tabbed browsing, follow these steps:

1. To open a new tab when you ⌘-click a link, activate the ⌘-click Opens a Link in a New Tab check box. As you come across links on pages, you can open the link in a new tab by holding down the ⌘ key when you click the link.

2. If you want new tabs to be selected, so the page on the tab is displayed, as soon as they are created, activate the When a New Tab or Window Opens, Make It Active check box.

 tip

The previously mentioned preference affects what the tab keyboard shortcuts do. If you don't enable this preference, you have to physically select a tab after you create it to view it. I have assumed that this preference is enabled for the rest of this section.

3. If you want to confirm when you close multiple pages at the same time, activate the Confirm Before Closing Multiple Tabs or Windows check box. If this isn't activated, you can close multiple pages without being prompted to confirm that action.

Using Cool Safari Tab Tricks

After you have enabled tabs, the Safari window contains a tab for each web page you have opened. To open a new tab, select File, New Tab, or press ⌘-T. Safari displays the Top Sites page by default, as shown in Figure 14.11.

tip

Notice the keyboard shortcuts at the bottom of the Tabs pane. These are important tips that help you work with tabs effectively. If you can't remember them, they are listed in the next section and in Table 14.1 at the end of this chapter. The keyboard shortcuts you see depend on the check boxes that are activated. For example, if you unactivate the first check box, you see a different set of actions for the keyboard shortcuts than you do with it activated.

Figure 14.11
Safari 4 displays the Top Sites page when you open a new tab.

Following is a list of tab tricks:

- Click a tab to view its web page. The tab currently being displayed is highlighted.

- To close a page, click the x button in its tab. The tab and page close.

- To open a page in a new tab and move to it, ⌘-click a link or bookmark.

- To open a new tab without viewing it, ⌘-Shift-click a link or bookmark.

- To open a link or a bookmark in a new window and view it, ⌘-Option-click it.

- To open a link or a bookmark in a new window but move the new window to the background, ⌘-Option-Shift-click it.

- To move into the next tab, choose Window, Select Next Tab or press Shift-⌘-].

- To move into the previous tab, choose Window, Select Next Tab or press Shift-⌘-[.

Okay, I have saved the coolest thing about Safari for this moment: Safari enables you to open as many pages as you want by clicking a single bookmark for a collection. Each page included in the group opens in a new tab. If you frequently open the same set of pages, you can click a single bookmark to open them all at the same time.

First, create the group of bookmarks you want to open:

1. Open the Bookmark window and create a folder in the Bookmarks Bar collection.

2. Activate the Auto-Click check box for the folder you created.

3. Place bookmarks for all the sites you want to open simultaneously in the folder you created in step 1.

Close the Bookmarks window and click the button on the Bookmarks bar for the folder you created in the previous steps. Every page opens in its own tab. Working with a set of web pages has never been so easy.

 *To learn how to use the Automator, **see** Chapter 25, "Making Your Mac Do the Work for You with the Automator," p. 515.*

 note

The previous four actions are reversed if you deactivate the When a New Tab or Window Opens, Make It Active preference. For example, you would ⌘-Shift-click a link or bookmark to open it in a tab and view it.

 tip

If you don't enable Auto-Click for a folder of bookmarks, you can open all the bookmarks it contains in tabs by opening its menu on the Bookmarks bar and choosing the Open in Tabs command. Also, you can open individual bookmarks within an Auto-Click collection by opening the collections menu on the Bookmarks bar and choosing the page you want to open.

tip

To make moving bookmarks into folders within collections easier, open a second Safari window and view the Bookmarks window. You can drag bookmarks from the first window onto the second to move them among collections.

 tip

You can use Automator to create an application that will open websites for you. You can add this application to your Login Items so they automatically open for you each time you log in.

Using Safari AutoFill

If you access services on the Web, such as travel planning, shopping, banking, and so on, you no doubt have a lot of experience filling out the same information time and time again. Completing a web form is fun the first time, but after completing your address, phone number, username, and password a few dozen times, it gets old. This is where Safari's AutoFill feature comes in. It enables you to complete various kinds of information automatically or at the click of the AutoFill button.

Using AutoFill, Safari can enter the following types of information for you:

- **Your Address Book information**—Safari can access the information stored on your card in your Address Book. This can include your address, phone number, website, and so on.

  ➡ *To learn how to configure the information on your card in your Address Book,* ***see*** *"Editing Your Own Address Card,"* ***p. 221.***

- **Usernames and passwords**—Safari can capture your username and password at many websites. When you return to those sites, your username and password are entered for you automatically.

- **Information entered on various websites**—As you provide information in other types of websites, Safari can gather this data and remember it so that the next time you visit a site, you can complete any information by clicking the AutoFill button.

Configuring AutoFill

First, you need to tell Safari which AutoFill features you want to use by configuring your AutoFill preferences:

1. Press ⌘-, to open the Preferences dialog box.

2. Click the AutoFill tab to open the AutoFill pane (see Figure 14.12).

Figure 14.12
Using Safari's AutoFill feature saves you a lot of typing.

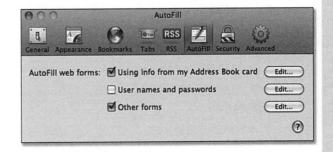

3. If you want Safari to be able to enter the information from your Address Book card, activate the Using Info from My Address Book Card check box.

4. If you want Safari to capture usernames and passwords at various websites you use, activate the User Names and Passwords check box.

5. If you want Safari to capture other types of information you enter on the Web, activate the Other Forms check box.

6. Close the Preferences dialog box.

Using AutoFill

Using AutoFill is straightforward.

To enter your personal information from your Address Book card, use the following steps:

1. Move to a web page that requires your personal information, such as name, address, and so on.

2. Click the AutoFill button on the Address Bar; select Edit, AutoFill Form; or press Shift-⌘-A. Safari will transfer the information from your card in your Address Book and place it in the appropriate fields on the web form.

3. Review the information that was entered to ensure that it is correct. AutoFill isn't perfect and sometimes web forms use slightly different terms for data.

To use the username and password feature, do the following steps:

1. Move to a website that requires a username and password.

2. Enter your username and password on the page.

3. Click Login. You will be prompted about whether you want Safari to capture the username and password for this site.

4. In the prompt, make one of the following choices:

   ▪ Click Yes if you want the information to be added to AutoFill.

   ▪ Click Not Now if you don't want the information to be captured at this time but want to be prompted the next time you access the site.

   ▪ Click Never for This Website if you don't want the information captured and never want to be prompted again.

If you click Yes, the next time you visit the website, your username and password will be filled in automatically. All you have to do to log in to the site is click the Login button or link.

 tip

If you click any of the Edit buttons, you can edit the AutoFill information for that area. For example, if you click the Edit button for the Address Book, the Address Book application will open and you will see your Address Book card in the edit mode so you can make changes to it. If you click Edit for user names and password, a sheet appears on which you see the websites for which Safari has remembered this information. You can remove individual sites by selecting them and clicking Remove.

 tip

If you find AutoFill consistently not entering specific information, add that information to your card in your Address Book.

 caution

The username and password feature is convenient, but you shouldn't use it unless you are the only one who uses your Mac OS X user account or the people who share your Mac OS X user account are very trustworthy. Because the usernames and passwords for your accounts are entered automatically, anyone who uses your Mac OS X user account and moves to the related websites can log in to your account on that website.

If you decide you don't want to provide automatic access to a specific website, you can remove that site's username and password:

1. Open the AutoFill pane of the Safari Preferences dialog box.

2. Click the Edit button next to the text User Names and Passwords. A sheet appears that lists each website and username you have captured in Safari.

3. Select the website you want to remove.

4. Click Remove. Continue removing websites until you have removed all the sites you no longer need.

5. Click Done and close the Preferences dialog box.

Using the AutoFill feature for other kinds of forms is similar to the first two. When you enable the Other Forms feature and enter information in websites, that information is captured. When you return to those sites in the future, you can enter the information again by clicking the AutoFill button; selecting Edit, AutoFill Form; or pressing Shift-⌘-A. You can edit the list of websites for which information is remembered by clicking the Edit button next to the Other Forms check box on the AutoFill pane of the Safari Preferences dialog box.

 tip

Click Remove All to delete all the websites for which you have captured usernames and passwords.

 note

If you don't turn off the username and password feature by deactivating the User Names and Passwords check box, you will be prompted by AutoFill the next time you visit any websites you deleted from the list.

Creating Web Widgets

Mac OS X's Dashboard feature is a great way to quickly get to specific information and tools. You can use Safari to add websites or parts of websites as widgets on your Dashboard so you can work with your custom web widgets just like other widgets on your Dashboard.

To create a web widget, do the following steps:

1. Move to the webpage you want to capture.

2. Select File, Open in Dashboard. The Dashboard capture bar appears along with the selection box that jumps to an element of the page that can be captured as a unit. The rest of the page is darkened to show it is not part of the capture (see Figure 14.13).

3. If the selected portion of the page is not the part you want, move the mouse pointer around the page. As you do, other sections of the page are highlighted.

    The capture tool is designed to capture specific document object model (DOM) elements of a page. As you move the pointer, the next closest DOM element is highlighted. These elements are rectangular boxes of various sizes; some will have content, others may not.

4. After the element you want to capture is selected, click it. Resize handles appear around the selection box, as shown in Figure 14.13.

5. Change the size of the selection box to include only the portion of the page you want to capture.

6. When the selection box reflects the widget you want to create, click the Add button. The widget is created, the Dashboard opens, and you see the widget you created (see Figure 14.14).

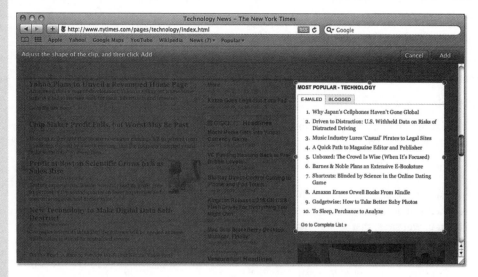

Figure 14.13
You can capture part of a web page and place it on your Dashboard with just a couple of mouse clicks.

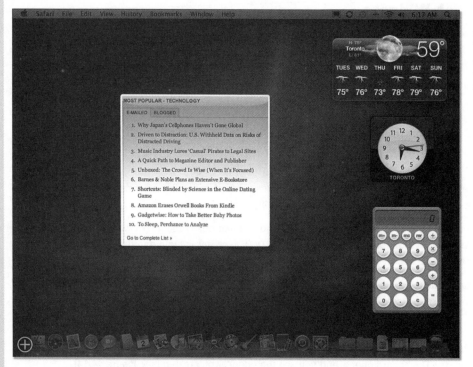

Figure 14.14
A section of a web page added to a widget on the Dashboard.

7. Click the info button (the lowercase "i") on the widget you created. The configuration controls appear.

8. Choose a theme for the widget by clicking it; themes change the borders of the widget.

9. If the widget includes audio, activate the Only Play Audio in Dashboard check box so that its audio only plays while the Dashboard is active. Otherwise, the widget's audio might play all the time, which is probably not what you want.

10. To change the size of the widget, click Edit and then resize it. Click Done.

11. When you're happy with the changes you made, click Done to save your changes and return to the widget.

> ➡ *To learn about the Dashboard,* **see** *Chapter 28, "Working with the Dashboard and Widgets," p. 561.*

Here are some tidbits about creating web widgets:

- Each time you open a web widget by opening your Dashboard, its content is refreshed.

- If changes are made to the layout or other aspect of a website on which you captured content, your widget may no longer work.

- To remove a web widget from your Dashboard, click the Manage Widgets button and click the x button on the widget. After you remove it, it is deleted and you have to re-create it to add it to your Dashboard again.

- Web widgets work best for viewing information that doesn't require authentication or for which a cookie stores any personalization information. Most sites that require secure logins can't be accessed using a web widget you create. To see if a site can be captured in a widget, try capturing its login box as a widget and then try to log in. If it works, you can log in into the site quickly by opening the widget and logging in. In most cases, you'll move to an error page or the actual login page, in which case you should just delete the widget.

- Most links in a web widget should take you to the appropriate place on the related web page. Some links might not work; it depends on how the page is built and how the widget was captured.

- Getting a web widget just right can be tricky. The only way to tell is to try capturing the widget you want. If it doesn't work the way you expect, try capturing more of the web page (remember you can use the widget's Edit button to change the size of the widget). For information pages, you'll usually get what you want on the first try. For pages with which you interact, a bit more experimentation may be required. In some cases, you won't be able to capture the part of a page that you want to be able to use, but at least it won't take very much work to find out.

Using Safari's Activity Viewer

As you move around the Web, Safari tracks the sites you have visited. You can view this information on the Activity window. To do so, select Window, Activity or press Option-⌘-A. The Activity window appears. In this window, you will see a list of the sites you have visited during the current browsing session. You can expand each site to see the individual pages you have visited and double-click any of these to return to that page.

Browsing Privately

As you travel around the Web, Safari helpfully tracks where you have been, usernames and passwords, cookies, AutoFill information, and other items to make using the Web more convenient. However, sometimes you might not want all this information recorded and would instead prefer to browse without any sort of record keeping on Safari's part. For example, you might be using a public Mac or be logged in under someone else's user account. In Safari terminology, this is called *private browsing*. When you browse privately, web pages you visit are not tracked in the History folder, items you download are removed from the Downloads window, any cookies stored on the Mac are deleted, information isn't retained for AutoFill, and your searches aren't saved.

To browse privately, choose Safari, Private Browsing. Click OK in the resulting prompt and private browsing will be in effect. When you are ready to resume normal browsing, choose Safari, Private Browsing again. Safari will clear any cookies and downloads stored during the private browse session and return to normal browsing mode.

Emailing Web Pages

When you surf, you'll likely encounter web pages you'd like other people to view. If you have Apple Mac configured as your default email client, then you can use Safari's built-in web page emailing ability, to easily send information about web pages to other people via email:

1. View the web page you want to send to someone else.

2. Choose File, Mail Contents of This Page or press ⌘-I if you want to send the actual contents of the web page to someone; choose File, Mail Link to This Page or press Shift-⌘-I if you want to send a link to the page. Your default email application opens, a new message is created, and the web page contents or a link to the page is inserted into the new message.

3. Address the email message, add any information you want, and send it.

Using Safari Keyboard Shortcuts

Table 14.1 lists keyboard shortcuts for Safari.

 note

Table 14.1 assumes you have enabled Safari's Tab feature.

Table 14.1 Keyboard Shortcuts in Safari

Menu	Command	Keyboard Shortcut
Safari	Preferences	⌘-,
Safari	Block Pop-Up Windows	Shift-⌘-K
Safari	Empty Cache	Option-⌘-E
File	New Window	⌘-N
File	New Tab	⌘-T
File	Open File	⌘-O
File	Open Location	⌘-L
File	Close Window	⌘-W
File	Save As	⌘-S
File	Mail Contents of This Page	⌘-I
File	Mail Link to This Page	Shift-⌘-I
Edit	AutoFill Form	Shift-⌘-A
View	Show/Hide Bookmarks Bar	Shift-⌘-B
View	Show/Hide Status Bar	⌘-/
View	Show/Hide Tab Bar	Shift-⌘-T
View	Show/Hide Toolbar	Shift-—-\
View	Stop	⌘-.
View	Reload Page	⌘-R
View	Make Text Bigger	⌘-+
View	Make Text Normal Size	⌘-0
View	Make Text Smaller	⌘-—
View	View Source	Option-⌘-U
History	Back	⌘-[
History	Forward	⌘-]
History	Home	Shift-⌘-H
History	Page SnapBack	Option-⌘-P
History	Search Results SnapBack	Option-⌘-S
Bookmarks	Show All Bookmarks	Option-⌘-B
Bookmarks	Add Bookmark	⌘-D
Bookmarks	Add Bookmark Folder	Shift-⌘-N
Bookmarks	Go to first bookmark	⌘-1
Bookmarks	Go to second bookmark	⌘-2
Bookmarks	Go to third bookmark	⌘-3
Bookmarks	Go to fourth bookmark	⌘-4
Bookmarks	Go to fifth bookmark	⌘-5

Table 14.1 Continued

Menu	Command	Keyboard Shortcut
Bookmarks	Go to sixth bookmark	⌘-6
Bookmarks	Go to seventh bookmark	⌘-7
Bookmarks	Go to eighth bookmark	⌘-8
Bookmarks	Go to ninth bookmark	⌘-9
Window	Select Next Tab	Shift-⌘-]
Window	Select Previous Tab	Shift-⌘-[
Window	Downloads	Option-⌘-L
Window	Activity	Option-⌘-A
Help	Safari Help	⌘-?

Downloading and Preparing Files

One of the best things about the Web is that you can download files from it. These files can be applications, graphics, audio files, text files, updaters, or any other file you can think of. Downloading files is simple; the only two areas that might give you some trouble are finding the files you download and preparing them for use.

The general process for downloading and preparing files is the following:

1. Locate the file you want to download.

2. Download the file to your Mac.

3. Prepare the file for use by decoding and uncompressing it.

There are two basic ways to download files. You can use a web browser to download files, or you can use an FTP client (or the Finder) to download files from FTP and other sites. Using a web browser to download files is simpler, but it is also slower. A dedicated FTP client can dramatically speed up file downloading.

Configuring a Downloads Folder

By default, your web browser stores files you download in the Downloads folder in your Home directory. If this isn't where you want downloaded files to be stored, you should create a folder into which your web browser will always download files. That way, you will always know where to find the files you download and they won't clutter your desktop.

After you have created your downloads folder, open the General pane of the Safari Preferences dialog box and use the Save Downloaded Files To pop-up menu to choose that folder.

 note

Because a directory is modified when you store files in it, you must use a directory that you have permissions to write to. On your Mac OS X startup volume, you are limited to downloading files to a directory within your Home directory. However, you can choose a location outside your Mac OS X startup volume if you want.

If you want other users of your machine to be able to access the files you download, you can use your Public folder as your downloads folder.

Downloading Files Using Safari

Downloading files is as simple as anything gets. Safari uses its Downloads window to show you information about the files you are downloading. To start the download process, just click the download link for the file you want to download.

Some sites simply provide the file's name as its link, whereas others provide a Download button. Whichever way it is done, finding the link to click to begin the download process is usually simple.

After you click the link to begin the download, the Downloads window opens showing the progress of the file you are downloading (see Figure 14.15). As a file is downloaded, you see its name, the download progress, and the file size. During the download process, you see the stop button for the files you are downloading; you can stop the process by clicking this button.

 tip

You can download multiple files at the same time. Start one; then, move back to a web window, move to the next, and start it downloading.

You can also continue to browse the Web while your files are downloading. The speed decreases a bit, but at least you can do something while the file is downloading. If you use a fast connection, you probably won't notice the slowdown.

Figure 14.15
The Downloads window provides the information and tools you need to manage your downloads.

When the download is complete, you will see the file's icon in the Downloads window. Also, the Stop button becomes the Find in Finder button, which contains a magnifying glass. Click this button to move to the file you downloaded in the Finder.

As you download files, Safari continues to add them to the list in the Downloads window. You can clear them manually by clicking the Clear button. You can have Safari remove them automatically by selecting either When Safari Quits or Upon Successful Download on the Remove Download List Items pop-up menu on the General pane of the Safari Preferences dialog box.

 tip

If the download process is interrupted for some reason (such as a connection problem or if you clicked the Stop button), the Stop button becomes the Retry button, which contains a circular arrow. Click this button to try to download the file again.

After the download is complete, Safari tries to prepare the file that downloaded so you can use it. Most of the time, this works automatically, but in some situations, you must perform this task manually. This process can be somewhat complicated depending on the file you download. If the file you are downloading contains an application, you may be warned about this and prompted to verify that you want to complete the download.

Preparing Files for Use

Most files you download are encoded and compressed. *Encoding* is the process of translating an application or other file into a plain-text file so it can be transferred across the Internet. *Compressing* a file is a process that makes the file's size smaller so it can be transferred across the Internet more quickly.

Before you can use a file you have downloaded, it must be decoded and it might also need to be uncompressed. Depending on the type of file it is, these two actions might be done at the same time or might have to be handled separately. An application is required for both tasks; a single application can usually handle them, but occasionally the file might need to be uncompressed with one application and decoded with another.

Understanding File Extensions for Compressed Files

Knowing what will happen in any situation requires that you understand the types of files you are likely to download. You can determine this by the filename extension. The most common extensions with which you will have to deal are listed in Table 14.2.

Table 14.2   Common File Extensions for Compressed or Encoded Mac Files

File Extension	What It Means	Comments
`.bin`	Binary file format	A common encoding format for the Mac.
`.gz`	Unix compression format	The dominant compression format for Unix files.
`.hqx`	Binhex encoding	Another very common encoding format for the Mac.
`.dmg`	Disk Image file format	A file that is a disk image and must be mounted with the Disk Utility application before it can be used.
`.pkg`	The package format	Package files are installed with the application installer.
`.sit`	StuffIt compression	One standard compression format for Mac files.
`.tar`	Tape Archive format	An archiving format for Unix computers that is used for some files you might want for Mac OS X.
`.zip`	Zip compression format	The dominant compression format for Windows PCs and Mac OS X's standard compression format.

If the file you download is in the `.bin`, `.hqx`, `.img`, or `.pkg` format, you don't need to do anything to prepare the file for use. Safari will handle that for you. Some of the other formats, however, will require some manual intervention to prepare the file for use.

Manually Preparing a File for Use

Although you can usually rely on Safari's preconfigured helper applications to handle most of the files you download, it is useful to know how to manually decode and uncompress files you download so you can handle them yourself and better understand how to configure a helper application to do it for you.

By default, Safari attempts to launch the appropriate helper application to handle files you download. If a file you download can be handled successfully by the helper application, it is prepared and a usable version of it is placed in the same folder into which it was downloaded.

If you download a `.zip` file, double-click it to uncompress it. A file or a folder containing usable files (if the `.zip` includes more than one file) will be created.

If you download a `.sit` or other file type, you'll need to also download and install a copy of the freeware StuffIt Expander to be able to expand and then use the file.

 note

You can get information about and download StuffIt Expander at www.stuffit.com.

Working with Plug-Ins and Helper Applications

Many file types are available on the Internet. In addition to HTML, JSP, GIF, JPEG, and other files that are used to present a web page, there are graphics, movies, sounds, PDFs, and many other file types you can open and view. Safari can't work with all these file types directly, and fortunately, it doesn't have to. Safari and other web browsers use plug-ins and helper applications to expand their capabilities so they can work with files they don't natively support.

Working with Plug-Ins

Plug-ins are software that can be incorporated into a web browser when it opens (thus, the term *plug-in*). Internet plug-ins enable applications to display files that are of the specific types handled by those plug-ins. For example, the QuickTime plug-in enables web browsers to display QuickTime movies.

Installing Internet Plug-Ins

As you travel around the Web, you might encounter file types for which you do not have the required plug-in. In that case, you must find and install the plug-in you need. Usually, sites have links to places from which you can download the plug-ins needed for the file types on the site. There are a couple of places in the system where plug-ins can be stored.

Plug-ins that are available to all user accounts are stored in the folder *Mac OS X*/Library/ Internet Plug-Ins/, where *Mac OS X* is the name of your startup volume.

You must be logged in under an Administrator account to store a plug-in in this directory.

Internet plug-ins can also be stored in a specific user account, in which case they are available only to that user. A user's specific plug-ins are in the location *shortusername*/Library/Internet Plug-Ins/, where *shortusername* is the short name for the user account.

To install a plug-in, simply place it in the directory that is appropriate for that plug-in (to be available either to all users or to only a specific user). Quit the web browser and then launch it again to make the plug-in active.

note

Some plug-ins are installed using an installer application, in which case you don't need to install the plug-in manually.

If you open the Internet Plug-Ins directories, you will see the plug-ins currently installed. Any plug-in installed in these folders can be used by a supported web browser.

Many plug-ins are available for web browsers. The QuickTime plug-in is installed by default so you can view QuickTime movies in web browsers. Additionally, the Shockwave Flash plug-in is installed by default, as is the Java Applet plug-in. There are many other plug-ins you might want to download and install.

You can see the plug-ins installed for Safari by selecting Help, Installed Plug-ins. A new window opens displaying all the installed plug-ins (see Figure 14.16).

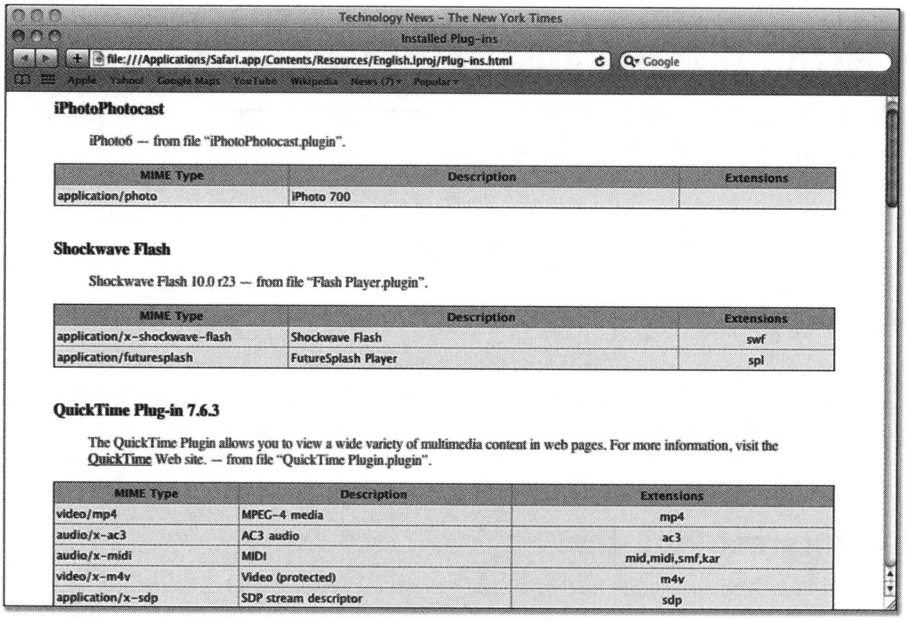

Figure 14.16
Safari's Installed Plug-ins window shows you all the plug-ins to which Safari has access.

When you attempt to view a file for which you do not have the appropriate plug-in, you see a warning dialog box that tells you what to do. Usually, you see instructions to help you find, download, and install the plug-in as well.

Using Internet Plug-Ins

After a plug-in is installed in the appropriate folder, it works with a web browser to provide its capabilities. When you click a file that requires the plug-in to be used, the appropriate plug-in activates and enables you to do whatever it is designed to do. For example, when you open a QuickTime movie, you see the controls that enable you to watch that movie within the web browser.

Working with Helper Applications

Although plug-ins provide additional capability by "plugging in" to a web browser, *helper applications* are standalone applications web browsers can use to work with files of specific types. Any application on your Mac can be used as a helper application.

Safari determines the helper applications it uses to open files based on the file type and filename extensions with which specific applications are associated via the Finder. For example, if PDFs are set to open in Preview, Safari launches Preview when you download a PDF file (assuming that the Open "Safe" Files After Downloading preference is enabled).

➡ *To learn how to associate files with applications,* **see** *"Determining the Application That Opens When You Open a Document," p. 138.*

MANAGING YOUR EMAIL

Managing Email with Apple Mail

Mac OS X ships with the Apple Mail application (which I'll just call Mail from now on), which is an elegant, full-featured, and easy-to-use email client. Mail offers a tidy, straightforward interface, but that surface simplicity hides a wealth of powerful and useful features. Covering all of those features would require a dozen chapters of this size, so I'll just hit the highlights here. These include configuring the Mail preferences, particularly the all-important task of setting up your email accounts; receiving email and sending your own messages and replies; using mailboxes and rules to organize your email; working with message attachments; and using Mail to follow your favorite RSS feeds.

Configuring Apple Mail

Before you can start using Mail to work with your email, you need to configure the accounts it uses. If you entered account information in the Setup Assistant when you installed Mac OS X, those accounts are configured for you already. For example, if you set up or entered the information for your MobileMe account in the Setup Assistant, your MobileMe email account is configured in Mail automatically.

If you are like most Mac users, you probably have more than one email account; you can use Mail to access any or all of them.

There are also several other areas that you don't necessarily have to configure to use Mail, but I have included them in the section "Configuring Email Accounts" so that all the configuration information is together for your reference.

Before proceeding to the next few sections, click the Mail icon in the Dock to launch Mail, and then open the Mail preferences by selecting Mail, Preferences (or by pressing ⌘-,).

Configuring General Mail Preferences

Using the General pane of the Mail preferences dialog box, you can configure the following preferences:

- **Default Email Reader**—Use this pop-up menu to select the email application that Mac OS X uses as the default. If you want to use Mail, you don't need to make a selection on this menu. If you want to use another application, choose Select on the menu and use the resulting sheet to select the application you want to use instead of Mail.

- **Check for New Messages**—Use this pop-up menu to determine how often Mail checks for new mail. Select Manually to disable automatic checking; otherwise, select the frequency with which you want Mail to check for new email automatically, such as Every 5 Minutes (the default interval).

- **New Messages Sound**—Use this pop-up menu to choose the sound that Mac OS X plays when new mail is received, or select None to disable the new mail sound. Mail can also play sounds for the following events: mail error and mail sent. To turn these sounds off, deactivate the Play Sounds for Other Mail Actions check box.

- **Dock Unread Count**—Use this pop-up menu to configure how Mail's icon on the Dock indicates when you have new mail and how many new messages you've received. Choose Inbox Only to have only unread messages in your inbox displayed on the icon. You can also choose All Mailboxes or, to disable the Dock indicator, choose None.

 tip

You can use custom mail sounds by selecting Add/Remove on the New Messages Sound pop-up menu and selecting the custom sound you want to use. Mail places the sound file you select in the `Library/Sounds` folder in your Home folder. You can then choose it on the pop-up menu in Mail and other applications, such as iChat.

- **Add Invitations to iCal**—Use this pop-up menu to determine how Mail handles iCal invitations you receive. Select Automatically to have them added to your iCal calendar when you receive them, or select Never if you don't want them added to your calendar.

- **Downloads Folder**—Use this pop-up menu to determine where Mail stores file attachments from the email messages you receive. Leave the default Downloads folder selected, or choose Other and then select a different folder.

- **Remove Unedited Downloads**—Use this pop-up menu to determine when Mail deletes file attachments that you haven't changed. The options are Never, When Mail Quits, and After Message Is Deleted.

- **If Outgoing Server Is Unavailable**—Use this pop-up menu to select what to do when the server you use to send email is not accessible. You can have Mail display a list of alternative servers, or have Mail automatically try to deliver the email again later.

- **When Searching All Mailboxes, Include Results From**—Use these check boxes to determine if the Trash, Junk, or Encrypted Messages folders are included in searches. If a folder's check box is activated, it will be included.

- **MobileMe**—Click this button to use MobileMe to keep your Mail information synchronized on each machine you use. Use the resulting MobileMe pane to configure the synchronization you want to use.

  ➡ *To learn how to use MobileMe to synchronize information,* **see** *"Using MobileMe to Synchronize Important Information on Multiple Macs," p. 435.*

Configuring Email Accounts

The most basic configuration for Mail is the email accounts you are going to access with it. Before you get started, gather the following information for each mail account you want to configure in Mail:

- **Account type**—There are four types of email accounts with which Mail can work. A MobileMe account is one provided by Apple's MobileMe servers. A Post Office Protocol (POP) account is provided by most ISPs. An Internet Message Access Protocol (IMAP) is similar to a POP account but offers additional features, and an Exchange account is provided by an Exchange server, which is used on many business networks.

> **note**
>
> When you use a MobileMe email account with Mail, it is configured as an IMAP account. In Mail, it is treated as its own category because it is part of your MobileMe account.

- **Your email address**—This should be self-explanatory.

- **Incoming mail server**—This is the address of the server that handles retrieving your email. For POP accounts, it often looks something like pop.isp.net.

- **Your email username**—This is your username for your email account, which might or might not be the same as your username for your Internet account. Typically, this is everything before the @ in your email address.

- **Your email password**—This is the password for your email account, which might or might not be the same as that of your Internet access account.

- **Outgoing email server or Simple Mail Transfer Protocol (SMTP) host**—This is the address of the server that handles sending your email.

- **SMTP port**—You need to know whether your SMTP server uses a port other than the standard port 25 (such as port 587).

- **SMTP Authentication**—You need to know whether your SMTP server uses authentication.

- **SMTP username**—This is the username for your SMTP server; it is usually the same as your email username, but it isn't always.

- **SMTP password**—Again, this is usually the same as your email password.

After you have gathered this information, you are ready to configure the email accounts. You can use the Accounts pane of the Preferences dialog box or the Add Account command.

To add email accounts to Mail, do the following:

1. Use either of the following techniques to get started:

   ■ If you have the preferences dialog box open, click the Accounts button to see the Accounts pane, and then click the Add Account button (the plus sign at the bottom of the list of accounts).

   ■ In Mail, select File, Add Account. Figure 15.1 shows the dialog box that appears.

Add Account

Add Account

You'll be guided through the steps to set up an additional account.

To get started, provide the following information:

Full Name:

Email Address: user@example.com

Password:

Cancel   Go Back   Continue

Figure 15.1
If you configured a MobileMe account when you installed Mac OS X, your MobileMe email account is configured in Mail automatically.

2. Enter the account information, including your full name, email address, and password.

3. Click Continue. For all account types except MobileMe, the incoming Mail Server sheet appears. For MobileMe accounts, Mail activates the information you entered and if it is correct, the account is configured and you move directly to the Conclusion sheet; skip to step 9.

4. Select the account type from the Account Type pop-up menu.

5. Enter a description of the account in the Description field.

6. Enter the Incoming Mail Server, enter your username (typically everything before the @ in your email address) and password, and then click Continue. Mail checks the connection using the

 note

What you enter in the Full Name field is what appears next to your return email address shown in the Email Address data field. If a recipient uses Mail, he sees your full name instead of your email address.

information you entered. If the information works, you see the Outgoing Mail Server sheet. If not, you'll need to correct it before you can move ahead.

7. Enter the SMTP server address for the account in the Outgoing Mail Server box. If an SMTP server is already configured, you can choose to use it by selecting it on the drop-down list.

8. If the SMTP server for the account uses authentication, activate the Use Authentication check box and configure the User Name and Password fields in the sheet; the username and password might or might not be the same as those for the incoming mail server. Click Continue when you are finished configuring the outgoing mail server. Mail checks the connection to make sure it can communicate with the server. If it can, you see the Account Summary sheet, which means the account has been configured successfully. If not, you'll need to correct the configuration until it can communicate with the server.

9. Click Create.

After you have created one or more accounts, you return to the Account pane and the accounts you have configured are shown in the left part of the pane. Next, configure mailbox behavior for each account.

Select the account you want to configure and click the Mailbox Behaviors tab. This tab provides several controls you can use to control how the account you are configuring behaves. The options you see depend on the type of account you are creating. For example, you see fewer options for a POP account than you do for other types. Because MobileMe accounts are popular with many Mac users, you see the options you can configure for MobileMe accounts in the following list and in Figure 15.2. You can configure the options on this tab for other account types in a similar way, although the specific options you have might be different:

- Use the check box in the Drafts area to determine whether messages are stored on the MobileMe server when you are writing them. This causes email that you are writing to be saved on the MobileMe server as you are writing it. If you write email offline, you don't want to select this. If you use a broadband connection to the Net, you can activate the Store Draft Messages on the Server check box to have your drafts stored online as you write them.

- You can use Mail to create and manage notes, which are text documents you can create and store within Mail. If you want your notes to be stored in your Inbox, activate the Store Notes in Inbox check box. If you leave this deactivated, you can access notes via the Notes folder.

- Use the controls in the Sent area to determine whether sent messages are stored on the server and when sent messages are deleted. Usually, you don't want to save sent messages on the server because those messages count against your total storage allowance for your account. If you do want sent messages to be stored on the server, activate the Store Sent Messages on the Server check box. Then use the Delete Sent Messages When pop-up menu to select how often the sent messages are deleted. The options are Never, One Day Old, One Week Old, One Month Old, or Quitting Mail.

- Use the Junk controls to configure how Mail handles messages that are classified as junk. Similar to the first two options, you can select to have junk mail stored on the server; if you select to allow this, use the pop-up menu to determine when junk mail is deleted from the server.

■ Use the Trash controls to configure how trash is handled. If you want deleted messages to be moved to the Trash mail box, activate the Move Deleted Messages to the Trash Mailbox check box. If you want deleted messages to be stored on the server, activate the Store Deleted Messages on the Server check box, and to determine when deleted messages are actually erased, use the Permanently Erase Deleted Messages When pop-up menu. The options are Never, One Day Old, One Week Old, One Month Old, or Quitting Mail.

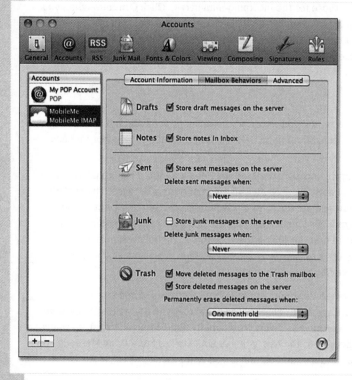

Figure 15.2
You can configure these special mail-box actions when using a MobileMe mail account.

Configure these behaviors for each account using similar options.

Finally, configure the Advanced options for each account using the following steps (again, these assume a MobileMe account; other account types might have different options):

1. Select the Account you want to configure and click the Advanced tab. Just as with the Mailbox Behaviors tab, the specific controls you see depend on the type of account you are configuring (see Figure 15.3).

2. Use the Enable This Account check box to enable or disable the account. If you disable an account, it won't be used.

3. Activate the Include When Automatically Checking for New Mail check box if you want this account always included when Mail automatically checks for mail. If you deactivate this check box, you must manually check for mail for this account.

Figure 15.3
These are the Advanced controls for a MobileMe email account.

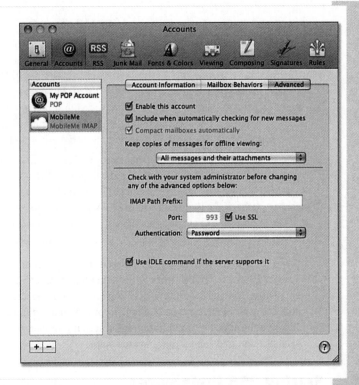

4. If enabled, activate the Compact Mailboxes Automatically check box to have Mail automatically compress your mailboxes to minimize the storage space they require.

5. Use the Keep Copies of Messages for Offline Viewing pop-up menu to determine what Mail does with the messages it receives when you are not connected to the Internet. For example, if you select All Messages and Their Attachments, all your messages and any attachments they contain are downloaded to your Mac so you can view them even if you aren't connected to the Net. If you select Only Messages I've Read, only the messages you have read are downloaded to your Mac. Choose All Messages, but Omit Attachments to download messages but not their attachments or Don't Keep Copies of Any Messages if you don't want any information to be downloaded to your Mac (you'll have to be connected to the Internet to be able to read messages).

6. Select another account or close the Preferences dialog box. Mail prompts you to save your changes.

> 🔍 **note**
>
> Other options are available at the bottom of the Advanced pane, but you aren't likely to use them unless you are specifically directed to do so by the administrator of the email system you are using.

IMAP Accounts

One area in which an IMAP account (such as a MobileMe account) is significantly different from a POP account is in how email is stored. Under an IMAP account (such as a MobileMe email account), mail is always left on the server until you delete it. The benefit of this is that you can access that mail from different machines without forwarding it to each machine or having duplicate copies (on the server and in the inbox in your email applications). As you learn later, when you work with an IMAP account that has a limited amount of storage for email messages, you have to be aware of how full your email storage is and make sure that you keep it under its limit.

When you use a POP account, the mail you read is actually downloaded to your Mac. So, a copy exists in both places. With POP accounts, you should activate the "Remove Copy from Server after Retrieving a Message" check box and select a timeframe for messages to be deleted on the pop-up menu. Otherwise, the email you read remains on the server, and you might download it again the next time you activate your email.

Using steps similar to these, you can add the rest of your email accounts to Mail to work with them all from the Mail application. As you read previously, the steps for a specific account depend on the type of email account you are adding. Just use the specific configuration information provided for each account and repeat the previous steps.

 note

Mail can't access an AOL email account. However, you should be able to add just about any other email account to it. In fact, Mail is pretty smart about some other email services. For instance, if you add a Google Gmail account, Mail automatically connects and adds all of the settings for you.

Setting RSS Preferences

You can use Mail and other applications to receive and read RSS feeds. The RSS preferences can be used to determine how RSS feeds are handled on your Mac.

➥ *To learn how to work with RSS feeds,* ***see*** *"Working with RSS Feeds,"* **p. 345**.

Setting Junk Mail Preferences

Use the Junk Mail pane to configure Mail's Junk Mail feature.

➥ *To learn how to configure and use Mail's junk mail feature,* ***see*** *"Handling Junk Mail,"* **341**.

Setting Fonts & Colors Preferences

Use the Fonts & Colors pane of the Mail preferences window to control how text appears in Mail windows:

- Use the various Select buttons to select the font and size for the Mailbox font, Message list font (the pane in which all the messages in a mailbox are listed), the message font (which is the font used for messages you read), the note font, and the fixed-width font.

- If you prefer a fixed-width font for plain-text messages, activate the Use Fixed Width Font for Plain Text Messages check box.

- If you want different levels of quoted text to use different colors, activate the Color Quoted Text check box and select the colors for each level using the pop-up menus.

Email Formats

Mail enables you to send and read email in two formats: plain text and Rich Text Format (RTF). (You can also read email in the HTML format, but you can't compose your own mail in this format.) Plain-text messages contain no formatting, but RTF messages can be formatted. Whether the formatting you apply in an RTF message will be seen or not depends on the email application the recipient of your email uses. Most can interpret RTF messages correctly, but others cannot.

Email purists prefer plain-text format because any email application can handle them and plain-text messages are quicker to compose and read (which is part of the point of email in the first place). Also, proper quoting is much easier with a plain-text message.

Many mailing lists enable you to select the format in which you receive messages. You often can select between the plain-text or HTML format. Selecting the plain-text format results in much faster performance, although you won't see all the bells and whistles that can be contained in an HTML email message. However, plain-text messages usually contain links to that content on the Web so you can easily view the specific content you want to see.

Setting Viewing Preferences

Using the Viewing pane of the Mail Preferences window, you can control the following viewing options:

- Use the Show Header Detail pop-up menu to determine how much information is shown in the header of email messages you receive. Your choices are Default, None, All, or Custom. If you select Custom, you can select the specific data you want to see in the header of your messages.

- Activate the Show Online Buddy Status check box if you want the status of people whom you have designated as being online buddies to be displayed. This helps you know when these people are online so you can chat with them.

- Activate the Display Unread Message with Bold Font check box if you want messages that you haven't read yet to appear in bold in the Mail List pane.

- Unactivate the Display Remote Images in HTML Messages check box if you want only the text portion of HTML messages that you receive to be displayed. If you receive a lot of

 note

Note that the Show Header Detail pop-up menu affects mail you have already downloaded. For example, you can select an email message to read and then select a level of header detail from the Show Header Detail pop-up menu to change the header information for the mail you are reading.

 tip

You can show all header information in messages by selecting View, Message, Long Headers or by pressing Shift-⌘-H.

spam, it's a good idea to deactivate this box so you can choose which images are displayed; otherwise, you might be unpleasantly surprised by images in spam messages.

- Deactivate the Use Smart Addresses check box if you don't want Mail to substitute a person's name (from the Address Book) for her email address when you receive mail from her.

> **note**
>
> Mail uses the Safari HTML rendering engine to display HTML messages. This improves the formatting you see when you view HTML messages and makes HTML messages fully interactive.

- Activate the Highlight Related Messages Using Color check box, and select a color by using the color button. *Threads* (a series of messages connected by replies to an original message) in your mailbox are highlighted with the color you select so you can spot related messages more easily.

Setting Composing Preferences

The Composing pane of the Preferences window controls various composing options, which include the following:

- Use the Message Format pop-up menu to set the default format for new messages you can create. Your options are Plain Text and Rich Text. You can override your default choice for specific messages.

- Select As I Type on the Check Spelling pop-up menu to have Mail check your spelling as you type messages. Choose When I Click Send to have Mail check spelling when you send a message, or Never to disable spell check.

> **tip**
>
> For example, if you select Plain Text as your default format, you can create a message in the Rich Text format by creating the message and selecting Format, Make Rich Text (Shift-⌘-T). If you select Rich Text, you can select Format, Make Plain Text (Shift-⌘-T) to create a plain-text message.

- Activate the Automatically check box and then select Cc: on the pop-up menu to include yourself in the Cc block of every message you send. If you prefer to include yourself on the address list for a message but hide your address from the other recipients, select Bcc: on the pop-up menu.

- Activate the Automatically Complete Addresses check box to have Mail look up addresses in your Address Book or on specific LDAP servers. Then click the Configure LDAP button and use the resulting sheet to configure the servers on which you want Mail to look up addresses.

- Activate the When Sending to a Group, Show All Member Addresses check box to list members of a group by their names in an email that you send to a group (rather than listing just the group name).

- If you want to highlight email addresses when you are sending them outside of safe domains, activate the Mark Addresses Not in This Domain check box and enter the domain you want Mail to consider safe in the box. For example, you might want to be careful about sending messages outside your work domain. In that case, you would activate the box and enter your company's domain (such as `company.com`) in the box. Whenever you address messages to someplace other than that domain, the address is highlighted in red.

■ Use the Send New Mail From pop-up menu to choose the account from which new email will be sent (your default account). You can choose Account of Last Viewed Mailbox to choose the account in which you most recently read email, or you can choose a specific account. This impacts only the default email account from which new email is sent. You can always override this choice when you compose a new message.

■ Use the Create Notes and To Dos In pop-up menu to choose the default account for notes and To Do items you create in Mail. The options are the same as for the default send account.

■ Use the controls in the Responding area to configure how Mail handles reply messages. To use the same mail format as the original message (such as plain text), activate the Use the Same Message Format as the Original Message check box. If you don't activate this, your reply uses your default format. To include the original message's text in your reply (which is a good idea so you can use quoting), activate the Quote the Text of the Original Message check box. Activate the Increase Quote Level box to have Mail indent each message's text by one level; this makes an email conversation clearer because you can more easily see the flow of the mail threads. If you choose to use quoting (which you should), use the radio buttons to determine whether the entire message is quoted or only the selected part. The second option is preferable because, if you don't select any text in the original message when you reply to it, the entire text is quoted, which is the same thing the Include All option does anyway. However, if you want to reply only to a specific part of a message, you can select it and only that part is included in the message. This provides better context for your reply.

Setting Signature Preferences

You can configure signatures to be attached to your email messages. You can have as many signatures as you would like, and you can select a default signature or select one each time you compose a new message:

1. Click the Signatures icon to open the Signatures pane of the Mail Preferences window. The accounts you have configured are shown in the far left pane. The list of signatures you have configured are shown in the middle pane, while the far right pane shows the detail for a selected signature (see Figure 15.4).

2. Select the account for which you want to configure a signature, or select All Signatures to make the signature available to all accounts.

3. Click Add Signature (+). A new signature appears in the center pane and its name is highlighted to indicate that it is ready to edit. Default text for that signature is shown in the far right pane.

4. Name the signature by typing a name in the highlighted area.

5. Edit or replace the signature text in the far right pane. You can use just about anything you'd like for your signature.

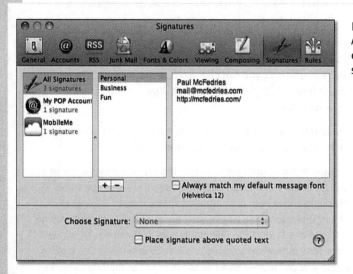

Figure 15.4
Adding a signature to your emails is easy to do and the signature can be shared across your email accounts.

6. If you want your signature to always appear in your default font, activate the Always Match My Default Message Font check box. Underneath this check box, you'll see what your default font currently is.

7. If you created signatures under the All Signatures category, drag them onto each account under which you want to be able to use them.

8. Select one of the email accounts in the far left pane.

9. If you want a signature to be added to messages from that account, select an option on the Choose Signature pop-up menu. You can choose a signature by name, or choose At Random to have Mail select from one of the signatures each time you create a new message, or In Sequential Order to have Mail choose each signature in the order in which they are listed. If you choose None, no signature will be added automatically. In any case, you can always choose from the available signatures on the Signature menu in the New Message window.

10. Activate the Place Signature Above Quoted Text check box, and your signature will be placed above any text that is quoted when you reply to a message. Signatures appear at the bottom of a message by default. When you use quoting, this can be odd because your signature appears after the quoted text instead of after the part you wrote. Use this check box to ensure that your signature appears after what you write and above the quoted text.

Here are a few more signature tips:

■ **Change signatures**—To change a signature, select it and edit it in the far right pane.

■ **Select a default signature**—When you have more than one signature created for an account, drag the one you want to be the default to the top of the Signature list.

■ **Copy a signature**—You can make a copy of a signature by selecting its text and selecting Edit, Copy. Then paste the text into a new signature. This is useful if you want to base a new signature on one you have previously created.

■ **Delete a signature**—You can delete a signature by selecting it and clicking Remove (-). After you confirm the deletion in the prompt, the signature is no longer available.

Setting Rules

You use the Rules pane to set up automated mail rules.

➡ *To learn how to create rules for your email,* ***see*** *"Configuring and Using Rules for Email," p. 339.*

Receiving, Sending, and Replying to Email

If you have used an email application before, such as Entourage or Eudora, using Mail to send, receive, and reply to email will be familiar to you after you learn about the Mail interface.

The main Mail window has four sections. The top section contains the Mail toolbar. The second section from the top is the Message List, in which you see the list of items in the selected mailbox. The lower section of the Mail window is the Reading pane in which you read a mail item that is selected in Message List. All your mailboxes are in the Mailbox pane, which appears along the left side of the Mail window (see Figure 15.5).

Figure 15.5
The Mail application uses four panes to enable you to browse, view, and organize your email.

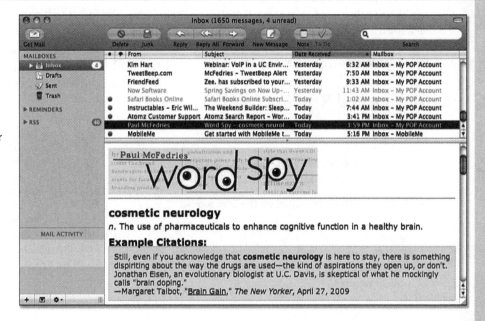

The Message pane of the Mail window behaves much like a Finder in List view. For example, you can change the width of the columns, sort the list of messages, and so on. The columns in the default Mail window are the following (from left to right in Figure 15.5):

- Message status

- Buddy availability

- From

- Subject

- Date Received

- Mailbox (this column only appears if you have multiple email accounts)

The Mailbox pane shows all your mailboxes. You can show the Mailbox pane by selecting View, Show Mailboxes (Shift-⌘-M). You can close the pane by selecting View, Hide Mailboxes (Shift-⌘-M). You can control the width of the pane by dragging the handle located at the bottom of the edge it shares with the other panes so it is the width you want it to be. At the bottom of the Mailbox pane you see Mail Activity, which displays the progress of Mail when it is sending or received email messages.

The Mailbox pane contains several mailboxes and folders by default. The Inbox is used to store all your received mail; within the main Inbox is a mailbox for each of your email accounts. You can expand or collapse the contents of a mailbox by using its expansion triangle. You also see Drafts, Sent, and Trash mailboxes; the purpose of each of these should be self-evident. You might also see Drafts and Sent Messages folders for specific types of email accounts.

 note

If you use a MobileMe, IMAP, or Exchange email account, the Drafts, Junk, and Sent Messages mailboxes appear and have folder icons. These are folders stored on your Mac, whereas the other mailboxes are stored online. If you configured a MobileMe email account to store messages online, they are stored in the online folders rather than those stored on your Mac.

Retrieving and Reading Email

There are several ways to retrieve email from your accounts, including

- Setting Mail to retrieve your mail automatically using the General pane of the Mail Preferences window

- Clicking the Get Mail button on the Mail toolbar

- Pressing Shift-⌘-N to get new mail in all your accounts

- Selecting Mailbox, Get New Mail in *accountname*, where *accountname* is the account from which you want to retrieve your mail

 note

The first three methods listed retrieve mail for all the email accounts you have configured in Mail (for those accounts that are enabled and that you set to be included in the Retrieve All action using that account's settings).

When you get mail, it is placed in the Inbox mailbox for the account to which it was sent. All email is accessible via the top Inbox account, which includes the contents of each account's inbox.

When you receive email, Mail's Dock icon indicates that you have new email and shows you the total number of new messages you have received. If you chose to have Mail play a sound when new mail is received, you hear that sound when mail is received. When you open the Mail icon on the Dock, a list pops up that shows you all the windows open in Mail, as well as some useful commands (see Figure 15.6).

 tip

You can temporarily hide the Reading pane by double-clicking the border between the Message List and the Reading pane. The Reading pane disappears and the Message list consumes the entire Mail window. Double-click the bottom of the Mail window to reopen the Reading pane. You can change the relative height of the two panes by dragging the resize handle located in the center of the bar between the two panes.

Figure 15.6
When you receive new mail, Mail lets you know how many messages you have received (four in this case); you can quickly access the mailboxes containing the new messages by opening the Mail icon on the Dock and selecting Inbox.

When you select Inbox on the Dock menu, you move into Mail to read your email; each unread message has a blue dot in the Status column to indicate that it is a new message. The number of new messages is also indicated next to the Inbox mailbox.

 tip

You can also create a new message or check for new email from the Mail Dock menu.

If you have more than one email account, each account has its own Inbox. To see all your inboxes, click the expansion arrow next to the Inbox icon (see Figure 15.7). The Inbox for each of your accounts appears. Select an Inbox to see the messages for that account only, or select the Inbox icon to see all your messages at the same time.

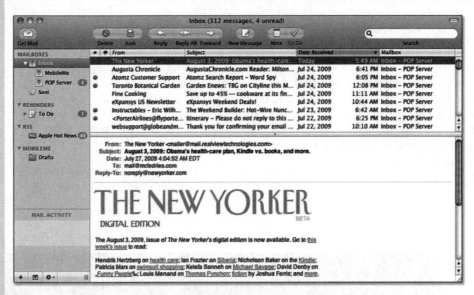

Figure 15.7
Each of my email accounts has its own Inbox, as you can see, listed under the Inbox icon.

Reading Individual Messages

To view the contents of a mailbox or folder, select it in the Mailbox pane. The Message list shows the messages contained in that mailbox or folder. To read a message, select it in the Message list and read it in the Reading pane.

To read your mail, use the following shortcuts:

- Scroll down in a message by pressing the spacebar.

- Move up and down the messages in the Message List using the up- and down-arrow keys.

- Double-click a message to read it in its own window.

 tip

In Mail, you can display the contents of more than one mailbox at a time. To do so, select File, New Viewer Window (Option-⌘-N). In the new Viewer window, select the mailbox whose contents you want to view. You can have as many Viewer windows open as you want. For example, you might select to have a Viewer window open for each of your mail accounts.

 note

You can see the activity of Mail as it downloads messages in a separate Activity window. To see the Activity window, select Window, Activity (or press ⌘-0).

Working with Email Threads

As you read and reply to messages, each message and its replies become a thread, as in a thread of conversation about a topic (or at least started from a topic). If the Highlight Related Messages Using Color preference is set, Mail highlights all the messages in a thread with the color you select (it is light blue by default). You can also select to organize a mailbox by threads so that all the mails that form a conversation are grouped together.

To organize messages in the Message List pane by threads, select View, Organize by Thread. A thread column is added to the left side of the Message List pane. Messages that are part of a thread are highlighted in the selected color and are grouped together. Select View, Organize by Thread again to return the Message pane to its previous organization. The messages in a thread are sorted just like other messages in the Message List pane.

Following are some thread tips (these apply when you use the Organize by Thread command):

- The first message in the thread is a summary of the other messages. Select that message to see each sender, title, and date of each message in the thread. At the top of the summary message is the name of the first message in the thread, who started it, and when the first message was sent.

- You can collapse a thread by clicking the expansion triangle next to the summary message. The thread collapses so you see only the summary message. You can also collapse a thread by clicking the up and down arrow icon in the Status column for a message in the thread.

- Select View, Expand All Threads to expand all the threads in a selected mailbox, or select View, Collapse All Threads to collapse all the threads in a selected mailbox.

 tip

Mail automatically tracks a list of people to whom you have sent email. This list is called the Previous Recipients list. When you enter an email address in the To field, Mail attempts to match what you are entering to the recipients on this list. If it finds a match, it fills in the rest of the address for you. You can view the list by selecting Window, Previous Recipients. On this list, you can view addresses of people who have sent you email or delete addresses from the list, or add addresses to your Address Book.

 tip

If the mailbox you are viewing has several messages in it, select those that are interesting to you; hold down the Shift key to select contiguous messages or hold down the ⌘ key to select messages that are not contiguous. Select View, Display Selected Messages Only. The other messages in the mailbox are hidden and you can quickly read the messages you selected (using the shortcuts mentioned in the previous list). To see all the messages in the mailbox again, select View, Display All Messages.

 note

If you don't organize by threads, messages in threads are still highlighted with the color indicated in Mail's preferences settings.

If the person who sent you a message is in your Address Book and has an image on the related address card, that image appears in the upper-right corner of the email message.

Writing and Sending Email

Writing email in Mail is also quite similar to other email applications. You can create a new mail message in several ways, including the following:

- Click the New button on the toolbar.

- Select File, New Message.

- Press ⌘-N.

- Right-click a name in the To, From, or Cc block for a message you are reading in the Reading pane and then select New Message on the resulting pop-up menu. A message is created and is addressed to the person whose name you clicked.

- Open Mail's Dock menu and select Compose New Message.

When you create a new message, you see the New Message window (see Figure 15.8). Creating the message is straight-forward. If the message is not already addressed, type the email address(es) in the To and Cc fields. Mail attempts to match what you type to the addresses in your Address Book or on the list of previous recipients that Mail maintains automatically. The addresses that match what you type appear on a drop-down list. You can move up and down this list with the up- and down-arrow keys. To select an address on the list, highlight it and it is entered in the message's address box. (If there is only one address for the name you type, it is selected by default.) You can enter multiple addresses in an address field by typing a comma and then repeating the previous steps to add more addresses. When you have added all the addresses in the To field, press Tab to move to the next field.

 tip

Mail defines the messages that make up a thread by a special header element. This means you can change the subject of a reply in a thread and Mail will still recognize that the message is part of the thread. However, not all applications can do this and sometimes header information is removed from a message; therefore, it is usually better to leave the subject as it was when the thread was started.

 tip

If you point to the From block on an email message and click, a pop-up menu appears. On this menu, you can see the email address of the person, chat with the recipient, create a new message, open the related address card (if the recipient has a card, that is), or create an address card. You can also create a smart mailbox for all the mail from that person (you'll learn about smart mailboxes later in this chapter).

Figure 15.8
If you have used other email applications, Mail's New Message window will no doubt look familiar.

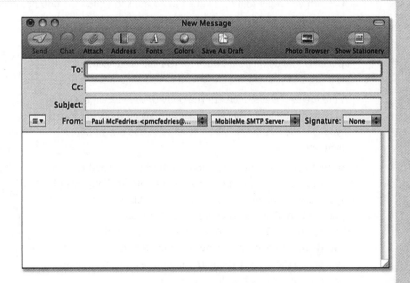

To use your Address Book to address a message, open the Address Book by clicking the Address icon on the New Message window's toolbar or by pressing Option-⌘-A. An Addresses window appears that contains the contacts in your Address Book. Browse or search the window to find the people or groups to whom you want to send the message. Select the person or group to whom you want to send mail, and click To or Cc to send those addresses to the respective fields in the New Message window.

Enter the subject of the message in the Subject field.

Select the account from which you want to send the mail using the Account pop-up menu (your default account is listed automatically). (If you have configured only one account, this menu isn't displayed.)

Mail uses the following three rules to determine the account that is used to send a new message:

- If you have selected a mailbox associated with an account (such as the Inbox for an account), that account is the default for a new message.

- If you selected a default account for new mail on the Composing pane of the Preferences dialog box, that account is used for new mail.

 tip
When an address is selected on the drop-down list that appears when Mail attempts to match the address you are typing, you can add it to the message and be ready to enter the next address by typing a comma.

 tip
You can add a Bcc (blind carbon copy) address line by selecting View, Bcc Address Field or by pressing Option-⌘-B. You can add a Reply To address line by selecting View, Reply-To Address Field (or by pressing Option-⌘-R). You can use the Reply-To Address Field to enter an address to which people should reply if it is different from the return address associated with your account.

■ When you reply to a message, the account to which the original message was sent is selected automatically.

Select the signature you want to use from the Signature pop-up menu. The default signature for the selected account is inserted, but you can use the menu to choose a different one.

There are two ways to create the body of the message. One is to just type the text and use Mail's formatting tools to format if you use the RTF format. The other is to use one of Mail's email templates.

To create your own message, move into the body and type your message. As you type, Mail checks your spelling according to your preferences. If you use the Check As I Type option, when Mail identifies a misspelled word, it underlines the word in red. You can Control-click or right-click a misspelled word to pop up a menu that enables you to change the word to the correct spelling, ignore the spelling, or learn the word that Mail thinks is misspelled.

 tip

You can also control Mail's spell checker using the Spelling commands on the Edit menu. You can open the Spelling and Grammar window by selecting Edit, Spelling and Grammar, Show Spelling and Grammar. You can configure the spell checking by selecting Edit, Spelling and Grammar, Check Spelling and then choosing the option you want, such as While Typing.

You can right-click or Control-click any word, misspelled or not, to perform a number of actions on it, such as searching for the word on your Mac using Spotlight, searching the Web via Google, looking up the word in the Dictionary application, and so on.

To use a template, do the following:

1. Click the Show Stationery button in the toolbar. The available templates appear below the header information.

2. Select a category to see the templates in that category.

3. Select a template, and it appears in the lower pane.

4. Change its content to be what you want it to be; some templates include images that you can't change (see Figure 15.9). You can change the template for a message without deleting any text you've input.

Right-click an empty section of the message body to open its contextual menu to gain quick access to various commands, such as formatting commands for an RTF message, Spell Checker controls, and quoting commands.

To send a message, do one of the following:

■ Click the Send button on the toolbar.

■ Select Message, Send.

■ Press Shift-⌘-D.

 tip

While you're composing a message, you can save it in the Draft mailbox by either selecting File, Save (⌘-S) or clicking the Save As Draft button on the New Message toolbar. You can leave a message you are working on in your Draft folder as long as you'd like. If you close it, you can open it to work on it again by selecting the Draft folder and double-clicking the message. As you work, Mail saves your messages as drafts periodically, but you can use the command to save them manually.

Figure 15.9
Mail's stationery enables you to create fancy emails with just a click.

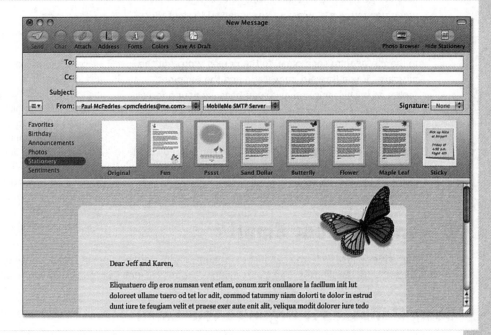

Replying to Email

Replying to messages you receive in Mail is also similar to other applications. By default, Mail marks the different levels of quoting with different colors along with a change bar. As with other applications, you can select the message to which you want to reply and click Reply on the toolbar; select Message, Reply; or press ⌘-R, which replies to only the sender of the message. You can also click Reply All; select Message, Reply All; or press Shift-⌘-R to reply to everyone to whom the original message was sent.

You can use the same tools to reply to a message as you use to write a new message.

You can also perform the following actions on mail you have received:

- **Reply with iChat**—Select Message, Reply with iChat or press Shift-⌘-I if the sender of the message is available via iChat.

- **Forward**—Select Message, Forward or press Shift-⌘-F to forward a message to other recipients.

- **Redirect**—Select Message, Redirect or press Shift-⌘-E to redirect the message to someone else. The difference

 note

You should always quote carefully in your replies. Quoting makes email much more effective because it gives the reader a good context for the information you are providing. Quoting in a plain-text message is much easier; formatting often gets in the way of clear quoting.

 tip

You can open a message's contextual menu to access many useful commands, such as Reply, Reply All, Forward, and so on.

between redirecting and forwarding a message is that when you redirect a message, the email address of the message's original sender's still appears in the From field so the person to whom you redirect the message can reply to the message to send email to the person who sent the message. If you forward a message and the recipient replies to it, the reply comes to you because your address becomes the From address on a forwarded message.

- **Bounce**—Select Message, Bounce or press Shift-⌘-B to bounce a message back to the sender. When you do so, the bounce message that is sent makes it appear as if your email address is not valid.

 note

You might be tempted to bounce spam email that you receive. However, this usually doesn't do any good because most spam includes a bogus return address, so your bounced message has no legitimate place to go. You can use the Bounce command to respond to email from legitimate organizations that have sent unwanted email to you. Hopefully, the bounce results in your address being removed from the related mailing list. Use Mail's Junk Mail feature to deal with spam.

Organizing Your Email

Mail provides many tools you can use to organize various aspects of your mail. These include using mailboxes, smart mailboxes, and smart mailbox groups, as well as automating your mail with rules.

Using Mailboxes to Organize Your Email

You can create your own mailboxes to organize your messages. The mailboxes you create are also shown in the Mailbox pane. You can also create nested mailboxes to create a hierarchy of mailboxes in which you store your messages.

1. Select Mailbox, New Mailbox or click the Add Mailbox button (+) at the bottom of the Mailbox pane to see the New Mailbox sheet.

2. On the Location pop-up menu, select the location of the mailbox you are creating. If you select On My Mac, the folder is created on your computer. If you use an IMAP or MobileMe account, you can select that account to create a folder on that account's server. (Remember that if you store the folder on a server, the contents of that folder count against your storage quota.)

3. In the New Mailbox sheet, enter the name of the mailbox you want to create. To create a nested mailbox, enter the name of each mailbox separated by a slash (/). For example, to create a mailbox called Receipts within a mailbox called Mail to Keep, you would enter `Mail to Keep/Receipts`.

4. Click OK.

The mailbox is created and appears on the Mailbox pane. If you have created a mailbox that contains other mailboxes, you can use its expansion triangle to expand or collapse it.

 tip

You can place a folder within another folder by dragging its icon onto the folder in which you want to place it.

You can move messages from one mailbox to another in the following ways:

- Drag and drop a message from the Message List pane to a mailbox.

- Drag messages from the Message List pane in one Viewer to the Message List pane in another Viewer; this copies the messages in the mailbox shown in the second Viewer window.

- Select messages and select Message, Move To; then select the mailbox to which you want to transfer the messages.

- Select messages and select Message, Copy To; then select the mailbox to which you want to create a copy of the selected messages.

- Select messages and select Message, Move Again to move the selected messages into the same mailbox into which you most recently transferred mail (Option-⌘-T).

- Open a message's contextual menu and select the Move To, Copy To, Move Again, or Apply Rules command.

- Select messages and select Message, Apply Rules (Option-⌘-L); then select a rule that transfers the messages.

Using Smart Mailboxes to Organize Your Email

You can use smart mailboxes to organize your email automatically based on criteria you define. For example, you might want to store all the email you receive from a group of people with whom you are working on a project in a specific folder. Rather than having to place these messages in the folder by dragging them out of your Inbox individually, you can create a smart mailbox so that mail you receive from these people is automatically placed in the folder. You can create smart mailboxes for many needs like the one mentioned here; if you can define a set of conditions for which you want something done, then you can create a smart mailbox to have the action you want to happen done for you automatically.

Smart mailboxes have the gear icon and are purple. To create a smart mailbox, complete the following steps:

1. If you want to create a smart mailbox based on the data in an existing message, select that message.

2. Select Mailbox, New Smart Mailbox or open the Add pop-up menu and select New Smart Mailbox. The Smart Mailbox sheet appears. If you selected a message in advance, Mail automatically includes the condition Any Recipient Contains *address*, where *address* is the address of the person who sent the selected message (see Figure 15.10).

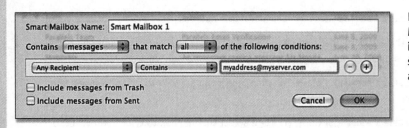

Figure 15.10
Mail automatically adds an initial condition to the smart mailbox if you select a message in advance.

3. Name the smart mailbox by typing its name in the Smart Mailbox Name box.

4. Select the first condition for the mailbox on the first pop-up menu in the conditions box; by default, this menu shows From, which bases the condition on the name or email address in the From field. There are many other choices, including Entire Message, Subject, Date Received, and so on.

5. Select the operand for the condition on the second pop-up menu. What you see on this menu depends on the condition you selected. Common choices include Contains, Does Not Contain, Is Equal To, and so on.

6. Enter the condition text or date in the text box.

7. To add another condition, click the + button.

8. Repeat steps 4–6 to configure the second condition.

9. If you have configured more than one condition, select All on the pop-up menu above the condition list if all the conditions must be true for mail to be stored in the smart mailbox, or select Any if only at least one of the conditions must be true.

10. If you want messages that are in the Trash folder to be included in the smart mailbox, activate the Include Messages From Trash check box.

11. If you want messages that are in the Sent folder to be included in the smart mailbox, activate the Include Messages From Sent check box.

12. Click OK. Mail creates the smart mailbox and populates the mailbox with any mail that meets its conditions.

 tip

To remove a condition, click the Remove (-) button next to the condition you want to remove.

 tip

To change the conditions for an existing smart mailbox, open its contextual menu and select Edit Smart Mailbox. Use the resulting Smart Mailbox sheet to make changes to the smart mailbox.

Using Smart Mailbox Folders to Organize Your Smart Mailboxes

If you want to organize your smart mailboxes, you can create a smart mailbox folder and then place your smart mailboxes within it (you can't put smart mailboxes within regular mailboxes/folders):

1. Select Mailbox, New Smart Mailbox Folder.

2. In the sheet that appears, name the new smart mailbox folder and click OK. The smart mailbox folder is created.

3. Drag smart mailboxes into the smart mailbox folder to place them there. When you do, an expansion triangle appears so that you can expand the folder to see its contents.

Configuring and Using Rules for Email

You can automate the handling of your email by configuring and using rules. For example, you could set up a rule where the Mail Dock icon bounces when you receive a message from a particular person or with a particular subject line. Mail comes with one predefined rule that looks for any messages from Apple and formats those messages to display with a blue background in the message list.

To create and implement rules, you use the Rules pane of the Mail Preferences window:

1. If you want to create a rule based on the data in an existing message, select that message.

2. Open the Mail Preferences window and click the Rules icon to open the Rules pane.

3. Click Add Rule to open a Rule sheet to define the rule you are creating. If you selected a message in advance, Mail automatically includes the condition Any Recipient Contains *address*, where *address* is the address of the person who sent the selected message.

4. Use the Description text box to enter a name for the rule.

5. Use the If pop-up menu to determine whether at least one criterion (select Any) or all the criteria (select All) in the rule must be met for the actions in the rule to be taken.

6. Use the first condition pop-up menu to select the item on which the rule will act. You can select any of the fields in a mail message. You can also select from various criteria, such as whether the sender is in your Address Book.

7. Use the Operator pop-up menu to select how the item relates to the value you enter (such as Contains, Is Equal To, and so on).

8. Enter the value for which the rule is implemented, if applicable, or use a pop-up menu to select a value. (Some conditions, such as Sender Is in My Address Book, don't require any values.)

9. To add more conditions, click the Add button (+) and repeat steps 6–8 to create additional conditions for the rule.

10. Use the Action area to select the action that will be performed by the rule, by making a choice from the first pop-up menu and making other choices from the other pop-up menus or fields related to that choice.

    The actions you can select are Move Message, Copy Message, Set Color of Message, Play Sound, Bounce Icon in Dock, Reply to Message, Forward Message, Redirect Message, Delete Message,

Mark as Read, Mark as Flagged, Run AppleScript, or Stop evaluating rules. You can include multiple actions in the same rule.

11. Click the Add button next to the action and repeat step 9 to create and configure additional actions. When you are done, review the rule you have created. For example, the rule shown in Figure 15.11 checks to see whether a message is from either Apple Developer Connection (which includes adc in its address) or iPhone Developer Connection (which has iphonedev in its address). For matching messages, the rule sets the message text to red, plays the Submarine sound, and bounces the Mail Dock icon.

 tip

You can remove conditions or actions by clicking the Remove button (–).

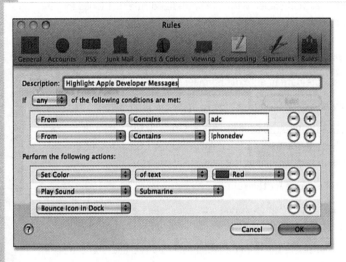

Figure 15.11
A typical Mail rule

12. Click OK. Mail creates the rule and prompts you to apply the rule to the messages in the current mailbox.

13. Click Apply to run the rule now, or click Don't Apply to skip this step. You return to the Rules pane and see the rule you created on the list of rules.

You can use the Edit and Duplicate buttons to edit or duplicate rules and the Remove button to delete rules.

Any future messages you receive that meet the criteria for a rule are acted upon by that rule. You can also manually apply rules to messages by selecting messages and selecting Message, Apply Rules (Option-⌘-L).

 note

If you apply a color in a rule, that rule appears in that color in the Rules pane. Messages already in a mailbox that meet the rule's criteria are also shown in the color applied by the rule.

 tip

Manually applying rules is a good way to test your rules to ensure that they do what you intended.

Handling Junk Mail

Unfortunately, no matter how careful you are with your email address, it might eventually get on a junk mail list. And after it gets on one such list, it will probably get on many, and your inbox will overflow with junk mail. Fortunately, Mail includes some built-in tools for dealing with junk mail.

You can configure Mail's Junk feature via the Junk Mail pane of the Mail preferences dialog box (see Figure 15.12).

Figure 15.12
Use the Junk Mail pane to configure Mail's junk feature.

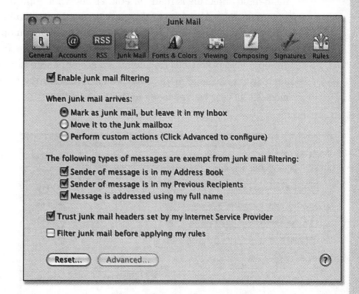

The Junk feature has four modes:

- **Disabled mode**—In this mode, Junk Mail filtering is inactive and doesn't do anything. You can disable Junk Mail filtering by deactivating the Enable Junk Mail Filtering check box.

- **Training mode**—In this mode (which is the default), Mail applies its Junk Mail rules to your messages. This causes Mail to color the message light brown, indicating that Mail thinks the message is junk. You use this mode to fine-tune Junk Mail filtering so that it correctly filters your messages to identify the junk. When you view a message that has been correctly identified as junk, don't do anything. When a message has been identified as junk but it isn't, click the Not Junk button. If you find a message that is junk, but Mail has not identified it as such, click the Junk button on the toolbar. You can place the Junk Mail feature in the Training mode by clicking the Mark as Junk Mail, But Leave It in My Inbox radio button.

- **Automatic mode**—After some time has passed and you are confident that Junk Mail filtering is working properly, you can move into Junk Mail's Automatic mode by clicking the Move It to the Junk Mailbox radio button. Mail creates a Junk folder in the Mailbox pane and asks you whether it should move all the identified junk mail to this folder. Click Yes. In Automatic mode, the Junk Mail filter moves all the messages it identifies as junk into the Junk folder. You should review the contents of this folder periodically to ensure that no messages you want to keep are in this folder by mistake. If there are messages you want, move them to a different folder. Then delete all the messages in the Junk folder.

- **Custom mode**—You use this mode to configure the rules used by the Junk filter. To activate this mode, click the Perform Custom Actions (Click Advanced to Configure) radio button. Then click the Advanced button to open the Advanced configuration sheet. You move to a Rules sheet and the default Junk rule is ready to edit, as shown in Figure 15.13. (Mail's Junk Mail feature is actually just a special mail rule.) You can change this mail rule just like any rule you create on the Rule pane to change how Mail handles junk mail. If you open the Junk rule, you see that this is simply a rule that acts on any messages that are from people who are not in your Address Book, are not on your Previous Recipient list, are not addressed to your full name, or are marked as Junk. In the Training mode, this rule changes only the color of the messages. In the Automatic mode, it moves the messages to the Junk folder.

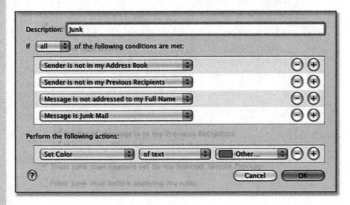

Figure 15.13
Use the Advanced configuration sheet to edit the default Junk rule.

By activating the related check box on the Junk Mail pane of the preferences dialog box, you can exempt email messages from the Junk Mail filter in the following situations:

- The sender of a message is in your Address Book.

- The sender of a message is on the list of Previous Recipients.

- The message is addressed to your full name (most spam uses an email address).

If your Internet service provider (ISP) provides junk mail headers that attempt to identify junk mail by its own rules and you want Mail to recognize and use those headers, activate the Trust Junk Mail Headers Set by My Internet Service Provider check box.

You can also specify if the Junk Mail filter should run before your other rules are applied. This makes sense, as spam should be removed or tagged as such before Mail does anything else with it.

If you click the Reset button, the Junk Mail feature is returned to its default state. This also removes any learning the filter has done, so you have to repeat the training process.

Sending and Receiving Files with Email

One of the most valuable uses of email is to send and receive attachments. Again, Mail handles file attachments similarly to other email applications you might be accustomed to.

Attaching Files to Your Email

Attaching files to messages you send can be done in the following ways:

- In the message to which you want to attach files, select File, Attach File (Shift-⌘-A). Then, use the Choose File sheet to select the files you want to attach.

- Click the Attach button on the New Message window's toolbar. The Choose File sheet appears; use it to select the files you want to attach to a message.

- Drag the files onto the New Message window.

When you place a file in a new message window, you see a thumbnail preview of the file with its icon, the filename, and its size in parentheses. If the file type is one that can be displayed in the message, such as a TIFF image or a PDF file, you actually see the contents of the file in the body of the message.

By default, Mail displays the contents of files you attach if it can. If the contents of the file are being displayed and you would rather see just an icon, open the file's contextual menu and select View as icon. The file is displayed as an icon instead. To view the file's content again, open the menu and select View in Place.

File attachments must be *encoded* before they can be sent. When a file is encoded, it is translated into a string of text. The application that receives the message must then decode that message so the files become usable. Encoding and decoding is handled automatically, and you can't select the encoding method used.

You should also compress files you attach to email messages. Under Mac OS X, you can compress any file in the Zip format using the Finder's Compress command. Simply select the files you want to attach to an email message, open the contextual menu, and select Compress. The files you selected are placed in a Zip file. You can then rename the file (don't change the `.zip` file extension) and attach the Zip file to the message you are sending.

Sending Windows-Friendly Attachments

Sending file attachments is simple except for one thing—the Windows versus Mac situation, which raises its ugly head in the area of file attachments, too. Basically, Mac and Windows operating systems use different file format structures. Mac files have two "forks," whereas Windows files have only one. This is sometimes a problem when you send files to Windows users because they end up with two files. One is the usable file and one is unusable to them (the names of the files are *filename* and *_filename*). Recipients can use the first one and safely ignore the second one. However, it is still confusing for them.

Mail includes a solution for this problem, which is called sending Windows-Friendly Attachments. This causes Mail to strip the second file away, so the Windows recipient receives only one file for each attachment.

However, Mac users who receive Windows-friendly attachments might lose some features, such as thumbnail preview or information about the file. In the worst case, the file might be unusable.

You can choose to attach files as Windows-friendly by activating the box in the Attach File dialog box. If you always want to send files in the Windows-friendly format, select Edit, Attachments, Send Windows Friendly Attachments.

Unless you always send files to other Mac users or only to Windows users, you have to decide whether to use the Windows-friendly option each time you attach files. You should either use this option when you send files to Windows users (if you don't know which type of computer the recipient uses) or not use it if you are certain the recipient uses a Mac.

Using Mail's Photo Browser

Because you're likely to use Mail to email photos that you manage in iPhoto, you can access the Photo Browser by clicking the Photo Browser button in the New Message toolbar. You can use the Photo Browser to easily find photos in your iPhoto Library and drag them onto a new message window to add them to an email you create. Use the Browser's tools to find the images you want to send and then drag them onto a new message window.

Using Files Attached to Email You Receive

When you receive a message that has files attached to it, you see the files in the body of the message. As when you send files in a message, you see the file's icon, name, and size. If the file can be displayed in the body, such as a TIFF or PDF, the contents of the file are displayed in the message. You can use the file attachments in the following ways:

- Select File, Save Attachments. Use the resulting sheet to move to a location and save the attachments.

- Select File, Quick Look Attachments. A Quick Look window appears and shows a preview of the document. Depending on the document type, you might be able to scroll and navigate the Quick Look to see more of the document.

- Click the Save button next to the attachment information at the top of the message. Use the resulting sheet to move to a location and save the attachments.

- Click the Quick Look button next to the attachment information at the top of the message. Depending on the document type, you might be able to scroll and navigate the Quick Look to see more of the document.

- If multiple files are attached, click the expansion triangle next to the attachment line in the message's header and work with each file individually.

- Double-click a file's icon to open it.

- Drag a file's icon from the message onto a folder on your Mac's desktop to save it there.

- You can open the attachment's contextual menu and select one of the listed actions, such as Open Attachment, which opens it in its native application; Open With, which enables you to select the application in which you want the file to open; Save Attachment; or Save to Downloads folder, which saves the attachment in your designated Downloads folder.

If the files you receive are compressed, you must uncompress them before you can open them.

> ➡ *To learn more about uncompressing files,* ***see*** *"Downloading and Preparing Files," p. 308.*

 tip

If the contents of the file are being displayed and you would rather see just an icon, open the file's contextual menu and select View as icon. The file is displayed as an icon instead. To view the file's content again, open the menu and select View in Place.

 tip

If you have trouble viewing a message and the folder into which you want to store the file attachments, double-click the message to open it in its own window. Then you can resize the window so you can more easily see the folder into which you want to drag it.

Working with RSS Feeds

RSS feeds are streams of information that change as times passes. Many websites, especially news sites, offer RSS feeds to which you can subscribe. You can use Mail to read RSS feeds, which is convenient because they are delivered to your Inbox automatically.

> ➡ *To learn more about RSS feeds,* ***see*** *"Browsing and Configuring RSS Feeds," p. 289.*

Adding RSS Feeds and Configuring Mail to Manage Them

To add an RSS feed to Mail, choose File, Add RSS Feeds. The RSS Feeds sheet appears. In the Collections pane, you see your bookmarks from Safari. At the top of this pane, the All RSS Feeds option is selected and you see all of the RSS feeds available to you in the right pane. To add one of these feeds, select it and click Add.

To enter the URL to a feed, click Specify the URL for a Feed in the RSS Feeds sheet; then enter the URL in the resulting Feed URL sheet (see Figure 15.14) and click Add.

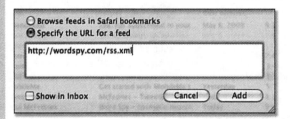

Figure 15.14
Adding RSS feeds to Mail makes keeping up with dynamic information easier.

All feeds appear in the RSS Feeds mailbox by default, but you can place them in your Inbox if you prefer. If you want feeds to appear in your Inbox, activate the Show In Inbox check box.

You can also move feeds from the RSS Feeds mailbox to your Inbox by clicking the Up arrow button that appears when you select a feed. Likewise, you can move a feed from your Inbox to the RSS Feeds mailbox by pointing to a feed in the Inbox and clicking the Down arrow button.

Lastly, configure your RSS feed preferences by opening the RSS pane of the Mail Preferences dialog box, shown in Figure 15.15. Use the following pop-up menus to configure how RSS feeds are managed:

- Use the Default RSS Reader menu to choose the application that you want to use by default to read feeds. The three options are Mail, Safari, or Other (which you can use to choose a different application).

- Use the Check for Updates menu to determine how frequently Mail checks for updates to your feeds. The choices are Manually, Every 30 Minutes, Every Hour, or Every Day.

- Use the Remove Articles menu to determine when Mail removes articles in your feeds. The options are Manually or after specific periods of time, such as a day, one month, two months, and so on.

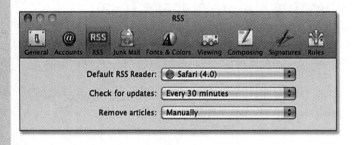

Figure 15.15
Use the RSS pane to configure Mail's RSS feature.

Reading RSS Feeds

After you add feeds to Mail, you can read them by selecting a feed in the Inbox if that is where it is stored or by selecting the RSS Feeds mailbox. The articles in the selected feed appear in the Message List. Choose one to read it in the Reading pane.

Apple Mail Keyboard Shortcuts

Table 15.1 shows keyboard shortcuts for the Mail application.

Table 15.1 Keyboard Shortcuts for Mail

Action	Keyboard Shortcut
Activity	⌘-O
Add Reply-To Header	Option-⌘-R
Add Sender to Address Book	Shift-⌘-Y
Address Panel	Option-⌘-A
Append Selected Messages	Option-⌘-I
Apply Bcc Header	Option-⌘-B
Apply Rules	Option-⌘-L
Attach File	Shift-⌘-A
Bigger	⌘-+
Bounce	Shift-⌘-B
Check Spelling	⌘-;
Copy Style	Option-⌘-C
Decrease Quote Level	Option-⌘-'
Delete	Delete
Erase Deleted Messages In All Accounts	⌘-K
Erase Junk Mail	Option-⌘-J
Find	⌘-F
Find Next	⌘-G
Find Previous	Shift-⌘-G
Forward	Shift-⌘-F
Get All New Mail	Shift-⌘-N
Go To In	⌘-1
Go To Out	⌘-2
Go To Drafts	⌘-3
Go To Sent	⌘-4
Go To Trash	⌘-5
Go To Junk	⌘-6
Go To Notes	⌘-7
Go To To Do	⌘-8
Hide Deleted Messages	⌘-L
Hide/Show Mailboxes	Shift-⌘-M

Table 15.1   Continued

Action	Keyboard Shortcut
Increase Quote Level	⌘-'
Jump to Selection	⌘-J
Mailbox Search	Option-⌘-F
Message Long Headers	Shift-⌘-H
Make Plain Text	Shift-⌘-T
Mark As Flagged	Shift-⌘-L
Mark As Junk Mail	Shift-⌘-J
Mark As Unread/Mark As Read	Shift-⌘-U
Move Again	Option-⌘-T
New To Do	Option-⌘-Y
New Message	⌘-N
New Note	Control-⌘-N
New Viewer Window	Option-⌘-N
Next Alternative	Option-⌘-]
Open Message	⌘-O
Paste as Quotation	Shift-⌘-V
Paste and Match Style	Option-Shift-⌘-V
Plain Text Alternative	Option-⌘-P
Preferences	⌘-,
Previous Alternative	Option-⌘-[
Raw Source	Option-⌘-U
Redirect	Shift-⌘-E
Reply All	Shift-⌘-R
Reply	⌘-R
Reply with iChat	Shift-⌘-I
Save As	Shift-⌘-S
Save	⌘-S
Select All Messages in This Thread	Shift-⌘-K
Send Again	Shift-⌘-D
Show Colors	Shift-⌘-C
Show Deleted Messages	⌘-L
Show Fonts	⌘-T
Show Spelling and Grammar	⌘-:
Smaller	⌘--
Use Selection for Find	⌘-E

CHATTING IN TEXT, AUDIO, AND VIDEO

Chatting with iChat

In these hyperconnected times, people still talk on the phone a lot because having a direct conversation with someone is the easiest and fastest way to resolve a problem, set up a get-together, or get an answer to a question. However, people use the phone a lot less often than they used to because many people consider a phone call to be a major interruption (which explains why we so often get a person's voice mail when we call).

Email has become the most popular of the Internet services because it's nearly universal (if you're on the Net, you almost certainly have an email account), and it solves the interruption problem: When someone receives your message, he or she can then read it and answer it when the time is right. Of course, your recipient's idea of the "right" time might be markedly different than your own, and you might end up waiting hours for a reply.

In the communications continuum, we need something that bridges the gap between the phone and email. That is, we need something that offers both the real-time immediacy of a phone conversation and the more casual style of an email exchange. That something is instant messaging (IM), which in its basic form is the exchange of text messages in real time. In Mac OS X, you perform these so-called text chats using the iChat application, as long as each person has a MobileMe, AOL Instant Messenger (AIM), Google Talk, or Jabber account.

However, iChat is a powerful messaging program that goes well beyond the standard issue text messaging. If you and another person have microphones and audio output equipment (sound cards and speakers or headsets), you can use iChat to conduct an audio chat with that person (a sort of telephone call over the Internet). If you and your friend have video equipment, as well (such as the iSight camera built into many modern Macs), you can also use iChat to conduct a video chat with that person. To chat with audio or video, both parties must be using a MobileMe account and must have a broadband Internet connection.

Configuring a Mac for iChat

If you are going to use iChat to have audio or video chats, you must have a FireWire or USB camera attached to your Mac. If you have a modern iMac, MacBook, MacBook Pro, or MacBook Air, an iSight camera is built-in. If you don't have one of these, you can use an external webcam or some FireWire camcorders for this purpose. You also need a broadband connection to the Internet. Finally, you need a Mac that's capable of handling the workload of a video chat. All modern Macs are videoconference capable. The best way to find out whether your Mac can handle a videoconference is to try it.

Connect the camera you are going to use to your Mac. If it is a camcorder, power it up and place it in camera mode.

If you don't have a FireWire camera or a broadband connection to the Internet, you can still use iChat for text chatting.

Getting Started with iChat

To get started, launch iChat by clicking the iChat icon on the Dock, and then use the following steps to configure it:

1. Review the information in the welcome screen and click Continue. The Account Setup window appears.

2. If you have a MobileMe account configured for the current user account, the account information is configured automatically. If not, enter the MobileMe, AIM, Google Talk, or Jabber account information in the window and click Continue.

3. If you specified a MobileMe account in step 2, iChat asks if you want to enable encryption. Unless you're exchanging state secrets (probably not a good idea over IM!), you don't need encryption (which slows chatting down ever so slightly), so click to deactivate the Enable iChat Encryption check box, and then click Continue.

4. Click Done. The basic configuration of iChat is complete and you see the main iChat interface.

 note

To use a camcorder for chatting, the camera must support play through, meaning the input coming through the camera's lens must play through the FireWire out port at the same time. If your camera doesn't offer this, you won't be able to use it to chat. Fortunately, many camcorders work with iChat.

 note

Many camcorders are set to go to sleep after a certain period of inactivity passes. When you are using a camcorder during a video conference, it thinks it is inactive because you aren't recording. When it goes to sleep, your conference suddenly ends. Use your camcorder's controls to set its sleep to a large value or to turn off its sleep mode.

 tip

If you want to apply for an iChat account, click the Get an iChat Account button and follow the onscreen instructions to register for a trial MobileMe account. The accompanying iChat account remains valid even if you let the MobileMe account expire.

Configuring iChat Preferences

iChat offers a number of preferences you can use to configure the way it works (select iChat, Preferences to open the Preferences dialog box). Here's an overview of the preferences you can configure:

- **General**—Use the General tab of the iChat Preferences dialog box to configure some general iChat behaviors (see Figure 16.1). The Settings check boxes enable you to configure various settings. For example, you can add the iChat status to the menu bar. Use the When Fast User Switching, Set My Status To pop-up menu to determine your iChat status when you switch to a different user account on your Mac. Use the radio buttons to determine what happens when you log in to your user account and your iChat status is Away; for example, you might want your status to be updated to Available automatically. Use the Save Received Files To pop-up menu to select a location in which you save files you receive via iChat.

Figure 16.1
Use the General pane to configure various iChat settings.

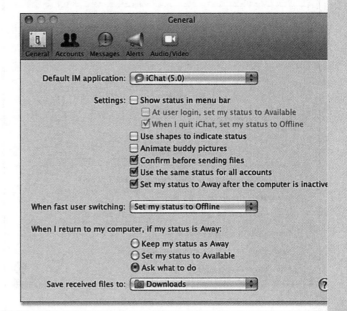

- **Accounts**—Use the Accounts pane to configure the accounts over which you want to chat. Click the Add button (+) at the bottom of the Accounts list to add new accounts. Select an account and use the tools that appear in the right pane of the window to configure it.

- **Messages**—The Messages pane enables you to set various formatting options for your messages (see Figure 16.2). Use the Set Font button to configure the font in which you want to view text messages. Use the balloon and font color pop-up

 note

You can have multiple accounts in iChat and have them logged in at the same time. In addition to MobileMe, AIM, and Google Talk accounts, if there is a Jabber server on your network, you can connect to it to chat with others. You can also enable Bonjour chatting so that you can communicate directly with others on your network that your Mac can discover.

menus to choose the color of those items. Activate the Reformat Incoming Messages check box and use the corresponding Set Font button and pop-up menus to have iChat reformat text you receive according to your preferences. In the lower part of the pane, you see various options for how iChat works. For example, if you want to save the transcript for chat messages, activate the Save Chat Transcripts To check box and use the Open Folder button to choose the location in which you want the transcripts to be stored. If you are a fan of tabbed web browsing, you will appreciate the Collect Chats in a Single Window feature. All of your chat sessions will be displayed as tabs in a window for the specific account you are using.

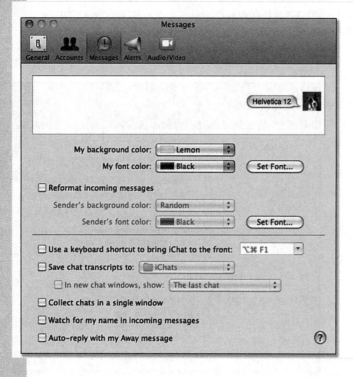

Figure 16.2
Using the Messages preferences, you can control the formatting used for chatting.

- **Alerts**—Use the Alerts pane to set the alerts and notifications iChat uses to get your attention. Select the event for which you want to configure an alert on the Event pop-up menu and then select the specific alert on the check boxes and pop-up menus to configure it. Repeat these steps for each event for which you want to set an alert.

- **Audio/Video**—Use these preferences to configure AV conferencing (see Figure 16.3). In this pane, you see the current image being received from the camera connected to your Mac. Just under the image is an audio meter that provides a graphic representation of the volume level being received. Choose the audio input on the Microphone pop-up menu; for example, to receive audio via the built-in mic, choose Internal microphone. If you have a Bluetooth headset, click the Set Up Bluetooth Headset button to configure it. If you want to set a bandwidth limit for conferencing, use the Bandwidth Limit pop-up menu to do so. Activate the Open iChat When Camera

Is Turned On check box to have iChat launch when you turn on your camera. Activate the Repeat Ring Sound When Invited to an Audio or Video Chat to be notified via a ringing sound when someone wants to conference with you.

Figure 16.3
Use the Video pane to configure AV conferencing.

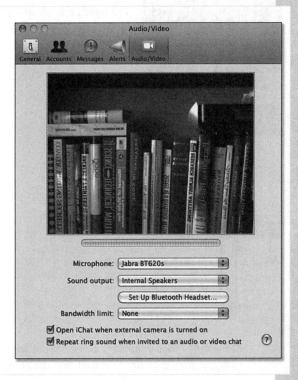

Setting Up Chatting Buddies

There are three sources of people you can chat with; in iChat lingo these are called *buddies*. One source is the people whom your Mac can see via Bonjour. The second source is people who are configured in your Address Book and have either a MobileMe email address, Jabber account, or an AIM screen name. The third source are the buddies you have defined with your MobileMe, AIM, or Google Talk accounts, as the info about these buddies is retained by these services so that you can log in from any computer and be able to access your buddies.

Examining the Buddy Windows

When you open iChat, you might see two windows: One is titled Buddy List (see Figure 16.4), and the other is titled Bonjour List. (If you don't see the Bonjour List, select Window, Bonjour List, or press ⌘-2. If iChat asks whether you want to log in to your Bonjour account, click Log In.) The people shown on the Bonjour list are found automatically when your Mac searches your local network for Bonjour users. You add people with whom you want to chat on the Buddy List. You can chat with people on either of these lists in the same way.

Status menu

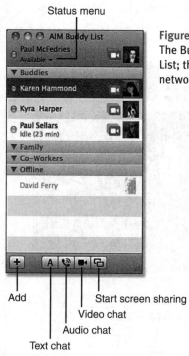

Figure 16.4
The Buddy List shows users who have been added to your permanent Buddy List; the Bonjour window shows users who are available to chat on your local network.

Add

Start screen sharing

Video chat

Audio chat

Text chat

At the top of each window, you see your information including your name, status, video icon (if you have a camera configured for use), and the photo associated with your name.

In the Buddy List window, buddies are placed into one of several categories. AIM Bots are those buddies who use AIM bots to chat. Buddies are your buddies who are currently online. There is a category for Family and a category for Co-Workers to easily get to these groups of contacts. If you chat with someone not on your buddy list, a new category called Recent Buddies will appear. The Offline category contains all your buddies who are currently offline. Use the expansion triangles to expand or collapse the categories.

Adding Someone to Your Buddy List

To add people to your Buddy list, do the following steps:

1. If you want to have the person's contact information available in your Address Book, add the person you want to place on your Buddy List to your Address Book; include either a MobileMe address or an AIM username.

2. In iChat, click the Add button (+) located in the lower-left corner of the Buddy List window and choose Add Buddy. The resulting sheet enables you to manually enter information or to choose a person from your Address Book.

3. To manually add a buddy, enter the account name, choose the type on the top pop-up menu, choose the Group in which you want the buddy placed (Buddies, Family or Co-Workers), and enter the first and last name. Skip to step 5.

4. To select the person you want to add to your Buddy List, click the expand button next to the Last Name field. The lower pane of the sheets expands and you see a mini-Address Book viewer. Search or browse for the person you want to add and select the name.

5. Click Add.

6. Repeat steps 2–5 to add more people to your Buddy list.

After you add buddies, you return to the Buddy List window and the new buddies appear in the appropriate sections when they are online or in the Offline section when they aren't.

Chatting with Text

Instant messaging is a preferred way of communicating for many people. Text chats are easy to do, fast, and convenient. Using iChat, you start your own text chats or answer someone's request to text chat with you.

Starting a Text Chat

You can text chat with another person by using the following steps:

1. Select the person in the Bonjour window or on the Buddy List. If the person is on the Offline list, she isn't available for chatting so you'll need to communicate some other way. Even if the person is online, make sure the status indicator shows that she is available for chatting before you initiate a chat session.

2. Click the Text Chat button, which is the A located at the bottom of the respective window. An empty Instant Message window appears. The name of the window is "Chat with *buddy*" where *buddy* is the name of the person with whom you are chatting.

3. Type your message in the bar at the bottom of the window. You can use the pop-up menu at the end of the window to add smileys to what you type.

4. When you are ready to send what you typed, press Return. You see the message you typed near your name at the top of the window. It is sent to the person with whom you are chatting.

   Your message appears in a text bubble on that user's desktop. When the user clicks the bubble, she is able to either decline the request, or accept your request, type a reply, and send it you (see Figure 16.5).

   When you receive a reply to your message, you see the person's picture along with the text she sent.

3

Figure 16.5
When you initiate a text chat request, the other person has the opportunity to accept or decline the request.

5. Type your response in the message box at the bottom of the window and press Return.

6. Continue chatting to your heart's content (see Figure 16.6).

 tip

Click the emoticon icon at the end of the text box to include a smiley with your text.

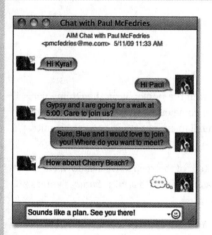

Figure 16.6
Text chats are a great way to communicate about the topics you care about.

7. When you are done chatting, let the person you are chatting with know and close the chat window. If you keep iChat open you could chat with that person again. If you quit iChat, or go offline, the person with whom you were chatting will see that your status has changed.

Answering a Text Chat Request

You saw earlier in Figure 16.5 that when a person wants to chat with you, a box will appear on your screen. Click it and it expands to a chat window. To accept the chat, click the Accept button, type your reply, and press Return to send it (you don't need to click the Accept button; you can just type and press Return to accept). If you don't want to talk, click Decline. If you want to block the person trying to chat with you, click Block.

If you accept the chat request, use the chat window just like when you start a session.

To end a session, close the chat window.

When someone leaves the chat, you'll see a status message saying so at the bottom of the window.

Chatting with Sound

Text chats are great, but audio chats are sometimes even better. Using an audio chat is pretty much like talking on the telephone.

To start an audio chat, select one or more people with whom you want to chat and click the Audio chat button. You see the Audio Chat window and invitations are sent to each buddy you selected. When a person accepts the invitation, you see their name above an audio level indicator and their image (see Figure 16.7). When you see that, start talking. Audio chats work just like talking on the telephone.

Figure 16.7
Audio chats allow you to talk with someone, or groups or people, just as if you were using a telephone.

Adjust the volume
Mute the sound
Invite someone to join the chat

To mute your microphone, click the Mute button, which looks like a microphone. When muted, the audio bar is filled and both the bar and button are orange.

Control the volume with the Volume slider.

To remove a person from an audio chat, point to their name and the x button that appears.

> 🔍 **note**
>
> If you are listening to iTunes when you start an audio or video chat, it automatically stops playing.

When someone wants to audio chat with you, you'll receive an invitation. Accept it and you'll join the chat.

Chatting with Video

If a person you want to talk to and see meets the requirements for AV chatting, click the camera icon next to the person with whom you want to conference or select one or more video-ready buddies and click the Video Chat button. A request for conference is sent to the buddies you selected. You also see a Video Chat window showing the image being transmitted by your camera.

The people with whom you are trying to communicate see a Video Chat invitation window. If they click your name in that window, it expands to show a Video Chat window on each person's machine. They can then select to Accept or Deny your request.

If a person accepts, you will see a message that video conferencing is starting. As other people accept, you see a video window for each (see Figure 16.8). You appear in a window as well; your window is highlighted.

Figure 16.8
When you have more than one person in a chat, each person appears in their own window.

Switch to full screen
Mute the sound
Invite someone to join the chat

Speak normally, and you should keep your movements a bit slower than usual so the motion is smoother on the other end. Depending on how many servers the data has to flow through and how fast each person's connection is, considerable delay might occur. You need to adjust your speech and movement to fit the specific conference in which you are participating. In most cases, this delay won't be a problem for you. To see the conference in full screen, click the Make Full Screen button.

To remove someone from the conference, point to their window and click the x button that appears.

To add more people to the conference, click the Add Buddy button and choose the person you want to invite to join you.

When you are done with the chat, close the window.

When someone wants to video chat with you, you receive an invitation similar to other invitations. You can accept it to start the conference or decline.

More iChat Ideas

Following are some additional iChat tidbits:

■ You can have multiple chats of various types going on with different people at the same time. Each chat appears in its own independent chat window unless you activate the Collect Chats into a Single Window check box on the Messages pane of the iChat Preferences dialog box.

■ Manage your status by clicking the pop-up menu next to your name at the top of the Buddy List. When the green dot appears, your status is online and people will be able to see you; when the red dot appears, you are unavailable for chatting. There are a number of status options that can appear for you as you see on the menu. For example, if you choose Current iTunes Song, the artist and song currently playing in iTunes will be shown when your status appears in other people's Buddy List. Choose Edit Status Menu to see a sheet on which you can customize your status menu.

■ Use your status settings to prevent unwanted interruptions. For example, if you are online, but busy with something, open your status menu and choose Away or one of the other unavailable statuses.

■ Right-click on a buddy on the Buddy List and choose Show Profile. You see the Info window, which has three panes. The Profile pane shows you the person's profile, including chat name account, capabilities, photo, and notes. On the Alerts pane, you can configure actions specific to that buddy, such as sounds that play when that person logs in. Use the Address Card pane to associate a card in Address Book or to enter additional information for the buddy.

■ To block someone with whom you don't want to chat, select the buddy and then select Buddies, Block, *buddy* where *buddy* is the name of the person whom you want to block.

■ Use the Video menu to configure and control various video and audio settings. For example, choose Video, Full Screen to put a video conference in full screen mode. Choose Video, Record Chat to record a chat session. Use the Enabled commands at the bottom of the menu to enable or disable the microphone, camera, and screen sharing feature.

■ To add effects to your image in a video chat, select Video, Show Video Effects. In the resulting Video Effects window, click the effect you want to apply.

■ You can add backgrounds to your video chat sessions. Select Video, Video Effects and a new window opens. You will see different special effects on the first page; use the arrows at the bottom corners to move to the next or previous pages. Page 3 of the video effects includes video clips you can use as backgrounds. For instance, a video of the Eiffel Tower or Yosemite can be used. Page 4 is where you can add your own still or video backdrops.

Just drag a photo or video file from iPhoto, iMovie, or the Finder onto one of the User Backdrop areas. Open the Video, Video Preview to see a preview of the backdrop; you will be asked to move out of the camera's view so that it will be able to replace the real background items behind you with the backdrop you have selected. After the backdrop has been applied, you can move back in front of the camera and initiate your video chat. You can change to another backdrop at any point after that, as iChat now knows enough about what is really behind you that it can replace those items with the backdrop you select.

Sharing Your Screen in a Chat

If you've ever tried to explain to someone how to do something on their computer or if you've ever tried to have someone explain to you what he is doing, you'll see why the ability to share screens in iChat is so useful.

To share your screen with someone, you need to first initiate a video chat with them. In addition, they must be using Mac OS X 10.5 or later. After you have established your video chat, go to the Buddies menu and select Share My Screen if you want that person to be able to remotely control your computer. If you want to control their computer, select Ask to Share Remote Screen from the Buddies menu.

After a screen sharing session has started, iChat will enable an audio chat between you and your buddy. You can then talk about what is being accomplished. A screen sharing session allows you to control your buddy's computer by giving you control of her keyboard and mouse; she will be able to see you doing whatever it is you are doing on her computer. You can copy files from her computer to yours, or from yours to hers. Anything she could do on her computer, you can do on her computer. The same is true if you had shared your screen with her.

Screen sharing has many practical applications, especially if you are trying to troubleshoot an issue on a remote computer. But there are security issues to be aware of. If you share your screen with someone, they have full access to everything you have access to. Be certain to only share with people that you know and trust.

Presenting in the iChat Theater

The ability to chat with someone via text, audio, or video can be very effective. But sometimes you need to be able to show someone a file or a presentation. iChat Theater provides you with the opportunity to share a file, photos, a presentation, or other type of document while you have a video chat with a buddy.

To see if the file you want to present will work in the iChat Theater, return to the Finder, click on the file, then click on the Quick View button in the Toolbar. If Quick View shows a preview of the file, it will work in the iChat Theater. If the file does not show a preview, but shows the icon for the file, it will not work.

To use the iChat Theater, you need to establish a video conference with your buddy. They do not need to have a video camera; you can create a one-way video chat with them. After you have established the video chat, go to the File menu and select Share a File with iChat Theater. You are presented with a standard Open dialog box; navigate to the file and click the Share button. Your buddy will then see the file that you have shared while they continue to hear you speaking in the chat. You will see a Quick View window of the file being shared. Depending on the file, you may be able to control what your buddy sees. For example, if you are sharing a Keynote slideshow you will be able to advance to the next slide. When you are done presenting the file, just close the Quick View window to return to your video conference.

When you are done sharing the document, close the Quick View window and your video conference will resume. If you have another file to present, you can follow the same steps to present another document to your buddy.

WIRED NETWORKING WITH MAC OS X

Networking and Mac OS X

If you have just a single Mac in your home or small office, and if you're the only person who uses that computer, your setup is inherently efficient. You can use the Mac whenever you like, and all the things you need—your applications, your printer, your CD/DVD drive, your Internet connection, and so on—are readily available.

Things become noticeably less efficient if you have to share the Mac with other people. For instance, you might have to wait for someone else to finish a task before you can get your own work done; you might need to have separate applications for each person's requirements; and you might need to set up separate folders to hold each person's data. User accounts and fast user switching in Mac OS X ease these problems (see Chapter 21, "Working with User Accounts"), but they don't eliminate them. For example, you still have to twiddle a thumb or two while waiting for another person to complete his work.

A better solution is to increase the number of Macs available. Now you have several computers kicking around the house or office, but they're all islands unto themselves. If you want to print something using another Mac's printer, you're forced to copy the file to a memory card or other removable media, walk that media over to the other computer, and then print from there. Similarly, if multiple computers require Internet access, you face the hassle (and expense) of configuring separate connections

So now you need to take the final step on this road: Connect everything together to create your own small network. This will give you all kinds of benefits:

- A printer (or just about any peripheral) that's attached to one Mac can be used by any other Mac on the network.

- You can transfer files from one computer to another.

- Users can access disk drives and folders on network computers as though they were part of their own computer. In particular, you can set up a folder to store common data files, and each user will be able to access these files from the comfort of her machine. (For security, you can restrict access to certain folders and drives.)

- You can set up an Internet connection on one device and share that connection with other machines on the network.

- You can set up a wireless portion of your network, which enables you to access other computers and the Internet from just about anywhere in your house or office.

Mac OS X supports both Ethernet (wired) networking and AirPort (wireless) networking. I cover the former in this chapter, and you learn about wireless networking with AirPort in Chapter 18, "Wireless Networking with Mac OS X."

There are two general steps to preparing a wired Ethernet network. The first is to connect the devices on that network using Ethernet cables, and this chapter assumes you've done that. The second is to configure the services you'll be providing on the network, which is what you'll learn here.

Mac OS X supports a variety, in both range and depth, of network services, as you can see in Table 17.1.

Table 17.1   Networking Services Provided by Mac OS X

Service/Protocol	Abbreviation	Function
Apple File Protocol	AFP	Enables file sharing on machines running Mac OS X, so this is the default protocol on most Macs.
AppleTalk	AppleTalk	Set of services used to communicate on Macs running older versions of the Mac OS or AppleTalk devices such as printers.
Bluetooth	Bluetooth	Enables Macs to communicate with various wireless devices, such as cell phones and PDAs.
Common Internet File System	CIFS	Provides remote file access on many platforms, such as Windows.
Dynamic Host Configuration Protocol	DHCP	Provides automatic assignment of IP addresses to devices on a network.

Table 17.1 Continued

Service/Protocol	Abbreviation	Function
Bootstrap Protocol	BOOTP	Enables computers to use the operating system installed on a different computer on the network to start up and operate.
File Transfer Protocol	FTP	Enables the fast transfer of files over TCP/IP networks.
Hypertext Transport Protocol	HTTP	Provides the transmission and translation of data between a web server and web client.
Internet Protocol	IP	Enables communication across a wide variety of devices and services.
Lightweight Directory Access Protocol	LDAP	Enables users to log on to a network and to locate resources, such as files and hardware devices, on a network.
Network File Service	NFS	Enables file sharing on Unix-compatible devices, such as Mac OS X computers.
Network Time Protocol	NTP	Synchronizes time across devices on a network.
Open Transport	OT	Another set of networking protocols that was introduced under earlier versions of the Mac OS.
Point-to-Point Protocol	PPP; PPPoE	Provides TCP/IP services over dial-up connections (PPP) and over Ethernet (PPPoE).
Printer Access Protocol	PAP	Provides services necessary to print to network printers.
Bonjour	Bonjour	Enables Bonjour-compatible devices on a network, such as computers and printers, to automatically discover and configure other Bonjour-compatible devices.
Service Location Protocol	SLP	Enables devices on a network to be discovered automatically.
Short Message Block	SMB	Enables Macs to connect to Windows and Unix file servers.
Transmission Control Protocol/Internet Protocol; User Datagram Protocol/ Internet Protocol	TCP/IP; UDP/IP	Enables the transmission across extended networks, such as the Internet. These protocols do not provide services in themselves but are the means by which data is transmitted across networks.
Web-based Distributed Authoring and Versioning	WebDAV	Extends HTTP to provide collaboration and file management on remote web servers. iDisk services are provided via WebDAV.

All the services listed in Table 17.1 can be useful, but in this chapter, you will learn how to implement the two services you are most likely to use: file sharing and FTP. After you've learned to configure these services, you can apply similar principles to configure additional services on your network.

Configuring and Using File Sharing

The Mac OS has long provided peer-to-peer file-sharing capabilities to enable Macintosh computers on a network to share files. Mac OS X provides robust file-sharing services along with more tools you can use to control and configure a network.

Under Mac OS X, you can share files with Macs running Mac OS X, Macs running OS 9 and earlier, Windows file servers, and Unix file servers. For Macs running earlier versions of the Mac OS (such as Mac OS 9), you can use AppleTalk to share files. For Windows and Unix, you can use SMB and CIFS services.

When connecting to other Macs for file sharing, the machines communicate through either AFP or TCP/IP. To log in to a Mac OS X file-sharing machine serving files via TCP/IP, that machine must have an IP address. Typically, this IP address is assigned as part of connecting that machine to the Internet, such as by a DHCP server provided by a router or an AirPort Base Station.

Mac OS X includes support for Bonjour, which enables devices to seek out other Bonjour-compatible devices on a network and automatically configure access to those devices. All Macs that have Mac OS X version 10.2 or later are Bonjour-aware and can therefore take advantage of this technology to easily and quickly connect to other Macs. However, other devices, such as printers, can also support Bonjour, so those devices can be configured automatically as well.

note

Support for SMB and CIFS enables you to integrate Macs onto Windows and Unix networks with no additional software installations. You can also integrate Windows computers into networks that mostly consist of Macs. See "Networking Mac OS X with Windows Computers," later in this chapter.

note

Peer-to-peer file sharing implies that the files being shared are stored on workstations that people use to accomplish work. The other type of file sharing is based on a server/client arrangement in which the primary purpose of the server machine is to provide network resources, such as files to share. The technology involved is similar. If you are managing a relatively small network, you are probably not likely to have a dedicated server on it, but that's okay because peer-to-peer file sharing works just as well for these kinds of networks.

note

Bonjour is also being used in some "non-computer" devices. For example, TiVos use Bonjour.

AppleTalk is the Mac's original network protocol and continues to be supported in Mac OS X. When you are connecting to Macs running OS version 8.6 or earlier, you have to use AppleTalk as support for file sharing over TCP/IP, which was added in Mac OS 9.0.

In Chapter 19, you will learn how to share an Internet account using a DHCP server. Such a server assigns IP addresses to the machines connected to it. The *D* stands for dynamic, meaning these addresses can change. This can make locating a specific machine by its IP address tough because each machine's address can be changed by the DHCP server. Fortunately, with most DHCP servers, you can choose to manually assign IP addresses to the devices attached to it. When you do this, machines have the same IP address even though they are using a DHCP server to obtain that address.

With Bonjour, you don't need to worry about the IP addresses of individual machines because your Mac seeks out the devices that are communicating on a network and automatically configures access to those devices.

To identify the current IP address of a Mac OS X machine, open the Network pane of the System Preferences application. Select a connection type from the Services list and the machine's current IP address will be shown in the Status section (see Figure 17.1).

 note

If other devices on your network, such as printers, have dynamic IP addresses assigned to them and you use the IP address to configure that device, you can lose the connection to those devices when the DHCP server assigns a new address to them. (This typically happens if the hub loses power for some reason or the device is removed from the network for a while.) In such cases, you need to reconfigure any computers that access the device with the new address assigned by the DHCP server. For such devices, consider assigning a static address that remains constant for that device.

Figure 17.1
On the Network pane, you see the current IP address of a Mac OS X computer; the address is shown next to the active network port (in this case, the address is 10.0.0.110).

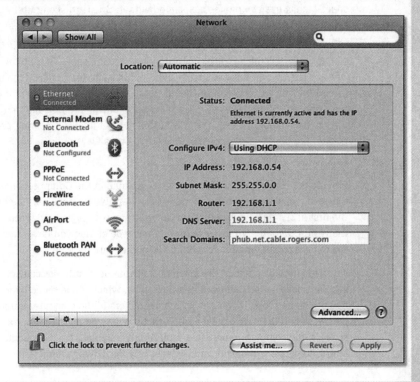

Configuring File Sharing on a Mac Running Mac OS X

To share the files stored on a Mac OS X machine, you must enable the Personal File Sharing service on that computer. This includes turning on the File Sharing service, naming the machine, and so on.

The following steps assume that a Mac has access to the network (via Ethernet or AirPort) and that the default security privileges are in place on the file-sharing machine. You can change the default privileges for items you share to make them more or less available, as you will learn in a later section of this chapter.

To provide file-sharing services from a Mac running Mac OS X, do the following steps:

1. Open the System Preferences application.

2. Click the Sharing icon to open the Sharing pane (see Figure 17.2). At the top of the pane is the computer's name and just below that, its hostname.

 tip

If your purpose in file sharing is one-way—for example, enabling others to download files from a specific machine but not to upload files to it—consider using FTP services on a machine rather than file sharing. You learn how to provide FTP services in a later section of this chapter.

What's in a Name?

Your Mac actually has two names associated with it. One is the computer name, which by default is a combination of the first user's name and the word *Computer*. The other name is that device's hostname, which is actually the name used when the device is accessed over a network.

By default, the hostname and the computer name are the same, except your Mac automatically removes any characters, such as spaces and uppercase letters, which aren't permitted in a hostname. Any changes you make to the computer name are automatically made in the hostname. However, you can manually set the hostname for a machine to be something different from its computer name. To do this, click the Edit button at the top of the Sharing pane. In the resulting sheet, enter the hostname of the Mac. The hostname always ends in **.local**.

---

3. Provide the computer's name by entering a name in the Computer Name text box; use a name that will help others on the network easily identify the machine. The default computer name is the first user's name entered when the machine was registered, with an apostrophe, an *s*, and the word *Computer* (where computer is the type of Mac you have) tacked onto it. You can use the default computer name or change it to one you prefer.

After you provide a name, the machine's hostname is automatically created. Some characters, such as spaces, aren't allowed in a hostname, which is the name by which the machine is identified on the network. If you enter such characters in the computer name, the machine name that people see on the network won't be exactly what you entered. For example, if you include a space in the computer name, it is replaced by a hyphen for the machine's network name. The Mac automatically removes and replaces any disallowed characters.

Figure 17.2
You enable the network services a Mac provides by using the controls on the Services tab of the Sharing pane.

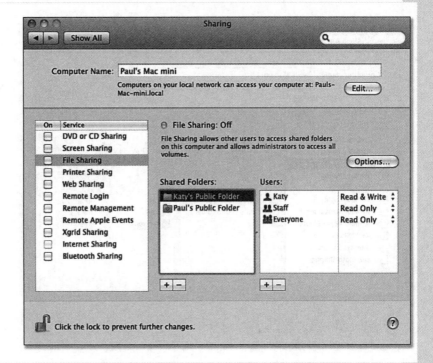

4. If you want to manually enter a hostname, click the Edit button; then, in the resulting sheet, enter the hostname for the machine and click OK. The extension .local is added to the hostname you type to indicate that the host is on the local network.

5. Activate the On check box beside File Sharing. After a moment or two, you see the AFP address of the machine and the browsing name (which is the name by which others on the network will be able to identify the computer when they browse the network), as shown in Figure 17.3.

Using Firewalls and Network Services

If you have a firewall installed on the machine you are configuring as a server, you must configure that firewall to allow the type of access needed for others to access it from the network. For example, to enable the machine to provide file-sharing services, you must configure the firewall to allow machines from the network to connect to the file server. With some firewalls, you can allow access to specific services, such as AFP, only from specific IP addresses. All other requests for services will be denied.

If you use the Mac OS X built-in firewall, the services you enable on the Services pane are allowed automatically. You can use the Firewall tab of the Security pane to manually configure the services that are allowed if you need to.

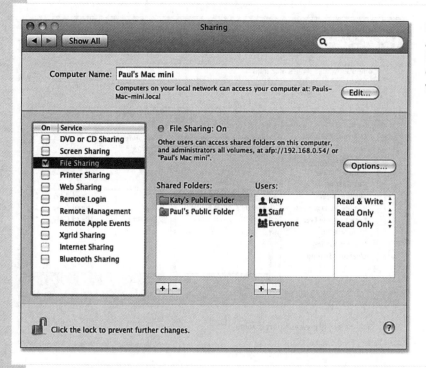

Figure 17.3
Activate the On check box beside File Sharing to enable file sharing for your Mac.

If you use another type of firewall or configure the built-in firewall using another method (such as the Unix commands), you must enable access to the services you are providing through that firewall.

Similarly, if some machines on your network are connected through an AirPort Base Station, you won't be able to access those machines from machines connected outside the network. Because an AirPort Base Station provides protection for the machines it connects, machines outside the network can't see any of the machines on the network.

Always be aware of the security settings of the networks you are configuring and using. Sometimes, you can waste a lot of time troubleshooting a network problem that is actually a case of things working just as planned (such as when you try to figure out why no one can connect to a machine protected by a firewall that isn't configured to allow those services to be accessed on the machine).

Accessing Shared Files from a Mac OS X Computer

There are two basic ways you can access shared files. One is to browse the network for available machines sharing files. The other is to move to the services on a machine directly using the URL for the specific service you want to access.

In either case, when you connect to a server, you must log in to that server to access its resources. You can log in under a user account that is valid for that server, or you can log in as a guest. When you log in under a valid user account, you have access to all the items on that machine just as if you were logged in to the machine directly (rather than over a network). If you are logged in as a guest, you can access only the items on the machine that allow public access, such as each user's Public folder.

note

To access a network resource by browsing, it must support Bonjour or SMB. If not, you have to access it by entering its URL via the Connect to Server command.

In Finder, the Shared section of the Sidebar always shows the network resources that are visible to your Mac (see Figure 17.4). You usually see two types of icons:

- Macs display an icon that indicates the type of Mac. For example, an iMac uses an icon that looks like an iMac, while a MacBook Pro displays a notebook icon.

- Windows PCs show a generic icon.

Figure 17.4
In Finder, the Shared section of the Sidebar shows an icon for each network computer your Mac can access.

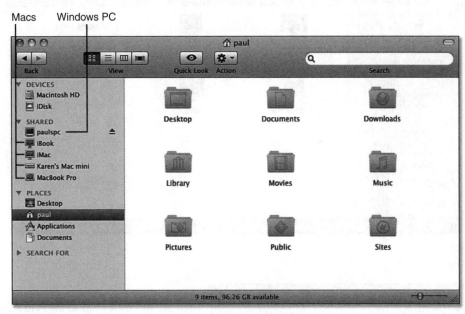

To access shared files stored on a Mac OS X computer that is sharing its files from a Mac OS X machine by browsing the network, do the following steps:

1. Open a Finder window and select Go, Network or press Shift-⌘-K. The Network directory will appear. Depending on the network to which you are connected, you will see a number of icons representing various network resources available to you.

2. To access other Macs providing services, open the Network icon if you see it; if not, the individual servers with which you can work will appear directly under the Network folder. In either case, you will see the names of the computers on your network that are providing services to you (see Figure 17.5).

3. Double-click the icon for the server and services you want to access. In most cases, Mac OS X connects you as a guest.

4. Click Connect As. The Connect to Server dialog box appears (see Figure 17.6).

 note

It can take a few minutes for your Mac to successfully browse the network to which it is connected. If you don't see the resources you think you should after you start the browse process, refresh the Network window by moving away from it and then back again or by clicking its icon to update the list of available network resources.

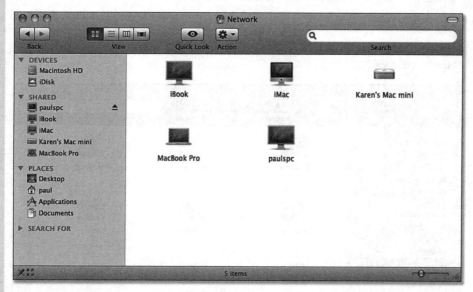

Figure 17.5
The Network folder provides access to other Macs providing services on your network; in this case, I can see an iMac on my network. Note you also see this iMac in the Shared section of the Sidebar.

Figure 17.6
You use this dialog box to log in to a server.

5. To log in as a registered user, which provides the same access to resources you would have when you log in directly to that machine, click the Registered User radio button and enter the username and password for the account under which you want to log in. Click Connect to connect to the server. A window appears that lists each volume or user's Home folder (which is the Home folder of the user account under which you logged in) you can access (see Figure 17.7).

6. Open the folders available via the shared resource to work with them. For example, you can open files, drag them to your Mac to copy them, and so on.

tip

Activate the Remember This Password In My Keychain check box in the Connect to Server dialog box to add a network resource's login information to your keychain. The next time you access that resource, the login information will be input automatically, so you can just click Connect to connect to it.

Figure 17.7
Log in to a network server to see its shared resources.

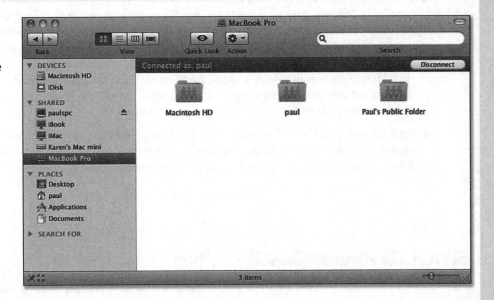

For more precise access to services on a Bonjour machine (such as to choose to access FTP services when file sharing and FTP are being provided) or to access services on a machine that doesn't support Bonjour, you can use a computer's address to access it manually. To do so, perform the following steps:

1. From the Finder, select Go, Connect to Server (⌘-K) or open the Finder's Dock menu and choose Connect to Server. The Connect to Server dialog box will appear (see Figure 17.8).

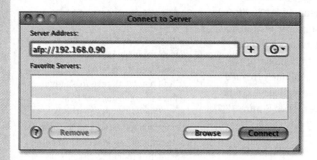

Figure 17.8
Use the Connect to Server dialog box to move to servers by entering their URL.

2. Type the server address you want to access in the Server Address box. The address you use depends on how you want to access the server. For example, to open all of a computer's resources, type its hostname, which is *hostname*.`local`, where *hostname* is the hostname of the machine you are accessing. To access file-sharing services, use the URL for File Sharing services, which will be something like `afp://192.168.0.55/`. You can obtain the address for the specific service you want to access on the Sharing pane of the System Preferences application on the computer you are accessing over the network. Select the specific service you want to access and the related address will appear at the bottom of the pane.

3. Click Connect. Your Mac will attempt to locate the resource via the address you entered. You can monitor the progress of this via the Connecting to Server progress window. If the connection is made successfully, you see the Connecting to Server dialog box (see Figure 17.9).

Figure 17.9
Notice the progress window that indicates the Mac is trying to connect to the specified URL. Use this dialog box to log in to a network server.

4. Enter the username and password for the account under which you want to log in and click Connect, or click the Guest radio button and click Connect instead. The server's volumes that you can access appear in the Select Volume dialog box (see Figure 17.10). The resources that appear depend on the user account under which you are logged in. If you logged in as a guest, you can access only public resources.

Figure 17.10
The machine called iMac has a number of volumes that can be mounted on the computer being used to access that server.

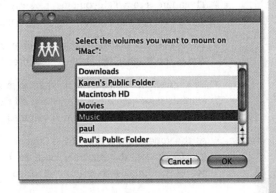

5. Select the volume you want to mount—hold down the Shift or ⌘ key to select multiple volumes—and click OK. A Finder window opens and the volume you chose to access appears (see Figure 17.11).

Figure 17.11
Finder displays the shared volume from the network server.

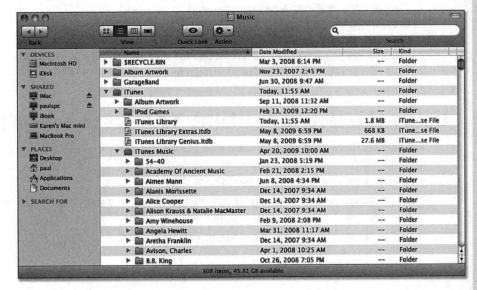

6. Access the network volumes just like those directly connected to or installed in your Mac.

Following are some additional tips about using a Mac OS X machine to access file-sharing services via the Connect to Server command:

- When you are logged in to a file-sharing machine, you can quickly choose other volumes to mount by clicking the server in the Shared section of the Sidebar. All of the volumes that you have access to are shown here, and you can then move to the resources you need.

- The address to which you most recently connected is remembered in the Connect to Server dialog box so you can reconnect to it by opening that dialog box and clicking Connect.

- To remove access to a network resource, click the Eject button shown next to it in the Shared section of the Sidebar, or select the mounted folder or volume and choose File, Eject or press ⌘-E.

- To log back in to the same file-sharing machine under a different user account, such as an administrator account, you must log off that machine and repeat the initial login process. You do this by ejecting all the mounted volumes provided by that server.

- At the upper-right corner of the Connect to Server dialog box is the Recent Servers pop-up menu (the Clock icon) that shows a list of the most recent servers you have accessed. You can select a server from this list to return to it, or you can clear the list by selecting Clear Recent Servers.

- Just below the Server Address box on the Connect to Server dialog box is the Favorite Servers list. You can add a server to your favorites list by entering its URL and clicking the Add to Favorites button (+). You can return to any favorite server by selecting it on the list and clicking Connect. Remove a favorite by selecting it and clicking the Remove button.

- You can place an alias to a networked volume on your Mac, such as by adding it to the Dock. When you open such an alias, you are prompted to log in to the server and, upon doing so, you can access that volume. If you add the password to your keychain, you will skip the login process.

> **tip**
>
> You can add a volume from a network server to the Login Items tab of the Accounts pane of the System Preferences application to mount that server each time you log in.

Using the Network Utility to Assess Your Network

The Network Utility application provides a set of tools you can use to assess the condition of communication across machines on your network as well as a set of tools that enable you to get information about various sites on your network and the Internet.

When you launch the Network Utility (Applications/Utilities), you will see a window with eight tabs, one for each service the application provides (see Figure 17.12).

Table 17.2 summarizes the tabs in the Network Utility application.

Figure 17.12
The Network Utility offers network information and troubleshooting tools.

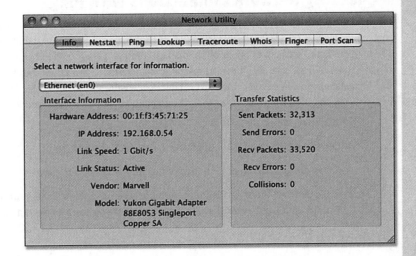

Table 17.2   Tabs in the Network Utility Application

Tab	Function
Info	Provides information about the interface selected on the pop-up menu. For example, you can get the IP address, connection speed, connection status, and hardware information. You also see the statistics about the transfers over the selected interface.
Netstat	Presents various statistics about the performance of the various network protocols. To access this data, select the Netstat tab, choose one of the options by selecting a radio button, and click Netstat. The data appears in the Netstat pane.
Ping	Contacts a specific server to assess network performance between the current Mac and a network resource. When you can't connect to a resource, ping its address to see whether your Mac can communicate with it. If the ping isn't successful, you will know that the machines are unable to communicate. If it successful, you know that the machines can communicate and the problem is related to the specific service you are trying to use.
Lookup	Provides various information about a specific Internet address. For example, you can enter a URL and get the IP address for that site.
Traceroute	Traces a specific route between machines and provides statistics about that route, such as the maximum number of hops needed.
Whois	Enables you to look up information about a domain or an IP address, such as to whom it is registered.
Finger	Reports information about a specific individual based on the person's email address.
Port Scan	Enables you to scan for open access ports on a specific domain or IP address.

Covering each of these services in detail is beyond the scope of this chapter, but the next couple of examples should be helpful in getting you started using this tool.

Checking Network Connections with Ping

Troubleshooting network problems can be difficult because identifying where the source of the problem is can be hard—for example, with the machine you are using, with the machine you are accessing, with an application, and so on. Ping is a way to check on the fundamental communication between two machines. If the ping is successful, you know that a valid communication path exists between two machines. If it isn't successful, you know that a fundamental problem exists with the communication between the machines, and this helps you know where to troubleshoot.

To ping a machine, perform the following steps:

1. Open the Network Utility application and click the Ping tab.

2. Enter the IP address or URL for the machine you want to ping.

3. Click Send an Unlimited Number of Pings to send a continuous number of pings, or click Send Only X Pings and enter the number of pings if you want to send a specific number.

4. Click Ping.

Watch the results in the lower part of the window. You will see your machine attempt to communicate with the machine whose address you entered. If they are able to successfully communicate, you see statistics about how fast the pings are (refer to Figure 17.13). If the pings are successful, you know the communication path between the machines is valid. If not, you know you have a fundamental connection problem between the two machines.

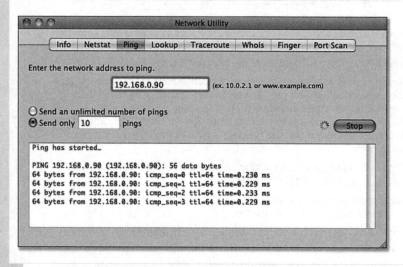

Figure 17.13
Ping is a useful way to test your connection to another machine (in this case, I pinged 192.168.0.90, which is another Mac on my network).

Tracing a Route with Traceroute

Sometimes looking at the specific route between two machines can help identify the source of problems you might be having:

1. Open the Network Utility application and click the Traceroute tab.

2. Enter the domain name or IP address to which you want to trace a route.

3. Click Trace. The lower pane of the window will be filled with information that shows each step of the path from your machine to the one whose information you entered (see Figure 17.14).

Figure 17.14
This Traceroute window shows the path from my machine to www.wordspy.com.

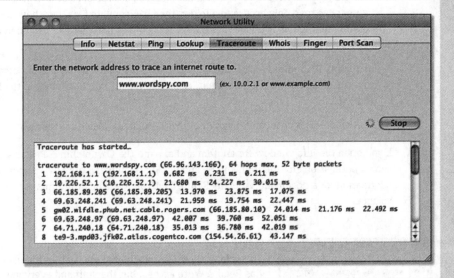

Understanding and Setting Permissions

Access to items on your Mac OS X machine, whether from the machine directly or over a network, is determined by the access privileges set for those items. Three levels of access privilege can be set for any item; these are the following:

- Owner

- Group

- Others

The owner is the owner of the item. When you are the owner of an item, this will be your short username followed by (Me).

The group is a set of users. By default, Mac OS X includes several groups for which various permissions are assigned to different volumes and directories. Many of these default groups look odd, and some are even nonexistent (for example, in certain places, you will see Members of group " "). You can also create your own groups and place users in those groups to provide access to a collection of people.

➡ *To learn about creating user groups, **see** "Creating Groups of Users," **p. 455**.*

Others include those users who are neither the owners nor members of a group.

For any object, there are four levels of access that can be assigned to people or groups:

- **Read & Write**—This is the broadest level of access and lets the user to whom it is assigned read and write to the item to which it is assigned.

- **Read only**—This privilege lets a user see items in a directory but not change them. For example, if a user has read-only access to a folder, they can copy its files, but they can't change the files stored in that folder. If this permission is applied to a file, the user can open the file, but not make any changes to it.

- **Write only (Drop Box)**—With this access, a user can place items in a directory but can't see the contents of that directory. By default, each user has a Drop Box folder in the Public folder in her Home folder.

- **No Access**—The user can't do anything with the item, including seeing it.

If you open the Info window for an item and expand the Ownership & Permissions area, the current access permissions for the item will be shown. For example, Figure 17.15 shows the Permissions information for a document, whereas Figure 17.16 shows similar information for the current startup volume.

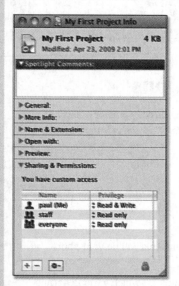

Figure 17.15
This Info window for a document shows that the user account paul (Me) has Read & Write access, but the staff and everyone accounts have Read only access.

There are several things you need to know about the Ownership & Permissions information shown in the Info window.

Figure 17.16
This info window for the current startup volume shows that only the root account (system) has Read & Write access, but the administrator account (admin) and the everyone account have Read Only access.

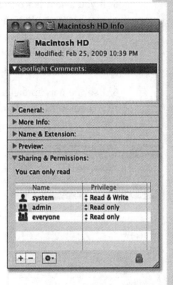

First, unless you are logged in under the root or administrator account, you can't use the pop-up menus to change the permissions assigned to items on the Mac OS X startup volume above the current user's Home directory. However, when you open the Ownership & Permissions area of the Info window for an item on another volume or within a user's Home directory, the pop-up menus become active and you can use them to change the privileges for the items that folder contains. You can select the user or group on the pop-up menu in the Name column and set the privilege for that user or group using the pop-up menu in the Privilege column.

You can add more users or groups to the list, or remove users or groups from the list, using the Add (plus) or Remove (minus) buttons at the bottom of the Info window.

Second, the groups you see in the Info window are default groups created when you install Mac OS X. The user accounts that are members of these groups can access the item with the group's privileges. You can use the Accounts pane of the System Preferences application to create and manage user groups.

To configure access privileges for most items, you need to either be logged in as an administrator or authenticate yourself in the Info window.

To set the access privileges for any item, perform the following steps:

1. Log in under an administrator or the root account.

2. Select the item for which you want to set permissions and press ⌘-I.

3. Expand the Ownership & Permissions section in the Info window.

4. If you are the owner of the item, use Privilege pop-up menu to set your access to the item.

5. If you select the Add button at the bottom of the Name column, you see the People tool. This tool presents all of the contact information in your Address Book along with all the user accounts and groups you have created on your Mac. Find the user with which you want to share the item, select it, and click Select. The person you selected will be shown on the user list and you can configure the user's permission.

6. Use the pop-up menu in the Privilege column to set the access permission for the user or group you selected (see Figure 17.17).

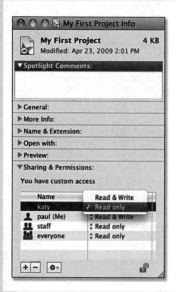

Figure 17.17
Use the pop-up menus in the Ownership and Permissions section of the Info window to set access permission for people and user groups.

7. To add additional users or groups, click the Add button (the plus sign). Then choose the user or group and select the access permission.

8. To remove a user or group from the list, select it and click the Remove button (the minus sign).

9. Continue adding, configuring, and removing users and permissions until you have configured all the permissions for the item.

 tip

Under Mac OS X, you can open multiple Info windows at the same time. This is a handy way to compare and contrast the permissions provided for different items.

Networking Mac OS X with Windows Computers

Because support for Windows and Unix file-sharing protocols is built in to Mac OS X, using a Mac on a Windows or Unix network is easy. It is simple to add a Windows computer to a Mac-based network.

Sharing Files with Windows Computers

You can use Mac OS X to access files provided on a Windows computer on your network via the SMB protocol without doing any additional configuration. To use files provided on a Windows or Unix network that uses SMB, perform the following steps:

1. Connect your Mac OS X machine to the network.

2. Open the Connect to Server dialog box and click Browse. Depending on the SMB servers on your network and how the network is configured, the SMB servers might or might not appear in the list of available servers when you browse the network, so you might have to enter the server address manually.

3. If you don't see the SMB server to which you want to connect, enter the address of the server to which you want to connect; the form of the address is smb://*ServerName*/*ShareName*/ where *ServerName* is the IP address for the Windows machine you are attempting to access, and *ShareName* is the name of the item being shared with you, such as a volume or folder.

 tip

To determine the IP address (*ServerName*) for a Windows machine, open the Command Prompt window, type **ipconfig**, and press Enter. The IP address of the Windows machine will be shown.

4. Click Connect. You are prompted to enter your workgroup/domain, username, and password for that server.

5. Enter the required information and click OK. You are logged in to the shared resource and can use the files it contains just like a Mac that is acting as a file server.

To enable Windows users to access files stored on your Mac, carry out the following steps:

1. Open the Sharing pane of the System Preferences application.

2. Click on the File Sharing service in the Services list. Click on the Options button.

 note

Connecting to Windows computers can be problematic depending on the specific network you are using. If the preceding steps don't enable you to connect to a Windows computer, try using the Apple support document located at the following address: http://docs.info.apple.com/article.html?artnum=106660.

3. On the resulting sheet, click the Share Files and Folders Using SMB (Windows) check box, as shown in Figure 17.18.

4. You must enable a user account for Windows sharing to be accessed from a Windows computer. Check the On check box for a user account that you want to be accessible from a Windows computer. A password sheet appears.

5. Enter the password for the account and click OK.

6. Repeat steps 4 and 5 for each account you want to enable.

7. When you have finished enabling accounts, click Done to return to the Sharing pane of the System Preferences application. Take note of the IP address to provide to users so they can access your Mac from their Windows computer.

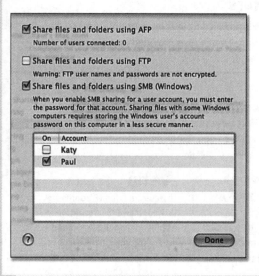

Figure 17.18
Activate the Share Files and Folders Using SMB check box to share your resources with Windows PCs.

8. Provide the user account, password, and address to the Windows users you want to be able to log in.

A Windows user can use the URL, username, and password you provided to log in to your Mac to share files just like Macs on your network (see Figure 17.19).

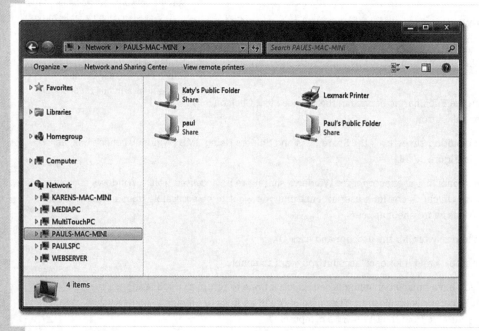

Figure 17.19
This Mac is being accessed from a Windows 7 computer.

Accessing Virtual Private Networks

Virtual Private Network (VPN) service enables networked computers to access file servers, email servers, and other network resources over a WAN connection just as machines connected via a LAN can. Using Mac OS X, you can connect a Mac to a VPN. To access a VPN, perform the following steps:

> **note**
>
> Before you will be able to access a VPN, you'll need to talk to that network's administrator to get all of the information you will need such as connection method, address, user name, password, and so on.

1. Open the Network pane of the System Preferences application.

2. Click the plus sign to Add a Service at the bottom of the Services list.

3. On the resulting sheet, select VPN from the Interface pop-up menu. When you do, you will be presented with two additional pop-up menus to work with.

4. Use the VPN Type pop-up menu to specify which VPN protocol to use. Your network administrator should specify which to use. L2TP over IPSec is more secure.

5. Enter a name for the service. This name will appear in the Services list on the Network pane.

6. Click the Create button. You will return to the Services list and the new VPN service will be selected.

7. Enter a Server Address. This can be in the form of a URL or an IP address.

8. You may need to enter an Account Name. Some VPN servers that you might connect to require this.

9. Click the Authentication Settings button to configure how you log in to the VPN. Use the information provided by your network admin to configure this sheet. Click OK when you are done.

> **tip**
>
> If you use VPN regularly, add the VPN status menu to the Finder menu bar by activating the Show VPN Status in Menu Bar check box in the Internet Connect window.

10. Click Connect. You will be connected to the VPN and should be able to access the resources on the remote network.

WIRELESS NETWORKING WITH MAC OS X

Networking the Wireless Way

Chapter 17, "Wired Networking with Mac OS X," was all about wired networking, where each computer and device connects to the network via a cable that runs from the device's network interface card (NIC) to a port on a switch or router. If you want maximum network speed, Ethernet, particularly Gigabit Ethernet, is the only way to connect.

However, sometimes a wired connection just isn't practical or even possible. For example, if your switch is in the den, how do you set up a wired connection for the computer in the bedroom next door? One solution is to drill holes in the adjoining walls and then snake a long Ethernet cable through the hole. That will work, but holes in the wall are rarely attractive.

Even more daunting, how do you connect a computer that's downstairs in the kitchen or even two floors down in the basement? Diehard Ethernet types might consider getting special outdoor Ethernet cables and poking more holes in the appropriate walls, but at some point the hole-making madness must stop. Finally, consider the simple scenario where you're tired of working in the den and you'd prefer to take your notebook Mac outside to enjoy the sunshine. Do you purchase a 200-foot cable for the privilege of occasionally working away from your desk?

A much more convenient solution in all these scenarios is to forego the cables and go wireless. It's not as fast as either Fast Ethernet or Gigabit Ethernet, but if you get the right hardware, it's fast enough, and it means that you can easily and quickly connect almost any computer or wireless device to your network. And wireless signals extend out of doors, so you can go ahead and enjoy the day.

Modern wireless networking can be both fast and reliable, particularly if you build your wireless network around Apple's AirPort technology, which is the subject of this chapter.

Understanding AirPort

AirPort is Apple's name for its implementation of IEEE 802.11a/b/g/n wireless standards, which are also the standards for Windows computers and other devices. That's good news because it means that AirPort devices are compatible with any networks or devices that implement these standards. So, you can use non-Apple devices on AirPort networks and use Airport-equipped Macs on non-AirPort networks as long as those networks comply with the 802.11 standards, which almost all do.

Like Ethernet, there are several flavors of AirPort. There are a number of technical differences between these types, but the most important one is communication speed:

- **AirPort**—This was the original incarnation and offered many wireless benefits. AirPort communicates at 11Mbps and is compatible with wireless devices based on the 802.11b standard. AirPort is no longer supported by modern Macs, which support AirPort Extreme instead. However, more modern AirPort technologies are backward compatible, so you can connect an AirPort Mac to a network using one of the newer standards and still enjoy its benefits (at a lower speed than the other types, but it works well enough).

- **AirPort Extreme**—This is the newer standard and offers even more benefits. The first is speed. AirPort Extreme communicates at 54Mbps, which is almost five times the speed at which the original AirPort communicates. AirPort Extreme is compatible with devices using the 802.11g Wi-Fi standard. Second, AirPort Extreme can support more computers at the same time than does AirPort. Third, AirPort Extreme enables you to share a USB printer or hard drive from an AirPort Extreme Base Station. Fourth, with AirPort Extreme, you can wirelessly link base stations together to expand the range of an AirPort network to cover large areas.

- **AirPort Extreme 802.11n**—This is the newest standard, and it supports the 802.11n specification, which is up to five times faster than 802.11g networks. The newest AirPort Extreme Base Station also has a much larger range than previous models, which is also good news.

Mac OS X supports all flavors of AirPort, but specific Mac models support either AirPort or one of the AirPort Extreme versions; in other words, older Macs can support an AirPort card, whereas all modern Macs support AirPort Extreme cards. The two cards are not interchangeable. To find out which flavor your Mac supports, check its documentation. All shipping Macs support AirPort Extreme.

Fortunately, even though the hardware for the two standards is different, it is compatible. AirPort machines can connect to AirPort Extreme networks, and vice versa. The primary difference is that AirPort networks are much slower than AirPort Extreme networks are. And, AirPort Extreme Base Stations offer more features than AirPort Base Stations do.

 note

Because it is based on the 802.11 standards, AirPort is compatible with 802.11 networks and devices. For example, you can connect an AirPort-equipped Mac to any wireless network that supports 802.11b, 802.11g, or 802.11n devices, such as those designed for Windows computers. Similarly, Windows machines equipped with 802.11b, 802.11g, or 802.11n devices can also access an AirPort network.

Because it is the newer standard, this chapter focuses mostly on AirPort Extreme. I do my best to use the term *AirPort Extreme* when discussing something that is specific to AirPort Extreme technology or *AirPort Standard* when referring to the older technology. When I use the term *AirPort*, I mean to refer to something that is applicable to both technologies.

AirPort functionality is provided through the following components:

- **AirPort-ready Macs**—If your Mac is AirPort ready, it has built-in antennas that are used to transmit and receive signals to and from the wireless network. The good news is that all modern Macs are AirPort-compatible and most include an AirPort card as standard equipment.

- **AirPort card**—To use AirPort, your Mac must have an AirPort card installed in it. If your Mac doesn't have a card, you can add one inexpensively because AirPort Extreme cards cost only about $49. AirPort cards are simple to install yourself. AirPort cards are standard on all current Macs, except the Mac Pro, which offers an AirPort card as an option.

- **AirPort software**—The AirPort software is necessary for Macs to communicate through the AirPort hardware. The software to configure and use an AirPort network is part of the standard Mac OS X installation.

- **AirPort Base Station**—An AirPort base station transmits the signals for the AirPort network. There are three basic types of base stations. The AirPort Extreme Base Station is a dedicated hardware device that contains ports for a cable or DSL modem, USB printer or hard drive, and up to three Ethernet devices. Another option is an AirPort Express Base Station, which performs a similar function to the full-size base station but doesn't offer as many features (for example, it has only one Ethernet port to which you connect a cable or DSL modem or a single Ethernet device). You can also configure any AirPort-equipped Mac to act as a base station by using Mac OS X's built-in Internet sharing capabilities.

 note

An AirPort Extreme or AirPort Express Base Station and an AirPort-equipped Mac OS X machine sharing its Internet connection are functionally identical from the perspective of providing an Internet connection (though using a dedicated base station offers many benefits). In this chapter, when I use the term *base station*, it can refer to any of these means of providing an AirPort network. When referring to a specific base station, I'll use the full name, such as AirPort Express Base Station.

An AirPort network provides access to a similar set of services that a wired network does, and the two networks can work together seamlessly. For example, computers connected to a wired network via AirPort can print to printers connected to the base station, use file sharing with Macs connected to the network wirelessly, and so on. If you connect a USB printer to an AirPort Extreme or Express Base Station, you can share that printer with any AirPort-equipped Mac. If you connect a USB hard drive to the USB port on an AirPort Extreme Base Station, you can share that drive with all the computers on the network, whether they connect via a wire or wirelessly.

➥ To learn how to configure file sharing over a network, **see** "Configuring and Using File Sharing," **p. 364.**

Upgrading with the AirPort Extreme 802.11n Enabler

As mentioned earlier, the latest incarnation of AirPort wireless technology supports 802.11n, and all new Macs that come with AirPort cards support 802.11n. However, many older Macs (even some that are fairly recent) only support 802.11g. How can you tell whether your Mac supports 802.11n? Here's the easiest way:

1. In Finder, select Applications, Utilities and then launch the Network Utility.

2. In the Network Utility window, select the Info tab.

3. Use the Select a Network Interface for Information pop-up menu to choose your wireless network interface.

The Model value tells you which 802.11 standards your AirPort card supports. In Figure 18.1, for example, this AirPort card only supports up to 802.11g.

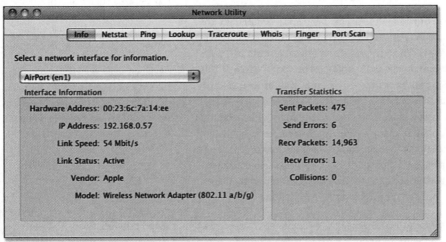

Figure 18.1
Use the Network Utility application to see which 802.11 standards your AirPort card supports.

Fortunately, many 802.11g Macs can jump up to 802.11n with a simple software upgrade. If your Mac has an AirPort Extreme card and an Intel Core 2 Duo processor, you can perform the upgrade, which requires a program called AirPort Extreme 802.11n Enabler for Mac. You have two choices:

- If you purchased a new AirPort Extreme 802.11n Base Station, the Enabler is included with the Base Station.

- Purchase the Enabler software from the Apple Store (it costs $1.99): http://store.apple.com/us/product/D4141ZM/A.

Setting Up an AirPort Base Station

Setting up an AirPort base station is slightly different depending on the type of base station you use: an AirPort Extreme or Express Base Station or an AirPort-equipped Mac OS X machine that provides Internet sharing.

There are many benefits to using an AirPort Extreme or Express Base Station to provide a wireless network. One is that they don't place any processing load on an individual Mac and are intended to run at all times, so the AirPort network is always available. They also provide the ability to share an Internet connection with devices to which they are networked using an Ethernet connection. One of the most important benefits of a base station is that they can shield your network from attack using Network Address Translation. The disadvantage of this device is its cost (currently $179 for an AirPort Extreme Base Station and $99 for an Express Base Station).

The benefit of using an AirPort-equipped Mac OS X machine as a base station is that you don't need to purchase any additional hardware (except for the AirPort card in the Mac that will act as the base station if it doesn't already have one). You get most of the functionality from an AirPort base station but don't have to support another dedicated device. Using this method does have several disadvantages, though. One is that it places additional processing load on the machine that acts as the base station. Another is that the network can be affected by the state of that machine. For example, if the machine is shut down or crashes, the network is taken down as well. Another is that a Mac acting as a base station doesn't support all the base station's features, such as the option to wirelessly link base stations together to increase the range of a network. Using an AirPort-equipped Mac isn't as secure as using a dedicated AirPort base station either.

 note

You can have multiple base stations operating in the same area at the same time to grow your AirPort network to be quite large.

Setting Up an AirPort Extreme Base Station

Apple's AirPort Extreme Base Station is a relatively simple device. It contains a transmitter that broadcasts the signal over which the network is provided. It has four Ethernet ports. One, the WAN port, is used to connect to a broadband Internet connection, such as a cable modem. The other three are used to connect to a wired Ethernet network or to Ethernet-equipped devices so the base station can also share its Internet and network connection with the devices connected to it via a network or directly to one of its Ethernet ports. Along with the power adapter port, it offers a USB port to which you can connect a USB printer or USB hard drive to share one of those devices with the network.

Setting up an AirPort Extreme Base Station consists of the following two tasks:

1. Install the base station.

2. Configure the AirPort network, including the Internet connection the base station will use to connect to the Internet.

Installing the Base Station

First, locate the device in a central area so it provides the maximum amount of coverage where you install it. In most houses, the AirPort Extreme Base Station provides adequate signal strength even if you locate it at one end of the house and place machines you want to network at the other end. However, the closer the machines are to the base station, the stronger the signal is.

Of course, a major consideration for the location of the base station is where your Internet connection will come from. If you use a cable modem, you need to locate the device so that you can connect the cable modem to it. If you use a DSL modem, you need to locate the base station relatively close to the phone line port to which the DSL modem is attached.

After you have placed the base station in its location, attach its power adapter to the station and plug it in to a wall outlet. Use an Ethernet cable to connect the cable or DSL modem to the WAN (Wide Area Network) Ethernet port.

You can connect an Ethernet device to each of the three LAN Ethernet ports on the base station. For example, you can connect a network printer, a computer, or to add more than three devices, connect one of the ports to an Ethernet hub.

If you want to share a USB printer with all Macs that can access the network, connect the printer's USB cable to the USB port on the base station. Likewise, you can connect an USB hard drive to the base station's USB port to share that drive on the network.

note

The machine you use to configure a base station must be AirPort-capable to be able to configure the base station wirelessly. It does not need to have an AirPort card if it is connected to the base station via Ethernet.

Configuring the Base Station

After you have installed the base station, you need to configure it. You can configure it manually through the AirPort Utility, or you can use the guided approach. With either method, you configure the base station from a machine with which it can communicate either via AirPort or through an Ethernet network.

Configuring the Base Station Using the Guided Approach

Use the following steps to configure the base station using the guided approach:

1. Open the AirPort Utility application (Applications/Utilities) to see the first window, which shows all the base stations with which the Mac can communicate (see Figure 18.2).

2. Select the base station that you want to configure.

note

The specific steps you use to configure a base station with the AirPort Utility depend on what you are doing. For example, you see different options when configuring a base station for the first time than you do when you are reconfiguring a base station. These steps provide an example of reconfiguring an existing base station, but the steps to configure a new one are similar, just in a slightly different order with differences in minor details.

Figure 18.2
Use the
AirPort Utility
application
to configure
AirPort base
stations.

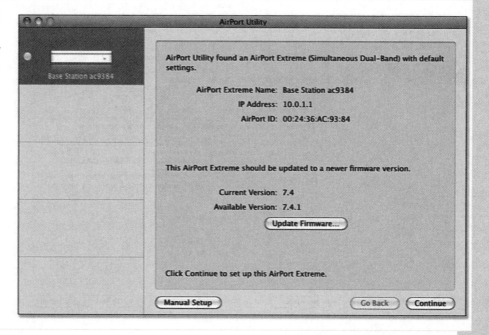

3. If you see a message that your base station firmware should be updated (as shown in Figure 18.2), click Update Firmware and then click Continue in the dialog box that appears. The AirPort Utility downloads and installs the new firmware, and then restarts the base station. When the base station reappears in the AirPort Utility, skip to step 5.

4. Click Continue.

5. Type a name for the base station, type the base station password (twice), and then click Continue.

6. Click the I Want to Create a New Wireless Network radio button and click Continue.

7. Enter the name for the wireless network you are creating. This is the name that you'll select to join a machine to the network.

8. Make sure the WPA/WPA2 Personal radio button is selected, as shown in Figure 18.3, and then type the network password (twice). You must specify a password that's between 8 and 63 characters long.

9. Click Continue.

 caution

If you are configuring a base station that has already been configured and is protected by a password, you have to enter that password before you can proceed.

If the base station you are configuring has outdated software installed on it, the AirPort Utility application attempts to update it. To do so, you must be able to connect to the Internet, which is sort of a Catch-22 in that it assumes that it is already configured and you are reconfiguring it. You can download the update to the Mac you are going to use to configure the base station and then the base station can update its software from there.

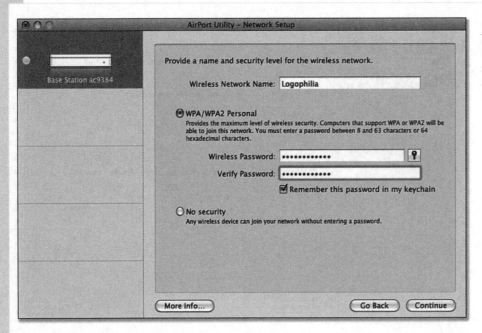

Figure 18.3
You should use WPA2 security on an AirPort network.

10. If you want to allow Macs and other devices to access the base station's Internet connection without also having access to your network, leave the Enable Guest Network check box activated, make sure WPA/WPA2 Personal is selected in the Guest Network Security pop-up menu, type the guest network password (twice), and click Continue.

11. Choose the radio button that corresponds to how you connect to the Internet. This is the same method that you'd use if you were connecting your Mac directly to the Internet, as described in Chapter 13, "Connecting Your Mac to the Internet." Click Continue.

➥ *To learn how to configure a Mac for the Internet, **see** "Connecting Your Mac to the Internet," p. 267.*

12. Enter your Internet connection data, as provided by your ISP, and then click Continue.

13. Click Update and then click Continue. AirPort Utility configures the base station according to the settings you entered. When the process is complete, the base station restarts and the network is available for use.

14. Click Quit.

 note

If you see an error message stating that the required AirPort hardware was not found when you started the AirPort Setup Assistant, see "No AirPort Hardware Is Found" in the "Troubleshooting" section at the end of this chapter.

If you can't access the base station because you don't know the password, see "I Don't Know the Base Station Password" in the "Troubleshooting" section at the end of this chapter.

Configuring a Base Station Manually

You should also know how to manually configure the base station. Manual configuration can be a better and more complete way to configure a base station, and there are some options you can only configure using the manual technique. If you want to change only one aspect of a base station's configuration, using the manual method is also the way to go. And, it can also be a faster way to configure a base station. For example, you need to manually configure a base station when you want to share an Internet account with other machines on an Ethernet network or to use the AirPort base station as a bridge between the wireless network and a wired one (for example, to allow AirPort-equipped machines to use a printer connected to a wired network). You also use the AirPort Utility application to configure a base station manually by performing the following steps:

1. Open the AirPort Utility (Applications/Utilities). You see all the base stations currently in range of the Mac you are using, whether they can communicate wirelessly or over an Ethernet connection.

2. Select the base station you want to configure and click Manual Setup (if there is only one base station in range, it is selected automatically).

   ➡ *If you get an error message when trying to configure your base station manually, see "I Can't Configure My Base Station Manually" in the "Troubleshooting" section at the end of this chapter.*

3. If the base station has been reset, you see a dialog box informing you that the base station has been reset and is not currently configured. (If the base station has not been reset, you won't have to do this step.) Click Automatic and then authenticate yourself using an administrator name and password. The software reconfigures the base station and restarts it. When it is complete, you return to the Select Base Station window. Click Manual Setup again.

 note

When you have problems with a base station, sometimes you must reset it so that it returns to its default settings (in effect, you start over).

If new AirPort firmware is available, the application will prompt you to download and install it. Do so and your base station's firmware will be updated and it will be restarted. You return to the Select Base Station window. Select the base station again and click Manual Setup.

You next see a window that has the base station name as its title that includes several tabs; some tabs also have subtabs (see Figure 18.4).

In the manual mode, the AirPort Utility has the following tabs:

- **AirPort**—Use this tab to configure various aspects of the AirPort network, such as the base station name and wireless network name.

- **Internet**—With this tab, you determine how the base station connects to the Internet and how it distributes addresses to the other devices on the network.

 note

The tabs you see depend on the type of base station you are configuring. For example, an Extreme Base Station has different options than does an Express Base Station. For example, an Express Base Station has the Music tab, which you can use to configure music broadcast from iTunes. The rest of this information reflects an AirPort Extreme Base Station.

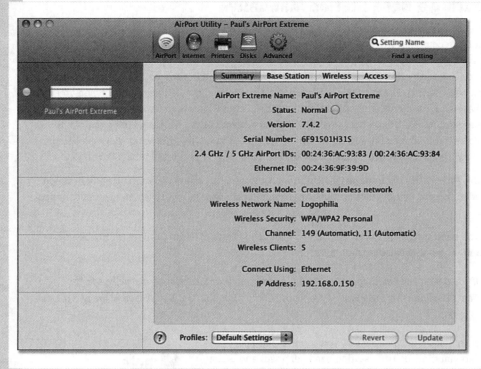

Figure 18.4
This Manual
Setup mode
enables you
to configure
all aspects
of a base
station.

- **Music**—On this tab (AirPort Express Base Station only), you configure AirTunes services to broadcast iTunes music to speakers connected to the base station.

- **Printers**—On this tab, you configure a printer attached to the Base Station.

- **Disks**—On this tab, you configure a hard disk attached to the Base Station.

- **Advanced**—While you are unlikely to need to use this tab, you should know in general what it does, which is to enable you to create logs to store messages that can be helpful in diagnosing network problems. You can also configure specific ports on the base station to provide access to devices outside the network. On the third subtab, you can configure PPP dial-in accounts.

Covering all these options is beyond the scope of this chapter, but the following steps demonstrate how to configure some of the most common settings.

 note

These steps assume the base station you are configuring has been configured previously. If not, the steps might be slightly different.

1. Select the AirPort tab if it isn't selected already. You see a number of subtabs.

2. Click the Summary tab to see the current configuration of the AirPort network.

3. Click the Base Station tab (see Figure 18.5).

Figure 18.5
Use the Base
Station tab to
configure the
base station
name, pass-
word, timer
server, and
whether it
can be con-
figured via
Ethernet.

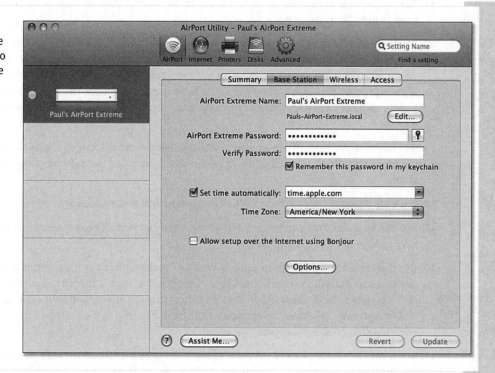

4. Enter the base station name (this is the name of the hardware, not the name of the network it provides) in the AirPort
   Extreme Name field.

5. To change the base station's password (not the network's
   password), use the AirPort Extreme Password and Verify
   Password fields and activate the Remember This Password
   in My Keychain check box.

6. To have the base station's time set automatically, activate
   the Set Time Automatically check box and choose the time
   server on the pop-up menu.

7. To allow the base station to be configured over its Ethernet
   WAN connection, activate the Allow Setup over the Internet
   Using Bonjour check box.

8. Click the Wireless tab. On this tab, you configure the wireless network being provided by the base station.

9. Use the Wireless Mode pop-up menu to determine if the
   base station is part of a WDS network.

10. Enter the network name in the Wireless Network Name field.

 tip

To enter the contact information for
the base station and its location,
click the Options button.

 note

If the base station is already providing a network and you change the
name or password of the network,
people who use the network need to
change the network they use. The
new network name appears as an
available network on the client
machines, but you must provide the
new password to those whom you
want to use the network.

11. Use the Radio Mode pop-up menu to determine the specific standards supported on the network, such as 802.11b/g compatible.

12. Use the Radio Channel Selection pop-up menu to select the channel over which the base station communicates. Generally, the default channel works fine, but if you are having trouble communicating with devices, you can try different channels to improve signal transmission and reception. If you have multiple AirPort networks in the same area, you can use the Radio Channel Selection pop-up menu to have each network use a different channel so that they don't interfere with one another.

13. Use the Wireless Security pop-up menu, Wireless Password field, the Verify Password field, and the Remember This Password in My Keychain check box to set the security of the wireless network.

14. Click the Wireless Options button. The Wireless Options sheet appears.

15. Use the Multicast Rate pop-up menu to set the multicast rate. Choosing a higher value improves performance but also reduces range.

16. Use the Transmit Power pop-up menu to change the strength of the base station's signal. If many base stations exist in the same physical area, reduce the signal strength to limit the interference of these stations with one another. You can also reduce the strength to limit the size of the AirPort network's coverage, for example, if the base station is in a small space and you don't want to extend the network past that space.

17. If you want to create a closed network, activate the Create a Closed Network check box. A closed network does not appear on other users' AirPort menus. To join closed networks, users have to know the name and password for that network (because they can't see the network on a menu). Using a closed network is a good way to keep your network more secure.

18. Activate the Use Interference Robustness check box to make the AirPort signal less sensitive to interference.

19. Click Done to save your changes and return to the Wireless tab.

20. Click the Internet tab and then the Internet Connection subtab.

21. Configure the base station for Internet access. This works similarly to configuring a Mac for Internet access. Choose the connection method from the Connect Using pop-up menu and then enter the settings you want to use in the lower part of the window. For example, if the Internet connection is provided via a cable or DSL modem using DHCP, choose Ethernet on the Connect Using pop-up menu and Using DHCP on the Configure pop-up menu. Enter the domain name in the Domain name field and a client ID if required.

> *For a more detailed look at how to configure an AirPort Extreme for the Internet, **see** "Using an AirPort Extreme Base Station to Share an Internet Connection," **p. 406**.*

 note

One additional control available for a base station's Internet access that is not present for a Mac is the WAN Ethernet Port pop-up menu. Use this to set the speed at which the base station communicates with a wired network over its WAN port. In most cases, the Automatic (Default) value is the best choice, but you can choose a specific speed.

22. Click the DHCP subtab to control how the base station provides IP addresses to the network (see Figure 18.6). If you want to use a specific set of IP addresses, use the DHCP Beginning Address and DHCP Ending Address text boxes to enter the starting and ending IP numbers you want to assign. As machines connect to your network, these IP addresses are assigned to each machine that connects (you have to have enough addresses in the range so one is available for each machine).

Figure 18.6
Use the DHCP subtab to configure the IP addresses the base station provides to the network.

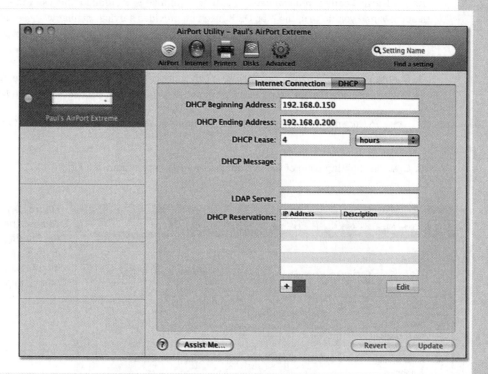

23. Use the DHCP Lease box and pop-up menu to set the number of hours for the DHCP lease on each machine. When this time passes, a new address is assigned to each machine. You can enter a DHCP lease message in the Message box.

24. Click the Printers tab.

25. Enter the name of the printer connected to the base station.

26. When you're ready to configure the base station, click Update. The base station is configured according to the settings you entered. When the process is complete, the base station restarts and the network is available for use.

27. Quit the AirPort Utility.

 note

To be able to print to a printer attached to a base station, each computer must have the printer driver installed on it.

 note

For more detailed information on AirPort, visit Apple's Knowledge Base at www.apple.com/support/ airport.

You can now access the Net and other network services from an AirPort-equipped Mac using the AirPort network. The base station also provides services to a wired network if it is connected to one.

Configuring an AirPort-equipped Mac to Act As a Base Station

As you learned earlier, you can use any AirPort-equipped Mac running Mac OS X to act as a base station. When you do this, the Mac OS X machine provides services similar to those that a dedicated base station provides, but you don't have as much control over the AirPort network.

To configure a Mac as a base station, perform the following steps:

1. Configure an AirPort-equipped Mac so it can connect to the Internet, for example, through DHCP services provided on an Ethernet network activate the AirPort connection via the Network pane.

   ➡ *To learn how to configure a Mac for the Internet,* **see** *"Connecting Your Mac to the Internet," p. 267.*

2. Open the Sharing pane of the System Preferences application (see Figure 18.7).

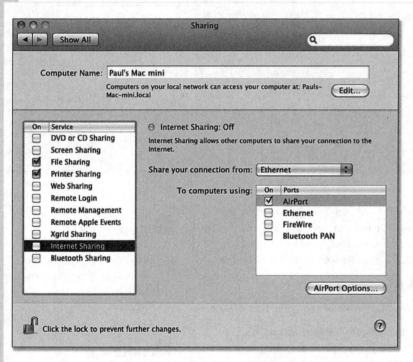

Figure 18.7
You use the controls on the Sharing pane to enable a Mac to share its Internet connection with other computers.

3. Select the Internet connection you want to share with other machines on the Share Your Connection From pop-up menu. For example, if your computer gets its Internet connection from a wired network, select Ethernet.

4. Select the type of connections with which you are going to share the machine's Internet connection by activating the appropriate To Computers Using check boxes. For example, if you want to share the connection with computers via AirPort, check AirPort, and if you want to share the connection via FireWire, activate the FireWire check box. You can choose more than one connection type with which to share the connection.

5. If you share the connection over AirPort, select AirPort and click the AirPort Options button. The AirPort network configuration sheet appears.

6. Edit the default network name as needed. The default name is the name of your computer, but you can make it something more interesting if you want to.

7. Unless you have multiple AirPort networks active in the same area or you experience interference that prevents your network from operating properly, leave the Channel pop-up menu set to Automatic. If you want to choose a channel manually, select it on the pop-up menu.

8. For a more secure network, check the Enable Encryption (Using WEP) check box.

9. Enter the network password in the Password and Confirm Password fields. This is the password users will enter to connect to the network.

10. Select an encryption key length on the WEP Key Length pop-up menu. The options are 40-bit and 128-bit. If only newer Macs running Mac OS X will be connecting to the network, select 128-bit. If you aren't sure which level of encryption other machines can support, select 40-bit. If you don't want to use the encryption at all, uncheck the Enable Encryption (Using WEP) check box.

11. Click OK. The Options sheet closes.

12. Check the Internet Sharing check box and then click Start when Mac OS X asks you to confirm. The Internet connection is shared with other computers via AirPort or built-in Ethernet.

13. Use the Other Services check boxes to configure other services you will provide over the network, such as File and Printer Sharing. Your Mac then begins providing services over AirPort and its network becomes available to AirPort-equipped Macs.

 note

You can choose to share a connection from a wired network to AirPort-equipped machines or from an AirPort-equipped machine to a wired network.

 note

WEP is an encryption strategy that attempts to provide wireless networks with the same level of protection that wired networks have. WEP does provide improved security compared to nonencrypted transmissions, but be aware that it does have some flaws as do almost all security measures. If the information transmitted over your network is very sensitive, you should use WEP to provide at least some protection.

 tip

If you'll be sharing the network with computers not running Mac OS X, make sure the password you create is 13 characters if you use 128-bit encryption or 5 characters if you use 40-bit.

 tip

If Printer Sharing is enabled, USB printers connected to the Mac acting as a base station are also available to the AirPort network. This is a great way to share USB printers with other Macs. Also, the AirPort menu on the menu bar on a Mac acting as a base station is different than the menu on a client machine. This menu also has different options than a client menu.

Using a Mac as a Base Station

One of the disadvantages of using a Mac as a base station is that the Mac must be on for the network to be available. If that Mac is turned off or crashes, the AirPort network is lost.

If the Mac that is acting as the base station goes into Sleep mode, its services are also lost. Use the Energy Saver pane of the System Preferences utility to ensure that the software base station machine never sleeps when you want the AirPort network to be available. Also, if Sleep interrupts AirPort network services, client machines might have to quit and then restart Internet applications, such as Safari, to resume using the network.

➡   *To learn how to control sleep,* **see** *"Managing Your Mobile Mac's Power," **p. 549.***

Connecting to an AirPort Network with Mac OS X

After an AirPort network has been established, you can access it from any AirPort-equipped Mac.

To access an AirPort network, you must configure a Mac OS X machine to connect to it.

You can do this in several ways. For example, you can configure a Mac's Airport using the AirPort tools on the Network pane of the System Preferences application, by completing the following steps:

1. Open the System Preferences application and click the Network icon to open the Network pane.

2. Click the AirPort option in the left part of the pane. The AirPort tools appear in the right part of the pane.

3. If AirPort is currently off, turn it on by clicking the Turn AirPort On button. AirPort services start. If your Mac has connected to a network, you see information about that network at the top of the pane.

4. To join a network, select the network's name on the Network Name pop-up menu and enter the password if the network requires one. The Mac joins the network (see Figure 18.8) and starts receiving services over the network.

5. If you want to be prompted to join new networks, activate the Ask to Join New Networks check box.

6. Activate the Show Airport Status in Menu Bar check box to put the AirPort menu on your menu bar. You can use this menu to quickly select and control your AirPort connection.

7. Click the Advanced button. You will see the Advanced options sheet, which you can use to configure additional aspects of your AirPort connection. It's unlikely you'll ever need to use most of these options, but they enable you to configure specific aspects of your connection, such as your preferred networks and the TCP/IP settings.

8. Click OK to close the Advanced sheet.

9. Click Apply and quit the System Preferences application.

 note

As your Mac connects to the network, the name of the network to which you are connecting briefly appears next to the AirPort icon in the menu bar.

Figure 18.8
Use the AirPort tools to
configure how your Mac
connects to AirPort net-
works.

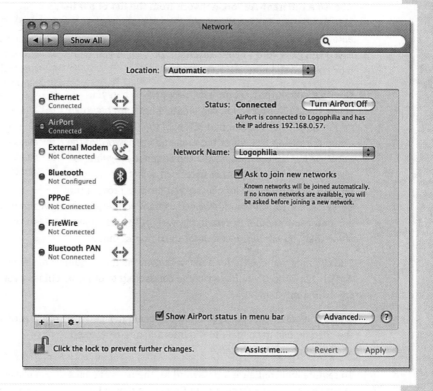

If you want to use an AirPort network other than your preferred
one, open the AirPort menu on the menu bar and select the
AirPort network to which you want to connect. If its password
is not already stored on your keychain, you will be prompted to
enter it. Do so and you will be logged on to that AirPort network.

You can use the AirPort menu on the menu bar to control
AirPort in several ways, including the following:

- **Measure the signal strength of the connection**—The
  "waves" emanating from the AirPort icon show the relative
  strength of the signal your Mac is receiving. As long as you
  see two or more waves, the signal you are receiving is
  plenty strong.

- **Turn AirPort on or off**—You can disconnect your Mac from
  the AirPort network and disable AirPort services by selecting Turn AirPort Off. Turn AirPort on again by choosing Turn
  AirPort On.

 tip

When prompted to enter your password, activate the Add to Keychain
check box to have Mac OS X remember the password so you don't have
to enter it again.

 note

If you can access an AirPort network
but can't access the Internet, see "I
Can't Access the Internet Through
AirPort Even Though I Can Connect
to the AirPort Network" in the
"Troubleshooting" section at the
end of this chapter.

- **Choose a different AirPort network from the list of available networks**—When you do so, you are prompted to enter the password for that network—unless you have saved the password to your keychain. Do so and you will move onto to the network you select.

- **Create a computer-to-computer network**—When you select Create Network, you can create a network between two or more AirPort-equipped Macs. In the Computer to Computer dialog box, enter the name and password of the network you are creating, select the channel you want to use, and then click OK. Other users can select the network on their AirPort menus (of course, you need to provide the password for your network to those users if you require one). When your Mac is hosting a computer-to-computer network, the AirPort icon changes to a Mac "inside" a quarter circle to show that you are in the computer-to-computer mode.

 note

Some AirPort networks are hidden (a closed network) and do not broadcast their identities. To join such a network, you must know the name and password of the network you want to join. To join a hidden network, select Other on the AirPort menu on the menu bar, enter the name and password for the network, and click OK.

The Channel you choose for a network controls the frequency of the signal used to create an AirPort network. If you have trouble connecting to other machines over the network you create, try a different channel.

When you create and use a computer-to-computer network, other AirPort connections, such as the one you use to connect to the Internet, are deselected and therefore can't be used.

To require and configure a password for the network, click Show Options in the Computer to Computer dialog box.

Check the Use Interference Robustness check box to make the network less susceptible to interference (it will have a smaller range).

 tip

Computer-to-computer networks are a great way to play network games. You can create an AirPort network and host a game. Other users can connect to the network and join the game by selecting your network using their AirPort controls.

Using AirPort is a great way to quickly create and use wireless networks. After you have connected to the Net without wires (especially when roaming with a mobile Mac), you won't want to settle for anything else.

Although this chapter has focused on using AirPort to access the Internet, an AirPort connection works just like any other network connection (such as an Ethernet connection). For example, you can access the files on another machine over an AirPort network just as you can with an Ethernet network.

 note

If you are getting no signal or a weak signal from the AirPort network you want to join, see "Weak Signal" in the "Troubleshooting" section at the end of this chapter.

Troubleshooting Your Wireless Network

Wireless networking is notoriously finicky to configure, and equally notoriously flaky to connect. (The major exception is the AirPort Extreme base station, which I've found to be gratifyingly easy to configure and amazingly reliable.) If you're having trouble with wireless networking, the next few sections offer some solutions.

No AirPort Hardware Is Found

When I launch the AirPort Utility, I see an error message stating that the required AirPort hardware can't be found.

If you have recently plugged in your AirPort base station, it usually takes a few minutes for the initial startup to complete, so wait a bit and then click Rescan to try again.

The AirPort software requires that you have an AirPort card installed on the machine you use to configure a base station. If an AirPort card is not found, the software won't run.

If you don't have an AirPort card installed in your Mac, you need to install one before running the AirPort Setup Assistant.

If you do have an AirPort card installed, it is not properly installed. Repeat the installation steps to ensure that the card is properly installed.

I Can't Configure My Base Station Manually

When I try to configure a base station manually, I get an error stating that the base station can't be configured.

This problem can occur for various reasons. First, try resetting the base station (see the next section). If that doesn't work, try opening the AirPort Setup Assistant and configuring the base station using the assistant. Then, go back into the AirPort Admin Utility and try to configure the base station again. This sometimes clears the error.

I Don't Know the Base Station Password

I can't access the base station because I don't know its password.

When you have trouble with an AirPort Base Station, you can reset it to its factory defaults by inserting a paper clip into the reset button hole on the bottom or back of the unit. Hold down the button for 5 seconds and the base station is reset—all settings are returned to the default and the password becomes `public`.

Weak Signal

My AirPort signal strength is low. Or, I can't find the network to which I want to connect.

Two primary factors affect the strength of the AirPort signal your Mac receives from a base station (hardware or software) or from Macs providing a computer-to-computer network. One is the distance from the base station to your Mac; the other is the amount of interference in the area.

If your Mac is within range of the base station you want to use, there should be no trouble getting a strong enough signal. If you are at the edge of or beyond that range, move your Mac closer to the base station or move the base station closer to you. You can also try repositioning the base station, because it can sometimes be affected by materials or other fields between it and your Mac.

If you are close to the base station but can't get a strong signal, try changing the frequency of the network in the event that it is being interfered with by another signal of some type.

➡ *To learn how to change an AirPort network's frequency,* **see** *"Configuring a Base Station Manually," p. 393.*

I Can't Access the Internet Through AirPort Even Though I Can Connect to the AirPort Network

My Mac is connected to an AirPort network, but I can't access the Internet.

If you are connecting to the Internet through a base station, the most likely cause is that the base station has lost its Internet connection. Use some means to confirm that Internet services are available to the base station, such as by using a machine connected independently or calling your service provider. If services are available, use the AirPort Admin Utility to check its configuration to ensure that it is correct. If all else fails, reset the access point.

If none of these steps works and you have a broadband modem connected to the base station that provides DHCP services, use the following steps to attempt to reset the connection:

1. Unplug the modem for at least 20 seconds, and then plug it back in again. This forces the modem to get a new address.

2. Reset the base station by pressing its reset button for 5 seconds.

3. Open the AirPort Setup Assistant and select the Join an Existing Network option.

4. Follow the onscreen instructions to update the base station.

SHARING AN INTERNET CONNECTION

Enabling Multiple Macs to Use a Single Internet Account

Setting up a network is all about sharing: files, folders, hard drives, optical drives, printers, and so on. One of the best things to share over a network is an Internet connection, because that means that you only need a single account with an ISP, and you only need to configure a single connection.

Most networks share an Internet connection using a router, or a hardware device that includes routing capabilities, such as the AirPort Extreme wireless base station that you learned about in Chapter 18, "Wireless Networking with Mac OS X." This involves the following general steps:

1. On your broadband modem, attach the cable that provides your ISP's Internet connection. For example, if you have an ADSL broadband modem, run a phone line from the nearest wall jack to the appropriate port on the back of the modem, which is usually labeled ADSL or DSL. Similarly, if you have a cable broadband modem, connect a TV cable to the cable connector on the back of the modem, which is usually labeled Cable.

2. Register the modem, if necessary. Nowadays, many ISPs insist that you register the broadband modem by accessing a page on the ISP's website and sometimes entering a code or the serial number of the modem. Read the instructions that come with your ISP's Internet kit to determine whether you must first register your broadband modem online. If you don't need to register, skip to step 5; if you do need to register, you must first connect the modem directly to a computer (instead of to your router, as described in the next step). Most broadband modems give you two ways to do this:

- **Ethernet**—All broadband modems have an RJ-45 port on the back that is labeled Ethernet, LAN, or 10BASE-T. Run an Ethernet cable from this port to the RJ-45 port on your Mac's network interface card (NIC).

- **USB**—Most newer broadband modems also come with a USB port on the back. If you're working with a Mac that doesn't have a NIC, or if the NIC already has a cable attached, you can use USB instead. Run a USB cable from the USB port on the modem to a free USB port on your computer. You also need to install the broadband modem's USB device driver, which should be on a CD that your ISP provided.

> **⚠ caution**
>
> Use either the Ethernet port or the USB port, but not both. Connecting both ports to your computer can damage the modem.

3. Turn on the broadband modem and wait until it makes a connection with the line. All broadband modems have an LED on the front that lights up to indicate a good connection. Look for an LED labeled Online, DSL, or something similar, and wait until you see a solid (that is, not blinking) light on that LED. You can now use a web browser to access the ISP's site (depending on the ISP, you may need to log on first) and register your modem.

4. Turn off the modem and disconnect the Ethernet or USB cable from your computer.

5. Examine the back of your router and locate the port that it uses for the Internet connection. Some routers label this port WAN, whereas others use Internet. On the AirPort Extreme Base Station, the Internet port is indicated by a circle of dots. (Some routers don't label the Internet port at all, but instead place the port off to the side so that it's clearly separate from the router's RJ-45 ports.)

6. With the broadband modem and the router turned off, run an Ethernet cable from the broadband modem's Ethernet port to the WAN port on the router, and run an Ethernet cable from your Mac's NIC port to an Ethernet port on the router.

7. You're now ready to turn on your devices. Begin by turning on the broadband modem and waiting until it has a solid connection with the line. Then turn on your router.

8. Access your router's configuration screen and set up your ISP's Internet settings. The router will automatically connect to the ISP. The front of the router should have an LED labeled WAN or Internet that will go solid when the Internet connection has been made.

The next section takes you through the details of configuring an AirPort Extreme Base Station to connect to the Internet. If you don't have a router on your network, you need to use a different method to share an Internet connection. In this chapter, you also learn how to share an Internet account using the following techniques:

- Using Mac OS X's built-in Internet sharing feature

- Using multiple IP addresses for a single account

Using an AirPort Extreme Base Station to Share an Internet Connection

Sharing an Internet connection through a router is the easiest way to get your networked Macs (and PCs) on the Internet, and if you have an AirPort Extreme, which includes built-in routing features, it's easier still because the AirPort Extreme is so easy to install and configure.

Before getting to the details, you should know a bit more about how IP addresses work when you have your base station connected to the Internet:

■ Your AirPort Extreme is given its own IP address—called the *public IP address* or the *external IP address*—from the pool of IP addresses controlled by your ISP. Internet data sent to any computer on your network is first sent to the router's public IP address.

■ Your AirPort Extreme assigns IP addresses to the computers on your network. In other words, when a computer logs on to the network, it is assigned an IP address from a pool of available addresses. When the computer logs off, the address it was using is returned to the pool. The system that manages this dynamic allocation of addresses is called the *Dynamic Host Configuration Protocol* (DHCP), and the computers or devices that implement DHCP are called *DHCP servers*. The AirPort Extreme Base Station can act as a DHCP server.

In most cases, the range of addresses is from 192.168.0.1 to 192.168.0.254. (On some routers, the range is from 192.168.1.1 to 192.168.1.254.) The router itself usually takes the 192.168.0.1 address (this is called its *private IP address*), and the pool of possible addresses is usually some subset of the total range, such as between 192.168.0.100 and 192.168.0.150.

The big advantage of this setup is that your network is never exposed to the Internet. All communication goes through the router's public IP address; so as far as, say, a web or email server is concerned, it's communicating with a device at that address. The router is able to get the correct data to your computer because when you initially request data, it adds your computer's private IP address and the number of the communications port your computer is using and stores this data in a *routing table*. When data comes back from the Internet, the router converts the public destination IP address of the data to the private address of your computer, a process known as *network address translation* (NAT).

 note

When a device such as a router is set up as the sole connection point between a network and the Internet, that device is called a *gateway*.

On your small network, the main function of a router is to be used as a gateway between your network and the Internet. Through the magic of NAT, your network cannot be seen from any device attached to the Internet; as far as the Internet is concerned, your network is nothing but a router. (For this reason, an Internet-connected router that performs NAT duties is sometimes called an *edge router*.) NAT, therefore, acts as a kind of simple *firewall*, a technology that prevents unwanted data from reaching a network.

How you configure your AirPort Extreme Base Station for Internet access depends on the type of connection your ISP requires: DHCP or Point-to-Point Protocol over Ethernet (PPPoE). The next two sections take you through each connection type.

Setting Up and Sharing a DHCP Internet Connection

If your ISP requires a DHCP Internet connection (as is the case with most broadband cable ISPs), follow these steps to configure and share the connection using your AirPort Extreme:

1. Connect your broadband modem to your AirPort Extreme Base Station, as described earlier in this chapter.

2. In Finder, select Applications, Utilities, AirPort Utility.

3. Select your AirPort Extreme in the list of AirPort devices.

4. Click the Internet tab.

5. Select the Internet Connection subtab.

6. In the Connect Using pop-up menu, select Ethernet.

7. In the Configure IPv4 pop-up menu, select Using DHCP. (If your ISP provided you with a static IP address, select Manually, instead, and then enter the address in the IP Address text box.)

8. Use the first DNS Server(s) text box to enter your ISP DNS server IP address. (If your ISP supplied you with two DNS server addresses, type the second address into the second text box.)

9. If your ISP supplied you with a domain name to use as part of the configuration, type it into the Domain Name text box.

10. If your ISP supplied you with a client ID to use as part of the configuration, type it into the DHCP Client ID text box.

11. Use the Connection Sharing pop-up menu to select Share a Public IP Address, as shown in Figure 19.1.

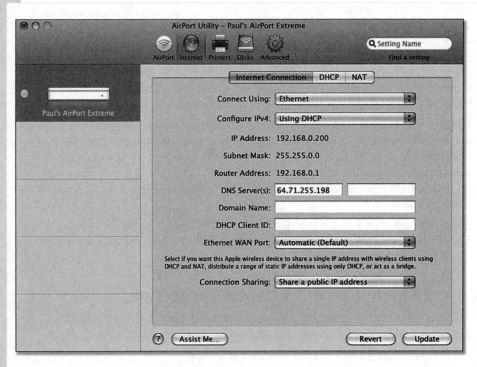

Figure 19.1
The Internet Connection tab filled out for a DHCP Internet connection.

12. Select the DHCP subtab.

13. Use the DHCP Beginning Address pop-up menu to select the first half of the IP addresses your AirPort Extreme will distribute: 192.168, 172.16, or 10.0.

14. Use the next text box to specify the third part of the distributed IP addresses (usually 0 or 1).

15. Use the next text box to specify the first IP address value the DHCP server will distribute.

16. Use the DHCP Ending Address text box to type the last value the DHCP server will distribute (see Figure 19.2).

Figure 19.2
Use the DHCP subtab to define the IP address that the AirPort Extreme's DHCP server will distribute to the network clients.

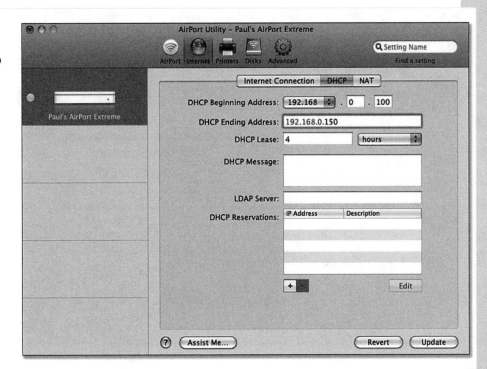

17. Click Update. AirPort Utility warns you that the device will be unavailable for a while.

18. Click Continue. AirPort Utility updates and then restarts your AirPort Extreme Base Station.

Setting Up and Sharing a PPPoE Internet Connection

If your ISP requires a PPPoE Internet connection (as is the case with many DSL broadband ISPs), follow these steps to configure and share the connection using your AirPort Extreme:

1. Connect your broadband modem to your AirPort Extreme Base Station, as described earlier in this chapter.

2. In Finder, select Applications, Utilities, AirPort Utility.

3. Select your AirPort Extreme in the list of AirPort devices.

4. Click the Internet tab.

5. Select the Internet Connection subtab.

6. In the Connect Using pop-up menu, select PPPoE. Figure 19.3 shows the resulting configuration of the Internet Connection tab.

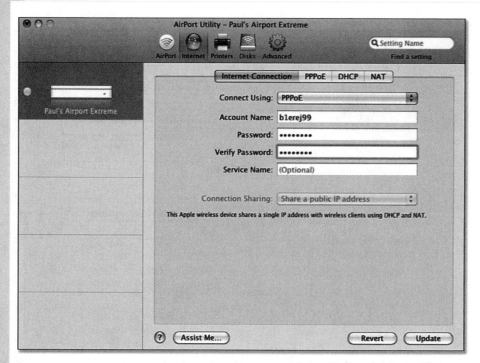

Figure 19.3
Select PPPoE in the Connect Using pop-up menu to configure the Internet Connection tab as shown here.

7. Use the Account Name text box to type the username or ID supplied by your ISP.

8. Use the Password and Verify Password text boxes to type the connection password assigned by your ISP.

9. Use the Service Name text box to enter the service name supplied by your ISP (if any).

10. Select the PPPoE subtab.

11. In the Connection pop-menu, select Always On.

12. Use the first DNS Server(s) text box to enter the IP address of your ISP's DNS server. (If your ISP supplied you with two DNS server addresses, type the second address into the second text box.)

13. If your ISP supplied you with a domain name to use as part of the configuration, type it into the Domain Name text box.

14. Select the DHCP subtab.

15. Use the DHCP Beginning Address pop-up menu to select the first half of the IP addresses your AirPort Extreme will distribute: 192.168, 172.16, or 10.0.

16. Use the next text box to specify the third part of the distributed IP addresses (usually 0 or 1).

17. Use the next text box to specify the first IP address value the DHCP server will distribute.

18. Use the DHCP Ending Address text box to type the last value the DHCP server will distribute.

19. Click Update. AirPort Utility warns you that the device will be unavailable for a while.

20. Click Continue. AirPort Utility updates and then restarts your AirPort Extreme Base Station.

Sharing an Internet Account with Mac OS X

Mac OS X includes a built-in DHCP server you can use to share a single Internet connection with other devices on your local network. And if the Macintosh on which you configure the DHCP server includes an AirPort card, you can also provide a wireless AirPort network without the use of an AirPort Base Station.

One advantage of this approach is that you don't need to add dedicated Internet sharing hardware (such as a router or an AirPort Base Station) to your network. A standard Ethernet router enables you to share your Internet account over an Ethernet network, and an AirPort card enables you to share that account over a wireless AirPort network. Another advantage is that it doesn't cost anything to share an account (assuming that you already have the connection hardware, such as for an Ethernet network).

 note

The function of the DHCP server is to provide and manage IP addresses to devices on the network. The DHCP server doesn't actually provide the Internet access itself; that comes from the connection method you use (such as a cable modem). The DHCP server manages the traffic between the Internet connection and the other devices on the network.

➥ *To learn how to configure the Mac OS X firewall,*
   see *"Defending Your Mac Against Internet Hackers,"*
   p. 723.

 note

You can use Mac OS X's built-in firewall to protect the DHCP machine from attacks from the Internet (and because it sits between the Internet and the other devices on your network, it protects those devices as well).

This approach does have one significant disadvantage and one minor drawback, however. The significant disadvantage is that the Mac providing DHCP services must always be running for the machines that share its account to be capable of accessing the Internet. If the DHCP machine develops a problem, no device on the network can access the Internet. Similarly, if the machine from which the account is shared goes to sleep or is shut down, the Internet connection is lost by all the computers on the network. The less significant issue is that the DHCP services do require some processing power. These services will most likely not result in any noticeable performance decrease, but if your machine already runs at its limits, asking it to provide these services might slightly slow down other tasks.

Configuring a Mac to provide DHCP services to a network requires the following general steps:

1. Connect the Mac to the Internet.

2. Install the network you will use to connect the Mac with other machines.

3. Configure the Mac to share its Internet account.

 note

DHCP servers are not platform specific. For example, if you have a DHCP server running on a Macintosh, you can connect a Windows computer to the network and use the same DHCP server to share the Internet account with it. Or, you can install a DHCP server on a Windows machine and use it to share the account with Macs on the network.

After you have configured the Mac for Internet access and connected it to other computers (with or without wires), you need to configure the Internet sharing services on it.

The three possibilities when you configure Internet sharing on your Mac are as follows:

- Your Mac is connected to the Internet via an Ethernet connection, and it has an AirPort card installed in it.

- Your Mac is connected to the Internet via Ethernet but does not have an AirPort card installed in it.

- Your Mac is connected to the Internet via an AirPort Base Station, in which case you can share the Internet account by connecting that Mac to other computers via Ethernet to share its account via an Ethernet network (you wouldn't need to share the Internet connection with the AirPort-equipped Macs because the base station already does that).

 note

AirPort Extreme Base Stations include Ethernet ports you can use to connect the base station to an Ethernet network. When you do this, the base station can also share a connection with machines connected to the Ethernet network. In that case, you don't need to use a Mac to share a connection.

When you configure Internet sharing on your Mac, it automatically determines which case is true for your machine and presents the appropriate options for you. To configure Internet sharing, use the following steps:

1. Open the System Preferences application and click the Sharing icon to open the Sharing pane.

2. Click Internet Sharing in the services list on the left side of the pane. What you see depends on how the Mac is connected to the Internet. For example, in Figure 19.4, you see the Internet Sharing configuration for a machine connected to the Internet via AirPort; you can tell this is so because AirPort is selected on the Share Your Connection From pop-up menu. In Figure 19.5, you see an example of a machine connected to the Internet via Ethernet. Because that machine also has an AirPort card installed in it, it can share its connection with other machines using both Built-in Ethernet and AirPort.

Figure 19.4
This Mac is connected to the Internet via AirPort.

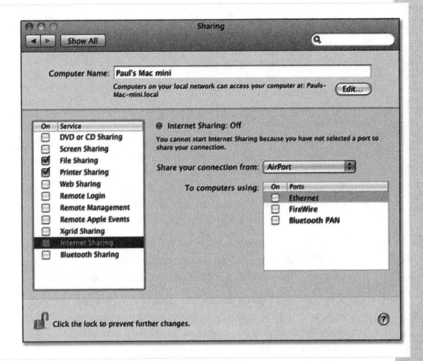

Figure 19.5
The Sharing pane shows a machine that is currently connected to the Internet via Ethernet, but that also has an AirPort card installed in it.

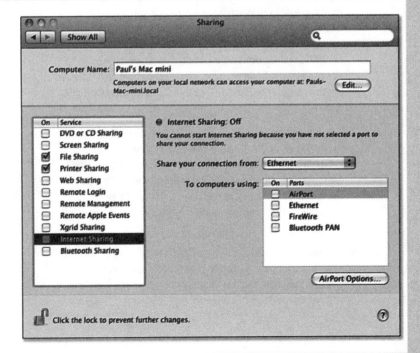

➧ *To learn how to configure your network settings,* ***see***
*"Managing Multiple Internet Accounts," **p. 279**.*

➧ *To learn how to use locations,* ***see*** *"Configuring and
Using Locations," **p. 557**.*

3. On the Share Your Connection From pop-up menu, select
the Internet connection you want to share. In most cases,
you will be connected by only one means, such as AirPort
or Ethernet, so the choice should be obvious. However, if
the Mac can connect in multiple ways, choose the option
you want to share. For example, if you are connected to an
Ethernet network that has Internet access and you also
have access to the Internet through an AirPort Base
Station, you can share either connection with other computers.

In the To Computers Using list are the means by which you can share the connection that you
selected with other computers. For example, in Figure 19.5, you can see that the Mac can share
its connection with other machines over Ethernet and AirPort.

4. Activate the On check box for the ports over which you
want to share the connection. For example, to share the
Mac's connection with computers via AirPort, activate the
On check box next to AirPort on the list of ports.

If you use an Ethernet port to share a connection, you
might see a sheet warning you that activating sharing
might cause problems for other ISP customers or violate
your service agreement (some providers prohibit sharing
an individual account on multiple machines, but most
allow a reasonable amount of sharing such as with five or
fewer computers). Read the dialog box and click OK to
close it.

5. If you activated AirPort in step 4, select AirPort and click
the AirPort Options button. Then configure the AirPort
network you are creating using the resulting sheet. For
example, you will name the network (if you don't want to
use the default name), choose a channel and password,
and so on. When you are done configuring the AirPort network, click OK.

6. Activate the check box next to Internet Sharing in the services list (you can't click the check box until you turn on at
least one port on the To Computers Using list). Your Mac
will start providing DHCP services.

 note

The ports you see listed in the To
Computers Using list will be those
that are active under your current
network settings (determined by the
location setting currently active). For
example, if in your current location,
the Built-in FireWire port is active,
that port will also be available for
you to share an Internet connection
with other computers.

 caution

Be careful about sharing an account
over the same port by which you are
receiving it. For example, if your Mac
is already getting an Internet connection through an Ethernet network, don't also share its Internet
connection with that same network.
For one thing, you don't need to
because the device providing the
connection to your Mac is already
sharing its connection with other
devices on the network. For another,
you can cause confusion for yourself
and potentially IP address conflicts
by sharing the same connection on
the same network. Generally, unless
you have multiple networks of the
same type operating in the same
location (such as more than one
AirPort network), a port that is
selected on the Share Your
Connection From pop-up menu
shouldn't also be turned on in the To
Computers Using list.

You might see a warning sheet that explains that activating sharing might disrupt services on the network. If you are administering the network, click Start in the sheet. If someone else administers the network on which you are sharing your connection, make sure you coordinate with that person before starting Internet Sharing.

Your connection will be shared with all the devices with which your Mac can communicate via the ports that you have turned on. For example, if your Mac is connected to a local network via Ethernet and you made that port active, other devices on the network can use the account via the DHCP services your Mac provides.

7. Quit the System Preferences application.

8. Configure the other devices on the network to obtain their IP addresses from a DHCP server. Those devices should now see your Mac and be able to access the Internet through the shared connection.

This section has focused on using Ethernet and AirPort to share a connection. That's because they are by far the most likely way you will do so. However, there are other ports by which you can share a connection, including FireWire and Bluetooth. Basically, you can share a connection via any means by which your Mac can communicate with other devices. Using these less common ports is really no different from using the ones described in this chapter. Just choose the appropriate port by which the sharing machine is accessing the Internet on the Share Your Connection From pop-up menu and turn on the ports through which you want to provide an Internet connection in the To Computers Using list.

 tip

If you share an Internet account over AirPort, an upward-pointing arrow is added to the center of the AirPort icon in the menu bar. This indicates that the connection is shared and that you can access the sharing controls from the menu.

 caution

If the machine sharing the connection goes to sleep or is shut down, the Internet connection is lost on the network and no other machine using the network can access the Internet. You should disable sleep using the Energy Saver pane of the System Preferences application when you use Internet Sharing.

Using Multiple IP Addresses to Share an Internet Account

With some broadband accounts, such as cable, you can purchase additional IP addresses (or DHCP names) so you can configure multiple machines to access the same account. The requirements to do this are an address for each device that will be using the account and an Ethernet or other network, which typically consists of a router with the cable or digital subscriber line (DSL) modem connected to the wide area network (WAN) port and each device connected to a local area network (LAN) port.

 note

Some Internet Service Providers use DHCP to provide IP addresses to you. In these cases, you assign a DHCP name to your computer. The ISP's DHCP server assigns IP addresses to you as you need them. To share an Internet account among several devices, you need a unique DHCP name for each device; you use this DHCP name to configure the network on each device.

To share an account using multiple IP addresses, do the following:

1. Contact your ISP to determine whether this option is available.

2. If it is, obtain additional addresses (or DHCP names); you will need one address for each machine or device (such as an AirPort Base Station) you want to share the account. You will probably need to pay an additional fee for each IP address you obtain.

3. Connect the cable or DSL modem to the WAN port on the router for your network.

4. Connect each device to a LAN port on the router.

5. Configure each machine with one of the available addresses (or DHCP names).

One advantage to this method is that you can use a standard Ethernet router to facilitate sharing the account; these routers are quite inexpensive and are simple to install and use. Setting up each device to use its address is straightforward as well. You simply configure each machine as if it were the only one using the account.

One possible disadvantage is that you might have to pay an additional fee for each address you use. The typical cost of additional addresses is $5–$7 per month per address on top of the address included with your base account. This can get expensive if you have several devices on your network; however, you can balance that cost against not needing a router (Ethernet or AirPort) that has Internet account sharing built in.

Another disadvantage is that you don't get any special features, such as a built-in firewall. The IP addresses that you configure on each machine are usually publicly accessible on the Internet, which means hackers can see them. You have to add protection for each device on your network in some other way.

Typically, using a router with built-in Internet sharing (such as an AirPort Base Station) or using a Mac to share its account is a more secure and easier-to-manage option. But, some providers require you to have a unique address for each machine that will be using the account, and this might be your only legal option.

Troubleshooting Internet Connection Sharing

If you have problems sharing your Internet connection, the next few sections offer some solutions that might help.

The Machines with Which I Am Sharing a Connection from My Mac Can't Connect at All

I have started Internet Sharing on a Mac, but other devices on the network can't access the Internet.

Attempt to connect to the Internet from the Mac that is sharing the account. If that machine can't connect, something has happened to its Internet connection. If that machine can connect, check that Internet Sharing is configured properly.

Then, check the Internet connection settings for each machine to make sure they are set to connect via a DHCP server.

➡ *To learn how to troubleshoot a Mac connected to the Internet,* ***see*** *Chapter 13, "Connecting Your Mac to the Internet," p. 267.*

The Machines with Which I Am Sharing a Connection from My Mac Have Lost Internet Access

The machines with which I am sharing an Internet connection were able to connect, but now they can't.

First, check whether all the machines with which the connection is being shared have this problem or only some do. If all the machines are unable to connect, the problem stems from the Mac sharing the account (see the next paragraph). If some of the machines with which the connection is being shared can access the Net, the problem lies with those machines. Check the configuration of those machines to ensure that they are configured to use a DHCP server. Also, check their network connections to make sure they are communicating with the network properly.

➡ *To learn how to troubleshoot a Mac connected to the Internet,* ***see*** *Chapter 13, "Connecting Your Mac to the Internet," p. 267.*

If none of the machines can access the Internet, something has happened to the Mac that is sharing the connection.

Make sure that the Mac is still running and that sleep is disabled. If both of these conditions are true, move to the next paragraph. If the Mac is shut down, restart it to restart Internet Sharing. If the Mac has gone to sleep, you need to wake it up to restart Internet Sharing.

Attempt to connect to the Internet from the Mac that is sharing the account, such as by opening a web browser. If that machine can't connect, something has happened to its Internet connection. If that machine can connect, reconfigure Internet Sharing.

➡ *To learn how to troubleshoot a Mac connected to the Internet,* ***see*** *Chapter 13, "Connecting Your Mac to the Internet," p. 267.*

I Get an Error Message Telling Me That Multiple Devices Have the Same IP Address

When I attempt to start up one of the devices on my network, I see an alert stating that a device has already been assigned the IP address and that IP services are being shut down. How do I correct this problem?

Two devices on the same network cannot have the same IP address. If you start up one device and see this error message, you have two or more devices trying to use the same address. Check the configuration of each device to see which devices are using that address (for Mac OS X machines, select the network service that is being used from the services list on the Network pane of the

System Preferences application to see how the computer is configured). Check that each device has a unique address, including an AirPort Base Station or other device that is sharing the account.

Occasionally, your router will "remember" the devices that are using specific IP addresses and you will see this error even though you made sure that each device had a unique address. If this happens, power down your entire network, including the router and all other devices attached to it. Wait a few seconds and power up everything again, starting with your broadband modem and router, then your computers. The error should be cleared as each device registers its unique address on the network.

Troubleshooting a Network Internet Connection

Troubleshooting a network connection to the Internet can be quite challenging. Your approach should be to eliminate potential sources of the problem one by one until you find the specific problem you are having.

If you are unable to connect to the Internet after you have installed and configured an Internet Sharing router, try the following steps:

1. Power down all the devices and the network, including the modem and router, wait a few seconds. Turn on the power to the modem and router first, then turn on your computers. This will often reset the network and restore access.

2. Check the modem to see if its status lights indicate it is connected to the Internet. If it isn't connected, check with the ISP to make sure service is currently available. If service is down, you'll need to wait until it's restored before you'll be able to connect. If service is available, the issue is with the modem. Your ISP may be able to remotely reconfigure the modem for Internet access. If that fails, the modem itself might have failed, in which case you need to repair or replace it.

   If the modem appears to be connected, the problem lies with a device on the network.

3. Check two or more devices on the network. If at least one computer can connect to the Internet, you know that account is available, therefore the problem lies with specific computers or with some other hardware connected to the network such as the router. If possible, try to connect with one device wirelessly and one connecting through the wired part of the network. This can identify which part of the network is having problems.

4. If you determine the problem is with a specific computer, reconfigure that computer to connect to the appropriate network.

5. If you determine the problem lies with part of the network, such as devices connected via a router, such as switches, check the devices to make sure they are still working. Most switches have status lights you can use for this. If the device seems to have a problem, remove its power and the restart it. This will often clear the problem.

6. If it appears that Internet service is available, but no device on the network can connect to it, connect the modem directly to a Mac and configure that Mac to access the Internet (make sure the Mac's firewall is turned on before you do this). Once the Mac can connect successfully, you know that the service is available and that the problem lies at the router or other part of the network.

7. Install the router that was connected to the modem again and configure it to connect to the Internet. Connect and configure the Mac you used in step 6 to the router to see if it can still connect. If it can't, the router is not working or is not configured correctly. You'll need to correct that problem to continue.

8. When the Mac can connect to the Internet through the router, start connecting other devices to the network one by one. Check each device for Internet connection.

9. Repeat step 8 for each device. If you discover a problem with a device, check its configuration and its connection to the Internet.

10. In some cases, you might need to configure your router to use media access control (MAC) address cloning. A MAC address uniquely identifies each node on a network. In some cases, you will need to clone, or copy, the MAC address of one of the computers on your network onto the router. See the instructions that came with the router to learn how to configure MAC cloning on your router.

 tip

You might be able to share an account using a software DHCP server even if you can't use a hardware device to do so. For example, try using the Mac's built-in Internet Sharing to share your account on a network. Connect the Mac directly to your cable or DSL modem and then use Internet Sharing to share the connection with the network. Remember to enable the Mac's firewall to protect it and your network from attacks from the Internet.

20

USING MOBILEME TO INTEGRATE A MAC ONTO THE INTERNET

Understanding MobileMe

These days, the primary source of online chaos and confusion is the ongoing proliferation of services and sites that demand your time and attention. What started with web-based email has grown to a website, a blog, a photo-sharing site, online bookmarks, and perhaps a few social networking sites, just to consume those last few precious moments of leisure time. You might be sitting in a chair, but you're getting run ragged anyway!

A great way to simplify your online life is to get a MobileMe account. For a Basic Membership fee ($99 per year currently), or a Family Pack membership, which consists of one main account plus four subaccounts ($149 per year currently), you get a one-stop web shop that includes email, an address book, a calendar, a Web Gallery for sharing photos, and a generous 20GB of online file storage (40GB with the Family Pack). The price is, admittedly, a bit steep, but it really is convenient to have so much of your online life in one place.

 note

If you don't want to commit any bucks before taking the MobileMe plunge, you can sign up for a 60-day trial that's free and offers most of the features of a regular account. Go to www.apple.com/mobileme/ and click the Free Trial button.

The web applications you get with MobileMe—Mail, Contacts, Calendar, Gallery, and iDisk—make up the "Me" side of MobileMe (because the web applications are housed on Apple's me.com site), but that's not the big news with MobileMe. The real headline-generator is the "Mobile" side of MobileMe. What's *mobile* is simply your data, particularly your email accounts, contacts, calendars, and bookmarks. That data gets stored on a bunch of me.com networked servers, which collectively Apple calls the *cloud*. When you log in to your MobileMe account at me.com, you use the web applications to interact with that data.

That's pretty mundane stuff, right? What's revolutionary here is that you can let the cloud know about all the other devices in your life: your Mac, your home computer, your work PC, your notebook, your iPhone, and so on. If you log in to your MobileMe account and, say, add a new appointment, the cloud takes that appointment and immediately sends the data to all your devices. Fire up your Mac, open iCal, and the appointment's there; switch to your Windows PC, click Outlook's Calendar folder, and the appointment's there; tap Calendar on your iPhone's Home screen and, yes, the appointment's there, too.

This works if you change data on any of your devices. Move an email message to another folder on your Mac, and the same message is moved to the same folder on the other devices and on your MobileMe account; modify a contact on your Windows PC, and the changes also propagate everywhere else. In each case, the new or changed data gets sent to the cloud, which then sends the data to each device, usually in a matter of seconds. This is called *pushing* the data, and the new MobileMe applications are described as *push email*, *push contacts*, and *push calendars*.

With MobileMe, you never have to worry about entering the same information into all of your devices. With MobileMe, you won't miss an important meeting because you forgot to enter it into the calendar on your work computer. With MobileMe, you can never forget data when you're traveling because you've got up-to-the-moment data with you at all times. MobileMe practically organizes your life for you; all you have to do is show up.

MobileMe promises to simplify your online life, but the first step to that simpler existence is to configure MobileMe on all the devices that you want to keep in sync. I'll just talk about configuring MobileMe on your Mac, but it's important to understand exactly which devices can do the MobileMe thing. Here's a summary:

- **Mac**—You must be running OS X 10.4.11 or later. To access the MobileMe web applications, you need either Safari 3 or later, or Firefox 2 or later.

- **iPhone or iPod touch**—MobileMe works with any iPhone or iPod touch that's running version 2.0 or later of the software.

- **Windows XP**—You must be running Windows XP Service Pack 2 or later. To access the MobileMe web applications, you need Internet Explorer 7 or later, Safari 3 or later, or Firefox 2 or later. For push email you need either Outlook Express or Outlook 2003 or later; for push contacts, you need either Windows Address Book or Outlook 2003 or later; for push calendar, you need Outlook 2003 or later.

- **Windows Vista and Windows 7**—Any version of Windows Vista and Windows 7 will work with MobileMe. To access the MobileMe web applications, you need Internet Explorer 7 or later, Safari 3 or later, or Firefox 2 or later. For push email you need either Windows Mail or Outlook 2003 or later; for push contacts, you need either Windows Contacts or Outlook 2003 or later; for push calendar, you need Outlook 2003 or later.

Configuring Your MobileMe Account on Your Mac

I'm assuming that you've already got a paid or free trial MobileMe account set up. (If not, go to http://www.apple.com/mobileme/ to get started.) After you've done that, your first chore is to configure your Mac with your MobileMe member name and password so that you can access the MobileMe services available via Mac OS X:

1. Open System Preferences.

2. Click MobileMe. The MobileMe window appears, as shown in Figure 20.1.

Figure 20.1
When you first open the MobileMe preferences, you need to enter your MobileMe member name and password.

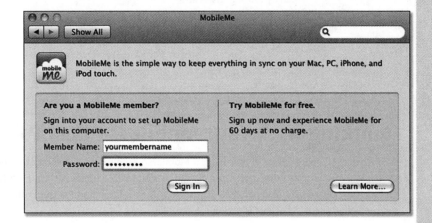

3. Type your MobileMe member name and password.

4. Click Sign In. Mac OS X signs in to your MobileMe account and then displays the full MobileMe preferences, as shown in Figure 20.2.

After you've completed these simple steps, your Mac will be able to access your MobileMe account automatically.

 note
Each user account on your Mac can have its own MobileMe account. The settings in the MobileMe pane of the System Preferences application of one account do not affect the other accounts. The steps to work with other MobileMe accounts are exactly the same as those to work with the first one you create.

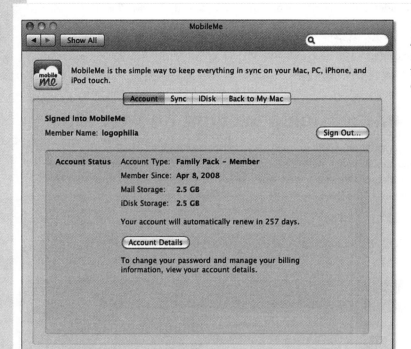

Working with Your MobileMe Email Account

One of the cool things about using a MobileMe account is that you get an email account with the distinctive "@me.com" domain. You can use MobileMe email accounts with Mac OS X's Mail application very easily. You can also access your MobileMe email via the Web, and you can add more email addresses to your MobileMe account.

Using Your MobileMe Email Account with Mail

To use your MobileMe email account with Mail, you need to configure that account in the Mail application. This is simple because support for MobileMe email accounts is built into Mail and adding a MobileMe email account requires only that you enter your MobileMe member name and password.

 *To learn how to configure email accounts in Mail, **see** "Configuring Email Accounts," p. 317.*

> **note**
>
> If you created or configured an existing MobileMe account when you installed Mac OS X, your MobileMe email account was configured in the Mail application for you automatically.

After you have set up your MobileMe email account in Mail, you use it just like other email accounts you have.

➡ *To learn how to use Mail, **see** Chapter 15, "Managing Your Email," p. 315.*

Accessing Your MobileMe Email Account from the Web

> **🔍 note**
>
> With a MobileMe account, you share your allocated disk space between your iDisk and email. You can choose the proportion of the space dedicated to each, as you' learn later in this chapter.

You can access your MobileMe email from any computer that has web access, which makes it convenient to use your MobileMe email account even if you aren't at your own Mac. To access your MobileMe email via the Web, perform the following steps:

1. Use a web browser to access www.me.com. The browser gets redirected to the MobileMe Login page.

2. Enter your member name and password and then click Log In.

3. In most cases you see the MobileMe Mail page automatically. If not, click the Mail icon (the envelope) in the MobileMe toolbar. Your MobileMe email Inbox appears (see Figure 20.3).

Figure 20.3
Using the MobileMe website is a great way to access your MobileMe email from any computer that can connect to the Web.

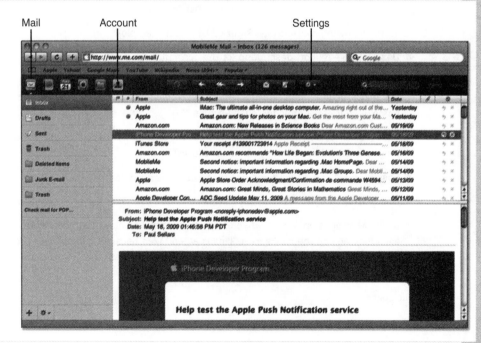

Mail   Account   Settings

Using the MobileMe website to access your email is similar to using the Mail application from the Mac OS X desktop. You can read your email, send email, organize it, and so on.

Accessing a POP Email Account Using MobileMe

Your MobileMe account is a convenient place to work with messages associated with your MobileMe email address, but you can also extend that convenience to another email account. That is, you can configure MobileMe to also check messages from some other account, even if it's not a MobileMe address. Note, however, that you can only check messages for this account; you can't send messages.

Follow these steps to add an external email account to your MobileMe inbox:

 note

To check another email account with MobileMe, that account must support the Post Office Protocol (POP). Most email accounts support POP, but not all. (For example, MobileMe accounts use Internet Message Access Protocol [IMAP], instead of POP.)

1. Click the Mail icon. The MobileMe Mail page appears.

2. Click the Actions icon (the gear) and then click Preferences. The Preferences window appears.

3. Click the Other tab.

4. Activate the Check Mail from an External POP Account check box. The window expands to display the controls for specifying the account particulars.

5. Fill in the following controls (see Figure 20.4 for an example).

   - **Description**—A short description for the account, such as "POP."

   - **Incoming Mail Server**—The name of the server your provider uses for incoming mail. It usually takes the form mail.*provider*.com or pop.*provider*.com, where *provider*.com is the domain name of your email provider (such as your ISP).

   - **User Name**—The name you use to log in to the account. This is most often your user name, but some providers require your email address.

   - **Password**—The password you use to log in to the account.

   - **Destination Folder**—Use this list to choose where you want the account's messages stored.

   - **Leave Messages on Server**—If you leave this check box activated, MobileMe leaves a copy of each message on the mail server. This is a good idea because it enables you to also download the messages to your regular email program. If you never do that, you should deactivate this check box to avoid messages piling up on the server.

6. Click Save.

Figure 20.4
You can con-
figure your
MobileMe
account to
check mes-
sages on
another
email
account.

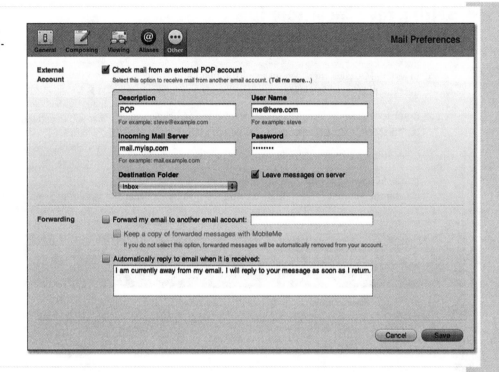

Using Your iDisk

iDisk is among the most useful things about having a MobileMe
account. The uses for an iDisk are almost limitless; the bottom
line is that your iDisk is additional disk space that you access
via the Internet. You can use this space to store any files you
choose. It is also vital to certain Mac OS X applications, such as
iWeb, because you store all the files you use on your web page
in the appropriate folders on your iDisk.

 tip

Although your iDisk isn't likely to be
large enough to perform system
backups, you can use it to back up
important documents. This keeps
them separate from your computer
and enables you to access them
from any Mac.

You can configure a Mac to create a local copy of your iDisk and
keep it synchronized with your online iDisk. This is especially useful when you work with the same
set of files from multiple locations, such as a work Mac and your home Mac.

When you purchase a MobileMe account, the combination of iDisk and email storage space is 20GB.
You can configure this to shift more space to the iDisk or to your email, and you can upgrade the
disk space available to your account.

Setting the Size of Your iDisk

In most cases, you should increase the size of your iDisk relative to the space used by your email account.

1. In MobileMe, click the Account icon (the head and shoulders in silhouette). MobileMe prompts you to log in again.

2. Enter your member name and password and then click Log In. The MobileMe Account page appears.

3. Click Storage Settings. The Storage Settings page appears.

4. In the Allocated column, use the Mail pop-up menu to choose the amount of storage space you want to use for mail, as shown in Figure 20.5.

tip

Only email that you store on the MobileMe server counts against the email portion of your MobileMe disk space. Make it a practice to download your MobileMe email to your Mac and to regularly delete your email to keep your disk use for email to a minimum so you can have more iDisk space.

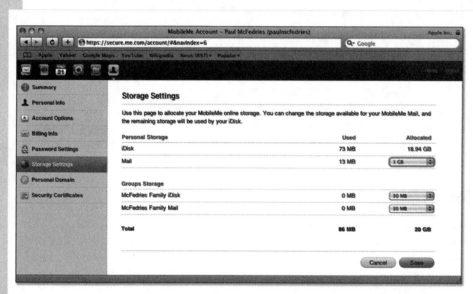

Figure 20.5
Using this page, you can set the balance of storage space between your iDisk and MobileMe email.

5. Click Save. Your MobileMe disk space will be allocated according to your selection.

Configuring Your iDisk

You can configure your iDisk for your Mac OS X user account by opening the iDisk tab of the MobileMe pane of the System Preferences application (see Figure 20.6).

tip

As you have probably figured out, you use the Account Settings web page to configure various aspects of your MobileMe account, such as changing your password, billing information, and so on.

Figure 20.6
Using the iDisk tab of the MobileMe pane, you can configure your iDisk.

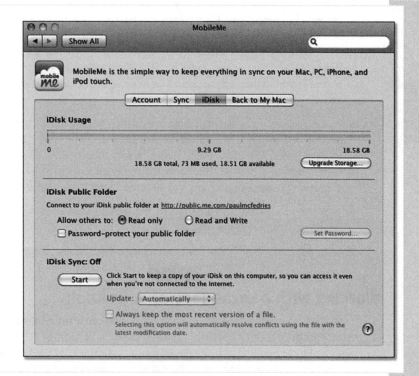

The most important configuration chore is determining whether you want to create a local copy of your iDisk on your computer. If you do this, you can work with the local copy just like other volumes on your computer. Then, you can either synchronize the local version with the online version manually or have your Mac do it automatically.

 tip

If the iDisk tab doesn't reflect your most recent account changes, quit the System Preferences application and restart it.

If you have a broadband connection, this is less important because there won't be as much difference accessing your online iDisk compared to the local copy. However, if you are going to work on files while they are on your iDisk (as opposed to just storing them there), using the local version will improve performance.

To configure your iDisk, perform the following steps:

1. Open the System Preferences utility and click the MobileMe button to open the MobileMe preferences.

2. Click the iDisk tab.

3. Use the iDisk Usage bar to assess the status of your disk space. The total length of the bar represents the current size of your iDisk, and the colored portion represents how much of that space is currently being used.

4. To create a copy of your iDisk on your Mac, click the Start button. This causes your Mac to download a copy of your iDisk so you can access it directly from your desktop. If you want your Mac to keep the local copy and the online iDisk synchronized at all times, click Automatically in the Update pop-up menu (this option should be selected only if you have a broadband connection to the Internet). If you prefer to manually synchronize your local and online iDisks, click the Manually button (this option should be selected if you have a relatively slow Internet connection).

5. To control whether others can input information to the Public folder on your iDisk, use the radio buttons in the iDisk Public Folder section. Click the Read Only button if you want users to only be able to read files in the Public folder on your iDisk but not be able to change any information there. Click the Read and Write button if you want them to also be able to change files there. If you chose the latter option, you should protect your iDisk with a password.

6. To protect your iDisk with a password, activate the Password Protect Your Public Folder check box and click the Set Password button.

7. In the resulting sheet, enter the password you want to use, confirm it, and click OK.

Working with a Local Copy of Your iDisk

If you chose to create a local copy of your iDisk, you can open it from the Finder by clicking its icon in the sidebar. You can also select Go, iDisk, My iDisk or press Shift-⌘-I (see Figure 20.7). In the resulting Finder window, you see the folders on your iDisk. At the bottom of the window, you can see the current space being used. While the local copy of your iDisk is being synchronized with the online version, you see the synchronization symbol rotating next to the iDisk icon.

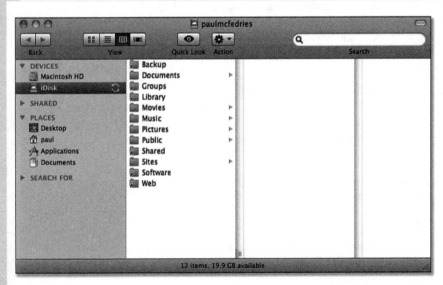

Figure 20.7
You can access your local copy of your iDisk by clicking its icon in the sidebar of a Finder window.

If you set the local copy of your iDisk for manual synchronization, you can perform the synchronization by clicking the
Synchronize Now button located to the right of the iDisk icon in
the sidebar. The two versions of the iDisk will be synchronized;
a progress bar at the bottom of the Finder window will inform
you about the status of the process.

 note

The local iDisk is actually a disk
image file called `Previous local`
`iDisk for username.dmg`, where
username is your member name.

Working with Your Online iDisk

If you choose not to create a local copy of your iDisk, you can still work with your iDisk from the
Finder. However, when you move files to and from the iDisk, you will actually be moving those files
across the Internet rather than just between locations on your hard drive. In most cases, you should
use a local copy instead. However, you can directly access your
online iDisk to work with it.

To do so, click the iDisk icon on the sidebar and the contents of
your iDisk will be shown in a Finder window.

If you have set your desktop preferences so that mounted disks
appear on your desktop, you will see a disk with the MobileMe
cloud icon—this is your iDisk. Your iDisk will also appear in the
Devices section of the sidebar.

➥ *To learn how to set the preference for disks being shown
on the desktop,* **see** *"Customizing the Mac OS X
Desktop," p. 15.*

tip

Look for the Synchronize symbol to
the right of the iDisk volume in the
sidebar of the Finder window to tell
the difference between the online
iDisk and a local copy of your iDisk.
If you don't see any symbol, you are
working with the online iDisk. If you
do see the Synchronization symbol,
you are working with a local copy.

Working with an iDisk

After your iDisk is mounted on your Mac (whether it is a local copy or the online version), you can
work with it just like the other volumes and disks on your machine. Open your iDisk and you will
see a number of folders, including the following:

- **Backup**—The Backup folder is where your data is stored if you use the Apple Backup application
  to back up your Mac via your iDisk.

- **Documents, Movies, Music, and Pictures**—These folders contain elements for web pages you
  might want to add to your MobileMe website using HomePage. For example, if you want to
  include a Pictures page on your site, you can store the images you want to include on the page
  in the Pictures folder.

- **Library**—The Library folder contains files that support the use of iDisk, such as application support files.

- **Public**—The Public folder is where you can store files you want other MobileMe users to be able
  to access via MobileMe or those you want to publish via a files web page so anyone can download them.

- **Sites**—The Sites folder is where you store your own HTML pages to be served from the MobileMe website.

- **Software**—The Software folder contains software you can download to your Mac. Apple stores system and application software updates here so you can easily access and download them. To see what software is available, simply open the Software folder. To download any of the files you see to your Mac, drag the file from the Software folder to a folder on your machine.

Accessing iDisks from the Go Menu

The iDisk commands on the Finder's Go menu are the following:

- **My iDisk**—This command opens your own iDisk.

- **Other User's iDisk**—When you select this command, you see the Connect To iDisk dialog box. Enter the member name and password of the user's iDisk that you want to access and click Connect. That iDisk is mounted on your Mac and you can work with it just like the iDisk that is configured as part of your MobileMe account. For example, if you have two MobileMe accounts, you can configure one iDisk as part of your Mac OS X user account and use this command to access the iDisk that is part of another MobileMe account.

- **Other User's Public Folder**—When you select this command, the Connect To iDisk Public Folder dialog box appears. Enter the member name of the user whose Public folder you want to access and click Connect. If the user has not selected the option to protect the Public folder with a password, that user's Public folder on her iDisk is shown in a Finder window. If the folder is protected with a password, enter the password and click Connect when prompted to do so.

tip

When you need to enter a password to access someone else's Public folder, your username is Public, which is entered for you. If you add the password to your keychain, you don't have to enter it again. The Public folder will be unlocked for you automatically when you access it.

Sharing Information on Your iDisk with Others

One of the most useful things about an iDisk is that you can place files in the Public folder and then share them with other users. You can do this in a couple of ways.

If the people with whom you want to share files are Mac users, they can access your files via the commands on their Mac's Go, iDisk menu. All you need to do is place the files you want to share in your iDisk's Public folder and then provide your MobileMe member name to the people with whom you want to share files. If you protect your Public folder with a password, you need to provide the password to them as well.

note

If you use a local iDisk and chose the Manual synchronization option, remember to synchronize your iDisk after you place new files in your Public folder for others to access.

You can also publish the contents of your Public folder so others can access it using a web interface. This means you can share files with anyone, whether they use a Mac or not.

> ➥ *To learn how to create a MobileMe website,* **see** *"Using MobileMe to Publish a Website,"* *p. 434.*

Upgrading Your iDisk

You might need to have more space available than the 20GB that is provided as part of a standard MobileMe account. In fact, if you want to create a website with lots of movies, music, and photos on it, up to 20GB might not be enough for you even if you've allocated most of your space to your iDisk. If you will be using the MobileMe backup application to back up your data, you are also likely to want more MobileMe disk space.

At press time, you could increase the total storage space for your MobileMe account to 40GB for an additional $50 per year, or to 60GB for an extra $109 per year.

To add more space to your MobileMe account, open System Preferences, click MobileMe, display the iDisk tab of the MobileMe pane, and then click the Upgrade Storage button. You'll move to the MobileMe website. Log in and you see the Account Upgrades dialog box. Click the Storage radio button for the amount of storage space you want to use, click Continue, and then follow the onscreen instructions.

After you have added more disk space to your MobileMe account, allocate the portion you want to make available to your iDisk.

Using Your iDisk to Work with the Same Files on Multiple Macs

If you regularly work on more than one Mac (such as one at work or school and one at home), you can use MobileMe to make sure you can access the same files on each Mac you use. To do this, perform the following steps:

1. Configure each Mac to use your MobileMe account.

2. On each Mac, configure your iDisk so you use a local copy and choose the synchronization option.

   You don't need to choose the same synchronization option on each Mac. For example, if one Mac connects via a broadband connection, you could choose the Automatic option. If another uses a slow connection, you could choose the Manual option for that Mac.

3. Store the files on which you are working in a folder on your iDisk. (Don't use the Public folder unless you want other people to be able to access these files.) As you save files, they will be saved on your iDisk.

4. When you are done working on a Mac for which the Manual synchronization option is active, synchronize the iDisk. The files on which you are working will be moved to the online iDisk.

5. When you get to a different Mac, synchronize the iDisk (if you have configured that Mac for automatic synchronization, you don't need to do this step). The files on which you work will be available in the Mac's iDisk folder.

 tip

After you have finished working on files and no longer need to access them, move them out of your iDisk so they no longer impact your available space.

Using MobileMe to Publish a Website

Using a MobileMe account, you can publish your own website. In brief, you add your own website files to the Sites folder on your iDisk to publish that site. For example, you can create your website using your favorite web page application and then post the site's files in the Sites folder on your iDisk. The iWeb application that is part of the iLife suite is perfect for this as it makes creating and publishing a website very easy.

You can use MobileMe to host *any* website you create using any other website editing tools, such as Apple's iWeb, Adobe's GoLive, or Macromedia's Dreamweaver. In this scenario, MobileMe acts just like any other web hosting service you might use.

The general process to get your customized website on the MobileMe site is the following:

 tip

Apple's iWeb application, part of the iLife suite, is about the easiest way to create and publish websites. iWeb is integrated with MobileMe, so to publish a site is literally a single click. The only downside to iWeb is that it is a template-based approach, so you have to work with the templates provided in the application. That isn't much of a limitation unless you like to design your sites from the ground up.

1. Create your website using the tools you prefer.

2. Test the site by accessing it while it is stored on your Mac. You can test a website by opening it from within a web browser. For example, open your site using Safari by selecting File, Open File. Then, maneuver to the home page for your site and open it. The site will work just as it will after you post it on your MobileMe website (except that it will be faster, of course). You should test your site in various browsers and operating systems to ensure that it can be viewed properly.

 note

Name the home page of your site `index.html`. This ensures that a viewer is taken to the right start page for your site when he moves to its URL.

3. Fix any problems you find.

4. When your site is ready to post, copy all its files and folders into the Sites folder on your iDisk.

5. Test your site again by accessing it over the Internet.

To access the website in your Sites folder, use the following URL: http://web.me.com/*yourmember-name*/. (For this to work, you must have named the home page for the site index.html.)

When you move to your MobileMe website URL, you see the page you named index.html.

Using MobileMe to Synchronize Important Information on Multiple Macs

You can also use MobileMe to keep important information synchronized on all the Macs you use. For example, you can make sure you have access to the same set of Safari bookmarks on each Mac you use. Similarly, you can keep the same set of information in the Address Book on each of your Macs. To synchronize your Macs, perform the following steps:

1. Click the Sync tab found on the MobileMe pane of the System Preferences application.

2. Activate the Synchronize with MobileMe check box as shown in Figure 20.8. Mac OS X enables the check boxes.

Figure 20.8
Use the options on the Sync tab to keep information on multiple Macs synchronized.

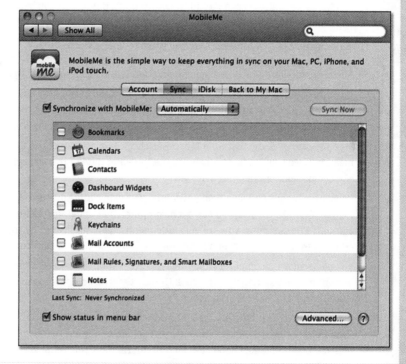

3. Use the Synchronize with MobileMe pop-up menu to choose the synchronization frequency. To have information synchronized constantly, choose Automatically. Other options include Every Hour, Every Day, Every Week, and Manually.

4. Activate the check box next to each type of information that you want to be synchronized. For example, to synchronize your Safari bookmarks, activate the Bookmarks check box. To synchronize your contact information, activate the Contacts check box.

5. Click Sync Now. The synchronization process starts and Mac OS X prompts you to choose how you want information to be synchronized.

6. Choose the synchronization option you want to use from the pop-up menu:

   ■ **Merge Data on This Computer and MobileMe**—This option adds new data on your Mac to that stored in your MobileMe account and adds data stored in your MobileMe account onto the Mac.

   ■ **Replace Data on MobileMe**—This option replaces all the related data in your MobileMe account with information on the Mac.

   ■ **Replace Data on This Computer**—This option causes data on MobileMe to replace the data currently on your Mac.

7. Click Sync. The data you selected to be synchronized will be moved to and from the Mac and MobileMe until it is synchronized according to the option you selected. From this point forward, it will be synchronized according to the option you selected on the pop-up menu.

8. Repeat steps 1–7 for each Mac you want to keep in sync.

The time and date of the last synchronization will be shown under the MobileMe icon.

If you configured the sync with something other than Manual, you don't need to bother with it any more; your Mac will keep its information in sync with what is on your MobileMe account. If you chose Manual, you'll need to click the Sync Now button to synchronize your Mac's information.

If you leave the Show Status in Menu Bar check box activated, the Sync menu appears in the Finder menu bar. On this menu, you can see the time and date of the last synchronization, choose the Sync Now command, or open the Sync tab.

You can manage the Macs being synchronized using the Advanced button of the Sync tab (see Figure 20.9). On the list, you see each computer that is being synchronized via the MobileMe account. The computer you are currently using will be indicated by the (This Computer) text. In addition to the computer name, you see the time and date of that computer's last synchronization.

You can remove a computer from the synchronization list by selecting it and clicking the Unregister button. In the resulting prompt, click Unregister. The computer is removed from the list and is no longer available for synchronization.

If you want to reset how data is being synchronized on a computer, select it and click the Reset Sync Data button. In the resulting sheet, you can configure the reset (see Figure 20.10). On the Replace pop-up menu, choose the kind of information you want to reset; choose All Sync Info to reset all the information you have chosen to sync. Click the left or right arrow to determine the direction in which you want to do the reset. To replace the data on the Mac with data on MobileMe, click the left arrow. To replace the data on MobileMe with data on the computer, click the right arrow. Then click Replace. The data will be reset in the direction you indicated.

Figure 20.9
Click Advanced in the MobileMe pane to see information about all the computers you are synching via MobileMe.

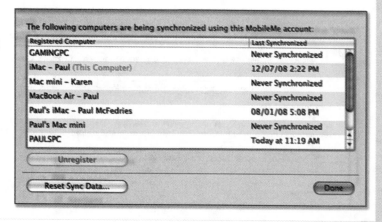

The following computers are being synchronized using this MobileMe account:

Registered Computer	Last Synchronized
GAMINGPC	Never Synchronized
iMac – Paul (This Computer)	12/07/08 2:22 PM
Mac mini – Karen	Never Synchronized
MacBook Air – Paul	Never Synchronized
Paul's iMac – Paul McFedries	08/01/08 5:08 PM
Paul's Mac mini	Never Synchronized
PAULSPC	Today at 11:19 AM

Unregister

Reset Sync Data...   Done

Figure 20.10
Use this prompt to reset the synchronization options for a computer.

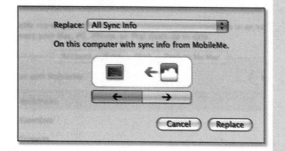

Replace: All Sync Info

On this computer with sync info from MobileMe.

Cancel   Replace

Accessing Your Mac Remotely with Back to My Mac

In Mac OS X 10.5 and later, you can use the Back to My Mac feature to access the data on your computer. Back to My Mac allows you to access files on the Mac OS X computers that use your MobileMe account. In addition, enabling the Screen Sharing services allows you to remotely control your Mac over the Internet. Back to My Mac requires a paid MobileMe account, and the Mac you want to access or control must be turned on and connected to the Internet. To enable Back to My Mac, perform the following steps:

1. Click the Back to My Mac tab found on the MobileMe pane of the System Preferences application (see Figure 20.11).

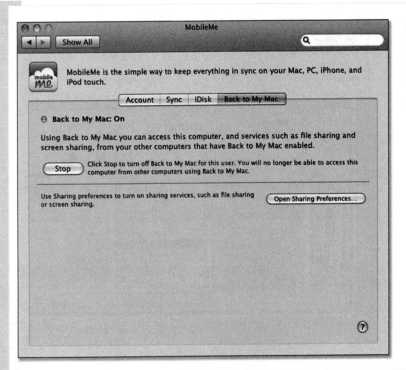

Figure 20.11
Back to My Mac enables you to share files with or remotely control any Mac configured with your MobileMe account.

2. If the Back to My Mac service is not enabled, click the Start button to enable it. You can see the status of the service at the top of the pane.

3. Click the Open Sharing Preferences button to move to the Sharing pane of the System Preferences application. Here you can configure the Screen Sharing and File Sharing services and turn them on so that you can remotely access this computer. Be sure to specify the accounts that can access this Mac remotely for Screen Sharing.

4. When you use another computer that is configured with your MobileMe account, the computer that has Back to My Mac turned on will appear in the Sharing section of the Sidebar.

5. Select the computer you want to remotely access. Click Connect As to access shared files on the remote Mac. You will be prompted to log in so that you can access the correct user account on the remote Mac. After you authenticated as a user on that computer, you will see the files you have access to, and you can copy files to and from the remote Mac.

 tip

If you do not see the remote Mac in the Sharing section of the Sidebar, open the Finder preferences and click on the Sidebar tab. Make sure that Back to My Mac is checked so that it will appear in the Sidebar.

6. To control the remote Mac, click Share Screen. Click As a Registered User and enter your username and password. You will then take control of the Mac. Note that this will take over control of the computer; if someone else is using that remote computer, this may be a bit of a shock. You could click By Asking Permission instead, which will ask the current user of that remote Mac if you can share the screen.

Back to My Mac offers a useful level of resource sharing. Because it is integrated with MobileMe, communicating with remote Mac OS X 10.5 and later computers is very easy to do.

WORKING WITH USER ACCOUNTS

Understanding Mac OS X User Accounts

Do you share your Mac with other people either at work or at home? Then you're no doubt all too aware of one undeniable fact of human psychology: People are individuals with minds of their own! One person prefers a constantly changing desktop background; another person likes to populate the menu bar with every available icon; yet another person prefers to have a zillion shortcuts on the desktop; and, of course, everybody uses a different mix of applications. How can you possibly satisfy all those diverse tastes and prevent people from coming to blows?

It's a lot easier than you might think. Mac OS X lets you set up a different user account for each person who uses the computer. A user account has a username (and an optional password) that uniquely identifies a person who uses the system. The user account allows that person to create their own version of Mac OS X, complete with interface customizations, system configurations, and their own private set of folders and files. The user account also enables Mac OS X to control the user's privileges; that is, the user's access to system resources (permissions) and the user's ability to run system tasks (rights).

There are several types of Mac OS X user accounts I'll address in this chapter:

- **Administrator** accounts have broad access to the system; the initial account set up by the Mac OS X installation application is of this type.

- **Clean** accounts are administrator accounts that you use solely for troubleshooting (this isn't a formal type, but rather a functional one).

- **Standard** user accounts don't have administrator permissions and can have other limitations as well.

- **Guest** user accounts are temporary accounts that don't have permanent resources on your Mac.

- **Shared** user accounts are intended to be used by multiple people.

- The **root** user account is the extremely powerful and equally dangerous account you use mostly for troubleshooting.

You can also create groups of user accounts to enable you to configure security properties to provide specific kinds of access to system resources, folders, and files.

Understanding Administrator Accounts

The account created when you installed Mac OS X is an administrator account. Administrator accounts are special because they provide wide access to the system and are one of only two accounts that can control virtually every aspect of Mac OS X (the other being the root account). A user who logs in as an administrator for your Mac can do the following:

- **Create other user accounts**—An administrator for your Mac can create additional user accounts. By default, these user accounts have more limited access to the Mac than does an administrator account, but you can allow other accounts to administer your Mac as well (so you can create multiple administrator accounts).

- **Change global system preferences**—The administrator can change global system settings for your Mac; other user accounts can't. For example, to change the network settings on your Mac, you must be logged in as the administrator (or you must authenticate yourself as an administrator).

- **Configure access to files and folders**—An administrator can configure the security settings of files and folders to determine who can access those items and which type of access is permitted.

- **Install applications**—Applications you install under Mac OS X require that you be logged in as an administrator or that you authenticate yourself as one.

When you are logged in under an administrator account, you can perform most of these actions without inputting more information because your account configuration gives you permissions to do so. However, when you are logged in under a non-administrator user account (and sometimes in specific situations while logged in under an administrator account), you need to authenticate yourself as an administrator to be able to complete the action.

You should limit who has access to the administrator accounts for your machine. If someone who doesn't understand Mac OS X—or who wants to cause you trouble—logs in with your administrator account, you might be in for all kinds of problems.

Understanding the Clean Account

There's one user account you should create, but seldom use. I call this the clean account, not because the others are dirty, but because no customization or personalization should be done under this account. It should remain in its just-created state so that all of the preferences and other files stored under it are as close to being in their default states as possible.

You use the clean account to troubleshoot problems. By logging in under the clean account, you can often isolate problems that are related to a user account preference or a change made by an application that only impacts the user account under which that change was made.

When a problem occurs, you log in to the clean account and attempt to replicate the problem. If it doesn't recur, you know that the issue is specific to the user account you were logged in under when it happened. If it recurs, you know that it is a system problem. This information can be critical to being able to solve a problem efficiently and effectively.

You should always create a clean user account on your Mac, whether you create any of the other types or not.

Understanding Standard User Accounts

When you share your Mac with others, you'll most likely want to provide them with non-administrator user accounts, which are called standard user accounts. Because these accounts don't have administrator permissions, the types of activities they can do are limited. For example, people using these accounts can't install applications or make certain changes that impact the system. This is a good thing because it prevents other people from making changes to your system without your knowledge or permission.

Understanding Managed Accounts

You can further limit the access of standard accounts too, such as using the Simple Finder or Parental Controls features to more extensively control the resources to which people using these accounts can access. When you limit an account like this, it becomes a managed account.

Understanding the Guest Account

The guest account is a good way to let people use your Mac on a temporary basis. You don't need a password to log in as a guest; all the user has to do is select the Guest account. After the user has logged in, she can access the Mac as if she were using a standard or managed account. The primary difference between the Guest account and other accounts is that as soon as the user logs off, all the information associated with that account is deleted so no permanent changes are made to your Mac.

You also use the guest account to allow others to connect to your Mac over the local network. When someone logs in as a guest they can access shared folders, as well as upload files to those public directories.

Understanding Sharing Only Accounts

Sharing only accounts are designed to allow a user to have access to your Mac over a network without being able to physically log in to your computer. Similar to a guest account, a sharing only account can access shared folders, as well as upload files to those public directories. However, the benefit of using a sharing only account is an added layer of security by requiring the person to know a username and password to access these resources. Depending on the environment your Mac is in, a sharing only account may be a more secure choice for providing others access to your files.

Understanding the Root Account

Because Mac OS X is based on UNIX, it includes the root account. In a nutshell, the root account is not limited by *any* security permissions. If an action can be done on your Mac, the root account can do it. This is both good and bad. It's good because you can often solve problems using the root account that you can't solve any other way. It's bad because you can also cause problems that it might not be possible to recover from, at least, not easily. For example, when you are using an administrator account, you have limited access to certain system files so there is no way you can delete them. However, under the root account, it's possible to do things that cause your system to become unusable.

Like the clean account, you'll likely only use the root account for troubleshooting. But, when you need it, you'll really need it.

Understanding User Groups

Mac OS X uses the group concept to assign permissions to access files and folders. You can create user groups and assign user accounts to those groups. This makes providing permissions simpler because you only have to choose one group to give the members of that group the appropriate permissions.

Creating and Configuring User Accounts

Hopefully, you are convinced that you need at least two user accounts on your Mac. Because one administrator account was created when you installed Mac OS X, you need to at least create one more administrator account to use as your clean account.

If you share your Mac with others, you can choose to create a user account for each person. Or, you can create a user account that several people share. This can be useful if there are people who use your Mac but don't necessarily need private folders or individual customization. For example, if you share your Mac with children, you might want to create a single user account for them to use.

The good news is that three of the four types I described earlier are created and configured using the steps you'll find in this section. (The root account is an animal of an entirely different type; you'll learn how to work with the root account later in the chapter.)

Creating User Accounts

To create user accounts, follow these steps:

1. Open the System Preferences application.

2. Click the Accounts icon in the System area to open the Accounts pane of the System Preferences application.

   Along the left side of this pane is the list of user accounts currently configured on the Mac. At the top of this list in the My Account section, the user account under which you are logged in is shown. If you've not created additional user accounts, this will be the account you created when you installed Mac OS X. Under the Other Accounts heading are the other user accounts that exist on the machine. Under each username, you will see the type of account it is, such as Admin, Managed, and so on. At the bottom of the user list is the Login Options button, and just below that are the Add User (+) and Delete User buttons (-). The right part of the pane shows the tools you use to configure the selected user account.

   Only an administrator can create or change user accounts. If you aren't logged in as an administrator for your Mac, you have to authenticate yourself as being an administrator before you can create an account. To do so, click the Lock icon located in the lower-left corner of the System Preferences window, enter the username and password for an administrator account, and click OK. This identifies you as an administrator so that you can make changes, such as adding and changing user accounts.

3. Click the New User button, which is the plus sign located under the list of users. A sheet appears in which you enter basic information for the user account you are creating (Figure 21.1 shows the sheet already filled in).

Figure 21.1
Use this sheet to specify the details for the new user.

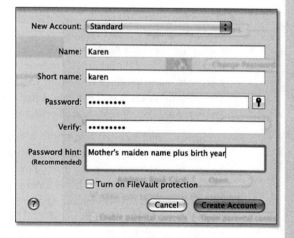

4. Choose the type of user to create on the New Account pop-up menu. If you want the new account to be an administrator account, select Administrator on the menu. Of course, you should only allow this on accounts you control or for people you trust not to cause you problems.

5. Enter the name for the user account in the Name box. The name is the "full" name for the user account; it doesn't have to be a real full name—the name can be pretty much whatever you want it to be.

6. Press Tab to move to the Short Name box. When you do, Mac OS X creates a short name for the user account. The short name is used for specific areas under that user account (such as the name of the user's Home folder) and for access to services provided under that account (such as the account's website). The short name can be used instead of the name to cut down on the number of characters you have to type in specific situations, for example, when you log in to the account (in which case the short name and name are interchangeable). However, the Home directory is always identified by the short name only.

7. Edit the short name as needed, for example, by replacing it if you don't like the one Mac OS X created for you automatically.

The short name can be as few as one character and can't contain any spaces, dashes, or other special characters (Mac OS X won't let you enter any characters that are unacceptable). Underscores are acceptable. You should adopt a general rule about the short name for an account, such as using the first initial of the first name and the complete last name. Keeping the short name consistent will help you deal with other user accounts more easily.

After it's created, you can't change the short name for a user account, so be deliberate when you create it.

 tip

You can use a user account for any purpose you want. For example, because each user account has its own website, you might want to create a user account simply to create another website on your machine. For example, you might want to create a user called "Group Site" (with a short name of "group_site") to serve a web page to a workgroup of which you are a member.

8. Create the password that the user will enter to log in under the user account. For better security, use a password that is eight characters long and contains both letters and numbers (this makes the password harder to crack). Passwords are case sensitive; for example, mypassword is not the same as MyPassword. If you want help creating a password, move to step 9 without typing a password. If you want to type it in without help, enter it in the Password and Verify fields and skip to step 16.

If you leave the Password field empty, a password will not be required to log in to the account. When you choose to do this, you will see a warning dialog box when you attempt to save the account. If you ignore this warning, the account is created without a password. When the user logs in to the account, he can select it on the list of user accounts and log in without entering a password. Obviously, this is not a secure thing to do, but it can be

 tip

You can remove a password from an existing account even though the system tells you this can't be done. Just remove the password, save the account changes, click Ignore in the warning dialog box, and then click OK in the dialog box that tells you this change won't be accepted. It is actually accepted and the account no longer requires a password.

useful nonetheless. For example, you might choose to create an account for children whom you don't want to have to use a password. When you create such "unprotected" accounts, you should use the Parental Controls tools to limit access to your Mac, such as by using the Simple Finder option.

9. Click the Key button to the right of the Password field. The Password Assistant opens (see Figure 21.2).

Figure 21.2
The Password Assistant can help you create passwords.

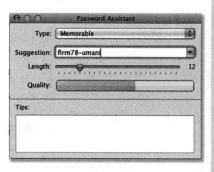

10. Select the type of password you want to create on the Type pop-up menu. There are several options:

- **Manual**—Enables you to type a password manually. When you choose this option, you can use the Password Assistant to help you gauge the quality of the password you create.

- **Memorable**—Creates a password that your Mac thinks users will be able to remember.

- **Letters & Numbers**—Creates a password consisting of letters and numbers.

- **Numbers Only**—Creates a password consisting only of numbers.

- **Random**—Creates a random password.

- **FIPS-181 compliant**—Creates a password that is compliant with the federal requirements for automatic password generation.

11. To create a password yourself, choose Manual and type the password in the Suggestion box. As you type, the Assistant will provide tips for you in the Tips box. It will also display the quality of the password on the Quality gauge. The more of the bar that is filled in with green, the more secure the password is. If the bar has red or yellow, the password you've created is not very secure. When you're satisfied with the password you've created, enter the password you've created in the Verify field and skip to step 16.

 note

If you close the Password Assistant before you create the user account, the password you entered manually will be deleted from both fields. Leave the Assistant open while you finish configuring the sheet.

12. To have the Assistant suggest a password, choose a type other than Manual. The Assistant will generate a password of that type in the Suggestion box.

13. Select the length of the password you want to create using the Length slider. The minimum number of characters is 8. The maximum is 31, but I suspect your users won't be happy with a password that long! More characters mean a more secure password, but also one that is harder to remember and type.

    After you choose the length, your Mac will generate a new password of the type you selected and it will appear in the Suggestion box.

14. If you don't like the suggested password shown, use the Suggestion pop-up menu to select another option. You can generate more suggestions by choosing More Suggestions.

    As you select passwords, the Quality gauge shows you a relative measure of the quality of the password you are choosing. The more of the bar that is filled with green, the more secure the password will be. Of course, this is from the security perspective, which isn't necessarily the same as the user's preferences.

15. When the Suggestion box contains the password you want to use, click in the Verify box and retype the password.

16. Move into the Password Hint field (press Tab) and enter a hint to remind the user what the password is. This reminder is optional; if a user fails to log in successfully after three attempts, this hint can appear to help him remember his password.

17. If you want the new account's Home folder to be protected with FileVault, activate the Turn on FileVault Protection check box.

> **note**
>
> If you have not turned off the Automatic Login mode and you create a new user account, you will see a dialog box asking whether you want that mode to be turned off. The account that is logged in automatically is also shown in this dialog box. (If you have disabled the Automatic Login mode already, you won't see this dialog box.)

➡ *To learn more about FileVault,* ***see*** *"Securing Your Mac with FileVault,"* ***p. 707.***

18. Click Create Account. (If you didn't enter a password, you are warned in a dialog box; click OK if you are sure you want to create a user account without a password.)

When you return to the Accounts pane, you see that the new user account you created appears in the Other Accounts list (see Figure 21.3). Under the account, you see the type of account it is.

Configuring User Accounts

After you have created a user account, you can configure it to determine the kind of access that account has to your Mac and to customize certain aspects of it.

When you select the account under which you are currently logged in (the one shown in the My Account area), the Password and Login Items tabs appear. You use these tabs to configure these elements of the current account.

Figure 21.3
The account called Karen has been created and is ready to configure.

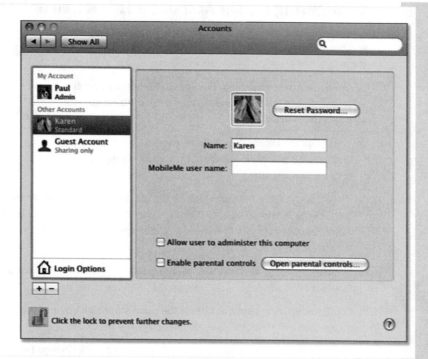

If you aren't logged in under the account you want to modify, you can configure the following aspects of that account:

- Account picture

- Account name (but not the short name)

- MobileMe user name

- Password (you can reset it for the user)

- Parental controls to limit the access of the account

- Administrator access

The following sections explain how to configure each of these areas for the current account as well as others you have created. You'll see notations about the differences in the steps.

Configuring a User Account's Full Name or Password

You can change the password for the current account or reset another account's password by performing the following steps:

1. Open the Accounts pane of the System Preferences application, unlock the pane, and select the user whose account you want to update.

2. To change the account's full name, enter a new full name in the Name box. (Remember that you can't change a user account's short name.)

3. If you are changing the password for the current account, click the Password tab and then click the Change Password button. If you are changing the password of another account, click the Reset Password button. The sheet that appears will look slightly different, but you use either version in a very similar way.

4. If you're changing the current account's password, enter the current password in the Old Password field.

5. Configure the new password using the same steps that you use when you create a password for a new user account.

6. If you're changing the current account's password, click Change Password or if you are changing another account's password, click Reset Password. The sheet will close and the new password will take effect.

7. To enable a user to administer your Mac, select the user and activate the Allow User to Administer This Computer check box.

 note

If a user account (other than the one you are currently using) is logged in to the Mac, you won't be able to make any changes to it. Log out of that account first and then change it.

Configuring a User Account's Picture

You can associate a picture with a user account. This picture shows up in a number of places, such as next to the user's account in the Login window, in the user's Address Book card, in their iChat sessions, and so on. There are two sources of images that you can use. One is the default images that are part of Mac OS X. The other is any other image that you create or that you download from the Internet. To configure a user's image, perform the following steps:

1. Open the Accounts pane of the System Preferences application and select the user whose picture you want to set.

2. Click the Image well, which is above the Name field (it will contain an image assigned by Mac OS X or selected when you created the first user account). The Picture sheet will appear (see Figure 21.4). At the top of this sheet, you'll see the Edit Picture command that you can use to customize the image. In the lower part of the sheet, you'll see all the default images from which you can choose.

3. To select a different default image, click the one you want to use. The current image will be replaced with the one you select.

Figure 21.4
On this sheet, you can select an image for a user account or click the Edit Picture link to open an image editor.

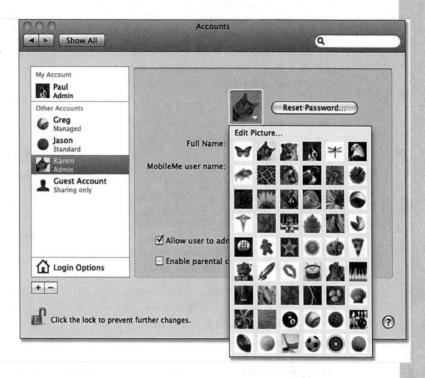

4. To capture an image to use or to choose one from an image file, click the Edit Picture command. The Image sheet appears (see Figure 21.5).

Figure 21.5
Use the Image sheet to create a more customized image for an account.

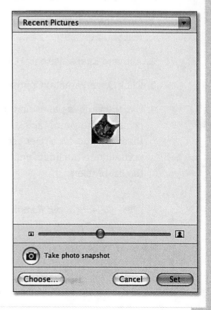

5. To place an image in the sheet, drag an image onto the image well in the center of the sheet, click Choose, and move to and select an image (such as one you've downloaded from the Internet), or click Take a Video Snapshot to capture an image from a video camera connected to your Mac (such as the iSight cameras that are built-in on most Macs).

The image formats you can use as the login picture include JPEG and TIFF. However, you can't use a GIF as a login picture.

6. When the image is shown in the image well, use the slider to crop the image to the part you want to use. Drag the slider to the right to zoom in on part of the image you want to use.

7. Drag the image around in the image well to select the portion of it to be used as the account's picture.

8. When the picture is what you want it to be, click Set. The image is shown in the image well on the Picture tab and is used for that user account.

 tip

If you have worked with other images recently, click the Recent Pictures pop-up menu at the top of the Images dialog box and select the image you want to use.

 tip

The default login pictures (those shown on the scrolling list) are stored in the directory *Mac OS X*/Library/User Pictures, where *Mac OS X* is the name of your Mac OS X startup volume. You can install additional images in this directory to make them available as part of the Apple Pictures collection.

Limiting Access of a User Account Using Parental Controls

You might want to limit the access a user has to your Mac. For example, if the user is a child, you might not want that child to be able to use certain applications or to burn CDs or DVDs. You can use the Parental Controls to set these kinds of limits on a user account. Follow these steps:

1. Open the Accounts pane of the System Preferences application and select the user whose access you want to limit.

2. Activate Enable Parental Controls.

3. Click Open Parental Controls. The Parental Controls pane appears.

4. Use the various panes and tools to set limits on the account. Because these controls are tightly connected to your Mac's overall security, they are covered in Chapter 37. After you've configured these controls for a user account, that account will only be able to perform tasks and access data according to the limits you set. In addition, the user will now be a managed account, as noted in the list of users.

➡ *To learn about Parental Controls in more detail,* **see** *"Using Parental Controls to Safeguard a Mac," p. 724.*

Configuring Your Address Book Card

In the Address Book application, each person has a card that provides her contact information. When you're viewing the user account pane for the currently logged-in account (the one listed in the My Account section), the Address Book Card Open button will appear. If you click this button, the Address Book application will open and you will move to your Address Book card. You can then edit your card as needed. After you've done this, your Address Book card will contain your current information, including the picture associated with your account. This is useful in a number of ways, such as including your picture in email sent with Mail.

➥ *To learn how to edit your address card information,* ***see*** *"Editing Your Own Address Card," **p. 221** (Chapter 10).*

Setting Applications and Documents to Open Automatically at Login

To make your Mac even more efficient, you can have applications automatically start or documents open when a user logs in to an account. And you can have a different set of applications start up for each user account; this lets you customize each user's startup experience.

To configure the startup items for a user account, perform the following steps:

1. Log in to the account for which you want to set the login items (you don't have to be logged in as an administrator to configure login items as you do to create user accounts or configure the Login window).

2. Open the System Preferences application.

3. Click the Accounts button, select the current user account, and then click the Login Items tab. The Login Items pane appears (see Figure 21.6). You place any items you want to open on the list to have them open when the user logs in. The order in which they are listed in the window determines the order in which they open (the topmost item opens first).

4. Click the Add button, which is the plus sign (+) at the bottom of the pane.

5. Use the Add sheet to move to the item you want to be opened at login, select it, and click Add. When you place an item in the window (by using the Add button or dragging it there), an alias to that item is created

6. If you want the item to be automatically hidden when it is opened, activate the item's Hide check box. This is useful for applications that you don't need to see right away but still want to open. For example, you might want to open your email application but leave it hidden until you receive new email.

 tip

You can also drag application or document icons directly onto the Login Items list instead of using the Add button.

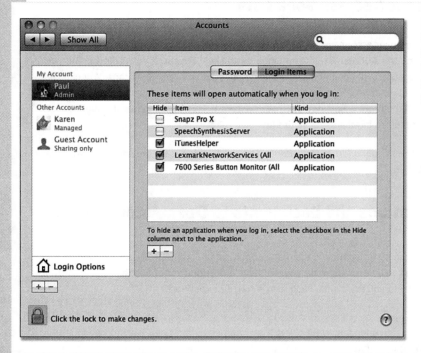

Figure 21.6
When you add applications or documents to the Login Items list, they automatically open when you log in.

7. When you have all the items in the window, drag an item up to make it open earlier in the process, or drag an item down to have it open later in the sequence.

8. To remove an application or document from the list (so that it doesn't open on login), select it and click the Remove button, which is the minus sign (–) at the bottom of the pane. This doesn't affect the item at all—it only removes it from the Login Items list.

9. Continue adding, removing, and rearranging items until all the startup items are listed in the window in the order in which you want them to open.

The next time the user logs in, the login items will open automatically, in the order you specified.

Enabling the Guest Account

A guest account enables someone to temporarily log in to your Mac without a password. Guest accounts have limited access to your Mac's resources, and any

 note

Some applications might rely on others to function. In that case, you want the dependent application to open after the application on which it depends, so it should be lower on the list.

 tip

Login items are a great way to customize your Mac for other users. Log in to the other accounts and create a set of login items for those users. The applications and documents will open for them automatically.

files or folders the guest user creates are deleted when the user logs out. The guest account is a good way to let someone use your Mac without making any changes to it. To enable the guest account, do the following:

1. Open the Accounts pane of the System Preferences application and unlock the pane.

2. Select Guest Account on the account list.

3. Activate the Allow Guests to Log In to This Computer check box. The Guest account is now ready to use.

If you want to allow a guest to be able to access shared folders on your Mac from across your network, leave the Allow Guests to Connect to Shared Folders check box activated.

Creating a Sharing Only Account

A Sharing only account is designed to be a more secure method for allowing others to connect to the shared folders on your Mac. Unlike a guest account, which anyone could attempt to use to connect to your shared folders, the sharing only account requires the person to know the username and password to gain access to the resources you are sharing.

You create a sharing account just like a standard user account, with a couple of differences. On the Account sheet, choose Sharing Only on the New Account drop-down list. Unlike with other accounts, you can't provide administrator permissions to a sharing account nor can you turn on FileVault protection or Parental Controls for them.

Creating Groups of Users

You can create a group and assign users to that group to configure permissions for folders and files. Groups make it easier to set the same level of access to specific objects for multiple people.

➡ *To learn more about setting permissions,* ***see*** *"Securing Your Mac with Privileges," **p. 307.***

To create a user group, do the following steps:

1. Open the Accounts pane of the System Preferences application and unlock the pane.

2. Click the Add Account button (the "+" sign).

3. On the Account sheet, choose Group on the New Account drop-down list.

4. Enter the name of the group in the Name field.

5. Click Create Group. You'll return to the Accounts pane and will see the user accounts, sharing accounts, and groups that can be placed into the group you created (see Figure 21.7).

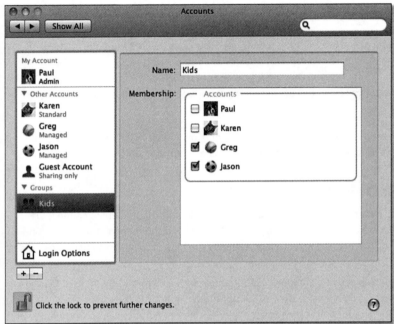

Figure 21.7
When you check the box next to a user account, sharing account, or group, it will be placed in the group selected on the account list.

6. Check the box next to each user account, sharing account, or group that you want to place in the group. When the group you created is assigned permissions, all the members of the group will get those permissions.

Resetting Your Password If You Forget Your Administrator Password

If you forget the password for your administrator account, you have two options. If you can remember the password for your clean account, log in under that account and reset your admin password. If you can't remember that password either or don't have a clean account (shame on you!), the process is slightly more complicated.

1. Restart your Mac from the Mac OS X installation disc. (You can insert the disc and use the Startup Disk pane to select it or restart your Mac while holding the C key down.)

2. After the installer application starts, choose Utilities, Reset Password.

3. Enter and verify the new password and click OK.

4. Quit the installer and restart your Mac.

5. As it restarts, hold the left mouse button down so the installation disc will be ejected. The Mac will restart from the previous startup disc and you should be able to log in using the new password.

Logging Out and Configuring Login Options

Under Mac OS X, rather than shutting the computer down, most of the time you will log out instead. When you log out, all the processes currently running are stopped and the user account is "closed." To log out of the current user account, select the Apple menu, and then select Log Out (or press Shift-⌘-Q). In the resulting confirmation dialog box, press Return or click Log Out (if you don't do this within one minute, the system logs you out automatically). The processes that are currently running are stopped (you are first prompted to save any open documents that have unsaved changes), and you return to the Login dialog box.

If you have enabled Fast User Switching (see "Enabling and Using Fast User Switching," later in this chapter), you can also select the Login window command on the User Switching menu to protect access to your account while keeping it logged in.

Configuring Automatic Login

When you started Mac OS X for the first time, you were in the Automatic Login mode. In this mode, you don't have to enter login information; Mac OS X does it for you. This means that you don't have to enter a username and password each time you start or restart your machine; by default, the first user account (created during the Mac OS X installation process) is used for the automatic login.

To configure the Automatic Login mode, use the following steps:

1. Open the Accounts pane of the System Preferences application and unlock the pane.

2. Click the Login Options button. The Login Options pane appears (see Figure 21.8).

 tip

Logging out and then logging back in is a lot faster than stopping and starting your machine. In fact, there aren't many reasons to shut down your machine. To secure your Mac when you aren't using it, just log out.

 caution

You should enable Automatic Login mode only if you are the only person who uses your Mac. If you enable Automatic Login mode with the administrator's account, you provide access to many of your system's resources, which is an unsecure way to operate. However, if you have a Mac in a secure location and are the only person who uses it, the Automatic Login mode eliminates the need to log in every time you start or restart the machine.

 tip

If you are going to enable Automatic Login mode, create a non-administrator account to use. That way, even if someone does get access to your Mac, he won't be able to use the administrator account. Of course, you might have to log out and then log back in as the administrator to perform certain tasks, but this strategy provides a good compromise between security and convenience.

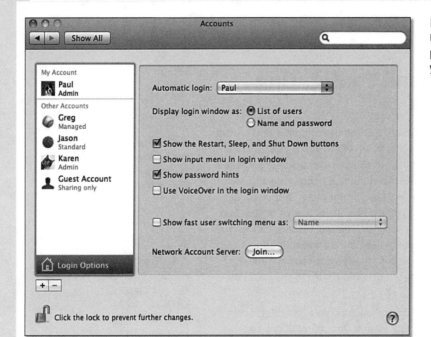

Figure 21.8
Use the Login Options pane to configure how you log in to your Mac.

3. To enable automatic login mode, open the Automatic Login pop-up menu and select the user account that should automatically be logged in. The password prompt sheet will appear, and the user account you selected on the pop-up menu is selected in the sheet.

4. Enter the password for the account that you selected in step 3.

5. Click OK.

The next time you start or restart your Mac, the account you specified is automatically logged in and you move directly to the desktop for that account.

This setting affects only the start or restart sequence. When you log out instead of shutting down or restarting, you still see the Login window again and have to log in to resume using the Mac.

To disable automatic login, choose Off on the Automatic Login pop-up menu.

Controlling How User Accounts Appear in the Login Window

You can configure several aspects of how user accounts appear in the Login window:

1. Log in under an administrator account, open the Accounts pane of the System Preferences application, and unlock the pane.

2. Click the Login Options button.

3. To display empty Name and Password fields in the Login window instead of a list of the user accounts you have configured, click the Name and Password radio button. When this button is selected, you have to type the name or the short name and password for an account to log in to it. To display the list of user accounts, click the List of Users radio button instead. With this option, each account (and its picture) appears onscreen. To log in, the user clicks her account, enters her password, and clicks the Login button.

Hiding the Sleep, Restart, and Shut Down Buttons

If you enable Automatic Login mode, you might run into trouble if you leave the Restart and Shut Down buttons in the Login window enabled. For example, suppose you're using your Mac and decide that you want to take a break for a while, but there are people nearby that you don't want to access the Mac while you step away. You log out, and your machine is protected, right? Not necessarily. If the Restart and Shut Down buttons are enabled, someone can restart the Mac from the Login window and then it would start up in the automatic account, giving the person access to the machine. Disabling these buttons prevents someone from using them to access an account that is automatically logged in to.

The previous scenario might make you pause to ask a question before you enable Automatic Login mode. If you do disable the Restart and Shut Down buttons and then log out, can someone simply press the hardware Restart or Reset button on the CPU to start up the Mac to automatically log in to the automatic login account? This would bypass the protection offered by disabling the buttons, right? Nope; when the Mac is not shut down properly (by using the Shut Down command), the automatic login feature is disabled when the machine is started or restarted the next time. So, if you have to use one of those buttons, you must log in the next time you start or restart the machine.

To disable the Sleep, Restart, and Shut Down buttons, do the following:

1. Open the System Preferences application, click Accounts, and then unlock the Accounts pane.

2. Click the Login Options button.

3. Deactivate the Show the Restart, Sleep, and Shut Down Buttons check box.

When the Login window appears, these buttons are hidden and the only way to use the Mac is to log in using a valid account. If you want these buttons to appear in the Login window again, simply check the check box. When these buttons do appear in the Login window, the related actions can be performed without being logged in to a user account.

Enabling and Using Fast User Switching

When a user logs out of his account, all documents are closed and all applications and processes quit. When a user logs in again, any of these must be restarted to get back to where the user was when he logged out. However, you can take advantage of *fast user switching*. What this means is that you can log in to another user account without logging out of the accounts that are currently logged in. This is very nice because you can leave applications and documents open in an account and display the Login window to prevent someone from using those items. And, another user can log in and work with his account. When he is done, you can log back in to your account and everything will be as it was when you left it. This saves a lot of time and hassle reopening items, and processes you are running can continue to run while another user is logged in to the machine.

To enable this feature, do the following steps:

1. Open the Accounts pane of the System Preferences application and unlock the pane.

2. Click the Login Options button.

3. Activate the Show Fast User Switching Menu As check box. A new menu appears in the upper-right corner of the desktop that enables other users to log in.

4. Use the pop-up menu to determine how the Fast User Switching menu appears on the Finder toolbar. Your options are

   ■ **Icon**—A silhouette appears at the top of the menu.

   ■ **Short name**—The short name of the user account that is currently logged in appears at the top of the menu.

   ■ **Name**—The full name of the user account currently logged in to appears at the top of the menu.

Then, logging in and out of accounts can be done fast and easily with the Fast User Switching menu (see Figure 21.9).

> **note**
>
> If your Mac has limited RAM, you might not want to enable Fast User Switching because applications running under other user accounts will consume resources even if your user account is the active one. This means performance might be slower for you because the applications under other user accounts are using RAM and so it isn't available to your applications.

Figure 21.9
The Fast User Switching menu enables you to log in to other accounts without logging out of the current one.

To log in under another account, select it on the menu. You see the Login window with the account you selected. Enter the password for the account and click the Log In button or press Return. After a cool, 3D spinning effect, that user is logged in and his desktop appears.

To temporarily block access to the current user account without logging out, open the Fast User Switching menu and select Login Window. The Login window will appear. You can leave the machine without worries that someone will be able to access your account. When you are ready to log in—or when anyone else is, for that matter—select the user account, enter a password, and click Login (you get to see the cool 3D spin again, too).

If another user account is logged in and you attempt to restart or shut down the machine, a warning dialog box appears that explains that other users are logged in and the action you are taking could cause them to lose data. If you enter an administrator username and password and click Shut Down or Restart, the other users are logged out and the action you want is performed. Be careful about doing this, though, because the other users can lose unsaved data.

 tip

If you create a user account without a password and enable the Fast User Switching feature, you can log in to the account without a password immediately by selecting it on the Fast User Switching menu. You will bypass the Login window altogether.

 note

On the Fast User Switching menu and in the Login window, users who are currently logged in have a circle with a check mark icon next to them.

Enabling the Root User Account

Because Mac OS X is based on Unix, a user account called root exists on every Mac OS X machine. The root account has permission to do everything that is possible; the root account permissions go way beyond even administrator account permissions. Because of this, logging in under this root account is very powerful, and it is also dangerous because it isn't that hard to mess up your system, delete folders (whether you intend to or not), and so on. However, because you sometimes need to log in under the root account to accomplish specific tasks, you should understand and become comfortable with it.

You should be logged in under the root account only for the minimum time necessary to accomplish specific tasks. Log in, do what you need to, and then log out of root again. This minimizes the chance of doing something you didn't intend to do because you forgot you were logged in under root.

 tip

You can jump quickly to the Accounts pane of the System Preferences application by selecting Account Preferences on the Fast User Switching menu.

caution

Be careful when you are working in your Mac under the root account. You can cause serious damage to the system as well as to data you have stored on your machine.

The root account is a very special user account, but it is still a user account. The full name of the root account is System Administrator, and its short name is root. One difference between the root account and other accounts is that the root account exists without having to create it. However, you have to assign a password to it before you can begin using it.

You can create a password for the root account by following these steps:

1. Open the Terminal application found in the Applications/Utilities folder.

   ➡ *To learn more about the Terminal application, **see** "Running Terminal," **p. 532**.*

2. At the prompt, type `sudo passwd root` and press Return. You'll see a prompt explaining that you are changing the password for the root account.

3. At the password prompt, enter an administrator password for your Mac and press Return. You'll be prompted to enter a new password for the root account.

4. Type the new password for the root account and press Return.

5. Type the new password a second time at the Retype New Password prompt and press Return. The new password is now set.

After you have created the root password, you can log in under the root account by performing the following steps:

1. Log out of the current account.

2. Log in under the root account. If the login window is configured to show user accounts, select Other on the list and then enter **root**, type the root password, and click Login. If the Login window just shows the User Name and Password fields, enter **root** and the password and click Login.

3. Confirm that you are logged in as root by opening the Home directory; root appears as the username and as the label of the Home folder in the Places sidebar (see Figure 21.10).

Figure 21.10
When you can see the Home directory for the root user, you are logged in as root.

Because the root account has unlimited permissions, you can add or remove files to any directory on your Mac while you are logged in under the root account, including those for other user accounts. You can also make changes to any system file, which is where the root account's power and danger come from.

Use the root account only when you really need to. Make sure that other people who use your Mac do not know the root password; otherwise, you might find yourself with all sorts of problems.

note

If you enable Fast User Switching, the root account isn't listed on the Fast User Switching menu. To log in to the root account, you must bring up the Login window by choosing Login Window on the Fast User Switching menu each time you want to log in as root.

tip

You can also log in to the root account directly in the Terminal window to enter Unix commands using the command line. This can be a faster way to enter a few commands if you are comfortable with the command-line interface.

MANAGING YOUR DESKTOP WITH EXPOSÉ AND SPACES

Taking Control of Your Desktop

Modern Macs now routinely ship with 2GB of RAM installed, and most of the latest iMac models come with 4GB to play with (and support up to 8GB). In other words, most Macs now have plenty of room in RAM to open as many applications as you need for working or playing.

The downside to having lots of applications on the go is that your desktop can get cluttered and crowded in a hurry, which can make finding the specific application or document you need a real needle-in-a-digital-haystack exercise. If you find that you're wasting lots of precious time trying to sort through that mess you call a desktop, it's time for some spring cleaning. I'm talking here about a couple of Mac OS X tools that can knock some sense into an out-of-control desktop:

- **Exposé**—This Mac OS X feature is a window management program that temporarily shrinks all your running windows and then arranges them on your screen so that nothing overlaps. This lets you see at a glance what's in each open window, and then you can select the one you want with a quick click of the mouse.

- **Spaces**—This Mac OS X feature lets you set up not just a single desktop, but a whole herd of them—up to 16 in all! These are called *spaces* and they act as virtual desktops. The idea is that you configure each space with a single application that has multiple windows, or with multiple applications that are related in some way.

This chapter introduces you to Exposé and Spaces. However, to fully appreciate the power and usefulness of these tools (or, on the other hand, to understand whether you need to use them at all), you should know the standard Mac OS X techniques for managing your desktop applications, so that's where we'll begin.

Managing Your Running Applications

If you have a single application on the go, and you have only a single window open in that application, there's really nothing to manage as far as your desktop is concerned, because you have just a single window open. These days, that's a pretty rare scenario, as most of us not only have multiple applications up and running, but also multiple windows open in many of those applications. To handle all those desktop windows, you need to know a few useful Mac OS X techniques, particularly how to switch between running applications and their windows, and how to temporarily hide an application that you won't be using for a while.

Switching Between Running Applications and Windows

If you've got two or more applications on the go (including Finder, which is always running), you need some way to switch from one application to another. The two most obvious methods are either to click inside an application's window, if you can see it, or to click the application's Dock icon. (Remember that Mac OS X displays a blue dot below the Dock icon of each running application.)

Those techniques work well, but they're not often the handiest. For example, if your hands are near the keyboard, you might prefer to keep them there to make the switch. In that case, your Mac offers you three keyboard techniques for switching applications:

- **Press ⌘-Tab**—This technique switches between the current application and the application you used most recently.

- **Hold down ⌘ and tap the Tab key**—The first time you tap Tab, you see a menu that shows an icon for each running application, as shown in Figure 22.1. With each subsequent press of the Tab key, Mac OS X highlights the next icon in the menu. When the application you want is highlighted, release ⌘ to switch to that application. Note, too, that if you prefer to cycle through the icons from right to left, hold down both Shift and ⌘ and then tap Tab.

- **Hold down Control and tap the F4 key**—This technique cycles through all the open windows in your running applications. For example, if you have two Safari windows open, you see both windows as you tap F4. When the application window you want is onscreen, release Control to switch to that window. If you want to cycle through the windows in the reverse order, hold down both Shift and Control and then tap F4. (Note that for all this to work, your Mac's keyboard must be configured to use F1 through F12 as standard function keys; see Chapter 30, "Working with Mice, Keyboards, and Other Input Devices," for more info.)

> **tip**
> When you have the menu of running application icons displayed, you can also switch to an application by clicking its icon.

➥ *See "Configuring a Keyboard," p. 593.*

Figure 22.1
Hold down ⌘ and tap the Tab key to cycle through the icons of your running applications.

On the other hand, if you're currently using the mouse, you might prefer a mouse-based technique for switching applications. That's no problem as long as you have a mouse with a scroll wheel in the middle:

- **Tap the scroll wheel**—Use this technique to switch between the current application and the application you used most recently.

- **Press down the scroll wheel and tilt it to one side**—When you press and hold down the scroll wheel, you see the same menu of running application icons as you saw earlier in Figure 22.1. Tilt the scroll wheel to the right to cycle through the icons left to right; tilt the scroll wheel to the left to cycle through the icons right to left. When the application you want is highlighted, release the scroll wheel to switch to that application.

 tip

If you have two or more windows open in a single application, hold down ⌘ and repeatedly press the backquote key (`) to cycle through the open windows. (Hold down Shift, as well, to cycle the windows in reverse.)

 note

Unfortunately, these techniques don't work with the scroll ball on Apple's Mighty Mouse.

Hiding a Running Application

If you've got a bunch of applications on the fly, your desktop can end up awfully messy. To reduce the clutter, you can remove an application from the desktop. If you won't need that application for a while, it's best just to quit the program to conserve your Mac's resources. Otherwise, a quick click of the application's Minimize button clears the application from the desktop and displays it as an icon on the right side of the Dock.

Actually, I should say that it clears the application's *current window* from the desktop. If the application has other windows open, they remain in place, and you won't be much better off. Ideally, you need a quick way to hide *all* the open windows in an application. Fortunately, your Mac gives you *three* ways to do this:

- Switch to the application and then press ⌘-H.

- Right-click (or Control-click) the application's Dock icon and then click Hide.

- Hold down ⌘ (or both Shift and ⌘), tap the Tab key until the application you want to hide is highlighted in the icon menu, and then press H.

Managing Open Windows with Exposé

The standard Mac OS X techniques for navigating running applications and open windows are handy, but they become less useful the more applications and windows you have on the desktop. You might very well find it useful to have multiple applications and multiple documents within each application open at the same time, but you might end up with dozens of windows open simultaneously with those windows layered one on another. Getting to the specific window you want can be difficult. That's where Exposé comes in. It's designed to help you quickly manage all the open windows on your desktop.

Using Exposé

Exposé is a window management program that offers a number of useful functions for managing your open windows. Exposé has four main features:

- **See all your open windows at the same time**—Press the F9 key on most Macs and Exposé temporarily reduces the size of the open windows and tiles them so that they can all be displayed on the desktop at the same time (see Figure 22.2). You can click a window to move into that window; the other windows return to their previous sizes and locations. You can also move into a window in which the cursor is located by pressing F9 again; if you don't point to a different window, pressing F9 will return you to your previous location.

 note

If you use multiple monitors and activate Exposé, the windows on all monitors shrink and remain on the monitor they were on when you activated Exposé.

Figure 22.2
Using
Exposé, you
can show all
open win-
dows on your
desktop at
the same
time.

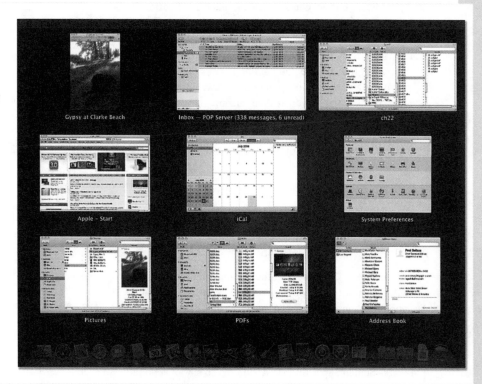

- **See all the windows in the current application at the same time**—Press the F10 key on most Macs and Exposé shows thumbnails of all the windows in the current application. Just as you can with the F9 key, you can point to a window to see its title, click it to move into it, and so on.

 tip

If you hold down the Shift key while you activate Exposé, you see its effects in slow motion. Why is this useful? I have no idea.

- **Hide all open windows and show the desktop**—Pressing F11 on most Macs and Exposé hides all the open windows by moving them off to the sides of the desktop, which means you see your desktop in all its beauty. This is useful if you have a bad case of desktop clutter and want to work on the desktop without closing or moving the current windows. You can return all windows to their previous locations by pressing F11 again. You can also open a desktop icon by double-clicking it; when you do, the other windows return to their previous locations. Another option is to click one of the window borders visible along the edges of your screen to return windows to their previous states.

■ **Cycle through the Open windows in each application—** Activate Exposé by pressing F9 or F10, then cycle through the set of open windows in each application by pressing the Tab or Shift-Tab keys (to move in the opposite direction). Each time you do, the next application becomes active and you see all its open windows. Windows open in other applications remain at their current sizes and are unselectable. When the window in which you want to work is exposed, click in it to deactivate Exposé and start using the application with which the window is associated.

Configuring Exposé

You can customize the following aspects of Exposé using the Exposé tab of the Exposé & Spaces pane of the System Preferences application (see Figure 22.3):

■ **Active Screen Corners**—Use the pop-up menu located at each corner of the preview monitor to set an action that happens when you move the cursor to that corner. The actions you can set are All Windows (the default F9 key), Application Windows (the default F10 key), Desktop (the default F11 key), Dashboard, Spaces, Start Screen Saver, Disable Screen Saver, and No Action (-). To set an action for a corner, select the action on the related pop-up menu. When you point to that corner of the screen, that action occurs.

■ **Keyboard**—Use the Keyboard pop-up menus to set the keys to activate each Exposé action. In addition to the keys on the menus, you can see other combinations by scrolling down the pop-up menu. If you hold down a modifier key (such as the ⌘ key), you can add that modifier to the shortcut.

■ **Mouse**—If you use an input device with more than one button, such as a two-button mouse, the Mouse pop-up menus appear. Use the Mouse pop-up menus to set Exposé actions for specific buttons on the device you use, such as the right button on a two-button mouse.

■ **Dashboard**—Use the pop-up menus to select which keyboard and mouse (if you have a mouse with multiple buttons) controls will activate the Dashboard.

 note

The Exposé keyboard techniques that I talk about in this section work on most keyboards but, unfortunately, not on all of them. For example, many Mac notebook keyboards don't support the standard Exposé keystrokes, and neither does the Apple Keyboard. If Exposé doesn't kick in when you press F9 (or when you press F10 or F11 to run Exposé's other features), you still have other options. First, there is another Exposé key you can use in place of F9: the F3 key. For F10 and F11 (or even F9, for that matter), you must also hold down the Fn key to run the Exposé features. Alternatively, consider configuring your Mac keyboard to use F1 through F12 as standard function keys, as I describe in Chapter 30. Finally, you can configure Exposé to use different keys altogether, as described in the next section.

Figure 22.3
The Exposé & Spaces pane of the System Preferences application enables you to customize various aspects of Exposé.

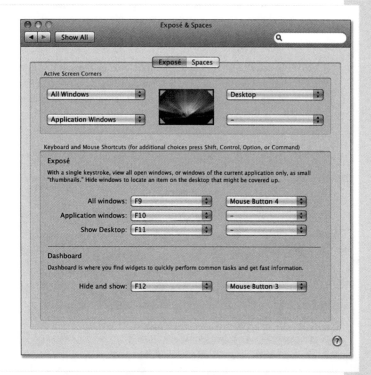

Creating, Using, and Managing Spaces

Being able to use Exposé to manage open windows and applications is nice, but if you use many applications and windows at the same time, you may still find it hard to pick out the window you want using the Exposé thumbnails. The Spaces feature enables you to create environments that contain specific applications so that you can easily switch between them. For example, you can create an Internet space that has all your Internet applications open and a Project space that contains applications and documents related to a project you're working on. When you want to move from the project to the Internet, you move into the Internet space and all your Internet applications are immediately available, and your project applications are hidden. Getting back to your project space is just as easy.

Enabling and Building Spaces

To get started with Spaces, you need to enable the feature and build your spaces. After you create spaces, you assign applications to those spaces; only applications that are bound to a space are available to you when you access that space. To enable Spaces and create spaces, perform the following steps:

1. Open the System Preferences application, click Exposé & Spaces, and then click the Spaces tab.

2. Activate the Enable Spaces check box, as shown in Figure 22.4. If you want to see the Spaces menu appear in the Mac OS X menu bar, activate the Show Spaces in Menu Bar check box, as well. You can use the Spaces menu to quickly switch from one space to another, so it's a good idea to activate the menu.

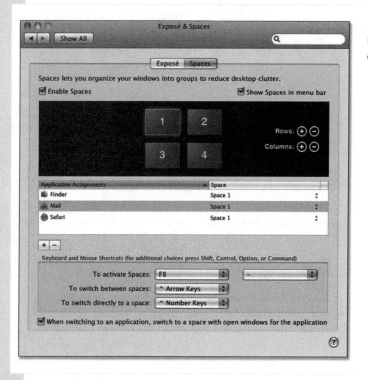

Figure 22.4
Use the Spaces tab to create and configure spaces on your Mac.

3. At the top of the pane, you see the preview window that shows a thumbnail of each space you have configured; initially there are four spaces arranged in a 2×2 grid. As you create spaces, you add them by row or by column. Below the preview window is the Application Assignments section; here, you see the applications that are part of the selected space. At the bottom of the pane are the controls you use to set keyboard shortcuts for specific actions.

4. Add applications that you want to be part of the spaces you are creating. There are several ways to do this:

   ■ Drag an application's icon from the desktop and drop it on the space in which you want it contained; when the icon is over a space, the space's thumbnail is highlighted to show you that you can drop it on the space.

- Drag an application's icon from the desktop and drop it on the application list. Then, choose the space in which you want the application to be used on the pop-up menu in the Space column (more on that in a bit).

- Click Add Application and use the resulting sheet to move to and select the application you want to add. Then use the pop-up menu in the Space column to choose the space in which you want that application to appear.

5. Add spaces by clicking the Add button in the Row section to add a new row of spaces or the Add button in the Column section to add a new column of spaces.

6. Add spaces until you've added all that you want to have available.

7. To remove spaces, you must remove an entire row or column by clicking the Remove button in the Row or Column section.

8. Use the pop-up menu in the Space column to assign an application to a space (see Figure 22.5). The choices on the menu are each space you've created and Every Space, which makes the application available in all spaces. When you select an application, the spaces to which it is assigned are highlighted in the preview window.

Figure 22.5
Assign applications to spaces to make them available when you choose a space.

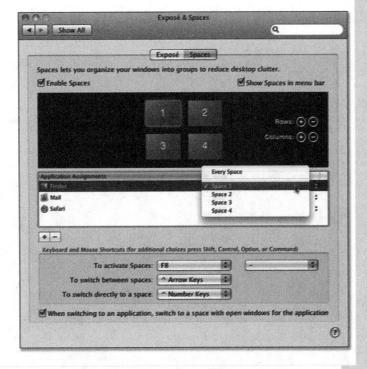

9. To remove an application from the list, select it and click Remove.

10. Use the To Activate Spaces keyboard pop-up menu to set the keyboard shortcut to activate Spaces.

11. If you have a multibutton mouse, use the To Activate Spaces mouse pop-up menu to set the mouse control to activate Spaces.

12. Use the To Switch Between Spaces pop-up menu to choose the keyboard shortcut to move among the spaces you have created.

13. Use the To Switch Directly to a Space pop-up menu to choose the keyboard shortcut you can use to jump directly into a space.

 tip

Hold a modifier key down to see more shortcut choices on these menus.

Using and Managing Spaces

After you've created spaces, you can use them to more efficiently manage your desktop. Here are some space pointers:

■ Press the keyboard shortcut you set for switching between spaces (the default is Control-Arrow key). The Spaces manager appears on the screen (see Figure 22.6). The manager has a box representing each of the spaces you've created. To jump to a space, keeping pressing the shortcut keys until the space you want to use is highlighted. When you release the keys, you jump into that space and return to the last application you were using in that space.

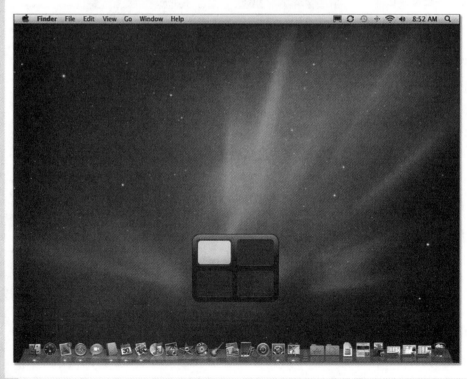

Figure 22.6
When you activate Spaces, you see the Spaces manager that indicates how many spaces are available to you.

- Press the keyboard shortcut for jumping directly to a space (the default is Control-number key) to move directly into a space. When you do, the Space manager will appear briefly, you move into the space you selected, and applications in that space are available to you.

- When you are in a space, you can open applications that aren't part of that space, just as you can when you aren't using Spaces. That application is available in the current space, but not in any others. If you open an application that is already assigned to a different space, you jump to the space in which it is assigned.

- The Finder is available in all spaces.

- If an application isn't running when you move into the space to which it is assigned, you need to launch the application to be able to use it.

- Spaces retain window configurations. If you use multiple monitors and have windows on each display in a space, they will resume their former positions as soon as you move back into that space.

- You can use the Dock to move into open or closed applications. If you open an application in a space, you move into that space. If the application is not part of a space, it opens as usual, but is available only when you are using the space you were using when you opened it. In other words, it is temporarily bound to the space you were using when you launched it.

- If you assign an application to all spaces, its windows will always appear in the same positions in all spaces.

- If you press the Spaces keyboard shortcut (the default is F8 or Fn+F8), you see large thumbnails of all your spaces (see Figure 22.7). In each space, you see smaller thumbnails of all the applications running in that space. If you use multiple displays, you see a thumbnail for each display. Click a space to move into it.

- To turn Spaces off, open the Spaces tab of the Exposé & Spaces pane of the System Preferences application and uncheck the Enable Spaces check box. All open applications will return to the desktop. You can start using your spaces again by checking the Enable Spaces check box.

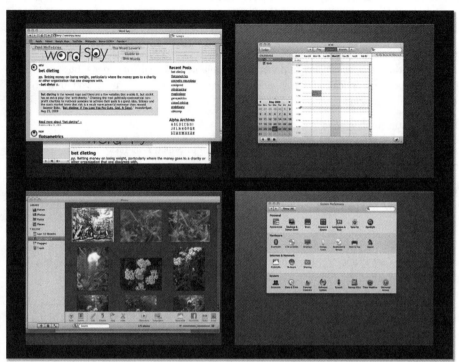

Figure 22.7
Pressing the
Spaces key-
board short-
cut shows
you all your
spaces.

MANAGING AND USING FONTS

Understanding the Architecture of Characters

Mac OS X has turned many otherwise ordinary citizens into avid amateur typographers. Mac users at cocktail parties the world over are debating the relative merits of serif versus sans serif fonts, expounding the virtues of typefaces with names like Futura and Herculanum, and throwing around font jargon terms such as *ascender*, *feet*, and *ligature*.

Okay, so most of us don't take fonts to that extreme. However, we certainly appreciate what they do to jazz up our reports, spreadsheets, and graphics. There's nothing like a well-chosen font to add just the right tone to a document and to make our work stand out from the herd.

This chapter shows you how Mac OS X and fonts work together. You learn just what fonts are and how Mac OS X sees them, and then you learn a few techniques for managing the fonts on your system.

I always like to describe fonts as the "architecture" of characters. When you examine a building, certain features and patterns help you identify the building's architectural style. A flying buttress, for example, is usually a telltale sign of a Gothic structure. Fonts, too, are distinguished by a unique set of characteristics. Specifically, four items define the architecture of any character: the typeface, the type size, the type style, and the character spacing.

Typefaces

A *typeface* is a distinctive design that is common to any related set of letters, numbers, and symbols. This design gives each character a particular shape and thickness (or *weight*, as it's called in type circles) that's unique to the typeface and difficult to classify. However, three main categories serve to distinguish all typefaces: serif, sans serif, and decorative.

- A *serif* (rhymes with *sheriff*) typeface contains fine cross strokes (called *feet*) at the extremities of each character. These subtle appendages give the typeface a traditional, classy look that's most often used for long stretches of text. In Mac OS X, Times New Roman is an example of a serif typeface (see Figure 23.1).

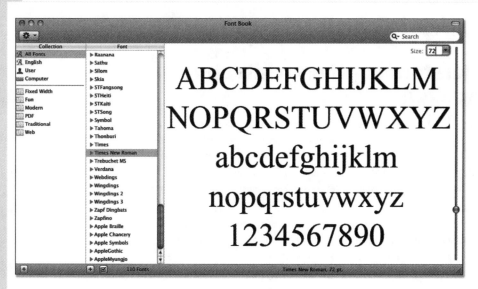

Figure 23.1
Times New Roman is an example of a serif typeface.

- A *sans serif* typeface doesn't contain these cross strokes. As a result, sans serif typefaces usually have a cleaner, more modern look that works best for headings and titles. Helvetica is an example of a common sans serif font in Mac OS X (see Figure 23.2).

- *Decorative* typefaces are usually special designs that are supposed to convey a particular effect. So, for example, if your document needs a fancy, handwritten effect, something like Brush Script MT is perfect (see Figure 23.3).

Figure 23.2
Helvetica is an example of a sans serif typeface.

Figure 23.3
Brush Script MT is an example of a decorative typeface.

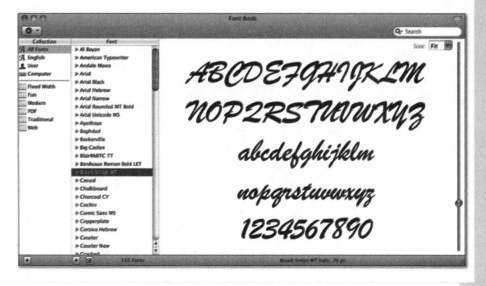

Type Size

The *type size* measures how tall a font is. The standard unit of measurement is the *point*; there are 72 points in an inch. So, for example, the letters in a 24-point font would be twice as tall as those in a 12-point font. Technically, type size is measured from the highest point of a tall letter, such as "f," to the lowest point of an underhanging letter, such as "g." (In case you're wondering, this book is laid out in a 8-point Glypha font.)

Type Style

The *type style* of a font refers to extra attributes added to the typeface, such as **bold** and *italic*. Other type styles (often called type *effects*) include <u>underlining</u> and ~~strikethrough~~. These styles are normally used to highlight or add emphasis to sections of your documents.

Character Spacing

The *character spacing* of a font can take two forms: *monospaced* or *proportional*. Monospaced fonts—also called *fixed width* fonts—reserve the same amount of space for each character. For example, look at the Courier New font shown in Figure 23.4. Notice how skinny letters such as "i" and "l" take up as much space as wider letters such as "m" and "w." Although this is admirably egalitarian, these fonts tend to look as if they were produced with a typewriter (in other words, they're ugly).

By contrast, in a proportional font, such as Times New Roman (shown earlier in Figure 23.1) or Helvetica (see Figure 23.2), the space allotted to each letter varies according to the width of the letter. This gives the text a more natural feel.

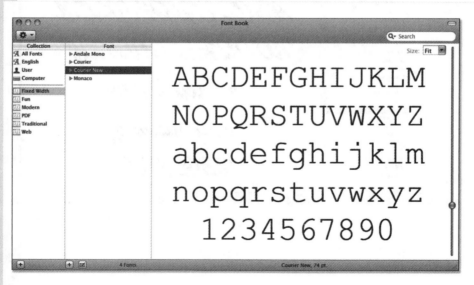

Figure 23.4
Courier New is an example of a monospaced font.

Installing and Managing Mac OS X Fonts

Mac OS X offers a lot of great features related to fonts. For example, the Quartz Extreme graphics layer renders Mac OS X fonts clearly at any size and makes using special font features such as kerning controls, ligatures, and so on, easy. You can configure and select fonts within applications using the Fonts panel. The Fonts panel offers several useful features, such as the ability to create and use sets of your favorite fonts.

➡ *To learn how to work with fonts using the Fonts panel, **see** "Using the Fonts Panel," **p. 485***

Mac OS X includes a large number of high-quality fonts in the default installation. You can also install additional fonts if none of the default fonts gives you the look you want.

You use the Font Book application (shown in Figures 23.1 through 23.4) to manage the fonts on your Mac. With the Font Book it is easy to group fonts together that you use often, quickly see a preview of a specific font, and manage the fonts that are available on your Mac.

Understanding Mac OS X Fonts

Fonts with the file extension .dfont are Datafork TrueType fonts that are single-fork files, meaning all the data for that font is stored in the single fork of its file. This is the native Mac OS X font format. However, under Mac OS X, you can also install and use any of the following types of fonts:

- Windows TrueType fonts (.ttf)

- TrueType collections (.ttc)

- OpenType fonts (.otf)

- Bitmapped fonts (.sfont)

- Fonts and font suitcases used by Mac OS 9 and earlier versions of the Mac OS (these might or might not have a filename extension)

 note

One advantage of the fact that Mac OS X font files provide all their information in a single fork is that these fonts can be shared with operating systems that do not recognize files with resource forks (Windows, Unix, and so on).

There are two locations in which fonts are installed under Mac OS X. To make a font available to everyone who uses your Mac, it is installed in the directory [*Mac OS X*]/Library/Fonts, where *Mac OS X* is the name of your Mac OS X startup volume. Within this directory are at least three types of font files. Those with the filename extension .dfont are the single-fork font files; you'll also see TrueType fonts, which have the .ttf extension. You might also see fonts whose names have other extensions or that do not have a filename extension (font suitcases).

 note

Under Mac OS X, you can install or remove fonts while applications are open; fonts you install instantly become available to the system and any active applications.

To make a font available only to specific users, it is installed in the following directory: /users/[*shortusername*]/Library/Fonts. A user's Library directory also contains the FontCollections folder. The FontCollections directory contains the set of font collections available to the user in the Font Book application and the Font pane.

note

Any user can install fonts into the Fonts folder in the Library folder in her Home directory.

Configuring Fonts with the Font Book

The Font Book enables you to manage all the fonts installed on your Mac. There are two levels of font groups you can use: libraries and collections. A *library* is a means of storing fonts on your computer or on a server; you can then access the fonts stored in those libraries. You can organize fonts into *collections* and then enable and disable individual fonts or font collections. Collections are a means to gather fonts into groups to make them easier to select and apply. For example, when you work with the Mac OS X Fonts panel, its fonts are organized by collection. You can use these collections to group fonts into smaller, focused groups to make font selection easier and faster.

Open a Finder window and select Applications, Font Book to open the Font Book window, which shows three panes by default (see any of the figures earlier in this chapter):

- **Collection**—This pane contains two sections. The upper section shows the libraries currently being managed by Font Book, while the lower section shows you the font collections on your Mac.

- **Font**—This pane shows the available fonts in the current library or collection.

- **Preview**—This pane shows a preview of the current font by rendering all the uppercase letters, lowercase letters, and numbers in that font.

Four libraries are available to you by default.

- **All Fonts**—This library contains all the fonts on your computer.

- **Default language (such as English)**—This library contains just the fonts for the main language you set for your computer and is named for the chosen language.

- **User**—This library contains fonts stored so that only the current user can access them.

- **Computer**—This library contains all the fonts on your Mac (in the default configuration, these are the same as those in the All Fonts library).

Some applications create collections that are installed by default, and you can create your own collections.

Working with Font Libraries

To view the contents of a library, select it on the library list at the top of the Collection column. The fonts it contains are displayed in the Font pane. You can also perform the following library actions:

- Create a new library by choosing File, New Library (or press Option-⌘-N). An empty library appears on the list; type the name of the new library and then press Return.

- Disable a library by selecting it and then selecting Edit, Disable *Library* (where *Library* is the library's name), or by pressing Shift-⌘-E. When you select a disabled library, the fonts do not appear in the Fonts pane. To enable the library, select it and then select Edit, Enable *Library*, or press Shift-⌘-E.

- Add fonts to a library by selecting it and then selecting File, Add Fonts or by pressing ⌘-O. Use the resulting Open dialog box to move to and select the fonts you want to add to the selected library.

- Delete a library by selecting it and then selecting File, Delete *Library* Collection (where *Library* is the library's name), or by pressing the Delete key. Confirm the deletion at the prompt and the library is removed from the Font Book window.

 note

The most likely use for a new library is to work with files that aren't stored on your computer. For example, if fonts are stored on a server on your network, create a library for those fonts and add them to it. To use the fonts stored on a server, you must be connected to that server via the network, even after you have stored the fonts in your Library.

Working with Font Collections

Font collections are groups of fonts created for any number of reasons, such as making it easier to select the fonts you use most frequently. You can use the default font collections included with Font Book and create your own collections.

To view the fonts that are currently part of a collection, select that collection on the Collection list. The fonts it contains are listed on the Fonts pane. You can view the typefaces provided with font families shown on the Fonts pane by clicking the expansion triangle next to that font (see Figure 23.5).

Figure 23.5
Click a font's expansion triangle to see the typefaces associated with that font.

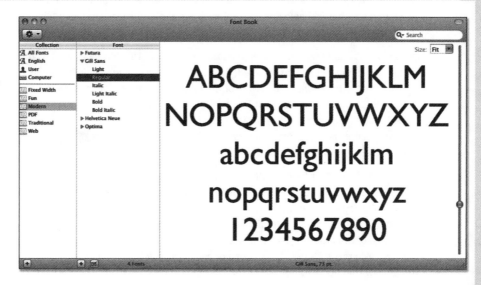

Creating a Font Collection

To create a font collection, follow these steps:

1. Click the New Collection button (the plus sign) below the Collection list. (You can also select File, New Collection or press ⌘-N.) A new collection appears on the list; its name is selected and ready for you to edit.

2. Type the name of the collection and press Return.

3. Open libraries or other collections, such as the All Fonts collection, to look for fonts to add to the collection you just created.

4. Drag a font from the Fonts pane and drop it on the new collection. You can drag an entire font family to add it to the collection or expand it and only drag the typefaces that you want to be available in the collection onto it.

5. Repeat steps 3 and 4 to add more fonts to the collection.

Editing Font Collections

After you have created a font collection, you can use the following techniques to edit the collection:

- Double-click the collection name and edit it.

- Select the collection; select a font you want to remove from the collection; and select File, Remove *font*, where *font* is the name of the font family or a specific typeface that you selected. Click Remove in the Confirmation dialog box; the font is removed from the collection (although the font remains installed on your Mac).

- Select a font family within a collection and choose Edit, Disable *font* Family, where *font* is the name of the font family you selected. Alternatively, select a font typeface and choose Edit, Disable *font*, where *font* is the name of the typeface that you selected. (In both cases, you can also press Shift-⌘-D). When Font Book asks you to confirm, click Disable. The word Off appears next to the font to indicate that it has been disabled, and you can no longer select the font within applications.

- Select a disabled font family within a collection and choose Edit, Enable *font* Family, where *font* is the name of the font family you selected. Alternatively, select a disabled font typeface and choose Edit, Enable *font*, where *font* is the name of the typeface that you selected. (In both cases, you can also press Shift-⌘-D). You can once again select the font within applications.

 tip

If a bullet appears next to a font's name, multiple versions of that font are installed. To remove the multiple versions, select the font and select Edit, Resolve Duplicates. This causes Font Book to turn off the duplicate fonts so that they won't clutter things up when you select a font.

 tip

To locate a specific font, select the All Fonts collection and type the font name in the Search tool on the Font Book toolbar.

 tip

You can move multiple fonts at the same time by holding down the ⌘ when you select each font you want to add to another collection.

 tip

If you use specific sets of fonts in specific applications, consider creating a font collection for each application and placing the fonts you use within it. Then, you can easily choose fonts from this group by selecting the application's font collection.

Configuring the Font Book Window

You can also configure the Font Book window itself in the following ways:

- Select Preview, Show Font Info. When you do, information about the selected font appears in the Preview pane.

- Change the size of the font preview in the Preview pane by either selecting a point size on the Size pop-up menu or by dragging the vertical slider along the right side of the pane. If you select Fit on the pop-up menu, the preview size is adjusted so you can see all of the preview within the pane.

- Change the relative size of the panes by dragging their resize handles.

- Change the configuration of the preview shown in the Preview pane by selecting one of the options on the Preview menu. The Sample option shows each letter and number in the selected font, whereas the Repertoire option shows all the characters included in the selected font. The Custom option enables you to type characters in the Preview pane to preview them.

 tip

The panes are limited to certain relative sizes. If you try to make a pane larger but are unable to do so, increase the size of the Font Book window itself and then make the other panes larger. You should then be able to resize the first pane.

 tip

If you have trouble with a font, try validating it by selecting it and then selecting File, Validate Font. Use the resulting Font Validation tool to check the font. When you do, the tool will report on the condition of the font.

Installing Fonts with the Font Book

You can use the Font Book to install fonts by performing the following steps:

1. Select or create the library into which you want to place the fonts and select File, Add Fonts (⌘-O). The Open dialog box will appear.

2. Move to and select the font you want to install.

3. Click Open. The font will be added to the selected library.
   You can add it to collections and work with that font within Font Book and from within applications.

tip

To see where a font is installed, select it and select File, Reveal in Finder (⌘-R). A Finder window opens that shows the location in which the file has been installed.

Using the Fonts Panel

The Fonts panel gives you control over the particular fonts used in your documents and also enables you to manage any font installed on your Mac, no matter which application you are using.

In most applications, you can open the Fonts panel by choosing Format, Fonts, Show Fonts or by pressing ⌘-T (see Figure 23.6).

Selected collection

Effects pane | Preview pane

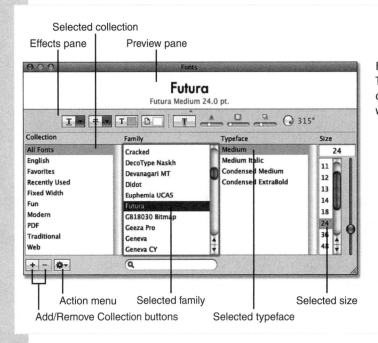

Figure 23.6
The Mac OS X Fonts panel provides complete control over your fonts within applications.

Action menu | Selected family | Selected size

Add/Remove Collection buttons | Selected typeface

The Fonts panel has a number of panes. You can choose to hide or display certain panes, while others are always visible. The various panes of the Fonts panel are the following:

- **Collections (always displayed)**—As you learned earlier, you can use collections to group fonts together. Font collections make selecting fonts easier because you can group fonts into collections, so you can select a set of fonts by choosing the collection in which those fonts are contained. The collections you see in the Collections pane of the Fonts panel include all those fonts and collections that are installed and enabled via the Font Book application. Applications can also provide distinct collections. For example, in TextEdit, you see the Favorites collection, which contains a set of fonts, typefaces, and sizes you

have added via the Add to Favorites action, and the Recently Used collection, which contains the fonts, typefaces, and sizes of text formatting you have recently applied in the current document.

 caution

Not all applications support the Mac OS X Font system. If an application doesn't use this system, it provides its own set of formatting tools that you use to format a document. For example, Microsoft Word does not support Mac OS X's font system, so you can't access the Fonts panel from within the application. If an application doesn't support the Mac OS X Fonts panel, you have to use its own font tools instead.

- **Family (displayed except when working with the Favorites and Recently Used collection)**— The Family pane lists all the font families that are part of the selected collection. You select the family you want to work with on the list of available families in the selected collection.

- **Typeface (always displayed)**—In the Typeface pane, you choose the typeface for the selected font family, such as Regular, Bold, and so on.

- **Size (always displayed)**—You choose the size of the font you are applying in the Size pane.

- **Preview (displayed when you select Show Preview on the Action menu)**—This pane, which appears at the top of the Fonts panel, provides a preview of the font you have selected.

- **Effects (always displayed)**—This pane provides buttons you use to configure underline, strikethrough, text color, background color, and text shadow effects.

The Action menu at the bottom-left corner of the panel provides access to the following commands:

- **Add to Favorites**—This command adds the current font, typeface, and size to the Favorites collection.

- **Show/Hide Preview**—This choice opens or hides the Preview pane.

- **Show/Hide Effects**—This command opens or hides the Effects pane.

- **Color**—Choosing this causes the Color Picker to open.

- **Characters**—This command opens the Character Viewer.

- **Typography**—This command opens the Typography panel that you can use to choose ligatures, adjust the space before and after characters, and shift the text baseline.

- **Edit Sizes**—Using this command, you can customize the sizes that appear in the Size pane.

- **Manage Fonts**—This command opens the Font Book, which enables you to manage the fonts installed on your Mac.

Previewing Fonts

If you select Show Preview on the Action menu, the Preview pane appears at the top of the panel. This pane provides a preview of the currently selected family, typeface, and size. You can use this preview to help you make better selections more quickly. To hide the Preview pane, select Hide Preview on the Action menu.

Using Font Favorites

When you select a font family, typeface, and size and then use the Add to Favorites command on the Action menu, that font is added to your Favorites collection. When you select the Favorites collection in the Fonts panel, you can quickly choose one of your favorite fonts to use; this saves you a couple of steps (see Figure 23.7).

Figure 23.7
When you add a font, typeface, and size to your Favorites collection, you can easily apply that formatting to selected text in a document.

Creating or Removing Font Collections

You can add or remove font collections from the Fonts panel. When you do so, the font collection is also added or removed to the Collections available in the Font Book application (which contains all the fonts installed on your Mac).

From the Fonts panel, you can make the following changes to the collections shown in the Collections list:

- Add new font collections

- Remove font collections

- Add fonts to collections

Although you can manage font collections from within the Fonts panel, you should generally use the Font Book application. This is because font collections are really a system-level resource, so it is better practice to manage them using a system tool—the Font Book.

Applying Effects to Fonts

Using the Effects tools, you can apply the following effects to selected text:

- Apply underline effects

- Apply strikethrough effects

- Apply color to text

 note

The capability to save specific combinations of family, typeface, and size as a favorite makes using specific fonts easy. This is much like the styles feature offered in Word and other text applications. By designating a combination as a favorite, you can reapply it quickly and easily. Unfortunately, you can't make changes to the favorite and have those changes be made wherever that favorite is used as you can with styles.

 tip

Using the Font Book, you can disable both font collections and individual fonts from within collections. This is the best technique because you can prevent collections and fonts from being available within an application but maintain those collections and fonts on your Mac.

■ Apply color to a document's background

■ Apply text shadow effects

> **note**
>
> You can also apply color effects by selecting Color on the Action menu.

To apply effects to text, do the following steps:

1. Select the text to which you want to apply the effects.

2. Open the Fonts panel.

3. Open the Action menu and select Show Effects (if the Effects pane isn't visible). The Effects pane provides a number of tools you can use to apply effects to your text (see Figure 23.8).

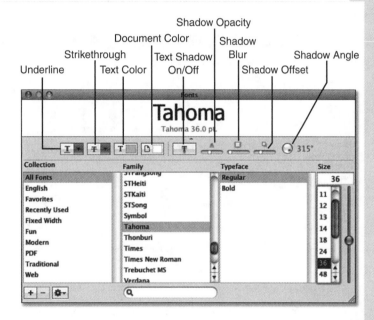

Figure 23.8
You can use the Effects pane to apply various effects to selected text.

4. Select from the underline effects on the Underline pop-up menu. The options are None, Single, Double, or Color. If you select Color, use the Color Picker to choose the color of the underline.

5. Select the strikethrough effects on the Strikethrough pop-up menu. The options are None, Single, Double, or Color. If you select Color, use the Color Picker to choose the color of the strikethrough.

6. Click the Text Color button and use the Color Picker to choose the text color.

7. Click the Document Color button and use the Color Picker to select the background color of the document on which you are working.

8. To apply a shadow to the text, click the Text Shadow button; when a shadow is applied, the button is blue.

9. Use the Shadow Opacity, Shadow Blur, and Shadow Offset sliders to configure those properties of the shadow.

10. Use the Shadow Angle wheel to set the angle of the shadow.

🔍 **note**

Unfortunately, you won't see the text effects you apply in the Preview pane of the Fonts panel. You need to be able to see the document you're working on to see the effects you apply.

Editing the Sizes That Appear on the Size Pane

If you select Edit Sizes on the Action menu on the Fonts panel, you see the Font Size sheet, which you can use to change the sizes that appear in the Size pane of the Fonts panel (see Figure 23.9).

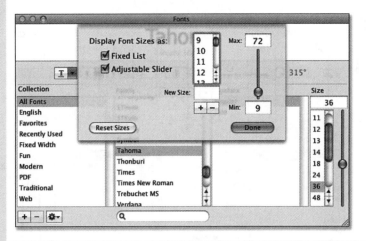

Figure 23.9
You can control the specific sizes of font that appear in the Fonts panel using the Font Size sheet.

Using the Font Size sheet, you can perform the following tasks:

- To add a size to the Size pane, enter the size you want to add in the New Size box and click + (the plus sign).

- To remove a size from the Size pane, select it on the size list and click – (the minus sign).

- To remove the list of fixed sizes from the Size pane, deactivate the Fixed List check box.

- To show the Size slider in the Size pane, activate the Adjustable Slider check box. Then, enter the minimum font size and maximum size to be included on the slider in the Min Size and Max Size text boxes.

- To reset the sizes to the default values, click the Reset Sizes button.

Save your changes by clicking the Done button. The sheet disappears and the changes you made are reflected in the Size pane.

Applying Typography Effects to Fonts

The Fonts panel enables you to apply some basic typography effects to text. To do so, use the following steps:

1. Open the Action menu and select Typography. The Typography tools appear (see Figure 23.10).

Figure 23.10
You can use the Typography tools to apply typography effects to text.

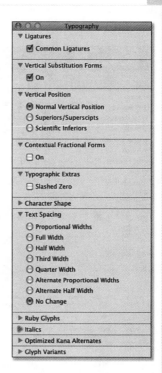

2. Use the resulting tools to apply a variety of typographical effects to the selected text.

Working with the Character Viewer

Special characters can be a pain to use because remembering which font family the character you need is part of is often difficult. The Character Viewer is designed to help you find special characters in various languages and quickly apply those characters to your documents. You can also add favorite characters you use frequently for even easier access.

> 🔍 **note**
>
> The specific Typography effects you see in the Typography window depend on the font family currently selected. Try selecting various families with the Typography window open to see the options that become available.

You can open the Character Viewer from within applications that use the Mac OS X Fonts panel, or you can install the Character Viewer menu on the Mac OS X menu bar.

Opening the Character Viewer from the Fonts Panel

To open the Character Viewer from the Mac OS X Fonts panel, select Characters on the Action menu. The Character Viewer will open (see Figure 23.11).

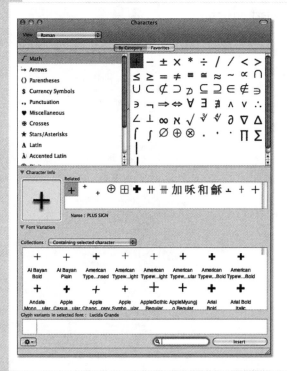

Figure 23.11
The Mac OS X Character Viewer enables you to efficiently work with special characters.

Installing the Character Viewer on the Finder Menu Bar

You can also install the Character Viewer on the Input menu on the Mac OS X menu bar so it is available in all applications, whether they use the Mac OS X Fonts panel or not. To install the Viewer, perform the following steps:

1. Open the System Preferences application.

2. Click the Languages & Text icon. The Languages & Text pane opens.

3. Click the Input Sources tab.

4. Activate the On check box next to Keyboard and Character Viewer.

5. Activate the Show Input Menu in Menu Bar check box and the Input menu appears on the Finder's menu bar. This enables the Input menu that appears on the right end of any application's menu bar, including the Finder (see Figure 23.12).

Figure 23.12

The Input menu enables you to access the Character Viewer from any application.

6. Check the boxes next to any languages you want to install on the Input menu.

After you have installed the Character Viewer on the Input menu, you can open it by selecting Input menu, Show Character Viewer.

Using the Character Viewer

The Character Viewer has two tabs. The By Category tab enables you to select and insert characters you need. When you find a character you use regularly, you can add it to the other tab, which is the Favorites tab, so you can grab it easily and quickly.

To find and use a character, carry out the following steps:

1. Open the Character Viewer (either through the Action menu in the Fonts panel or from the Mac OS X Input menu).

2. On the Character Viewer, select the language sets you want to view on the View pop-up menu. For example, to see Roman characters, select Roman.

3. Click the By Category tab and choose the category of character you want to view in the left pane. For example, select Math to view mathematical symbols.

4. Click the character you want to work with.

5. Expand the Character Info section to see a large version of the selected character along with its name. You also see characters that are related to the selected character. You can choose to work with one of the related characters by clicking it. The one you click becomes selected, even if its not in the currently selected category.

6. To apply different fonts to the character, click the expansion triangle next to the Font Variation tab. Select the font collection you want to use on the Collections pop-up menu. Then, click the font you want to apply to the character you selected. When you expand the Font Variation section, a preview pane appears; this shows a preview of the character

 tip

To limit the fonts shown in the Font Variation pane to only those that contain the character you are working with, select Containing Selected Character on the Collections pop-up menu. The character is shown with the fonts that contain it.

you have selected along with its name. You can see a version of the character in each font family in the collection selected on the Collections pop-up menu.

7. Continue adjusting the character until it is the way you want it.

8. Click Insert with Font. The character is pasted into the active document at the insertion point.

 note

If you don't apply a font to the character, the Insert with Font button is just the Insert button.

 tip

You can search for special characters by description or code using the Search tool that appears at the bottom of the Character Viewer window.

MAKING YOUR MAC ACCESSIBLE TO EVERYONE

Understanding Universal Access

Although the physical world has, over the past few years, striven to increase access for the disabled (in the form of Braille elevator buttons, wheelchair ramps, and handicapped parking spaces, to name just a few changes), the virtual world of the computer interface has been a more difficult challenge. That's not surprising because the typical computer interface offers small text and objects, occasional audio feedback, and the need for precision when performing actions such as mouse clicks, all of which makes life difficult for people who are visual-, hearing-, or mobility-impaired.

Fortunately, the computer industry in general, and Mac OS X in particular, have made great strides in recent years toward the goal of making computers universally accessible. In Mac OS X, this goal is realized using the aptly named Universal Access feature, which is found on the Universal Access pane of the System Preferences application.

You normally use Universal Access to make your Mac more accessible to users who have various physical or mental challenges. However, even if you don't have such challenges or don't provide technical support to other users who do, you can use the Universal Access tools to make your Mac better suited to the way in which you like to work. For example, using the Zoom feature, you can zoom using the same keyboard shortcut in any application.

Setting up Universal Access involves configuring any or all of the following areas:

- **Seeing**—Using the Seeing controls, you can configure visual aspects of your system. You can use VoiceOver to have your Mac speak interface elements, and you can use zoom to increase the size of items on the screen. You can change the display to be white on a black background or grayscale. You can also configure the display's contrast.

- **Hearing**—The Hearing controls enable you to set the screen to flash when an alert sound plays.

- **Keyboard**—Using the Keyboard controls, you can configure Sticky Keys, which enable users to choose key combinations by typing only one key at a time. You can also provide assistance to users who have difficulty with initial or repeated keystrokes with the Slow Keys feature. Slow Keys enables you to set a delay for the time between when a key is pressed and when the input is accepted by the system.

- **Mouse**—The Mouse controls enable you to control the mouse by using the numeric pad on the keyboard and to control the size of the cursor that appears on screen.

 note

On mobile Macs, the Mouse controls are the Mouse & Trackpad controls.

This chapter takes you through the configuration of all these aspects of Universal Access. To get started, open System Preferences and click the Universal Access icon.

Configuring and Using Seeing Assistance

The Seeing assistance functions are designed to make the Mac's display more visible to users who have difficulty seeing the screen. There are three basic areas of configuration: VoiceOver, Zoom, and Display. You start configuring all of these areas by moving to the Universal Access pane of the System Preferences application and clicking the Seeing tab, shown in Figure 24.1.

note

If you have an assistive device, such as a Braille display, you can activate the Enable Access for Assistive Devices check box to enable that device. You can also display the Universal Access status in the menu bar by activating the Show Universal Access Status in the Menu Bar check box.

Understanding and Using VoiceOver

VoiceOver causes your Mac to speak the current position of the VoiceOver cursor in the interface so that you can tell where you are on the screen even if you can't see it clearly. For example, if you have VoiceOver active when you open the Universal Access pane, your Mac would speak the following text to you, "System Preferences, Universal Access, Toolbar" because that is the first interface element that gets selected with the VoiceOver cursor when you open that particular pane. VoiceOver also speaks commands you issue when you activate them. When VoiceOver is active, your Mac will also speak the contents of dialog boxes and other interface elements.

You can customize VoiceOver to work in very specific ways by using the VoiceOver Utility.

Figure 24.1
The Seeing tab of the Universal Access pane enables you to configure how your Mac displays information and to have the OS use VoiceOver to speak interface elements.

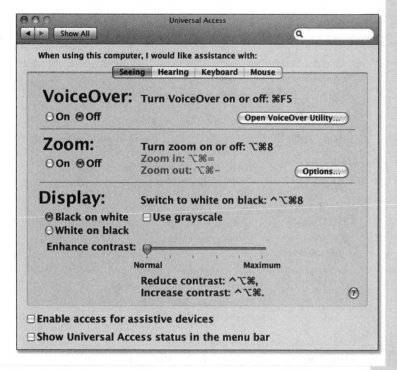

Using Default VoiceOver Settings to Have Your Mac Speak to You

To turn VoiceOver on, use the following steps:

1. Open the System Preferences application and click the Universal Access icon to open the Universal Access pane.

2. Click the Seeing tab.

3. Click the On radio button in the VoiceOver section. The first time you do this, the Welcome to VoiceOver dialog box appears.

4. If you want to learn more about VoiceOver, press the Spacebar; otherwise, press V to start using VoiceOver. On the screen, you see the VoiceOver cursor (which is a box around the specific interface element currently selected; see Figure 24.2) and the Mac speaks its current location to you.

VoiceOver cursor

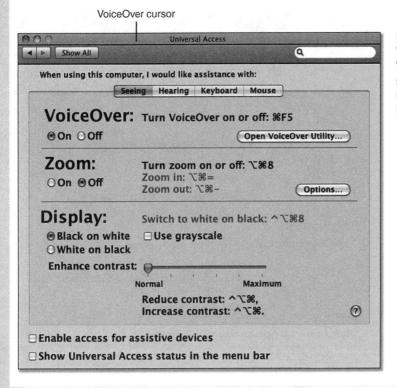

Figure 24.2
When VoiceOver is active, the VoiceOver cursor is used to speak a specific part of the interface (in this case, the Back button).

After you have activated VoiceOver, your Mac begins to speak to you. Each time something changes, the Mac always speaks the current location of the VoiceOver cursor. You navigate the interface by pressing the Control-Option-Arrow keys to move the VoiceOver cursor around the screen. Each time the cursor moves onto a new element, the element's name is spoken as it becomes highlighted by the cursor (that is, when the VoiceOver cursor is placed around the element).

When you change applications, VoiceOver speaks the application name and the current location of the VoiceOver cursor within that application.

If you move into an editable text field, your Mac speaks each letter of the text as you move onto it.

By default, the position of the mouse cursor is not tied to the VoiceOver cursor. To activate a command or control, you must still use the mouse cursor to point to it. The idea is that you use the VoiceOver cursor to point to interface elements so

 note

When something appears on the screen that needs your input, such as a sheet, your Mac will speak the words "interactive dialog" to let you know that such an element has appeared on screen.

 note

If you move around quickly, your Mac might not be able to speak each element as you move to it. It will continue speaking each element you have moved the cursor over until it catches up with you.

that you know what they are because the Mac will speak them. When you want to activate an element, you still select it with the mouse cursor. For example, suppose you are looking at a screen with tabs on it. You can use the Control-Option-Arrow keys to move the VoiceOver cursor to each tab. When you find the tab you want to move into, you would move the mouse cursor to the tab and then click the mouse button to open the tab.

Using the VoiceOver Utility to Configure VoiceOver

VoiceOver is a useful tool even when you use its default configuration, but you can also customize it in many ways by using the VoiceOver utility. To access this utility, click the Open VoiceOver Utility button on the Seeing tab. The VoiceOver Utility has nine sections, each of which enables you to configure a specific aspect of how VoiceOver works (see Figure 24.3).

Figure 24.3
The VoiceOver Utility enables you to customize nine aspects of how it works.

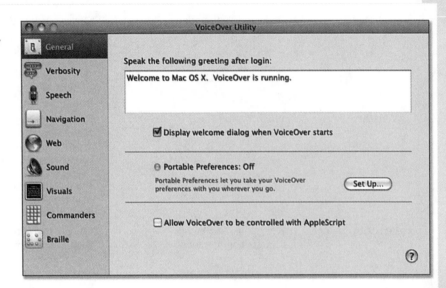

Unfortunately, going into the details of each control in the VoiceOver Utility is beyond the scope of this book. However, Table 24.1 provides a description of some of the configuration tools available to you.

Table 24.1 Useful VoiceOver Utility Configuration Controls

Section	Control	What It Does
General	Login Greeting box	This field contains the text that is spoken when you turn on VoiceOver and log in; you can change the text to change the greeting.

Table 24.1   Continued

Section	Control	What It Does
General	Portable preferences	Allows you to select what this Mac should do if it detects portable preferences. VoiceOver allows you to save your preferences to removable media so you can take those preferences and apply them on other Macs you might use.
Verbosity	Punctuation	Use this to determine how punctuation is spoken to you; for example, choose None to prevent any punctuation from being spoken or All to have all punctuation spoken.
Verbosity	Repeated Punctuation pop-up menu	Choose how you want your Mac to speak repeated punctuation, such as Spoken with Count, which causes your Mac to speak the punctuation followed by the number of times it appears (for example, "Comma, three").
Verbosity	While Typing Speak pop-up menu	Choosing Every Word causes your Mac to speak every word as you type it; choosing Every Character causes your Mac to speak each character you type; choosing Characters & Words causes your Mac to speak both; choosing Nothing turns off this feature.
Verbosity	When Text Attributes Change pop-up menu	When a text attribute changes, such as something being bolded, your Mac can speak the attributes, play a tone, or do nothing; make your selection using this menu.
Verbosity	When Encountering a Misspelled Word pop-up menu	Your Mac can alert you to spelling errors by either playing a tone or speaking the attributes of the spelling error.
Verbosity	When Encountering a Link pop-up menu	Use this to choose how your Mac acts when a link is encountered; choices include Do Nothing, Speak Link, Change Pitch, and Play Tone.
Verbosity	Read Numbers As pop-up menu	You can specify if the Mac should read numbers as words or as digits.

Table 24.1 Continued

Section	Control	What It Does
Verbosity	When Reading a Capital Letter pop-up menu	Use this to choose how your Mac speaks when it reaches an uppercase letter; choices include Do Nothing, Speak Cap, Change Pitch, and Play Tone.
Verbosity	When Deleting Text pop-up menu	If you would like your Mac to warn you when you are deleting text, you can select from changing the tone when the text is read, playing a tone, or speaking the change.
Verbosity	Words Are Separated By pop-up menu	Select from punctuation and whitespace, or just whitespace to help your Mac know how to treat words as it reads them.
Verbosity	Announcement Settings tab	This tab opens the Announcement Settings pane.
Announcements pane	Announce When Mouse Cursor Enters a Window check box	When this box is checked, your Mac will tell you when the mouse cursor moves into a different window by speaking the window name (and application name if applicable).
Announcements pane	Announce When a Modifier Key Is Pressed check box	This causes your Mac to speak when you press a modifier key, such as the ⌘ key.
Announcements pane	Announce When the Caps Lock Key Is Pressed check box	This causes your Mac to speak when you press the Caps Lock key.
Announcements pane	Speak Header When Navigating Across a Table Row check box	This causes your Mac to speak the headers in the table as you move across a row.
Announcements pane	Automatically Speak Text in Dialog Boxes	Your Mac will read dialog boxes to you when this is checked.
Announcements pane	When Status Text Changes Under VoiceOver Cursor	If you have a status window open and there is a change to the status, you can either play a tone or have that change spoken.
Announcements pane	When Progress Indicator Changes Under VoiceOver Cursor	When a progress indicator appears during a lengthy operation, you can either play a tone or have the progress updates spoken.
Announcements pane	Speak Text Under Mouse After Delay check box and slider	Check the check box and your Mac will speak the element at which the mouse cursor is currently pointing; use the slider to set the amount of time between when you point to something and when your Mac speaks it.

Table 24.1 Continued

Section	Control	What It Does
Speech	Mute Speech	Select this check box to temporarily stop the speech on your Mac without turning off VoiceOver.
Speech	Default Voice	Select the voice that your Mac should use to speak the VoiceOver elements. Use the additional controls to change the rate, pitch, and volume of the voice.
Speech	Pronunciation	This pane provides you with a number of special characters, abbreviations, and terms. You can then modify how each should be pronounced when spoken by your Mac. Use the Add button at the bottom of the pane to add specific items that you want to have pronounced correctly.
Navigation	Initial Position of VoiceOver Cursor pop-up menu	Select whether VoiceOver should initially be positioned on the first item in the window or on the keyboard focus.
Navigation	Keyboard Focus Follows VoiceOver Cursor check box	This keeps the keyboard focus in synch with the VoiceOver cursor; when you move the VoiceOver cursor, the keyboard focus moves too.
Navigation	Mouse Cursor Follows VoiceOver Cursor check box	This makes the mouse cursor always be in the same location as the VoiceOver cursor.
Navigation	Mouse Cursor Follows VoiceOver Cursor	Selecting this check box will make your mouse cursor move automatically to where you have the VoiceOver cursor.
Navigation	VoiceOver Cursor Follows Mouse Cursor	If you want the VoiceOver cursor to follow your mouse, select this check box.
Navigation	Insertion Point Follows VoiceOver Cursor check box	This control causes the insertion point to be in the same location as the VoiceOver cursor.
Navigation	VoiceOver Cursor Follows Insertion point	You can have the VoiceOver cursor move to where the insertion point is for entering text by clicking this check box.

Table 24.1 Continued

Section	Control	What It Does
Web	Web Navigation radio buttons	Choose DOM navigation to move through a web page via its DOM (Document Object Model) elements or Group navigation to move via the groups on a page.
Web	When Loading a New Web Page	Use these check boxes to activate a web page summary, cause Voice Over to automatically move to a new web page when it loads, and to automatically speak the web page.
Web	Navigate Images	Use this pop-up menu to decide whether you want to navigate all images, only images that have descriptive text, or no images.
Web	Only Navigate Images with a Description	If you check the Navigate Images check box, this check box includes only images with a description that can be read to the viewer.
Sound	Mute Sounds check box	Allows you to temporarily mute the VoiceOver sounds without changing your VoiceOver preferences.
Sound	Enable Positional Audio check box	If you are listening through headphones or very good speakers, this selection will let you hear a relative position in stereo where an element is on your Mac's screen.
Visuals	Show VoiceOver cursor check box and slider	With the box checked, the VoiceOver cursor appears as a box on the screen; use the slider to change its size.
Visuals	VoiceOver Menus Magnification slider	This slider changes the font size used on the VoiceOver menu.
Visuals	Caption Panel tab	Opens the Caption Panel pane.
Caption Panel pane	Show Caption Panel check box and slider	With the box checked, VoiceOver will display a panel at the bottom of the screen that shows what it most recently spoke; use the slider to set the size of the panel.
Caption panel pane	Rows in Caption Panel slider	Use this to set the number of rows allowed in the Caption Panel.
Caption Panel pane	Caption Panel Transparency slider	Use this to determine how transparent the Caption Panel is.
Braille Panel	Braille Panel tab and slider	Opens the Braille Panel pane.

Table 24.1 Continued

Section	Control	What It Does
Braille Panel pane	Show Braille Panel	When you use this pop-up menu to turn on the Braille panel, a black panel appears near the bottom of the screen with the Braille characters for the words your Mac speaks in VoiceOver. Use the slider to control how large the panel is on your screen.
Braille Panel pane	Braille Panel Transparency slider	Allows you to select how transparent the Braille Panel should appear on screen.
Commanders, NumPad pane	Enable NumPad Commander check box	Activate this check box to use the numeric keypad to navigate on the desktop; when this setting is activated, you can use each key's pop-up menu to determine how that key navigates.
Commanders, Keyboard pane	Enable Keyboard Commander check box	Activate this check box to use the keyboard to navigate on the desktop; when this setting is activated, you can use each key's pop-up menu to determine how that key navigates.
Braille	Braille Translation pop-up menu	Displays American English as the language supported by the Braille display connected to the Mac.
Braille	Show Contracted Braille	Select this check box to specify if VoiceOver should contract words not shown by the VoiceOver cursor, as well as display words in the cursor in uncontracted Braille.
Braille	Status Cells check boxes	Use the check boxes to specify how status windows should be shown and in what style for the connected Braille display.
Braille	Show Status On radio buttons	Select which side the status messages should appear on the Braille display connected to your Mac.
Braille	Displays tab	The Displays tab opens a pane that allows you to change which Braille display keys map to specific VoiceOver functions. You can use this sheet to add or remove mappings, as well as modify existing input key mappings.

Understanding and Using Zoom

The Zoom function enables you to zoom in on the screen to make things easier to see.

Using Zoom

First, activate zoom by using the following steps:

tip
You can also turn Zoom on or off by pressing ⌘-Option-8.

1. Open the Seeing tab in the Universal Access pane of the System Preferences application.

2. Click the On radio button in the Zoom section.

After Zoom is turned on press ⌘-Option-= to zoom in or ⌘-Option-− to zoom out (see Figure 24.4). When you are zoomed in, you can move around in the display by moving your mouse.

Figure 24.4
Here, I have zoomed in on the Zoom controls.

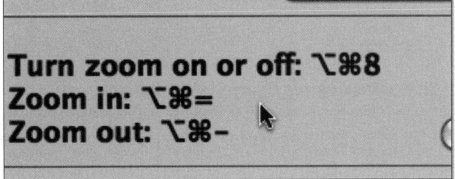

Configuring Zoom

There are several options you can configure for Zoom as listed in Table 24.2. You can access these controls by clicking the Options button in the Zoom section. When you do, the Options sheet appears. Choose the options you want and click Done to save them.

Table 24.2 Zoom Controls

Control	What It Does
Maximum Zoom slider	Sets the amount of magnification that can be achieved by pressing the Zoom In keys once.
Minimum Zoom slider	Sets the amount of magnification that can be achieved by pressing the Zoom Out keys once.
Show Preview Rectangle When Zoomed Out check box	When this is checked, a black box will appear around the mouse cursor; this box shows the area that will be zoomed in on when the zoom in keys are pressed when no zoom is currently applied; the box disappears when you zoom in.

Table 24.2 Continued

Control	What It Does
Smooth Images (Press Option-⌘-\ to turn smoothing on or off) check box	When this is checked, your Mac will smooth zoomed images; you can turn this on or off using the keys listed.
Zoom Follows the Keyboard Focus check box	When this option is checked and you zoom, the zoom focus occurs for the area of the screen that you are focused on using the keyboard.
When Zoomed In, the Screen Image Moves radio buttons	Choose Continuously with Pointer to have the zoomed image move with mouse movements; choose Only When the Pointer Reaches an Edge to have the image moved only when the mouse cursor reaches the edge of the image or screen; choose So the Pointer Is at or near the Center of the Image to always keep the cursor near the center of the image
Use scroll wheel with modifier keys to zoom check box and field	Check this box to use the scroll wheel on a mouse to zoom and enter the modifier key you'll use to activate zoom.

Understanding and Using Display Options

The Display options section of the Seeing tab enables you to configure the following settings:

- **Black on White**—Check this check box to use the default black text on a white background in Mac OS X screens.

- **White on Black**—This check box causes your Mac to display white text on a black background.

- **Use Grayscale**—This check box removes the color from the display and instead uses shades of gray.

- **Enhance Contrast**—Use this slider to change the contrast of the display. Contrast is the visual difference between the light and dark elements presented onscreen.

 tip

Use the keyboard shortcuts listed next to the Display options on the Seeing tab to be able to turn them on or off quickly.

Configuring and Using Hearing Assistance

The Hearing tab of the Universal Access pane enables you to have your Mac display an onscreen visual alert when it needs to get your attention (see Figure 24.5). To set this, open the tab and activate the Flash the Screen When an Alert Sound Occurs check box. When your Mac plays the alert sound, it will also flash the screen. Click the Flash Screen button on the Hearing tab to see what the flash alert looks like.

Figure 24.5
If you prefer your Mac to flash the screen when it needs your attention, use this check box to make it so.

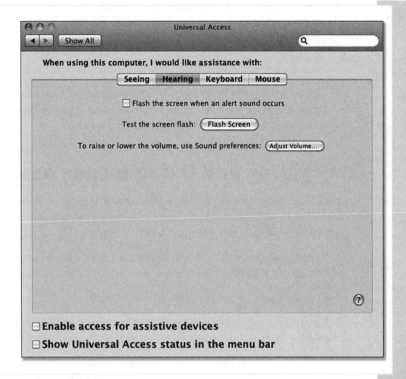

Configuring Keyboard Assistance

The Keyboard tools make your Mac easier to control for those who have difficulty manipulating the keys on the keyboard. There are two general features: Sticky Keys and Slow Keys. Sticky Keys helps users press more than one modifier key at a time because each key pressed "sticks" on. You can also configure Slow Keys to tailor how keys can be pressed to register them with the system. To configure the Keyboard settings, perform the following steps:

1. Open the Keyboard tab on the Universal Access pane of the System Preferences application.

2. Click the Sticky Keys On radio button to activate that feature.

3. If you want users to be able to turn on Sticky Keys by pressing the Shift key five times, activate the Press the Shift Key Five Times to Turn Sticky Keys On or Off check box.

4. If you want audio feedback when the modifier key is set, activate the Beep When a Modifier Key Is Set check box.

5. If you want each key press to be shown on the screen, activate the Display Pressed Keys on Screen check box.

6. Turn Slow Keys on by clicking the Slow Keys On radio button.

7. To play a key sound each time a key is pressed, activate the Use Click Key Sounds check box.

8. Use the Acceptance Delay slider to set the amount of time a key must be pressed before it is registered. Move the slider to the left to increase the delay between the time the key is pressed and when it is registered as a key press by the system.

Configuring and Using Mouse Assistance

Mouse Keys enables users to control the location of the pointer by using the numeric keys on the keypad; this can be useful if a person has difficulty manipulating a mouse or trackpad. To configure Mouse Keys, perform the following steps:

1. Open the Mouse (or Mouse & Trackpad on a mobile Mac) tab of the Universal Access pane of the System Preferences application.

2. Click the On radio button to turn Mouse Keys on.

3. If you want users to be able to turn on Mouse Keys by pressing the Option key five times, activate the Press the Option Key Five Times to Turn Sticky Keys On or Off check box.

4. Use the Initial Delay slider to set the amount of time a key must be pressed before the pointer starts moving. Move the slider to the left to make the pointer start moving sooner when a key is pressed or to the right to increase the delay.

5. Use the Maximum Speed slider to determine how fast and far the pointer moves when a key is pressed. Drag the slider to the right to increase the speed of movement or to the left to decrease it.

6. To change the size of the pointer on the screen, use the Cursor Size slider. Drag the slider to the right to increase the size of the cursor (see Figure 24.6).

7. If you are using a mobile Mac you can activate the Ignore Trackpad When Mouse Keys Is On check box so that moving your hand across the trackpad does not interfere with using the keyboard to navigate.

Figure 24.6
You can increase the size of the cursor if someone who uses your Mac has difficulty seeing the standard pointer.

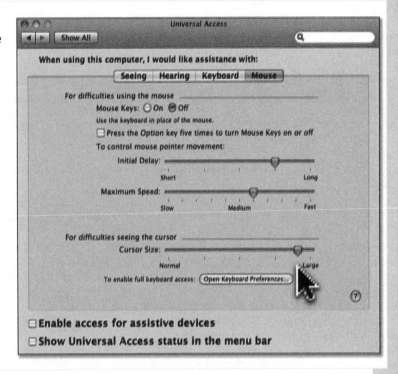

Configuring and Using Speech Recognition

Mac OS X has built-in support for speech recognition. This works both ways—you can speak to your Mac to issue commands and your Mac can read onscreen text to you. Whether controlling your Mac with speech works for you or not depends on a lot of variables, such as your speaking voice, the position of your mouth relative to your Mac's microphone, the microphone itself, and so on. Also, don't expect your Mac to start working like the computer on the Starship Enterprise; it will take some time for you to get voice recognition working effectively.

Configuring Your Mac for Voice Control

To configure speech recognition on your Mac, perform the following steps:

1. Open the Speech pane of the System Preferences application.

> **note**
>
> I've tried several voice recognition systems, including the Mac's built-in one. Frankly, beyond the initial gee-whiz factor of being able to speak a command and have the computer respond by doing something, I have found that using the keyboard and mouse is a much more effective way to work. But, you might want to experiment to see if it works better for you, particularly if you have special needs when it comes to interacting with your Mac. This section will get you started, but it is certainly not intended to explain all the details.

2. Click the Speech Recognition tab and use the controls to configure how speech recognition works. This pane has two tabs: Settings and Commands (see Figure 24.7). Use the Settings tab to configure basic settings of speech recognition.

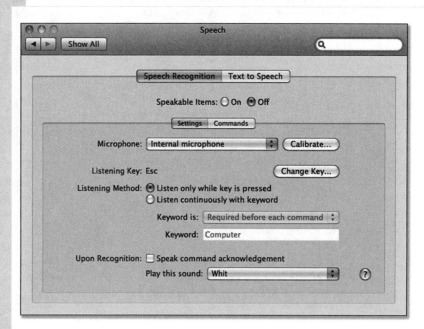

Figure 24.7
Use the Settings tab of the Speech Recognition pane to configure how your Mac listens to you.

3. Use the Microphone pop-up menu to choose the microphone you want to use. The options you have will depend on the configuration of your system.

4. Click the Calibrate button. The Microphone Calibration window will appear (see Figure 24.8).

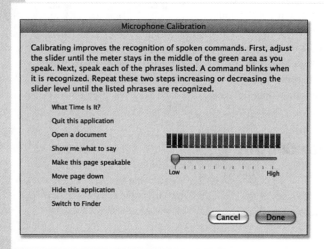

Figure 24.8
Using the Microphone Calibration window, you adjust your microphone's input to easily pick up spoken commands.

5. Speak into the microphone and drag the slider to the left or right until your voice is mostly registered near the center of the green band above the slider.

6. Speak each phrase listed along the left edge of the window. If the phrase is recognized by your Mac, it will flash. If it isn't recognized, adjust the slider and repeat the phrase until it is.

 tip

When you speak to your Mac, you'll probably have to slow down and make sure you enunciate each word more clearly than you probably do in normal conversation.

7. Continue this process until you can speak all of the phrases and have them recognized without changing the slider.

8. When your Mac registers each phrase when you speak it, click Done. The Microphone Calibration window will close.

9. By default the listen key is Esc; if you want to change this, click Change Key and choose the key you want to use. The listen key makes your Mac listen for spoken commands.

10. If you want to press the listen key before you speak a command, click the Listen Only While Key Is Pressed radio button. With this setting active, you must press the listen key before you speak a command.

11. If you want your Mac to listen continuously for commands, click the Listen Continuously with Keyword radio button. Then, choose when the keyword is required on the Keyword Is pop-up menu. Then enter your keyword in the Keyword field. The default is Computer, which means you need to say the word "Computer" to get your Mac to listen to your commands, but you can change this to something else if you prefer to use a different term.

12. If you want your Mac to acknowledge your command by speaking it, activate the Speak Command Acknowledgment check box. When your Mac acknowledges your command, it will speak the command it thinks it heard.

13. Use the Play this Sound pop-up menu to choose the sound you want your Mac to play when it recognizes a command.

14. Activate speech recognition by clicking the Speakable Items On radio button at the top of the pane. A sheet appears that provides some tips for success; read these tips and click OK. A round feedback window will appear on the desktop. In the center of this, you see either the current listen key or the phrase you need to speak (see Figure 24.9). When your Mac is listening to you, the lower part of this window will show you how the sound is being registered.

Figure 24.9
The feedback window indicates that the word "Computer" needs to be spoken before voice commands.

15. Click the Commands tab. You use this pane to determine the command sets you can speak (see Figure 24.10).

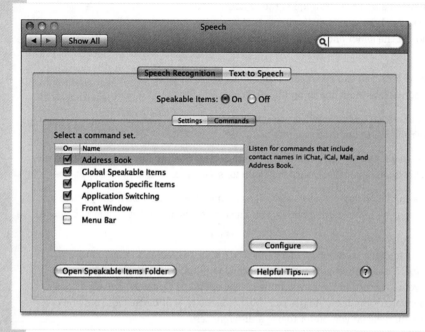

Figure 24.10
Use the Commands tab to choose command sets that you want to be able to speak.

16. Select a command set, such as the Font Window set. A description of the commands appears to the right of the list.

17. To activate a command set, activate its check box. You will then be able to speak the commands in that set. You are ready to start talking to your Mac.

Using Speech Recognition

After you have configured speech recognition, it will either be easy to use or extremely frustrating depending on how well your Mac recognizes the commands you speak. The only way to find out is to try it.

If you configured speech recognition to require the listening key, press it and speak a command. If your Mac recognizes the command, it will act on it and provide you with the feedback you configured it to, such as repeating the command or playing the sound you selected.

If you have your Mac listen continuously, speak the keyword you set and then speak the command. If your Mac recognizes

 tip

If a command set has additional configuration options, the Configure button becomes active when you select that command set. Use this button and the resulting sheet to set options for the command set.

 note

There are a number of commands available in the Speakable Items folder. When you activate the Global Speakable Items command set, these commands will be available to you. To see these commands, click the Open Speakable Items Folder button. A Finder window will appear and you will see Speakable items available to you. (For kicks, check out the "Tell me a joke" command.)

the command, it will act on it and provide you with the feedback you configured it to, such as repeating the command or playing the sound you selected.

If your Mac does nothing, it doesn't recognize the command. This can be because it didn't "hear" you, didn't understand what you said, or the command you spoke isn't a Speakable command.

If you find speaking commands useful, you can continue to talk to your Mac to control it. However, if you are like me, you will quickly grow tired of trying to get it to work reliably and even if you do get it to work well, it is still faster to use your hands to control your Mac. But, this can be kind of fun to play around with.

> **tip**
>
> To see which commands you can speak, click the arrow at the bottom of the feedback window and select Open Speech Commands window. In the Speech Commands window is the list of commands you can speak. When you open an application that supports speech recognition, that application appears in the Speech Commands window and the list of spoken commands it supports is shown.
>
> If you double-click the feedback window, it moves to the Dock.

Using Text to Speech

As you saw earlier in this chapter, using VoiceOver, your Mac can speak to you. The Text to Speech feature takes this concept much further and can be used across many applications and OSes to have your Mac speak to you.

To configure Text to Speech, perform the following steps:

1. Open the Text to Speech tab of the Speech pane of the System Preferences application.

2. Select the voice you want your Mac to use on the System Voice pop-up menu and then set the rate at which the voice speaks using the slider. Click the Play button to hear a sample.

3. If you want your Mac to speak alerts to you, activate the Announce When Alerts Are Displayed check box and use the Set Alert Options button to open a sheet that enables you to configure the voice used, the alert phrase, and the delay time. Click OK to set the options you selected.

4. If you want applications to speak when they need your attention, activate the Announce When an Application Requires Your Attention check box.

5. If you want to be able to quickly have your Mac read selected text to you, activate the Speak Selected Text When the Key Is Pressed check box. In the resulting sheet, type the key combination you want to use to cause your Mac to read text you select and click OK.

> **tip**
>
> You can change this key combination later by clicking the Set Key button.

Your Mac will start speaking to you when the conditions you selected occur, such when an alert is played.

If you enabled the Speak Selected Text feature, you can select any text and press the keyboard shortcut to cause your Mac to read it.

In applications that support text-to-speech, you can have your Mac read to you by choosing Edit, Speech, Start Speaking. You can shut your Mac up by choosing Edit, Speech, Stop Speaking.

> **tip**
>
> Your Mac can speak the time to you, as well. Use the Date & Time Preferences pane to configure this option.

MAKING YOUR MAC DO THE WORK FOR YOU WITH AUTOMATOR

Getting to Know Automator

If there were such a thing as a Most Underrated Player award for Mac OS X utilities, Automator would win it hands down. Most Mac users barely even know the application exists, and the rest shudder at the very thought of actually using it. However, Automator is actually one of the most useful of the Mac OS X utilities. And, as an added bonus, it's also quite easy to use. In fact, in just a few minutes you'll have learned enough to have Automator performing tasks that duplicate some fancy utilities from third-party vendors (programs that other less adventure-some folks are shelling out big bucks for). This chapter explores Automator by showing you how to create and run your own workflows, and by giving you a lot of examples that put your newfound knowledge to good use.

Understanding Automator's Workflows

Besides the proverbial paperless office, the other thing we were sup-posed to have by now (at least according to the so-called "futurists" of 50 years ago) was an automated home where little Robbie-the-Robot types would whisk around taking care of all our dirty work.

Well, although we've actually seen some progress on that front (see the Roomba vacuum cleaner), we're still a long way from that pipe dream. However, you can get one step closer by automating your Mac house by creating *workflows* that whittle long-winded, repetitive tasks down to a single action. For example, suppose you regularly send files to another person via email. To perform that task, you probably use the following general steps:

1. Select the files you want to send.

2. Archive the selected files into a Zip file.

3. Open Mail.

4. Create a new message.

5. Add the recipient's address.

6. Type a subject line.

7. Attach the Zip file to the email.

8. Type some text into the message.

9. Send the message.

Running through all those steps is fine every once in a while, but if you do this several times a week or more, it gets old pretty fast. However, you can combine all these steps into a single work-flow file, and then run the whole thing at once whenever you need to. (In fact, I show you how to build this workflow later in this chapter; see "Sending Files via Email.")

The secret to creating these Mac robots is the Automator utility. The idea is that, using a simple drag-and-drop interface (no programming!), you can add and configure each step in the process, until your workflow is complete. Then, later, you can double-click the resulting workflow file to run the entire sequence with little or no intervention on your part.

Understanding the Automator Utility

Before getting to the specifics of building your own workflows, let's take a second to look around the Automator window. First, launch the program by selecting Finder, Applications, Automator, and then click Choose to select the Workflow starting point. The Automator window has several panes (see Figure 25.1):

- **Library**—This is the pane for the Library of applications that Automator can work with.

- **Actions/Variables**—This is the pane to the right of the Library. When you click the Actions but-ton, this pane shows the functions that the selected Library application can run; when you click the Variables button, this pane shows a list of information items that you can pass from one application to another.

- **Information**—When you click an action or variable, this pane shows a description of that item.

- **Workflow**—You use this pane to build and configure your workflow.

Figure 25.1
Automator makes creating complex programs easy because you can drag steps onto the Workflow area of the Automator window.

Library   Actions/Variables   Workflow

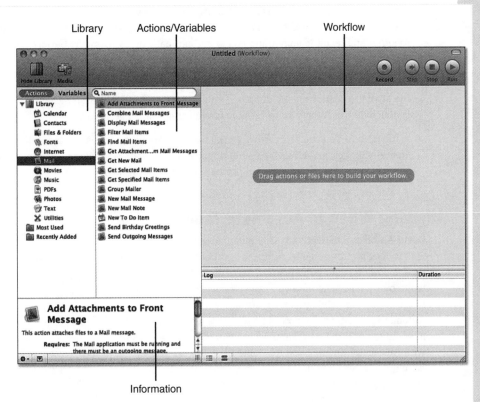

Information

Understanding how Automator works requires that you understand the following concepts:

- **Actions**—These are the basic building blocks of any automated workflow. An *action* is a single step that is performed when your automated tasks run. Actions can be relatively simple, such as asking the user to input text, or complex, such as applying photo editing tools to a series of files. Each application supported by Automator supports a number of individual actions.

- **Input**—Some steps require input, which is something that is needed for the action to be performed. For example, if an action applies to a file, that file is the input of the action. Different actions require different kinds of input. Automator helps you understand what kind of input an action requires.

- **Output**—Most actions end up providing output, which is the result of that action. For example, if an action makes a change to a file, that changed file becomes the output of the action. When actions are linked together, the output of one action becomes the input to the next one.

- **Workflow**—A *workflow* is a series of actions you save to automate work, i.e. a script of actions that you want to be able to run easily. A workflow consists of one or more steps that are linked together and result in something you would normally do by manually performing each step. You can save workflows so you can run them from within Automator, edit them, and so on.

- **Variables**—Variables represent attributes that are part of a workflow. You use a variable when the attribute changes. For example, if you want to perform an action based on today's date, you can include the Today's Date variable when configuring a workflow.

- **Application**—You can also save a workflow as an application. You can run the applications you create with Automator just like other applications on your Mac. When you run an application you have created, the actions you programmed are performed.

Knowing When to Automate Tasks

Using Automator is relatively easy given how powerful it is. Still, it does require some learning, so you need to balance the time and effort required to learn to use Automator to create workflows against the time you save by automating your Mac. In the beginning, while you are learning how to use Automator, it might take more time to create a workflow than it would to perform tasks manually. As you get more proficient with Automator, though, you'll be able to create workflows more quickly, which in turn will improve your overall efficiency in getting things done on your Mac.

Good candidates for automation with Automator are any series of steps you find yourself performing repeatedly. The steps you perform manually can be exactly the same, or you might perform the same series of steps but use different files or folders each time. In such cases, the time you invest in creating an Automator workflow can pay off because you can have your Mac repeat those steps for you.

 note

Automator can record what you are doing on your Mac and create a workflow from those steps. To do this you must first access the Universal Access pane of the System Preferences application and activate the Enable Access for Assistive Devices check box so that Automator can record what you do with the mouse and keyboard. When the steps have been recorded, you see a new Action called Watch Me Do that you can incorporate into a workflow.

Perhaps the most important consideration when deciding to automate is that the applications you use during the steps you are automating must be supported by Automator and, more specifically, the individual actions you perform must be available in Automator for that application.

Understanding Actions That Are Supported by Automator

Each application supported by Automator has one or more actions that you can use in your workflows. Some applications, such as the Finder, support many actions, whereas others support only a few. If all the steps you need to perform to complete a task are available as actions, you can automate a task. You can also create actions by recording them. If neither of those approaches work, you need to use a different automation tool.

To see which actions are supported, select an application on the Library list. The actions supported for that application will be shown in the Action pane (see Figure 25.1, which shows the actions supported by Mail).

When you select an action on the Action pane, information about the action is shown in the Information pane located at the bottom of the Action pane of the Library window. This information includes a summary of what the action does along with its input and output. For example, when you select the Finder's Create Archive action, you see that this action creates a zip format archive (.zip) from the files specified. Its input is the files to be archived. The output, called `result`, is the archived file.

To understand an action in more detail, drag it from the Action pane and drop it onto the Workflow area (see Figure 25.2). The action is added to the workflow, and you see its details. The action's title bar has the expansion triangle at the far left to show or collapse the detail of the action, the action's title is in the center, and the delete button is on the right side. In the action's window, you see the tools you use to configure the action; these depend on the specific action you are using. These tools can include text boxes, check boxes, and pop-up menus.

Figure 25.2
Drag an action into the workflow area to see its details.

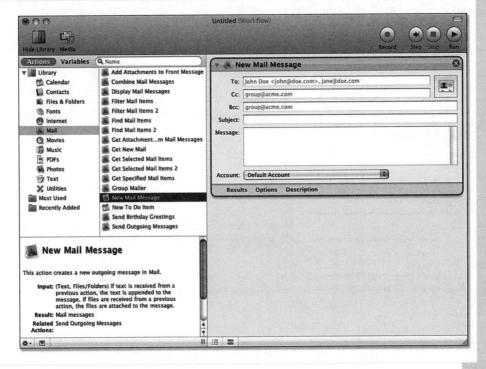

Understanding Action Inputs and Outputs

Some actions are self-contained and require no input when you run the workflow. For example, if you use the New Mail Message action and fill in all the fields in the workflow area, Automator uses that data each time you run the workflow.

However, many actions accept input, so you can customize an action by sending it the output of some other action. For example, you can see in the Information pane shown in Figure 25.2 that the New Mail Message action takes two types of input: Text and Files/Folders. Text input goes into the message itself, so you could use the Ask for Text action to prompt for some text, and then have that text output sent to the New Mail Message action.

This is what I've done in Figure 25.3. You can see that I've added the Ask for Text action above the New Mail Message action. Notice that Automator connects the two actions using a downward-pointing arrow to indicate output and a semicircle to indicate input.

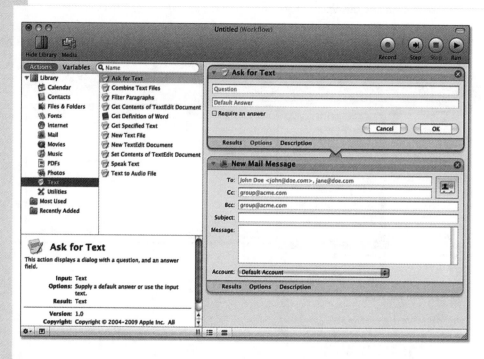

Figure 25.3
To build a workflow, you drag actions onto it.

Understanding Variables That Are Supported by Automator

Some applications can use variables to represent attributes that are used in a workflow. To see the list of available variables, click the Variables button at the top of the Library pane. The Library pane will display different categories of variables, such as Date & Time, System, User, and Utilities. Clicking on a category will display the variables that are available. Select a variable to see more information about it in the bottom of the Library window. Variables allow you to use their values in your workflow.

Creating Your Own Workflows

Any type of programming, which is what you are doing when you use Automator, requires that you follow a logical path (well, logical to your Mac anyway) that ends up in the result you want. This isn't always easy to do. For best results, you should tackle any automation project by performing a series of steps, as you will learn in the following sections.

Designing a Workflow

The first step when creating any workflow is to determine the tasks you want to automate. You need to identify the applications those tasks involve and the specific steps that are required. For best results, you should manually perform each step that is required to complete these tasks and document what you do during each one. Create a list of specific applications the tasks involve and the specific steps performed in that application. This might seem tedious, but creating a workflow that actually does what you expect will be much easier if you take the time to design it before you jump into Automator and start dragging steps into a workflow.

A less systematic approach is to just use trial and error. You can sometimes develop workflows effectively by just adding an action at a time running the workflow after each to make sure it does what you expect.

A third approach is to try to record a workflow. Even if this doesn't result in the end product, it will often add most of the actions you need so that you can just refine them to complete the workflow.

Building a Workflow Manually

To build your workflow, perform the following general steps:

1. Use your design document to identify the first step that needs to be done.

2. In the Library pane, select the application you use to perform that step. Then select the specific action that should occur during the step.

3. Drag the action into the Workflow area.

4. Configure the action for the workflow.

5. Refer to the next step in your workflow design document.

6. Repeat step 2.

7. Drag the action into the Workflow area. The output of the previous step will be become the input of the step you just placed in the workflow.

8. Check the output/input connection to ensure they match. For example, if the previous step outputs a file or folder, the input of the next step should be a file or folder.

9. Repeat steps 5–8 to systematically create the workflow to match your design.

10. Select File, Save to open the Save As sheet, type a name for the file, make sure that Workflow is selected in the Type pop-up menu, and then click Save.

Recording a Workflow

You can also build a workflow by recording actions you perform. When viewing a workflow, click the Record button and then perform the steps you want to record. As you perform them, they are added to the workflow. After the steps have been added, you can configure them and refine the workflow by recording more tasks or adding and configuring actions manually.

Testing and Editing a Workflow

After you have created the workflow, you should go through a testing process to ensure that the workflow works as you expect it to. It is typical that it won't work quite right at first, so plan on needing to edit it a few times before you get it working properly. The general steps to test and edit a workflow are the following:

 note

If a step fails, you'll usually see an error message that should help you figure out what went wrong.

1. Click the Step button. The workflow executes the next action.

2. Check the results of the action. Did the action perform as you expected? Do you see a green checkmark beside the Results area of the action?

3. If the action didn't work properly, edit the action to fix the problem, then perform steps 1 and 2 again.

   To help in the troubleshooting process, click an action in the workflow and select Show Results from the Action menu, or click the Results button on the action. The action's tools are replaced by the results of the action. This can be extremely useful when troubleshooting a workflow.

4. Repeat steps 1–3 top step through the entire workflow.

5. Click the Run button to test the entire workflow. If it works properly, you are done.

6. If the workflow doesn't result in what you expect, repeat steps 1–5 until it does.

You should expect to spend some time testing and editing a workflow until it does just want you want it to. You can increase the odds of your workflow working right the first time by designing it in a good amount of detail before you start creating it. Generally, the more prep work you do designing and documenting your workflow, the less time you will have to spend testing and editing it.

Saving a Workflow as an Application

After your workflow does what you want it to, you can save it as an application. You can then run the workflow by launching the application, which you do just like other applications on your Mac, such as by double-clicking it, putting it on the Dock and clicking its icon, adding it to your Login Items so it runs when you log in, and so on.

To save a workflow as an application, follow these steps:

1. Open the workflow you want to save as an application.

2. Choose File, Save As. The Save As sheet appears.

3. Name the application (you can use the same name as the workflow if you want because they are different types of files, so you don't have to worry about replacing the workflow).

4. Choose the location in which you want to save the application you are creating. Consider creating a folder in which to store all your applications so you can locate them easily. For example, you might want to create a folder called My Applications within the Applications folder.

5. On the Type pop-up menu, select Application.

6. Click Save. An application is created from the workflow.

Learning How to Automate Your Mac by Example

When you understand the general way Automator works and how you should go about building workflows, the only way to really learn how to create your own workflows is to start creating them. The first few you create might take a while, but as you gain more experience with Automator, you'll become more proficient creating new workflows. To get started, you'll find two sample workflows in this section that you can re-create on your Mac. Doing this will give you some experience using Automator; you will then be ready to start designing and creating your own workflows.

Opening Websites

If you visit the same websites regularly, you can create a workflow and application that opens Safari for you and takes you to as many websites as you'd like. To create this workflow, perform the following steps:

1. Launch Automator and select Workflow as the starting point.

2. In the Library list, click Internet. Automator displays a list of Internet-related actions.

3. Double-click the Get Specified URLs action. Automator adds the Get Specified URLs action to the workflow pane on the right side of the window.

4. Click Add to add a new URL.

5. In the new URL, double-click the URL name text, type the name of the site, and then press Tab to select the text in the Address column.

6. Type the address of the site and then press Return.

7. Repeat steps 4–6 to add all the sites you want to open.

8. Double-click the Display Webpages action. Automator adds the Display Webpages action to the workflow pane, as shown in Figure 25.4. This action takes the addresses in the Get Specified URLs action and displays them in Safari.

 tip

You can also add a website by opening it in Safari and clicking the Current Safari Page button. The URL of the current web page is added to the URL list.

 tip

To remove a URL, such as the Apple home page, select it from the list of URLs and click the Remove button.

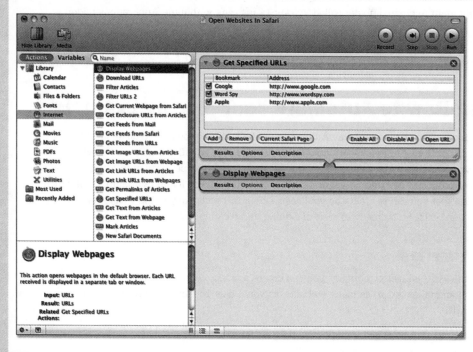

Figure 25.4
Automator passes the Get Specified URLs addresses to Display Webpages to open the sites in Safari.

9. In the Library, click Utilities.

10. Double-click the Launch Application action.

11. In the list, click Safari. This ensures that Safari becomes the active window when you run the workflow.

12. Select File, Save, type a name in the Save As box, and then click Save. Automator saves your workflow file. Figure 25.5 shows the completed workflow.

**Figure 25.5
The final
workflow.**

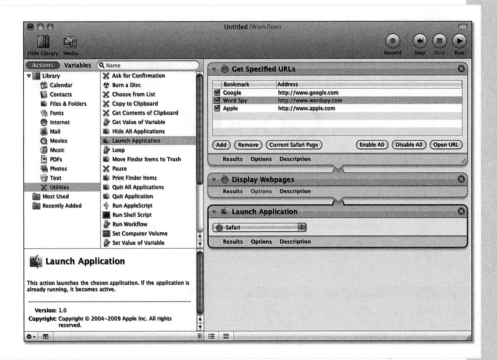

When you run this workflow, Safari launches and opens each URL in a separate window. Chances are this isn't the behavior you want; that is, you're more likely to want to open each URL to appear in a separate tab in a single window. That's easy to fix with a single Safari tweak:

1. Start Safari.

2. Select Safari, Preferences.

3. Select the General tab.

4. In the Open Links from Application section, click the In a New Tab In the Current Window radio button.

Quit Safari and then run your workflow again. This time you see the sites open in tabs, as shown in Figure 25.6.

Figure 25.6
Run the workflow, and you now see each site appear in its own tab.

Sending Files via Email

For this example, suppose that you regularly send files to someone via email (maybe you are an author and you send your chapters to your editor). You can create a workflow that will archive files you select into a Zip file, create and address an email, and attach the Zip file to the email. Here's how to create this workflow:

1. Launch Automator and select Workflow as the starting point for a new workflow. (If you already have Automator running, select File, New—or press ⌘-N click Custom, and then click Choose.)

2. In the Library pane, click Files & Folders.

3. Drag the Get Selected Finder Items action onto the workflow or double-click it to add it to the workflow. This action gets items you have selected in the Finder and passes them to the following action.

4. Add the Create Archive action (which creates a Zip archive of files or folders) to the workflow. (If you're clicking and dragging, be sure to place it after the Get Selected Finder Items action.) Notice that the Get Selected Finder Item output type (Files/Folders) matches the Create Archive input type (also Files/Folders).

5. In the Save As box of the Create Archive, enter a name for the archive file that will be created.

 tip

Check out the Options for actions by clicking the Options button. There are a number of useful selections on the resulting menu, such as Show This Action When the Workflow Runs.

6. Use the Where pop-up menu to choose the location in which the archive file will be saved (see Figure 25.7).

Figure 25.7
So far, this workflow takes selected Finder items and saves them in a Zip file called "Archive" in the folder called "Projects."

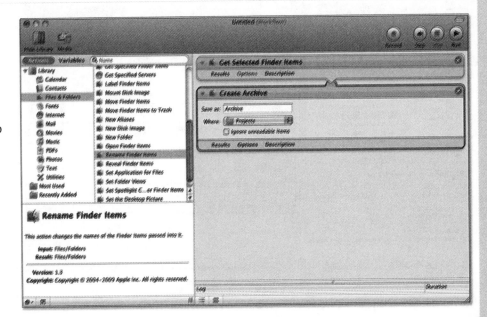

7. Add the Rename Finder Items action to the workflow and place it after the Create Archive action. (A warning sheet appears, explaining that this action will change the name of the Finder Items, and presents you with an option to add a copy action; click Don't Add.) Because you're going to be using this workflow many times, you don't want each file to have the same name or they'll get replaced each time the workflow runs. This is why you need to add an action to rename the file.

8. Use the tools in the Add Date or Time to Finder Item Names action to configure the name of the archive file created. For example, you can add the date or time to it, make it sequential, and so on. Choose Make Sequential on the top pop-up menu; the tools in the action change to reflect the selection you made. To have a sequential number added after the name separated by an underscore, choose Underscore on the Separated By pop-up menu. Enter the first sequential number you want to be used in the Start Numbers At box (see Figure 25.8).

It's a good idea to test workflows as you create them, so test what you've done so far.

 tip

You can double-click an action's title bar to collapse or expand it.

9. Move to the Finder and select a couple of files.

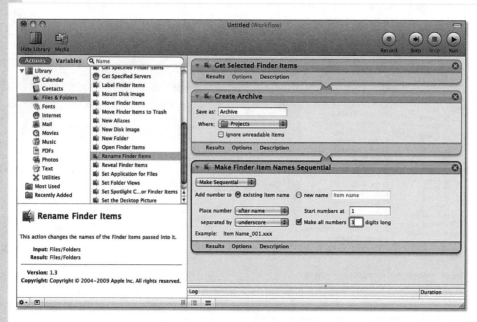

10. Move back to the workflow and click the Run button. The workflow runs. If it can't complete for some reason, you see information about what happened. If it does complete, you hear the whistle tone. Look in the save location you configured. You see the file the workflow created (see Figure 25.9).

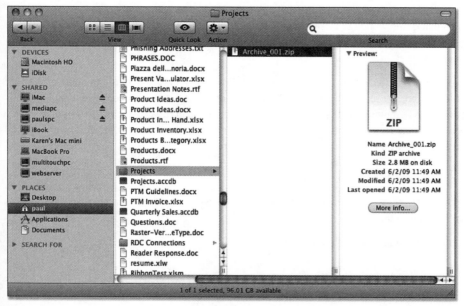

The file that was created is a .zip file containing the files that were selected when you ran the workflow.

Now, add the actions to send the archived file.

11. Move back to the workflow.

12. Select the Mail application and then drag the New Mail Message action into the workflow and place it below the Rename Finder Items action. Notice that the output of the Make Finder Item Names Sequential action (Files/Folders) fits with the input of the New Mail Message action.

13. Enter the email address for the person to whom you want to send the file in the To box or click the Address Book icon to select an address in your Address Book.

14. Type a subject for the message in the Subject field.

15. If you want some text to appear in the message every time, enter it in the Message box.

16. Choose the email account that should be used to send the message on the Account pop-up menu.

17. Review the workflow to see whether the actions you need it to run are available, configured, and in the correct order (see Figure 25.10).

Figure 25.10
This workflow creates an archive of selected files and emails them.

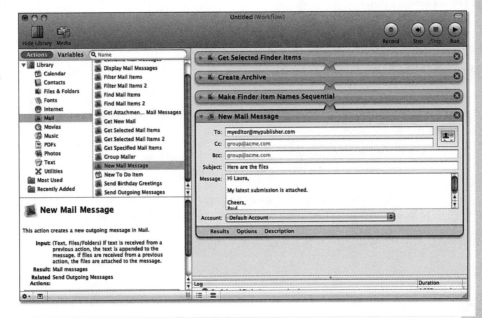

18. Save the workflow.

Now that you have created the workflow, it is time to test it by performing the following steps:

1. Move to the Finder and select one or more files.

2. Move back into Automator and click Run to run the work-flow. The workflow runs; when it completes, you see a new email message with the default text entered and the archive file attached (see Figure 25.11).

 caution

You should always save a workflow before you run it. If it doesn't work properly, Automator might quit, in which case you could lose your workflow.

Figure 25.11
The workflow took selected files, created a .zip file containing them, and then attached that file to a new Mail message.

3. If the result is correct, you can save the workflow as an application. If not, you need to troubleshoot it until it does work as you want.

After the workflow creates the email message and attaches the file to it, you can edit the message as needed before you send it. The workflow won't actually send the message, so you need to click Send to send it.

WORKING WITH THE MAC OS X COMMAND LINE

Using the Unix Command Line with Mac OS X

As you learned earlier in the book, Mac OS X is running on top of a version of the Unix operating system. This means that Mac OS X can use many Unix applications. It also means you can enter Unix commands directly in the command-line interface to manipulate your system. In fact, in some situations, using a Unix command might be the best way you can accomplish a task (such as deleting a rogue file that you can't delete by dragging it to the Trash).

Unix is a very powerful language/operating system; however, it is also complex, and many of its commands require you to use complicated syntax to get them to work properly. Unix commands are incomprehensible to most people when they first encounter them, so don't expect to be able to figure out how a particular command works without some help. Mostly, you will learn about commands you want to use from various Unix resources (such as this chapter, other books, websites, and Unix manual pages). You might find using the command line to be so counter to the Mac OS X interface experience that you don't want to use it; this is fine because few situations exist in which it is required in everyday Mac use. However, if you want to master Mac OS X, you should become familiar with the command line and learn some basic Unix commands. You might find that Unix provides ways of doing things that are both powerful and efficient.

There is so much you can do with Unix that there is no way you can learn how to work proficiently with it in the few pages of this chapter.

To become even remotely fluent in Unix, you need to do some additional learning outside of this book. What you can learn here is generally how the command-line interface works, and you also learn how to use some basic Unix commands as examples. In the "Unix Resources" section at the end of the chapter, I provide references for you so you can learn more about using Unix.

 note

Hostname is the name of the machine that is hosting your Unix session. When you are running a Unix session from your local machine, this will be your computer's name (with punctuation marks removed and spaces replaced by dashes) for most default configurations. If you are providing services over the network, the computer's network name is used.

Running Terminal

Use the Terminal application (open Finder and select Applications, Utilities) to enter Unix commands in the command-line interface (see Figure 26.1). When you first open it, the Terminal window is simple; you see your last login date and time, the hostname, the user account under which you are logged in, and the command prompt.

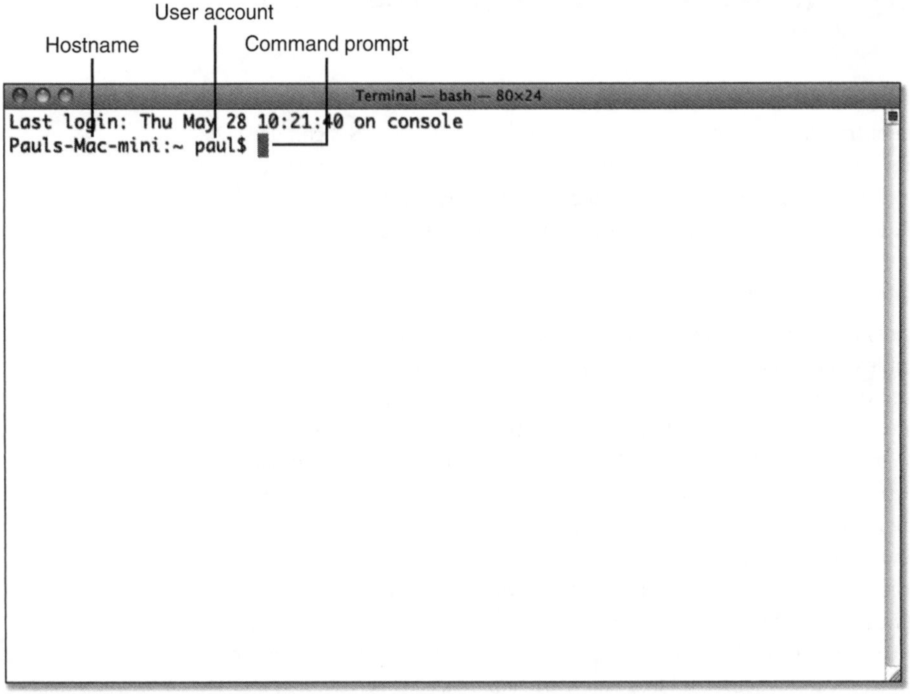

User account

Hostname   Command prompt

```
● ● ●                    Terminal — bash — 80×24
Last login: Thu May 28 10:21:40 on console
Pauls-Mac-mini:~ paul$ █
```

Figure 26.1
The command-line interface in Terminal isn't much to look at, but it is very powerful.

Understanding Shells

In Unix, the *shell* is the user interface you use to interact with Unix. You can use different shells for the same set of Unix tools; each shell will have slightly different features, but they all work somewhat similarly (although the specific commands you use can differ). You can change the specific shell you use if you find one that offers features in which you are interested.

The default shell for working with Unix under Mac OS X is called bash (see the Terminal title bar in Figure 26.1). Other shells are available, but bash is a good place to start.

 tip

The default Terminal text size is a bit on the small side. To increase the text size, select View, Bigger (or press ⌘-+) until the text is the size you want.

Understanding Unix Command Structure

To enter commands, you type them at the command prompt. All Unix commands use a specific syntax and consist of the following three parts:

- **Command**—The command is the specific action you want to take, such as listing the contents of a directory using the ls command.

- **Options**—You add options to a command to make the command work in a specific way. To add an option to a command, type a hyphen followed by a letter. The options you can use are specific to each command. For example, when used with the ls (list) command, the -l option tells Unix to list the contents of the directory in the long format.

- **Argument**—The argument is the "thing" on which the command will be executed, such as a file or directory. For example, to list the contents of a directory called mydirectory, the argument would be that directory name and the path to that directory.

 note

There are different shells installed in Mac OS X by default, and you can also download additional shells. After you download and install the shell, you use the Terminal's Preferences to set the shell you want to use. The details of using different shells are beyond the scope of this chapter. See some of the references listed at the end of this chapter for help.

When you enter specific commands, you might not use options or arguments; in some cases, you won't use either and will simply enter the command by itself.

You can run several commands in sequential order by separating the commands with a semicolon, as in command1; command2. Terminal runs the commands in the order you enter them.

You can send the output of one command to be the input of another command by separating them with the pipe symbol (¦), as in command1 ¦ command2. This is called *piping*.

 note

Unix is case sensitive, so you must always follow the case conventions for specific commands. Most of the time, you will type everything in lowercase letters for commands and options, but paths can include both uppercase and lowercase letters.

When entering commands, you frequently need to use the path to a directory or file you want to manipulate. The path is the means by which you locate a file in the hierarchy; levels of the hierarchy are indicated by the slash (/). Also, Unix uses relative pathnames. When you refer to something within or below the current directory, you need to enter only the portion of the path from the current directory to the subdirectories and files rather than the full path from the top level of the hierarchy. For example, to refer to a directory called `projects` within your `Documents` folder when you are currently in the `Documents` directory, you would enter the path `projects`. When you want to move above or outside the current directory, you must type the full path. In Unix, full paths always start with `/`.

Unlike graphical interfaces, such as Mac OS X, Unix does not like spaces in filenames, volume names, or paths. To enter a space in one of these, use the backslash (\) followed by the space. For example, to refer to the volume called Mac OS X, you would enter `/Mac\ OS\ X`.

To get to the root of the startup volume, the path is simply `/`. However, unless you are logged on under the root account, you won't be able to do anything with the files and directories you see using a command line because of the system security.

One of the best ways to become familiar with entering pathnames is to drag items from a Finder window onto the Terminal window. When you do so, the pathname to that item is entered in the Terminal. You can use this trick to make entering paths easier because you can drag the item onto the prompt after you have entered a command and option to quickly add the argument to complete the command. And, after you drag several onto the window, you will get a good idea of how to type pathnames at the prompt manually. Follow these steps:

1. In a Finder window, open the Home directory for your user account.

2. Open a new Terminal window from within the Terminal application by selecting Shell, New Window, Basic (or press ⌘-N). A new Terminal window appears.

3. Drag the Documents directory from the Finder window onto the new Terminal window. The path to the directory is shown at the prompt (see Figure 26.2). (Note that you can't drag the folder from the Places sidebar; you must drag it from a Finder window.)

 note

The full path to your Home directory is /*startupvolume*/Users/*short-username*/, where *startupvolume* is the name of your Mac OS X startup volume and *shortusername* is the short username for your account. However, because you can use relative paths, you can leave out the first / and the name of your Mac OS X startup volume to get to this directory. You need to add only the volume name when you are working outside the current volume.

 tip

When using the Terminal, you can have multiple windows open at the same time. Each window is independent, so you can have multiple sessions running independently. You can save each session separately too, which you will learn about later in this chapter.

 note

If you deal with Unix systems outside of Mac OS X, you will notice that paths almost never include spaces. Unix can have trouble properly interpreting spaces, so you can run into problems if the path you want to use includes spaces. Generally, if you plan to use Unix frequently, you should include underscores when you name your files and directories instead of spaces. Or, you can simply drag the object into the Terminal window and let the Mac enter the path for you. Spaces will be replaced by a backslash and a space (\ ).

Figure 26.2
You can
quickly enter
a path at the
prompt by
dragging an
item from a
Finder win-
dow into the
Terminal; in
this case, I
dragged the
Documents
folder from
my Home
directory into
the Terminal
window.

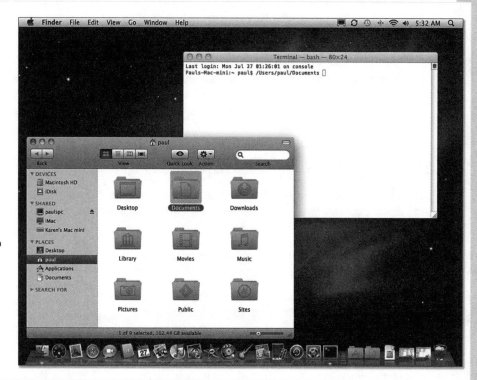

Understanding Unix Applications

Because Unix has been around so long, thousands and thousands of Unix applications are available. You can run many of these under Mac OS X, and the OS includes several of these applications as part of the standard installation. For example, the Apache web server application enables you to host your own web pages. Mac OS X comes with a couple of Unix text editors, which are vi (Visual Editor) and emacs (an abbreviation of editing macros).

➡ *To get some examples of running these Unix applications, **see** "Working with Basic Unix Applications," p. 544.*

Understanding Shell Scripts

You can invoke a series of commands using a shell script; you can save the script and run it at any time to save yourself from having to retype the commands over and over. You create a script using the same syntax as in regular Unix commands. The difference is that you save those commands to a text file. When you want to run the commands, you execute the file instead. You can also run scripts that others have written just as easily.

The details of writing and running scripts are beyond the scope of this book. See the references listed at the end of this chapter for information about creating and using shell scripts.

Understanding Unix Flavors

Finally, you should be aware that various versions of Unix are available. And, different releases of different versions exist as well. Mac OS X is built upon a version of the Berkeley Software Distribution (BSD) version of Unix called Darwin. As this version is updated, the version that is part of Mac OS X is updated as well.

Learning Unix by Example

Many Unix commands are available, and there is no way you can do more than scratch the surface in a single chapter. However, you can learn how Unix commands work in general by trying some specific examples of useful Unix commands.

➡ *For references in which you can learn more Unix commands, see "Learning Unix," p. 547.*

Each of the following sections provides information about specific commands. For each command, you see four areas of information about that command: a general description of what the command does; the command's syntax and some of the useful options for that command; a more specific description of the command's effect; and the steps you can take to use the command.

> **note**
>
> For the commands in this section, you won't see all or even many of the options that are possible for each command. You need to access a more detailed reference for that type of information, such as the command's manual pages (see "Using the Manual," later in this chapter).

Learning About the Environment

When you are troubleshooting, it can be helpful to understand the environment in which you are running Unix. You can use the uname command to get information about the computer on which you execute the command. Or, you might need to check this information to make sure some software or hardware is compatible with your system:

Command: uname
Options: -a provides all the information about your machine; -s shows the operating system name; -n lists the machine name
What it does: Provides information about various aspects of the machine on which you are running Unix

1. Launch the Terminal application and at the command prompt, type **uname -a**; then press Return. You see various items of information about your machine, such as the core operating system (Darwin), the version of the kernel you are running, and so on (see Figure 26.3).

Figure 26.3
The uname command provides information about the machine on which you are running Unix.

```
Terminal — bash — 80×24
Last login: Mon Jul 27 01:26:01 on console
Pauls-Mac-mini:~ paul$ uname -a
Darwin Pauls-Mac-mini.local 10.0.0 Darwin Kernel Version 10.0.0: Sat Jul 18 23:3
5:54 PDT 2009; root:xnu-1456.1.22~1/RELEASE_I386 i386
Pauls-Mac-mini:~ paul$ ▊
```

2. Type **uname** **-s** and press Return. You see only the core operating system (Darwin).

3. Type **uname** **-n** and press Return. You see the name of the machine hosting the Unix session.

Command: env
What it does: Provides extensive information about your Unix session (your Unix environment)

Type **env** and press Return to see environment information that includes your Home directory, the shell you are running, the username you are using, the language being used, the application you are using to enter Unix commands, and so on.

Viewing the Contents of Directories

You will frequently need to move up and down the directory structure to work with specific files or other directories. Unix has many commands that enable you to do so, including

Command: pwd
What it does: Shows you the full path to your current location

Use the pwd command when you aren't sure about the directory you're currently working in. When you run the command, you see the full path of the current directory. This can be helpful if you become confused about where you are as you move around the directories.

Command: cd *pathname*
What it does: Changes your directory location to *pathname*

1. Type **cd** **Music**. The prompt changes to *computername*:Music to indicate you're now in the Music directory in your Home directory.

 tip

If you're running multiple Terminal sessions, rather than having multiple Terminal windows scattered around your desktop, you can use a single window and display each session in its own tab, much like the web page tabs you probably use in the Safari web browser. Select View, Show Tab Bar (or press Shift-⌘-T) to display the tabs. You can then select Shell, New Tab, Basic (or press ⌘-T) to open a session in a new tab.

 note

When a specific command is listed in a step, you should ignore the period at the end of the command. For example, in the following steps, don't type the period after the command cd Music in step 1.

2. Type **cd /Users/*shortusername***, where *shortuser-name* is the short username for your account. This moves you back into your Home directory. You include /Users/ because you are moving above the Music directory and so need to include the full pathname.

Command: ls
Options: -F differentiates between files and directories; -1 shows full information for all the files in the directory
What it does: Lists the contents of a directory in various formats and with varying amounts of information

1. Use the cd command to move into the directory you want to work with.

2. Type **ls**. You see a multiple-column view of the directory; files and directories are listed by name.

3. Type **ls -F**. You see the same list as before except that now directories are indicated by a / after their names.

4. Type **ls -1**. You see the contents of the directory listed along with a lot of information about each file and directory within the current directory (see Figure 26.4). If there are many items, the information scrolls so quickly that you might not be able to see all of it. In step 5, you learn how to use piping to remedy this.

5. Type **ls -1 ¦ more**. This time, the same list appears, but the display stops when the screen is full and you see the colon (:) prompt at the bottom of the window. Press the spacebar to see the next screenful of information. When you see the regular prompt, you can scroll the window using the scrollbars to see all the items in the window.

The permissions string you see at the start of each item in the full listing indicates how the item can be accessed. The first character indicates whether the item is a file (-) or a directory (d). The next three characters indicate what the owner of the file can do; r is for read, w is for write, and x is for execute. If any of these characters is the hyphen (-), that action can't be taken. The next three characters indicate the permission that the group has to the file. For example, if these characters are r - x, other members of the group can read, not write, and execute the file. The last three characters indicate what everyone else can do.

 tip

The ~ in a pathname represents your Home directory, so ~/Music means you are in the Music directory that is within your Home directory. This can help you take some shortcuts when entering paths, as you see in the next step.

Also remember that the forward slash (/) in a path indicates a change in level in the hierarchy. For example, if you're in your Home directory and type cd /Music, you get a message telling you that no such directory exists. When you enter the forward slash, Unix looks back to the highest level in the structure, and because there's no directory called Music at that level, you get the error. Leaving the / out indicates that Unix should look in the current directory, which is where the directory is actually located.

 note

In a pathname, the tilde character (~) indicates that you are in your Home directory. In step 2, you could have just entered cd ~ to move back into your Home directory. Also, if you're in a directory and you want to move up a level, type cd .. and press Return.

 note

Although most commands and options are in lowercase, they aren't always. For example, the -F option is different from the -f option (both are valid for the ls command).

 tip

If you type the command ls -la, you also see the invisible files in a directory.

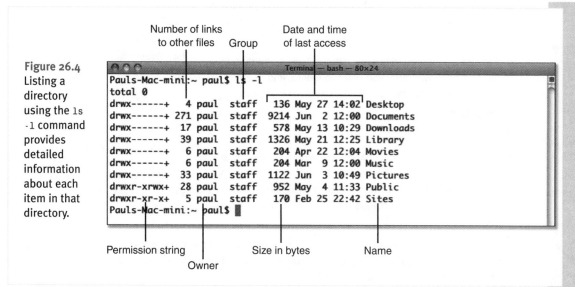

Figure 26.4 Listing a directory using the ls -l command provides detailed information about each item in that directory.

Number of links to other files

Group

Date and time of last access

Permission string

Owner

Size in bytes

Name

The execute permission applies to a directory. To access a directory, you must have both read and execute permission. If you also have w permission, you can change the contents of the directory as well.

Command: file *filename*

What it does: Indicates what type of file *filename* is

 tip
To clear the screen and get a fresh prompt, press Control-L.

Type **file**, followed by the filename you would like information about (it's often easiest to drag the file from the Finder and drop it next to the command rather than typing the pathname to that file), and press Return. Information about the file is displayed.

Changing the Contents of Directories

You can use Unix commands to change the contents of directories as well. For example, you can delete files using the rm (remove) command. This can sometimes be faster than using the Trash. Once in a while, you might not be able to use the Trash to get rid of a file; you can often use the Unix commands to accomplish the task when other means fail.

Command: rm

Options: -i prompts you before deleting each file; -r removes the entire directory

What it does: Deletes everything that you indicate should be deleted

1. Use the cd and ls commands to find a file you want to delete.

2. Type **rm *filename***, where *filename* is the name of the file you want to delete, and press Return. The file is deleted.

3. Type **rm -i** *filename* and press Return. You're prompted about removing the file; type **Y** to remove the file or **N** to cancel.

4. Type **rm -r** *directoryname*, where *directoryname* is the name of a directory you want to delete, and press Return. The directory and all its contents are deleted.

Command: cp
What it does: Copies a file

1. Type **cp** *filename filenamecopy*, where *filename* is the name of the file you want to copy and *filenamecopy* is the name of the file to which it be copied; then press Return. The first file is copied into a new file that has the second name you typed.

2. Type **cp** *filename path*, where *filename* is the name of the file you want to copy and *path* is the location in which you want the copy to be created; then press Return. A copy of the file is placed into the location you specified.

Command: mv
What it does: Moves a file or directory

Type **mv** *filename path* and press Return. The file or directory *filename* is moved to the location *path*.

Command: mkdir
What it does: Creates a directory (folder)

1. Use the cd command to move into the directory in which you want to create a new directory.

2. Type **mkdir** *directoryname* and press Return. A new directory with the name *directoryname* is created in the current directory.

note

You can't remove the current directory unless you enter the full path to it.

tip

The asterisk (*) is a wildcard character. For example, to delete all the files in a directory that have the file extension .tiff, you can type rm *.tiff.

Using the Manual

All Unix commands have a manual associated with them. This manual lists the syntax for the command and defines its options; manuals can be a good reference when you're using a specific command but can't remember an option or the command's exact syntax. Many manual pages also provide some explanation about how the command works.

Command: man
What it does: Brings up the manual pages for the command you enter

1. Type **man ls** and press Return. The first page of the manual for the ls command appears (see Figure 26.5).

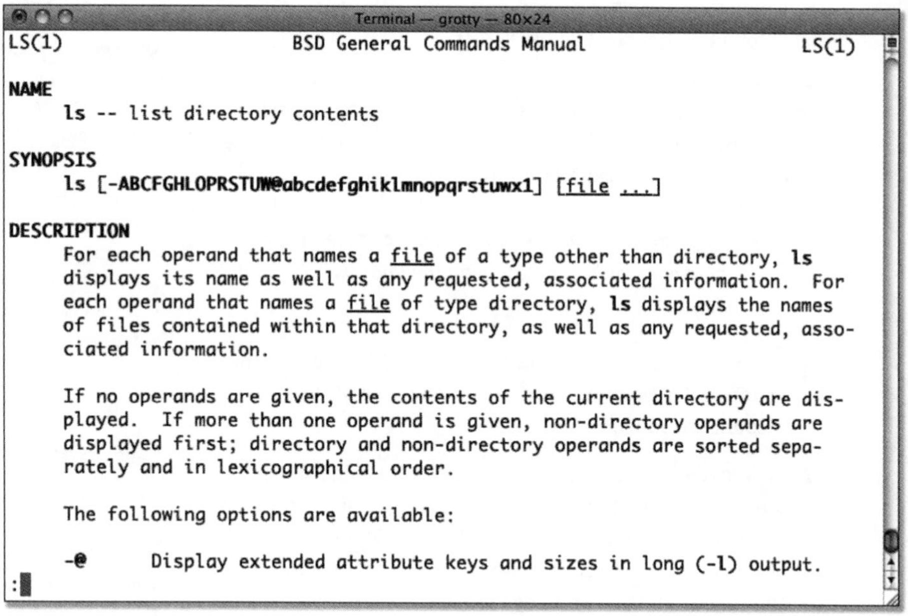

Figure 26.5
You can get extensive information about any command by using the man command.

```
● ○ ○                    Terminal — grotty — 80×24
LS(1)                    BSD General Commands Manual                    LS(1)

NAME
     ls -- list directory contents

SYNOPSIS
     ls [-ABCFGHLOPRSTUW@abcdefghiklmnopqrstuwx1] [file ...]

DESCRIPTION
     For each operand that names a file of a type other than directory, ls
     displays its name as well as any requested, associated information.  For
     each operand that names a file of type directory, ls displays the names
     of files contained within that directory, as well as any requested, asso-
     ciated information.

     If no operands are given, the contents of the current directory are dis-
     played.  If more than one operand is given, non-directory operands are
     displayed first; directory and non-directory operands are sorted sepa-
     rately and in lexicographical order.

     The following options are available:

     -e        Display extended attribute keys and sizes in long (-l) output.
:
```

2. Press the spacebar to move to the next page.

3. Continue reading the manual pages until you have the information you need.

4. Press Q to return to the command prompt.

It is a good idea to take a look at the manual pages for any Unix commands you use. Pay special attention to the list of options that are available for the command.

Using Superuser Commands

As you learned earlier in the book, the root account is the fundamental user account that can do *anything* under Mac OS X. The root account has more access to the system than even an administrator account does. Using this account can be hazardous to your system because, when you're under root, the OS assumes that you know what you're doing and doesn't provide any checks on your activities. You can easily delete things you don't mean to or mess up the system itself.

 note

Some Unix applications provide manual pages using the help argument. For example, `perl --help` brings up information about the Perl application.

 tip

Pressing the spacebar moves you down the manual page one screen's worth at a time; you can move down a manual page one line at a time by pressing the Return key instead.

However, when you need to use a specific command at a specific time that you can't do under another user account, it can be helpful to enter commands as root.

Command: sudo
Option: -s, which runs the command in the default shell
What it does: Gets you into the root account so you can enter a command that you can't enter under another account

➥ *For help activating the root account and creating a password for it, **see** "Enabling the Root User Account," p. 461.*

1. Open a new Terminal window or a new tab in an existing window. The prompt shows the short name of the user account you're logged in under.

2. Type **sudo -s** and press Return. If you're using the sudo command for the first time in a session, you may see a warning regarding what you're about to do and be prompted to enter your password; enter your password and press Return. If you have logged in as root previously, you won't have to enter the password again. When the sudo command is successful, the prompt shows the shell you're using (see Figure 26.6).

caution
Be very careful about the commands you enter while logged in to the root account. You can potentially do damage to your system—even an errant keystroke could result in unexpected and undesired results. You should use the root account only when you really have to, and even then, you need to be very careful about the commands you enter while you're working on the root prompt.

note
Not all account types can access the root account. You must be logged in as an administrator account to be able to properly run the sudo command.

```
● ○ ○              Terminal — bash — 80×24
Last login: Wed Jun  3 11:43:51 on console
Pauls-Mac-mini:~ paul$ sudo -s
Password:
bash-3.2# ▮
```

Figure 26.6
The bash-3.2# prompt indicates that you're logged in under the root account; be careful when you see this prompt.

To return to the previous account, type **exit** and press Return. You'll return to the prompt showing your previous user account. You should do this as soon as you finish entering commands under the root account to lessen the chance that you'll do something you don't intend.

Killing a Process

When a process (such as a running program or system service) goes wrong, it can cause problems, such as hanging, or it might start consuming tremendous amounts of processing power, thus bringing your system's performance to a crawl. You can tell that a process has gone out of control by monitoring its percentage of CPU usage. If this number gets high and stays there, the process is likely hung.

The top command allows you to view information about the different applications and processes that are running on your Mac. Because the information generated by the top command is dynamic, you should open it in a Terminal window and then open another window or tab to enter commands. Under Mac OS X, there are several ways to stop an out-of-control process. For applications, you can use the Force Quit command. At the process level, you can use the Process Viewer to force a process to quit. You can also use the powerful Unix command kill to stop a running process.

Command: kill *ProcessID*
Option: -9 kills the process no matter what; -3 quits the process
What it does: Stops the process with the ID number *ProcessID*

1. Launch the Terminal.

2. Type **top**. You see a listing of all the processes currently running on your Mac (see Figure 26.7). Use the information in the table to identify the problematic process, such as one that is consuming an unreasonable amount of processing power. In this example, assume that Safari has gone out of control (as you can see in the figure, Safari is using 99.9% of the CPU, so it might have a problem). In the figure, Safari's process ID number is 57156.

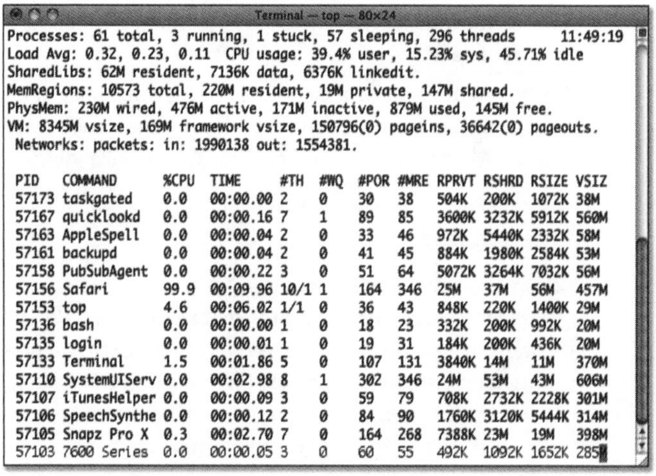

Figure 26.7
This top window shows all the processes running on your Mac; you can use the process ID with the kill command to stop any running process.

3. Open a new tab by selecting File, New Tab (⌘-T).

4. Type **kill -9 57156**. (Of course, you would actually type the process number for the process you want to kill.) The -9 option specifies that the computer cannot ignore the kill command.

5. Switch back to the Terminal tab showing top. The process that you killed no longer appears in the process list. You can use the same steps to kill any process by using the process ID of that process.

You can stop the top process by pressing Control+C.

note

If the process you're trying to kill is an Administrator process, you have to use the sudo -s command to get into the root account before you use the kill command.

Working with Basic Unix Applications

You learned earlier that several Unix applications are included with Mac OS X. Although you're not likely to use these instead of your Mac OS X applications for your everyday work, sometimes these applications can be quite useful. For example, you might want to use the vi text editor to create shell scripts. A couple of simple examples show you how such applications work.

Editing Text with vi

The Unix application vi is a basic text editor. You can use it to create and edit text files, but it is most useful for creating shell scripts. You're unlikely to use it to create text documents, but you can use it to create plain-text documents if you would like.

The vi program has two modes: Edit and Command. In Edit mode, you can enter and edit text. In Command mode, you can issue commands to the program. Try the following:

1. Type **man vi**. Read the manual pages to get an idea of how vi works.

2. Open a new Terminal window (⌘-N) or a new Terminal tab (⌘-T) and type **vi** and the name of the text file you want to create, such as vi mytextfile.txt. The program opens, the file is created in the current directory, and you see a screen containing tilde symbols in the editing area. At the bottom of the screen, you see the vi command line.

3. Type **i** to enter Insert mode.

4. Type your text.

5. Press Esc to move into Command mode. While you're in Command mode, you hear an alert sound if you try to type anything that isn't a recognized vi command; you also see a prompt at the bottom of the vi window telling you that the text you typed isn't a recognized command.

tip

To save long manual pages for a command, use the man command on that command and press the spacebar to reveal the entire text of the manual pages. Select the manual text you want to save in a file and select File, Save Selected Text As. Name the text file and save it. You can then refer to that file when you need help with that command.

note

Determining which mode you're in can be confusing. When you enter Command mode, the cursor appears to jump back a couple of spaces and the bottom line of the window is empty. You can then type a command. If you see text on the screen when you type, you're in Edit mode. You also see -INSERT- at the bottom of the screen.

6. Type **:w** and press Return to write the text to the file you created. At the bottom of the vi window, you see confirmation that the text has been written to the file (see Figure 26.8).

Figure 26.8
The message at the bottom of this vi window indicates that one line of text has been written to the file mytextfile.txt.

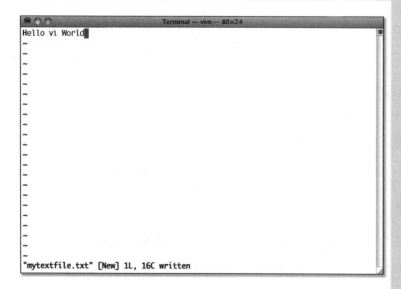

7. To continue adding text to the file, type **a**. The command line disappears and the cursor becomes active after the last text you entered.

8. Continue adding text and writing it to the file.

9. When you're done, press Esc to enter Command mode; then type **:wq** and press Return to quit vi. You return to the command line.

Because GUI text editors are available, you might not want to use Unix text editors such as vi, but for short, plain-text documents, such as a shell script, these editors can be useful.

To edit an existing file with vi, type **vi *filename***, where *filename* is the name of the file you want to edit, and press Return. The file opens and you can begin editing it.

If you intend to use vi, make sure that you read its manual pages in detail; vi has many commands available, but they are hard to figure out without help.

Compressing, Uncompressing, and Extracting Files

Unix has some built-in programs to enable you to work with compressed files, including the following:

- To compress a file, type **compress *filename***. The file named *filename* is compressed and a .Z is appended to its name.

- To uncompress a file, type **uncompress *filename***, where *filename* is the name of the compressed file. The file is uncompressed.

- You can also use the gzip compression application by typing **gzip** *filename*. Uncompress the file using the gun- zip command. gzip offers various options; check its manual pages to see them.

note

The tar command also has various options; check its manual pages for help.

Many Unix files are archived in the tar (tape archive) format before they are compressed. After you compress such files, you see a file that has the .tar extension. You can extract a tar file using the command tar xvf *filename*, where *filename* is the name of the tar file.

Unix Resources

Using Unix proficiently requires some additional learning—Unix is a very complex and sophisticated tool that you should become familiar with to master Mac OS X. To help you get slightly farther along that road, in this last section of the chapter you learn some keyboard shortcuts that help you use the Terminal application more efficiently. I also provide you with a few references to websites and books that can help you learn Unix in more depth.

Using Terminal Keyboard Shortcuts

Table 26.1 lists keyboard shortcuts for the Terminal application.

Table 26.1 Terminal Keyboard Shortcuts

Action	Shortcut
Use Selection for Find	⌘-E
Find Next	⌘-G
Find	⌘-F
Find Previous	Shift+⌘-G
Jump to Selection	⌘-J
Line Down	⌘-Down arrow
Line Up	⌘-Up arrow
Clear Screen	⌘-L
New Command	Shift+⌘-N
Next Page	Spacebar
Cycle Through Windows	⌘-'
New Window Basic	⌘-N
New Tab	⌘-T
Export Selected Text As	Shift+⌘-S
Export Text As	⌘-S
Send Reset	⌘-R
Set Title	Shift+⌘-T
Show Inspector	⌘-I

Learning Unix

The following list describes websites for learning more about Unix:

- www.ee.surrey.ac.uk/Teaching/Unix/—Site name: Unix Tutorial for Beginners. This is a nicely organized and fairly extensive reference site.

- freeengineer.org/learnUNIXin10minutes.html—Site name: Learn Unix in 10 minutes. This is a short but clear Unix tutorial.

- www.comet.ucar.edu/strc/unix/index.htm—Site name: SOO/STRC Unix Resources. This is a page containing links to other Unix learning sites.

The following list describes some recommended books for learning more about Unix:

- *Sams Teach Yourself Unix in 10 Minutes*—Author: Robert Shimonski. This is a good "fast and easy" entry into the world of Unix.

- *Sams Teach Yourself Unix in 24 Hours, Second Edition*—Author: Dave Taylor. This contains 24 one-hour lessons to get you into Unix.

- *The Complete Idiot's Guide to Unix*—Author: Bill Wagner. This book's friendly approach to Unix is good if you prefer a less structured approach than the *Sams Teach Yourself* books.

- *Practical Guide to Unix for Mac OS X Users*—Authors: Mark G. Sobell, Peter Seebach. This is a comprehensive Unix reference aimed at Mac OS X users. This is a good resource to have when you become comfortable with Unix and want to explore it in great detail.

USING THE MAC OS X NOTEBOOK FEATURES

Using Mac OS X on a Mobile Computer

Whether you have a MacBook, a MacBook Pro, or a MacBook Air, using Mac OS X on your notebook isn't fundamentally different than using it on a desktop system. You interact with the same desktop, run the same applications, deal with the same types of files and folders, and set most of the same preferences. This is good news if you're moving from a desktop machine to a notebook (or adding a notebook to your Mac collection), because it means there's only a small learning curve ahead of you, as you see in this chapter.

Managing Your Mobile Mac's Power

The factor that makes a mobile Mac mobile is the capability to run using battery power. This is obviously an advantage, but it also adds another task for you, which is managing that power so you maximize your battery life and thus your working time while on the move.

Monitoring Battery Status

On a mobile machine, Mac OS X displays the battery status icon in the menu bar by default, and you use this icon to monitor the current power state of your Mac. When the battery is fully charged and you're running on the AC adapter, you see the plug icon, as shown in Figure 27.1.

Battery status icon

Figure 27.1
The battery status icon on the menu bar keeps you informed of the power state of your mobile Mac.

When you switch to battery power, the battery status icon's plug changes to a solid black rectangle. This rectangle represents the amount of power you have left. At first, the rectangle fills the icon because you have 100% power. As you use your Mac, the battery slowly drains, and this drain is represented by the rectangle shrinking within the battery status icon. For example, when your Mac's battery power reaches 50%, the rectangle takes up only half the icon (see Figure 27.2).

Figure 27.2
When the Mac is running without AC, the battery status icon shows a graphic representation of the remaining battery power.

When you plug the power adapter back into the Mac, you see a lightning bolt inside the battery status icon (see Figure 27.3) to indicate that the battery is charging.

Figure 27.3
When you connect the Mac to a power source again, the battery status icon displays a lightning bolt while the battery is recharging.

Using the Battery Status Menu

The battery status icon is useful for getting a general overview of the current state of the battery. To get a bit more detail, click the battery status icon to open the battery status menu. As you can see in Figure 27.4, the first item in the menu gives you an approximation of the amount of time you have left before running out of battery power. The second items tells you the current source of power for your mobile Mac (Power Adapter or Battery).

You can also use this menu to configure the battery status icon:

- Select Show, Time to show the time remaining for the battery or for the charging process next to the icon.

- Select Show, Percentage to show the percent of power remaining for the battery (see Figure 27.4) or for the charging process next to the icon.

- Select Show, Icon Only to show just the icon.

 note

When you are running on battery power and choose to show time or percentage, the first item on the battery status menu is always the opposite of what you have selected to display with the icon. For example, when you choose to display percentage on the icon, the time is shown on the menu (see Figure 27.4), and the reverse. If you don't show time or percentage with the icon, you still see the time remaining on the menu.

Figure 27.4
Click the battery status icon to display the battery status menu.

Maximizing Battery Life

The ultimate and constant challenge of using a mobile Mac when running on the battery is to make your power last as long as possible. You should consider the following steps to maximize your battery life:

- **Dim your screen**—Your Mac's screen is a major source of power consumption. If you dim the screen, it requires less power and thus extends your battery life. To dim your screen, use the Brightness slider on the Displays pane of the System Preferences application or the appropriate function key. Dim the display as much as you can while still being able to see it comfortably. For example, when you are traveling on a darkened airplane, you can set your display brightness to a lower level than when you are using it in a well-lit room.

- **Configure the Energy Saver pane for the work you are doing while you are on the move**—Use the Energy Saver

 tip

To remove the battery status icon and menu from the menu bar, open the Energy Saver pane of the System Preferences application and deactivate the Show Battery Status In the Menu Bar check box.

tip

Recent notebook Macs have dedicated function keys to control screen brightness, typically F1 to lower brightness and F2 to increase it. When you press one of these keys, an onscreen level indicator pops up to show you the relative brightness level and how you are changing it.

pane to configure your mobile Mac's power usage to maximize battery life. You learn how this works in the next section ("Configuring Power Use").

- **Avoid applications that constantly read from a CD or DVD**—The CD or DVD drive is another major source of power use. If you can copy files you need onto your hard drive and use them from there, you will use power at a lower rate than if your Mac is constantly accessing its removable media drive. In some cases, such as when you are watching a DVD movie, this isn't possible. At other times, however, you can store the files you need on the hard drive. For example, when you want to listen to music, you can add the songs to your iTunes Music Library so you don't need to use the CD or DVD drive.

- **Turn off AirPort if you don't need it** —When AirPort is on, it regularly checks for available wireless networks, which drains the battery. If you don't need to connect to a wireless network, turn off AirPort to conserve energy. Click the AirPort status icon in the menu bar and then click Turn AirPort Off. (If you aren't displaying the AirPort status icon, open System Preferences, click Network, click AirPort, and then click Turn AirPort Off.)

- **Turn off Bluetooth if you don't need it**—When Bluetooth is running, it constantly checks for nearby Bluetooth devices, and this also drains the battery. If you aren't using any Bluetooth devices, turn off Bluetooth to save energy. Click the Bluetooth status icon in the menu bar and then click Turn Bluetooth Off. (If you aren't displaying the Bluetooth status icon, open System Preferences, click Bluetooth, and then deactivate the On check box.)

- **Put your Mac to sleep whenever you aren't actively using it**—You can put your Mac to sleep by selecting Apple menu, Sleep, by pressing Option-⌘-Eject, or by closing your mobile Mac's lid. Your Mac instantly wakes up when you open it or press a key, so putting it to sleep frequently doesn't cause a lot of wasted time for you.

 note

When your Mac sleeps, all active processes are stopped, the screen goes dark, and the disk or disc drives stop. This reduces your Mac's power use to the bare minimum. A Mac in Sleep mode can survive a long time, but of course, it can't do anything while it is asleep. You need to strike a balance between the length of pauses in your work and the sleep time.

Configuring Power Use

 tip

One of the most important power management tasks is to actively use the Mac's Energy Saver pane of the System Preferences application. This enables you to customize your Mac's energy settings to maximize battery life for the type of work you are doing. Follow these steps:

Because the screen is such a major consumer of power, you should have the display sleep after only a few minutes of inactivity when you configure your mobile Mac for operating in battery power.

1. Open the System Preferences application and click Energy Saver. (You can also click the battery status icon and then click Open Energy Saver.) The Energy Saver preferences appear, as shown in Figure 27.5.

Figure 27.5
Use the Energy Saver preferences to configure your Mac's power usage.

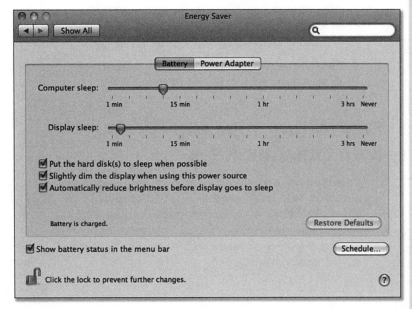

2. Click the Battery tab.

3. Use the Computer Sleep slider to control the amount of idle time before the entire system goes to sleep. Setting a shorter sleep time causes your Mac to sleep frequently, thus conserving battery power. But this can also interrupt your work. Set the Sleep slider to a value that is just longer than normal pauses in your work.

4. Use the Display Sleep slider to set the amount of idle time before the screen goes dark.

5. Unless you have a very good reason not to, leave the Put the Hard Disk(s) to Sleep When Possible check box activated. The hard disk is another major consumer of power, and putting it to sleep saves significant amounts of energy. This setting causes your Mac to put the hard drives to sleep when they aren't actively being used, which is a good thing when your goal is to minimize power consumption.

6. By default, Mac OS X automatically dims the display to conserve power when you switch to the battery. If you find the dimmed screen hard to read, deactivate the Slightly Dim the Display When Using This Power Source check box.

 note

Normally, when you're running on battery power you want the screen to sleep rather than have the screen saver kick in because the screen saver consumes battery power for processing and screen display. Therefore, it's a good idea to set the Display Sleep value to a lower idle time than your screen saver.

 note

When your battery power starts getting low (about 10% remaining), you start to see low-power warning dialog boxes. If you continue to use your Mac to lower power levels, eventually the screen dims. When your Mac is on its last electron, it goes to sleep, which prevents you from losing any data. The only way to revive your Mac is to connect it to the power adapter.

7. If you leave the Automatically Reduce Brightness Before Display Goes to Sleep check box activated, Mac OS X dims the display automatically before it puts your Mac to sleep. This saves a bit of battery power, but it's also a useful indicator that display sleep mode is about to start, so if you want to keep reading what's on the screen, jiggle the mouse to return to normal brightness.

8. If you also want to configure power options for when your Mac is using the AC adapter, click the Power Adapter tab and then repeat steps 3–7.

Controlling Your Mobile Mac with Function Keys

As with all Mac keyboards, the function keys on a mobile Mac are the top row of keys, and they usually show both an icon and standard function key text. On mobile Mac keyboards, the function keys run F1 to F12. Table 27.1 presents a summary of the special features associated with F1 through F12 on modern notebook Mac keyboards.

 caution

The function key associations for the special features listed in Table 27.1 are standard on current Mac notebook keyboards, but Apple seems to change them regularly. So your old Mac keyboard might not be set up this way, and it's quite possible that future keyboard designs might change this layout yet again.

Table 27.1 Special Features Associated with Standard Function Keys

Key	What the Icon Represents
F1	Reduce screen brightness
F2	Increase screen brightness
F3	Launch Exposé
F4	Launch Dashboard
F5	Reduce keyboard brightness
F6	Increase keyboard brightness
F7	Skip to beginning of current media track or to previous media track
F8	Play/pause current media
F9	Skip to next media track
F10	Toggle volume mute
F11	Reduce volume
F12	Increase volume

What if you want to use a key as a standard function key? For example, in some applications pressing F1 invokes the Help system. To get a standard function keystroke (such as F1) instead of a special function, hold down Fn and press the key (for example, Fn+F1).

Using and Configuring the Trackpad

If you have a MacBook, MacBook Pro, or MacBook Air, you can always connect an external mouse, but you might prefer just to use the trackpad. If so, it helps to know how to use the hidden features of the trackpad. You saw earlier that you can unlock the trackpad's ability to display shortcut menus, but it also has a few other features:

 tip

If you prefer to have F1, F2, and so on work as standard function keys without having to hold the Fn key down while you press them, open the System Preferences application, click the Keyboard icon, and then click the Keyboard tab. Activate the Use All F1, F2, etc. Keys as Standard Function Keys check box. If you do this, you have to hold down the FN while pressing the appropriate hardware control key (such as F1 to lower the screen's brightness).

- **Two-finger scrolling**—If you need to scroll a window or document, don't bother dragging the scroll bar. Instead, drag two fingers along the trackpad: drag them left and right to scroll horizontally; drag them up and down to scroll vertically. (Or, if you prefer, place two fingers on the trackpad and then drag just one finger to scroll.)

- **Dragging**—To drag an object with the trackpad, press and hold the trackpad button and then drag a finger along the trackpad.

- **Control+scroll**—Use this technique to zoom the Mac window. Hold down Control and drag two fingers toward the top of the trackpad to zoom in; hold down Control and drag two fingers toward the bottom of the trackpad to zoom out.

If you've got a Mac notebook with a multi-touch trackpad (such as the MacBook Air or the latest MacBook and MacBook Pro models), you get even more techniques to play around with:

- **Pinch and spread**—Use these techniques to zoom in on or out of an object such as a photo or a web page. To pinch means to move two fingers closer together on the trackpad to zoom in; to spread means to move two fingers apart on the trackpad to zoom out.

- **Rotate**—Use this technique to rotate an object such as a photo clockwise or counterclockwise. Place two fingers on the trackpad, about an inch apart. Drag the fingers clockwise on the trackpad to rotate the object clockwise; drag your fingers counterclockwise on the trackpad to rotate the object counterclockwise.

- **Three-finger navigation**—Use this technique to move from one object to the next in applications that can display multiple objects. For example, if you have multiple photos open in the Preview application, swipe three fingers quickly across the trackpad to the right to navigate to the next item; swipe three fingers to the left to navigate to the previous item.

- **Invoke Exposé**—Place four fingers on the trackpad and swipe down to launch Exposé and tile the open windows; swipe down to use Exposé to display the desktop.

- **Switch applications**—Place four fingers on the trackpad and swipe left or right to display icons for your running applications. Then use a single finger to drag the mouse pointer to the application icon you want, then click to switch to the application.

The techniques above are built into the trackpad, but they don't represent everything you can do with a modern trackpad. Open System Preferences and click the Trackpad icon to display the Trackpad preferences, as shown in Figure 27.6.

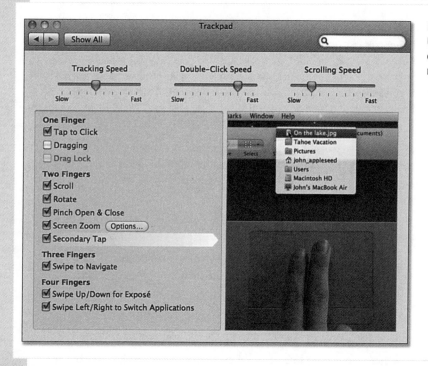

Figure 27.6
Use the Trackpad preferences to configure your mobile Mac's trackpad.

Here are the trackpad features you can activate using these preferences:

- **Trackpad clicking**—Although older Mac notebooks support trackpad clicking, many recent models do not. Instead, you have to click the button. However, Mac OS X provides a solution. In the Trackpad preferences, activate the Tap to Click check box.

- **One-finger dragging**—The two-finger drag methods explained earlier work, but it would be easier if you could just use one finger to do it. In the Trackpad preferences, activate the Tap to Click check box, and then activate the Dragging check box. You can now drag windows and other objects without having to hold down the trackpad button. To do this, move the mouse pointer over the object and double-tap the trackpad, but leave your finger on the trackpad. (If you take your finger off, your Mac assumes you're double-clicking.) Drag your finger along the trackpad to drag the object along with it.

- **Drag Lock**—If you've got a long way to drag something, even the simple one-finger drag might not work very well. To work around this, you can use the Drag Lock feature. To turn this on, activate the Tap to Click check box, activate the Dragging check box, and then activate the Drag Lock check box. To use Drag Lock, position the mouse pointer over the object and double-tap the trackpad, but leave your finger on the trackpad. Drag your finger along the trackpad to drag the object along with it. After you've dragged the object, you can remove your finger, and then resume dragging at any time because your Mac is "locked" in drag mode. To exit drag mode, tap the trackpad.

- **Right-clicking**—You might have noticed that the button below the trackpad doesn't right-click, which means you need to hold down Control and click any part of the button to bring up a short-cut menu. Fortunately, you can configure the trackpad to display shortcut menus without need-ing to press the Control key. In the Trackpad preferences, activate the Secondary Tap check box. What you've done here is configured your Mac notebook to display a shortcut menu by tapping the trackpad with two fingers instead of just one.

Configuring and Using Locations

As you move your mobile Mac around, you will probably want to connect to different networks from different locations. For example, you might use an AirPort network to connect to the Internet at home, an Ethernet network to connect when you are at work, and a wireless hotspot when you are on the road.

The Mac OS X Location Manager feature enables you to config-ure multiple network configurations on your Mac. You can then switch among these configurations easily (rather than having to manually reconfigure your Mac each time you change loca-tions).

note

You can have more than one active port on the same machine, meaning you can have different means of con-necting to a network active at the same time (such as AirPort and Ethernet). You don't need to have a location for each active port. You should use locations when you want to be able to switch easily among different *sets* of active ports.

Creating a New Location

To configure a new network location, use the following steps:

1. Open the Network pane of the System Preferences application.

2. On the Location pop-up menu, select Edit Locations. The Locations sheet appears. In the pane, you see the locations on your Mac.

3. Click the Add Location button (the plus sign) at the bottom of the Locations. A new location is created and its name is highlighted to show you it can be edited.

4. Type a name for the new location (see Figure 27.7) and then press Return.

Figure 27.7
Use the Location sheet to create a new location.

5. Click Done. The sheet closes and you return to the Network pane with the new Location automatically selected in the Location pop-up menu.

6. Click Add Service (the plus sign). Mac OS X prompts you to select an interface.

7. Choose a network interface (such as AirPort or Ethernet), type a name for the service, and then click Done.

8. Repeat steps 6–8 to add any other services you need for this location.

9. Configure each service for the location. For example, select Ethernet and then use the tools in the right pane of the window to configure the Ethernet connection for the new location.

➡ *For help configuring an Internet connection, **see** Chapter 13, "Connecting Your Mac to the Internet," **p. 267.***

➡ *For help configuring an Ethernet network connection, **see** Chapter 17, "Wired Networking with Mac OS X," **p. 361.***

➡ *For help configuring an AirPort connection, **see** Chapter 18, "Wireless Networking with Mac OS X," **p. 385.***

10. Open the Action menu at the bottom of the Services pane and choose Set Service Order.

11. In the resulting sheet, arrange the order of the connection methods in the list to be the order in which you want your Mac to try to connect to the network. Drag the first method you want to be tried at the top of the list, the second one in the second spot, and so on. For example, if you

want to use Ethernet first and then AirPort, drag Ethernet to the top of the list and place AirPort underneath it. When your Mac connects to the network, it will try these connections in the order in which they are listed. When you're done, click OK. When you return to the Network pane, you see the services in the order you configured them.

12. Click Apply to apply your new location settings.

Changing Your Mac's Location

To change the location your Mac is using, open the Network pane of the System Preferences application and choose the location you want to use on the Location pop-up menu. If the Apply button becomes active, click it to Apply the location; some configuration changes require this while others don't.

Editing or Deleting Locations

You can edit or remove locations by following these steps:

1. Open the Network pane of the System Preferences application.

2. Select Edit Locations from the Location pop-up menu. The Locations sheet appears.

3. Select the location you want to change.

4. Rename the location by selecting it, pressing the Return key, entering the new name, and pressing Return again.

5. Delete a location you no longer use by selecting it and choosing Delete Location (minus sign).

6. To duplicate a location select it, open the Action menu at the bottom of the Locations pane, and choose Duplicate Location; you can then rename it to something that describes that location.

7. Click Done. You return to the Network pane.

8. Make any other changes to the location selected in the Location pop-up menu and click Apply.

9. Close the System Preferences application.

➡ *To learn how to use FileVault,* **see** *"Securing Your Mac with FileVault,"* **p. 707**.

 tip

To protect your mobile Mac's data in the event someone swipes it, use Mac OS X's FileVault feature to encrypt your data so anyone who takes your mobile Mac won't be able to use its data.

Keeping Your Files in Sync

As you move around with your mobile Mac, you'll find all kinds of great things to do with it. Some of these might even involve work. If you work on files on your mobile Mac, it is highly likely that you will want to move those files to or from another Mac, such as your desktop Mac. There are a lot of ways to accomplish this:

- Store the files you are going to share between your mobile Mac and other machines on your MobileMe iDisk. Then set your iDisk to synchronize automatically on all machines. The same versions of those files will be accessible on all your Macs automatically (and they will be backed up on your iDisk, too).

  ➡ *To learn how to use an iDisk,* ***see*** *"Using Your iDisk,"* **p. 427.**

- Before and after a session on your mobile Mac, connect the mobile Mac to the network that your desktop Mac is on and use file sharing to move the files back and forth between the machines. (Make sure you move the correct version so you don't accidentally replace a newer version with an older one.)

- Email files to yourself. This is easier to do if you have more than one email account. For example, use a MobileMe email account for your regular email and another account just on one machine. You can send files to yourself via that address. The big problem with this method is that most email gateways allow only relatively small files to be sent (usually less than 5MB).

- Put files on CD, DVD, or an external hard drive (an iPod is excellent for this), and then copy them onto a different machine.

One of the harder aspects of keeping files synchronized between a mobile Mac and other machines is knowing exactly which files changed during your most recent use of the mobile Mac. With Mac OS X's smart folders, you can make even this easy to do:

1. Create a new smart folder.

2. Configure it to find files whose Kind is Documents and that were Last Modified Within Last 2 Days (or some other timeframe that you choose).

3. Save the smart folder.

Each time you open this smart folder, you will see the document files that have changed within the timeframe you specify. This makes it simple to know which files you need to move to your desktop Mac or other location.

  ➡ *To learn how to configure and use smart folders,* ***see*** *"Searching Your Mac with Smart Folders,"* **p. 97.**

WORKING WITH DASHBOARD AND WIDGETS

Using Dashboard and Widgets

Your Mac comes equipped with about 20 or so mini-applications called *widgets* that perform very specific tasks such as showing the weather, displaying stock quotes, or making simple calculations. Instead of cluttering your desktop with these widgets, Mac OS X gives you a separate layer of screen real estate called Dashboard. When you invoke Dashboard, your Mac sends your desktop and its windows into the background, and brings Dashboard and its widget collection into the foreground.

Activating and Deactivating Dashboard

Mac OS X gives you three main ways to activate Dashboard:

- Press F4. (On older Mac keyboards you can usually invoke Dashboard by pressing either F12 or Fn+F12).

- Click Dashboard icon on the Dock.

- Click the scroll ball on Apple's Mighty Mouse.

 tip

If you're having trouble launching Dashboard via the keyboard on your mobile Mac, you can find out which key or key combination your Mac uses. Run System Preferences, click Exposé & Spaces, and select the Exposé tab. In the Dashboard section, check the key listed on the Hide and Show pop-up menu to determine what the default Dashboard activation key is on your Mac.

Whichever method you use, Dashboard appears and it displays its open widgets, as shown in Figure 28.1.

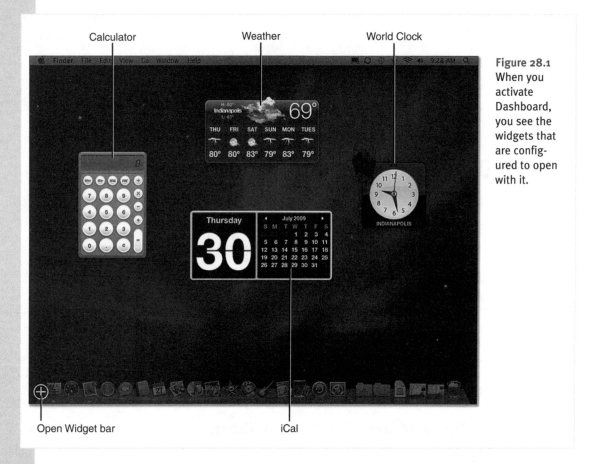

Calculator   Weather   World Clock

Open Widget bar   iCal

Figure 28.1
When you activate Dashboard, you see the widgets that are configured to open with it.

When you are done using the widgets, you deactivate Dashboard by pressing the default hot key (usually F12), by clicking the desktop outside of any open widget, or by clicking the Mighty Mouse scroll ball. All the widgets disappear and you return to your Mac's desktop.

Configuring the Widgets That Open When You Activate Dashboard

By default, on most Macs you see the Calculator, Weather, iCal, and World Clock widgets when you activate Dashboard. However, as mentioned earlier, Mac OS X comes with more than 20 widgets, so you can configure which widgets open when you activate Dashboard. Here are the steps to follow:

1. Activate Dashboard.

2. Click the Open Widget bar button (pointed out in Figure 28.1). The Widget bar opens and you see some of the widgets that are currently installed on your Mac (see Figure 28.2). The Widgets

appear in alphabetical order from left to right (with the exception of the Widgets widget, which is always the first one in the list).

Close buttons

Figure 28.2
The Widget bar shows the widgets that are currently installed on your Mac.

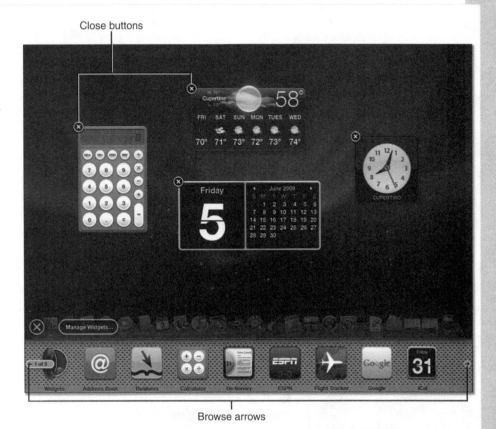

Browse arrows

3. Scroll through the installed widgets using the Browse arrows. At the bottom of each widget's icon, you see the widget's name.

4. To have a widget open when you activate Dashboard, click its icon on the Widget bar or drag it from the Widget bar onto the screen and then drop the widget where you want it to appear.

5. If the widget isn't in the right location, drag the widget to your preferred spot on the screen.

6. To close a widget that you don't want to open when you activate Dashboard, click the widget's Close button, which is the "X" located in the upper-left corner of each widget's window.

 tip

You can open multiple instances of the same widget at the same time by continuing to click its icon or dragging it from the Widget bar onto Dashboard. Each time you do so, a new version of that widget appears. This is useful for some widgets such as the Weather widget if you are interested in information about the weather in more than one area.

7. Repeat steps 3–6 to configure Dashboard to your liking.

8. Close the Widget bar by clicking the Close button, which is the X located just above the Widget bar. The next time you activate Dashboard, you will see and can use the widgets as you configured them.

 tip

You can close a widget whenever Dashboard is active by holding down the Option key and then hovering the mouse pointer over the widget to display the Close button. Click the button to close the widget.

Using and Customizing Useful Widgets

Mac OS X includes a number of useful widgets along with some that aren't so useful. In this section, you'll find a mini-review of some of the default widgets I think are worth using.

➡ *To learn how to remove widgets that you don't use,* **see** *"Removing Widgets from Dashboard," 572.*

➡ *To learn how to install widgets in Dashboard,* **see** *"Finding and Installing More Widgets," 572.*

 tip

You don't need to close the Widget bar. When you deactivate Dashboard, the Widget bar is closed automatically. The next time you activate Dashboard, the Widget bar remains closed.

Using the Widgets Widget

The Widgets widget, which is the first one on the Widget bar even though it isn't the first one alphabetically, enables you to use a widget to manage the widgets on your Dashboard (see Figure 28.3).

Figure 28.3
You can use the Widgets widget to manage your widgets.

Widget available only
under current user account

Here are some notes to bear in mind about this widget:

- The widget's list shows all of the widgets installed under the current user account. You can scroll the list or resize the widget to see more or fewer of the available widgets.

- Choose how you want the list sorted by choosing Sort by Name or Sort by Date on the drop-down list at the top of the widget.

- You can disable a widget by deactivating its check box. Dashboard closes the widget if it's currently open, and removes it from the Widget bar. However, this doesn't actually remove the widget from your computer. You can restore a widget by activating its check box again.

- Widgets marked with a red circle with a line in it (see Figure 28.3) are available only under the current user account.

- You can look for more widgets on Apple's website by clicking the More Widgets button (see "Finding and Downloading Widgets," later in this chapter).

Using the Address Book Widget

The Address Book widget enables you to access information in your Address Book more quickly than by using the Address Book application itself. The Address Book widget provides a number of useful tools as you can see in Figure 28.4 and in the following list:

- View a contact's information in the Address Book widget's window. If not all of a contact's information fits in the window, use the scroll arrows that appear to move up and down in the contact's information.

- Browse contact information by clicking the Previous or Next buttons.

- Search for a contact by typing the name of the contact in the Search tool. As you type, the contacts in the window are reduced to include only those that meet your search text. You can only search by name. When the list contains the contact whose information you want to view, click it and the contact's information fills the widget.

- Use the linked information for a contact to perform an action. For example, click an email address to send an email to the contact (when you do this, Mail opens and a message to the recipient is created). Similarly, if you click an address, your web browser opens and the address appears on a Google map.

- To view unlinked information (such as a telephone number) at a larger size, click it. Dashboard magnifies the information on the screen.

Figure 28.4
The Address Book widget is a quick way to view and work with a contact's data.

Using the Calculator Widget

The Calculator widget is simple, but useful. When it appears on the screen, you can use it to perform basic calculations (see Figure 28.5). You can "press" the Calculator's keys using the mouse or the keyboard.

Figure 28.5
Use the Calculator widget to make simple calculations.

Using the iCal Widget

The iCal widget presents an onscreen calendar that you can use to view dates, such as today's date or any date in the past or future (see Figure 28.6). You can see the iCal events you've scheduled for today when you click the date on the left side of the widget.

Today — Previous month — Next month — Today's events

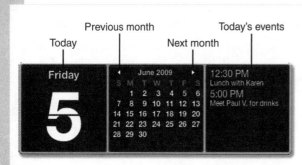

Figure 28.6
You can view today's iCal events by clicking a date in the iCal widget.

Here are some iCal widget pointers:

- Click the date shown on the left side of the widget to expand it to show the month and click again to show the iCal events pane. Keep clicking to collapse the widget again.

- Move ahead or back by a month in the calendar using the Next or Previous buttons or the left and right arrow keys.

- When you expand the widget to see all three panes, the iCal events for the selected date are shown in the far right pane. Unfortunately, only events on the current date are displayed; you have to go into the iCal application to look at events for future dates.

Using the Dictionary Widget

The Dictionary widget is a handy way to access the Mac OS X Dictionary application. You can use the widget both for its dictionary and thesaurus functions. You can also search Apple resources with it. To use this widget, perform the following steps:

1. Activate Dashboard, open the Widget bar, and click Dictionary to open the widget.

2. Use the pop-up menu to choose the mode you want to use: Dictionary, Thesaurus, or Apple.

3. Use the Search box to type the word you want to look up. As you type, the widget finds words that match your search text.

4. If a list of words appears, click the word you want to look up. The word's definition (or synonyms) and other information appears in the widget window, as shown in Figure 28.7.

 tip

The Dictionary widget is one of the few whose window you can resize by dragging its Resize handle.

Figure 28.7
Type a word to look it up in the Dictionary widget.

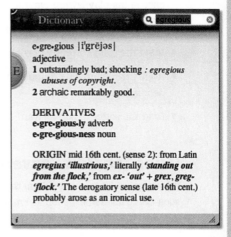

5. To move back to the list of words, click the Back button. Your original search term appears in the Search box again.

6. If the Scroll bar appears instead, use it to move up and down the window to view the entries that meet your search criteria.

Using the iTunes Widget

You can use the iTunes widget to view and control music playback via iTunes. To use it, open iTunes. When iTunes is running, you can use the iTunes widget to select and play music (see Figure 28.8).

Song information

Volume wheel   Slider

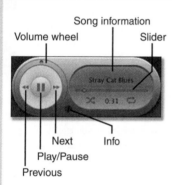

Next   Info

Play/Pause

Previous

Figure 28.8
Use the iTunes widget to take control of your music.

To use the iTunes widget, bear in mind the following notes:

- To choose a playlist, click the Info button. The Select Playlist pop-up menu appears. Use this to choose the playlist you want to hear. Click Done to move to the widget's controls.

- Use the Play/Pause, Previous, and Next buttons to control the music.

- View the song currently playing in the Song information area.

- Adjust the volume by dragging the Volume wheel clockwise to increase it or counterclockwise to decrease it.

- Drag the slider to fast forward or rewind in a song.

Using the Unit Converter Widget

If you ever need to convert from the English system to the metric or vice versa or perform other such unit conversions, such as among different currencies, the Unit Converter widget can take all the work out of the process for you. To use this handy widget, perform the following steps:

1. Activate Dashboard, open the Widget bar, and click Unit Converter to open the widget.

2. Choose the type of unit you want to convert on the Convert pop-up menu. There are many options from which you can choose, including Area, Currency, Energy, and Time.

3. Use the lower-left pop-up menu to choose the specific unit you want to convert. The options you see depend on what you selected on the Convert pop-up menu. For example, if you choose Temperature, the options on this menu are various units of temperature, including Fahrenheit, Celsius, and so on.

4. Use the lower-right pop-up menu to choose the unit into which you want to convert the measurement.

5. Type the data you want to convert in the lower-left box. The converted measurement is shown in the lower-right box (see Figure 28.9).

Figure 28.9
Use the Unit Converter widget to convert weights, measures, and many other units.

Using the Weather Widget

The Weather widget displays current weather conditions and temperature forecasts for a location you select. To use it, perform the following steps:

1. Activate Dashboard and, if the Weather widget isn't already displayed, open the Widget bar, and click Weather to open the widget.

2. Move the pointer over the widget. When you do, the Info button appears in the lower-right corner.

3. Click the Info button to display the widget's configuration tools.

 tip
If you choose a conversion for which data is provided by a third-party, such as Currency, click the Info button to see who is providing the data.

 note
Many widgets, such as the Weather and World Clock widgets, require an Internet connection to work.

4. Use the text box to enter the city or ZIP code for which you want to see weather information. The simplest approach is to enter the ZIP code, but you can enter the city and state if you don't know the ZIP code. When you enter a city's name, a list pops up that shows you all the cities that might match your search. Click the city you want to use.

5. Choose the unit of temperature you want to be displayed on the Degrees pop-up menu. The options are Fahrenheit and Celsius.

6. If you want lows to be included in the 6-day forecast, activate the Include Lows in 6-Day Forecast check box.

7. Click Done. You'll see the city you selected and an icon representing the current weather conditions in that area. Also displayed are the current temperature and the current day's temperature forecast (see Figure 28.10).

Figure 28.10
The Weather widget supplies forecasts for places large and small, such as Pigeon Forge, Tennessee.

Here are a few tips to help you make the most of the Weather widget:

- To hide or show the 6-day forecast, click the widget's window.
- You can track the weather in multiple areas at the same time by opening multiple Weather widgets and configuring each one for the location you're interested in.
- Click the city shown in the Weather widget window to open the Yahoo! Weather site.

Using the World Clock Widget

This simple widget displays the current time in a city of your choice.

1. Activate Dashboard and, if the World Clock widget isn't already displayed, open the Widget bar, and click World Clock to open the widget.

2. Move your mouse pointer over the widget and then click the Info button that appears in the lower-right corner of the widget.

3. Choose the continent in which you are interested on the Region pop-up menu.

4. Choose the city on the City pop-up menu.

5. Click Done. The World Clock widget displays the current time in the city you selected (see Figure 28.11).

Figure 28.11
Use the World Clock widget to keep track of the time in your favorite cities.

Configuring Widgets

In a couple of the previous examples, you saw a step to click a widget's Info button. Some widgets have configurable options, such as setting a location or information source, configuring the information displayed in the widget's window, and so on. Not all widgets have the Info option, but many do. The button is located in various places on different widgets, so there's really no way to know where to look for it on any given widget.

To see if a widget has options, move the pointer over the widget in which you are interested. If it has options, you see the Info button appear; this button is usually a lowercase "i" sometimes inside a circle, sometimes not (see Figure 28.12).

Info

Figure 28.12
This Twitter widget has options.

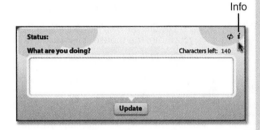

When you click the Info button, the widget's configuration tools appear (see Figure 28.13). You can use those tools to make the widget work or look the way you want it to. When you're finished making changes, click the Done button and the widget is updated accordingly. You should always check out the Info options for any widgets that you use often because they usually provide options to make widgets even more useful to you.

Figure 28.13
Check out the options for any widgets you use regularly.

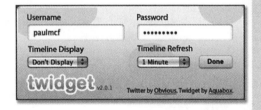

Configuring Dashboard

There are a couple of things you can do to configure Dashboard itself. You can change its hot key and active screen corner and you can remove any widgets you never use.

Setting Dashboard's Hot Key and Active Screen Corner

You can change the default hot key and active screen corner for Dashboard by following these steps:

1. Open System Preferences and then click Exposé and Spaces. The Exposé and Spaces preferences appear.

2. Click the Exposé tab.

3. In the Dashboard section, use the Hide and Show pop-up menu to choose the new hot key.

4. Use the second Hide and Show pop-up menu to choose which mouse button controls Dashboard (if you have a multi-button mouse connected to your Mac, of course).

5. In the Active Screen Corners section, select Dashboard in the pop-up menu that corresponds to the screen corner you want to use to invoke Dashboard. For example, to invoke Dashboard when you move the mouse pointer to the lower-right corner of the screen, select Dashboard in the lower-right pop-up menu.

Removing Widgets from Dashboard

Some of the widgets that come with Mac OS X probably won't be useful to you. You can remove any widgets you won't use by performing the following steps:

1. Open the Widgets folder that is located in Library folder of your startup drive.

2. Drag the widget you don't want to use out of the Widgets folder. If you might want to install it again sometime, save the widget file. If not, you can delete it.

3. Restart your Mac. The undesirable widget no longer appears in Dashboard.

 note

You have to authenticate yourself as an administrator to be able to remove widgets. And if you remove them, no one who uses your Mac can use the widgets you remove. If you think you might use a widget someday, just remove it from Dashboard instead of deleting it from your Mac.

 caution

There's no easy way to recover a built-in Mac OS X widget if you delete its file, so it really is best to save the file in some other location just in case you need it later.

Finding and Installing More Widgets

Some of the default widgets are more useful than others. The good news is that your Dashboard isn't limited to just these widgets. You can add widgets to your Mac in three ways. The first is by capturing sections of web pages as a widget. The second is to download widgets from the web and install them on your Mac. The third is to program your own widgets. In the remaining sections of this chapter, you learn about the first two options. The third one is beyond the scope of this chapter, but if you search the web, you'll find a lot of information about how to create your own widgets.

Building Your Own Widgets with Web Clips

What do you do if you come across a chunk of a web page that you want to save for later use? For example, you find a compelling YouTube video, an engaging Flickr photo, an important craigslist ad, a funny cartoon, or a useful list of links. Saving bits of web pages for easy reuse has never been easy, but Safari offers a method that makes saved web page parts just a click or two away.

The feature that accomplishes this is Safari's Open in Dashboard feature, which can save part of a web page to Dashboard's Web Clip widget. You can then access the page piece at any time just by opening Dashboard.

First, here are the steps to follow to add part of a web page to Dashboard's Web Clip widget:

1. From the web page with the content you want to save, choose File, Open in Dashboard. Safari grays out all of the page except for a small selection window.

2. Click the part of the page that contains the content you want to save:

   - To save an image, click the image and Safari automatically selects the entire image.

   - To save a video, click the video playback window and Safari automatically selects the window.

   - To save any other content, click anywhere within the content (see Figure 28.14).

Figure 28.14
This tag cloud
will make a
handy widget.

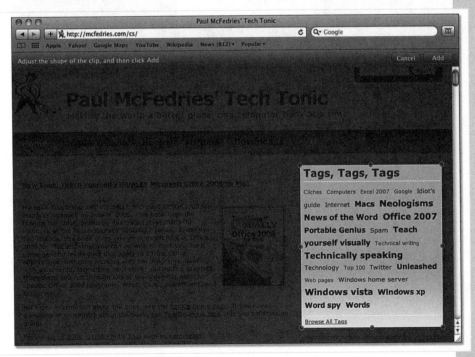

3. Use the handles that appear around the clip to adjust the size and shape of the clip, if necessary.

4. Click Add. Safari opens Dashboard and loads the clip, as shown in Figure 28.15.

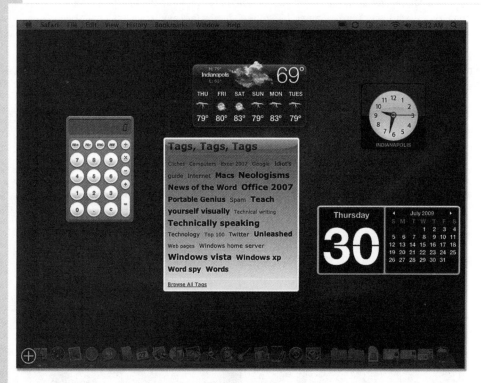

Figure 28.15
Here's the tag cloud as a Web Clip in Dashboard.

After you've created a Web Clip widget, you can use that widget just like other widgets—well, mostly anyway. The links in the widget take you to the related information on the source web page. Some notes about this feature follow:

- The Web Clip captures a static portion of the web page based on what you select. If the information changes on the source web page, it might shift what's shown in the widget you create.

- Capturing part of a web page can be complicated. It works fine with some parts of some pages, but might not work with everything you try. It depends on how the page is configured, the part you select, and so on. Don't be too surprised if a widget you create doesn't work exactly as you expect. If not, just delete it and try again.

- Widgets that you create have an Info button. Click this button to change the theme for the widget (which changes how the widget is framed) or to edit it by changing the part of the page that is selected.

Finding and Downloading Widgets

Dashboard can also be expanded with new widgets that you download from the Internet.

1. Activate Dashboard and open the Widget bar.

2. Click the Widgets widget.

3. Click the More Widgets button. Your default web browser opens and you see Apple's Dashboard Widgets web page (see Figure 28.16).

Figure 28.16
Apple's
Dashboard
Widgets
page is home
to hundreds
of widgets.

4. Browse or search until you find a widget you want to try.

5. Download the widget. In most cases, you're prompted to install the widget after it has been downloaded.

6. Click Install at the prompt. Move to Dashboard to see the new widget that you installed.

7. Click Keep to keep the widget or Delete to get rid of it. If you click Keep, the downloaded widget is installed on your Dashboard.

Installing Third-Party Widgets

If you download a widget from the Apple Dashboard website, you don't need to do any installation as it is automatically recognized and installed, as you learned in the previous section. However, you'll find widgets in other locations as well.

There are two ways widgets from other sources can be installed. One is to use an installer if one was provided with the widget. Otherwise, just place the widget file in the Widgets folder that is in the Library folder on your startup disk or in the Library folder in your Home folder; restart your Mac and then use the Widget bar to open and use the new widget. If it is installed in the startup disk's Library folder, the widget is available to everyone who uses your Mac. If it is installed in the Library within a user's Home folder, it is only available to that user.

 tip

When you install a widget from the Apple website, it is installed only in the current user's Widgets folder. To make it available to all your users, move it from the Widgets folder in the user's Home folder to the Widgets folder in the startup disk's Library folder.

29

RUNNING WINDOWS AND WINDOWS APPLICATIONS

Choosing How to Run Windows on a Mac

Unlike in those ubiquitous Apple commercials where a Mac and a PC are always together, these two worlds don't often collide in real life. The planet is divided (albeit rather unequally) into Mac and Windows camps, and it's a rare user who has a foot in both. However, the Mac and Windows worlds do intersect, and here are just a few examples:

- **No Mac version of the software you need**—Thanks to the popularity of Windows, the vast majority of software developers create programs for Windows, so Windows has by far the largest collection of available applications. Because many developers don't bother creating Mac versions of their programs, often there's no Mac equivalent of a particular type of software. In that case, you need Windows in order to run one of those non-Mac programs.

- **The Mac equivalent just isn't the same for you**—If you use Windows at work, or if you used to run Windows at home, you might have a favorite Windows program that doesn't have a Mac version. There may be Mac applications that do something similar, but you really like the version you were using on Windows. In that case, you need Windows in order to install and run that program.

- **Better gaming opportunities**—If you like to play games, you probably already know that the Mac isn't a great gaming platform. Windows is very game-friendly, however, and not only do most games run better under Windows than under Mac, but many (perhaps even most) of the best games don't have Mac versions. In that case, you need Windows for the optimum gaming experience.

- **Access to the full Microsoft Office suite**—If you're an Office user, you already know that the Mac version of Office doesn't come with Outlook (it has Entourage, instead) or the Access database program. If you really need to use either or both of these programs, you need Windows in order to install Office 2007, Office 2003, or some other version of Office for Windows.

- **Viewing the Windows Internet platforms**—If you develop content for the Web, it's crucial to know what your content looks like on all the most popular platforms. And given that Windows is the most popular operating system in the world, you'd be remiss in your duties if you didn't fire up your site (or whatever it is) using the Windows versions of Internet Explorer, Safari, and Firefox. In that case, you need Windows in order to view your content in these programs.

In all these examples, you probably only need to use Windows every now and then, or just for short periods each day. Buying a separate PC to run Windows will set you back hundreds of dollars (at least), which is more than likely wasteful for something that you won't be using all that often. On the other hand, of the two methods for running Windows on your Mac that I talk about in this chapter, one (Boot Camp) comes free with Mac OS X (versions 10.5 and later) and the other (Parallels Desktop) costs just $79.99 at the time of this writing. (In all cases, you also need a copy of Windows XP Service Pack 2 or later, Windows Vista, or Windows 7, so be sure to add that into your budget.) Either way, running Windows on your Mac is much more economical than using a separate PC, and you don't have to clutter your desk with multiple monitors, keyboards, and mice.

Understanding Boot Camp

The option that is native to Mac OS X is running Windows via Boot Camp. When you use this option, you can choose to boot your Mac up in the Mac OS or in Windows. When you boot up in Windows, you have a fully-functional Windows PC on your hands (it will probably outperform many dedicated Windows machines too). This option is great because it provides you with the ability to run Windows and its applications on your Mac. And you don't have to pay anything else for the Boot Camp software because it's built into Mac OS X. However, this method has one significant flaw: You have to restart your computer each time you want to switch from Mac to Windows and then back again. If you run Windows applications only very rarely, this might not be so bad, but if you regularly run a couple of Windows applications, you waste a lot of time restarting the computer.

Understanding Virtualization Software

The second option is to use virtualization software. This approach provides a virtual environment (also called a virtual machine) in which you install and run Windows. Because the virtualization software is just another application running on

 note

To run Windows on a Mac, you do have to purchase a *full* copy of Windows to install whether you use Boot Camp or a virtualization application. The cost for this varies depending on the version of Windows you purchase and how you purchase it. If you are getting Windows only to run specific applications, see if the applications you need are supported on Windows XP. If so, you might be able to save a few dollars using this older version of Windows. At press time, a full version of Windows Vista Home Basic Edition was about $180. If you're only going to be using Windows to run Windows applications, the basic edition should be sufficient. Make sure you get a full version; an upgrade version won't work.

the Mac, you can switch to it as easily as moving to any open Mac application. So, you can leave Windows running all the time and jump into it when you need it. This makes using Windows much more convenient than the Boot Camp option. Surprisingly, the performance of Windows in the virtual environment isn't noticeably slower than running it under Boot Camp or even on some Windows hardware. The only downside is the cost of the virtualization software itself. If you use Windows more than rarely, the time you save switching back and forth more than makes up the cost of the software. Plus, with a virtual approach, you can easily share data and files between the Mac OS and Windows.

In the remainder of this chapter, you'll get information about each of these methods so you can choose the one that works the best for you.

Using Boot Camp to Run Windows on a Mac

Following are the general steps to get Windows running under Boot Camp:

1. Run the Boot Camp Assistant to prepare your Mac for Windows and install it.

2. Install Windows.

The next couple of section take you through the details.

Running the Boot Camp Assistant and Installing Windows

The Boot Camp Assistant prepares your Mac for a Windows installation. One of the things it does is partition a hard drive to create a volume on which Windows will be installed and from which you'll boot up when you want to run Windows. To use the Boot Camp Assistant, do the following:

1. Open Finder, select Applications, Utilities, and then open Boot Camp Assistant. You see the first screen of the assistant (see Figure 29.1).

 caution

You must activate a copy of Windows to keep it running for more than 30 days. When you do this, the copy of Windows you run is registered to the specific computer on which you activate it as a means to limit illegal copies of Windows. Unfortunately, you can only activate Windows under one environment (Boot Camp or a virtual machine) on the same computer. Don't activate your copy of Windows until you're sure which method you are going to run it under (Boot Camp or a virtual machine) because you'll have to pay for a new copy of Windows to activate it under a different scheme (or try to explain the situation to Microsoft to get the previous activation "undone" so you can activate it under a different environment).

 note

To get support for Boot Camp, visit www.apple.com/support/bootcamp/.

 caution

Part of the Boot Camp preparation is to partition your Mac's internal hard drive. Before you do this, make sure you have all your data backed up in case something goes wrong.

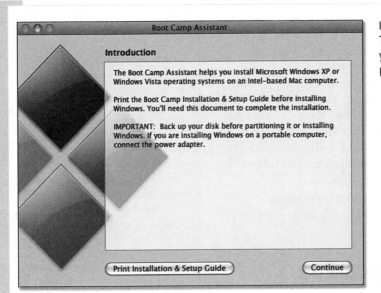

Figure 29.1
The Boot Camp Assistant walks you through the process of preparing for Boot Camp.

2. Click Continue. You see the Create a Partition for Windows screen (see Figure 29.2). On the left, you see the partition for Mac OS X while on the right you see the partition for Windows, which is a minimum of 5GB.

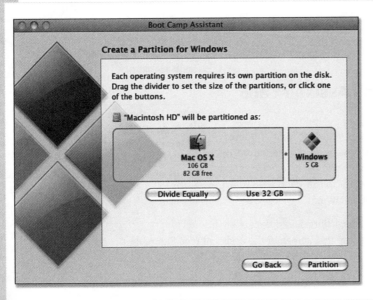

Figure 29.2
In order to run Windows under Boot Camp, you must create a Windows partition on your Mac's internal hard drive.

3. Set the size of the Window partition by dragging the Resize handle between the two partitions to the left, clicking the Divide Equally button to divide the disk in two partitions, or clicking the Use 32 GB button to set the Windows partition at 32GB. The 32 GB option is a reasonable size for many Windows environments, but remember that you'll be limited to the partition's size when you run Windows, so make sure you allow plenty of space if you are going to install a lot of Windows applications.

4. Click Partition. The partition process starts and you see its status in the window. When the process is complete, you're prompted to insert your Windows installation disc (see Figure 29.3).

Figure 29.3
When you see this screen, insert your Windows installation disc to start the installation process on the partition you just created.

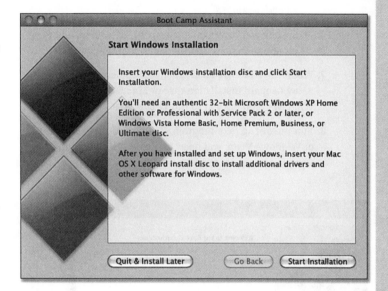

5. Insert the Windows installation disc, wait until it is mounted on the Mac, and then click Start Installation. The Mac restarts and boots from the Windows installation disc. The installation application starts installing files; you see the progress at the bottom of the blue Windows Setup screen.

6. Follow the Windows installation screens as they appear. Here are some things to bear in mind:

   - When the Windows setup program asks you where you want to install Windows, be sure to choose the BOOT-CAMP partition.

      Windows 7 and Windows Vista—Choose Disk 0 Partition 3 BOOTCAMP.

      Windows XP—Choose C: Partition 3 <BOOTCAMP>.

 tip
Boot Camp formats the BOOTCAMP partition using the FAT32 file system, which is fine for Windows XP partitions that are 32GB or less, but won't work for Windows 7 or Windows Vista, which require a different file system called NTFS. During the Windows 7 or Vista installation, when you get to the Where Do You Want to Install Windows? dialog box, click the BOOTCAMP partition, click Drive Options, and then click Format.

■ When the Windows XP setup program asks you to select a file system, be sure to choose one of the format options, such as Format the Partition Using the FAT File System.

■ The Windows Setup program automatically reboots your Mac a few times during the installation, and each time you'll see a screen that says `Press any key to boot from CD or DVD`. Don't press any key when you see this message, or the installation process will start all over again.

■ Specify your username, password, time zone, and any other preferences that the setup program asks for.

7. When the Windows installation is complete, insert your Snow Leopard installation disc or Mac OS X Disc 1. Windows prompts you to run `setup.exe`.

8. Run the `setup.exe` program. If you're running Windows 7 or Windows Vista, you need to provide User Account Control credentials to continue. The Boot Camp application appears, as shown in Figure 29.4.

 caution

In the Windows XP installation, do not choose the option that says Leave the Current File System Intact (No Changes). For the Boot Camp partition to work with XP, it must be formatted during the installation.

 note

Another of the benefits of using a virtualization approach is that the virtualization software does almost all of the Windows configuration for you automatically, making installing Windows much easier and faster.

Figure 29.4
Insert your Mac OS X DVD to run Boot Camp in Windows.

9. Click Next. The License Agreement dialog box appears.

10. Select the I Accept the Terms in the License Agreement option, and then click Next.

11. Make sure the Apple Software Update for Windows check box is selected, and then click Install. Boot Camp installs Apple Software Update for Windows.

12. Click Finish. Boot Camp lets you know that you need to restart the computer to put the changes into effect.

13. Click Yes to restart your Mac.

14. Restart the Mac and hold the Option key down.

15. Choose the Mac OS X startup volume and press the Return key. The Mac starts up under Mac OS X again.

> **note**
>
> Some wireless keyboards or mice won't be recognized during the startup process. If yours isn't, connect a wired keyboard to control the startup process.

Switching Between Mac OS X and Windows

In an ideal world, you switch between Mac OS X and Windows by restarting the Mac and then booting into whichever operating system you want to use. Unfortunately, right after you install Windows via Boot Camp, you find that you're living in a Windows world. That's because Windows somewhat rudely sets itself up as the default startup volume. This means that every time you restart your Mac, it always boots you directly into Windows.

Not to worry; there are a couple of ways that you can work around this problem.

First, you can follow these steps to exit Windows and boot directly to Mac OS X:

1. Click the Boot Camp icon that appears in the Windows notification area.

2. Click Restart in Mac OS X, as shown in Figure 29.5. Boot Camp asks you to confirm.

Figure 29.5
To get back to the friendly confines of Mac OS X, click the Boot Camp icon and then click Restart in Mac OS X.

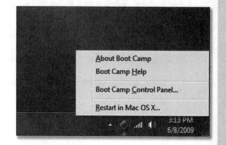

3. Click OK. Boot Camp shuts down Windows and then boots into Mac OS X.

If your Mac is off and you want to boot into Mac OS X, it seems awfully inefficient to have to boot into Windows first. Fortunately, you don't have to do this. Instead, you can invoke the Startup Manager, and you can then choose whether you want to boot to Mac OS X or Windows.

Here are the steps you need to follow to switch between Mac OS X and Windows using the Startup Manager:

1. Start your Mac.

2. Hold down the Option key until you see the Startup Manager. All you see are two hard disk icons: one for Macintosh HD and one for Windows.

3. Double-click the Macintosh HD icon. Alternatively, if you want to boot into Windows, double-click the Windows icon.

Yes, you have to follow these steps every time you start your Mac. See the next section for a way to avoid this.

Reinstating Mac OS X as the Default OS

If you usually boot to Mac OS X and only boot to Windows occasionally, it's a hassle to have to invoke Startup Manager every time you want to use Mac OS X. To fix this, follow these steps:

1. Boot to Mac OS X.

2. Click System Preferences in the Dock. The System Preferences appear.

3. Click the Startup Disk icon. The Startup Disk preferences appear.

4. Click Mac OS X Ver on Macintosh HD (where Ver is your OS X version number).

 tip

If you decide that you don't want to use Boot Camp to run Windows, launch the Boot Camp Assistant, click Continue, choose Create or Remove a Windows Partition, click Continue, and then click Restore. Mac OS X deletes the Windows partition and recovers the hard disk space. Any files you've stored on the Windows partition are lost, so make sure they're backed up before doing this.

Using Parallels Desktop for Mac to Run Windows Virtually on a Mac

Following are the general steps to get Windows running under a virtual environment:

1. Purchase, download, and install the virtualization software.

2. Configure a virtual environment and install Windows.

3. Run Windows in the virtual environment.

There are several virtualization applications available, but the one that works best for me is Parallels Desktop for Mac. This application is simple to install and configure and it performs very well. It has a lot of great features, including the ability to easily share data and files between the Mac OS and Windows. You can download and try it before you purchase the application; at press time, it costs about $80 to continue using the application beyond the 15-day trial period. The remainder of this section focuses on using Parallels Desktop for Mac.

 note

For more detailed information about Parallels and to download a trial version, visit www.parallels.com/en/products/desktop/.

Installing Parallels Desktop

To install Parallels Desktop, perform the following steps:

1. Move to www.parallels.com/products/desktop/.

2. Click the Download Trial link. This moves you to the download page.

3. Download the Parallels Desktop for Mac installer.

4. While you're waiting for the download to complete, click the Get Trial Key link.

5. Create a new account to request the activation link be sent to your email address. The activation code will be emailed to the address you entered.

6. When the download process is complete, move back to the desktop, double-click the Parallels Desktop icon, and then click Install.

7. Follow the on-screen instructions to complete the installation.

8. Click Close to quit the installer. You're ready to launch Parallels and activate the program.

9. Launch Parallels Desktop (Applications folder unless you chose a different installation location). You're prompted to enter an activation code.

10. Click Activate Product. The Activation Key sheet appears.

11. Enter the activation key, your name, and click Activate. You see the Welcome to Parallels Desktop window.

Configuring a Virtual Machine and Installing Windows

Each OS you run under Parallels has its own virtual machine for which you can set various settings, such as the amount of disk space dedicated to that machine, where the machine is stored, and so on. Before you can install Windows, create and configure a virtual machine for it.

Parallels Desktop 4 includes a new operating system detection feature that can examine your Windows installation disc and detect the OS automatically. To set up a virtual machine using operating system detection, follow these steps:

1. Launch Parallels Desktop if you haven't done so already.

2. In the Welcome to Parallels Desktop window, click Run Windows on Your Mac. The New Virtual Machine Assistant window appears, and displays the Operating System Detection dialog box shown in Figure 29.6.

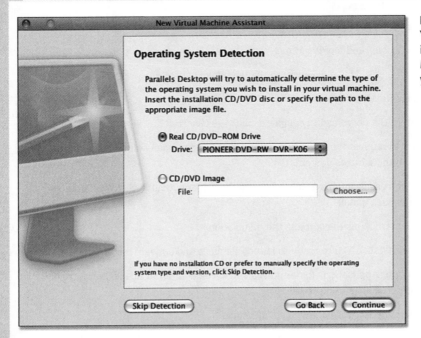

Figure 29.6
You can save time by having the New Virtual Machine Assistant detect your Windows OS.

3. Insert your Windows installation disc and wait until the disc mounts.

4. Make sure the Real CD/DVD-ROM Drive radio button is selected.

5. Click Continue. The New Virtual Machine Assistant examines the disc and then displays the Detected System dialog box (see Figure 29.7).

6. Use the Name text box to name the virtual machine; the default name is the name of the detected version of Windows, but you can call it something else if you'd like.

7. Leave the Enable File Sharing check box activated if you want to share your Mac Home folder with the Windows virtual machine.

 note

If the New Virtual Machine Assistant fails to detect the Windows OS, click Go Back and then click Skip Detection to display the Select Operating System Type and Version dialog box. In the Type pop-up menu, choose Windows, and in the Version pop-up menu, choose your Windows version. Click Continue to display the Virtual Machine Type dialog box, click Typical, and then click Continue.

8. Leave the Enable User Profile Sharing check box activated if you want to share your Mac's desktop and user folders with the Windows virtual machine.

9. Click More Options.

10. If you want a Parallels icon on your desktop, leave the Create Icon on Desktop check box activated.

Figure 29.7
These settings configure several important aspects of your Windows virtual machine. These include the ability to share files with the Mac OS and if other users will be able to access the virtual machine.

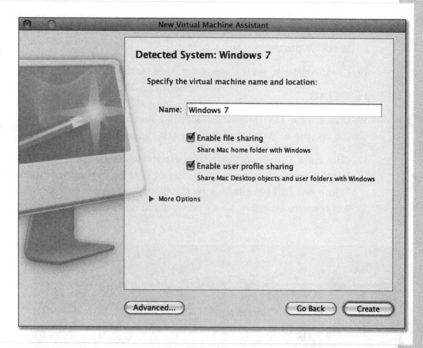

11. To enable other users on your Mac to access Windows, activate the Share Virtual Machine with Other Mac Users check box.

12. Click Advanced. The New Virtual Machine Assistant displays the Advanced settings, shown in Figure 29.8.

Figure 29.8
Use the Advanced settings to configure the CPUs and RAM for your virtual machine.

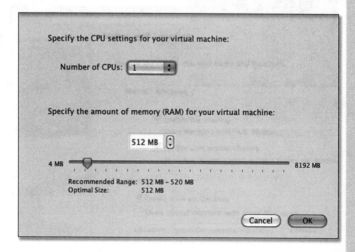

13. If your Mac has a dual-core processor (or you have a multi-core Mac Pro), use the Number of CPUs pop-up menu to choose how many CPUs you want the Windows virtual machine to access. Choose a higher number for better performance, particularly if you won't be running Mac and Windows programs at the same time.

14. Use the slider to set the amount of RAM for the virtual machine.

15. Click OK.

16. Click Create. The New Virtual Machine Assistant creates the virtual machine and then displays the Prepare to Install Operating System dialog box.

17. Click Start. The virtual machine starts and launches the Windows installer. You see the Parallels Desktop window with various Windows installer messages as the installation progresses (see Figure 29.9). You can expect the installation process to take 45 or more minutes to complete, and it is resource intensive, so it's better if you don't use your Mac for anything else while it runs.

Figure 29.9
The Windows Setup program runs inside the Parallels Desktop window.

Windows will start and stop a time or two, and you see a variety of messages from Windows itself and from Parallels Desktop. Read and respond to the messages as seems best; in most cases, you just click OK at various prompts.

After the basic installation process and initial Parallels Desktop configuration are complete, you see the Windows Welcome screen in the virtual machine window.

18. Log on to Windows to display the Windows desktop (see Figure 29.10).

Figure 29.10
Windows 7 running on a Mac inside a Parallels Desktop virtual machine.

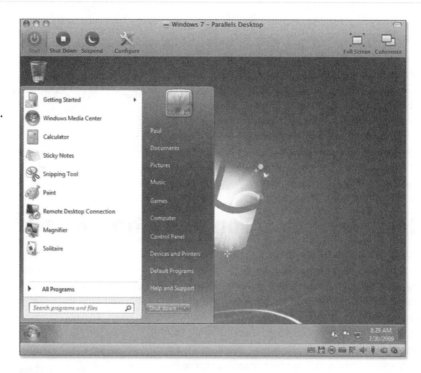

19. Install Parallel Tools by choosing Virtual Machine, Install Parallel Tools. These tools ensure that all device drivers are installed correctly, and they make it easier to share data between Mac OS X and Windows.

Running Windows

To run Windows under Parallels Desktop, you have two choices:

- If you chose to display an icon for the Windows virtual machine on the Mac desktop, double-click that icon.

- Launch Parallels Desktop, select File, Open, use the Open dialog box to click your Windows virtual machine, and then click Open.

 note

One of the great things about Parallels Desktop is that the Windows environment gets its network settings from the Mac. So if the Mac on which you install Parallels is connected to a network and the Internet, the Windows environment is also connected without any additional configuration by you. Also, because the Windows environment gets its connection from the Mac, any protection from hacking through the network (such as NAT protection from an AirPort Extreme Base Station) is also applied to the Windows environment.

There isn't much difference between running Windows in a virtual machine and running it on a Windows PC. However, you can jump back to the Mac by switching to the specific application you want to run, for example, by pressing ⌘+Tab. You can leave Windows running as long as you need to; if you won't be using it for a while, it's a good idea to shut it down to maximize the resources available to the Mac OS.

Parallels Desktop has a lot of great features that you can use to make Windows work the best for you. For example, you can use the Coherence mode so that the Parallels window disappears and all you see on the Mac desktop is the Windows Start menu and any Windows applications you are running. You can also run Parallels in full screen mode, which is especially useful if you have two displays connected to your Mac because you can run the Mac OS on one display and have the Windows environment fill the other. For additional information, see the documentation included in the Parallels installation disk image.

 note

Only one environment can be using a CD or DVD at the same time. If you've inserted a CD or DVD, but don't see it on the Mac desktop, the odds are that Windows is running and the disc is mounted there, which makes it unavailable to the Mac. Stop the Windows environment and the disc will appear on the Mac desktop.

Protecting Windows on a Mac from Attack

Running Windows, whether via Boot Camp or a virtual machine, is hazardous. There are thousands and thousands of viruses, trojan horses, worms, and other threats to the Windows OS and to the files you store under it. One of the first things you should do when you get a Windows environment running is to install security software on it. At the least, you need a package that protects Windows from viruses, but that is really only the basic protection you need. The application you get should also protect Windows from other threats as well, such as worms and macro viruses. Because there are so many Windows computers and so many threats to those computers, there are many Windows security applications from which to choose. Here are a few to check out:

- Norton Internet Security (www.symantec.com/index.jsp)

- McAfee Internet Security Suite (http://mcafee.com/us)

- Avast! Antivirus (www.avast.com)

- AVG Internet Security (http://free.grisoft.com/)

Make sure in whichever software you use that you configure it to automatically update its virus definitions frequently because new Windows viruses emerge constantly, so you need to ensure your security software is as current as possible.

 caution

It's not clear if the threats to Windows on a Mac also expose the Mac OS and its files to attack. There's no doubt some clever hacker is working on a way to attack the Mac OS through Windows running under Boot Camp or a virtualization application to show it can be done if for no other reason. Protecting the Windows environment from attack should also lower the already small chance that the Mac environment can be attacked via Windows.

30

WORKING WITH MICE, KEYBOARDS, AND OTHER INPUT DEVICES

Choosing an Input Device

An *input device* is any device you use to move data into your Mac. Some input devices enable you to input data to create documents, images, movies, and so on. The other type of data input devices enables you to control your Mac.

In the context of this chapter, the term *input device* refers to the essential devices you use to input data and to control your Mac. Other sorts of input devices used only for data input, such as cameras, scanners, and so on, are covered elsewhere in this book.

There are two types of essential input devices: keyboards and mouse devices. However, many varieties of each device exist, and in the case of mouse devices, some of the varieties are hardly recognizable as being a device of that type. There are other types of input devices you might want to use, such as a graphics tablet.

Many of the devices described in this chapter use the USB interface.

 note

Introduced in Mac OS X version 10.2 was the built-in handwriting recognition system called Ink. Now called Inkwell, this technology allows you to use a tablet to write or draw and the Inkwell system converts your writing into text and graphics. Because of space limitations, I can't provide detail about using Inkwell in this chapter. However, if you have a graphics tablet, you can use the Ink pane of the System Preferences application to configure Inkwell. Then, you can write on your graphics tablet to input text and graphics and to control your Mac.

Since Mac OS X version 10.2, Mac OS X has supported wireless devices that use Bluetooth technology. Many of these devices are available, including keyboards, mouse devices, PDAs, cell phones, and so on. Bluetooth enables your Mac to wirelessly communicate with multiple devices at the same time.

Choosing, Installing, and Configuring a Keyboard

The keyboard is one of the most fundamental, and at the same time, simplest devices in your system. You are likely to spend most of your "Mac" time pounding on its keys, so it pays to make sure you have a keyboard you like.

Choosing and Installing a Keyboard

All Macs come with a keyboard of one type or another, so if you are happy with the keyboard that came with your Mac, there is no need to consider another type. The most recent Apple Keyboard combines a very nice feel with good ergonomics and features. The Apple Keyboard also provides several control keys, which are the mute, volume, and eject keys; these are located along the top of the number pad. And it looks pretty cool, too. Apple has also recently introduced the Apple Wireless Keyboard, which connects to your Mac using Bluetooth wireless technology.

However, other types of keyboards are available, such as those designed for maximum ergonomics, to provide additional controls (such as an Internet button), and so on.

Many modern keyboards use the USB interface, so installing a keyboard is a trivial matter of plugging it in to an available USB port. Some keyboards are wireless; two basic types of these devices are available. One type includes a transmitter you plug in to a USB port. The other type, such as the Apple Wireless Keyboard, uses Bluetooth. The advantage of Bluetooth is that you don't consume a USB port and can communicate with many Bluetooth devices at the same time. The disadvantage is that your Mac must have a Bluetooth module built in or have a Bluetooth adapter installed.

If at all possible, you should obtain a wireless keyboard; being without wires is very freeing, especially if you move your keyboard or mouse around much. And who needs all the clutter that so many wires bring? If you use a USB-based wireless keyboard, connect its transmitter to a USB port and then use its controls to get the transmitter and keyboard communicating. If you use a Bluetooth keyboard, use the Bluetooth configuration tools to install and configure it.

➡ *To learn more about Bluetooth devices, **see** "Choosing, Installing, and Using Bluetooth Devices," p. 601.*

If the keyboard you select includes additional features, such as additional buttons and controls, it probably also includes software you need to install. This typically adds a new pane to the System Preferences application that you use to configure the device. An example of this is provided in the next section.

Configuring a Keyboard

With the Keyboard pane of the System Preferences application, you can change the key repeat rate and the delay-until-repeat time. You can also configure the function keys and set the language in which your keyboard is configured. Here's how:

1. Open the System Preferences application, click the Keyboard icon to open the Keyboard pane, and click the Keyboard tab if it isn't selected already (see Figure 30.1).

Figure 30.1
Use the tabs on the Keyboard preferences pane to configure your keyboard.

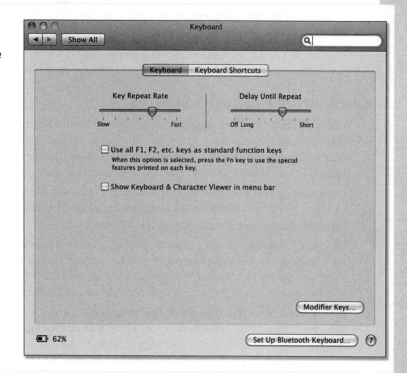

2. Use the Key Repeat Rate slider to set how fast a key repeats itself. Move the slider to the right to cause keys to repeat more quickly.

3. Use the Delay Until Repeat slider to set the amount of time it takes for a key to repeat itself. You can test your settings in the text area below the sliders.

4. If you prefer to use your keyboard's Fn (F1, F2, and so on) keys as standard function keys rather than to invoke the special features printed on each key, activate the Use All F1, F2, Etc. Keys as Standard Function Keys check box.

5. If you want easy access to the Character Viewer and the Keyboard Viewer utilities, activate the Show Keyboard & Character Viewer in Menu Bar check box.

6. Click the Modifier Keys button. The Modifier Keys sheet appears.

7. For each of the four modifier keys (Caps Lock, Control, Option, and Command), select the action that you want to occur when you press that key. The options are one of the modifier keys or No Action. For example, if your keyboard preference is such that the Control key is more convenient for you, you might want to set it to be the Command key since you use that key more frequently. You can select No Action to disable a key.

8. Click OK to set your preferences and close the sheet.

 note

If you rarely use the Caps Lock key, but find that you often press it accidentally and end up with a string of uppercase letters, consider either disabling the key or using it as an alternate ⌘ key.

Configuring Keyboard Shortcuts

One of the best things you can do to increase your personal productivity is to learn to use keyboard shortcuts, and I've shown you many Mac OS X shortcuts throughout this book. You should take the time to learn and practice the shortcuts for the OS, as well as shortcuts for any applications you use frequently. The Mac Help Center also lists some keyboard shortcuts if you need to look them up.

Using the Keyboard Shortcuts tab of the Keyboard pane, you can configure many of the available keyboard shortcuts. You can enable or disable some of the standard keyboard shortcuts and add keyboard shortcuts for commands in applications you use.

Using the Full Keyboard Access feature, you can access the interface elements with the designated keys. Open the Keyboard pane of the System Preferences application and click the Keyboard Shortcuts tab (see Figure 30.2). You see a list of standard Mac OS X keyboard shortcuts in a number of areas, such as Screen Shots, Universal Access, Keyboard & Text Input, and so on.

Disable any of the listed shortcuts by deactivating the shortcut's check box. Typically, you would do this when that shortcut conflicts with a shortcut in an application you use. For example, the default shortcut to capture the screen to an image file is Shift-⌘-3. However, one of the most popular Mac screenshot applications—Snapz Pro X—also uses this shortcut by default. So if you use Snapz Pro X instead of the Mac OS X built-in shortcut, you'd disable the default screenshot shortcut so it won't interfere with the default Snapz Pro X shortcut.

 *To see an explanation of the standard keyboard shortcuts you can configure and use,* **see** *"Getting the Most from Keyboard Shortcuts," p. 606.*

In the Keyboard & Text Input section, many of the commands start with the phrase Move Focus To. Moving the focus means highlighting the item that you want to access via the keyboard. For example, if you want to use the keyboard to access a menu command for which a keyboard shortcut isn't defined, you can press Control-F2 (the default) to highlight the first item on the active menu bar, which is always the Apple menu. Then use the right arrow key to select the menu you want to open. Then press the down arrow key to open the menu and move to the command you want to activate. Press Return to activate the command.

For more on navigating the screen using the keyboard, **see** *"Using Keyboard Navigation," p. 607.*

Figure 30.2
Use the Keyboard Shortcuts tab to configure your own keyboard shortcuts.

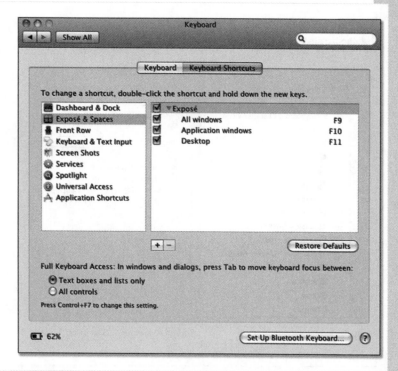

Configuring Your Keyboard's Language Settings and the Input Menu

You can configure the languages you use for the keyboard along with other input preferences using the International pane of the System Preferences application. You can also configure the Input menu, which enables you to quickly choose among languages and select some other handy keyboard tools:

1. Open the Language & Text pane of the System Preferences application.

2. On the Language tab, move the language you want to be the default to the top of the list by dragging it there. Move the other languages on the list to set the order in which they are used.

3. Click the Input Sources tab. Use this area to show the Input menu on the Finder menu bar and to configure the items you see on it (see Figure 30.3).

4. Activate the Show Input Menu in Menu Bar check box.

5. Activate the boxes next to the other languages you want to be available on the Input menu.

6. Activate the Keyboard & Character Viewer check box to add that to the menu. The Keyboard Viewer shows you the keys for a selected font; the Character Viewer enables you to select, configure, and use special characters like accent marks.

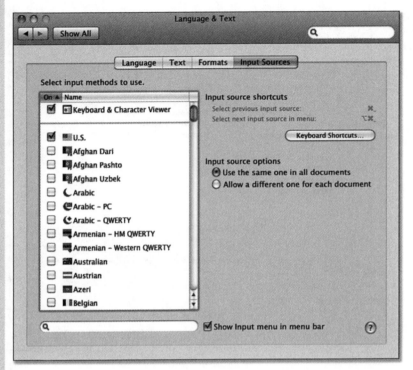

Figure 30.3
You can configure the Input menu with the Input Sources tab of the International pane.

7. If you want to change the keyboard shortcuts for selecting the source on the Input menu, click Keyboard Shortcuts and use the controls you learned about in the previous section to set the appropriate keyboard shortcuts.

When you open the Input menu, which is indicated by a flag representing the language you have made the default, you will see the items you configured there (see Figure 30.4). You can change the current input source, which is indicated by the check mark, to a different one by selecting a different source on the menu. You can open the Character Viewer or Keyboard Viewer by selecting the command from the Input menu for the item you want to show. If you select Show Input Source Name, the source name appears as the menu title in addition to the flag icon.

Figure 30.4
The Input menu enables you to select the language setting for your keyboard and open the Character Viewer and Keyboard Viewer.

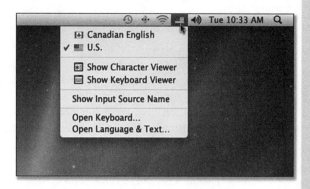

Choosing, Installing, and Configuring a Mouse

When the Mac was first introduced, its mouse separated it from all the computers that came before it, and those that came after it, for a long time. Until Windows and other platforms adopted the mouse as one of their primary input devices, the Mac and its mouse really stood out from the crowd. Now, Apple's Mighty Mouse stands out because its design and controls are quite different from most other mice.

Choosing and Installing a Mouse

All desktop Macs come with the Apple Mighty Mouse. This is an optical mouse, which means it uses light to translate your movements into input information (as opposed to the rolling ball in previous generations of mouse devices). The Apple Mighty Mouse uses the entire top half as its two "buttons," which makes using it even easier, and it shares the same clear or white plastic look as the Apple keyboard. It also includes a tiny scroll ball that you can use to scroll vertically or horizontally and you can press the ball down for an additional button control. There is yet another button at the base of the mouse on each side (though there are two buttons, they perform the same action).

Whatever mouse you use, I strongly recommend that you get a mouse that has at least two buttons. The ability to right-click things to activate contextual menus and to perform other commands is much more convenient than using a key and clicking the single mouse button. Plus, if you use a mobile Mac, you might want to add a mouse for those times when you are using your notebook at a desk.

There are three main considerations when choosing a mouse.

One is its comfort in your hand. Mouse devices come in various shapes and sizes. Using one that is suited to your own hand cuts down on fatigue in your hand and lower arm.

Another factor is the number of buttons and other features on the mouse. Apple's mouse devices all provide four mouse buttons, but other mouse devices come with even more or fewer buttons. These buttons can be programmed to accomplish specific tasks, such as opening contextual menus. Also, most mouse devices include a scroll wheel that enables you to scroll in a window, such as a web page, without moving the mouse (the Mighty Mouse's scroll ball enables you to scroll in two directions).

Because support for a two-button mouse with a scroll wheel is built in to the OS (even though you won't find this indicated on the Mouse pane of the System Preferences application unless you have such a device installed), you should get at least a two-button mouse. This makes opening contextual menus, which are used throughout the OS and in most applications, much easier. Even better, get a mouse that includes a scroll wheel or a scroll ball like the Mighty Mouse has. This makes scrolling much more convenient and faster at the same time.

Third, you need to decide whether you want a wireless mouse. Because of the amount of time you spend moving a mouse, you should really consider a wireless mouse. Getting rid of the wire provides much more freedom of movement for you. As with keyboards, two types of wireless mouse devices are available—those that use a USB transmitter and those that use Bluetooth (such as Apple's Wireless Mouse).

Like installing a keyboard, installing a mouse isn't hard.

If you use a wired mouse, just plug it in to an available USB port; Apple keyboards include USB ports that you can use for this. If you use a USB-based wireless mouse, plug its transmitter in to an available USB port and use its controls to get the mouse and transmitter communicating.

If you use a Bluetooth mouse, use the Bluetooth configuration controls to set it up.

➡ *To learn more about Bluetooth devices,* **see** *"Choosing, Installing, and Using Bluetooth Devices," p. 601.*

 note

Apple's wireless keyboard and mouse use Bluetooth to communicate with a Mac. You must purchase these devices separately. Hopefully, someday soon Apple will include Bluetooth support into all Macs and include the wireless keyboard and mouse for all desktop models.

Configuring a Mouse

Configuring a mouse is much like configuring a keyboard; however, if you use a mouse that offers additional features, you need to install and configure the software that comes with that device first to take advantage of all its features. Without this software, the second button and scroll wheel will likely work as you expect, but more advanced features might not work.

To configure an Apple Mighty Mouse, do the following:

1. Open the Mouse pane of the System Preferences application (see Figure 30.5).

2. Use the Tracking slider to set the tracking speed of the mouse. A faster tracking speed means that the pointer moves farther (faster) with less movement of the mouse.

3. Use the Scrolling slider to set the speed at which the scroll ball scrolls. Moving the slider to the right makes the scroll action faster, meaning you move up or down or across the screen faster.

Figure 30.5
In System Preferences, open the Mouse pane to configure your mouse.

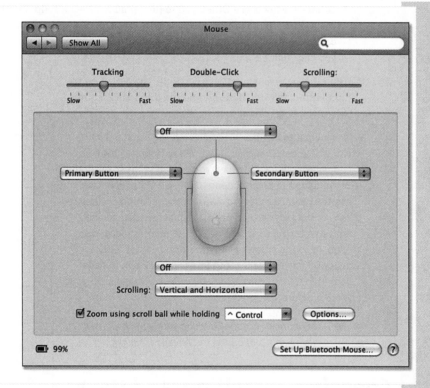

4. Use the Double-Click slider to set the rate at which you have to click the mouse buttons to register a double-click.

5. Click the pop-up menu for the left mouse button and choose the action that you want to be performed when you click the button. For example, if you want the left button to be your primary button, choose Primary Button (which is the default). Other actions include:

- **Secondary button**—Choose this to have a button perform the secondary action, such as opening an item's contextual menu.

- **Exposé**—Choose Exposé actions to trigger Exposé. The All Windows option minimizes all windows on the desktop; the App Windows minimizes all windows open in the current application and presents them on the desktop; and the Desktop option shows the desktop.

- **Dashboard**—Choose this option to open the Dashboard when you press the button.

- **Application Switcher**—This option causes the Application Switcher to open so that you can quickly move among your open applications.

- **Spotlight**—This action moves you into Spotlight so you can search for information.

■ **Other**—If you choose Other, you're prompted to select a script or other executable file to associate with the button. For example, if you've created an application with Automator, you can associate it with a mouse button so it runs when you click that button.

6. Using the same menu options, configure the action for the right button, the side buttons, and the scroll ball button (when you press on the scroll ball).

7. If you want to be able to zoom using the scroll ball, activate the Zoom Using Scroll Ball While Holding check box and choose the modifier key you'll need to press to trigger zooming on the pop-up menu. Click the Options button and use the resulting sheet to control how zooming occurs. You can control how the screen image moves when zoomed (stays with pointer, moves when the pointer reaches an edge, or so the pointer is always at the center of the image). Activate the Smooth Images check box to have your Mac smooth zoomed images. Click Done to save your zoom preferences.

➥ *For information about working with a trackpad, **see** "Using and Configuring the Trackpad," **p. 555**.*

Choosing, Installing, and Using a Trackball

Trackballs are really upside-down, roller-bearing mouse devices. Instead of the ball being inside the body (modern mice don't use a ball any more, but I'm sure you get the idea), the ball is on the top of a trackball style mouse and you move just the ball instead of the mouse body. Trackballs have several advantages over mouse devices. Because you don't actually move the trackball itself, it takes up less space than a mouse does. And you don't have to lift it up to move it when you run out of room or reach. Because your hand remains stationary, you don't rub the sensitive areas of your wrist across the edge of your desk, which can lead to damage of the tissues in your forearm. Trackballs also have more than one button, and you can program the other buttons to perform various functions. For example, you can set a button to add a modifier key when you click with the trackball. In addition, trackballs can move the cursor either more quickly to cover

 note

Mobile Macs use a trackpad instead of a mouse (although you can connect a mouse to one of these machines just as you can any other Mac).

 note

Two of the best input device makers are Logitech and Kensington. You can learn more about their products at their websites: www.logitech.com and www.kensington.com.

 caution

If you experience fatigue or pain when using any input device, make sure that you experiment to see whether you can find a more comfortable position for the device. If you can't, consider replacing the device with another type that is more suited to you. Discomfort, even of a mild nature, can indicate that some damage is being done to your body. If this happens over a long period of time, you can end up with serious health problems.

If you do experience problems, consider obtaining several different devices and set up positions among which you can rotate so you can avoid repeating exactly the same actions over an extended period of time. For example, you might want to have both a mouse and a trackball and switch between those devices every so often more screen real estate or more slowly to give you more precise control than a mouse.

Choosing a trackball is similar to choosing a keyboard or mouse (except that desktop Macs don't ship with a default trackball). Look for one that fits your hand and has the features you want—such as the number of buttons it has.

Installing trackballs is also similar to installing keyboards and mouse devices. You attach the device through an available USB port and then install and configure its software. Some of these devices are wireless and are set up similarly to wireless keyboards and mouse devices.

Providing Universal Access

You can use the Universal Access pane of the System Preferences application to configure input devices in different ways to enable those with disabilities to be better able to use a Mac. For example, you can use the Sticky Keys feature to cause a series of modifier key presses (such as ⌘ or Option) to be treated as if those keys were pressed at the same time. You can also use Mouse Keys to enable the pointer to be moved with the keyboard for folks who have difficulties using a mouse.

➡ *For the details of configuring Universal Access,* **see** *Chapter 24, "Making Your Mac Accessible to Everyone," p. 495.*

Choosing, Installing, and Using Bluetooth Devices

Bluetooth is a wireless communication standard used by many devices, including computers, keyboards, mouse devices, personal digital assistants (PDAs), cell phones, printers, and so on. Mac OS X is designed to be Bluetooth capable so your Mac can communicate with Bluetooth devices, such as to synchronize your iCal calendar on your Mac with the calendar on your Palm PDA.

Preparing for Bluetooth

Two elements are required to be able to use Bluetooth devices:

- The software component, which is installed as part of Mac OS X.

- The hardware component, which is the transmitter and receiver that sends and receives Bluetooth signals. Most Mac models have this device built in. For those models, you don't need anything else. For models without this, however, you need to obtain and install a Bluetooth USB adapter. This device connects to a USB port and enables a Mac to send and receive Bluetooth signals (see Figure 30.6).

Figure 30.6
For less than $40, you can add Bluetooth support to any Mac that has USB ports and is running OS X.

Bluetooth communication is set up between two devices—a single device can be communicating with more than one other Bluetooth device at the same time. Each device with which your Mac communicates over Bluetooth must be configured separately so your Mac recognizes that device and that device recognizes your Mac.

Two steps are involved in setting up Bluetooth. First, configure Bluetooth for your Mac using the Bluetooth pane of the System Preferences application. Then configure your Mac to work with each Bluetooth device you want to use.

Configuring Bluetooth on Your Mac

When your Mac recognizes that it has the capability to communicate via Bluetooth, the Bluetooth pane appears in the System Preferences application (see Figure 30.7). Use this to configure the general aspects of Bluetooth on your Mac and to see the list of devices your Mac recognizes.

note

If your Mac isn't capable of using Bluetooth, the Bluetooth pane won't appear in the System Preferences application.

Figure 30.7
Use the Bluetooth pane of the System Preferences application to control general aspects of Bluetooth on your Mac.

Use the Bluetooth pane to configure your Mac's Bluetooth configuration. It includes the following controls:

tip

In most cases, the default settings will work for you. You should try to configure a Bluetooth device before you adjust your Mac's Bluetooth settings. If it doesn't work properly, come back to these controls to make adjustments.

- **Bluetooth Power**—Use the On check box at the top of the pane to turn Bluetooth services on or off. Obviously, Bluetooth has to be turned on for your Mac to be able to communicate with Bluetooth devices.

- **Discoverable**—Activating this check box makes your Mac "discoverable" by other devices because your Mac transmits signals that other devices can detect. If you don't want this, you can deactivate the check box. For example, if you work in a area in which there are many Bluetooth devices, you might want to hide your Mac so other devices won't be able to detect it. You can still connect to your configured Bluetooth devices when this box is unchecked; your Mac just won't be capable of being detected by other devices automatically.

- **Devices List**— If you have already configured your Bluetooth devices to communicate with your Mac, you see them in this list (assuming they are turned on). If you have not yet paired your device to your Mac, you can click Add (the plus sign) to open the Bluetooth Setup Assistant to guide you through this process.

- **Advanced**—Several additional configuration options are available on the Advanced sheet of the Bluetooth pane. If your primary keyboard and mouse connect to your Mac with Bluetooth, you can have the Bluetooth Setup Assistant start automatically if your Mac doesn't recognize a keyboard or mouse. You can make sure that your keyboard or mouse can wake your Mac. You can even share your Internet connection with Bluetooth devices. Explore the Advanced sheet to see what settings make the most sense for your computer.

- **Bluetooth menu**—Activate the Show Bluetooth Status In the Menu Bar check box to add the Bluetooth menu to the menu bar.

Many Bluetooth interactions allow the transfer of files between the devices. Configure this using the Sharing pane of the System Preferences application (see Figure 30.8). For example, you can use these settings to move files from your Mac to a Bluetooth cell phone or PDA.

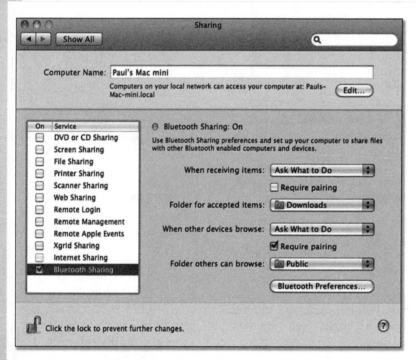

Figure 30.8
Use the Sharing pane of the System Preferences application to configure file transfers over Bluetooth.

Installing a New Bluetooth Device

Before your Mac can communicate with a Bluetooth device, that device must be configured on your Mac. And because Bluetooth devices are paired, your Mac must also be configured on the Bluetooth device with which you are communicating. After you have established a pair, your Mac can communicate with its partner via Bluetooth, and vice versa.

To set up a new device, use the Bluetooth Setup Assistant. The general steps to do this are the following:

1. Open the Bluetooth Setup Assistant by either clicking the Add (+) button on the Bluetooth pane of the System Preferences application or selecting Set up Bluetooth Device on the Bluetooth menu. The Bluetooth Setup Assistant opens (see Figure 30.9).

Figure 30.9
The Bluetooth Setup Assistant walks you through the steps required to set up a Bluetooth device.

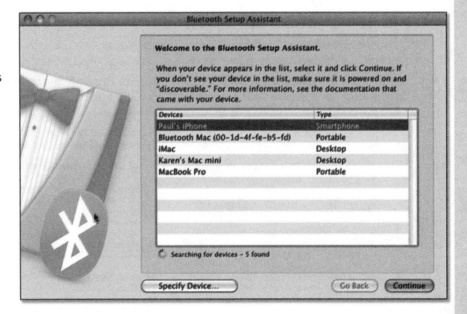

2. If you see your device in the list (it might take a minute or two for your Mac to discover it), skip to step 5; otherwise, click Continue.

3. Select the type of Bluetooth device you want to set up, such as Mouse, Keyboard, Mobile phone, or one of the other devices listed, and then click Continue. Your Mac searches for available Bluetooth devices.

4. If the device is not auto-discoverable (most mice and keyboards are not), press the communicate button on the device. This causes the device to start broadcasting a Bluetooth signal that your Mac can detect. As your Mac discovers devices, they are listed in the search results pane of the Bluetooth Setup Assistant window. The devices should be easily recognizably by their names, such as Kensington PocketMouse For Bluetooth when a mouse of that type is detected.

5. Select the device you want to configure and click Continue.

6. Follow the onscreen instructions to configure the device. When the process is complete, the devices can communicate. When Bluetooth devices are connected as a trusted pair, the same passkey is required on each device for those devices to communicate. Depending on the device, you may need to enter a passcode the Mac generates and shows in the assistant window on the device or enter a passcode the device generates on the Mac. When dealing with a mouse, keyboard, or other "dumb" device, this is done automatically and you'll seem to skip over this part of the process.

   When the process is done, you see the Conclusion screen in the assistant.

7. Click Set Up Another Device to configure another Bluetooth device or Quit to stop the assistant.

Working with Bluetooth Devices

After you have configured a Bluetooth device to work with your Mac, use the device's applications or controls to communicate with your Mac or use a Mac application to work with the device.

For example, one of the most useful Bluetooth devices is a Bluetooth-capable cell phone. You can use the iSync application to synchronize the phone's contact list with your Address Book so that you have the same information available on both devices. Because you can communicate wirelessly, you don't need to bother connecting any wires to synchronize. You can also transfer files between the two devices, such as to install applications on the cell phone if it supports them.

Although synchronizing a cell phone wirelessly is one of the most useful Bluetooth-enabled tasks, it isn't the only one. Consider the following examples:

- Using wireless keyboards and mouse devices

- Printing wirelessly

- Connecting to the Internet through a Bluetooth modem or cell phone

- Communicating with other Bluetooth-equipped Macs to share files

- Transferring photos wirelessly from a Bluetooth digital camera

Getting the Most from Keyboard Shortcuts

Using keyboard shortcuts is a great way to work both faster and smarter. Mac OS X includes support for many keyboard shortcuts by default. As you have seen throughout this book, many areas of the OS and within applications provide keyboard shortcuts you can use.

Using Keyboard Navigation

One of the least used, but most useful, aspects of using keyboard shortcuts is keyboard navigation. You can use the keyboard to access almost any area on your Mac in any application, including the Finder. For example, you can open any menu item by using only keys even if that item does not have a keyboard shortcut assigned to it.

First, configure keyboard navigation:

1. Open System Preferences, click Keyboard, and then click the Keyboard Shortcuts tab.

2. Review the list of shortcuts in the Dashboard & Dock, Exposé & Spaces, and Keyboard & Text Input sections to make sure the ones you want to use are enabled (see Table 30.1 for the default shortcuts).

3. If you want to use a keyboard shortcut that is different from the default, click the default shortcut, wait for a moment for it to become editable, and change it to a new combination.

Table 30.1   Keyboard Navigation and Dock, Exposé, and Dashboard Keyboard Shortcuts

Shortcut	What It Does	Default Keyboard Shortcut
Move focus to the menu bar	Opens the first menu on the current menu bar; use the Tab or arrow keys to move to other menu items.	Control-F2
Move focus to the Dock	Makes the Dock active; use the Tab or arrow keys to move to icons on the Dock.	Control-F3
Move focus to the active window or next window	Moves into the currently active window or takes you to the next window if you are already in a window.	Control-F4
Move focus to the window toolbar	If you are using an application with a toolbar, such as the System Preferences application, this makes the toolbar active. Use the Tab or arrow keys to select a button on the toolbar.	Control-F5
Move focus to the floating window	If you are using an application that has a floating window, this takes you into the floating window so that you can control the corresponding application.	Control-F6

Table 30.1 Continued

Shortcut	What It Does	Default Keyboard Shortcut
Move focus to next window in active application	Moves you among the open windows in any application, such as the Finder, Word, and so on.	⌘-`
Move between controls or text boxes and lists	If the Text Boxes and Lists Only check box is activated, when you are viewing windows or dialog boxes with controls, pressing the Tab key moves you among only the text boxes and lists in that open window or dialog box. If the All Controls check box is activated, pressing Tab moves you among all the elements of the window. This command changes the mode. You can uncheck its check box to disable this action entirely.	Control-F7
Move focus to window drawer	If the application you are using has a drawer, such as iDVD, this moves you into that drawer so you can use its tools.	⌘-Option-`
Move focus to status menus in the menu bar	If you have enabled additional menus in the Mac OS X menu bar, such as the Displays menu, this command enables you to open them.	Control-F8
Automatically hide and show the Dock	Hides or shows the Dock.	⌘-Option-D1
All windows	Causes Exposé to present reduced versions of all open windows on the desktop.	F9
Application windows	Causes Exposé to present a reduced version of all windows currently open in the active application on the desktop.	F10
Desktop	Moves all open windows off the desktop.	F11

Table 30.1 Continued

Shortcut	What It Does	Default Keyboard Shortcut
Dashboard	Opens the Dashboard.	F12
Spaces	Moves your Mac into Spaces mode	F8
Show Spotlight Search field	Opens the Spotlight.	⌘-Spacebar
Show Spotlight window	Opens the Spotlight results window	⌘-Option-Spacebar

Using the shortcuts in Table 30.1, you can move to and select just about anything you can see. For example, to select a menu command, press the Focus on Menu shortcut (Control-F2 by default) and use the right arrow or Tab key to move to the menu on which the command is located. Use the down arrow key to move to the command on the menu that you want to select, and press Return to activate the command.

As another example, when you are working with an application that has a toolbar, press the shortcut for the Move Focus to the Window Toolbar command, use the Tab key to select the tool you want to use, and press Return to use it.

 note

If you use a mobile Mac, some of the defaults might be different from those listed in Table 30.1. Check the Keyboard Shortcuts pane to see the current shortcuts for your specific system.

Adding Keyboard Shortcuts for Application Commands

You can add keyboard shortcuts for commands within Mac OS X applications using the following steps:

 note

Some applications don't support all aspects of keyboard navigation. For example, in some versions of Microsoft Word, you can't select radio button options using the arrow keys, which is too bad.

1. Open System Preferences, click Keyboard, and then click the Keyboard Shortcuts tab.

2. Click the Add Shortcut button (+) at the bottom of the pane. The Add Application sheet appears.

3. Select the application for which you want to create a shortcut on the Application pop-up menu. If the application for which you want to create a shortcut isn't listed, select Other and use the Open Application dialog box to select the application. To create a shortcut for all applications, select All Applications.

 tip

To type an ellipsis, use the Character palette to select it or press Option--.

4. In the Menu Title box, type the exact command name for which you want to create a shortcut. If the command contains an ellipsis, you need to include that as well.

5. In the Keyboard Shortcut field, press the key combination for the shortcut that you want to use to access the command. You need to be careful not to use a keyboard shortcut that is used elsewhere or you might get unexpected results. Figure 30.10 shows a completed sheet that applies the keyboard shortcut Shift-⌘-X to Safari's Close Tab command.

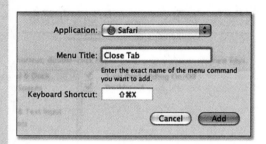

Figure 30.10
Using this simple sheet, you can add a keyboard shortcut for any command in any application.

6. Click Add. When you return to the Keyboard Shortcuts tab, the shortcut you added is listed under the related application under the Application Keyboard Shortcuts section.

7. If the application for which you configured a shortcut is currently running, quit and restart it. If it isn't currently running, open it. The keyboard command you created will be shown next to the command on the application's menu and you can execute the command by pressing the keyboard shortcut.

 tip

You can expand or collapse the applications listed in the Application Keyboard Shortcuts section to see all of the keyboard shortcuts configured using this tool.

31

WORKING WITH YOUR MAC'S DISPLAY

Getting the Most out of Your Mac's Displays

Most improvements to productivity save you only a few seconds here and a few seconds there. However, save a few seconds a few dozen times a day, and you're finishing your day thirty minutes earlier than usual. These improvements are almost always marginal, but occasionally you come across a new way of doing things that offers a radical increase in efficiency. Over the past few years, study after study has shown that you can greatly improve your productivity by doing one thing: adding a second monitor to your system. This makes sense because you can have whatever you're working on displayed on one monitor, and your reference materials (or your email client or whatever) on the second monitor.

The good news is that you can easily add a second display to all Macs except the Mac mini; if you have a Mac Pro, you can even add up to eight displays.

In the next section, you learn how to configure a Mac's display. From there, you learn about adding and configuring a second display to your system to expand your desktop real estate (or even more if you have a Mac Pro). And for maximum effectiveness, you learn how to synchronize the color across the various devices you use with your Mac.

Configuring a Mac's Display

Use the Display pane of the System Preferences application to configure the displays connected to your Mac. If you use a single display, this pane has two tabs—Display and Color, as shown in Figure 31.1. If you use multiple displays, the pane also includes the Arrangement tab, which you learn about later in this chapter.

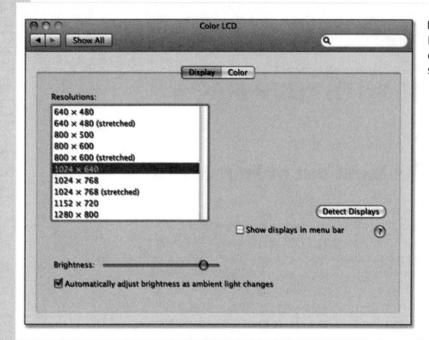

Figure 31.1
If your Mac has a single display, you see this version of the Display pane.

Use the Display tab to configure the resolution, color depth, refresh rate, and, depending on the display you are using, the rotation and the brightness of the display. The specific options you have depend on the graphics card and display you are using. In any case, you use the menus, sliders, pop-up menus, and other controls to configure the display. Generally, you should use the highest resolution that is comfortable for you to view. Then, choose the largest color depth and highest refresh rate that are available at that resolution. Finally, set the brightness to a comfortable level for you.

Configuring Resolution

A display's resolution is the number of pixels (picture elements) shown in the horizontal direction by the number of pixels in the vertical direction. For example, a setting of 1024×768 means the display presents 1024 pixels horizontally and 768 pixels vertically.

When you increase the resolution for a display, the objects on the screen get smaller. That's because a display has a fixed physical display size, such as a 23-inch Apple Cinema HD Display. As you increase a display's resolution, the number of pixels displayed on the fixed screen area of the display increases. This means that each pixel gets smaller. Higher resolutions display more information in the same physical space, requiring that the information is smaller.

Setting the resolution of a display is a matter of personal preference, but generally you can use higher resolutions on larger displays. For example, on the 24-inch iMac, a resolution of 1920×1200 is comfortable for many people. On smaller displays, such as a 13-inch MacBook, 1024×768 might be appropriate. The resolution also depends on the sharpness and clarity of the display. Higher-quality displays, such as those produced by Apple, can display higher resolutions more clearly so that they are more comfortable to view.

All displays also have a maximum resolution that can be used. This maximum is determined by the Mac's video capabilities and the display's hardware. For example, a 24-inch iMac can display resolutions up to 1920×1200, whereas a 13-inch MacBook's maximum resolution is 1280×800.

You can resize your Mac's resolution on the fly (you don't have to restart for the change to be applied) by simply clicking the resolution that you want to try on the Display pane. The display is immediately resized according to the resolution you selected. So trying different resolutions to see which works best for you is easy. The trade-off is between more screen space at higher resolutions versus everything appearing smaller. Find the best fit for the type of data you work with and your eyesight.

Some displays support a "stretched" resolution, such as 1024×768 (stretched). This takes the standard 1024×768 resolution and "stretches" pixels in the horizontal direction so the image fills a widescreen display. (If you use a nonstretched resolution on these displays, black vertical bars appear on each side of the screen.)

 note

The "standard" resolution for Macs has continued to increase along with the size and clarity of displays. For most of the Mac's early life, the standard display resolution was 640×480 (which also happens to be the resolution of non-HD television). When Macs included larger screens and bigger displays became available, this increased to 800×600. Currently, the minimum resolution you likely use on most displays is 1024×768. In fact, some applications, such as iMovie, won't even run at 800×600 or less.

Configuring Color Depth

Select the color depth on the Colors pop-up menu. In almost all cases, you should select Millions. However, if you use an older graphics card and display, you might have to settle for Thousands.

Select the highest refresh rate available on the Refresh Rate pop-up menu. If you use a digital signal with a flat-panel display, the Refresh Rate pop-up menu is grayed out because refresh rate isn't applicable to these displays when you use a digital signal over the DVI interface.

Configuring Rotation and Brightness

If your display supports multiple orientations, you usually see a Rotation pop-up menu, which has four values: Standard, 90 Degrees, 180 Degrees, and 270 Degrees. Choose the rotation value that corresponds to the display's current orientation.

Some displays support software brightness controls, in which case you see a Brightness slider on the Display pane. If you don't see this, use the physical controls located on the display itself to set its brightness (and contrast, if applicable). If you do see the Brightness slider in the Display pane, move it to the right to increase the brightness of the display or to the left to decrease it.

note

Non-Apple displays provide hardware controls for a lot of display settings, such as brightness and contrast, color adjustments, and so on. If you use one of these displays, check out its configuration menu to see what options you have.

Using the Displays Menu in the Menu Bar

Activate the Show Displays in Menu Bar check box to turn on the Displays menu in the menu bar. You can configure a display, such as setting its resolution, by selecting the resolution you want to use from the Displays menu (see Figure 31.2).

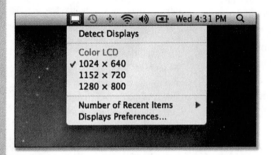

Figure 31.2
The Displays menu on the menu bar makes it easy to configure the display.

On the Displays menu, use the Number of Recent Items menu to set the number of resolution settings to display. For example, if you select 3 on this menu, the Displays menu on the menu bar shows the three most recent settings you have selected. This makes changing among your most commonly used resolution settings even easier.

You can also select the Displays Preferences command to open the Display pane of the System Preferences application. Other commands appear on the menu when you have multiple displays connected to your Mac. You learn about those commands later in this chapter.

After you have configured the Display tab, use the Color tab to select a ColorSync profile for your display.

➥ *To learn more about ColorSync,* **see** *"Synchronizing Color Among Devices," **p. 622.***

Setting Up and Using Multiple Displays

To create the greatest amount of desktop working space, consider adding multiple displays to your system. With the Mac OS, you have always had the capability to have two or more displays working at the same time, with each display showing different portions of the desktop. For example, you can display a document on one display and all the toolbars and palettes you are using on a second. Or you might want to have a document open on one screen and your email application open on the other.

With all Macs except the Mac mini it is easy to connect a second display to your system to give yourself even more working room. If you have Mac Pro, you can use up to eight displays at the same time.

Installing a Display

Installing a display requires two steps. First, connect the appropriate cable to the display and the Mac. Second, install any software that was provided with the display (you won't need to do this for most displays, such as Apple displays). Some displays include a ColorSync profile; if yours does, you should install and use it. If you have to install an additional graphics card in a Mac Pro, the graphics card you install might also have software that provides its special features.

➥ *To learn more about ColorSync, **see** "Synchronizing Color Among Devices," **p. 622**.*

The details of these steps depend on the kind of Mac you have. Each type is covered in the following sections.

Installing a Second Display for Macs with a Built-In Display

In addition to their internal displays, newer iMacs, MacBooks, and MacBook Pros have a Mini DisplayPort port, while older machines come with a Mini-DVI port. To attach a display to this port, you either need a newer Apple LED Cinema Display, which supports Mini DisplayPort, or you need one of Apple's adapters. There are three types, and the type you need depends on the type of display you are going to connect:

- If you have a DVI display, you need either the Mini DisplayPort to Dual-Link DVI Adapter or the Mini-DVI to DVI Adapter.

- If you use a VGA display, you should get either the Mini DisplayPort to VGA Adapter or the Mini-DVI to VGA Adapter (see Figure 31.3).

- If you want to connect your older Mac to a television or other video device, you need the Mini-DVI to Video Adapter (as I write this, there is no video adapter for the Mini DisplayPort interface).

Each of these is available from Apple or other retailers.

Figure 31.3
With a Mini-DVI to VGA Adapter, you can easily connect a second display to older iMacs, MacBooks, and MacBook Pros that use the Mini-DVI port.

Connect the mini-DVI end of the adapter to the mini-DVI port on your Mac. Connect the other end to the display. If you are using the Video Adapter, you can use its S-video connector or the composite (RCA) video connector depending on the input port available on the video device you are using.

On an older MacBook Air, the display connection is a Micro-DVI port. To connect the MacBook Air's Micro-DVI port to a DVI port on an external display, use the Micro-DVI to DVI adapter that comes with the MacBook Air package. (If you can't find yours, you can buy one from the Apple Store or a Mac dealer for about $19.) To connect the MacBook Air to an external display that offers only a VGA connector, use the Micro-DVI to VGA adapter, as shown in Figure 31.4, which comes in the MacBook Air box. To connect the MacBook Air to an external display that only offers either Composite or S-Video connectors, use the Micro-DVI to Video adapter, which is available from the Apple Store or most Apple retailers.

Figure 31.4
With a Micro-DVI to VGA Adapter, you can connect a second display to your older MacBook Air.

Installing a Second Display for Mac Minis

The most recent version of the Mac mini is designed from the ground up to support two displays because it comes with two video output ports: one Mini DisplayPort and one Mini-DVI. (As an added bonus, the new Mac mini even comes with a Mini-DVI to DVI Adapter right in the box.) This means you can connect one display to each port, although you'll probably need an adapter for the Mini DisplayPort interface (unless you have a newer Apple LED Cinema Display, which supports the Mini DisplayPort natively.)

The older Mac mini is the most limited model with respect to displays. That's because the older Mac mini only has one DVI

 note

There are a lot of splitters and other specialized devices that enable you to connect more than two displays to iMacs, MacBooks, MacBook Pros, and MacBook Airs. Some of these devices also enable you to connect two displays to a Mac mini. Providing details about these devices is beyond the scope of this chapter, but if you do a quick search of the Web, you'll find a lot of information about this topic.

port, so it is the only Mac that doesn't support multiple displays out of the box. However, you can use Apple's DVI to Video Adapter to connect the Mac mini to a television or other video device. This can be useful to view the mini's output over a big screen TV, but isn't all that useful for working with your Mac because it doesn't expand your working space.

Installing Multiple Displays for Mac Pros

The Mac Pro is definitely the most expandable in all ways, including multiple display support. All Mac Pro models support two displays out of the box. For even more displays, you can add more graphics cards to a Pro, with each supporting up to two displays for a grand total of eight displays.

The specific number and type of displays a Mac Pro supports depend on the video cards installed in it. The current low-end (which is a relative term) graphics card includes one Mini DisplayPort and one dual-link DVI port. You can connect a display to each port; you can connect one of Apple's monster 30-inch cinema displays to the dual-link port. Other cards include two dual-link ports if you want to use two of the 30-inch displays.

After you've connected displays to both ports on the Pro's first graphics card, you can add additional graphics cards to work with more than two displays.

Many graphics cards are available, each offering differing levels of performance and special features. When choosing a graphics card, consider the following factors:

- **Mac OS X compatibility**—Not all graphics cards are Mac OS X–compatible, so any that you consider should be.

- **Performance**—Graphics cards offer varying levels of performance, such as 2D and 3D acceleration and the display resolution they support. The amount of memory installed on a card is a large determinant of this performance, with more memory being better. Common memory amounts are 256MB or 512MB. Generally, you should obtain the highest-performance card you are willing to pay for.

- **Video interface support**—Most modern graphics cards support the DVI interface used by almost all flat-panel displays. Some offer support for multiple interfaces, such as DVI and VGA.

- **Special features**—These include video digitizers that enable you to digitize video from analog sources, TV tuners that enable you to watch TV or the output from a VCR on your display, and other features for which you might have a use.

 note

If software is provided for the card, such as drivers and applications, you should install the software before you install the card. However, check with the instructions that came with the card to see the order in which the manufacturer recommends the items be installed.

Installing a PCI Express graphics card in a Mac Pro is a relatively easy process.

To install an additional graphics card, do the following:

1. Turn off and unplug the Mac Pro.

2. Put the Mac Pro upright on a solid surface, preferably one where the computer is within easy reach.

3. Pull up the lever on the back of the Mac Pro. This unlocks the side panel, which is the panel on the left when you're looking at the back of the Mac Pro.

4. Open the side panel from the top, and then pull the panel away from the case.

5. Touch something metal to ground yourself.

6. Remove the two screws that hold the slot bracket, as shown in Figure 31.5, and then remove the bracket.

Figure 31.5
Remove the two screws that hold the slot bracket.

7. Place the new graphics card so that its bracket is flush with the open slot cover, and slowly slide the card toward the slot.

8. When the card's connectors are touching the slot and are perfectly aligned with the slot opening, place your thumbs on the edge of the card and press the card gently but firmly into the slot.

9. Reattach the slot bracket.

10. Close the case.

11. Attach displays to the DVI ports of the graphics card.

12. Restart your Mac.

 tip

The easiest way to tell whether or not the card is completely inserted into the slot is to look at the portion of the bracket that touches the case. If that portion isn't flush with the case, the card isn't fully inserted.

Working with Two (or More) Displays

After your Mac is connected to multiple displays, you need to configure the displays to work together. When you have more than one display installed, one of the displays is the primary display. This is the display on which the menu bar, Dock, mounted volumes, and other desktop items are displayed. The rest of the displays contain the windows that you place on them.

To view items on more than one display, do the following:

1. Open the Display pane of the System Preferences application. When you do so, you see a Display pane on each display. On the primary display, this is included in the System Preferences application window. On the other displays, this is an independent window with the name of the display at the top of the window. The settings shown in each Display pane are those that are currently being used for that display. On the primary display, a third tab called Arrangement appears in the Display pane (see Figure 31.6). The Display pane on the other displays contains the normal tabs, but it does not contain any part of the System Preferences interface (see Figure 31.7).

 tip

The Display preferences window for each display is independent. By default, each Display preference window appears on the display it controls. If you want to move all the open Display preference windows together, click the Gather Windows button. This stacks all the open Display preference windows under the current one.

Figure 31.6
This Display pane contains the Arrangement tab, which means it is for the primary display.

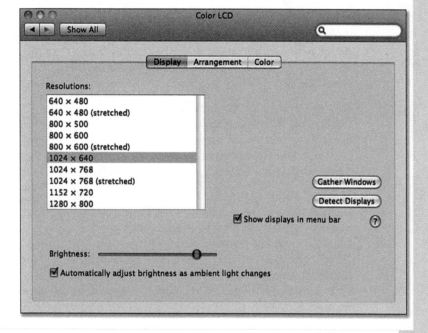

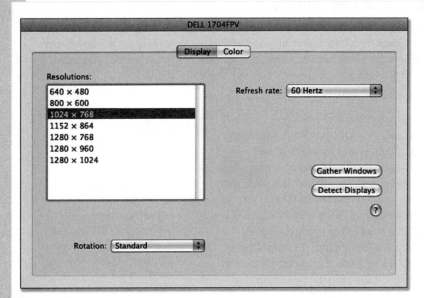

DELL 1704FPV

Display | Color

Resolutions:

640 × 480
800 × 600
1024 × 768
1152 × 864
1280 × 768
1280 × 960
1280 × 1024

Refresh rate: 60 Hertz

Gather Windows

Detect Displays

Rotation: Standard

Figure 31.7
This Display pane is
shown on a secondary
display.

2. Set the resolution, color depth, and refresh rates for each
   display using its Display pane. You can use different settings for each display; for example, if one display is larger
   than the other, you might want a higher resolution on the
   larger display.

3. Click the Arrangement tab on the primary display's
   Display pane. You see a graphical representation of the
   displays attached to your system (see Figure 31.8). The
   primary display is indicated by the menu bar across the
   top of the display window (on the left display in Figure
   31.8).

4. Organize the displays by dragging them on the pane so
   they correspond to the physical arrangement of the displays. For example, drag the display you want to display
   "to your left" to the left side of the pane. This configures
   the virtual desktop so you move the mouse pointer to the
   left to work on the left display. The display icons should be in the same orientation as the physical displays.

tip

If you want your Mac to detect the
displays you have attached to it,
click the Detect Displays button (it
won't be available in all circumstances). The name shown at the top
of the System Preferences application and each Display settings window (there's one for each display)
should identify the display you are
using. Similarly, if you connect
another display to your Mac but it
doesn't become active, click the
Detect Displays button. Your Mac
should recognize and start using the
additional display.

Figure 31.8
This system has two displays attached to it with the primary display located on the left.

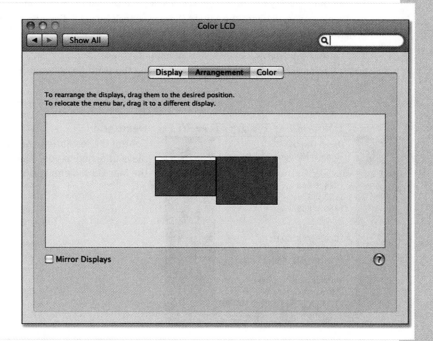

5. Set the primary display by dragging the menu bar onto it. The menu bar, Dock, and other elements move onto the primary display.

Because the desktop stretches across all the displays connected to your system, they act as one large desktop. You can drag windows, palettes, and other elements from one display to another by moving them from one side of the desktop to the other. You can move between the displays by moving the pointer across the divide between them. For example, you might have an image open in Photoshop on one display and all the Photoshop palettes on another. Or, you can have a Word document open on one display and a web browser on another.

You can have multiple displays show the same image by turning on display mirroring. When you do this, each display shows the same desktop. You are limited to the same amount of working space, but that same space is displayed on multiple displays. This is especially useful when you connect a projector to one video port and use a display on the other. You can work using the display while the audience sees what you are doing via the projected image.

Or, if you connect a mobile Mac to an external display, you can have that display face the audience while you work on the internal display.

 note

If a display supports additional features, controls for those features may appear in the Display pane. For example, in Figure 31.7 you can see that the display can be rotated and the current orientation of the display can be selected on the Rotate pop-up menu.

 note

You can drag windows between the displays, but the menu bar and Dock always remain on the primary display.

To configure display mirroring, set the displays to the same resolution. In the Arrangement tab of the Display pane, activate the Mirror Displays check box. All displays connected to the machine then display the same image.

If you add the Displays menu to your menu bar, you can control display mirroring, the resolution, and the color depth of each display by choosing the setting you want from the menu (see Figure 31.9).

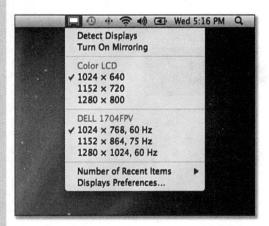

Figure 31.9
Control the resolution and other settings of all the displays attached to your Mac from the Displays menu in the Mac OS X menu bar.

Synchronizing Color Among Devices

One of the most challenging aspects of creating color documents for output on paper or electronically is maintaining consistent color among the images and text in those documents. Each device you use, such as displays, printers, scanners, cameras, and so on, can have a slightly different interpretation of particular colors and can use a different color space. This makes creating a document that contains the exact colors you really want difficult.

Apple's *ColorSync* technology is an attempt to solve this problem. With ColorSync, you configure a ColorSync profile for each device with which you work. If all your devices use a ColorSync profile, the colors across the elements of your document should be more consistent because ColorSync translates colors across different color spaces.

The two general steps to use ColorSync are the following:

1. Use the ColorSync Utility to select and configure a ColorSync profile for each device you use.

2. To select the ColorSync profile for a project, use the color management features of the application in which you want to create that document.

Configuring ColorSync

To configure a ColorSync profile for your devices, do the following:

1. Open the ColorSync Utility (found in Applications, Utilities). The first time you run this, you're prompted to run Profile First Aid, which attempts to repair the various profiles stored on your Mac.

2. Click Verify. The Profile First Aid utility runs and finds all the profiles stored on your Mac. It looks for problems and reports any it finds.

3. Click the Devices button to open the Devices pane. On this pane, you see the list of devices with color implications connected to your Mac, such as cameras, printers, displays, and so on (see Figure 31.10).

Figure 31.10
Expand a device type to see a list of devices of that type connected to your Mac.

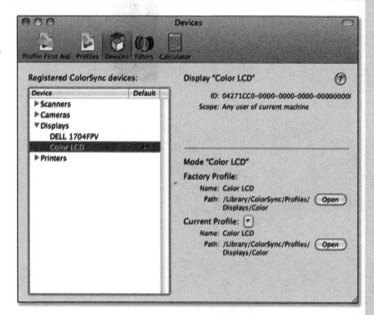

4. Choose the device you want to configure. The current ColorSync profile for that device is shown.

5. To select a different profile, click the Current Profile pop-up menu and choose the profile you want to use. If the one you want to use is not shown on the menu, choose Open and then move to and select the profile you do want to use.

6. Repeat steps 4 and 5 for each device you want to use with ColorSync.

Using ColorSync

After you have installed and configured your device profiles and workflows, the way you use ColorSync depends on the particular applications you use. For example, you can employ the ColorSync profiles when you print a document by using the ColorSync option on the Options pop-up menu in the Print dialog box. Other applications, such as Photoshop, enable you to employ more sophisticated ColorSync features.

WORKING WITH YOUR MAC'S SOUND

Understanding Mac Audio

Sound is an important part of any Mac. From alert sounds that tell you something is happening to being able to enjoy DVD movies, it's important that you have sound capabilities that match what you want to do. Sound goes both ways; you probably want to connect a speaker system to get sound out of your Mac and you might want to use input devices so that you can record various audio on your Mac.

Understanding Audio Output Options

You're likely to use your Mac for a lot more than just work. From listening to music and watching video with iTunes to enjoying DVDs with DVD Player to creating your own masterpieces with iLife applications, sound is a very important component of your system. Modern Macs support at least three audio output options, and the Mac Pro supports even more than that.

When it comes to Mac audio, there are two fundamental options you can choose: analog sound or digital sound. Adding good-quality analog sound to your Mac is easy and inexpensive. But, most Mac users should opt for digital sound instead. Digital sound enables your Mac to take advantage of the highest-quality speakers along with benefits such as surround sound so that your Mac's sound quality can rival that of a home theater system.

When it comes to getting sound from your Mac, your options include the following:

- **Built-in speakers**—iMacs, MacBooks, MacBook Airs, and MacBook Pros include built-in speakers. The speakers in some iMac models are pretty good, but they don't come anywhere close to the sound quality you can get with even a basic set of external analog speakers, and completely pale in comparison to a set of digital surround sound speakers.

- **Analog speakers**—Analog speakers connect to the Mac's audio minijack port. You can find very high-quality analog computer speakers, some of which rival their home stereo counterparts in sound quality. Analog speakers tend to be inexpensive, but they don't provide you with surround sound capabilities.

- **Digital speakers**—For Mac users who are interested in high-quality audio for music, video, movies, and so on, a digital sound system is the way to go. All Macs support digital sound output so you can connect a set of digital speakers (such as a 5.1 surround sound system) to any Mac to enjoy all the quality that digital sound offers. Several ways to do this are explained in this chapter.

 note

Mac Pros and Mac minis include a single speaker built in, but unless you have absolutely no interest in sound quality, you won't want to rely on these speakers to hear what your Mac puts out.

Choosing Speakers

As with other system components, choosing speakers is primarily a task of balancing how much you want to spend versus how demanding you are in terms of quality. At the low end, you can get a basic analog set that has two speakers. For a little more you can get an analog set that also includes a subwoofer. From there, you can move up to more advanced digital systems such as a 5.1 speaker set that includes six speakers to provide full surround sound.

A mind-boggling variety of speaker systems are available, and there's no way to provide even a reasonable overview of them in this short chapter. So, I'll stick with some general guidelines about how to choose a speaker system.

First, assess your Mac's current capabilities. If you use a Mac with built-in speakers that sound fine to you, and you don't use your Mac for movies, the built-ins might be good enough.

Second, determine how important sound quality is for you. If you don't really care that much, you can get a basic set of speakers, such as a 2.1 system and you'll probably be satisfied. If you use your Mac to listen to and watch content and you care about quality, you want to move toward the middle and upper end of the spectrum by obtaining at least a 5.1 sound system for your Mac.

Third, set a budget. Quality speaker systems can get expensive. Decide how much you want to spend and let that drive your selection of speakers (of course, you'll want to do some shopping to make sure you get the best speakers available for your budget). To get a good quality 5.1 system, you can expect to pay about $350.

Installing Speakers

Figuring out which speakers to add to your system is a lot more complicated than installing them. Even though the installation procedure depends on the kind of system and Mac you are using, none of the options require much in the way of time or effort.

Installing Analog Speakers

Analog speakers are the simplest to install. If you have a two-speaker set, you want to place one speaker on your right and one on your left, preferably at ear level. If you have a three-speaker set, you want to place the bass unit on the ground or on your desktop. Connect the input line for the speaker set (which should be connected to one of the satellite speakers or to the bass unit) to the audio output minijack on the Mac. Connect the speakers to the bass and power the system. That's all there is to it.

Installing Digital Speakers Using the Mac's mini-Toslink Digital Audio Out Port

All modern Macs include a combo analog/digital audio-out minijack port. To connect a digital speaker system to the Mac, you need a cable that has a mini-Toslink connector on one end; typically, the cables you use include an adapter that connects to one end of the cable. What's on the other end of the cable needs to be determined by the input connector on your speaker system. There are two basic options: digital coax or Toslink (which is often called optical digital). If you use a 5.1 system, it probably includes a control unit with the input jacks; which cable you need to get is determined by the jacks available on the control unit.

The most difficult part of installing a 5.1 or higher sound system is being able to place the speakers in appropriate locations so you get the maximum benefit of surround sound. Generally, you want to arrange the speakers so that they are all at ear level. With a 5.1 system, you have three front speakers, which are arranged one on the left, one in the center, and one on the right. You have two or more rear speakers, which should be arranged similar to the front speakers, except behind you; these are often the tricky ones depending on how hard it is to route speaker wires to the speaker locations. You usually want to place the bass unit on the floor; where it is in location to you really doesn't affect the sound.

After you've placed the speakers, you need to connect their wires together at a central point; typically, you connect them to the bass speaker along with power. Then you connect the bass input wire to the control unit and use the cable you purchased to connect the control unit's input jack to your Mac's output.

Installing Digital Speakers with a Mac Pro

The Mac Pro includes digital output ports. One is the same mini-Toslink port included on all Macs. The other is a full-sized Toslink port. The capabilities of these ports are similar, so you can use either port to connect a set of digital speakers to a Mac Pro. Otherwise, the steps are the same as described in the previous section.

Installing Digital Speakers Using USB

Some speaker systems use USB to connect a Mac. These systems are limited to two- or three-speaker sets, but if you don't have a need for more advanced audio capabilities, they might be a good choice for you.

A more likely option for USB sound is to connect a USB adapter to a Mac and then connect the speaker system to the adapter. You might use such an adapter when the Mac's built-in audio capabilities are not sufficient for your needs, such as if you want to use specific types of microphones to input sound to your Mac.

Installing Digital Speakers Using a PCI Express Card (Mac Pro)

If you use a Mac Pro, you can install a high-end audio PCI Express card and then connect the speaker system to that card. Mac Pros (and other Macs for that matter) have pretty good audio capabilities built in, so you likely only need to add such a card for specific purposes, which are beyond the scope of this chapter.

Understanding Audio Input Options

There are many situations in which you want to be able to put sound into your Mac. If you use GarageBand, you want to record instruments and vocals. You might want to add narration to a slideshow you create in iPhoto. Or, you might want to be able to use iChat for audio and video conferencing.

The options for inputting sound to a Mac range from the simple to complex. On the simple side, you can use the microphone built in on iMacs, MacBooks, MacBook Airs, and MacBook Pros to record voice narration or other sounds.

You can also attach sound input devices to either USB ports or to the Mac's input sound jacks. For example, you can attach the output of another device, such as a portable cassette recorder, to a Mac's audio input jack to be able to record the device's output on the Mac. Like the audio output jack, the input jack is a combo analog and digital port. To use its digital capabilities, you need to obtain a cable with a mini-Toslink adapter to be able to connect a device to that port digitally.

As with other areas, Mac Pros include the most sophisticated sound input capabilities and include both the standard analog/digital input port along with a full Toslink digital input port. You can also install many kinds of audio PCI Express cards for more sophisticated capabilities.

Choosing and installing audio input devices is more complex than choosing a speaker system simply because there are so many more options. The options are also more complicated because there is a large variety of audio sources from which you might want to input sound.

If you want to record only voice input, the Mac's built-in microphone or a simple USB headset microphone probably meet your needs just fine. If you want to record output from other devices, you can probably connect their output to the Mac's input minijack using a cable similar to one you use to connect speakers to the output minijack. Being able to record multiple or MIDI instruments requires either a USB adapter or a sound card (Mac Pro only).

After you've installed an input device, you can use its output in a variety of ways, such as recording narration for your projects.

Controlling a Mac's Audio

After you've set up a Mac for sound output and input, it's time to take control of all that audio.

There are three ways to control audio on a Mac. First, you can use the Sound pane of the System Preferences application to configure general sound properties for the system. Second, all applications that have audio components provide audio controls; at the least, they enable you to configure the relative volume level of that application's output (versus the overall system volume setting), but most provide other controls as well, such as enabling you to choose an input source for applications in which you can record sound. The third way is to use audio hardware connected to your Mac; for example if you use an external speaker system, it probably has volume controls (most 5.1 systems include a remote to enable you to control output volume, input source, settings, and so on).

In the remainder of this section, you discover the details of using the Sound pane of the System Preferences application to control your system's audio. The other means of controlling audio depend on the specific applications or hardware with which you are working.

The Sound pane of the System Preferences application has three tabs: Sound Effects, Output, and Input (see Figure 32.1). Each tab controls a specific aspect of a Mac's audio.

Figure 32.1
The Sound Effects pane of the System Preferences application provides complete control over your Mac's sound effects, such as the alert sound.

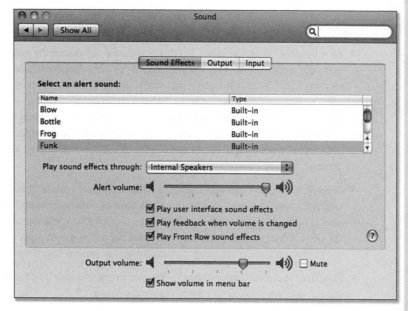

At the bottom of the Sound pane, you can use the Output Volume slider to set the general sound level for your system, or you can mute it by activating the Mute check box. You can also choose to install the Volume menu on the Mac OS X menu bar by activating the Show Volume in Menu Bar check box. If you do so, you can set the volume level by clicking the speaker icon on the menu bar and setting the volume level with the slider.

If your Mac is connected to a digital sound system, these controls are disabled because you control the system volume with that system's controls.

 note

You can also control volume using controls within specific applications, such as iTunes or iMovie. When you do so, the volume control in the application changes the volume of that application's output relative to the system volume level.

When you use the volume controls on an Apple keyboard, you change the system volume level.

Configuring Sound Effects

On the Sound Effects tab, you can configure several aspects of the sound effects your Mac uses to communicate information to you.

When a Mac needs your attention, such as when an error has occurred, it plays the alert sound. Select the alert sound you want to use by selecting it on the list shown in the Sound Effects pane. You then hear a sample of the sound you select.

➥ *To learn how to add and use custom alert sounds,* **see** *"Installing Additional Alert Sounds,"* *p. 632.*

The rest of the Sound Effects tab offers the following preferences:

- **Play Sound Effects Through**—On this pop-up menu, choose the output device on which you want the alert to be played. The options on the menu are determined by the output devices connected to your Mac. If your Mac can output sound through different devices simultaneously, such as via internal speakers and a sound system connected to a USB port, you can select the system on which you want the sounds to be played. This prevents you from being jarred by an alert sound when listening to loud music or movies. If a Mac is connected to only one sound output system, such as to a digital speaker system, you have to have alert sounds played on that device.

- **Alert Volume**—Use this slider to set the volume level of alerts. If you have alerts play through internal speakers while other sound plays through external speakers, you likely need to set the alert volume level relatively high to be able to hear it over the sound coming from the external speakers. If you play all audio through one device, you might want to test the volume level of the alert sound while listening to other content at typical sound level.

- **Play User Interface Sound Effects**—If you activate this check box, you hear sound effects for various actions, such as when you empty the Trash.

- **Play Feedback When Volume Is Changed**—If you activate this check box, you hear a sound when you change the system volume level using the volume keys on your keyboard. The louder the volume setting, the louder the feedback sound. You also see a visual slider appear briefly on the screen to show you the relative sound level you are setting.

■ **Play Front Row Sound Effects**—If you activate this check box, Front Row uses its cool sounds when you activate it, open menus, and so on.

Controlling Sound Output

Use the Output tab to select and configure the output devices you want to use to play all sound other than system alerts (see Figure 32.2). The list of devices through which you can play audio appears at the top of the pane. Select the device you want to use to play sound and then configure the settings for that device if additional controls appear under the device list. The settings you have depend on the device you have installed. For example, with analog speakers, you can control the balance of the satellite speakers using the Balance slider. If you connect a digital system or other device that Mac OS X doesn't recognize, the message "The selected device has no output controls" appears to let you know that you use the device's controls to configure it, such as to select specific output settings.

 note

Some hardware devices include control panels you can use to perform detailed configuration of those devices. In such cases, a pane is added to the System Preferences application for that device. Open its pane to configure it.

Figure 32.2
The Output tab of the Sound pane of the System Preferences application enables you to select and configure a Mac's sound output.

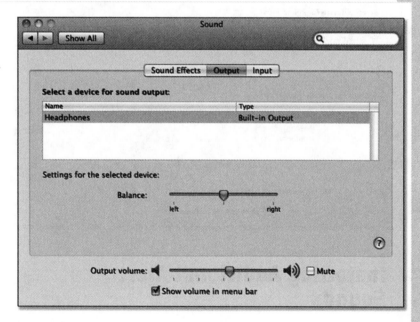

Controlling Sound Input

Use the Input tab to configure sound input devices, such as an internal microphone, the audio in port, or a USB microphone (see Figure 32.3). A list of all sound input devices appears in the upper part of the pane. To capture input from a device, select it on the list. Then use the Input Volume slider to set the input volume level for the selected device. Use the Input Level display to monitor the input volume being received by the input device. The "blips" show you how loud the input sound is. A blip remains at the highest level of sound input to show you where the maximum is. Generally, you should set the level so that most of the sound is coming in at the middle of the slider's range.

 note

Using the Sound pane only configures the general system settings. When you use sound in other applications, make sure you configure the audio settings for that specific application. For example, when you record narration in an application, use its controls to select the appropriate device and to set the input volume level and other settings.

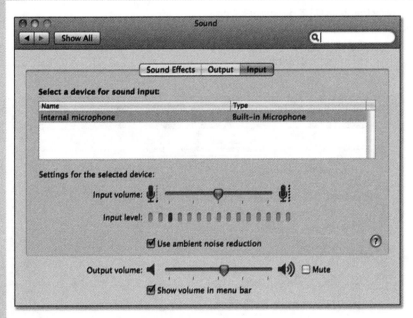

Figure 32.3
You can use the Input tab to set the input volume for devices you use to record sound or for other reasons (such as speech recognition).

Installing Additional Alert Sounds

Mac OSX includes a number of default alert sounds from which you can choose. However, you can also create your own alert sounds if you want your Mac to sport a unique way of communicating with you.

Under Mac OS X, system alert sounds are in the Audio Interchange File Format (AIFF). This is a good thing because you can use many sounds as your alert sound, and using

 note

Under Mac OS X, AIFF files have the `.aiff` filename extension. By default, iTunes appends the `.aif` filename extension to files when you convert them to the AIFF format. Be sure to add the second *f* to the filename extension for the sound you want to add as an alert sound. If you don't, the file is not recognized as a valid alert sound.

iTunes and other applications, you can convert or record almost any sound into the AIFF format and use that sound as a custom alert sound.

There are two basic ways in which you can add alert sounds. You can add them to specific user accounts or to the system so they are accessible to everyone who uses your Mac.

Perform the following steps to add an alert sound to a specific user account:

1. Create or download the AIFF files you want to add to your available alert sounds.

2. Log in to the user account under which you want to make the alert sounds available.

3. Drag the new alert sounds to the following directory: /*shortusername*/Library/Sounds. The new alert sound is available to that user account on the Alert Sounds list in the Sound pane of the System Preferences application.

You can also add alert sounds to the system so they are available to all the user accounts on your machine. However, to do this, you must log in under the root account.

➡ *To learn how to enable and log in under the root account,* ***see*** *"Enabling the Root User Account," **p. 461**.*

To add alert sounds to your system, do these steps:

1. Create or download the AIFF files you want to add to your alert sounds.

2. Drag the AIFF file into the directory *Mac OS X*/System/Library/Sounds, where *Mac OS X* is the name of your Mac OS X startup volume.

3. You are warned that the Sounds directory cannot be modified. Click Authenticate and enter an administrator username and password to finish moving the files. The new sounds are available on the Alert Sounds list on the Sound pane of the System Preferences application.

 note

If the System Preferences application is open when you install a new alert sound, you must quit and restart it to see the new sound on the list.

When you install your own system alert sounds in the alert sound list, the type for the sounds you add is Custom instead of Built-in. Built-in sounds are stored in the Sound folder in the System Library folder instead of the user's Library folder.

 caution

You can't modify files or directories that are within the Mac OS X system directory without authenticating as an administrator or being logged in under the root account. Be careful when you are logged in under the root account because you can change anything on your system, including changing vital system files in such a way that your Mac fails to work. You can also delete any files on the machine while you are logged in as root.

 note

The alert sounds you add to the system when logged in under the root account are Built-in, just as the alert sounds that are installed with Mac OS X.

33

INSTALLING, CONFIGURING, AND USING PRINTERS

Finding, Installing, and Using Printers

If you want to get your work out on paper, you can use many types of printers to get the job done. Under Mac OS X, you install and manage printers using the Print & Fax pane of the System Preferences application, the Printer Browser, and the Printer Setup Utility application. And Mac OS X includes support for a large number of printers by default.

There are two ways you can connect a printer to your Mac: directly or through a network. To connect a printer directly to your Mac, attach the printer cable to the appropriate port on your Mac (USB or Ethernet). How you connect a printer to your network depends on the type of network you are using. If you are using an Ethernet network, you can attach a cable from the nearest hub or print server to your printer. You can also choose to share either type of printer over a wired or wireless network. If your network includes an Apple AirPort Base Station or an AirPort Express Base Station, you can connect a USB printer to the base station's USB port on either kind of base station or to one of the Ethernet ports on the AirPort Base Station.

Mac OS X supports several printer communication protocols, including, IP Printing, Open Directory, Bonjour, direct connection through USB, and Windows Printing.

Using Bonjour enables your Mac to actively seek devices to which it is networked. In the case of Bonjour printers, your Mac can discover the printers it can access and automatically configure itself to use those printers. No configuration on your part is required. However, printers have to be Bonjour-capable for this to work.

Configuring Printers

There are many types of printers you can use with Mac OS X. In this section, you learn how to work with the most common types of printers.

Configuring a Local USB Printer

Support for many USB printers is built in to Mac OS X. After you connect your USB printer, follow these steps to configure it:

1. If the printer has Mac OS X–compatible software, install it—support for many printers is built in to the operating system.

2. Open System Preferences and click Print & Fax. The Print & Fax preferences appear (see Figure 33.1).

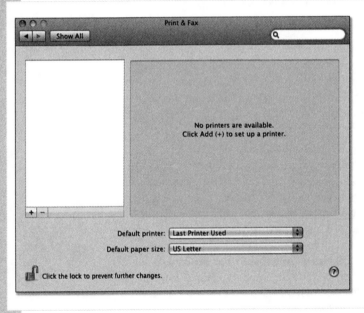

Figure 33.1
Use the Print & Fax pane of the System Preferences application to configure the printers your Mac uses.

3. Click the Add Printer button (the plus sign). The Printer Browser appears and immediately seeks out all the printers it can find. At the top of the browser, you see buttons for each type of printer that Mac OS X supports, including Default, which finds all the printers your Mac can access; IP, which you use to configure printers via their IP addresses; Windows, which you select to find and configure printers on Windows PCs, and so on. When you select one of these types, the browser's lower pane is reconfigured for the type of printer you selected.

4. For a printer connected to your Mac's USB port, select the Default button in the toolbar. The list of printers shown in the lower pane of the browser is refreshed (see Figure 33.2).

Figure 33.2
The Printer Browser finds printers connected to your Mac.

5. Select the printer you want to configure by clicking its name in the list. Information about that printer is gathered, and Mac OS X attempts to choose the best driver software for it, which is shown on the Print Using pop-up menu (see Figure 33.3).

Figure 33.3
Mac OS X can configure most printers automatically, as it did for this one when I selected the Epson Style CX4600 on the printer list.

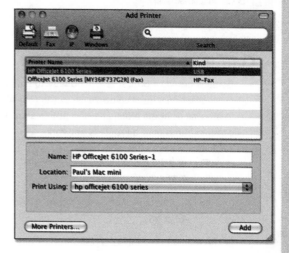

6. If you don't want to use the default printer name shown in the Name box, select it and type a new name.

7. If the default location isn't what you want, select it and change that, too.

8. If Mac OS X found a driver for your printer and selected it on the Print Using pop-up menu, leave that selection as it is; if a driver wasn't found, open the pop-up menu and choose the appropriate driver. If you can't find a driver for your printer, you need to get one from the printer's manufacturer.

9. Click Add. You return to the Printer List on the Print & Fax pane and the printer you selected and configured appears on the list (see Figure 33.4).

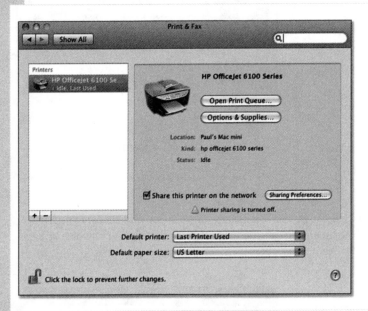

Figure 33.4
A new printer has been installed on this Mac.

Configuring a Network Printer

Using a network printer is a good way to share a printer among multiple users; with the rise of home networks and the decrease in the cost of networkable printers, installing networked printers in a home or home office is also a practical option. Using an AirPort Base Station, any USB printer can be shared over a wireless network.

➡ *To learn how to establish a wired network, **see** Chapter 17, "Wired Networking with Mac OS X," p. 361.*

➡ *To learn about sharing a printer via AirPort, **see** Chapter 18, "Wireless Networking with Mac OS X," p. 385.*

In the following example, a printer is installed on a small Ethernet network. The steps to configure such a printer are:

1. Connect power to the printer.

2. Connect the printer to an Ethernet hub.

3. If the printer has Mac OS X–compatible software, install it—support for most laser printers is built into the operating system.

4. Open the Print & Fax pane of the System Preferences application.

5. Click the Add Printer button (the plus sign). The Printer Browser appears and begins to search for printers with which your Mac can communicate. The printers it finds are shown on the printer list.

6. Select the printer you want to install. Mac OS X attempts to find the driver and configure the printer. If it can do so, you see the printer's name, its location, and the driver Mac OS X has selected.

7. If you don't want to use the default printer name shown in the Name box, select it and type a new name.

8. If the default location isn't what you want, select it and change that, too.

9. If Mac OS X found a driver for your printer and selected it on the Print Using pop-up menu, leave that selection as it is; if a driver wasn't found, open the pop-up menu and choose the appropriate driver. If you can't find a driver for your printer, you need to get one from the printer's manufacturer either on the disc that accompanied the printer, or on the manufacturer's website.

10. Click Add. You return to the Printer List on the Print & Fax pane and the printer you selected and configured appears on the list. The printer is ready to print your documents (see Figure 33.5).

Figure 33.5
This printer is connected to a hub on a local network.

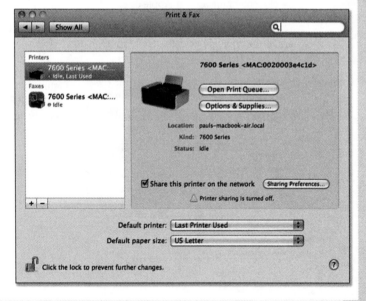

Configuring Other Types of Printers

Mac OS X supports many types of printers connected in a variety of ways. Although you are most likely to use a printer connected directly to your Mac or through a network—in which case the Printer Browser likely does most of the configuration work for you—you might have a more unusual situation, such as wanting to use a Windows PC's printer.

In the event that the Printer Browser doesn't automatically find and configure a printer, you can use its advanced tools to do the configuring:

1. Open the Print & Fax pane of the System Preferences application and click the Add Printer button (the plus sign). The Printer Browser appears.

2. If the printer you want to install doesn't appear in the list, click the button for the type of printer you want to configure. Commonly used options are in the following list:

   - **IP** If a printer is installed on a network, but the browser doesn't find it automatically, you can use this tool to configure a printer by entering its IP address on the network. The only challenge of using this option is determining the printer's address. Most network printers have a function that prints the printer's current configuration options, including its IP address. See your printer's documentation to determine how to print this information.

   - **Windows** If your Mac is connected to a Windows printer, use this tool to configure it.

   - **AppleTalk** AppleTalk is a local network protocol that can also be used by a Mac to communicate with a printer. For you to use AppleTalk, AppleTalk services must be enabled on your Mac. When you select the AppleTalk tool, your Mac identifies all the printers with which it can communicate via AppleTalk.

After you select a tool, the browser is reconfigured with the controls you use to configure printers of the type you selected (see Figure 33.6).

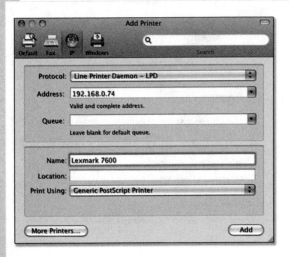

Figure 33.6
Use the IP Printer tool to configure a printer based on its IP address.

3. Use the tools on the browser to configure the printer. Each offers a different tool set, but the general tasks are the same. Select the printer you want to configure, choose its driver, name it, and so on. For example, to configure an IP printer, you select the protocol on the Protocol pop-up menu, enter the IP address, and choose a queue for that printer. Then, name it, create a location name, and choose its driver. Other tools have similar tasks.

4. Click Add. The printer is installed on your Mac and you see it on the Printer List on the Print & Fax pane of the System Preferences application.

Managing Printers

Manage the printers with which your Mac can work using the Print & Fax pane of the System Preferences application (see Figure 33.7). In the left part of this pane, you see the printers installed on your Mac. For the selected printer, you see information pertaining to its location and status, and you have access to other options in the area to the right of the Printers list. At the bottom of the pane are a number of controls you can use to set your printing preferences. These include the following:

Figure 33.7
Use the Print & Fax pane to set printer preferences for your system.

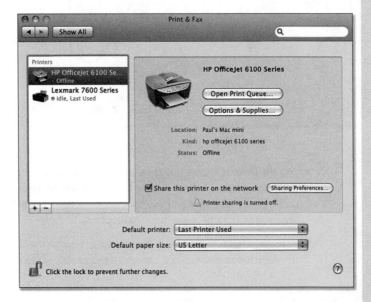

- Select a printer and click the Delete button (-) to remove the printer from the list of available printers.

- Select a printer and click Open Print Queue to open its Print Queue window (more on this later in the chapter; see "Printing Under Mac OS X").

- Select a printer and click Options & Supplies to open its Info sheet (see Figure 33.8). This sheet has four tabs. Use the General tab to update the printer's name and location information. You also see configuration information for the printer, such as the version of the driver being used, its URL, and so on. Use the Driver tab to change the driver being used for the printer and to configure additional options it supports, such as paper trays, memory configuration, and the like. The Supply Levels tab provides you with information about the consumables for your printer (if supported.) This is a handy way to find out how much ink is left in one of your printer's cartridges. When you click the Supplies button, Mac OS X opens your default web browser and attempts to locate supplies for the printer, such as ink cartridges, in the Apple Store. In the Utility tab (not available with all printers), click Open Printer Utility to open the utility program that was installed along with the printer.

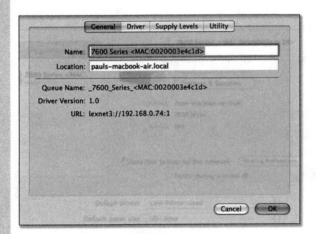

Figure 33.8
The Options & Supplies sheet enables you to configure additional options for a selected printer.

- Use the Default Printer pop-up menu to determine which printer is selected automatically in the Print dialog box. The Last Printer Used selection causes the dialog box to remember the last printer you printed with. If you choose one of the installed printers, that printer is selected each time you print (it becomes the default printer).

- Use the Default Paper Size in Page Setup to choose the default size of paper that is selected in the Page Setup dialog box for the selected printer when you print.

Working with Shared Printers

Under Mac OS X, you can share printers connected to your Mac over wired and wireless networks, as well as those connected directly to your Mac through USB or Ethernet. If your Mac can communicate with a printer, it can also share that printer with other computers with which it can communicate. You can also access printers being shared with you.

Sharing a Printer Connected to Your Mac

To share a printer, perform the following steps:

1. Install and configure the printer you want to share on your Mac.

2. Open the Sharing pane of the System Preferences application. On this pane, you see the list of services you can share on your Mac.

3. Activate the Printer Sharing check box.

4. Activate the check box next to each printer you want to share (see Figure 33.9). The selected printers are now accessible to other Macs on the same network.

 note

You can also share printers that are connected to your Mac through a network connection, but you don't need to do this. Instead, just install the network printer on each machine from which it should be available.

Figure 33.9
The printers connected to this Mac can be used by other Macs on the same network.

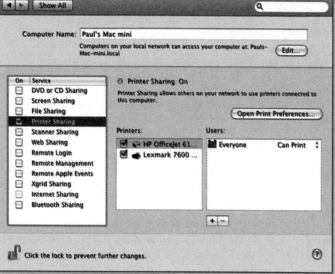

When you share a printer, the Mac from which it is being shared must be running for the printer to be available to other computers on the network. If it isn't, the printer won't be accessible to those other Macs.

tip

If your network includes an AirPort Extreme or AirPort Express Base Station, you can connect a USB printer to the Base Station to share it.

Adding Shared Printers to Your Mac

To access printers being shared on a network, use the following steps:

1. Open the Print & Fax pane of the System Preferences application.

2. Click the Add Printer button. The Printer Browser appears and searches for printers with which your Mac can communicate. Printers that are being shared with your Mac have Bonjour Shared or Shared Printer in the Kind column (see Figure 33.10).

Figure 33.10
Shared printers show either Bonjour or Shared Printer in the Kind column.

3. Select the shared printer you want to be able to access.

4. Change the name and location if you want to; in most cases, you should leave the default selections.

5. If your Mac was able to find a driver for the printer, leave the default driver as the selection on the Print Using pop-up menu. If no driver was found, use the pop-up menu to select a driver for the printer.

6. Click Add. The shared printer is added to the printer list and you are able to print with it just like the printers connected directly to your Mac or that are connected to your network.

Printing Under Mac OS X

In all Mac applications that support printing, you initiate a print job by selecting File, Print, or by pressing ⌘-P. When you print a document, you see the print dialog box for the current printer; the printer shown on the Printer pop-up menu is determined by the preference you set (either the last printer you used or the default). You can choose any other printers that are installed on your Mac or those being shared on the network by using the Printer pop-up menu (see Figure 33.11). The Print dialog box contains a variety of pop-up menus and other tools you can use to configure a print job.

Figure 33.11
The list of printers available to your Mac, including any that are being shared with you over a network, is shown on the Printer pop-up menu.

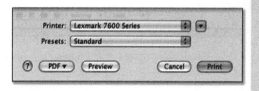

There are two versions of the Print dialog box. The smaller version is shown in Figure 33.10. If you click the expansion triangle next to the Printer pop-up menu, the dialog box expands to the version shown in Figure 33.12.

Figure 33.12
Click the expansion triangle beside the Printer pop-up menu to expand the Print dialog box and see its extra options.

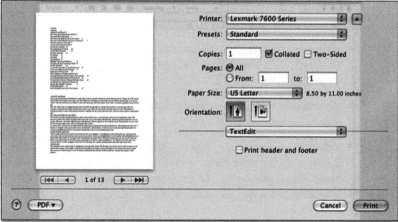

The specific options you see in the Print dialog box depend on the printer you are using and the application from which you are printing. Select the settings you want to configure from the third pop-up menu (counting the Printer and Preset pop-up menus as the first and second ones) and then configure those settings with the controls that appear in the lower part of the dialog box. Depending on the printer and application you are using, the options you have can include the following:

- **Printer**—You can use this pop-up menu to select a printer to which to print. You can also open the Printer Browser by selecting Add Printer. You can open the Print & Fax pane of the System Preferences application by choosing Print & Fax Preferences.

- **Presets**—You can switch between the standard settings for the selected printer, or you can save a custom configuration and switch to that one.

- **Copies & Pages**—These controls enable you to set the number of pages you want to print and choose the part of a document you want to print. Several applications also show a mini-preview of a document on the left side of the Print dialog or sheet.

- **Two-Sided**—If a printer is capable of duplexing, you can select the check-box to save paper when printing.

Most applications have specific print settings that you can configure, as well. A pop-up menu with the name of the current application appears on the Print dialog box or sheet and allows you to adjust the following print options:

- **Layout**—These commands enable you to control how many pages print per sheet of paper, the direction in which your document layout prints, and whether a border is printed.

- **Scheduler**—This pane enables you to schedule a print job.

- **Paper Feed**—These controls enable you to select a paper tray for the print job, or you can choose to do a manual feed.

- **Print Settings**—Controls in this pane enable you to choose a paper type and select from the print modes offered by a printer (such as color, black and white, draft, and so on).

- **Image Quality**—These controls enable you to determine the quality with which images are printed—to save toner, for example.

- **ColorSync**—This pane enables you to choose ColorSync options for the selected printer.

- **Summary**—The Summary area displays a description of the print job you have currently configured. This can be useful if you have configured a complex print job and want to check it before you run it.

 tip

In the Copies & Pages pane for most printers, you have the option to collate documents by checking the Collated check box. If you have ever had to hand-collate a large document, you will really appreciate this feature.

Some applications allow you to preview a print job by clicking the Preview button. The document opens in the Preview application and appears as it does in the printed version. When you're ready to print, you can print it from that application. You can also see a preview by clicking the PDF pop-up menu and selecting Open PDF in Preview.

When you are ready to print, click Print or press Return.

After you have sent a document to a printer, the print proxy application for that printer opens. You know this because the Printer's icon opens on the Dock and begins to bounce; you can click this to open the printer to access its queue application (see Figure 33.13). You can also monitor the status of print jobs by opening the Print & Fax pane in System Preferences and then either double-clicking the printer in the printer list or clicking the printer and then clicking Open Print Queue.

With this tool, you can perform the following tasks:

- Click a print job and click Hold. The printer temporarily stops printing the current job and continues printing any other pending print jobs.

- Click Resume and the current job on hold starts printing again.

- Click Pause Printer to pause all current and pending print jobs.

Figure 33.13
Clicking the printer's icon on the Dock opens the queue for that printer.

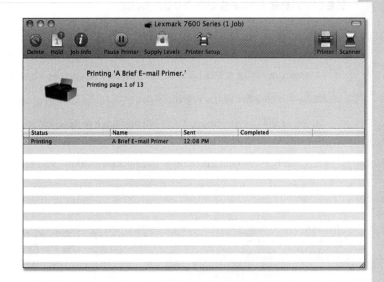

- Click Resume Printer and the currently paused printer starts printing again.

- Click the Info button to open the Options & Supplies information for the printer.

- Click Printer Setup to open the printer's utility software.

- Move print jobs up or down the list to change the order in which they print.

- Select a print job on the list and click Delete to remove the job from the queue.

 tip

Some additional actions can be useful for some printers. For example, you can click the Supply Levels button to check the amount of ink left in a printer's cartridges if that action is supported by the printer you are using.

Sending Faxes with Mac OS X

With the rise of email, faxing documents isn't something you are likely to need to do that often, but it can come in handy from time to time. Mac OS X has the capability to send and receive faxes. Of course, to use this capability, your Mac must have a modem installed and that modem must be connected to a working phone line. With the rise of broadband, this isn't always the case. Modern Macs don't include a dial-up modem by default; it is an optional device.

 note

If you're like me and no longer have a dial-up modem, but you need to send a fax, check out the email-to-fax services that are available. These services allow you to send and receive faxes via an email application. You can find a lot of these services to choose from by doing a quick web search.

Receiving Faxes on Your Mac

To configure your Mac to receive faxes, do the following steps:

1. Connect your Mac's dial-up modem or fax printer to a working phone line.

2. Open the Print & Fax pane of the System Preferences application.

3. Select your fax in the Printers list.

4. Enter the phone number to which you have connected your Mac's modem in the Fax Number field.

5. Click Receive Options to open the Receive Options sheet.

6. Activate the Receive Faxes on This Computer check box, as shown in Figure 33.14.

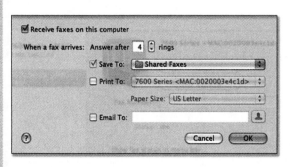

Figure 33.14
Use the Receive Options sheet to set up your Mac to receive faxes.

7. Use the Answer After field to set the number of rings before your Mac answers the phone. Make sure this number is set before any answering machine or voice mail picks up the call.

8. If you want the fax to be saved as a file, activate the Save To check box and select the location in which you want fax files to be saved on the pop-up menu.

9. If you want the fax to be printed, activate the Print To check box and select the printer to which it should be printed on the pop-up menu.

10. If you want the fax sent via email, activate the Email To check box and type the email address (or click the Addresses icon and select the recipient from the Addresses dialog box).

11. Click OK.

12. If you want to be able to control faxing from the desktop, activate the Show Fax Status In Menu Bar check box. The Fax menu is added to the Mac OS X menu bar.

When the phone number to which your Mac is connected receives a call and the number of rings you set have occurred, your Mac answers the phone and attempts to receive a fax. If it receives one, it is saved or printed as indicated by your configuration choices.

 tip

If you want to share your Mac's faxing capability, for example when it is the only Mac connected to a phone line, activate the Share This Fax On the Network check box.

Sending Faxes from Your Mac

You can send faxes from within any application on your Mac as easily as you can receive them.

Open the Print dialog box and then click the PDF menu. Choose Fax PDF and use the resulting tools to configure and send the fax.

Creating a PDF File

Portable Document Format (PDF) files are one of the most useful ways to output documents for electronic viewing. Any PDF document can easily be read by anyone using any computer platform. PDF documents maintain their appearance because they do not rely on fonts and other aspects of the system on which they are viewed.

Under Mac OS X, PDFs are a native file format. You can create PDFs from within any Mac OS X application, and you can read PDF files with the Preview application.

note

The free Adobe Reader application is also available for Mac OS X. This application offers more features for viewing PDFs than does Preview, but either application get the job done. To download a copy of Adobe Reader, visit get.adobe.com/reader/.

To create your own PDF file, follow these steps:

1. Open the document for which you want to create a PDF.

2. Select File, Print, or press ⌘-P.

3. Open the PDF pop-up menu and choose Save as PDF. The Save dialog box appears.

4. Name the document and select a location in which to save it. Use the filename extension `.pdf`.

5. Complete the fields that appear for the PDF, which are Title, Author, Subject, and Keywords. This information is associated with the PDF file and is available to anyone who accesses the PDF.

6. Click Security Options. The PDF Security Options dialog box appears (see Figure 33.15).

Figure 33.15
You can secure a PDF you create using the Security Options dialog box.

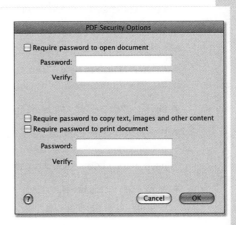

7. To require that the viewer enter a password to be able to view the PDF, activate the Require Password to Open Document check box and enter the password in the Password and Verify boxes. In order to open the document, you need to provide the password you create to the people whom you want to be able to access it.

8. To protect content from being copied, activate the Require Password to Copy Text, Images and Other Content check box. With this box checked, viewers cannot select and copy the document's content and paste it into other documents.

9. If you want to restrict the PDF from being printed unless the viewer has the correct password, activate the Require Password to Print Document check box and enter the password in the Password and Verify boxes. This can be the same as the open password or it can be a different one.

10. Click OK. The options you selected are set and the dialog box closes. You return to the Save dialog box.

11. Click Save. The PDF is created in the location you specified with the settings and other information you configured.

One thing to note is that creating a PDF in this way does not always create or preserve any hyperlinks in a document. For example, if you create a PDF of a web page in Safari, the links on that page will be functional. However, if you create a text document that contains a table of contents in which the entries are hyperlinked to the sections in the document, the resulting PDF may not contain active links. Being able to create a PDF from any document using the Print command is useful when you want to send your documents to other people.

 tip

Creating a PDF version of a document is also a great way to capture versions of that document at specific points in time for archival purposes.

To create PDFs that contain hyperlinks and other electronic document features, you may need to use a more sophisticated application. For example, Adobe applications can save documents in PDF format and preserve hyperlinks within those documents. Or, you can use the full Acrobat application to create more sophisticated PDFs from any application.

In addition to a standard PDF document, there are a number of other options on the Print sheet's pop-up menu:

- **Open PDF in Preview**   This command creates a temporary PDF of the page and opens the Preview application.

- **Save as PostScript**   This creates a PostScript file for the document.

- **Fax PDF**   This command presents you with the dialog boxes to specify the fax number to send the document to, as well as add a cover page. When you are ready, click Fax. Note that you must have a fax modem connected to your Mac for this option to work.

- **Mail PDF**   This creates a PDF of the document and attaches it to an email message in your default email application.

- **Save as PDF-X**   This commands saves the document in the PDF/X format which adds information intended to improve the reliability of printing the document. This format is intended to be used when the desired output of the document is a high-quality printed version. PDF/X files can be sent directly to a printer and be rendered more reliably than standard PDF files.

- **Save PDF to iPhoto**   This creates a PDF version of the document and adds it to iPhoto.

- **Save PDF to Web Receipts Folder**   This create a Web Receipts folder in your Documents directory (if it does not already exist.) This is a handy place to store all of the receipts for those late-night Amazon.com buying sprees.

- **Edit Menu**   Use this command to edit the contents of the PDF menu. You can use the Add Command button (the plus sign) to add commands to the menu or the Remove Command button (the minus sign) to remove commands from the menu. These tools enable you to configure the menu so that it contains only those commands that you use regularly.

USING DATA STORAGE DEVICES

Using Disks and Discs

Working with hard drives, CDs, DVDs, and other similar types of storage devices is an important part of using Mac OS X. The following bullets provide information about some useful disk- and disc-related tasks:

- You can control whether mounted disk, disc, and volume icons are automatically shown on the desktop using the Finder Preferences window (select Finder, Preferences and click the General tab). In the Show These Items on the Desktop section, activate the check box beside each type of storage device you want to see on the desktop: Hard Disks; External Disks; or CD, DVDs, and iPods. (If you chose not to have disk icons mounted on the desktop, you can access the mounted disks and volumes using the Computer folder and the Sidebar.)

- You can eject removable disks by dragging them to the Trash; selecting them and selecting File, Eject; pressing ⌘-E or your Apple keyboard's eject button; using the contextual menu's Eject command; or using the Eject icon that you can place on the Finder toolbar. You can also eject any ejectable item by clicking the Eject button that appears next to that item in the Sidebar. You should always eject any kind of disk before you disconnect it from your Mac; if you don't, some or all of the data it contains might be damaged.

 tip

When you select a mounted volume (such as a CD), the Trash icon on the Dock becomes an eject symbol to indicate you are unmounting a volume rather than deleting it.

- To erase a disk under Mac OS X, use the Disk Utility application (Applications/Utilities). Open the application, select the disk you want to erase, click the Erase tab, select the format on the Volume Format pop-up menu, enter the volume name, and click Erase.

- Disk Image is a file type that mimics the behavior of a disk. When you open a disk image, it acts just as if it were a real disk. Disk images are most commonly used to distribute applications. When a disk image is mounted, you can open it as you would a physical disk, eject it, and so on.

➥ *To learn more about disk images,* **see** *"Installing Mac OS X Applications,"* **p. 128.**

➥ *To learn how to configure the action when you insert blank media,* **see** *"Configuring Disc Actions,"* **p. 661.**

Installing and Using a Hard Drive

Your Mac's hard drive is one of its most important devices, and its performance and operation have a major impact on the performance and operation of your system. At some point, you may want to increase the amount of hard disk space available to you. Adding more hard drive space is relatively simple in most cases and offers many benefits to you.

Installing an External Hard Drive

Installing an external hard drive is very simple. Connect the power supply to the drive and to an electrical outlet, if needed (some drives take their power from the interface). Then, connect a FireWire, USB 2.0, or FireWire 800 cable to the drive and your Mac.

After you have connected the drive and powered it up, the installation part is complete (easy installation is a good reason to use an external drive). Because FireWire and USB are hot swappable, you don't even need to shut your Mac down to connect it to an external hard drive. However, you should immediately initialize and partition the disk before you place any data on it. (See "Initializing and Partitioning a Hard Drive," later in this chapter.)

Installing an Internal Hard Drive

Installing an internal hard drive is a bit more complicated than installing an external drive, but it is still relatively easy to do.

Before you get started, read through the instructions contained in your Mac's user manual. Then do the following:

1. Get the drive ready to install by configuring it as a slave drive (if necessary); see the instructions that came with the drive for help with this. Typically, this involves configuring jumper clips on specific pins at the back of the drive. Most of the time, these pins are already set in the appropriate configuration.

 note

Because I don't recommend that most users replace a hard drive in most Macs, this section provides information only on adding additional hard drives to a Mac Pro. If you are comfortable enough working inside a Mac to be able to replace a hard drive, you probably don't need any help doing so.

2. Back up the data on your Mac (just in case).

3. Turn off and unplug the Mac Pro.

4. Put the Mac Pro upright on a solid surface, preferably one where the computer is within easy reach.

5. Pull up the lever on the back of the Mac Pro. This unlocks the side panel, which is the panel on the left when you're looking at the back of the Mac Pro.

6. Open the side panel from the top, and then pull the panel away from the case.

7. Touch something metal to ground yourself.

8. Locate the hard disk bay where you want to install the hard disk. Figure 34.1 shows the Mac Pro's four hard disk bays.

Figure 34.1
The Mac Pro's disk drive bays

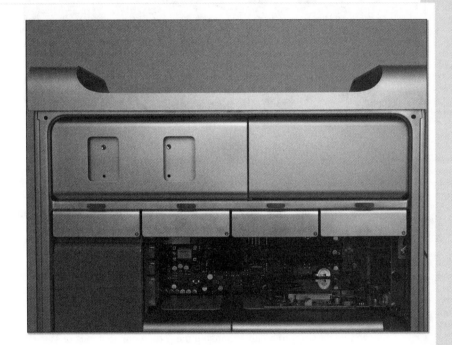

9. Pull out an empty hard disk bay bracket.

10. Remove the four screws from the bracket.

11. Take your new hard disk and line up the four holes on the bottom of the disk with the four holes in the bracket.

12. Use the screws to attach the hard disk to the bracket.

13. Slide the bracket back into the bay (see Figure 34.2) until the hard disk connectors snap into place.

Figure 34.2
After you've attached the hard disk to the bracket, slide the bracket back into the bay.

14. Replace the side panel and push the latch down.

15. Power the Mac up.

The Mac should restart normally. When it boots up, you might not notice any difference because you can't use the drive until you initialize it, as described next.

Initializing and Partitioning a Hard Drive

Before you use a hard drive, whether it is internal or external, you should initialize it (you have to initialize most internal drives before you can use them, but most external drives can be used out of the box). You can also partition a hard drive to create multiple volumes on a single drive (for example, you might want to be able to install more than one instance of Mac OS X on a single disk).

When you partition a hard drive, logical volumes are created for each partition on the disk. For most practical purposes, a logical volume looks and acts just like a separate hard drive. There can be some small performance advantages to partitioning a disk, or you might choose to partition it to help you keep your system organized. The most likely reason to partition a drive is to be able to run more than one version of the Mac OS on your computer—each version needs to be installed on a separate volume. For example, you should create at least one partition to install an alternate startup version of Mac OS X in case your primary stops working correctly.

One of the results of partitioning a drive is that all the volumes outside of the startup volume are not a part of the default Mac OS X organization scheme. This can be a benefit or a problem depending on what you are doing. For example, documents you store on a separate volume aren't secured using Mac OS X's default permissions, as documents you store within your Home folder are. If you want to provide broader access to files, this is a good thing. If you don't want people to be able to access these documents outside the control of Mac OS X's security, it isn't.

Be aware that when you partition a drive, the size of each partition becomes a size limitation, just as if the volume was a separate disk. If your partition sizes are too small, you might run out of free space in a specific volume even though the disk on which that volume is stored still has plenty of space. Generally, you should keep your partitions pretty large. If you run out of space on a partition, you have to delete files from it or re-partition the disk, which means that you must start over and reformat the disk (resulting in all files being erased). Unless you have a very specific reason to do so, you typically shouldn't partition a drive into more than two volumes. If you aren't going to have multiple versions of the Mac OS installed, you might not want to use multiple partitions at all.

To initialize and partition a disk, perform the following steps:

1. In Finder, select Applications, Utilities and then launch Disk Utility. In the Disk Utility window, you see two panes. In the left pane, you see the drives installed in your system (the drives are labeled by their capacities and types). Under each disk, you see the volumes into which that disk has been partitioned.

2. Select the drive with which you want to work. At the top of the right pane are five tabs; each tab enables you to view data about a drive or to perform a specific action. At the bottom of the window, you see detailed information about the drive with which you are working, such as its connection bus, type, capacity, and so on (see Figure 34.3).

Figure 34.3
The Source pane of the Disk Utility application shows one internal hard drive, and one external FireWire drive. Information about the selected drive appears at the bottom of the window.

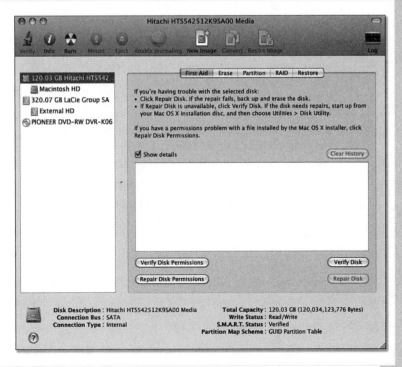

3. Click the Partition tab. In the left part of this pane, you see a graphical representation of the partitions on the disk. If the disk is currently partitioned, you see its current partitions. If you are working with a new disk or one with a single partition, you see one partition called "Untitled" (if you've not named it before). In the right part of the pane, you see information about the selected volume, such as its name, current format, and size.

4. Select the number of partitions you want to have on the drive by using the Volume Scheme pop-up menu. You can choose Current, which leaves the partitions as they are, or the number of partitions you want from 1 to 16. After you choose the number of partitions, each partition is represented by a box in the disk graphic shown under the Volume Scheme pop-up menu. The partitions are called `Untitled 1`, `Untitled 2`, and so on.

note

Another reason you might want to partition a hard drive is to more easily share files with other users of your Mac. Because volumes outside the startup volume don't use Mac OS X's default security settings, it can be easier to provide access to a volume that all users share. For example, you might want to store files related to an iMovie project that other people are helping you with. They can then access these files without needing access to your Home folder.

5. Select a volume by clicking its box. The volume's partition is highlighted and information for that volume is shown in the Volume Information area.

6. Name the selected volume by typing a name in the Name box. As you type the name, it appears in the partition's box.

7. Select the format type from the Format pop-up menu. You should almost always select Mac OS Extended (Journaled) or Mac OS Extended. The journaling option is the best choice if it is available because it improves Mac OS X's capability to recover from unexpected power losses and other such circumstances. For each of these options, you can choose Case-sensitive. If you select a Case-sensitive format, file names are case sensitive meaning that a file called `filename.file` is not the same as a file called `FileName.file`. In most cases, you should choose Mac OS Extended (Case-sensitive, Journaled) to take advantage of the most sophisticated format option.

note

The other format options include MS-DOS, Unix File System, and Free Space. These are useful in some special circumstances. For example, if you are going to run a Unix OS system (apart from Mac OS X) on your machine, you might want to use the Unix File System for one partition.

8. Enter the size of the partition in the Size box. You can also set the size of a partition by dragging its Resize handle in the Volumes pane.

9. Select the next partition.

10. Repeat steps 6–8 for each of the volumes (see Figure 34.4).

caution

Partitioning a drive erases all the data on it. If the drive has data on it, make sure you back it up before you partition the drive.

Figure 34.4
This drive contains two volumes after it has been partitioned; one called Data and the other called Backups.

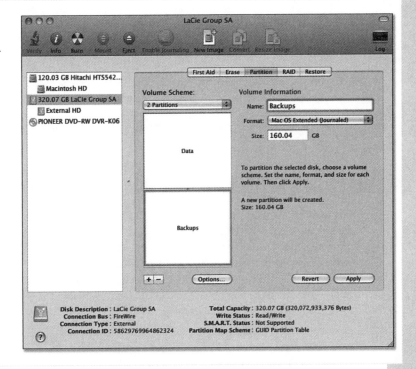

11. Click Options. The Options sheet appears (see Figure 34.5). If you want to use the disk as a startup disk for a PowerPC Mac or with any other kind of Mac, click Apple Partition Map. If you want to use the disk for a Windows startup disk, click Master Boot Record. If you are using an Intel Mac, leave the default GUID Partition Table option selected. Click OK.

Figure 34.5
If you use an Intel Mac, you won't need to choose one of the other options when you partition a drive.

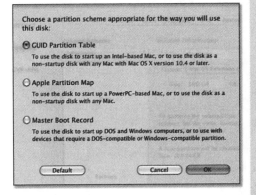

12. Click Apply.

13. If you are sure that you want to initialize and partition the drive, click Partition in the Warning sheet. You return to the Disk Utility window and a progress bar appears in the lower-right corner of the window. You can use this to monitor the process.

You can also use Disk Utility for various other tasks, such as erasing a disk or a volume, managing disk images, disk maintenance, and creating a RAID disk.

 To learn how to use Disk Utility for disk maintenance tasks, **see** *"Maintaining Your Disk Drives," p. 675.*

Working with Optical Discs

CDs and DVDs are the dominant removable media storage devices for Macs. They offer many benefits including large capacity per disc, inexpensive media, and ease of use. All modern Macs include an optical disc drive that reads CDs and DVDs and at least writes to CD too. Most Macs include an Apple SuperDrive that also writes to DVD in a variety of formats.

Before you burn your own discs, you should understand the type of drive your Mac has because that determines what kind of media you can use. CDs can hold about 700MB of data. Single-layer DVDs can hold up to 4.7 GB of data, and dual-layer discs can hold more than twice as much data.

> ### 🔍 note
> Just as with hard drives, third-party DVD-R/DVD-RW drives are available. However, because Apple's optical disc technology works so well and is included with Mac hardware and as part of Mac OS X, Apple's technology is the focus of this section.

Assessing Your Mac's Disc Drive

There are a number of ways to determine which type of optical drive your Mac has.

All modern Mac models come with some version of the SuperDrive, which reads CDs and DVDs, and can write to CDs and DVDs, including dual-layer DVDs; there are some speed differences among the drives in some models, with the higher-end Macs having faster drives.

> ### ⚠️ caution
> Before purchasing a large number of discs, purchase a single disc from various manufacturers rated for your drive's speed and try to born them with the application you intend to use to make sure they work properly.

You can check the documentation that came with your Mac to determine which formats it supports. For example, if your Mac includes an 8x SuperDrive with 2.4x Dual Layer burn, you can use single-layer DVDs, dual-layer DVDs, and writable CDs (you can also use erasable versions of these formats).

You can also assess your Mac's drive using the System Profiler.

1. Choose Apple, About This Mac.

2. Click More Info. The System Profiler launches.

3. Open the Hardware branch and click the Disc Burning category in the left pane. In the right pane, you see the formats your Mac's drive supports.

4. To see information about the performance you achieve with specific media, insert a disc into the drive and choose View, Refresh (or press ⌘-R). Under the Media section, you see the type of media along with whether it is erasable and the write speeds it supports. (In Figure 34.6, you can see that a DVD+R DL disc is in the Mac's drive.)

 tip

Any media you purchase should match one of the supported formats shown for your drive. For example, to burn to a dual-layer DVD, the +R DL format should be listed in the DVD-Write section.

Figure 34.6
This Mac can read and write CDs and DVDs.

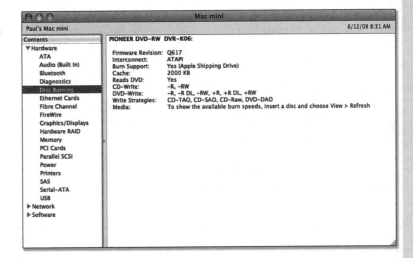

Configuring Disc Actions

You should configure Mac OS X to work with the disc drive you have installed. Do this through the CDs & DVDs pane of the System Preferences application.

Open the System Preferences application and click the CDs & DVDs icon to open that pane (see Figure 34.7).

5

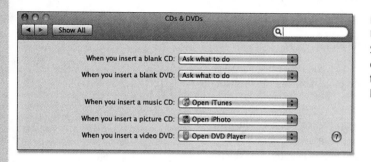

Figure 34.7
Use the CDs & DVDs pane of the System Preferences application to configure the actions your Mac takes when you insert CDs and DVDs of various types.

Use the When You Insert a Blank CD and the When You Insert a Blank DVD pop-up menus to select the action you want your Mac to take when you put a blank CD or DVD into your machine. (If your Mac's drive doesn't support DVD burning, you see only the CD menu.) You have the following options:

- **Ask What to Do**—When you insert a blank disc, your Mac prompts you and provides an Action pop-up menu containing a list of possible actions from which you can choose (see Figure 34.8).

Figure 34.8
Use the Action pop-up menu to choose what you want your Mac to do when you insert a blank disc.

The Action pop-up menu contains a set of choices similar to those on the When You Insert a Blank Disc pop-up menus on the CDs & DVDs pane, such as Open Finder or Open iDVD (when you insert a blank DVD and iDVD is installed on your Mac). You can make the action you select on the Action pop-up menu the default (checking the Make This Action the Default check box in the prompt window does the same thing as selecting that option in the CDs & DVDs pane). The Eject, Ignore, and OK buttons in the dialog box do what you expect (eject the disc, ignore it, or implement the changes you make, respectively).

Because the Ask What to Do option provides the most flexibility, I recommend that you choose this option. However, for specific situations, the other choices might be more appropriate for you.

- **Open Finder**—When this option is the default or if you select it in the Action dialog box, the blank disc is mounted and a burnable folder is created. You can then use the Finder to name the folder, add content to it, and burn the disc. If you usually burn discs from the Finder and don't like to be interrupted by the Action dialog box, this option is probably for you.

- **Open iDVD**—When a DVD is mounted, iDVD becomes the active application. If you mostly burn DVDs using iDVD, this setting can make the process more convenient. (iDVD must be installed on your Mac for this to appear.)

- **Open iTunes**—When a DVD or CD is mounted, iTunes becomes the active application. If you regularly burn discs for your iTunes content, this might be your best choice.

- **Open Disk Utility**—You can also burn discs using the Disk Utility application. If that is your preference, you can choose this option to have Disk Utility launch when you insert a recordable disc into your Mac's drive.

- **Open Other Application**—You can use this option to select a different application to open when a disc is inserted.

- **Run Script**—With this option, an AppleScript you select is launched when you insert a blank disc. After you select the script you want to launch, it appears on the When You Insert a Blank CD/DVD pop-up menus. If you have a custom burn process implemented through an AppleScript, this is the option you should choose.

- **Ignore**—When you insert a blank disc, your Mac takes no action. In fact, this disc is not even mounted in the Finder. You have to manually take some action later, such as opening an application that can burn DVDs, to do something with the disc. If you prefer to keep blank discs in your Mac and don't want to be interrupted when you insert them, this might be the option you want to choose.

 tip

Use the other pop-up menus on the CDs & DVDs pane to set default actions for specific kinds of discs. For example, if you want iTunes to launch when you insert a music CD, choose Open iTunes on the When You Insert a Music CD pop-up menu.

Burning Discs from the Finder

After you have configured your Mac, burning discs from the Finder is very straightforward, as the following steps demonstrate (these steps assume that you have selected the Ask What to Do option; however, using the Open Finder option works similarly). Do the following:

➡ *To learn how to use Disk Utility to burn discs,* ***see*** *"Burning CDs/DVDs with Disk Utility,"* ***p. 665.***

1. Insert a blank disc into the drive. You are prompted to select an action (refer to Figure 34.8).

2. Select Open Finder on the Action pop-up menu, and then click OK. The blank disc is mounted on your desktop and you see a burnable folder icon on the Sidebar.

 caution

Because burning CDs or DVDs from the Finder is a single session, you can burn to a disc only once. After it has been burned, you won't be able to add files to it (unless it is a rewritable disc, in which case you can erase it and burn a new set of files to it). Make sure you have all the files on the disc that you want before you burn it. If you want to burn to a disc in more than one session, use Disk Utility instead.

3. Select Untitled CD or Untitled DVD on the Sidebar or double-click the disc's icon on the Desktop to open it in a Finder window (see Figure 34.9).

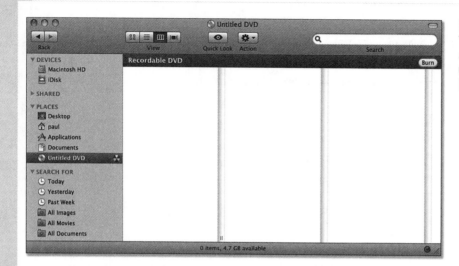

Figure 34.9
The selected burn-able folder called `Untitled DVD` is a blank DVD.

4. Select the burnable folder on the Sidebar, open its contextual menu, and choose the Rename command. The disc's name becomes editable.

5. Type a name for the disc and press Return to save the new name.

6. Drag the folders and files you want on the disc to the mounted disc, just like any other volume to which you can copy or move files. Aliases to those files and folders are created on the disc.

7. Arrange and organize the files as you want them to be on the disc (see Figure 34.10). At the bottom of the Finder window, you see the amount of space still available for more files.

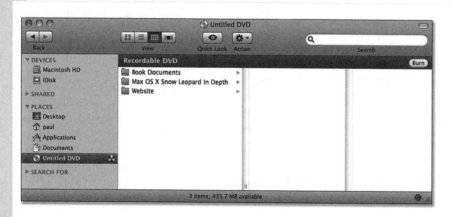

Figure 34.10
After you add files and folders to the burn folder, Finder uses the status bar to display how much disc space you have left.

8. When you are ready to record the files on the disc, click the Burn button in the disc's window. (You can also select the disc and choose File, Burn Disc, or click the Burn button next to the disc in the Sidebar.) The Burn Disc dialog box appears (see Figure 34.11).

Figure 34.11
Use the Burn Disc dialog box to name your disc.

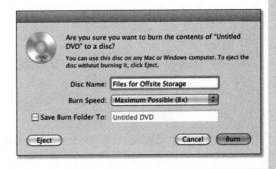

9. If you want to name the disc with a different name than it currently has, type the name of the disc in the Disc Name field. You can choose most any name you'd like. If you plan to share the disc with people who use other kinds of computers, keep the name relatively short, such as fewer than eight characters.

10. Select the speed at which you want to burn the disc on the Burn Speed pop-up menu. In most cases, choose the fastest speed available. However, if you are having problems burning discs at your drive's maximum speed, you can try to burn at a lower speed, which might solve the problems.

11. If you want the data saved to a Burn folder, so you can make multiple copies of the disc for example, activate the Save Burn Folder To check box and name the Burn folder (the default name is the name of the current disc, but you can rename it if you want to).

12. Click Burn. If the files fit onto the disc, the burn process starts. If not, you see a prompt explaining that the selected files are too large for the disc; you need to remove some of the files until they fit on the disc and then start the burn again. As it proceeds, you see a progress window as the data is prepared and the disc is recorded and verified. When the process is complete, the disc is mounted on your Mac and is ready to use. The time it takes to burn a disc depends on the amount of data, type of disc, and the speed of your system. Fortunately, you can work on other tasks during the burn process.

 tip

In the CD Burn progress window, click the Stop button (the *x*) to abort the burn process. This might destroy the disc if the burn process is under way, so most of the time, it's better to just let the process complete unless you are using erasable media.

Burning CDs/DVDs with Disk Utility

In addition to helping you maintain your disks, Disk Utility can also burn CDs and DVDs. It is especially useful when you want to burn a CD or DVD from a disk image file. Another great use of this utility is to back up image files for the applications you download from the Internet; rather than keeping a folder of these items on your hard drive, you can use Disk Utility to burn a folder of images onto a CD or DVD.

The benefit to burning a disk image onto a CD or DVD using Disk Utility rather than just using the Finder is that, when you use Disk Utility, the image is mounted when you insert the CD—you don't have to first open the disk image file to mount it.

Creating a Disk Image to Burn

Before you can burn a disc using Disk Utility, you create a disk image containing the folders and files you want to place on the disc using the following steps:

1. Open Finder, select Applications, Utilities, and then launch Disk Utility.

2. Click the New Image button on the toolbar. The New Image sheet appears.

3. Use the Save As text box top to name the disk image, and choose where you want to save it.

4. Name the volume you are creating by typing a name in the Name field. The name of the volume becomes the name of the disc you burn it onto.

5. Use the Volume Size pop-up menu to choose the size of the disk image. Because you are going to burn the image to disc, you want to choose one of the disc options, such as 663 MB (CD-ROM 80 min) if you're putting the image on CD, or 4.6 GB (DVD-R/DVD-RAM) if you're putting the image on a single-layer DVD.

6. Choose the format on the Volume Format pop-up menu. You have the same options as when you format a hard disk. In most cases, you want to use one of the Mac OS Extended formats.

7. If you want to protect the contents of the image with encryption, choose the level of encryption you want to use on the Encryption pop-up menu.

8. On the Partitions pop-up menu, select CD/DVD.

9. Leave Read/Write Disk Image selected on the Image Format pop-up menu.

10. Click Create. The disk image is created and mounted on your Mac; you can access the disk image just like other volumes such as hard disks (see Figure 34.12).

11. Open the disk image by selecting it on the Sidebar and drag folders or files onto it to add them to the image. Do this until all the files and folders you want to put on disc are part of the disk image. You are limited to the size of the image you selected using the Volume Size pop-up menu; for example, if you selected the 663 MB option, the files can't consume more than 663MB if you want them to fit on a single disc. If you try to place more files on the disk image than fit, you're prevented from moving the files onto the image and a warning prompt appears.

 tip

One of the best reasons to use Disk Utility to burn CDs or DVDs is that you can leave a disc open so you can burn to it multiple times. When you use the Finder, you can have only one recording session for a disc. When you use Disk Utility, you can choose to make a disc *appendable*, meaning you can burn to it more than one time.

 tip

To see how large a disk image currently is, select it in the Sidebar and use its contextual menu to choose Get Info. In the resulting Info window, expand the General section. In the middle of this section, you see the size of the image listed next to the text Capacity.

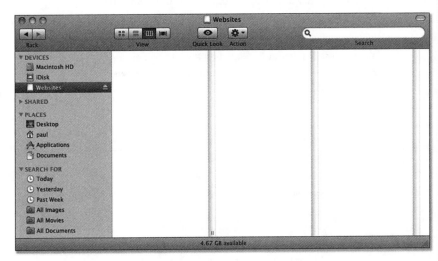

Figure 34.12
The disk image called Websites is mounted and can be used just like other volumes available to this Mac.

Burning a Single Disk Image on CD or DVD

To put a disc image on CD or DVD using Disk Utility, do the following:

1. Open Finder, select Applications, Utilities, and then launch Disk Utility. If you have worked with the disk image recently, it's listed in the lower part of the left pane of the Disk Utility window (which Disk Utility calls being *attached*); you can skip to step 4. If it isn't listed, you need to locate it using Disk Utility.

2. Locate the disk image by choosing File, Open Disk Image. The Select Image to Attach dialog box appears.

3. Move to and select the disk image you want to place on disc; then click Open. The image you selected is attached to Disk Utility and you see it in the left pane of the window.

4. Select the disk image you want to burn to disc.

5. Choose Images, Burn. (You can also press ⌘-B or click the Burn button.) The Burn sheet appears.

6. Insert the disc on which you want to burn the image. The drive is prepared and the Burn button becomes active if the disc has enough space to hold the image. If not, you see a message saying so; click Cancel and use a smaller disk image or use a larger capacity disc. Then start the burn process again.

 tip

Disk images are separated from physical disks by the dividing line that appears in the left pane of the Disk Utility window when at least one disk image is attached. Anything above the line is a volume on a physical disk of volume; anything below the line is a disk image.

 note

If the disk image is currently mounted, you see its mounted icon below the disk image file itself. You need to select the image file, not the mounted icon.

 tip

If you have more than one drive that can burn discs available to you, choose the drive you want to use on the Burn Disc In pop-up menu.

7. Click the downward-facing triangle next to the Burn Disc In text to see additional options (see Figure 34.13).

8. Set the burn speed by using the Speed pop-up menu. In most cases, Maximum Possible is the best choice. However, if you have problems burning discs, a slower speed might help.

 tip

If you move files from the disk image into the Trash, empty the trash to see the image's current size.

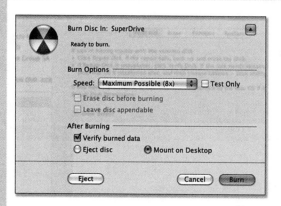

Figure 34.13
Use the options on this sheet to configure a burn session.

9. If you want to test the burn process without actually burning the disc, check the Test Only check box. If the test is successful, you can come back and burn the disc; if not, you need to fix any issues you encounter. This can be a good way to prevent wasting discs during the burn process.

10. If you are burning to an erasable disc, activate the Erase Disc Before Burning check box to erase the disc before you burn to it.

11. If you want to be able to add more data to the disc at a later time, activate the Leave Disc Appendable check box. This is one of the best reasons to use Disk Utility to burn discs; you can add data to discs during multiple burn sessions.

12. Make sure the Verify Burned Data check box is activated to have your Mac verify the disc after the burn is complete; if you are confident and want to save some time, you can uncheck this box.

13. Click the Eject Disc radio button if you want the disc ejected when it has been burned, or click the Mount on Desktop radio button if you want the disc to be mounted instead.

14. Click Burn. You see the Progress window that displays the progress of the burn.

15. When the process is complete, you hear a tone and the finished prompt appears; click OK and the disc is ejected or mounted on the desktop, depending on the option you selected in step 13 (Figure 34.14 shows the disc mounted).

 tip

To unattach disk images from Disk Utility, select the disk image file and press Delete or drag its icon out of the window. This does not delete the image file itself—it just removes it from the Disk Utility window.

Figure 34.14
Here, I have placed a disk image (called Websites) containing website files on a DVD; above the DVD of the same name, you can also see the disk image which is still mounted.

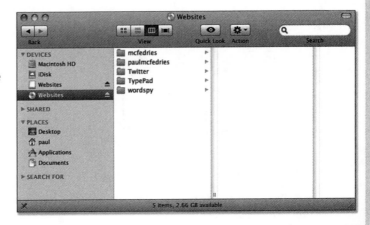

If you leave a disc appendable, you can repeat these steps to add disk images to it. When you append files to a disc, the Burn button becomes the Append button to indicate that you are adding files to the disc rather than burning it for the first time.

Burning a Folder on CD or DVD

Using the following steps, you can create a disk image from a folder and then burn that image onto a disc:

1. Gather all the files you want to put onto a disc in a single folder.

2. Open Disk Utility.

3. Select File, New, Disk Image from Folder.

4. Move to and select the folder from which you want to create an image.

5. Click Image. You see the New Image from Folder dialog box (see Figure 34.15). Use this dialog box to name the disk image and choose the options for the image.

6. Name the disk image file and select the location in which you want to store it.

7. On the Image Format pop-up menu, select a format for the image you are creating:

   ▪ The Read/Write option creates an image you can add more files to later.

 caution

If you want a disk image to mount when you insert the disc on which you want it burned, burn only one disk image on the disc. If you add multiple disk images to the same disc, only the one you most recently burned is accessible in the Finder. You should use the multiple session option only when you are burning other types of files onto a disc or when you are adding files to the same disk image.

 tip

You can use Disk Utility to erase CD-RW or DVD-RW discs. To do so, launch the application, insert the CD-RW or DVD-RW you want to erase, select the icon for the disc drive, and use the tab's tools to erase the disc. You can also erase such discs by activating the Erase Disc Before Burning check box in the Burn sheet.

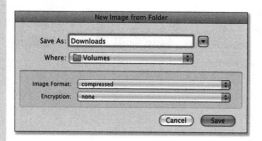

Figure 34.15
The New Image From Folder dialog box enables you to configure a disk image you are creating.

■ The Read-Only option creates a "closed" image to which files can't be added later.

■ The Compressed option creates a compressed version of the folder so you can get more files in a smaller space.

■ The DVD/CD Master option creates a disk image ready to be put on disc, so choose that one if you want to put the folder on a disc.

■ The Hybrid Image (HFS+/ISO/UDF) option creates a file that can be used with other systems (not just Macs).

8. Use the Encryption pop-up menu to choose an encryption scheme for the image file if you want to protect the data it contains. If you select none, the image is not encrypted.

9. Click Save. You see a Progress window as the image file is created. When the process is complete, the disk image you created is shown in the Source pane.

10. Select the disk image you just created and follow the steps in the previous section to put that image on disc.

Burning a Volume on CD or DVD

You can also create a disk image from an entire volume. Then you can place that image on a disc for backup or other purposes. The steps you follow are very similar to those in the previous section. The only difference is that you select the volume from which you want to create a disk image and then select File, New, Image from *volume* where *volume* is the name of the volume you selected. That volume is then selected and you move to the Convert Image dialog box.

35

MAINTAINING YOUR MAC

Basic Mac Maintenance

Time and effort that you have to spend troubleshooting problems is time and effort you don't have available to accomplish what you want to accomplish. To minimize the time you have to spend solving problems, you should take specific steps to maintain your Mac. In this chapter, I describe the following preventive maintenance chores:

- Maintaining your system software
- Maintaining your hard disks
- Maintaining alternative startup volumes and discs
- Building and maintaining a Mac toolkit
- Maintaining your applications

Maintaining your Mac in good condition with these tasks isn't terribly difficult, and the effort you do put in pays off in having to spend less time and effort solving problems.

This list should certainly get you started with good Mac maintenance practices. A couple of other areas are equally or more important to keeping your Mac working and in good condition. These topics are so important that the next two chapters are dedicated to them.

➥ *To learn about the most important Mac maintenance task you can and should do,* **see** *Chapter 36, "Backing Up Your Mac,"* **p. 689.**

➥ *To learn how to prevent problems using Mac OS X's security features,* **see** *Chapter 37, "Securing Your Mac,"* **p. 705.**

Using Software Update to Maintain Your System Software

Apple regularly updates Mac OS X (and other applications, such as the iLife applications) to solve problems, enhance performance, and introduce new features. Keeping track of the updates manually would be time-consuming. Fortunately, you don't have to. You can use the Software Update tool (which consists of a pane in the System Preferences application and the Software Update application) to check, download, and install updates to Mac OS X and related software (including firmware updates, updates to Apple applications you use, and so on).

Configuring Software Update

To configure Software Update, follow these steps:

1. Open the System Preferences application, and then open the Software Update pane (see Figure 35.1).

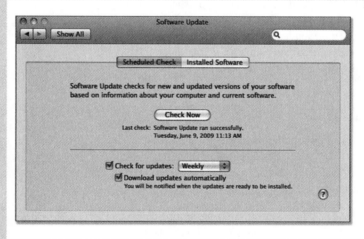

Figure 35.1
The frequency with which you check for updates depends on your connection to the Net; for most people, weekly updates are sufficient.

2. Use the check boxes, pop-up menu, and other buttons to configure the Software Update schedule (the options are described in the following bulleted list).

When configuring Software Update, you have the following options:

- **Check for Updates**—Use this check box to determine whether your system automatically checks for updates when you have a network connection. If you leave this check box activated, use the pop-up menu to set the checking frequency: Daily, Weekly (the default), or Monthly.

- **Download Updates Automatically**—If you leave this check box activated, Software Update automatically downloads important updates (such as updates to the OS) without bothering you first. When the update has been downloaded and is ready to be installed, you're prompted to allow the operating system to start the installation process.

- **Check Now**—Click this button to manually check for updates. The Software Update window appears and you see a progress bar to indicate how the process is proceeding. If no updates are available, you see a message saying so along with the date and time at which you last checked for updates. If updates are available, the Software Update application opens.

- **Installed Software**—Click this tab to see the history of all the updates Software Update has installed for you and when they were installed.

Working with Software Update

When you have configured your system to check for updates automatically and at least one update is available, you see the Software Update dialog box shown in Figure 35.2. (You also see this dialog box if you click Check Now in the Software Update pane of the System Preferences application, and at least one update is available.) You have three options:

note

Whether the Download Updates Automatically option is good for you or not mostly depends on the type of Internet connection you have. If you have a broadband connection, this option doesn't hurt because you aren't tying up a phone line while updates are downloading. You can just choose not to install any updates you don't want to. If you use a dial-up connection, it is better not to download updates in the background because some of the updates are quite large and you might tie up a phone line for a long time downloading an update you aren't going to install anyway.

- **Show Details**—Click this button to see the list of available updates (see Figure 35.2).

- **Not Now**—Click this button to skip the installation of the available updates.

- **Install**—Click this button to start the installation of the available updates.

Figure 35.2
You see this dialog box if Software Update has updates available for you to install.

You can jump straight into the Software Update application (without opening the Software Update pane first) by selecting Apple menu, Software Update. The application launches and immediately checks for updates. If any are available, the Software Update window appears and you see the list of available updates, as shown in Figure 35.3.

In the top pane of the application's window you see a list of the available updates, which includes the update name, its version number, and its size. Here are two things to note about this list:

- If you select an update, information about that update appears in the lower pane of the window.

- If you see a grey circle with a white triangle inside (for example, see the iLife Support and Digital Camera Raw Compatibility Update items in Figure 35.3), it means Mac OS X will restart your Mac after it has finished installing the update.

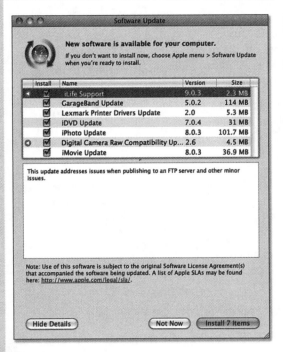

Figure 35.3
The Software Update application manages the download and installation of available updates for you.

Use the check boxes in the Install column to decide which updates you want to download and install. All the updates are selected by default, but if there are any you don't want to install right now, deactivate the check box beside each of those updates. (If you don't want to install anything right now, click the Not Now button.) When you're ready to begin, click the Install *X* Items button (where *X* is the number of Install check boxes you left activated).

Occasionally, updates are released that are of no value to you, such as updates for languages you don't use, devices you don't have, and so on. Software Update regularly reminds you of these updates until you download them. However, if you see an update that you are sure you won't want to download and install, you can have Software Update ignore that specific update. To do so, use the following steps:

1. In the Software Update application, select the update you want to ignore.

2. Select Update, Ignore Update or press the Delete key.

 note

As with other application installs, you have to authenticate yourself as an administrator to be able to install updates via Software Update. Depending on the type of update you install, you might have to agree to a license before the update can be installed on your computer (such as a new version of an iLife application).

 tip

Ignoring an update removes it from the list of available updates. If you don't want to install a specific download, just uncheck its check box. To install that update, check its box before you click the Install button.

3. Click OK in the resulting warning sheet. The update is removed and you're no longer prompted to download the current or future versions of the update you ignored.

You can see ignored updates again by selecting Software Update, Reset Ignored Updates. All the updates you have ignored are added back to the Software Update application and you are prompted to download and install them again. You can't choose to restore a single update; you have to restore them all. Of course, you can choose to ignore specific updates again to remove them from the list.

 note

If you want to manually check for Apple software updates, go to www.apple.com/support. Use the tools on the Apple Support pages to locate and download updates. For example, in the Downloads section, you see a list of the current updates that are available.

After you have downloaded and installed an update, use the Installed Updates tab of the Software Update pane of the System Preferences application to verify that the updates were installed.

Seeing Installed Files

To view all installs that have been done on your Mac, including but not limited to software updates, open the folder `Mac OS X/Library/Receipts`, where `Mac OS X` is the name of your Mac OS X startup volume.

In this folder, you see all the installs that have been performed on your Mac. Most are in `.pkg` files, but you can't open these to reinstall the software. Because they are receipts, they are for information purposes only.

Maintaining Your Disk Drives

Maintaining your disk drives goes a long way toward maximizing performance and preventing problems. You can use the Mac OS X Disk Utility application to do basic disk maintenance and repair. For maximum performance, you can also consider defragmenting and optimizing your disks.

Checking and Repairing Disks with Disk Utility

Among other things, the Disk Utility application (located in the Applications/Utilities folder) enables you to check for problems with your disks and then repair problems that are found.

➡ **See** *"Initializing and Partitioning a Hard Drive,"* **p. 656.**

To check and repair a volume, perform the following steps:

1. Launch Disk Utility. In the left pane of the window are all the disks mounted on your Mac, including drives installed in your computer and those that are connected via FireWire or USB. Each volume on each disk is

 note

A volume is a disk that has been partitioned into two or more partitions. Each partition behaves as if it were on a separate hard disk. There are several reasons you might want to partition a disk into multiple volumes, such as for organization purposes or to create multiple startup volumes. See Chapter 34 for more information.

listed under that disk's icon. You also see any disk images that have been mounted on the machine.

2. Select a disk, a volume on a disk, or a disk image you want to check. When you select a disk or volume, a number of tabs appear in the right pane of the window. How many tabs appear depends on what you select:

 note

Even if a disk has only one volume on it, you see that disk's volume listed under the disk's icon.

- If you select a hard disk, the following tabs appear: First Aid, Erase, Partition, RAID, and Restore.

- If you select a mounted volume, CD, or DVD, you see the following tabs: First Aid, Erase, and Restore.

- If you select a disk image, the First Aid, Erase, and Restore tabs appear.

3. Check the bottom of the Disk Utility window for information about the disk, volume, disc, or image you selected. Again, what you see here depends on what you have selected:

If you select a hard drive, you see the disk type, connection bus (such ATA for internal drives or USB for an external drive), connection type (internal or external), capacity, write status, S.M.A.R.T. status, and partition map scheme (see Figure 35.4).

 note

In this context, *volume* and *partition* are the same thing. When you partition a disk, each partition becomes a mounted volume on that disk.

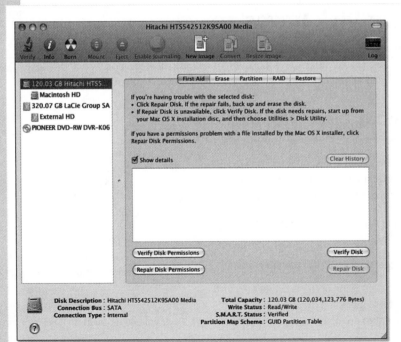

Figure 35.4
At the bottom of the Disk Utility window, you see information about the selected hard disk; the name of the window is the name of the selected disk or volume.

■ For most disks, the S.M.A.R.T. status provides an indication of the disk's health. The status is Verified if the disk is in good working condition or About to Fail if the disk has problems. If a disk doesn't support S.M.A.R.T., the status is Not Supported.

■ If you select a volume on a disk, you see various data about the volume, such as its mount point (the path to it), format, whether owners are enabled, the number of folders it contains, its capacity, the amount of space available, the amount of space used, and the number of files it contains (see Figure 35.5).

Figure 35.5
A partition on a disk has been selected and information relevant to a volume is now shown at the bottom of the Disk Utility window.

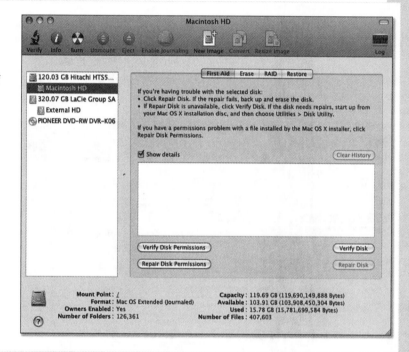

■ If you select a CD or DVD disc drive, you see the drive's specifications and the types of discs with which the drive can work.

■ If you select a mounted CD or DVD, you see where the disc is mounted and its name, its format, its write status, the numbers of folders it contains, the disc's capacity, the available space, the used space, and the number of files stored on it.

■ If you select a disk image, you see its description, size of the image file, write status (mounted or not), connection bus, and where it is located (the path to it).

 note

S.M.A.R.T. stands for self-monitoring analysis and reporting technology. Most modern disk drives support this technology, which means potential problems with a disk are identified and reported before the problem occurs. The goal of this technology is to enable you to repair a disk before you lose any data or at least transfer the data on that disk to another disk.

4. Click the First Aid tab to see some information explaining how Disk Utility works.

5. Click Repair Disk. The application checks the selected disk or volume for problems and repairs any it finds. If you select a volume on a disk, the application checks all the volumes on that disk automatically. As Disk Utility works, you see progress messages in the First Aid pane. When the process is complete, a report of the results appears (see Figure 35.6).

⇥ *To learn how to run a Unix disk repair utility during startup,* **see** *"Starting Up in Single-User Mode," **p. 124***.

note

You can't repair a disk with open files, which means you can't do these tasks with your Mac OS X startup volume. You can verify your startup volume to learn about any issues on that disk. To repair that volume, restart your Mac from the Mac OS X installation CD and select Disk Utility from the Installer menu. Or start up your Mac from an alternate startup volume, which should be part of every Mac user's toolkit.

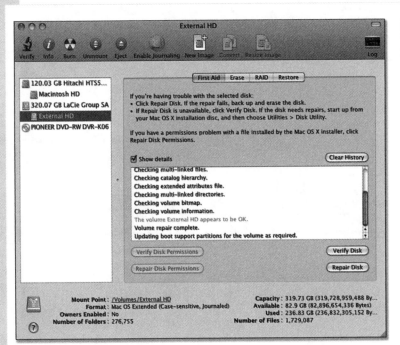

Figure 35.6
The selected disk appears to be okay.

You can choose to verify a volume rather than to repair it. When you do so, the application finds problems with the disk and reports back to you. You then have to tell the application to repair those problems. Generally, you should use the Repair button to save the extra step and because you always choose to repair problems Disk Utility finds.

note

For the Mac OS X startup volume, you never really need to run Disk First Aid. That is because the disk is checked and repaired during startup. You can also run a Unix disk repair utility during startup.

➡ *To learn how to use the Disk Utility to initialize and partition hard disks,* **see** *"Initializing and Partitioning a Hard Drive,"* **p. 656** .

You can also use Disk Utility to check or repair the permissions on the startup volume you are using. This can solve access problems with specific files on the machine when you don't have the required permissions. Even if you aren't currently having permissions related problems, it's a good idea to do the following steps periodically as part of your disk maintenance tasks:

1. Select your current startup volume (if your startup disk has more than one volume, you have to select the startup volume, not the disk on which the volume is stored).

2. Click Repair Disk Permissions. The application starts searching for permission problems and repairing those it finds. As it works, you can view the status of the process in the window. When the process is complete, you see the results in the information window on the First Aid tab.

You can use the Verify Disk Permissions button to find permission problems. Then you have to tell the application to repair them. As with disk problems, you almost always repair any problems the application finds, so you can save yourself a step by using the Repair button instead.

 tip

Disk Utility has a toolbar, which you can configure by Control-clicking it and using the resulting pop-up menu to configure the toolbar.

Erasing Disks with Disk Utility

You can also use Disk Utility to quickly erase and reformat volumes or erasable disks (such as CD-RW discs):

1. Select the disk, disc, or volume you want to erase.

2. Click the Erase tab.

3. Choose the format you want to use for the volume on the Volume Format pop-up menu. The format options are Mac OS Extended (Journaled), Mac OS Extended, Mac OS Extended (Case-sensitive, Journaled), or Mac OS Extended (Case-sensitive). If you select a disk, you also see the MS-DOS File System format.

4. Name the volume in the Name field.

5. Click the Security Options button. The Secure Erase Options sheet appears (see Figure 35.7).

There are four options you can choose to determine how your Mac handles data it is erasing:

 tip

If you select a volume, you can use the Erase Free Space button to remove files that you have deleted from the volume to make them harder or impossible to recover using data recovery tools. When you click the Erase Free Space button, you can use the resulting sheet to choose how you want to overwrite the free space. There are three options, with each providing a different level of security.

- **Don't Erase Data**—This option makes the data unviewable from the Finder but leaves the data physically on the disk. As your Mac needs to write more files to the disk, it overwrites the erased space. Until the data is overwritten, that data can be recovered (unerased) using an application designed to recover data.

■ **Zero Out Data**—This option writes zeros in all sectors on the disk.

■ **7-Pass Erase**—This option writes random data over the entire disk 7 times.

■ **35-Pass Erase**—This option writes random data over the entire disk 35 times.

The purpose of the last three options is to prevent data on the disk from being restored after you erase it. For example, if you were transferring a disk to someone else, you would want to select one of these options so that the data you had on the disk could not be recovered. The more overwrites you choose, the more secure the erase and the longer the process takes. If you are maintaining control of the disk, you probably don't need to choose one of the secure erase options, but using the Zero Out Data option doesn't add a lot of time to the process, so it isn't a bad choice.

If you want to use one of these options, click its radio button and then click OK.

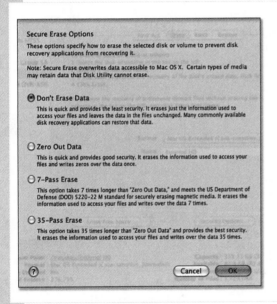

Figure 35.7
When you erase a volume or disk, you can choose the security with which you erase that volume's data.

6. Click Erase. The confirmation sheet appears; if you are sure you want to erase the disk, click Erase again. The drive's or volume's data is erased and is formatted with the options you selected.

 tip

You can get detailed information about a device or volume by selecting it and clicking the Info button on the toolbar.

Enabling Journaling with Disk Utility

Under Mac OS X, disks can use the Mac OS (Journaled) file format. This format provides a journal function that tracks activity that has taken place in the main areas of the disk. This log helps recreate the data on the disk and makes repair operations more successful. In most cases, you should use this option because it gives you a better chance of recovering data and disks if you have problems. As you saw in the previous section, you can select the Journaled format when you erase a disk or volume. You can also enable journaling on an existing volume without erasing or reformatting it. To do the latter, use the following steps:

1. Select the volume on which you want to enable journaling.

2. Click the Enable Journaling button on the toolbar. (Alternatively, select File, Enable Journaling, or press ⌘-J.) The journaling information begins to be tracked for the selected disk or volume. (If this option is inactive, it means that journaling is already enabled or it can't be activated on the current disk, in which case, you have to erase the disk to activate journaling.)

Defragmenting and Optimizing Your Hard Disks

As you save files to a disk (again, this means any kind of disk you have mounted on your Mac, except for CD-ROMs, DVD-ROMs, and other locked disks from which you can only read data), data is written to the disk. The Mac is also frequently writing other sorts of data (such as preference changes and other system-level data) to the startup disk. As data is written to a disk, it is written in the next available space (called a *block*). After the data is laid down, the Mac returns to what it was doing. When it is time to save more data, the next batch is written in the next open space, and so on. Think of this as the Mac putting all the data down in a straight line (yes, the disk is round, but it is easier to think of it this way), one chunk after another.

As files are opened and closed, data from different files is laid down in the next available space so that, instead of all the data from one file being in a continuous block, it can be stored in blocks located in various spots around the disk. In this state, the data is *fragmented*. Although fragmentation is a normal part of the way disk drives function, excessive fragmentation can slow down the disk. Things slow down because the drive head must read data from all the blocks that make up a particular file. As those blocks become more numerous and are spread out around the disk, it takes longer and longer to read all the data for that file.

You use a process called *defragmentation* to correct this condition. You need a disk maintenance program to do this, such as Tech Tool Pro. What the defragmentation process does is pick up all the data blocks for each particular file and write them in a continuous block. It does this for every file on the disk. After the data is laid out nice and neat, the drive performs faster because it doesn't have to move as far to read and write the data for a particular file.

 note

To learn more about Tech Tool Pro, visit www.micromat.com.

Because a hard drive is made up of a round disk that spins at a constant speed, it takes longer to read and write data to various parts of the disk. Data near the center is read more quickly than data out near the rim. Data can be written to the disk in such a way that the access speed of the drive is *optimized*.

To do this, the data that is used constantly but not changed much—such as the system software and applications—is stored near the center of the disk. The documents and other data that are infrequently used are stored out toward the edge of the disk. This arrangement speeds up the disk because access to the most frequently used data is faster, and keeping the static data together means it does not become fragmented. Thus, the data is read and written in an optimized (for speed) fashion. You also need a disk maintenance tool to optimize a disk.

Usually, defragmentation and optimization are done at the same time using the same tool. The steps to perform these tasks depend on the particular software you use. Generally, this is not complicated and is a matter of choosing the drives you want to defragment and optimize and clicking Start.

Defragmentation and optimization are somewhat controversial topics. Many experts believe they do little to no good, but others believe you can gain some performance and reliability improvements by performing these tasks on your disks regularly. Personally, I think you can better spend your time by keeping your disks well organized and using Disk Utility to check them every so often rather than worrying about squeezing a few microseconds of performance out of them. But you might want to obtain and use a disk maintenance application, such as TechTool Pro, if getting the best possible performance from your disks is important to you. These applications also provide additional troubleshooting tools that can be useful.

Cleaning Up Your Drives

You can do a lot for the performance of your disks by simply keeping them cleaned up. The more data on your drive, the less room you have to store new files. If your disks get too full, their performance slows down significantly. More data means there is more information for your Mac to manage, and thus it has to work harder and uses more resources. You can also run into all kinds of problems if you try to save files to disks that are full to the brim; how full this is depends on the size of the files with which you are working.

Learn and practice good work habits such as deleting files you don't need, uninstalling software you don't use, and archiving files you are done with (such as on a DVD). Regularly removing files that you no longer need from your hard drives goes a long way toward keeping them performing well for you, not to mention maximizing the room you have to store files you do need.

 note

Many disk maintenance applications enable you to retrieve files you have deleted (an undelete or recover function). This is possible because during normal deletes (when you empty the Trash) the file is removed from the active system but might still exist on the disk in some form. The only way to be permanently rid of a file so it can't be recovered is to write over the area in which that file was stored with other data. To do this, you need an application that writes zeros or other bogus data over the location where the file you are deleting is stored. Typically, disk maintenance and other tools enable you to "really" delete files that you don't want to be able to be recovered. In Mac OS X, you can also do this by using the Finder's Secure Empty Trash command or by erasing a disk with Disk Utility (see "Erasing Disks with Disk Utility," earlier in this chapter).

Maintaining Alternative Startup Volumes

One of the most important tasks you need to be able to do reliably and quickly is to start up from an alternative startup volume. There are several situations in which you might need to do this. For example, if you find problems on your current startup volume, you need to start up from another volume to repair the startup volume. If something happens to your startup volume such that your Mac can no longer use it, you need to use an alternative startup volume to keep your Mac running. An alternate startup volume can also be very helpful when you are troubleshooting problems.

Several possibilities exist for alternative startup volumes; you should maintain at least one, and preferably two, of the following options

- **Your Mac OS X installation disc**—You can always use the disc that contains the Mac OS X installer as a startup volume. It contains the basic software you need to start up your Mac and accomplish a limited number of activities, such as reinstalling the operating system. The downside to this is that any updates you have applied to your active system are not included in the version on the installation disc. If the version of Disk Utility on the installation disc is too far removed from the version of the OS installed on your Mac, it is possible (but not likely unless you are using a very old installation disc) that Disk Utility on the disc is incompatible with the OS version installed on your startup disc. The biggest drawback to this option is that you can't really use your Mac while it is started up with the Mac OS X installation disc. You can only install system software or use Disk Utility and the other tools that are available on the Installer's menu.

- **An alternative Mac OS X installation on a different volume**—You should install a backup installation of Mac OS X on a different volume from the one that you use for your primary system—if you can spare the disk space required to do so. Ideally, this alternative volume is also located on a separate disk (not just a separate volume) from your primary installation. For example, if you have an external USB or FireWire hard drive, you can install Mac OS X on it so you can also use it as a startup volume.

- **Third-party application discs**—Many third-party applications, such as disk maintenance, antivirus, and backup software, include discs that contain system software you can use to start up your Mac. These discs also enable you to run the application software so you can correct a problem that has prevented you from starting up your system from the primary startup volume.

> **tip**
>
> If you choose to install a backup version of Mac OS X on an alternative startup volume, you should delete any applications in that Mac OS X installation that you won't need when you are starting up from that volume. This reduces the storage space it consumes. You also should start up from that volume and run Software Update periodically to keep the alternative startup volume's OS software current. Plus, this ensures that you can actually start up from that volume before you need to actually do so, such as when there is a problem with your primary startup volumes.

To start up your Mac from an alternative volume, restart the machine and hold down the Option key. After a few moments, each valid startup volume appears. Select the volume from which you want to start up and click the arrow pointing to that volume. The volume you selected is used to start up your Mac. Depending on the type, such as a full installation of Mac OS X on a volume or the Mac OS X installation disc, you can access various functionality from full Mac OS X capabilities (a full install on an alternative volume) or at least attempt to repair the startup volume itself (using the installation disc).

If your Mac is hung, meaning it won't respond to any commands, such as the Restart command, press and hold its Power button down until the machine shuts down. Press the Power button again to restart it and hold the Option key down so that you can select an alternate startup volume.

You can start up your Mac from a disc installed in it, such as the Mac OS X Installation disc, by holding down the C key while the machine is starting up.

A third approach is to use the Startup Disk pane of the System Preferences application to choose the volume you want to use to start up your Mac. Of course, your Mac has to be running to be able to do this.

tip

If you use a wireless keyboard and mouse, keep wired versions handy. In some cases, you might not be able to use a wireless device to control system startup by pressing the Option key down. You would then need to attach a wired keyboard and mouse to start up your machine from an alternate volume.

Maintaining Your Applications

Along with the system software, you should also maintain the applications you use. It is good practice to regularly check for updates for the applications on which you rely. There are several ways to do this, including the following:

- **Software Update**—Mac OS X's Software Update function also updates any Apple software installed on your computer, such as the iLife applications.

- **Automatic update features**—Most modern applications include the capability to go online to check for updates, automatically or manually. For example, most Adobe applications can check for updates to keep you informed when new versions or patches are available. You should configure your applications to check for updates periodically, just as the Software Update application checks for updates to Mac OS X.

- **Company mailing lists**—Some publishers maintain a mailing list for each application. Updates are announced in the mailing list, and the link to get to the update is provided.

- **Company websites**—Software publishers announce updates to their applications on their websites. Typically, you can check for and download updates from the Support area of a publisher's website.

- **Mac news**—Many Mac news sites and mailing lists include information about updates to popular applications.

- **Version Tracker**—Most Mac applications are listed on www.versiontracker.com. You can regularly check this site to look for application updates and patches.

note

As with the system software, it is sometimes wise to let a few days or a week pass after an update to an application is released before you download and install it in case problems are introduced by the update.

You should also organize your applications and ensure that you have all the registration and serial number information you need for each application. It is amazing how easy it is to lose this information; getting it from the publisher can be a time-consuming task (and if you have to relicense the software, it can be expensive). Consider making a list of each application along with its serial number or registration number and keeping that list with the original installation discs or the discs containing the installers and updaters you make for your applications. When you need to reinstall an application, this list can be a great timesaver.

Downloading Applications

If you obtain an application by downloading it rather than getting it on a disc, you should save the application installer so that you can reinstall it even if the publisher withdraws the installer for some reason (for example, sometimes the installer for one version is removed if a newer version is released). You can save hard drive space by burning these installers on a DVD or CD disc and storing that disc with your other application discs.

You should also maintain the installer for any updates or patches you download and install so you can return the application to its current condition if anything happens to the version you have installed on your hard drive.

Building and Maintaining a Mac Toolkit

One of the best maintenance-related tasks you can do is to assemble and maintain a Mac toolkit. In times of trouble, this toolkit can enable you to get back to work quickly. Not having to find your tools in times of trouble also reduces the stress you experience. Following are some fundamental items you should keep in your toolkit:

- **Your system configuration**—When you need help or are considering adding something to your system, having a detailed understanding of your system is very important. Use the System Profiler application (in the Applications/Utilities folder) to generate a report on your system. Print that report and keep it handy (in case you can't generate it when you need it).

  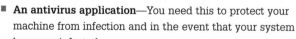 *For more information about Apple System Profiler,* **see** *"Using System Profiler to Create a System Profile," p. 737.*

- **Up-to-date backups**—Your toolkit should include everything you need to restore as much of your system as possible. This includes all your data, applications, and so on.

- **A disk maintenance application**—You need one of these applications to solve disk problems you might encounter. Examples are Disk Utility (included with Mac OS X) or Tech Tool Pro.

- **An antivirus application**—You need this to protect your machine from infection and in the event that your system becomes infected.

- **Your Mac OS X installation disc**—Sometimes, this is the only thing that gets your Mac started again.

 caution

When selecting a disk maintenance application, make sure you get one that is written for the specific version of Mac OS X that you are using. Using one designed for an older version of the OS can be harmful to your Mac and its data.

■ **Your original application installers on CD or DVD (even if you downloaded the installer originally), serial or registration numbers, and updates**—You should maintain the current versions of all your applications by maintaining the discs on which they came. You should also create CDs or DVDs containing updates to those applications along with any applications you download from the Internet. Finally, be sure you have a list of the serial or registration numbers for your applications so you can restore them if needed.

Consider devising some secure way to record passwords, usernames, serial numbers, and other critical data so you don't have to rely on memory to retrieve such information when you need it. Although keeping such information in hard copy is usually not advised, some people find it safer to develop and use some sort of code for this information and then have a hard copy of the encoded information handy.

Going Further with Disk Utility

Disk Utility is a very powerful and useful application. Covering all its functionality is beyond the scope of this chapter, but it is covered again in several other chapters for a variety of purposes. Following are some hints about other tasks for which you can use it:

■ **Create disk images**—You can create disk images from files, folders, or even drives and volumes. Just as with other disk images you work with, you can easily put your disk images on CD, use them to quickly re-create a set of data in multiple locations, and so on. The commands you use to create and work with disk images are on the File and Images menus.

■ **Burn CDs and DVDs**—Disk Utility enables you to burn CDs or DVDs from disk images. You can also use it to create multisession discs so that you can burn to a disc more than once. First, create a disk image for the files you want to put on disc. Then use the Burn button or the Burn command on the Images menu to access the application's burn functionality.

To remove a disk image from Disk Utility, drag its icon out of the application window or select it and press Delete.

■ **Work with disk images**—As you mount disk images in Disk Utility, it tracks those images in the lower part of the left pane so you can work with them again by selecting them. This makes accessing these images simple.

■ **Mount, unmount, or eject volumes**—You can use the mount, unmount, and eject buttons and commands to perform those actions for disks, discs, volumes, and disk images.

■ **Restore any folder, volume, or disk**—You can create a disk image from any source (such as a folder or volume) and use the application's command to restore that information on a disk. For example, if you want to replicate a set of software on multiple machines, you can create a disk image and use the Restore function on each machine to re-create that data. After you have created the disk image, use the Restore tab to restore it.

■ **Access a log file**—As you perform actions with it, Disk Utility maintains a complete log of the actions it performs (see Figure 35.8). To access this log, select Window, Show Log, press ⌘-L, or click the Log button in the toolbar. The Log opens and you can view its contents. This provides a complete history of your disk maintenance tasks.

Figure 35.8
Disk Utility's log shows you all the actions it has performed along with the results of those actions.

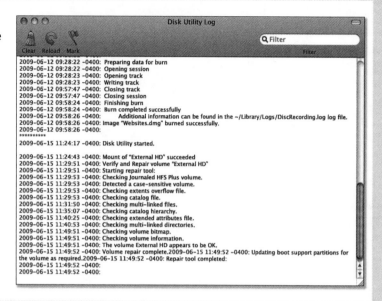

- **Configure RAID disks**—Redundant array of independent disks (RAID) is a scheme whereby multiple disks can be linked to work together for performance and reliability reasons (for example, disks can be mirrored so the same information is always stored on more than one disk in case of disk failure). You can use the RAID tab in Disk Utility to configure RAID services on a machine.

BACKING UP YOUR MAC

Backing Up Your System

If you use a computer, at some point, your system will crash, a disk will fail, you'll delete files that you really didn't intend to, or some other problem will occur and you will lose data you would rather not lose—maybe not today or tomorrow, but it *is* the inevitable nightmare. Think of the information you have on your Mac at this very moment that would be difficult—if not impossible—to reconstruct if your computer destroyed it. This data might be a report for work, a school project, your tax information, a complex spreadsheet, or even the great American novel on which you have been working. To be more specific, think about all the content you've purchased from the iTunes Store. If you lose that content and don't have it backed up, you need to pay for the content again. Even worse, imagine that you have 5,000 photos in your iPhoto Library covering the last five years. Now imagine that the disk on which these images are stored crashes. Without a backup, there's simply no way to recover that kind of data, and your photos are gone forever.

Whatever the information, rest assured that someday, somewhere, somehow you will suddenly lose it. When that happens, you will want to be able to restore all the information on your Mac so you can quickly re-create your data. Backing up is the means by which you ensure that you can always preserve most of your work, no matter what happens to your Mac.

Backups: Insurance for Your Data

You need a good backup for more than just catastrophic failures of your hardware. Perhaps you accidentally delete a file right before you need it. If you have a backup, you can quickly recover it. Or perhaps you edited a document and discovered that all your changes were actually worse than the original. You can use your backup to bring the file back to the way it was. And if your Mac is ever stolen or destroyed, your backup enables you to recover from potential disaster.

Although backing up your data is strongly recommended by computer authors, experts, and support personnel, it is a task that many Mac users never do for a variety of reasons. Some people don't back up data because they think their systems are infallible and won't crash. Still others are confused about how to make a backup of their system, or they lack the hardware and software necessary to maintain good backups. And then there are always those who simply don't believe that protecting their data is enough of a priority to waste their time on it. Trust me, the first time you lose something you can't re-create, such as important photos, you'll wish you'd backed up your Mac. Why wait for the inevitable? Better to get backed up now so you don't have to face losing your data.

Defining a Backup Strategy

One of the first things you need to decide is what data on your machine needs to be backed up. The following list describes the three general categories of data you should consider backing up:

- **Documents, photos, movies, music, and other important data you create or purchase**—These items are, after all, the reason you use a Mac in the first place. You should back up all your own data because it doesn't exist anywhere other than on your computer. If you lose important data, it might be impossible to re-create. Even if you are able to re-create it, you'll waste a lot of valuable time redoing what you have already done. Other data, such as your photos, simply can never be re-created. Still other data, such as music you have purchased from the iTunes Store, costs money to replace.

- **System files**—You should have installation discs that contain your Mac OS software, so you usually don't risk losing the Mac OS software itself. What you do risk losing is any customization you have done, updates you have installed, and so on. If you have adjusted any settings or added any third-party software, all the settings you have changed are lost in the event of a major failure.

  Additionally, don't forget about all the configuration information you have on your machine. For example, if you lose your system for some reason, you might lose all the configuration you have done to make your Mac connect to the Internet. You might also lose all the serial numbers of your software, which you have to re-enter if you need to reinstall it.

- **Applications and other third-party software**—As with the OS software, you probably have discs containing much of your third-party software. What you lose if you have a failure without a backup is the customization of those applications. Plus, you have to reinstall that software —not an easy task if you have a lot of applications installed on your Mac. In any case, it can be very time-consuming to reinstall your applications. Don't forget about all the updates you have applied to these applications. If you lose your system, you have to do that all again, too.

In conjunction with the kind of files you back up, several types of backups you can make include:

- **Full backup**—In a full backup, you back up each and every file on your system. The advantage of doing full backups is that restoring your entire system, as well as just particular parts of it, is possible.

- **Selected files only**—Using this scheme, you select particular files to back up; usually these are your important data (documents, photos, music, and so on) and some of your customization files (for example, preferences files). The advantage of this scheme is that you can make a backup quickly while protecting the most important files on your computer.

- **Incremental backup**—This scheme combines the first two techniques in that all files are backed up the first time, but after that, only files that have changed are backed up until the next full backup. This scheme protects all your files but avoids the time and space requirements of doing a full backup each time.

 note

You probably obtain a lot of your software by downloading it from the Web. If you lose the installers or patches you download without having a backup, you have to download them again—assuming they are still available, of course. Sometimes, the version you want to use has been replaced by a newer version you don't want to use or pay for. And, occasionally, software moves from shareware to commercial, in which case it becomes unavailable to download again without paying for it. You should keep backup copies of any software installers or updates you download so you can reinstall that software if you need to—whether it is still available from the original source or not.

What you decide about the type of data you back up and how you back it up should determine the type of backup system you develop and use. For example, if you decide that you don't mind having to reinstall applications and reconfigure settings or you mainly use small document files, you might be able to simply copy your document files onto a DVD or other removable media drive. If you have a great deal of data to protect, you need to implement a more sophisticated system.

If you can assemble the hardware and software required to do incremental backups, you should use this approach. It is the only one that is practical for frequent backups and also protects all your data.

Ideally, you want your backup system to work without any supervision or intervention by you. This is called an *unattended* backup because you don't even need to be there for the system to work. You can set the system to automatically back up during times when you are not working on your Mac. This is not only convenient, but it also means that because you don't have to *do* anything, you can't forget or be too lazy to keep your backups up to date.

Lastly, you need two basic types of backups. One is "short term," meaning that you back up daily (or more frequently) to protect your data over the short term, which can mean from a few days to a month; you keep these backups easily accessible from your Mac so that you can quickly restore files. The other is "long term," meaning that you capture snapshots of your data at specific points in time and store those in safe locations, preferably away from your Mac in case something really bad happens to it. You're likely to use different hardware and software for each of these types.

Backing Up Your Mac with Time Machine

Mac OS X includes its own backup software called Time Machine. Using Time Machine, you can automate the backup process and easily restore any data included in your backups. Time Machine is designed to work with Apple's iLife and other Mac OS X applications, so it's ideal to back up your iTunes and iPhoto content along with your documents. It's also smart enough to not waste backup space on files such as temporary Internet files. You can also determine how frequently backups are made and how long they are kept.

The primary limitation of Time Machine is that you can only use it to back up to a hard drive, so you must have a dedicated hard drive to be able to use it. Time Machine is also somewhat limited as backup software because you can only have one backup active at a time. However, it is very easy to use, which is important for backup software, and you can automate the backup process. Time Machine also makes restoring files very easy. For some applications, such as Address Book, you can even restore individual data records.

If you do use Time Machine, you really shouldn't rely on it as your only backup solution. You should back up so that you can store long-term backups away from your Mac; however, for everyday, short-term backups, it's ideal.

Configuring Time Machine

To configure Time Machine, perform the following steps:

1. Open the System Preferences application and click Time Machine. The Time Machine pane opens (see Figure 36.1).

Figure 36.1
With Time Machine, backing up isn't hard to do.

2. You can either slide the switch to turn Time Machine on, or click the Select Backup Disk button.

3. In the resulting sheet, select the drive you want to use to store your backup files.

4. Click Use for Backup. You return to the Time Machine Pane where the top portion allows you to modify your settings. The bottom portion of the pane notes the frequency of the backups. Time Machine creates an hourly backup for the past 24 hours, daily backups for a month, and weekly backups, assuming your backup drive has enough storage space.

>
> **⚑ caution**
>
> You'll lose any existing data on the drive when you use it for Time Machine backups, so make sure the drive doesn't contain any information you want to keep. If it does, copy the data to your main hard drive.

5. Click on the Options button. Use the exclusion list to exclude files from the backup process. By default, the drive you are using to back up is excluded because it would make no sense to back up a drive onto itself.

In an ideal world, you'd have such a large backup disk that you could back up all of your files indefinitely, but for most Mac users, that won't be the case. If it isn't true for you, you need to exclude files that don't really need to be in your short-term backups. One candidate is your Applications folder, which tends to be pretty large.

Make sure any files you exclude from your short-term backup are backed up in some way, such as on DVD or with the original installation discs.

To exclude files from the backup, click the Add button (+) and use the resulting sheet to move to and select the files you want to exclude. You can exclude entire volumes or choose specific folders to exclude the contents of those folders from the backup.

To include files in a backup again, select the folder on the exclusion list and click the Remove button (-). The folder you selected is removed from the exclusion list, which means it's included in the backup.

You can see how large the files excluded from the backup are by looking just above the exclusion list toward the right side of the pane. The amount shown next to "Total Included" tells you how much room your back up is going to require.

You can decide if you would like to be warned when old backups are deleted by Time Machine. It is a good idea to have your long-term backup completed before Time Machine deletes any older backup files.

>
> **◉ note**
>
> If the data you selected to back up doesn't fit on the backup disk, Time Machine aborts the backup process and warns you about the situation. You need to exclude more data from the backup until it does fit. If the data you want to back up consumes a large part of the space available on the backup disk, you won't be able to maintain backups for very long, so you should consider using a larger backup disk.

6. When you've excluded all the files you want to, click Done. The backup process runs at the next scheduled time (see Figure 36.2). The first time you run a backup, it takes a longer time because every file in the backup has to be copied to the backup drive. Subsequent runs will be faster because only changed files will be copied.

Figure 36.2
The Time Machine pane provides status information and the option to change the hard drive used for backup files.

When the backup process is complete, the time and date when it was completed is shown in the status area at the top of the pane.

After you've configured Time Machine, it handles the backup process for you and keeps your backup fresh according to the parameters you set.

Restoring Files with Time Machine

A backup system is something you need to have in place but hope you never have to use. But, losing data is inevitable, so you're going to have to use your backup system to recover the data you've lost. Time Machine makes restoring files relatively easy, at least when you understand its unique interface.

There are two basic sources of data you can recover with Time Machine: files in the Finder or data within applications. Time Machine works very similarly for both kinds.

 tip

If you make significant changes to your data, such as downloading photos from a camera or making purchases from the iTunes Store, and the next backup time doesn't occur for a while, click the Time Machine icon in the menu bar and then click the Back Up Now command to immediately add the new data to your backups. If you don't see the Time Machine icon, open System Preferences, click Time Machine, and then activate the Show Time Machine Status in the Menu Bar check box.

Restoring Files from the Finder with Time Machine

To restore files from your backup, perform the following steps:

1. Open the Finder window showing the location of the files you want to recover (this step is optional because you can navigate the Finder from within Time Machine).

2. Launch the Time Machine application (in the Applications folder or click its icon on the Dock). Time Machine fills the entire desktop on the primary monitor and makes all other displays dark (see Figure 36.3). Depending on the desktop resolution and window size of the folder in focus, that folder might be resized in the Time Machine window, but it remains in focus. Along the bottom of the window, you see the Time Machine menu bar.

Figure 36.3 Time Machine takes a bit of getting used to, but once you do, you can quickly recover files and data.

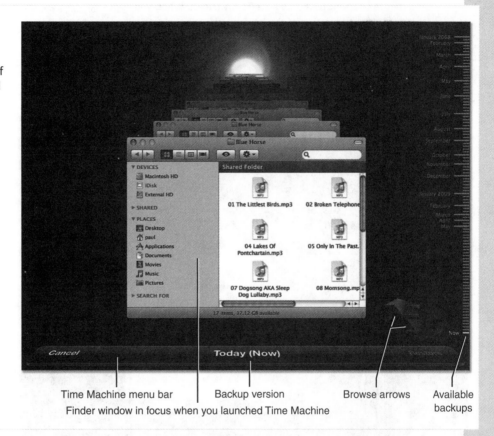

Time Machine menu bar   Backup version   Browse arrows   Available backups

Finder window in focus when you launched Time Machine

The Time Machine interface is quite different than other applications. The general concept of how it works is that you browse through the backups for the item in focus until you get to the files you want to restore. When you see the files or folder you want to restore, select the version you want to restore and click the Restore button located at the right end of the menu bar (this button becomes active only when you've selected something that can be restored).

The first task is to locate the specific version of the files that you want to recover. You can do this by browsing with the browse arrows or using the backup bars along the right side of the screen to choose a specific backup (by date and time) from which you want to restore a file.

3. Browse through the backups by clicking the backward-facing arrow to move to older versions of the backup or the forward-facing arrow to move to newer versions of the backup. Or, point to

the Available backups bar along the right side of the screen and click a date and time to jump to that version of the backup. As you point to versions, the magnifying effect is applied to make it easier to see the specific version you are working with.

The version of the backup that is currently in focus is shown in the center of the menu bar. When you are looking at the current files, this says Today (Now). When you are looking at a version of the backup, you see the date and time of the version in focus.

 note

To quit Time Machine without performing a restore, click the Cancel command.

4. When you've reached the version of the backup from which you want to restore the file, move to the file's or folder's location in the Finder window (see Figure 36.4).

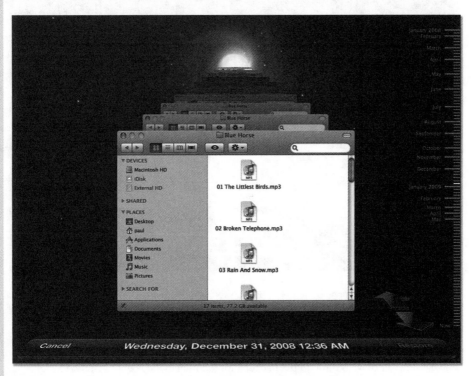

Figure 36.4
Time Machine enables you will to move back in time to recover files and folders that have been lost.

5. Select the file or folder you want to restore and click the Restore command. The file or folder is restored to your desktop in the state it was in for the backup version you selected. Time Machine quits and you return to the Finder with the recovered files and folders available for your use.

 note

If you restore a file to a location that already has a file with that name, you will be prompted to select if you want the restored file, the existing file, or both. Selecting both keeps the existing file and saves the restored file with "(original)" added to the name.

Restoring Data from within Applications with Time Machine

With certain applications, mostly Apple applications that manage data such as iPhoto, Address Book, and so on, you can also use Time Machine to restore data within those applications. For example, if you accidentally delete photos from iPhoto, you can use Time Machine to retrieve them from one of your backups.

To restore data from within an application, perform the following steps:

1. Make the application containing the data you want to restore active.

2. Launch Time Machine. The application appears and you see the application's window in the Time Machine space (see Figure 36.5).

Figure 36.5
Time Machine allows you to recover data that you may have deleted within Apple's applications.

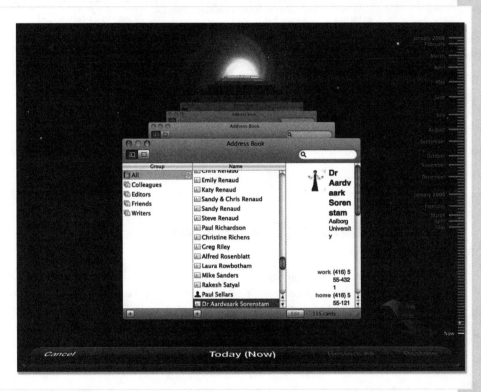

3. Move back through the available backups until you see the data that you want to restore.

4. Select the data you want to restore and click Restore. The selected data is added to the application. For example, if you select an address card, it is added to Address Book. If you select photos in iPhoto, they are added to your iPhoto Library.

Managing Your Time Machine Backups

Time Machine stores each backup on the selected backup disk. The backups are stored in a folder called Backups.backupdb. If you open that folder, you see a folder for the disks you are backing up. Open that folder to see folders for each version of the backup that Time Machine is managing (see Figure 36.6). You can open these folders to access files that are stored within them; this means that you can try to manually recover files from these folders if Time Machine loses track of them for some reason.

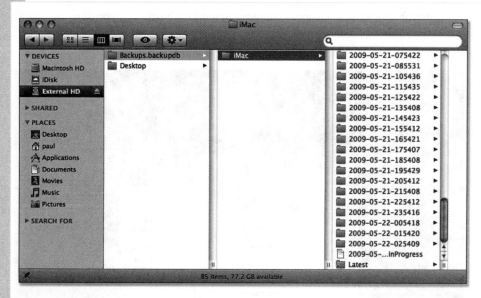

Figure 36.6
The various versions of your backups are stored in folders on your backup drive.

As time passes and the number of backups increases, the backup drive becomes full. When that happens, Time Machine starts dropping versions of the backups, starting with the oldest first. It attempts to keep all backups for as long as indicated on the Time Machine pane, but if your drive doesn't have enough room, you're prompted to let Time Machine delete versions that it doesn't have room to store. If this happens frequently, you need to get a larger backup drive or reduce the size of the files included in the backups.

Backing Up Your Mac with Apple's Backup

Time Machine is great for short-term backups that you want to keep active. However, you should also create backups that are more permanently stored and that you can keep in a location away from your Mac. To do that, you need a different application.

Apple's Backup application is capable backup software that enables you to back up to various kinds of media, including hard drives, DVD, CD, and iDisk (which takes the idea of remote storage of your data to a new level). You can also automate backups, and you can even configure different backups, such as a long-term backup and a short-term backup, and Backup manages each of them for you, so you can rely on Backup as your primary backup solution. The good news is that if you are a MobileMe member, you get Backup for free. If you aren't, you need to get a different application because Backup is not available to nonmembers.

Obtaining and Installing Backup

To get a copy of Backup, move to the MobileMe website and log in to your account. Move to the iDisk page, select the Software folder, and then download the Backup application. Launch the installer and work through its steps to install Backup on your Mac.

tip

A very good backup system is to use Time Machine for your short-term backups, because it is so easy to configure and restore files when you need them, and Backup for long-term backups because you can back up to DVD.

Configuring Backups with Backup

To configure a backup, perform the following steps:

1. Launch Backup, found in the Applications folder.

2. The first time you launch Backup you're presented with the welcome sheet, which includes four different backup plans with descriptions of the plans to help you select the best fit for your needs (see Figure 36.7).

Figure 36.7
Backup provides a number of templates you can use to quickly create a backup configuration.

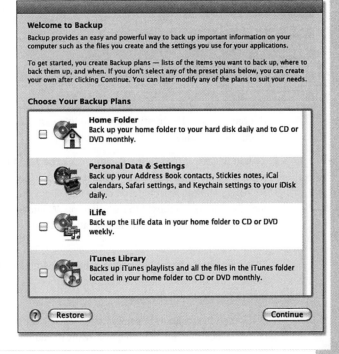

Welcome to Backup

Backup provides an easy and powerful way to back up important information on your computer such as the files you create and the settings you use for your applications.

To get started, you create Backup plans — lists of the items you want to back up, where to back them up, and when. If you don't select any of the preset plans below, you can create your own after clicking Continue. You can later modify any of the plans to suit your needs.

Choose Your Backup Plans

Home Folder
Back up your home folder to your hard disk daily and to CD or DVD monthly.

Personal Data & Settings
Back up your Address Book contacts, Stickies notes, iCal calendars, Safari settings, and Keychain settings to your iDisk daily.

iLife
Back up the iLife data in your home folder to CD or DVD weekly.

iTunes Library
Backs up iTunes playlists and all the files in the iTunes folder located in your home folder to CD or DVD monthly.

Restore   Continue

3. Activate the check box beside the plan you want to use and click Continue. The plan is created and the options that came from the template or that you selected are shown when you double-click the plan (see Figure 36.8). At the top of the plan window, you see three tabs. The Back Up tab enables you to configure the backup. The History tab shows you when the backup has run. Use the Restore tab to restore files from previous backups.

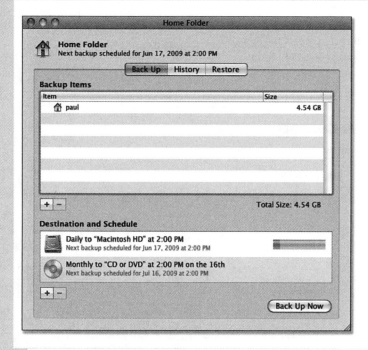

Figure 36.8
The plan window enables you to configure and use a backup plan.

The Back Up tab has two panes. The Backup Items pane shows the items that are included in the backup. The Destination and Schedule pane shows where the backups are stored and how often the plan backs up to each location.

4. To add folders or files to the backup, click the Add button (+) at the bottom of the Backup Items pane. Use the resulting sheet to move to and select folders or files you want to include. Anything marked with a green circle and check mark is included in the backup; if a folder is included, all its contents are included too. When you've selected all the content you want to add to the backup, click Done.

5. To remove items from the backup, select the items you want to remove and click the Remove button (-) at the bottom of the Backup Items pane.

6. To change the location or schedule for the backup, double-click the location and schedule you want to change or to

 tip
You can also remove folders and files from the backup in the Add Item sheet by selecting them and activating the Do Not Include This Folder or the Do Not Include This File radio button.

add a new location and schedule to the backup, click the Add button (+) at the bottom of the Destination and Schedule pane. The Choose a Destination and Schedule sheet appears (see Figure 36.9).

Figure 36.9
Use this sheet to choose a location and schedule for your backups.

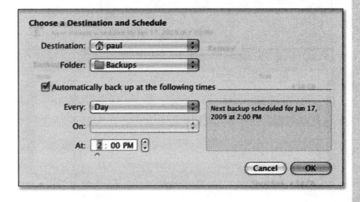

7. Choose the volume on which you want the backup to be stored on the Destination pop-up menu. You should choose a destination different than the volume on which the information you are backing up is stored so that problems that wipe out what you are backing up don't also destroy your backup.

8. Choose the folder in which you want the backups stored on the Folder pop-up menu. Click Choose Location and then move to and select the folder you want to store the backup in or use the New Folder button to create a new folder.

9. To enable automatic backups, activate the Automatically Back Up at the Following Times check box, choose the frequency on the Every pop-up menu, choose the day the backup runs (all options except Daily on the Every pop-up menu), and the time for the backup. Click OK to save the changes.

10. Repeat step 9 to create as many locations and schedules for the backup that you need. For example, you might want to make a daily backup to hard drive and a monthly one to DVD.

11. If you want to run a backup immediately, select the location to which you want to back up and click Back Up Now. The configuration you selected runs and the backup is created.

12. Close the plan. Move to the Backup window in which you see all of the backup plans you've created (see Figure 36.10).

 tip

You can create as many backup plans as you need to protect your data. For example, you might want to have a backup that runs frequently (unfortunately, daily is as frequent as you can run backups in Backup) and stores important files on a hard drive while another stores all your files on disc and runs monthly.

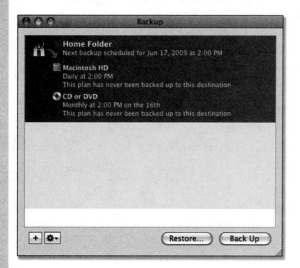

Figure 36.10
The Backup window shows all of the backup plans you've configured.

Backing Up with Backup

After you've configured backups, they run according to the schedules you've set. If a backup is stored on a CD or DVD, when it runs, you're prompted to insert the appropriate kind of disc.

You can manually run a backup by launching the Backup application, selecting the backup plan you want to run, and clicking Back Up. If the backup has more than one location, choose the location you want to run on the location sheet.

After the backup runs, the time and date of its last operation are shown under the plan in the Backup window. You can also open a plan and click the History tab to see when its been run.

If a backup fails, it's marked with an exclamation point icon in the Backup window. Click it to move to the plan's History tab where you see the backup that failed. Select it and click View Details to open a log file. Sometimes the information you see is useful, and sometimes it isn't. The most common cause of a failure is not having enough room on the selected destination.

 tip

To remove a backup plan, select it in the Backup window, open the Action pop-up menu and choose Remove. The backup is removed from the Backup application and is no longer used. If the backup is stored on a hard drive, look in the location in which it was stored and delete any files associated with the backup if you no longer need them.

Restoring Files with Backup

To restore files from a Backup backup, do the following:

1. Launch Backup.

2. Select the plan from which you want to restore files and click Restore. The Restore tab for the selected backup appears.

3. Select what you want to restore on the Previous Backups list.

4. If you want to restore the files to a location other than the one from which they were copied, check the Restore to an Alternate Location check box and choose the location to which you want the files restored.

5. Click Restore Selection. The selected files are restored from the backup to their previous location or to the location you selected.

 tip

If your Backup installation is lost (such as when a hard drive fails and you have to use a new one) such that you no longer see the plans in Backup, you can still restore files. Re-install Backup and launch it. Choose Plan, Restore from Backup. Then move to and select the backup from which you want to restore files.

Using a Backup System

I can't emphasize enough how important it is to maintain good backups for your data. Here are a few tips to keep in mind:

- **Develop your own strategy based on the hardware and software you have or plan to purchase**—At the least, make sure your critical files, such as photos, iTunes content, and financial data, are protected with good backups.

- **Make sure that backing up is easy**—If you have to do a lot of work to back up or if it takes a lot of your time, you won't end up keeping up-to-date backups. Ideally, you want to be able to do unattended backups; Time Machine and an external hard drive make it so.

- **Be consistent**—Whatever strategy you decide on, keep up with it. Old, out-of-date backups are not much better than no backups.

- **Always refresh your backups before you install any new software or make major changes to your system**—This enables you to recover data if the changes you make to your system cause problems.

- **Be sure to test your backups regularly**—Pretend that you've lost some very important files and try to restore them to ensure that everything is working properly. If you don't, you might get a nasty surprise when you need to restore some data "for real." You need to know your backup system has a problem before you need to use it. If you don't regularly test your backups, you are asking for trouble.

- **Maintain your equipment**—Almost all equipment needs some kind of maintenance now and again, so follow the manufacturer's guidelines to keep your system in top condition. Hard drives can fail, so check the ones you use for backing up periodically to make sure they are still working (see previous bullet).

 note

Archiving is slightly different from backing up. Backing up is done mostly for the "active" data on your Mac, whereas archiving is done with data you don't really need to work with any more. Fortunately, you can use your backup system to archive data as well. For archiving smaller documents, a CD drive is a good choice because the media is very cheap and relatively permanent. For larger amounts of data, a DVD is a good way to archive. When you archive, you should use a solution that won't degrade over time, which is why optical media such as CD and DVD are good choices. After you've archived data and checked to make sure that you can recover that data from the archive, you can delete the files from your working drive to free up some space.

- **Maintain more than one set of backups**—Create multiple copies of your backups in case something happens to one set.

- **Keep a set of backups offsite**—Keep a copy of your backups in a different location than your Mac is in. This saves you in the event of a catastrophic event such as fire or theft. This is especially important for data you can't replace, such as photos and financial data.

Restoring a Disk or Files

Using Disk Utility, you can create and save a disk image of a folder, volume, or disk. (A disk image is a file type that can be mounted and used just like a physical volume, such as a hard drive.) You can then use Disk Utility's Restore feature to restore the entire volume or specific files that are part of that disk image. This is, in effect, backing up specific parts of your system. You can choose folders, volumes, or an entire disk. To do this, you first use Disk Utility to create a disk image of the volume or folder you want to back up.

When you need to restore a file, you select the disk image you created and use the Restore tab to restore it or specific files it contains.

Although this approach has the benefit of using tools always available under Mac OS X, it does have several major drawbacks. This first is that you have to manually update the disk images you save. The second is that you still have to have the space to store those images (of course, you don't want to store them on the same volume as the files they include). However, you can use this technique to back up files if you don't have a better solution or to archive them.

SECURING YOUR MAC

Making Your Mac More Secure

Your Mac can never be too secure. There are just too many threats out there, and too many ways that the defenses in Mac OS X can be breached.

If that sounds strange, it's probably because everyone assumes that Macs are super-secure right out of the box. Yes, Macs *are* secure by default, but they're not impregnable by any means. For example, the reason we don't see many Mac viruses and spyware is that, yes, a Mac system isn't as welcoming as, say, a Windows PC, but it's also because virus and spyware authors prefer to target Windows PCs with their massive numbers of users.

Also, most people assume that security means being secure from Internet-based attacks, but you also need to be concerned with protecting your PC from direct attacks: that is, when an unauthorized *cracker* (which I define as a hacker who has succumbed to the Dark Side of the Force) sits down at your keyboard and tries to gain access to your system. Sure, it may be unlikely that a malicious user would gain physical access to the computer in your home or office, but it's not impossible.

Online crackers specialize in breaking into systems ("cracking" system security, hence the name), and at any given time hundreds, perhaps even thousands, of crackers roam cyberspace looking for potential targets. If you're online right now, the restless and far-seeing eyes of the crackers are bound to find you eventually.

The crackers are armed with programs that automatically search through millions of IP addresses (the addresses that uniquely identify any computer or device connected to the Internet). The crackers are specifically looking for computers that aren't secure, and if they find one they'll pounce on it and crack their way into the system. If all this sounds unlikely or that it would take them forever to find you, think again. Tests have shown that new and completely unprotected systems routinely get cracked within 20 minutes of connecting to the Internet!

So how do your thwart the world's crackers? I often joke that it's easy if you follow a simple four-prong plan:

- Don't connect to the Internet. Ever.

- Don't install programs on your computer. No, not even that one.

- Don't let anyone else work with, touch, glance at, talk about, or come with 20 feet of your computer.

- Burglar-proof your home or office.

The point here is that if you use your computer (and live your life) in an even remotely normal way, you open up your machine to security risks. That's a bleak assessment, for sure, but fortunately it doesn't take a lot of effort on your part to turn your computer into a maximum security area. The security techniques in this chapter will get to that goal.

Securing Your Mac with User Accounts

You should create user accounts for everyone who uses your Mac. In addition to the features user accounts provide, such as a website and well-organized file storage, user accounts prevent unauthorized users from changing the system configuration of your machine. And you can use parental controls to define how users are able to use your Mac.

➡ *To learn how to limit how your Mac is used by others,* **see** *"Using Parental Controls to Safeguard a Mac,"* **p. 724.**

Securing Your Mac with Privileges

For those who access your Mac over a network and for those who share your machine, you can control the access to specific items by setting privileges for those items. You can control access in several levels of privilege from not being able to even see the item to being able to read and write to it.

➡ *To learn how to configure privileges,* **see** *"Understanding and Setting Permissions,"* **p. 377.**

Securing Your Mac with the Security Pane

The Security pane of the System Preferences application enables you to protect your Mac in three ways. One is by using the FileVault feature that encrypts all the files in your Home folder; these files can't be used unless you input your login password or the master password for your Mac. The second way is through the configuration and use of Mac OS X's firewall. The third way is by configuring various security settings for your Mac.

Securing Your Mac with FileVault

Mac OS X's FileVault feature encrypts all the files in your Home folder with 128-bit encryption. Such files can't be opened unless one of two passwords is entered. One password is the one you use to log in to your account. The other is a master password you set for your Mac; with this password, you can decrypt any encrypted files on your Mac, regardless of the user account with which those files are associated.

FileVault is valuable for those times when you aren't logged in to your account and someone else has access to your machine. For example, suppose someone steals your MacBook. Although she can't access your user account without your login password, she could connect the machine to a FireWire drive with Mac OS X installed and start up from that volume. Because the files on your MacBook startup volume are not protected any more (the OS on the computer to which the MacBook is connected is running the show), they are accessible. If FileVault is not on, these files are not encrypted and can be used, but if FileVault is on, these files are encrypted and are useless.

After being configured, FileVault works in the background and you won't notice it doing its job unless you try to open encrypted files without knowing one of the two passwords. In that case, you definitely notice it working.

The following steps demonstrate how to configure FileVault:

1. Open the System Preferences application, click the Security icon, and then click the FileVault tab (see Figure 37.1).

2. Click the Set Master Password button and then enter your administrator password. The master password enables you to decrypt encrypted files for all users.

3. Enter the master password in the Master Password field and enter it again in the Verify field.

4. Enter a hint for the master password in the Hint field.

5. Click OK to set the master password.

 caution

According to Apple, FileVault can interfere with backups because it makes your Home folder appear as a single file to the backup system. This can make the individual files impossible to restore. When using FileVault, be sure you test your backup system to ensure that you can still recover files if you need to.

 tip

Click the key button next to the Master Password box to open the Password Assistant. You can use this tool to generate passwords based on specific criteria, such as type and length. When you have configured a password, it is placed in the box for you. You then have to type it in the Verify box.

 note

To use FileVault, a user account must have a password. If you didn't configure a password for your user account, or for any other user account, you need to do so before you can activate FileVault.

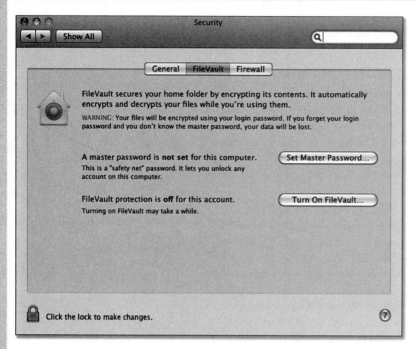

Figure 37.1
Use the FileVault feature
if you want to encrypt the
files in your Home folder
so they can't be used
without a valid password.

6. Click the Turn On FileVault button. If there currently isn't a password for the user account, the warning sheet appears and you can use the Password sheet to create one. If the user account already has a password, the service starts up and you are prompted to enter your password.

7. Enter your user account's login password and click OK. You see a warning sheet that explains what you are doing and that activating this service can take a while (you can't log out of your account until the service has been turned on).

8. Click the Turn On FileVault button. The FileVault window appears; you can't do anything else on your Mac until FileVault has started up. This window shows you the progress of the encryption process. If you have a lot of data in your Home folder, this process can take quite some time. When the process is complete, you see the Login window.

9. Log back in to your account. You shouldn't notice any difference, but all your Home folder files are encrypted and won't be accessible unless a valid encryption password has been entered.

 tip
If you also want Secure Erase (which overwrites deleted data so that it can't be recovered as easily), check the Use Secure Erase check box.

 note
If you want this feature to be active for multiple user accounts, you must log in under each account and turn on FileVault.

When you log in to your account (or any other user whose account is protected by FileVault), the files in your Home folder are decrypted automatically, so you won't need to do anything else to access them. You can turn off FileVault again by clicking the Turn Off FileVault button and entering your login password.

If another user on your Mac turns on FileVault and subsequently forgets her password, you can use your FileVault master password to reset that user's password. You do this by trying to log in to that user's account. The login will fail, of course (since the password is lost), but that's okay. After the third unsuccessful attempt, click the Forgot Password button, then enter the FileVault master password, click Continue, and then type a new password for the user.

 caution

FileVault applies only to each user account in which it is activated. And it works only on the files in each user's Home folder. Files stored outside the Home folders for which it is activated are not protected.

Securing Your Mac with the Mac OS X Firewall

 note

When a user account is protected by FileVault, its Home folder icon looks like a cross between the normal Home folder icon and a safe.

If your Mac is connected to the Internet, it's critical that it be protected from Internet attacks. There are number of ways to accomplish this. Ideally, you connect your Mac to the Internet via a network hub that protects it from attack. However, if you connect your Mac directly to the Internet or just want a double-layer of protection, you can configure Mac OS X's built-in software firewall to guard your Mac from attack.

➡ *To learn more about protecting your Mac from Internet attacks,* ***see*** *"Defending Your Mac Against Internet Hackers," p. 723.*

You can enable your Mac's firewall by doing the following:

1. Open the System Preferences application.

2. Click the Security icon to open the Security pane.

3. Click the Firewall tab.

4. If the Firewall setting is currently Off, click Start. Mac OS X activates the firewall.

5. Click Advanced. Mac OS X displays the Advanced firewall settings sheets, as shown in Figure 37.2). If you have services that you have turned on in the Sharing pane of the System Preferences application, those services appear in the list.

6. To prevent all connections to your Mac, activate the Block All Incoming Connections check box. With this active, you won't be able to accept any connections between your Mac and network services, so you should use this only when you have a Mac that you want to completely isolate. If you block all connections, skip the rest of these steps.

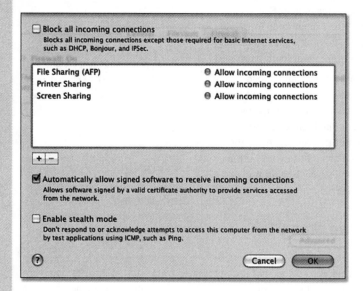

Figure 37.2
Use the Firewall's Advanced settings to configure your Mac's built-in firewall.

7. If you want to add another program to the list of applications that are allowed to accept network or Internet connections through the firewall, click the Add button (+), select the application, and then click Add. A pop-up menu appears for each application (see Figure 37.3), and you use that pop-up menu to determine the connections that are allowed: Choose Allow Incoming Connections to enable your application to communicate with other network resources; or choose Block Incoming Connections to prevent an application from any communication across the network.

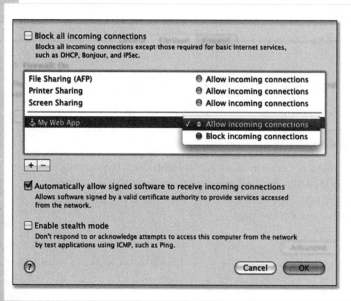

Figure 37.3
You can add applications that require Internet or network connection to the firewall list.

8. By default the firewall allows incoming connections from applications that have a valid security certificate. If you don't want to allow such programs through the firewall, for some reason, deactivate the Automatically Allow Signed Software to Receive Incoming Connections check box.

9. To put your Mac into stealth mode, where the computer doesn't respond to probe requests such as pings, activate the Enable Stealth Mode check box.

10. Click OK to put the new settings into effect.

Only the connections for the services and applications you allow are permitted to access your Mac. All others are denied. This prevents most of the kinds of attacks you are likely to experience.

 note

If you have trouble with some network or Internet services, make sure you check the firewall configuration to ensure it isn't configured to prevent the kind of service you are trying to use.

Securing Your Mac with Security Settings

Several other security settings are available on the General tab of the Security pane (see Figure 37.4).

Figure 37.4
Check out these general security settings to protect your Mac.

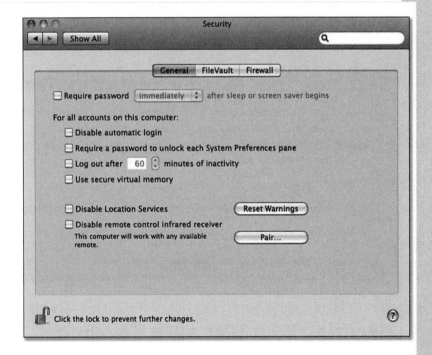

These features are described in the following list:

- **Require Password *X* After Sleep or Screen Saver Begins**—If you activate this feature, a user account's login password is required to stop the screensaver or wake up the Mac from sleep.

This setting impacts only the account that is currently active; if you want this to be required for each user account, you need to log in to each one and set it for that account.

- **Disable Automatic Login**—Activate this check box and the automatic login feature is turned off. This means that someone has to log in into your Mac manually to be able to use it.

- **Require a Password to Unlock Each System Preference Pane**—When you check this box, an administrator password must be entered to make changes to any of the System Preferences panes.

- **Log Out After *X* Minutes of Activity**—Activate this check box to log out the current user account after the specified amount of inactivity has occurred.

- **Use Secure Virtual Memory**—Activate this check box to use secure storage for data written to disk when virtual memory is required.

- **Disable Location Services**—Activate this check box to prevent location-aware applications from using the data provided by a location device (such as a GPS sensor) attached to your Mac. If you have previously allowed applications to use your location, click Reset Warnings to remove that data.

- **Disable Remote Control Infrared Receiver**—If you activate this check box, your Mac's infrared receiver is disabled so that it can't be accessed via infrared (such as through its remote control). You can also use the Pair button to associate a specific remote control with your Mac.

Securing Your Mac by Removing Trash Securely

Normally, when you delete files they are deleted from the system, but the data for those files might or might not be overwritten by other data. If not, files you've deleted can sometimes be recovered by software restoration tools. If you want the files you delete to be overwritten with random, system-generated data so they can't be recovered, follow these steps:

1. Switch to Finder.

2. Select the Finder, Secure Empty Trash command. Finder prompts you to confirm.

3. Select Secure Empty Trash. Mac OS X cleans out the Trash folder securely.

This causes the files you delete to be overwritten so they can't be recovered. It takes a bit longer to empty the trash because your Mac has to overwrite the space on which the files you deleted are stored.

Securing Your Mac with Keychains

For security and other reasons (such as making online shopping more convenient), you need usernames and passwords to access network resources, whether those resources are on a local network or the Internet. After using even a few of these, you may have a large collection of usernames and passwords. Remembering these can be a challenge. Fortunately, your Mac lets you store all your usernames and passwords along with other information you might want to secure in a keychain. You can then apply your keychain to whatever resource you want to use and the appropriate information is provided so you can access what you need. All you need to remember is the password that unlocks your keychain. By default, this is the same as your login password so that your keychain is used automatically. After you have added a password to your keychain, you can access the related resources without entering your keychain's password (because it is entered when you log in).

You can configure other keychains so that you can gain automatic access to secured resources during each working session. To secure those resources again, you can lock your keychain, which means the password must be entered for that keychain to use it again.

A keychain is created automatically for each user account you create. However, you can create additional keychains for specific purposes if you need to.

Many types of resources can be added to your keychain to enable you to access them, including the following:

 note

Safari can also remember usernames and passwords for sites you visit so you don't have to enter this information each time you log in. This saves a lot of time and keystrokes (assuming you can even remember all your usernames and passwords, of course). What actually happens is that Safari creates an item within the Passwords category in your keychain in which all your web username and passwords are stored. When you return to a page for which you have had Safari remember your login information, it uses the data stored in the keychain to input the appropriate data for you.

- **AirPort network password**—When you add an AirPort network password to your keychain, you can join the network by selecting it via the AirPort controls. The network's password are added to your keychain automatically.

- **Application password**—Some applications require passwords to perform specific tasks. One notable example is the iTunes Store function. When you have your iTunes Store password added to your keychain, you can purchase songs with a single click of the mouse button.

- **AppleShare password**—Any passwords you use to access network volumes can also be added to your keychain.

 note

You can store information that you want to secure using notes. For example, if you want to store your credit card information so it can't be accessed unless you are logged in to your user account, you can add it to your keychain. When you need that information, you can open the secured note containing your credit card information in your keychain.

- **Internet password**—When you need to enter passwords for Internet services, such as email accounts, adding them to your keychain makes accessing those services much more convenient because you never have to enter the password manually.

- **MobileMe password**—When you enter your MobileMe password in the MobileMe pane of the System Preferences application, it is added to your keychain so you can work with your iDisk from the desktop without having to log in to your MobileMe account each time.

- **Secure note**—These enable you to store information securely.

■ **Internet and web form password**—When you access your account on secure websites, you can add your usernames and passwords to your keychain. When you visit those sites again (via Safari), you can log in just by clicking the Login button because your username and password are entered automatically.

> ⚠ **caution**
>
> Having passwords in your keychain is convenient, but it's also a security risk because it enables anyone who has physical access to your computer to log in to those resources. If other people have access to your Mac, do not add passwords for sensitive resources to your keychain.

Viewing and Configuring Your Keychains and Keychain Items

Access your keychains through the Keychain Access application by doing the following:

1. Open the Keychain Access application (Applications/Utilities folder). When the application opens, two panes appear (see Figure 37.5). In the left pane is a list of categories for all the keychains that are installed under your user account. These categories include All Items, which contains all keychain items you can access; Passwords, which contains passwords for network, application, and Internet resources; and so on. Select a category and the keychain items it contains appear in the right pane of the window. You see information related to each keychain item, such as its name, its kind, the date it was last modified, when it expires, and the keychain in which it is stored.

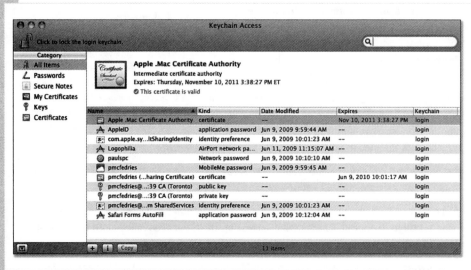

Figure 37.5
Over time, your keychain may have quite a few keys installed on it.

2. To view all the keychains your user account can access, click the Show Keychains button at the bottom of the Keychain Access window (see Figure 37.6). The Keychains pane appears at the top of the left side of the window.

> **tip**
>
> The Passwords category contains several subcategories. To view them, expand that category by clicking its expansion triangle.

Figure 37.6
Here, you can see that this user has several keychains available; only the Login keychain is currently unlocked.

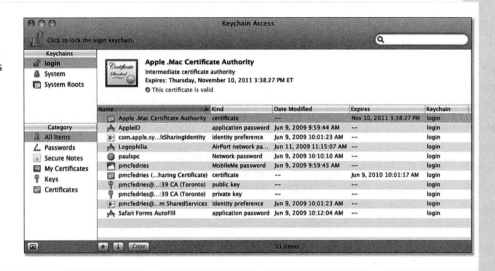

3. To get summary information about a keychain item, select it. A summary of the item appears at the top of the window, including the kind of item it is, the user account with which it is associated, the location to which it relates, and the modification date.

4. With the item still selected, click the Information button (the *i* located at the bottom of the Keychain Access window). The Information window appears. This window has two tabs: Attributes and Access Control (see Figure 37.7). The Attributes tab presents various information about the item, such as its name, its kind, the account, the location of the resource with which it is associated, comments you have entered, and the password (which is hidden when you first view an item). The Access Control tab enables you to configure how the item is used.

Figure 37.7
The Information window provides detailed information about a keychain item.

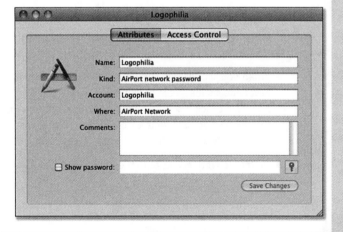

5. To see the item's password, activate the Show Password check box. You are then prompted to confirm the keychain's password (you learn more about this in the next section).

6. Confirm the password by entering it at the prompt and choosing to allow access to the item (the options you see are explained in the next section). When you return to the Attributes tab, you see the item's password.

7. Click the Access Control tab. At the bottom of the tab, you see a list of the applications that have access to the keychain item. Use the access controls in the pane to control which applications can access this item and how they can access it.

8. To allow access to the item by all applications, select the Allow All Applications to Access This Item radio button. You see a warning that access to the item is not restricted. This means that all applications are able to use the item. With this option, you can't configure the other options because they don't apply. If you want to configure access for specific applications, continue with the rest of these steps.

9. To allow access by specific applications but require confirmation, select the Confirm Before Allowing Access radio button, and activate the Ask for Keychain Password check box if you want to be prompted for your keychain's password before access is allowed. (If you don't select this option, the item is accessed automatically.)

10. To enable an application not currently on the list to access the keychain item, click the Add button (+) and select the application to which you want to provide access.

11. To remove an application's access to the item, select the application and click Remove (-).

12. Click Save Changes to save the changes to the keychain item.

 note

Sometimes you have to click the Options button to be able to add an item to your keychain. For example, when you mount a network volume, click Options to reveal the Add Password to Keychain check box.

Adding Items to a Keychain

You can add items to a keychain in several ways, including the following:

- When you access a resource that can provide access to a keychain, such as a file server, look for the Add to Keychain check box. When you check this, an item for that resource is added to your keychain. This is the most common and easiest way to add items to a keychain.

- Drag a network server onto the Keychain Access window.

- Drag the Internet Resource Locator file for a web page onto the Keychain Access window.

- Manually create a keychain item.

⚠ caution

Not all applications support keychain access. If a particular application or resource doesn't support keychains, you won't be able to access that resource automatically. However, you can still use Keychain Access to store such an item's username and password for you, thus enabling you to recall that information easily. This also stores it more securely than writing it down on a piece of paper.

To manually add a password item to your keychain, perform the following steps:

1. Open Keychain Access (Applications/Utilities).

2. View the keychains installed for your user account and select the keychain to which you want to add the item (your default keychain, which is the login keychain unless you have changed it, is selected automatically).

3. Select File, New Password Item. (You can also press ⌘-N or click the Add button (+) below the Name column.) The New Password Item sheet appears.

4. Enter the name of the item in the Keychain Item Name box. If you are adding an Internet resource, such as a web page, enter its URL.

5. Enter the account name or username for the item in the Account Name box. This is the name of the user account with which the keychain item is associated.

6. Enter the password for the item in the Password box. If you want to see the password as you type it, activate the Show Typing check box. This helps you confirm you are entering the correct password. Otherwise, you see only bullets as you type. You see an indication of the strength of the password you create in the lower part of the sheet.

7. Click Add to return to the keychain's window and see the new item you added. You can access that item using your keychain. You can view and configure the new item using the steps in the previous section.

To add a secure note to a keychain, use the following steps:

1. Open Keychain Access.

2. Select the keychain to which you want to add the note (your default keychain is selected automatically).

3. Select File, New Secure Note Item (or press Shift-⌘-N). The New Secured Note sheet appears.

4. Enter the name of the note in the Keychain Item Name box.

5. Enter the information you want to store in the Note box. This a freeform text field so you can enter anything you want.

6. Click Add to return to the Keychain Access window where you see the new note you added.

To view a secure note, double-click it and click the Show Note check box. You see the note in the window.

 tip
Click the Key button to open the Password Assistant to help you configure a password for the item.

 tip
You can set the default keychain for your user account by selecting the keychain you want to make the default and choosing File, Make Keychain *keychainname* Default, where *keychainname* is the name of the keychain you have selected.

 note
If you select a keychain that is currently locked, you have to unlock it before you can add items to it.

Adding a Keychain

You might want to add keychains to your current account, which you can do using the following steps:

1. Open Keychain Access (Applications/Utilities).

2. To add a keychain, select File, New Keychain or press Option-⌘-N. You see the New Keychain dialog box.

3. Move to the location in which you want to save the keychain, name it, and click Create. (By default, keychains are stored in the Keychains folder in the Library folder in your Home folder. In most cases, you should store new keychains in this folder.) You are prompted to create the password for the keychain.

4. Enter the password for the keychain in the Password and Verify fields; then click OK. The new keychain is added to the list of available keychains, and you can work with it just like those already on the list.

Using Keychains

When you have a keychain configured for an account and it is unlocked, you can access the items it contains without entering your username or password. For example, when you open a server, it opens for you immediately.

To prevent a keychain from being accessed, lock it. Do so by opening the Keychain Access application, selecting the keychain, and selecting File, Lock Keychain *keychainname*, where *keychainname* is the name of the keychain. You can also do so by pressing ⌘-L or clicking the Lock button (the padlock) on the toolbar.

To unlock a keychain again, select it, click the Unlock button or press ⌘-L, enter the password for that keychain, and click OK.

When an application needs to access a keychain item and it is not configured to always allow access, you see the Confirm Access to Keychain dialog box, which prompts you to enter a keychain's password and choose an access option. When prompted, you have the following three options:

 note

You might want to move a keychain between user accounts so you don't have to re-create the items it contains.

 tip

An exception to where you keep your keychains might be when you want to enable others to import your new keychain into their accounts, in which case you should store it in a location accessible to others, such as your Public folder. For example, you might want to create a keychain with website items on it. You could provide this to other users who would then be able to access the items contained in the keychains you install.

 tip

Click the Key button to open the Password Assistant to use it to create a password for the keychain you are creating.

 note

By the way, this is how Mac OS X can access your .Mac account without you having to log in each time. When you create a .Mac account, it is added to the keychain for the Mac OS X user account related to it. Mac OS X can use this keychain to access the .Mac account without requiring that you log in manually.

- **Deny**—If you click this, access to the item is prevented.

- **Allow Once**—A single access to the item is allowed. The next time you attempt to access it, you see the prompt again.

- **Always Allow**—Access to the item is always allowed.

Going Further with Keychains

Keychain Access is actually a fairly complex application that can do more than just what I have room to show you in this section. Following are some pointers in case you are interested in exploring on your own:

 note

The first time you access keychain items after the OS has been updated, such as through the Software Update application, you see the Confirm Access to Keychain prompt, even for those items for which you have selected the Always Allow option (such as the first time you check your email after upgrading the OS). This is normal behavior. Just select the Always Allow option to re-enable that behavior.

- Your keychains are stored in the Library/Keychains folder in your Home directory. You can add a keychain from one account to another account by exporting the keychain file (use the File, Export Items command) to a location that can be accessed by the second account. (For example, you can copy your keychain into the Public folder of your Home directory to enable other users to add that keychain to their own accounts.) To add a keychain to a user account, open Keychain Access under that account and use the File, Import command. This is useful if you want to use the same keychain from several accounts. You can't export all keychains, so you have to try one to see whether you can export it.

- Delete a keychain either by selecting it and selecting File, Delete Keychain *keychainname*, where *keychainname* is the name of the keychain.

- If you select Edit, Change Settings for Keychain *keychainname*, where *keychainname* is the name of the keychain, you can set a keychain to lock after a specified period of time or lock when the Mac is asleep.

- You can synchronize keychains on different computers by using MobileMe.

- If you select Edit, Change Password for Keychain *keychainname*, where *keychainname* is the name of the keychain, you can change a keychain's password.

- Choose Keychain Access, Preferences. On the General tab, activate the Show Status in Menu Bar check box. This adds the Keychain Access menu to the Mac's menu bar. From this menu, you can lock or unlock keychains and access security preferences and the Keychain Access application.

- If you select Edit, Keychain List or press Option-⌘-L, you see the Configure Keychain sheet. You can use this to configure keychains for a user account or the system. For example, you can check the Shared check box to share a keychain between user accounts.

- If you select Keychain Access, Keychain First Aid or press Option-⌘-A, you see the Keychain First Aid dialog box. You can use this to verify keychains or repair a damaged keychain.

- In the keychain access prompt, you can click the Show Details button to expose the details of the keychain access being requested.

Defending Your Mac from Internet Attacks

The Internet is a major source of threat to the health and well-being of your Macs and the network to which they are connected. You face two fundamental types of threats: viruses and hackers. Although viruses receive more media attention, defending against viruses is easier than defending against attacks from hackers. However, with some relatively simple activity, you can protect yourself from both threats. The next few sections provide you with these security details.

Defending Your Mac from Virus Attacks

No matter what level of computer user you are, because of the extensive media hype about viruses, you are likely to be keenly aware of them. Although many viruses are relatively harmless, some viruses can do damage to your machine. Part of practicing smart computing is understanding viruses and taking appropriate steps to protect your machine from them.

Understanding the Types of Viruses

Although there are many types of individual viruses, there are two major groups of viruses of which you need to be aware:

- **Application viruses**—These viruses are applications that do *something* to your computer. What they do might be as harmless as displaying a silly message or as harmful as corrupting particular files on your hard drive.

 caution

Under previous versions of the Mac OS, there were many fewer viruses on the Mac platform than for Windows or other operating systems. And, as of the release of Mac OS X, version 10.6, this is still the case. However, because Mac OS X is based on Unix, Unix viruses can be a threat to machines running Mac OS X. Until this threat is more fully understood, Mac OS X users would do well to pay additional attention to virus threats.

- **Macro viruses**—A macro virus can be created in and launched by any application that supports macros (such as the Microsoft Office applications). When you open a file that has been infected by a macro virus, that virus (the macro) runs and performs its dirty deed.

Covering the multitude of viruses that are out there is beyond the scope of this book and, besides, there is no real need to become an expert on the viruses that exist. It is more important to understand how to protect yourself from these viruses and be able to recover from an infection should one occur.

Preventing Virus Infection

The best way to avoid viruses is to avoid files that are likely to have viruses in them. The following are some practices to help you stay virus-free:

- Find and use a good antivirus software program; keep the virus definitions for that application up to date.

- Be wary when you download files from any source, particularly email. Even if an email is apparently from someone you know, that doesn't mean the attachments it contains are safe. Some users unknowingly transmit infected files to you (especially beginning users). Some viruses can use an email application to replicate themselves. Before you open any attachment, be sure it makes sense given who the sender appears to be.

- When you do download files, download them from reputable sites, such as magazine sites or directly from a software publisher's site. These sites scan files for viruses before making them available so your chances of getting an infected file are lower. Remember the expression, "Consider the source."

- After you download a file, run your antivirus software on it to ensure that it isn't infected. Most programs let you designate the folder into which you download files and automatically check files in this folder.

Identifying Virus Infection

Even with good preventive measures, your Mac might occasionally become infected. Hopefully, you find out you have been infected by being notified by your antivirus software—that means it is doing its job. But if you suddenly notice that your computer is acting peculiarly, you might have become infected. What does acting peculiarly mean? Viruses can have many different effects on your computer; some of the more common effects are the following:

- **Weird messages, dialog boxes, or other unexpected interface elements**—Sometimes viruses make themselves known by presenting something odd onscreen. So, if you suddenly see a strange dialog box, you might have stumbled across a virus (for example, one of the Word macro viruses causes a happy face to appear in Word's menu bar). They can also cause menu items to disappear or be changed in some way.

- **Loss in speed**—Viruses often make your computer work more slowly.

- **Disappearing files**—Some viruses cause files to be deleted or hidden.

- **Errors**—Many viruses cause various errors on your computer and prevent applications from working properly. If you haven't changed anything on your machine for a while and you suddenly start experiencing errors, you should check your computer for a possible infection.

 note

The first time an application opens, Mac OS X presents a dialog box to you informing you about this. If you recognize the application because you are trying to open, allow it to open and move along. If you don't recognize the application, it could be a virus. Deny it permission to open until you check it out to make sure it's something you want to use. It's easy to get in the habit of allowing applications by default, but you should pay attention to these warnings because they could save you a lot of trouble.

Using Antivirus Software

Although the best defense against viruses is being very careful about the files you transfer onto your machine, you should also obtain and use a good antivirus application. Good antivirus applications generally perform the following functions:

- Monitor activity on your computer to identify potential infection

- Periodically scan your drives to look for infections

- Notify you if an infection is discovered

- Repair the infected files and eliminate the virus

- Delete infected files if repairing them is impossible

- Enable you to identify particular folders that should be scanned automatically, such as the folder into which you download files

- Update themselves automatically

As with previous versions of the Mac OS, there are several major antivirus applications, including Norton AntiVirus for Mac and Virex.

These applications provide most of the features in the previous list, and they work well. You should obtain and use one of these applications to protect your Mac against viruses and to repair your Mac should it become infected.

 note

Most viruses are identified by their code. The antivirus software knows about the virus's code through its virus definition file. As new viruses appear, this virus definition file needs to be updated so that the new viruses can be recognized as being viruses. You can usually obtain an updated virus definition file from the website of the manufacturer of your antivirus software. Most programs automate this process and can update the virus definition at intervals you set.

note

One of the important things to look for in an antivirus program is that it can detect and repair macro viruses. Macro viruses are easy to create and spread, and some of them are quite nasty.

Viruses and You

Viruses are less of a problem than they appear to be from the tremendous amount of media hype they receive, especially for Mac users. Most of the time, you can protect yourself from viruses by being very careful about the files you receive in email or download from the Web. Because the only way for a virus to get onto your machine is for you to accept a file in which it is contained, you can protect yourself from most viruses by using common sense. For example, if you receive an email containing an oddly titled attachment (such as the famous I Love You file), you should either request more information from the sender before you open the file or simply delete the message. And you should *never* open an attachment that comes from an unknown sender.

This is one case in which being in the minority as a Mac user is beneficial. The vast majority of viruses are designed for Windows machines and have no effect on a Mac.

Defending Your Mac Against Internet Hackers

If you have a broadband connection to the Internet such as a cable or DSL modem, being attacked by hackers is a much more real threat than are viruses. And with a broadband connection, you *will* be attacked, daily if not hourly or even more frequently. Hackers are continuously looking for machines they can exploit, either to do damage to you or to use your machine to do damage to others (such as using your machine to launch a spam attack). Most of these attacks are carried out by applications, so they can be both automatic and continuous.

There are two fundamental ways you can prevent your Mac from being hacked through your broadband Internet connection: Use a hardware firewall on a router or server to isolate the machines on your network from the outside world, or use a software firewall to protect each machine on the network from attack.

 caution

Never expose a machine containing sensitive or production data to a broadband connection without protecting that machine from network attack. Doing so makes everything on such a machine vulnerable to exposure to a hacker, and the machine itself can be used to carry out attacks on other networks and machines.

Using a Hardware Firewall to Protect Your Network

You can isolate the machines on your network from attack by placing a physical barrier between them and the public Internet. You can then use a Dynamic Host Configuration Protocol (DHCP) server that provides network address translation (NAT) protection for your network, or you can add or use a router that contains a more sophisticated firewall to ensure that your network can't be violated. A benefit to these devices is that you can also use them to share a single Internet connection.

 note

One of the easiest and best ways to protect machines on a local network from attack and to share an Internet connection is to install an AirPort base station. These devices provide NAT protection for any computers that obtain Internet service through them, and for most users, this is an adequate level of protection from hacking.

Using a Software Firewall to Protect Your Network

You can also install and use a software firewall; a software firewall prevents unexpected access to your Mac from the Internet. Software firewalls can be quite effective and might be the best solution if you have only a single Mac connected to the Internet.

A software firewall works by blocking access to specific ports on your Mac; these ports are linked to specific services. If hackers can access these ports on your machine, they can use them to attack your machine directly to launch attacks on other computers, servers, and networks (such as denial-of-service attacks, in which a system is overloaded by repeated requests from many machines).

 caution

Unlike a hardware firewall or NAT router, a software firewall must be installed on each computer attached to your network.

➡ *To learn how to configure and use Mac OS X's built-in firewall, **see** "Securing Your Mac with the Mac OS X Firewall," p. 709.*

Using Parental Controls to Safeguard a Mac

In addition to protecting your Mac itself from attack, you can also protect individual users from various kinds of danger by blocking specific types of access for individual accounts. For example, you might want to control the kind of email a child who uses your Mac receives. You control various types of access to your Mac and to the Internet via the Parental Controls pane of the System Preferences application.

Using Parental Controls to Limit a User's Access to the Mac

You can limit a user's access to your Mac's resources using the tabs on the Parental Controls pane of the System Preferences application.

Use the System tab to control how users can interact with the system by doing the following:

1. Open the System Preferences application and click Parental Controls. The Parental Control window appears.

2. In the user list in the left pane of the window, select the user whose access you want to limit.

3. If the user account is not already a managed account, click Enable Parental Controls. Mac OS X displays the Parental Controls tabs.

4. Click the System tab (see Figure 37.8).

 note

The first time you select a user, you have to click the Enable Parent Controls button before you are shown the detail page with the tabs.

Figure 37.8
Use the System tab to determine what kind of system resources a user can access.

5. To limit the user to the Simple Finder, activate the Use Simple Finder check box.

The Simple Finder provides the most basic level of access. As you might expect from its name, the Simple Finder provides a less complex interface for a user and greatly restricts what that user can do. When a user is logged in with the Simple Finder, the Dock contains only five icons: Finder, My Applications, Documents, Shared, and Trash. These are the only areas the user can access. For example, under the Simple Finder, a user can store documents only in his Documents folder and can't open other folders. The only Finder commands the user can access are Sleep, Log Out, About Finder, the Hide/Show Finder commands, and Close Window. The Simple Finder makes your machine more secure because it limits the actions of a user so severely. Using the Simple Finder can be a good choice if the user for whom you are creating an account has minimal computer skills, such as for very young children or someone who is totally new to the Mac.

6. To limit the user to specific applications, activate the Only Allow Selected Applications check box. Then activate the check box next to each application on the application list to enable the user to use it or uncheck a box to prevent a user from using that application.

On the list, applications are grouped; expand a group to see the applications it contains. You can enable or disable all of the applications in the group by using its check box or expand a group and check or uncheck individual applications.

note

Apple applications are grouped pretty well, such as the iLife applications. Most other applications appear in the all-inclusive Other category.

7. Activate the following check boxes to determine if the user can perform the related actions or not:

- **Can Administer Printers**—This control allows or prevents a user from being able to configure printers.

- **Can Burn CDs and DVDs**—This one is easy to figure out; if enabled, the user can burn discs. If not, the user won't be able to write to CD or DVD.

- **Can Change Password**—If enabled, the user can change their password.

- **Can Modify the Dock**—If this is enabled, the user can configure his Dock.

To limit when a user can use a Mac, do the following:

1. Open the Parental Controls pane of the System Preferences application, select the user whose access you want to limit in the user list in the left pane of the window, and click the Time Limits tab (see Figure 37.9).

2. To limit the time the user can access the Mac on weekdays, activate the Limit Computer Use To check box in the Weekday time limits section of the pane and set the amount of time on the slider.

3. To limit the time the user can access the Mac on weekends, activate the Limit Computer Use To check box in the Weekend time limits section of the pane and set the amount of time on the slider.

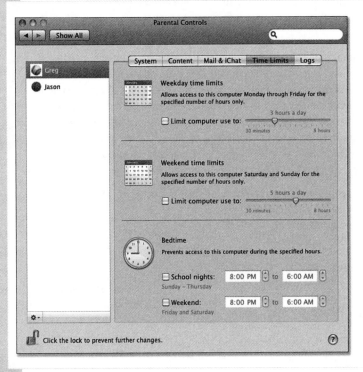

Figure 37.9
Use the Time Limits tab to determine when a user can use a Mac.

4. To set an off-limits period for weekdays or weekends, use the controls in the Bedtime section. Activate the School Nights check box and enter times during which the computer can't be used by the user. Activate the Weekend check box and set times to limit its use on Friday and Saturday nights.

After you set time limits, the user won't be unable to use his user account outside of the limits you set. If you have your Mac configured to show the list of users on the login window, a note next to the username indicates when that user can log in again. If a user is logged in and has a Bedtime set up, he is warned a few minutes before that time that his computer time is almost up. An option is displayed to add more time, which requires an administrative password to confirm. After the Bedtime limit is reached, the user is locked out of his account. When he can log in again, he is able to pick up where he left off.

Limiting the Web and Dictionary Content Your Mac's Users Can Access

The Web is often a great place to be, but it can also be a dangerous or disgusting place to be as well. You can protect users by limiting the websites they can visit by doing the following steps:

1. Open the Parental Controls pane of the System Preferences application, select the user whose access you want to limit in the user list in the left pane of the window, and click the Content tab (see Figure 37.10).

Figure 37.10
Use the Content tab to limit access to Dictionary and website content.

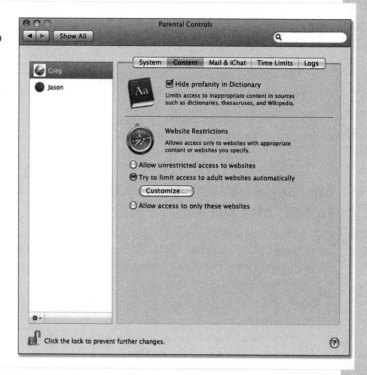

2. To hide profanity in the Dictionary, activate the Hide Profanity in Dictionary check box.

3. To determine web content the user can access, choose one of the following options:

   ■ **Allow Unrestricted Access to Websites**—This option doesn't prevent access to any websites.

   ■ **Try to Limit Access of Adult Websites Automatically**— Mac OS X will try to prevent the user from accessing websites that have adult content, such as porn sites.

   ■ **Allow Access to Only These Websites**—If this is enabled, you can configure a specific list of URLs that the user can access by doing the rest of these steps.

 tip

To organize the bookmarks, first click the Allow Access to Only These Websites radio button. You can then click the Add button and choose Add Folder. Name the new folder. You can use these folders to organize the bookmarks you create.
Unfortunately, you can't drag bookmarks around the list to place them in folders. You must create the folder first and then create the bookmark in it.

4. If you selected the Allow Access to Only These Websites option, a list of kid-friendly sites appears below the radio button. These are the sites that the user is allowed to access. To add to this list, click the Add button (+) and choose Add Bookmark. The bookmark sheet appears.

5. Enter the site title and URL and then click OK. The website is added to the list of approved sites.

6. Repeat steps 4 and 5 until you've added all the websites that you want the user to be able to access.

7. To remove a site from the list, select it and click the Remove button (-).

The user is only able to access web pages for which you have configured bookmarks. If the user attempts to access any other pages, such as by entering a URL, that access is blocked.

tip

You add websites to the approved list by dragging the URLs from the Safari Address bar or from the Bookmarks page in Safari and dropping them onto the Content pane (drag them onto a folder to place them there).

Limiting Email and Chat Access of Others to Your Mac's Users

You can determine from which email addresses a user can receive email to shield that user for unwanted emails. You can also allow a user to chat only with specific people. Set this up with the following steps:

1. Open the Parental Controls pane of the System Preferences application, select the user whose access you want to limit in the user list in the left pane of the window, and click the Mail & iChat tab (see Figure 37.11).

2. Activate one or both of the check boxes for Limit Mail or Limit iChat.

note

The Parental Controls tools are designed to work with Apple applications, such as Safari and iChat. If you allow the user to access other applications, such as Instant Messenger, the Parental Controls tools doesn't prevent access to whatever resources the user wants. For maximum protection, you need to limit the user to Safari, Mail, and iChat.

3. Click the Add Email Address button (+) located at the bottom of the allowed email list. The Add sheet appears. There are two ways to add people to the approved list. One is to create the person's information in the sheet (step 5), while the other is to select a person from your Address Book (step 6).

Figure 37.11
Use the Mail & iChat tab to prevent users from communicating with anyone except those people on the approved list.

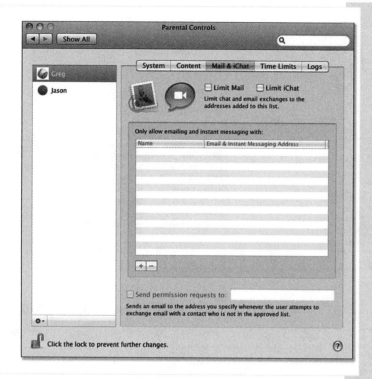

4. Enter the first and last names of the person with whom you are going to allow email or chat and then enter the email address in the box below the name fields. Use the pop-up menu to choose email, AIM, or Jabber. You need to enter an email address or username for each of the options you want to allow. Activate Add Person to My Address Book to add the person whose information you are entering to your Address Book. Click Add to add the person to the approved list.

5. Click the expansion triangle next to the Last Name field. Use the resulting Address Book browser to select the person you want to add to the approved list and click Add (see Figure 37.12). The person and all their email addresses are added to the approved list.

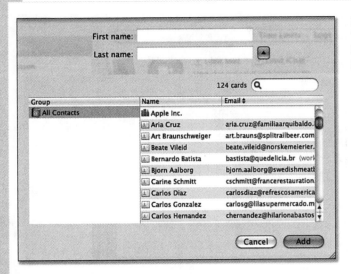

Figure 37.12
You can add people to the approved list by selecting them in your Address Book.

6. To remove someone from the list, select the name and click Remove (-).

7. If you want to receive a permission email each time an email from an address not on the list is received, activate the Send Permission Requests To check box and enter the email address where you want the permission emails to be sent in the box. If you approve the contact, the email address is added to the approved list.

Any email or chat requests addressed to the user from addresses not on the approved list you configured are rejected. If you enabled the permission email option, a permission email is sent to the address you configured. If permission is granted via that email by clicking the Always Allow button, the email or chat request from the unlisted address is allowed, as are future emails or chat requests from the same address (it is added to the list of allowed email addresses).

 tip

You can prevent additional emails from the same address by clicking the No Longer Allow button in the permission email.

Viewing Logs of User Activity

If you want to view the activity of a user account, perform the following steps:

1. Open the Parental Controls pane of the System Preferences application, select the user whose access you want to limit in the user list in the left pane of the window, and click the Logs tab. In the Logs pane, you see the categories of logs you can view: Websites Visited, Websites Blocked, Applications, and iChat.

2. Select the category in which you are interested, such as Websites Visited.

3. Select the timeframe you want to view on the Show Activity For pop-up menu.

4. Choose how you want the information grouped on the Group By pop-up menu.

5. In the Logs pane, you see the user's activity for the category you selected.

6. To prevent further activity with a resource, select it on the list and click Restrict. The user can no longer access the resource.

7. To view a resource, select it and click Open. You move to the resource, such as website, you selected.

SOLVING MAC PROBLEMS

Handling Mac Problems

Even though Mac OS X is a very stable and reliable operating system, you'll inevitably experience problems. You might experience application crashes or hangs, or an application just might not work the way it is supposed to. You might even experience minor annoyances, such as having to do something in several steps that should require only one. In any case, eventually you'll run into a situation that requires you to troubleshoot and solve a problem.

Dealing with a problem, especially related to Mac OS X, can be intimidating even if you are a power user because there is so much going on that you might not understand. Although the top-level Mac interface is relatively intuitive, the Unix underpinnings of the OS have a tremendous amount of complexity. Nowhere is this more apparent than when you are trying to solve a problem. As you use the various tools that are part of Mac OS X to diagnose and solve a problem, you are likely to run into information that doesn't make much sense to you—unless you have lived in the Unix world for a long time, in which case you feel right at home.

Fortunately, you don't need to be a Unix expert to be able to

 note

If there is one troubleshooting trick or technique that I would classify as critical, it is the ability to accurately and completely (and calmly) describe a problem you are experiencing, whether you are telling someone about it or writing to them. Not only does this help your own troubleshooting work, but it also is vital when you need help from someone else. Unfortunately, many requests for help provide only partial or incomplete information, which makes it almost impossible to provide the correct help.

troubleshoot and solve Mac OS X problems. Mostly, what is required is the ability to carefully observe what is happening and to follow logical trails. Being able to communicate clearly with other people is also very important when you need to get help.

From the title of this chapter, you might be under the impression that you'll be seeing many solutions to specific Mac problems you might encounter. Unfortunately, there simply isn't room in this book to provide lists of problems and solutions that would be detailed enough to help you with the specific problems you'll face.

Instead, the purpose of this chapter is to help you learn *how* to troubleshoot Mac OS X problems in general. You can then apply the techniques and tools you learn about in this chapter to any problems you face; these techniques help you solve problems on your own. In the long run, the strategies you need to know to solve problems are much more useful to you than lists of problems that might or might not include those you actually experience.

 note

The goal of this chapter is to help you learn general problem-solving techniques, but solutions to some specific problems you might encounter are explained in the "Troubleshooting" sections in Chapters 13, 18, and 19 of this book.

Understanding the Causes of Problems

The causes of the problems you experience can be one—or a combination—of five general types of problems:

- User error

- Bugs

- Conflicting software

- Attacks on your system

- Hardware failures

Each of these problems is detailed in the sections that follow.

User Error

Many problems are the direct result of a user (this means you) doing something improperly—or not doing something properly. Some of the things you might do to cause problems for yourself are the following:

- **Not following instructions**—This is the big one. At times, you can cause your own problems simply because you fail to follow instructions provided with software or hardware. You should become a believer in the old adage, "if all else fails, follow the instructions."

- **Operating a machine past its limits**—If you know that a particular application requires a computer with an Intel processor, but you try to run it on a G3-equipped Mac, you are bound to have troubles. If you live on the edge of your machine's capabilities, you'll have more problems than you might with a more capable machine. This is especially important related to a computer's RAM. Most minimum RAM requirements are understated; add as much RAM to your Mac as it can handle and you can afford.

■ **Not doing proper maintenance on your system**—If you don't keep an eye out for patches and updates to Mac OS X as well as the applications you use, you might experience more problems than you have to. Take advantage of the many ways in which you can keep your system up to date. For example, Mac OS X's Software Update feature can help you keep your operating system and all your Apple applications current automatically.

■ **Not keeping enough free space on a drive**—This is a fairly common cause of problems. All drives need to have free space to be capable of storing files, sometimes temporarily. If a drive is full, or very close to being full, you'll have problems as you try to store more data on it. This can be a problem under Mac OS X because virtual memory is always on—low disk space can cause problems related to insufficient RAM as well.

➥ *See Chapter 36, "Backing Up Your Mac," p. 689.*

 note

Proper maintenance includes maintaining good backups of your data, applications, or (even better) your entire system. Using a Mac without a backup system is like playing Russian roulette. Much of the time, you'll be fine. But sometimes you lose, and when you get caught without a backup, you lose big.

Bugs

Sometimes the cause of a problem is a bug inherent in the design of the products involved. The bug can be a design flaw, a manufacturing problem, or a conflict with some other part of your system. Although companies often do the best they can to prevent bugs, there is usually no way to prevent all the possible bugs in a product. Many bugs aren't revealed until a piece of software or hardware is combined with some other pieces of hardware or software.

Conflicting Software

One of the most common causes of problems is conflicting software. Conflicts are often associated with system-level applications and resources because they modify the low-level operations of the system. However, applications can also conflict with one another and cause you headaches.

Because Mac OS X features protected memory, these types of conflicts are much less common under Mac OS X than they were under previous versions of the Mac OS. Because of protected memory, you aren't likely to experience many conflicts between applications. However, there is still the potential for conflict between software that modifies the system and the core OS or software that uses hardware components of your system, such as heavy use of disks.

Attacks on Your System

The two primary sources of attacks on your system come from the outside: viruses and hackers. Viruses can cause all sorts of problems from simple and silly messages appearing to strange dialog boxes to major system crashes and even data deletions or hard disk failures. Viruses that do serious damage have traditionally been fairly rare on the Mac, but because Mac OS X is based on Unix, it remains to be seen whether viruses will be a more significant source of concern than they have been for Mac users traditionally. Fortunately, viruses are among the easier problems to avoid. On the other hand, if you use a broadband connection to the Internet, your Mac will be subjected to all sorts of hackers who want to do damage to you or others. These are definitely the more serious of the two possible sources of attacks.

 note

Although attacks are normally associated with someone from outside your local network, this is not always the case. Sometimes, even unknowingly (such as in an email-based virus attack), users on your local network can wreak havoc on your system. The proper use of user accounts and permissions and a bit of paying attention can go a long way toward preventing incursions on your Mac from a local user.

➡ *To learn how to defend yourself against these attacks,* **see** *"Defending Your Mac from Internet Attacks,"* **p. 720.**

Hardware Failures

The most unlikely cause of problems is a hardware failure. Although hardware does fail now and again, it doesn't happen very often. Hardware failures are most likely to occur immediately after you start using a new hardware item or close to the end of a hardware item's useful life. Sometimes, you can induce a hardware failure when you upgrade a machine or perform some other type of maintenance on it—for example, if you install new RAM in a machine but fail to seat a RAM chip properly.

The most common problems associated with hardware devices are actually related to the device drivers that enable the OS to communicate with the device.

Preventing Problems

It is better to prevent problems than to try to solve them. Following are three techniques you can employ to minimize the problems you experience:

■ **Maintain your Mac properly and protect it**—This goes a long way toward minimizing your problems.

➡ *For information about protecting and maintaining your Mac,* **see** *Chapter 35, "Maintaining Your Mac,"* **p. 671.**

■ **Be cautious about upgrades, updaters, and other changes to the system software or applications**—Generally, you should wait a period of time after an upgrade is released before putting it on your system. You should always carefully evaluate the benefits of a new version of an application versus the potential for problems it might introduce. This holds true for updaters and patches as well. If you are not experiencing the problems that are solved by an updater or a patch, you might be better off without it.

You should try to keep a log that records the date and time when you make significant changes to your system, such as adding new software, changing network settings, and so on. Such a log can help you identify possible causes of problems when a time lag exists between when you make a change and when problems occur. Mac OS X's Software Update feature maintains such a log for you automatically. But when you make changes outside of that tool, you have to record the relevant information manually.

 tip

If you support more than one computer, you should have a test system on which you can install new software to test for a while before exposing other systems to it.

■ **Make as few changes as possible at one time**—There are at least two reasons you should make changes to your system (such as installing software, making major configuration changes, and so on) incrementally. The first and most important is that making multiple changes at one time can obscure the cause of problems. For example, if you install three or four applications at once and then experience problems, determining which of the applications you installed is causing the problem can be difficult. The second reason is that sometimes making multiple changes at once can cause problems for you. When you change something significant, go slowly and take one step at a time. Introduce additional changes only after you are fairly sure that the changes you previously introduced are working properly.

Assessing Your Mac

Key to troubleshooting and solving problems that you can't prevent is being able to accurately and precisely assess how your Mac is performing and knowing the specific configuration of your system. Mac OS X offers many diagnostic tools that can help you; however, several of these tools are quite complicated. Still, even if you are not able to interpret all their output, people who are trying to help might be able to, so even in this case it is useful for you to know how to use them. And, you should understand how to use these tools before you need them.

 note

If you choose Apple menu, About This Mac, you see a window displaying the version of the Mac OS X you are running, the amount of RAM installed in your machine, the specific processors it contains, and the current startup disk. You can also click the Software Update button to move to that pane in the System Preferences application or click More Info to move into the System Profiler.

Using System Profiler to Create a System Profile

Mac OS X includes the System Profiler application. This application enables you to get a detailed view into your system at any particular point in time.

To create a profile of your system, launch System Profiler (Applications/Utilities directory). The System Profiler provides a window with two panes (see Figure 38.1). In the left pane is a list of areas about which you can get information, including Hardware, Network, and Software. Each of these sections is broken down into component areas. For example, the Hardware

 tip

If you click the Mac OS X version number shown in the About This Mac window, you see the specific build number of the version you are using. Click this information and you see your Mac's serial number. Click it again and you return to the Mac OS X version information.

section is further organized into various aspects of your system, such as ATA, Audio, Bluetooth, Diagnostics, and so on. The Software area is organized into Applications, Extensions, Fonts, and so on. When you select an item in the left pane, detailed information about that item appears in the right pane. For example, in Figure 38.1, the Hardware item is selected, which provides an overview of a machine's hardware configuration.

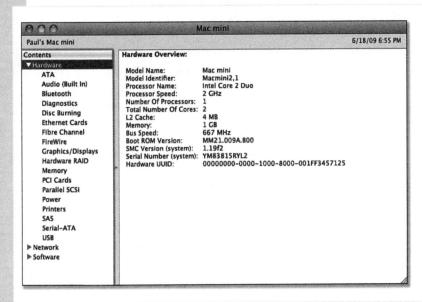

Figure 38.1
The System Profiler provides detailed information about the hardware and software that make up your system.

Click the category for the part of the system about which you want information. For example, to see the memory configuration of your machine, click the Memory category. In the right pane is each memory slot the machine contains. When a chip is installed in a slot, you can select the chip and see detailed information about it in the lower part of the pane (see Figure 38.2).

Three views are available in System Profiler; you can select the view on the View menu. The Full Profile (press (⌘-3) is the default view and provides the most information. The Mini Profile (press ⌘-1) hides details under the Software and Network categories; you can expand these sections to view the detail. The Basic Profile (press ⌘-2) includes more detail in the Hardware and Network sections but no additional detail in the Software section. There's really no reason to use any view other than the Full Profile. After all, you use the System Profiler to get information, so why not get as much as is available?

 tip

You can also open the System Profiler by clicking the More Info button that appears in the About This Mac widow.

 tip

Click the expansion triangle next to a category to expand or collapse its detail.

Figure 38.2
The Memory category enables you to get information about the memory configuration of your Mac.

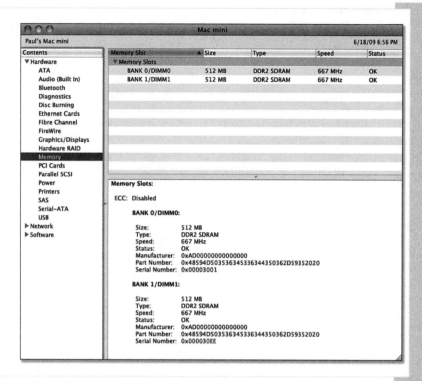

The categories available in System Profiler in the Full Profile view can include those shown in Table 38.1.

Table 38.1 System Profiler in the Full Profile View

Category	Subcategory	Summary
Hardware	None	This area provides an overview of the hardware that is part of your machine. You see the type of Mac, the CPU(s) it includes, cache information, memory details, and other hardware information.
Hardware	ATA	Use this category to view detailed information about the ATA disk or disc drives in your Mac.
Hardware	Audio (Built In)	Use this section to view information about the audio capabilities of your Mac. For example, you see the type of Line In port your Mac has; Combo means that it's both an analog and a digital port.
Hardware	Bluetooth	If your Mac supports Bluetooth, this tool provides a lot of information about it, such as the Mac's current settings, the services that are enabled, and the devices with which the Mac is paired.

Table 38.1 Continued

Category	Subcategory	Summary
Hardware	Diagnostics	This section provides information about diagnostics that your Mac sometimes runs, such as those that occur during the self-test when you power up your Mac.
Hardware	Disc Burning	Use this to view information about CD or DVD burners in your system or that are connected via FireWire or USB.
Hardware	Ethernet Cards	This section lists the wired and wireless Ethernet controllers installed in your Mac.
Hardware	Fibre Channel	This section applies if you use Fibre Channel to link machines together.
Hardware	FireWire	This provides information about your Mac's FireWire ports including the devices that are currently connected. If a FireWire device is connected to your Mac, but is not listed in this section, you know there is a problem with the device or the cable connecting it to your Mac.
Hardware	Graphics/Displays	This section provides details about the graphics cards installed in your Mac and the displays connected to those cards.
Hardware	Hardware RAID	If you have a Mac with a hardware RAID, you can gather information about it in this category.
Hardware	Memory	Use this category to view detailed information about the composition of your machine's RAM memory.
Hardware	PC Cards	If you use a mobile Mac and PC cards, you can view information about them here.
Hardware	PCI	This area provides information about PCI cards you have installed in your Mac. If you have physically installed a card, but it is not listed here, the card is not working. The most likely cause is that the correct driver isn't installed.
Hardware	Parallel SCSI	Here you see information about any SCSI devices included in your system.
Hardware	Power	This area displays the current power settings for your Mac, such as sleep time.
Hardware	Printers	This provides information about any printers with which your Mac can communicate.
Hardware	SAS	Serial Attached SCSI devices are listed in this part of the report.
Hardware	Serial-ATA	In this area, you see information about serial ATA drives connected to your Mac or installed in it.
Hardware	USB	This particularly useful section shows all the USB devices attached to your system. If you are having trouble with a specific device, use this information to see whether your Mac recognizes a device properly. You can also see the speed at which USB devices are communicating with your Mac.

Table 38.1   Continued

Category	Subcategory	Summary
Network	None	This category provides an overview of your Mac's current network connections.
Network	AirPort Card	View this to see the type of AirPort card installed in your Mac and the current AirPort network you are using, along with other AirPort information.
Network	Firewall	This area provides information about the firewall configured for your Mac.
Network	Locations	This section provides a list of all the locations configured on your Mac. If you select a location in the upper pane, details about it are shown in the lower pane.
Network	Modems	This provides information about modems installed in or connected to your Mac, such as an internal dial-up modem, or an external modem, such as a cable modem to which your Mac is directly connected.
Network	Volumes	This section provides information about network volumes that are currently mounted on your Mac, such as your iDisk.
Network	WWAN	This area provides data on Wireless Wide Area Network (WWAN) connections.
Software	None	This provides an overview of your system software, including version and build, kernel version, boot volume (startup volume), computer name, and current user.
Software	Applications	This category displays information about the applications installed on your startup volume. The upper part of the pane shows the application name, version number, and modification date. If you select an application, in the lower part of the pane you see its version, modification date, location, Info String (which is usually a copyright statement from the manufacturer), the location in which it is stored, and the kind of application it is.
Software	Extensions	Here, you see the Mac OS X extensions installed on your startup volume. This information can sometimes be useful when troubleshooting. For example, you can determine if an extension associated with a piece of hardware is currently recognized by your system.
Software	Fonts	This provides the details about all the fonts on your Mac. Select a font listed in the upper pane to see more details about it in the lower pane.
Software	Frameworks	This category lists the Mac OS X frameworks installed on your startup volume. In the upper pane, you see the name of the framework, its version, and when it was last modified. If you select a framework, in the lower part of the pane you see its version, modification date, location, Info String (which can sometimes tell you more about the framework), and whether it is private.

Table 38.1 Continued

Category	Subcategory	Summary
Software	Logs	This section provides access to various logs the system and some applications keep to record significant events, such as crashes. Each log can be selected to reveal its details. In the upper pane are all the logs available to you. For each log, you see its name, a description, its size, and when it was last modified. If you click a log, its information is displayed in the lower pane. The specific information you see depends on the log you select.

Some of the information in these logs is quite technical. However, you can often review the logs for a specific point in time during which you were having trouble, to assess what was happening with your system. For example, you can see significant events that occurred or didn't occur successfully. This can often reveal the source of a problem. Also, if you need to ask for help, accessing these logs can enable you to provide more specific information to the person trying to help you and might result in a problem being solved more quickly.

Other logs, such as those for applications, are quite easy to understand and often reveal information about problems you have experienced. |
Software	Managed Client	This portion of the report details the preferences that your Mac receives when it is connected to the Workgroup Manager functions of a Mac OS X Server.
Software	Preference Panes	This list shows you all the preference panes currently installed in the System Preferences application. Select a preference pane in the upper pane of the window to see details about it in the lower pane.
Software	Startup Items	This list shows all processes that start up when your Mac does. As with other panes, select the item that interests you in the upper pane and view the details in the lower pane.
Software	Sync Services	This list shows a log of the synchronization services active on your Mac, including calendars and address books.
Software	Universal Access	This list displays the current settings for the Mac's Universal Access features, such as cursor magnification.

You should periodically save a Profiler report, called a *profile*, to disk and print it. Then, if you need to get help with a problem but can't open System Profiler at the time, you can use the saved version or the hard copy of the profile to help troubleshoot the issue. You can also email the profile file to people trying to help you solve a problem. To save a profile for your system, do the following steps:

1. Launch the System Profiler.

2. Select File, Save As.

3. In the resulting Save sheet, name the file, choose a location in which to save it, and select the file format in which you want to save the profile. The options are System Profiler 4.0 (XML), Rich Text Format (RTF), and Plain Text. The format you choose depends on how you are going to use

the profile. In most cases, you should choose System Profiler or Rich Text because the resulting profile retains some formatting.

4. Click Save. The profile is saved in the format you selected.

5. Open the profile to view it (see Figure 38.3).

Figure 38.3
Here is a profile saved in the RTF format.

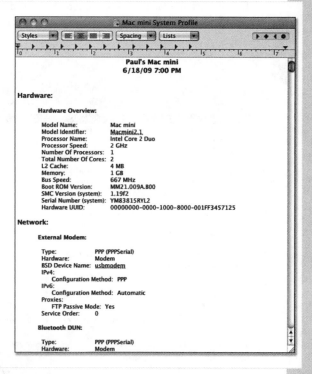

The System Profiler menus contain some additional commands that might be useful. For example, View, Refresh causes System Profiler to refresh all its information.

Using Activity Monitor to Understand and Manage Processes

To provide services, your Mac runs a lot of processes. These processes fall into many categories. User processes are those that are related to specific user accounts, such as running an application. Administrator (also called root) processes are those that are fundamental to the OS and are controlled by it, such as the Desktop database.

 tip

When you need help from Apple, you can send a Profile by choosing File, Send to Apple. Click the Send to Apple button in the resulting sheet and your profile is transmitted to Apple. An Apple representative can access the profile to help you solve a problem. Apple can also use the profile to help identify bugs and other issues with Apple software, including OS X.

The Activity Monitor application enables you to get detailed information about any process running on your Mac at any point in time. This information can be useful when it comes time to troubleshoot your system. You can also use the Activity Monitor to kill any running process; this is useful when a process is hung and needs to be stopped.

The following steps walk you through using the Activity Monitor:

1. Open Activity Monitor (Applications/Utilities directory). You see the Activity Monitor window, which provides a listing of all the processes on the machine (see Figure 38.4).

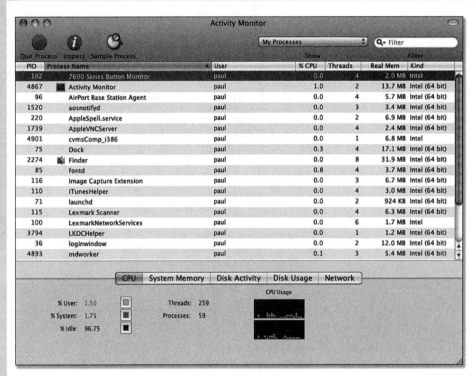

Figure 38.4
Activity Monitor enables you to get detailed information about any process on your Mac.

2. Select the category of process you want to view from the pop-up menu at the top of the window. There are many options from which to choose, and the option you choose depends on the types of processes in which you are interested. For example, select My Processes to see the processes that are related to your user account. The processes shown in the window are refreshed according to the category you select.

tip

One of the more useful process categories to view is the Active Processes option. This shows only processes that are currently doing something. When you are troubleshooting, these are typically the processes in which you are interested.

For each process shown in the Activity Monitor window, you can see the following information (you may need to expand the column to see the full name):

- **PID**—This column shows the Process ID number. Each process running on your Mac is assigned a unique ID number. This number can change each time the process is started.

- **Process Name**—Unlike process number, a process's name is constant.

- **User**—This identifies the specific user running the process. If you choose All Processes in the pop-up menu, then in addition to the user accounts on your machine, you also see processes with root as the user. These are processes that are part of the OS and are started and managed by your Mac when it starts up.

- **CPU**—This percentage indicates the amount of CPU processing that a process is consuming. This is one of the more useful pieces of data. Any process should be consuming a small percentage of the available CPU processing power. If a process is consuming a large amount, such as something more than 90%, over a long period of time, that usually indicates the process is having trouble and should be stopped.

- **# Threads**—Processes can run in different execution channels—called *threads*—within the processor. This column indicates how many threads a process is using.

- **Real Mem**—This column displays the amount of real memory—that is, how much physical RAM—is being used by the process.

- **Kind**—This column indicates whether the process is designed for Intel processors or PowerPCs. If you have an Intel Mac, you want more processes to be of the kind Intel to get the best performance. Older applications are likely to have the type PowerPC. They probably work fine on an Intel Mac, but won't perform as well as Intel processes do.

The following list outlines some additional process tasks you can perform in Activity Monitor:

- **Open a sheet that enables you to quit a process normally or to force it to quit**—Select a running process and either click Quit Process or press Option-⌘-Q to open this sheet. You can use this to stop a process that is hung. For hung processes, use Force Quit; for processes that are running normally, use Quit.

- **Sort the processes shown in the window**—Do this by clicking the column by which you want them sorted. The current sort criterion is shown by the highlighted column name. You can reverse the direction of the sort with the sort order button that is located next to the column heading.

- **Find specific processes**—Do this by typing in the Filter box. The list is reduced to only those processes that contain the text you type.

 tip

Sorting the window by the Real Memory or CPU column is useful because you can see which processes are consuming the most system memory or processing power. If a process is consuming a large amount of memory (such as 80%), that can indicate something is wrong with the application that is generating the process.

- **Open the Inspector window**—When you double-click or select a process and then either click Inspect or press ⌘-I, the Inspector window opens and you see additional information about the process, including the parent process and recent hangs (see Figure 38.5). You can click the Memory tab to see detailed memory usage information for the process. Click the Statistics tab to get information about the threads, CPU time, and other technical specifications. Click Open Files and Ports to see the open files and network ports related to the process. Click the Quit button to open the Quit/Force Quit sheet.

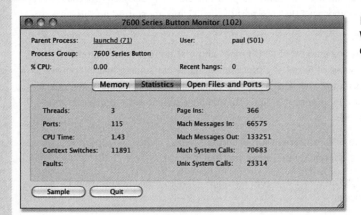

Figure 38.5
With the Process Inspector, no process can hide.

- **Change the rate at which process information is updated**—Do this by selecting View, Update Frequency; then select the frequency you want to use, such as Very Often (every 0.5 seconds) or Less Often (every 5 seconds).

 tip

If you click the Sample button, you see yet another window that provides even more technical information about a process.

Using the Activity Monitor to Monitor System Activity

Using the tabs along the bottom of the Activity Monitor application enables you to gain insight into the following system activities:

- **CPU**—You can monitor the CPU activity of the processors in your Mac. This gives you a good idea of the resources being used at any moment in time. When CPU usage becomes close to the upper limit, this usually indicates a problem.

- **System Memory**—Using this tool, you can view the usage of various types of system memory, such as physical RAM and virtual memory. You can also view the free memory of your system, which can be useful to determine whether you need to add more memory resources to your Mac.

- **Disk Activity**—This tool enables you to view the performance of your machine when reading and writing data to disk.

- **Disk Usage**—This area enables you to see the space breakdown of a selected disk (see Figure 38.6). This is particularly useful to make sure your disks aren't running close to their maximum capacity.

- **Network**—This tool provides information about the communication across your network interface, such as via Ethernet.

 note

Virtual memory is your Mac using its hard drive as it uses real memory—to temporarily store data with which it is working. Virtual memory is much slower than real RAM, but you usually have a lot more available to you. Fortunately, Mac OS X takes care of managing both kinds of memory for you.

Figure 38.6
The Disk Usage information shows that the disk called Macintosh HD currently has about 103GB of free space: time for a little housekeeping.

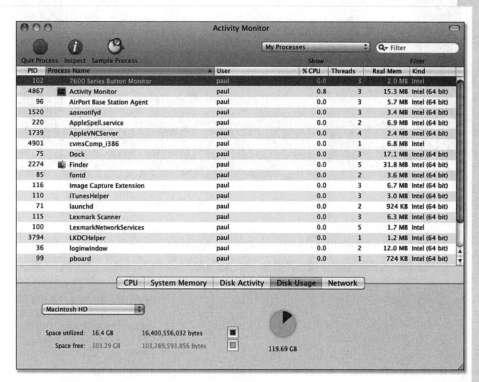

Using Activity Monitor, you can display system activity monitoring information on your desktop in a number of ways. For example, you can display CPU usage information on the desktop and display an icon showing other information on the Dock (see Figure 38.7). The monitoring options you have are listed in Table 38.2.

CPU Usage

Figure 38.7
Several options are available for real-time performance monitoring from the desktop, such as viewing CPU usage on the Dock.

Table 38.2 Monitoring Options in Activity Monitor

Menu	Command	Keyboard Shortcut	What It Does
Window	Activity Monitor	⌘-1	Opens the Activity Monitor window.
Window	CPU Usage	⌘-2	Opens a window on the desktop containing a bar for each processor that graphically displays its activity level. This is disabled if the Dock icon is showing CPU usage.
Window	CPU History	⌘-3	Opens a window that tracks processor activity over time.
Window	Floating CPU Window, Show Horizontally	⌘-4	Opens a bar showing activity for each processor. The bar appears in the lower-left corner of the desktop and is oriented horizontally.
Window	Floating CPU Window, Show Vertically	⌘-5	Opens a bar showing activity for each processor. The bar appears in the lower-left corner of the desktop and is oriented vertically.

Table 38.2 Continued

Menu	Command	Keyboard Shortcut	What It Does
Window	Floating CPU Window, None		Closes the Floating CPU window.
Window	Keep CPU Windows on Top		When this option is selected, all CPU monitor windows always appear on top of other windows. When this option is not selected, the CPU monitoring windows can be hidden by other windows.
View	Clear CPU History	⌘-K	Starts the CPU history over again.
View	Columns, *Column*, where *Column* is the name of an Activity Monitor column		Enables you to show or hide all the columns Activity Monitor can display.
View	Dock Icon, Show CPU Usage		Shows a CPU Usage window on the Dock (as shown in Figure 38.7).
View	Dock Icon, Show CPU History		Shows a CPU History window on the Dock.
View	Dock Icon, Show Network Usage		Shows a Network Usage window on the Dock.
View	Dock Icon, Show Disk Activity		Shows a Disk Activity window on the Dock.
View	Dock Icon, Show Memory Usage		Shows a Memory Usage window on the Dock.
View	Dock Icon, Show Application Icon		Shows the Activity Monitor icon on the Dock instead of a monitoring window.
View	Update Frequency, *Frequency*, where *Frequency* is the frequency you choose		Changes the frequency at which the Activity Monitor monitors processors. The frequency can be 0.5 seconds, 1 second, 2 seconds, or 5 seconds.

Monitoring is available only while Activity Monitor is running. When you quit the application, all monitoring disappears. If you want to display the monitoring tools but hide the Activity Monitor window itself, you can minimize or close the Activity Monitor window.

 tip

When you choose a frequency, it affects only the monitoring of processes. The monitors always display information in real time.

Viewing System Activity with Top

The Top window is a Unix window that provides detailed information about the current operation of your Mac. To access it, open a command-line application such as Terminal, type **top**, and press Return.

The Top window provides detailed information about your system, although not in the most easily understood format (see Figure 38.8). At the top of the Top window, you see a summary of the activity on your machine; the lower part of the window lists all the running processes and detailed information about each.

```
● ● ○                    Terminal — top — 83×27
Processes: 58 total, 3 running, 1 stuck, 54 sleeping, 234 threads        05:38:11
Load Avg: 0.17, 0.05, 0.02  CPU usage: 0.48% user, 1.92% sys, 97.59% idle
SharedLibs: 5276K resident, 6368K data, 0B linkedit.
MemRegions: 5881 total, 152M resident, 14M private, 103M shared.
PhysMem: 203M wired, 399M active, 196M inactive, 797M used, 227M free.
VM: 131G vsize, 1041M framework vsize, 90744(0) pageins, 6276(0) pageouts.
Networks: packets: 712720/345M in, 470045/98M out.
Disks: 107788/1588M read, 471843/5479M written.

PID   COMMAND     %CPU  TIME     #TH  #WQ #POR #MRE RPRVT  RSHRD  RSIZE  VPRVT
4942  top         3.5   00:00.65 1/1  0   24   33   888K   264K   1456K  17M
4939  bash        0.0   00:00.02 1    0   17   24   336K   244K   1016K  17M
4938  mdworker    0.0   00:00.06 3    1   48   62   1328K  9208K  3132K  30M
4937  login       0.0   00:04.18 1    0   22   53   392K   244K   1416K  18M
4936  mdworker    0.0   00:00.12 3    1   50   60   1408K  8372K  3116K  31M
4934  Terminal    0.5   00:00.95 5    1   108  107- 4480K- 14M    12M-   34M-
4932  quicklookd  0.0   00:00.16 6    2   85   102  3096K  7752K  8604K  566M
4925  ocspd       0.0   00:00.01 1    0   23   27   512K   304K   1140K  17M
3795  check_afp   0.0   00:00.51 4    1   34   42   584K   244K   1100K  29M
3794  LKDCHelper   0.0   00:00.01 1    0   23   36   380K   244K   1216K  28M
2274  Finder      0.0   00:25.77 4    1   188  293  11M    39M    32M    53M
1739  AppleVNCServ 0.0   00:00.50 4    1   65   59   880K   300K   2424K  31M
1738  RFBRegisterM 0.0   00:00.01 2    1   27   31   436K   372K   1748K  27M
1712  socketfilter 0.0   00:18.95 4    2   48   54   1652K  5932K  3064K  30M
1520  aosnotifyd  0.0   00:00.89 3    1   46   158  2040K  6112K  3488K  31M
220   AppleSpell  0.0   00:01.13 2    1   33   56   3524K  9468K  7104K  29M
124   SystemUIServ 0.0  00:47.94 3    1   270  279  11M    38M    21M    63M
```

Figure 38.8
Using Top can be a bit intimidating, but the information it provides is worth getting to know.

In the summary area of the window, you can see how many processes are running versus the number sleeping, how many threads are running, the average loads, and the percentage of CPU usage of user processes versus system usage. The PhysMem information contains data about your RAM. For example, the amount shown as active is the RAM currently being used by running processes. The VM information provides data about the virtual memory being used.

 note
You can get similar information in an easier-to-use format by using Activity Monitor.

In the lower part of the window, you see a table that provides data on each process that is similar to the information in the Activity Monitor. For example, you see the PID, which is the same Process ID as is displayed for a process in the Activity Monitor. You can also see the percentage of CPU use, the processor time, and other more technical information. Much of this information may not be useful to you, but it can be useful to others when you are trying to get help.

You can save the information seen in the Top window by selecting the information in the window and selecting Shell, Export Selected Text As. This text file can be useful or can be provided to someone else when you are getting help with a problem.

 tip
To stop the Top process, press Control-C.

Using the Console to View Logs

The Console application (Applications/Utilities) provides a window to which Mac OS X writes system messages you can view, most notably various logs your Mac creates as it works (or doesn't work as in the case of crash logs). These messages are mostly error messages; some of these can be useful when you are troubleshooting problems. Console messages can be helpful to understand what was happening when something went wrong and when you are communicating a problem to someone else.

You can choose the log that is displayed in the Console window in a number of ways:

- **Click the Show Log List button in the toolbar**—You see a list of all available logs organized into categories, as shown in Figure 38.9. You can expand a category to show the logs contained in that category. When you select a log, it appears in the Console window.

Figure 38.9
The Console
enables you
to view the
contents of a
log in detail.

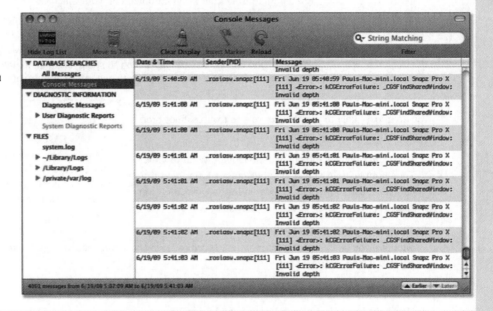

- **Select File, Open Console Log (or press Shift-⌘-O)**—This opens the Console log. Or, you can select Open System Log (or press Option-⌘-O) to open the System log.

- **Select File, Open Quickly**—Then choose the log you want to see on the hierarchical menu that appears.

A number of logs are available through the Console, and each provides a specific type of information, as you can see in Table 38.3.

Table 38.3 Logs Available in the Console

Log Name	Information It Provides
Console Messages	This log lists events related to the core operation of your Mac, such as when specific events occurred. Reviewing this log can sometimes give you insight into failed processes that might be causing problems for you, but that you might not be aware of because an application didn't crash.
All Messages	Whereas the console.log displays mostly errors, the system.log shows all events that have occurred for the system, such as when specific processes start up. You see the date and time for each event.
~/Library/Logs	This category of logs provides information related to your user account (indicated by the ~). The specific logs you see in this category depend on what you are running at any point in time. You always see the CrashReporter log for each application that has crashed. You might also see logs for various processes, such as the MirrorAgent.log when you are using an iDisk that is synchronized on your Mac.
/Library/Logs	This category presents a set of logs related to the system. These include various error logs along with logs for various system services.
/private/var/log	This category contains many logs related to various processes. For example, you can choose the install.log to see a list of all installations you have done on your Mac or ftp.log to see information related to FTP access of your machine.

You are most likely to use the Console to troubleshoot problems. To do so, use the following steps:

1. Open the Console and choose the log you want to view. For example, if an application has crashed, find that application's crash log, which is located in the CrashReporter category within the ~/Library/Logs set of logs.

2. Examine the information you see. At the top of the log window, you see summary information. Moving down the screen shows you the very technical log detail (see Figure 38.10).

3. Save a copy of the log by selecting File, Save a Copy As.

4. Name the log, select a save location, and press Return.

5. In the Console, click the Clear Display button on the toolbar. The log's information is erased.

6. Repeat the steps that lead to the crash if you can. If not, just keep doing what you were trying to do.

7. If the crash occurs again, repeat steps 1–4 to view the crash log. Compare the log to what you viewed in step 2. This might tell you whether it is the same problem or not.

8. If you can't solve the problem on your own, save the new log information so you can provide both logs to whomever you contact for help.

 note

You must be logged in under an account to see its logs. Even if another user is currently logged in while you are using your user account, you still see only your logs.

Figure 38.10
This Crash
Reporter log
shows infor-
mation about
a crash of the
Address
Book appli-
cation.

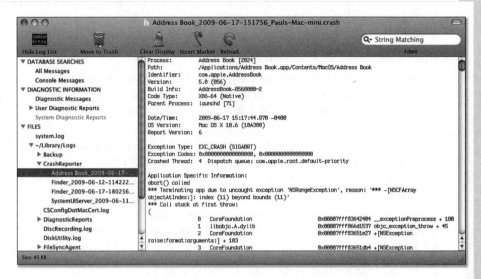

If you aren't very technically inclined, the information you see in the logs won't be understandable. However, you can still glean useful information such as the general cause of a problem and specific information about the time it occurred. That information often helps you pinpoint exactly what was happening when a problem occurred, which is often critical to being able to solve it.

Here are a few other Console tips:

- You can open multiple Console windows at the same time by selecting File, New Log Window or pressing ⌘-N. This is useful when comparing different logs.

- You can reload the information in a log by viewing it and clicking the Reload button; by select-ing File, Reload; or by pressing shift-⌘-R.

- You can get rid of old logs by selecting them and clicking the Move to Trash button.

- You can use the Filter tool to search for specific log items.

Solving Problems

If you understand the general techniques you should use when troubleshooting, you can handle most of the problems you are likely to encounter. The general process of solving problems can be broken down into four phases:

1. Implementing a workaround

2. Troubleshooting and describing your problem

3. Fixing problems yourself

4. Getting help

You should work through these phases in the order in which they are listed. Doing so helps you solve your problem as efficiently as possible.

Implementing a Workaround

One of the tough things about troubleshooting is that you usually have to do it at an inconvenient time—for example, in the middle of a big project. At times like these, you are likely to feel stress, which can lead to frustration, which in turn often leads to hasty actions. Haste often drives you down the wrong path.

Effective troubleshooting requires a cool head. The best approach when you are working under a deadline is to find a quick workaround for the problem that enables you to complete the job you need to get done immediately. Then you can come back and really fix the problem later when you are more in a "troubleshooting" frame of mind.

There are many types of workarounds you might be able to implement to get you working well enough to meet your immediate needs. Some examples are the following:

- **Use a different application to complete the project**—If your trouble is with a specific application, use an alternative one to get the project done.

- **Log in from a troubleshooting user account**—Some problems are related to corrupted preferences and other files that are part of your user account. If you followed my recommendation to create an alternative user account, log in under that account and try to complete your work.

- **Restart from an alternative startup volume**—If the problem is related to the system itself, use one of your alternative startup volumes until you have time to fix your current one.

- **Use a different Mac**—If you use your Mac for important work, you should consider having a backup machine so you can switch to it in times of trouble.

Troubleshooting and Describing Your Problem

When you start to troubleshoot, the most important thing you can do is to understand your problem in as much detail as possible. This understanding enables you to know what you need to do to correct the problem. As you gain insight into your problem, you should be able to describe it in detail; this helps you get assistance from others if you are not able to solve the problem yourself.

Use the assessment tools, such as the System Profiler and Activity Monitor, that you learned about earlier in this chapter to help you understand what is happening.

Putting the Problem in Context

Many problems are triggered by something you do (this doesn't mean you cause the problem, but that some action you take initiates the problem). When a problem happens, think about what you were doing immediately before the problem occurred. The following are some questions you need to answer:

- Which applications and processes were running (not just the particular one with which you were working)?

- What, specifically, were you trying to do (print, save, format, and so on)?

- Have you made any changes to the computer recently (installed software, changed settings, and so on)?

The answers to these questions provide significant clues to help you figure out what is triggering the problem. Identifying the trigger goes a long way toward identifying the cause.

Using Your Troubleshooting Account

Some problems you encounter might be related to files that are associated only with a user account. Examples of these include preference files for applications, other application support files, and so on. One of the best troubleshooting steps—which can also be a workaround—is to create a troubleshooting user account. Keep this account as basic as you can, meaning don't install applications that modify the system (such as applications associated with specific hardware) while logged in under this account. Leave all its settings in their default configurations, such as login items, preferences, and so on. Keeping the account free of any extra applications and settings is the reason I also call this a *clean* account.

➥ *For more information about clean accounts,* **see** *"Understanding the Clean Account," **p. 443**.*

When you encounter a problem, log in under your troubleshooting account. If the problem goes away, you know that it is related to the user account under which you were logged in when the problem occurred. This can give you a good idea of where to start solving the problem. If the problem doesn't go away, you know that it is a more general issue.

 tip

Your troubleshooting account should have administrator privileges.

Trying to Repeat the Problem

When a problem occurs, you should recover the best you can and then try to make the problem happen again. Try to re-create everything that was happening when the problem first appeared.

If you can replicate the problem, figuring out what is happening is much easier. The hardest problems to fix are those that occur only occasionally or intermittently.

caution

Obviously, you shouldn't intentionally re-create a problem in such a way that you lose data. Make sure that your data is safe by having a good backup before you do much troubleshooting.

Describing the Problem in Detail

After you have developed an understanding of how and when the problem is happening, write down a description of the problem. Be as detailed as you can. This description helps you decide on the best course of action, and if you are unable to solve the problem yourself, you'll be in an excellent position to ask for help.

Use the Console to save logs related to the problem and the System Profiler to create a report about your system's configuration. This creates much of the detail that enables you or someone else to solve the problem.

Fixing Problems Yourself

After you have described your problem, you should have some idea of where it lies. The four general areas in which you may experience problems are applications, system, hardware, and during startup.

Correcting Application Errors

Application errors usually fall into one of the following categories:

- **The application hangs**—Sometimes application errors cause your application to hang. Fortunately, because Mac OS X has protected memory, a hung application usually affects only the application itself and your other applications continue to work normally. You are likely to lose unsaved data in the hung application, but at least your losses are limited to a single application.

- **The application quits unexpectedly**—Sometimes, the application you are using suddenly quits. You might or might not get an error message saying something like, The application has unexpectedly quit because of an error. When this happens, you lose all the changes you made to the open document since the last time you saved it.

- **The application behaves erratically**—Many times, errors occur that prevent you from doing what you want to do— whether using a particular function of the software, printing, saving files, and so on.

Obviously, application problems are usually unpredictable. And when they happen, there isn't much you can do to recover your unsaved data (if you are saving frequently, you limit your losses when the inevitable does happen). With an application problem, your real task is to figure out how to *prevent* future occurrences of the problem.

Mac OS X includes a crash reporter feature. When an application crashes, the crash reporter appears. At the top of this window, you can enter information about what you were doing at the time of the crash. When you have described this in as much detail as possible, you can send the information to Apple. Apple collects this information and uses it to identify problems that need to be fixed.

 note

When you see an error alert that provides an error ID number, you should make a note of it. Although the number is not likely to be meaningful to you unless you have seen it before, it might be very meaningful to someone else when you ask for help.

 tip

Some applications, such as Microsoft Office, have a recover feature that attempts to recover documents on which you were working when the application crashed or hung. This sometimes works and sometimes doesn't. However, you should take a look at recovered documents when you restart the application to see how much of your work you can restore.

Typically, there are many things you can try to correct an application error. Following are the general tasks you should attempt to get the application working properly again.

The Application Hangs

When an application is hung, your only option is to force it to quit. You can do this by bringing up the Force Quit Applications window by pressing Option-⌘-Esc or by choosing Apple, Force Quit. Select the application you want to force quit and click Force Quit. After you confirm that you really do want to force the application to quit, Mac OS X shuts it down. You can also use the Activity Monitor to force an application to quit—the benefit of the Activity Monitor is that you can see all the processes that are running along with their status. If other processes are also hung, you can see them by looking at the Activity Monitor window. This can provide important clues as to the source of the problem (where two or three hung processes are gathered, there is likely a problem in their midst).

After you unhang the application, try to replicate the conditions under which it hung. If the problem is repeatable, it is either a bug in the application or a conflict with another part of the system.

Try running the application by itself while re-creating the situation in which the problem occurred (use your problem description to do this). If the hang doesn't occur again, you know that the problem is some type of conflict with another part of your system—be aware that this is much less likely to occur under Mac OS X than with previous versions of the OS.

If the hang is repeatable, the most likely solution is to install an update to the application. Visit the support area of the manufacturer's web page to see whether the problem you have is a known one. If so, an update is probably available to correct it. If not, report the problem to tech support to see what the application's manufacturer recommends.

> ➥ *To learn how to capture screenshots,* **see** *"Capturing Screen Images," p. 265.*

 tip

When an error dialog box appears or an application hangs, it can be useful to capture a screenshot so you can reproduce it later when you are writing down the description of your problem. In the case of a hung application, capturing a screenshot can help you re-create at least a screen's worth of data if you lose it all. Sometimes this can be helpful (such as for a table of data). To capture a screenshot, use the Grab application or download and use the much more capable Snapz Pro X.

The Application Quits Unexpectedly

When an application unexpectedly quits, you should do the same tasks as when it hangs—except that you don't need to force it to quit because it already has. When an application quits, you see a dialog box that enables you to reopen the application. If it reopens, continue working—while saving frequently, of course.

If the application quits again, restart your Mac and try again using a different file (if the application involves working with a

 note

Although Mac OS X's protected memory guards applications, unexpected quits and other issues can impact the application's memory space. Because of this, you should save all work in open applications and restart your Mac when you experience an application quitting or hanging.

file). If you are able to work with a different file, you know the issue is specific to the file you were using when it quit. If it continues to quit, the most likely solution is to get an updated version of the application from the manufacturer.

The Application Behaves Erratically

If the application isn't working as you expect it to, the most likely causes are that the application has a bug or you aren't using it in the way it was intended.

Eliminate the second possibility first. Check the application's documentation, help, or readme files to ensure that you are doing the task in the way the manufacturer intends. If you ask for help for something that is covered in the application's documentation, the responses you get might be embarrassing or unpleasant.

If you seem to be using the application properly, a likely cause is a bug and the solution is to get an update from the manufacturer.

Correcting System Errors

System errors can be tougher to solve because they are usually harder to isolate. Even so, your goal should be to isolate the problem as much as you can. If you have carefully investigated and described your problem, you should have some idea where it originates.

Your first step should be to ensure that your system software is current—use the Software Update tool to check this.

The following list provides some general things to try for various sorts of system errors:

- If the problem seems to be related to a disk, run Disk Utility or other disk maintenance application to correct it. The problem might be related to the disk being too full, so check that as well.

  ➥ *To learn how to use Disk Utility for disk repair,* ***see*** *"Checking and Repairing Disks with Disk Utility,"* **p. 675.**

Many Unix commands can be helpful when you are trying to solve system problems, such as getting rid of files you can't delete in the normal way and working with directories.

  ➥ *To learn how to use some basic Unix commands,* ***see*** *Chapter 26, "Working with the Mac OS X Command Line,"* **p. 531.**

 tip

Applications under Mac OS X are like applications under other versions—they don't always work as they should and sometimes crash or hang, in which case you lose any changes you have made since you last saved your document. Make it a practice to save your documents frequently; make sure you take advantage of auto-save features to automate this task, such as in Microsoft Office applications. You can also use automation tools, such as QuicKeys, to save any documents at regular intervals. Of course, you should always back up your data at regular intervals.

 tip

Occasionally, an application's preferences can become corrupted, and cause problems for you. One way to eliminate this as a cause of a problem is to log on under your troubleshooting user account. If the problem doesn't occur under that user account, the cause might be corrupted preference files. Log back in to the previous user account and delete preferences related to the application that are stored in that user account's Library folder. Preference files have the extension .plist, so look for the name of the application and that extension to find its preference files.

- If the problem seems to be related to a specific user account, try repeating the same action under a different account. If the problem goes away, you know that something is wrong in the user account configuration.

  The best option for this is to use your troubleshooting user account to assess this. Because this account should have few or no third-party software programs installed, it often helps you determine whether a problem is part of the system or is related to something happening under a specific user account.

  Some troubleshooting tasks are possible only when you are logged in to your Mac as root. Logging in as Root can be dangerous, so you should know what you are doing before you try any action under the root account.

  ➥ *To learn about logging in as root,* ***see*** *"Enabling the Root User Account," **p. 461.***

- If the problem is more general, you might have to reinstall the system or specific components of it.

Correcting Hardware Errors

Hardware problems are almost always caused by one of the following two conditions: improperly installed hardware or problematic drivers.

Eliminate the first cause by reviewing the steps you took to install the hardware. Check out the instructions that came with the device to make sure you are following the manufacturer's recommendations.

If the hardware is an external device, check the cable you used to connect it; if you have another cable, try that. If the device is connected to a hub, reconnect it to a port on the Mac itself.

If the hardware is internal, repeat the installation process to ensure that it is correct.

 tip

A good way to check whether a device is successfully communicating with your Mac is to use the System Profiler. Use the bus type information (such as FireWire) for that device to see whether the device with which you are having trouble is listed.

The most likely cause of hardware problems is a faulty or buggy driver. Your only solution to this problem is to get an updated driver from the manufacturer. Visit the manufacturer's website for help or use the related application's check for updates command.

The hardware might simply be defective. Although this doesn't happen very often, it can occur. If none of the other solutions works, you might be left with this possibility, in which case all you can do is exchange the unit for a different one or repair it. Hardware failures are most likely to occur immediately after installing and starting to use a device or at the end of its useful life.

Correcting Startup Problems

One of the worst problems you can have is when your Mac won't start. This can be caused by many things, including software conflicts, buggy software, disk problems, failed hardware, or a combination of all of these. Instead of loading the system, the machine just sits there and flashes a broken folder icon, meaning your Mac can't find a suitable System folder to use to start up the machine. (If the system doesn't try to start up at all, but you just hear the chimes of death, that means you definitely have a hardware problem.)

If the startup problem is because of failed hardware, you have to correct the issue before you can get going again.

If the startup problem is related to your system software, the best solution is to start up from an alternative startup volume. Just like the troubleshooting user account, maintaining an alternative startup volume, with as little modification as possible, enables you to get back to work as quickly as possible and fix the problems with your regular startup volume when you have time to do so.

If you have an alternative startup volume available, use it to start up your Mac. Run Disk Utility on your normal startup volume to see if it can find and correct issues.

 note

Make sure you start up under your alternative startup volume every so often and update its software so its system stays current. This ensures it is ready to use when you need it.

If you do not have an alternative startup volume, you can start up from the Mac OS X installation DVD. When the Installer opens, you can use the Utility menu to run Disk Utility on your normal startup volume. Be aware that the version of OS X on your installation DVD is likely older than the version you are currently using. This can sometimes cause problems, but you might not have a choice if you don't have an alternative startup volume to use.

If you can't repair the disk on which OS X is installed, you might have to reinstall the system. Try using the Archive option so that you maintain your user accounts; this might not work if the version of OS X you are currently using is much newer than the one on the DVD, but it is worth a shot.

 note

If you have a backup of your entire system when it was working properly, you can restore that version instead of reinstalling a new one. The advantage of this is that you won't have to reinstall your third-party software.

Getting Help for Your Problem

Unless you can instantly see how to solve your problem or one of your tools takes care of it, you will probably need to get help. There are plenty of sources for troubleshooting help, including the following:

- Manuals and online help
- Technical support from the manufacturer
- Websites, many of which include forums that can be used to look for help
- Magazines
- Troubleshooting software
- Mailing lists
- Co-workers and other people you know personally

Table 38.4 lists some specific sources of online help with Mac OS X issues.

Table 38.4 Sources of General Help for Problems

Source	Contact Information	Comments
Apple	www.apple.com/support	Apple's support pages are a great source of information about problems, and you can download updates to system and other software. You can search for specific problems. You can also read manuals and have discussions about problems in the forums available here. If the problem you are having seems to be related to the OS, Apple hardware, or an Apple application, this should be your first stop.
MacFixIt	www.macfixit.com	This is a good source of information related to solving Mac problems. Access to much of the information is not free, but you can get help on literally every aspect of using a Mac. Most of the information comes from Mac users, and you can ask specific questions—although the answer to your question is probably already available. You can get access to some current information free; however, you must pay to access older information maintained in an exhaustive set of archives. The fee is quite reasonable for the quality of the information to which you have access.
MacInTouch	www.macintouch.com	This site offers a lot of Mac news that can help you solve problems, especially if those problems are solved by a software update of which you are unaware.
MacWorld	www.macworld.com/news	Another source of Mac news. Be aware that some of this "news" is press releases from various companies. However, you sometimes learn useful information from press or marketing information.
Version Tracker	www.versiontracker.com	You can quickly find find out whether updates have been released for applications with which you are having trouble.

INDEX

How can we make this index more useful? Email us at indexes@quepublishing.com

FREE Online Edition

Your purchase of **Mac OS X Snow Leopard In Depth** includes access to a free online edition for 45 days through the Safari Books Online subscription service. Nearly every Que book is available online through Safari Books Online, along with more than 5,000 other technical books and videos from publishers such as Cisco Press, Addison-Wesley Professional, Exam Cram, IBM Press, O'Reilly, Prentice Hall, Que, and Sams.

SAFARI BOOKS ONLINE allows you to search for a specific answer, cut and paste code, download chapters, and stay current with emerging technologies.

Activate your FREE Online Edition at www.informit.com/safarifree

> **STEP 1:** Enter the coupon code: GGFKYFA.

> **STEP 2:** New Safari users, complete the brief registration form.
> Safari subscribers, just log in.

If you have difficulty registering on Safari or accessing the online edition, please e-mail customer-service@safaribooksonline.com